PUBLIC OPINION

PUBLIC OPINION

BY

WILLIAM ALBIG

Associate Professor of Sociology,
University of Illinois

FIRST EDITION
SECOND IMPRESSION

McGRAW-HILL BOOK COMPANY, INC.

NEW YORK AND LONDON

1939

301.154
A335p

THE MAPLE PRESS COMPANY, YORK, PA.

PREFACE

The discussion of public opinion and of the opinion process offers many difficulties. There is the tangled, matted field of opinion theory. It is a field cluttered with the stumps of the once mighty theoretical particularisms, a field in which a dense underbrush has grown, in which there are confusing brambles of terminological disputation and an infinite thicket of psychological descriptions. It is not to be readily cleared by the beavering tactics of a petty scholarship or by little brush pickers or small, controversial conflagration makers. It calls for a master synthesizer, who, stoutly implemented with tools of original keenness, can cut a clear path to the other side. While awaiting such a man, perhaps we can beaver a little.

For the most part I have used simple, nontechnical terms in this discussion. But not in all cases. At the present time, no one can write on the field of public opinion in terms satisfactory to all his readers. If an author uses simple terms, satisfactory to the general reader, he ignores the pyramid of language hastily thrown up in recent years by the specialist in this field. These special terms are invented ostensibly to provide an exact definitive terminology of non-emotion-arousing words suitable for use among scientists. The absence of most of these terms would provide the basis for an indictment of the author as an outsider, an outlander, a stranger to the code of the jousts. As language is truly a bond of unity, he might be expelled into the outer darkness. On the other hand, if the author bandies about this esoteric jargon too freely, there is no doubt as to where the general reader would willingly consign him. Therefore, I have attempted to use certain of the special terms, developed in recent years, where such words seemed to make for clarity and objectivity. Elsewhere I have eschewed such terms and striven for relative simplicity.

There is one phrase that I would define briefly at this point. Throughout this book I have referred to the "common man." I mean the unintellectual man—unaware of intellectual traditions and the history of thought. As Harvey Fergusson has written, "By the common man I mean the man who is so absorbed in the immediate and personal ends of living that he cannot view his destiny with any intellectual detachment. Such a man is capable of receiving doctrines upon authority and accepting them, but he is typically not capable of making hypotheses on his own account."

v

I have not approached the subjects of growth of communication, the emergence and organization of propaganda, the control of newspapers, radio and motion pictures, the questions of restriction and censorship, the conscious manipulation of legends, and the like as "problems" or as "menaces." My objective, I hope maintained with some consistency, has been to direct the attention of the student of public opinion to the development of these phenomena as related to other aspects of the social process. To emphasize programs of "reform" in these fields is absurdly to simplify the processes. This is not to say that we have not had occasion to suggest procedures which might be helpful in controlling these processes, but simply to emphasize that such suggestions are not high-lighted and that "problems" are not the central thesis of this volume. I have not thought it necessary or desirable to indicate my own position on all the controversial topics with which we shall deal. I hope that that position is frequently implicit in the method of discussion of the particular item— or that it may be assumed from the underlying viewpoints of this work.

The reader may feel that in several chapters of this volume I have been unnecessarily discursive and that I have strayed from the central topics under discussion. In such instances, it was my purpose to place these topics in their settings. However, I may have been overzealous in describing the terrain at the side of the road.

It is customary, not only in the teaching profession but in popular learning in America, to emphasize two procedures that I have attempted to avoid in this volume. One is to shock, the other to edify. Indeed, these methods are so common that any serious exponent of relatively impartial description of the social process finds himself baffled at times by the persistent demand of his auditors that they be shocked into attention and then led into "the way."

The contemporary writer of a volume that may find some use as a text finds himself embarrassed by the need to indicate his sources and give adequate appreciation to the originators, or at any rate users, of ideas that he has found helpful, while at the same time avoiding a too liberal sprinkling of references and footnotes lest he incur the charge of an absurdly vain pedantry. I have not coyly hidden all footnotes and references at the ends of chapters or at the end of the book, so that the eyes of students might be untroubled and their minds unperturbed by the obtrusion of the mechanics of scholarship. Sources and references are working tools. However, the reference lists for reading on various topics have been placed at the end of the volume. Any student of public opinion has a debt to acknowledge for the bibliographical labors of H. D. Lasswell, R. D. Casey and B. L. Smith in the preparation of their annotated bibliography, *Propaganda and Promotional Activities;* to H. L. Childs for his *A Reference Guide to the Study of Public Opinion;* and to

Kimball Young and R. D. Lawrence for their *Bibliography on Censorship and Propaganda.*

I hope that the experimental studies referred to in various sections of this book will be superseded within a very short time. Speculation on these topics is rife, and experimental data in parts of this field have been presented at an accelerated pace during the past ten years.

I have no apologies to offer for the various stories and anecdotes that are strewn through the pages of this book. I am well aware of the limitations of such material. Stories sometimes distort meanings, divert the attention or unstabilize the judgment by laughter. But they add interest for the reader and sometimes really illustrate. They are painfully objectionable only to the experts in any field.

It is customary for an author to express appreciation and gratitude to his wife for patience and forbearance with his aberrations during periods of intensive writing, or for sympathetic silence while he expounded certain points, or for critical comment, or for typing and clerical assistance. I am indebted to Helen H. Albig on all counts. I am under obligation to my colleague Professor E. T. Hiller for reading Chapters III, XI, XII, XIV and XV; to Professor D. R. Taft for reading Chapters III, XI, XII, XIV, XV and XX; and to Donald Coney, Librarian of the University of Texas, for reading Chapter III. Before my fireside, my colleagues E. A. Ahrens, R. E. Crist, H. F. Underhill and W. G. McAllister listened patiently to the reading of various sections of this volume during the past winter.

WILLIAM ALBIG.

URBANA, ILL.,
February, 1939.

CONTENTS

LIST OF TABLES

LIST OF FIGURES

CHAPTER I

THE NATURE OF PUBLIC OPINION

The discussion of human affairs, of personal relationships and of public issues and actions is persistent in all societies. Such discussion deals with all subjects about which there is information in the group. It is conducted in all groups, among the simple and the sophisticated, the ignorant and the learned, the common man and the expert. Discussion utilizes all the means of communication—speech, gesture, print and picture. The process of discussion is intensified by the appearance of unusual information or occurrences, by controversy and by conflict. It is said that "a happy people have no history." A people or group in essential agreement have little to discuss except the sporadic individual variations from the norm. In the simple folk societies such is normally the case. In such a situation, knowledge is limited by the common traditions of the folk, the happenings of the immediate area and the occasional infiltration of alien lore. Today, in the great society, the common man has access to a multitudinous and detailed bulk of information. He has that portion of the accumulated learning of his culture to which he is exposed and the news of the day which is purveyed by newspaper and gossip, by pictures and motion pictures, by radio and all other means of communication. During the past generation, this news has expanded enormously, as to both the size of the geographic areas from which it is drawn and the scope and variety of its subject matter. Discussion is greatly intensified.

Upon this mass of information, the common man projects those scales of value with which he has been equipped. Standards limit his discussion to some extent. Certain topics are not discussible in some groups, although in our day everything is discussible somewhere. Where popularly accepted standards can be applied to the various items of information, there need be no discussion, as there is only one value or principle involved. There is no debate, no controversy. Hence, there is no opinion. An opinion is some expression on a controversial point. Opinion is some form of expression (verbal or other behavior); and it deals with the controversial (not with materials considered as proved or generally believed to be true).

In a period of rapidly changing standards, the range of opinion topics rapidly widens as values are less absolute. In the morning's newspaper, the reader comes upon two columns of news and a full page of pictures

1

dealing with a New York City suicide, who, by vacillating for ten hours on an exposed building ledge, became national news even before he jumped. The reader may express opinions on the ethical justification of suicide, on the mental normality or abnormality of a suicide, on the viciousness of the gaping spectators, on the methods used to dissuade the jumper, and the like. The reader is in the process of developing opinions on this and many other topics in the morning's paper. On innumerable subjects, he is asked to form opinions. Competitive appeals by various interest groups assail, distract and confuse him. He is admonished, persuaded and cajoled. In the thinking of the common man there is much confusion. Villagers, with the codes that were the product of the village, are engulfed in cities, where complex indoctrination confuses those trained to the slow pace of decision in agrarian communities. In the primary group of the family and in intimate association, man functions on the basis of the rules, the traditions of the folk culture and also of procedures developed in his own experience of association. These relations are carried on in a vital consensus in which the loves, hates, fears and sympathies are a common, oft-repeated pattern. He is accustomed to the development of opinions regarding variant behavior and thought.

In many of his secondary-group relationships in modern life, however, neither the patterns of the traditional culture nor his own experience offer sharp, clear-cut ways of life. Yet, under democracy, he is called on to develop opinions and make decisions. His fumblings in this field, his economic and political ineptitudes, his lack of grasp of essentials, his following of personal phantoms when he should be occupied with abstract realities make the common man a creature for the satirical thrusts of the more informed observer. Modern authoritarian rulers also express distrust of his capacity. As the number of secondary associations in which the average man is involved has increased, the breach has widened. And the mounting disdain of the intellectual is increasingly in evidence. The common man exhibits a preference for the opinion process and decision relating to personal and private problems and issues. He would "win friends and influence people." He would survey the problems of personal relationships and values. This has always been the despair of the political reformer under democracy. As man in the mass has been thrust into situations in which opinions and decisions about economic issues were required of him, the despair of the theorists has frequently been abject. In the rising tide of popular decision many saw the "revolt of the masses." The people were projecting personal and individual values upon the larger scene. Former President A. Lawrence Lowell of Harvard University recently wrote, "Truly the future has less to fear from individual than from cooperative selfishness." Yet that the common man, with guidance and adequate information, can be trained to function satisfactorily in the realm of public affairs is the premise of democracy. He should be properly trained under democratic education and then turned loose upon the sacred icons. The remainder of this volume will be concerned with the discussion of the opinion process in large publics. We shall note at least some of the elements involved in that process, thus indicating some of the resources and liabilities of large publics for realistic decisions.

THE MEANING OF PUBLIC OPINION

There has been little agreement among sociological theorists, political scientists and social psychologists on the exact meaning of "public opinion." The term has been loosely used, sometimes in reference to widespread beliefs, "climate of opinion," consensus, the mores and the more settled convictions of a group; at times, to the process of developing opinions, as distinguished from the product; elsewhere, to statements which are the result of a reasoned, logical process as contrasted with those which have been arrived at by illogical means; and the like. We shall not attempt a historical résumé of the various meanings that commentators of differing schools of thought and of different periods have ascribed to this term.[1] Let us consider merely a few of the more important recent distinctions and definitions.

Our position is that opinion is any expression on a controversial topic. Public opinion results from the interaction of persons upon one another in any type of group. The opinion process occurs in groups varying in size from two to the largest number ever responding to common stimuli on a controversial issue. Publics are simply large groups. At any time there may be a prevailing or dominant view existing in a group, but there are also any number of other opinions maintained by the members of that

[1] In spite of the widespread use of the term "public opinion" during the past two centuries, there is surprisingly little analytic writing concerning its meaning, its constituent elements and the opinion process. For outstanding discussions in different periods, see: Mackinnon, W., *On the Rise, Progress, and Present State of Public Opinion in Great Britain*, Saunders and Otley, London, 1828; Bagehot, W., *Physics and Politics*, Chap. 5, 1872; Thompson, G. C., *Public Opinion and Lord Beaconsfield*, vol. I, pp. 29–40, 1886; Tarde, G., *L'Opinion et la foule*, 1901; Dicey, A. V., *Law and Public Opinion in England*, 1905; Bryce, J., *The American Commonwealth*, vol. II, pp. 261–403, 1889; Cooley, C. H., *Social Organization*, Chaps. 12, 13, 34, 1909, *Social Process*, Chap. 31, 1918; Lowell, A. L., *Public Opinion and Popular Government*, 1913, *Public Opinion in War and Peace*, 1923; King, C. L., *Public Opinion as Viewed by Eminent Political Theorists*, University of Pennsylvania Lectures, 1916; Lippmann, W., *Public Opinion*, 1922; Dewey, J., *The Public and Its Problems*, 1927; Carr, L. J., in Cooley, Angell and Carr, *Introductory Sociology*, Chaps. 22, 23, 24, 1933; Harris Foundation Lectures, *Public Opinion and World Politics*, University of Chicago Press, 1933; Wilson, F. G., *The Elements of Modern Politics*, Chaps. 10, 11, 1936; Bauer, W., "Public Opinion," *Encyclopaedia of the Social Sciences*, 12: 669–674.

group. There may or may not be a majority expressing a common opinion. The opinion process is the interaction occurring within a group on a controversial issue. The group opinion is the product of that interaction, the resultant expression including all the positions maintained by members of the group. This group opinion is not static but is in flux as new elements are introduced into the discussion. The opinion process in the group may be a reasoned, logical analysis and procedure. In large groups it is more often involved in sentiment, emotion, casual impressions and various illogical elements. Let us amplify these statements.

Opinion is expressed through some of the means of communication. On the basis of the expressed opinion one may and does assume attitudes, mind-sets, beliefs and other subjective states, but the opinion is expression on a controversial issue. "There can be no such thing as opinion without stating the content of the opinion in language form. The response of individuals to this common stimulating situation may be either verbal or nonverbal. It may, for example, be a grimace, gesture or emotional expression. This reaction, however, must be capable of being readily translated into words, such, for example, as expressions of agreement or approval."[1] The trucking code of a few years ago placed a license fee on all vehicles engaged in paid transportation. A Maine farmer, who also pushed a wheelbarrow from the depot to the post office in his little town, objected to this tax. What did he do? "He didn't evade. He didn't chisel. He didn't grouse much. He went to the authorities, paid his $3 in three well-worn greenbacks, and took out a trucking license for his wheelbarrow. He may not have known what 'reductio ad absurdum' meant but he knew how to do it. Having fastened his license to his wheelbarrow, and paraded it twice daily before the village, he hit upon a better scheme. His little daughter has a trained rooster. Hitched to a cart, the rooster draws two or three letters daily to a neighbor. My friend tried to take out a rooster license under the Trucking Code."[2] Opinion may achieve expression in any understandable and translatable act. Opinion expression is behavior. But this does not mean that opinions can be adequately described in behavioristic terms. By no means. Any fruitful examination of expression of opinion must relate the opinions to the subjective states out of which the opinions have emerged. "The extreme behaviorist assumes that there is only one way in which physical processes can be studied, namely through outward action. Now an object that is immediately presented may produce outward activity without either understanding or belief."[3] If ten people say that they do not like Italians, that is an expression of opinion. We may record that

---

[1] Allport, F. H., "Toward a Science of Public Opinion," *Pub. Opin. Quar.*, 1: 1: 14.
[2] Canham, E. D., in the *Chris. Sci. Mon.*, July 11, 1934.
[3] Eaton, R. M., *Symbolism and Truth*, p. 25, 1925.

expression on any type of detailed test that has been created. But the reasons for that dislike may be so varied and diverse that in a changing situation one of those individuals may change his opinion statement within an hour, whereas another holds to his position for a lifetime. The record of opinion statements is a record of behavior, but that is simply a starting point for the description of the opinion process. To proclaim, as does the behaviorist, that he is concerned only with overt verbal behavior in this field is to depart very far from science, which is the description of reality.

An opinion is an expression about a controversial point. ⟩"An opinion may be defined as the acceptance of one among two or more inconsistent views which are capable of being accepted by a rational mind as true."[1] It may thus be distinguished from a demonstration or proof. There are certain relations, though fewer than commonly supposed, that are generally accepted as proved. A child may give a unique answer to the problem of three times three. But his answer is in error; it is not an opinion. It is variation from established truth. Now, of course, almost all our knowledge is relative, but that residue which is generally accepted at any given time is not the subject of opinion. In addition to the generally accepted demonstrations and proofs, there are those propositions which, within the limits of any group, are accepted as unquestionable. These, too, are not the subject of opinion within that group. Opinions emerge at controversial points, when the old, accepted patterns break down, when doubt has risen, when the tenets of any group are questioned. When there is an awareness of discrepancy, the situation is defined, solutions are presented and opinions are formed.

Opinion may be defined as contrasted to the noncontroversial, but what is a *public* opinion? This is a controversial concept. There are many opinions on public opinion. And real issues are involved. What constitutes a public? In sociological speculation, "public" is made synonymous with "group." In all groups there are some controversial issues. Therefore, the opinion process is operative to a greater or less extent in all groups, from a primary group engaged in gossip and discussion to an international organization. The limits of a group are defined in terms of those who participate therein. "In defining the public as those persons who have the right of participation, we have reached, perhaps, a reasonable interpretation. Such a view leaves the problems of the formation and expression of opinion in psychological terms to the further discussion of opinion itself."[2] But what is *the* public opinion? There is no agreement among the theorists on the nature of the public opinion. The Round Table on the Measurement of Opinion of the American Political Science Association, after agreeing that opinion need

[1] Lowell, A. L., *Public Opinion in War and Peace*, p. 12, 1923.
[2] Wilson, *op. cit.*, p. 247.

not be the result of rational process, that it need not include an awareness of choice and that it must be sufficiently clear or definite to create a disposition to act upon it under favorable circumstances (all of which are statements on the nature of opinion), state as further and undecided problems, "(1) whether there is or must of necessity be a single public opinion or whether there may be a number of public opinions on a given question; (2) whether opinion is public because of the subject matter to which it relates or of the kind of persons who hold it; (3) what part of the public must concur to make it public opinion; and (4) must there be acquiescence by those who do not agree?"[1]   From the viewpoint of public as group, a public opinion is the expression of all those members of a group who are giving attention in any way to a given issue.   The public opinion includes the expression of the majority (if there be a majority) and the minority or all the minorities at any given time.   If the differences are so great and persistent that the minorities will not acquiesce to function with the majority, then there is no public—there are several publics.   Thus Dr. Lowell quite properly points out that the "opinion of a majority is not always public."[2]   Publics exist only when the constituent members will function together.   In order to have public opinion, "A majority is not enough, and unanimity is not required, but the opinion must be such that while the minority may not share it, they feel bound, by conviction not by fear, to accept it; and if democracy is complete the submission of the minority must be given ungrudgingly."[3]

There is another problem as to the nature of the public opinion, a haunting and confusing subject for the social theorist.   F. H. Allport has referred to it as the personification of public opinion, the personification of the public and the "group fallacy" of the public.   "Public opinion, according to this fiction, is thought of as some kind of being which dwells in or above the group, and then expresses its view, upon various issues as they arise.   The 'voice of public opinion,' or the 'public conscience,' are metaphors of this sort. . . . A related fiction is one in which the notion of a collective, super-organic being is applied not to the opinion process itself, but to the public which holds it. . . . Somewhat less mystical, but equally uncritical, is the usage of those who renounce the idea of a collective entity or group mind, holding that when they say 'the public' they mean individuals; but who, nevertheless, go on employing such phrases as 'the public wants so and so' or 'the country voted dry.' "[4]

[1] *Am. Pol. Sci. Rev.*, 19: 126.

[2] Lowell, A. L., *Public Opinion and Popular Government*, pp. 4–10, 1913.

[3] *Ibid.*, p. 15.

[4] Allport, *op. cit.*, pp. 7 and 8.   For a critical discussion of this problem, see Allport's article and also Lundberg, G. A., "Public Opinion from a Behavioristic Viewpoint," *Am. Jour. Sociol.*, 36: 387–405.

We have here the old problem of the "individual" and "society," which has been recast in myriad forms. The controversy has often become heated conflict, and the intensity of academic jousting has sometimes appeared to be maintained by what seemed suspiciously like a willful misinterpretation of terms and concepts. One form in which the dichotomy has been stressed is that of individual and group opinion. Public opinion, it is maintained, is something more than individual opinions. It is true that there is continuity of habitual ideas, of beliefs and standards. These are brought to bear on each issue as it arises. But the process occurs in individuals. Is not public opinion simply the individual opinions which exist and are expressed after some form of interaction on the issue before that particular public or group? Otherwise, we go into some form of mysticism about group mind, group soul, the collective unconscious of the psychoanalysts, and the like. In the public there is a great body of traditional beliefs, feelings and ideas. There are also habitual customs, practices and various types of behavior. These have continuity as they are incorporated into the responses of successive generations of individuals. They are superindividual only in the sense that the particular individual did not create them.

Great confusion in terms has occurred because "public opinion" has been used by one group of writers as a label for the content of group opinion (that is, the statements of all the members of the group at any given time), whereas another group of writers refers to public opinion as the process of opinion formation.[1] C. H. Cooley wrote, "Public opinion, if we wish to see it as it is, should be regarded as an organic process, and not merely as a state of agreement about some question of the day."[2] Certainly statements of opinion can be understood only in relation to the interaction that preceded the statement, but, as a matter of labels, we shall designate the formation of opinions as "opinion process." But on active issues, individual opinions may change rapidly. There is constant flux. A record of opinion at a given time may be true only momentarily. To make a record by means of opinion tests simply freezes the process. It is as if I could suddenly freeze the water and the fish in a bowl before me. It might be noted that a number of fish had their mouths open in an identical manner. I count and classify mouth positions. All sense measurements inform me that the fishes' mouths are identical. Yet, on return to fluidity, one fish takes a gulp of water, one a gulp of food and two snap at each other's tails. The opinion process is the subject of the bulk of this volume, but most specifically of Chap. XIII on Opinion Change.

[1] Carr, L. J., has stated this issue clearly in "Public Opinion as a Dynamic Concept," *Sociol. Soc. Res.*, 13: 18–30.

[2] Cooley, C. H., *Social Process*, p. 378, 1918.

Beliefs and Consensus

There are relatively stable beliefs which, at any given time, are not involved in the opinion process. A state of agreement following an opinion controversy is a consensus. It is a relatively quiescent period in the flux of social change. Every existing belief has been questioned at some time in the history of a culture. "Every consensus is a won agreement; to realize it as such requires a background of awareness of disagreements from which the harmony has emerged."[1] And, of course, large publics are not commonly aware of the history of their cherished beliefs and so regard them as universally true and self-evident.

A consensus may be achieved within groups widely differing as to size, maturity and the degrees of complexity of their psychological processes. Experts achieve consensus on theories. The history of ideas illustrates the starts and stops of the professional thinker. Publics reach consensus on ethical, political and economic issues. Even large publics may be in substantial agreement. There is then consensus of the type that Montesquieu designated as the *esprit général*, that Rousseau spoke of as the *volonté générale* and that the English theorists called "public will." The ethical consensus which W. G. Sumner labeled the "mores" are states of agreement and are outside the realm of opinion. Among the bulk of the inhabitants of Mississippi, a public opinion on intermarriage between whites and blacks cannot be said to exist. The subject is not discussible; it is part of the mores. The nineteenth-century social theorists quite generally included both the materials on which consensus existed and also the controversial items as part of the general content of public opinion. A. V. Dicey writes of public opinion as a body of convictions and beliefs and prejudices, as well as of what he calls crosscurrents due to controversy. But we may logically distinguish between consensus and opinion. Plato confined opinion to that which is subject to change. Opinions are developed about admittedly controversial topics, whereas, in belief or consensus, "an idea fills the mind to the exclusion of possible alternatives."

In modern life, awareness of other and conflicting beliefs has made for relativism. Certainty has been extensively undermined. The enlargement of communication first brought the variant beliefs, codes and standards to the attention of the professional thinker and then, to some extent, popularized such knowledge. The areas of certainty were narrowed. "In order to show the vanity of all efforts to found rationally an absolute and universal morality, the varieties and contradictions of moral rules actually recognized at various times and in various societies had to be systematically described."[2] At the close of the nineteenth century such

---

[1] Kallen, H. M., "Consensus," *Ency. Soc. Sci.*, 4: 225.
[2] Znaniecki, F., *The Method of Sociology*, p. 113, 1934.

comparative studies were made in large numbers. The results were partly popularized. Thus, the field of opinion widens, and the sphere of consensus diminishes.

PUBLIC OPINION AND THE AVERAGE

Will the resultant expressions of opinion, which appear after the opinion process in any group, be the average of individual opinions at the time when the process started? Obviously not, for the opinion process has introduced new elements; the convincing opinions of the better informed, the prejudices and emotional responses aroused during the interaction, the injection of personal prestige into the process, and the like. Will the result be above or below the average, as measured by realistic judgment and conclusions? In the absence of relatively exact, analytic interpretations of the opinion process in large publics, the answer will depend on the faith of the commentator in the capacity of the common man. A century ago, W. A. Mackinnon declared, "Public opinion may be said to be that sentiment on any given subject which is entertained by the best informed, most intelligent, and most moral persons in the community, which is gradually spread and adopted by nearly all persons of any education or proper feeling in a civilized state."[1] C. H. Cooley states, "There is a widespread, but as I believe a fallacious, idea that the public thought or action must in some way express the working of an average or commonplace mind, must be some kind of a mean between the higher and lower intelligences making up the group. . . . A little common-sense and observation will show that the expression of a group is nearly always superior, for the purpose in hand, to the average capacity of its members."[2] But another group of writers, in depreciation of the judgment and capacity of the common man, maintains that the opinions of the wiser members of a society are usually ignored and that the level of majority opinion and decision is very low indeed.

PUBLIC OPINION, REASON AND THE ILLOGICAL

Confidence in the power of reason has waxed and waned throughout the history of thought. Rationalism "aims to regulate individual and social life in accordance with principles of reason and to eliminate as far as possible or to relegate to the background everything irrational."[3] P. A. Sorokin isolates the upward movements of rationalism as from 540 to 450 B.C.; the second half of the fifth and first half of the fourth century B.C. (Socrates, Plato, Aristotle); about 200 B.C.; about 80 B.C.; the twelfth, thirteenth and first half of the fourteenth centuries; the first

---

[1] Mackinnon, *op. cit.*, p. 15.
[2] Cooley, C. H., *Social Organization*, pp. 123, 124, 1909.
[3] Groethuysen, B., "Rationalism," *Ency. Soc. Sci.*, 13: 113.

half of the fifteenth century; the sixteenth and first half of the seventeenth centuries; and the end of the eighteenth and beginning of the nineteenth centuries.[1]   Faith in the capacity of the common man to form his opinions on the basis of rational principles has fluctuated in like manner.   During the last period of rationalism the great societies were emerging.   Social and psychological thinking of the late eighteenth and early nineteenth centuries was dominated by the concept of reason and by the assumption that man is a rational animal.   In politics there was the emergence of democracy and faith in the rational man.   Economic assumptions posited rational choices, and philosophy assumed the calm deliberation of goods and ills.   Rational capacity was believed to be inherent in the individual, to be cultivated by education and enlightenment.   The optimism of the nineteenth century was based upon this faith.   Knowledge could solve everything, and with industry it was yours.

Then another "flight from reason" began.   Darwinian evolution linked the species, and there was no reason to believe that instinctive drives might not dominate reason in man.   Psychology was providing a description of man's thinking that made the doctrines of "rational man" appear to be speculative wishful thinking.   It was increasingly assumed that the older breed of political and economic theorists had erred in regarding man as a purely rational being.   In the twentieth century the flight from reason gathered momentum.   In literature, an increasing number of influential writers rejected the primacy of the intellect and denied, as Aldous Huxley said, "that there is an intrinsic superiority in mental, conscious, voluntary life over physical, intuitive, instinctual life."   The cult of D. H. Lawrence was built upon the assumptions about deep, instinctive drives, the voice of the blood, the final reality of deep-seated, primal, emotional urges.   Considerations of orderly and logical analysis were supplanted by emphasis upon nerves, instinct, emotion, intuitive sensual memories, and the like.   Psychology disparaged the amount and thoroughness of rational and logical thinking.   Emotional drives were emphasized, the instinct theories proliferated, behaviorism and conditioning were extensively described, emotional linkages with verbal and personal symbols were illustrated, the tricks of the mind in rationalizing and stereotyping were gleefully exhibited, the unconscious was uncovered and other psychological partial descriptions were paraded.[2]   The political theorist applied a portion of these doctrines to political functioning and public opinion.   The first incisive analysis was Graham Wallas's *Human Nature in Politics* (1908).   His thesis was that "political thinking in the past has assumed a degree of intellectuality in mankind that mankind

---

[1] Sorokin, P. A., *Social and Cultural Dynamics*, vol. II, Chap. 1, 1937.

[2] The psychological contributions to the understanding of the opinion process are reviewed in Chaps. IV and V.

never really possessed. The human nature with which he is concerned is the pre-rational and non-rational behavior which complicates political processes everywhere."[1] Harold Laski declared that formal doctrine and popular opinion were rationalizations of deeper drives in men. These rationalizations were the orientations of each era to the new set of living conditions. There were many emulators of such writings.

Political practitioners provided anti-rationalistic and anti-intellectualistic ideologies in support of the new authoritarian states organized about Fascist, Nazi and Communist doctrines. There was a remarkable growth of bigotry and intolerance, of avowed faith in violence and of the consciously organized management of opinion through propagandas that promulgated conclusions and depreciated appeals to reason. There was a widespread decline in the prestige of reason.

During the past fifty years there has been a vast increase in organized special pleading. Reform groups were perfecting their techniques of popular appeal. Conflicting doctrines were seeking a hearing. Commercial advertising was creating markets for the distribution of the growing number of consumers' goods. Newspapers and other media of communication fought for circulations. All of these showed by their practices that their directors had decreasing faith in the effectiveness of rational appeals. In commercial advertising, there is a score of attempts to influence buying by emotional appeals to one analysis of the quality of the product. Commenting on these trends, a philosopher states, "If, in the name of reason, you summon a man to alter his fundamental purposes—to pursue, say, the general happiness rather than his own power—you will fail, and you will deserve to fail, since reason alone cannot determine the ends of life."[2] We shall examine the different facets of this problem in the various chapters of this book. Those who maintain that the only proper way to influence a human being is to encourage him to think for himself and who have faith in his capacity to do so effectively are in combat with the pragmatic practitioners of power by any means.

THE IDEOLOGY

Popular opinions do not exist as separate, disjointed, unrelated items. Although the opinions of the common man are by no means totally consistent, there are underlying systems of thought. During the past century, general popular thought systems have been increasingly referred to as "ideologies." Confusion and glaring inconsistencies have become evident in popular thought and action as the common man has had access to conflicting ideologies in religion, politics and economics.

[1] Wallas, G., *Human Nature in Politics*, p. 21, 1908.
[2] Russell, B., "Power over Opinion," *Sat. Rev. Lit.*, Aug. 13, 1938, p. 13.

A consideration of the life of an individual, a people or an age must begin with an inventory of its systems of thought. There are always complexes of popular convictions and beliefs that are fundamental and decisive for the life of a time. Underlying such popular thought are the systems provided by the professional philosopher, theologian, political theorist and economist.[1] When both the professional thinker and the common man considered such beliefs as emanations from God, from nature or from underlying, immutable truth, they believed that the statements of their opponents or enemies were lies, errors, misinterpretations and misconceptions resulting from the activities of the devil or from the faulty perceptual or conceptual apparatus of misguided souls. There were absolutes, and the righteous and favored people received them. All others were in error and in some way personally responsible for their derelictions from the truth or for their failures to achieve it. On the other hand, ideology implies a system of ideas related to the life situations of its creators. As such it is changing, relative and nonabsolute. "The ideas expressed by the subject are thus regarded as functions of his existence. This means that opinions, statements, propositions and systems of ideas are not taken at their face value, but are interpreted in the light of the life situation of the one who expresses them. It signifies further that the specific character and life situation of the subject influence his opinions, perceptions, and interpretations."[2] In the ideology, certain distorted and partially untrue conceptions of persons are regarded as legends, certain theories as myths, and postulates and assumptions as "guiding fictions."

Such a relative conception of human thought could not develop until very recently in the history of thought. The sociology of thought remains a startling view to many social theorists, and the concept has scarcely penetrated to the common man, except in the form of Marxian dialectics that brand opposing doctrines as class ideologies. Nor is it a comfortable or comforting doctrine to masses of mankind who still prefer to quest for the absolutes with self-styled infallible guides. In an Oxford Group Movement, they quest for absolute honesty, absolute purity, absolute unselfishness and absolute love. Hitler, Mussolini and other dictators who have tinkered together certain dogmatic absolutes for the masses have proved once more that there is a persistent popular cry of, "What shall I believe to be saved?" Nor is the quest only among the simple-minded. An Oxford scholar recently declared to Wickham Steed, "I believe in the State Absolute, and demand Absolute values."[3] Hegel has

---

[1] Prof. Sorokin, *op. cit.*, vol. II, has provided a study, largely quantitative, of the fluctuations and trends in such systems.

[2] Mannheim, K., *Ideology and Utopia* (English trans.), p. 50, 1936. Quoted by permission of Harcourt, Brace & Company.

[3] *Chris. Sci. Mon.*, Mar. 24, 1934.

cast a long shadow over large sectors of modern thought. As A. N. Whitehead has written, "Man has always sought the perfect, harmonious and orderly universe."[1] And John Dewey notes, "There is something deep within human nature itself which pulls toward settled relationships. Inertia and the tendency toward stability belong to emotions and desires as well as to masses and molecules."[2] But, in spite of the desire for absolutes and the "quest for certainty," the relative nature of thought systems and the relationships between thought and group interests become increasingly apparent in our diversified world.

The concept of ideology arose in western Europe when various popular thought systems were obviously in conflict as religious, political and finally economic controversies engaged the attention of the common man. Suspicion of the quality of the adversary's thinking found justification in branding that thinking as "ideological," that is, as partial, incomplete and limited by his time and place, his station and class. The seventeenth century had a phrase, "climate of opinion." It was beginning to be recognized that ideas had a setting, and that "whether arguments command assent or not depends less upon the logic that conveys them than upon the climate of opinion in which they are sustained."[3] Bacon wrote of the "idola," the idols, phantoms, preconceptions, the illusions of the populace. These erroneous notions were derived sometimes from "human nature," sometimes from society or tradition.[4] Glimmerings of the concept of ideology were appearing in various writings. Montesquieu, in the narrow world of the eighteenth century and with scanty knowledge of civilizations other than the European and the Classical, tried to show the trends of civilization and to make people conscious of the fact that men's mentalities were conditioned by the systems in which they lived. Social organization was becoming more intricate; classes and interest groups were arising. Not only was the "thought of the palace one thing and that of the public square another,"[5] as Machiavelli had noted, but there were also various groups with diverse ways of thinking. "The modern conception of ideology was born when Napoleon, finding that this group of philosophers was opposing his imperial ambitions, contemptuously labelled them 'ideologists.' Thereby the word took on a derogatory meaning which, like the word 'doctrinaire,' it has retained to the present day. . . . What is depreciated is the validity of the adversary's thought because it is regarded as unrealistic."[6] The derogatory connotations of

[1] Whitehead, A. N., *Science and the Modern World*, p. 230, 1925.
[2] Dewey, J., *The Public and Its Problems*, p. 213, 1927.
[3] Becker, C. L., *The Heavenly City of the Eighteenth-century Philosophers*, p. 5, 1932.
[4] Mannheim, *op. cit.*, p. 55.
[5] *Ibid.*, p. 56.
[6] *Ibid.*, p. 64. Quoted by permission of Harcourt, Brace & Company.

ideology were furthered in the Marxian writings. Marx discussed religion, law and systems of thought as ideologies beneficial to the capitalists. Marxian thought placed emphasis upon class position and class interests in thought.

But ideology was not only an intellectual weapon but also a valuable conceptual tool. Thought is conditioned by time and place and by group interests. Certainly this is not equally true of all kinds of thought. Scientific thought, theological thought and philosophy have their own histories and deep roots. But popular thought on political and economic issues is especially ideological. And class interests are apparent. If in the United States a scientific report of governmental experts on the breeding conditions of frogs is ridiculed by a portion of the press as the study of the "love life of the frog," and the activities of unemployed white-collar workmen engaged under government auspices in gathering statistical information on a variety of social relations is "boondoggling," whereas a three-year investigation of shaving sponsored by soap manufacturers at Mellon Institute resulting in the conclusion that "preparation of the face is important" is reported as a scientific achievement, it is evident that an ideology is involved. When the psychologist S. D. Porteus, in giving tests to Australian primitives, refused to help them answer the questions and solve the problems of the tests, they were aggrieved and resentful. Accustomed to a communal and cooperative life (and he had been initiated as a member of the tribe), they resented his emphasis on individual achievement. The climate of opinion differed. Values in a culture provide a frame of reference for thinking. In Spain, the Jesuits have left marks on the national character. Indirectness and cleverness are esteemed in conversation; frankness is considered unpardonable naïveté. It is difficult for an American or European, with his conceptions of sovereignty and of executive power, to grasp the psychological attitude of the Japanese people toward their mikado. There is no parallel, no Western analogy. The ideologies differ. The concept of ideology is a useful way of thinking about popular complexes and systems of ideas. As relativism in the description of thinking, it illumines many otherwise unintelligible differences between classes, interest groups and entire cultures.

A popular ideology must be simple and must be adapted to simple mentalities. As a public creed it must be implemented with symbols of a readily comprehensible type. "Thus it is that most of man's behavior is symbolic of the various characters which he assumes. This is true not only of his behavior as a warrior or a priest, but extends even to such practical concerns as eating and drinking, with their little rituals of highly decorated tables and service. The words, ceremonies, theories, and principles and other symbols which man uses make him believe in the

reality of his dreams and thus give purpose to his life."[1] So the ideology
is couched in symbols to which the believer may respond. Mussolini
writes, "There must be music and banners to kindle enthusiasm. The
mob is loose and dispersed as a shoal of fish until they're well disciplined
and led. They don't need to know; but the faith that moves mountains
must flash from the orator's soul into their own, like the radio that can
excite the world with a mighty thought. Really the tendency of our
modern folks to believe is . . . quite past belief."[2] The ideology is
expressed in personal symbols, emblems and language forms.[3] The uses
of slogans, catchwords, cries and other popular verbal symbols are
meaningful in their particular contexts. The associated emotional
responses are usually ill-understood by those of another time who may
attempt to understand the potency of these phrases. Indeed, it is with
great difficulty that we achieve any true appreciation of past symbols or of
those of an opposing ideology. In a religious, fear-ridden public of the
seventeenth century, the cry of popery aroused emotional responses which
today can be understood only by the meticulous historian. When words
are redefined and used as symbols of an ideology, confusion is compounded.
The Marxian made "bourgeois" synonymous with "capitalist." But
this term, originally meaning "city dweller," had come to mean "middle-
class citizen," as opposed to nonurban elements, the aristocracy, and the
peasants, before Marxian jargon made an epithet of it. The puerilities,
the vacuousness, the ambiguities and the absurd simplifications of popular
ideological symbols alienate the intellectual analyst. In satiric mood,
H. D. Lasswell outlines the specifications for an American *Das Kapital*.

(1) The title must be a slogan. The title *Capital* has become a diagnosis
and by implication a prescription; for if capital is to blame for our plight, capital
must be crushed. An example of what to avoid is V. Pareto's *Treatise on Sociology*, regardless of the brilliance of analysis. (2) The book must be thick.
Thickness conveys authoritativeness and discourages reading by the masses who
must revere the book as a symbol. (3) The book must be systematic and
quantitative ("scientific"). The analytic pattern of thinking has now become
so current in society that the volume must appear to possess imposing categories
and sub-categories. It must be studded with charts, graphs, tables, footnotes,
and other impressive impedimenta of exactitude. (4) The vocabulary must be
more than analytic—it must be ethical, legalistic (constitutional), technological,
sporting, individualistic, nationalistic. (5) The selected "facts" must allude
mainly to American experience. (6) The key words and the style must be
invidious. Terms like "unearned increment," "surplus value," "leisure class"
can be handled with appropriate innuendo. (7) The volume as a whole should

[1] Arnold, T. W., *The Symbols of Government*, Preface, 1935. Quoted by permission
of Yale University Press.
[2] Mussolini, B., *Cur. Hist.*, 45: 4: 81.
[3] Personal symbols are discussed in Chap. VI, language symbols in Chap. IV.

be ambiguous, obscure, and somewhat contradictory. This facilitates the redefinition of the book to serve the purposes of the self-selected revolutionary elite. (8) The style must be dull, in order to reduce the danger that the work will be extensively read or that the illusion of comprehension should sprout too widely and too readily without aid of centralized interpreters. (9) The prescription should be activistic; join a specific organization, obey the revolutionary elite, prepare for revolutionary acts![1]

A political, religious or economic ideology is first inculcated by persuasion. If its principal tenets fulfill needs that are widespread, the ideology wins adherents. The political theories accepted at any time and place are those which promise fulfillment of the hopes and utilitarian interests of some class or group. After a system becomes dominant, as did the Roman Catholic church or the contemporary Fascist, Nazi and Communist doctrines, it is imposed by force. The viewpoints are crystallized into principles. Then violence, the venting of fierce partisan hatreds and the "liquidation" of those who espouse other principles ensue. Physical coercion may be used sincerely, ruthlessly, cruelly and without compunction. Afterward, a genuine belief may be engendered in the majority, making force unnecessary.

The relative nature of ideologies does not mean that some systems of thought are not superior to others as adaptations to reality or that we can comfortably find rest in irrationality and skepticism as to all popular thought. The thinking of large publics is conditioned by their time and culture, but the awareness that such is the case may provide a bulwark against the more extreme illusions. Adversaries may be understood. Fervid adherence to a particular ideology cuts communication and isolates the convert. Awareness of ideologies may restore communication. We must reiterate, moreover, that not all thinking can be considered ideological. In the final chapter of this volume we shall return to this problem.

[1] Lasswell, H. D., *World Politics and Personal Insecurity*, p. 219, 1935. Quoted by permission of the McGraw-Hill Book Company, Inc.

CHAPTER II

THE DEVELOPMENT OF PUBLIC OPINION

As a member of large publics, modern man has a mass of information about many facts, systems of ideas, fragments of information, ideologies and news. Most of this information is shallow, unrelated to any deep roots in integrated thought systems. It is predigested, simplified and served to him in catchwords and other simple symbols. A great deal of it is inaccurate. To a considerable extent it is a mental conglomerate, chaotic and transient. Much of his information is presented to him for a purpose, the furtherance of the interests of some organized group. There is great emphasis on publicity, some of it presumably in the public interest, such as publicity about government, income-tax returns, stock ownership, securities, and the like (although the campaigns for such publicity are by no means disinterested from the viewpoint of their proponents). Other types of publicity, advertising and propaganda are obviously in the interest of the sources from which they emerge. But in all cases there is a vast to-do about informing the general public. Today the struggle for power is conducted by interest groups implemented with the newer means of communication, the popular press, motion pictures and radio. Interest groups are more varied, better organized and very effective in winning large publics. They struggle with one another in a competitive attempt to inject their viewpoints in the various media of communication. It has been estimated that over one-half of the stories in an issue of a conservative newspaper emanated from a publicity agent or publicity organization.[1] Dictators meticulously organize propaganda bureaus, economic groups develop publicity organizations and individuals retain publicity agents to present their viewpoints and personality to large publics. How has this scramble for publicity come about? Why does it seem imperative to so many groups that they should have a public hearing? What changes in social organization have accompanied the rise of contemporary public opinion?

If we identify "public" with "group," it is evident that there are innumerable publics differing as to size, organization, methods of communication and systems of control and guidance existing therein. If we reserve the term "public" for the numerically larger groups, we still have an amazingly large number of publics organized about some common interest.

[1] Gruening, E., "Publicity," *Ency. Soc. Sci.*, 12: 701.

Elsewhere, we shall attempt to classify them.[1] The individual in modern society is a member of some, usually of numerous, large groups. He will have membership in some groups whose interests are partially antipathetic to those of other groups of which he is also a member. His expressions of opinion on the same issue may differ in various groups. Such inconsistent memberships have been described by F. H. Allport as due to the "partial inclusion" of the individual in his groups.[2] How has the individual become so atomized in his social relationships?

The term "public opinion" was coined in the late eighteenth century. It appeared at that time because large publics were coming into existence owing to the rapidly increasing populations; their geographic concentration in cities where large mobs, crowds and assemblages made possible the speeding-up of the opinion process; the development of the means of communication, especially of printing, by which tracts, pamphlets and posters could be duplicated in larger numbers; the increase in literacy. At the same time the importance of the individual citizen's opinions and decisions was emphasized, owing to the rise of rationalism and of political democracy. The enlightenment of public opinion became a creed, a faith and an objective. Public opinion was not a new phenomenon, but the theorists' preoccupation with the opinion processes of the masses emerged during the eighteenth century when there was the maximum confidence in the judgment of the common man.

In earlier times and in primitive and folk societies, innovations are usually dealt with by the application of customary rules, rather than by discussion and the formation of opinions. The mores, the beliefs, the consensus and the customary procedures are invoked. There is little of the dynamic opinion process. "There exist many communities in which public opinion—if by that term be meant speculative views held by the mass of the people as to the alteration or improvement of their institutions—can hardly be said to have any existence. The members of such societies are influenced by habits rather than thoughts."[3] Of course, there are great variations among types of primitive societies and of folk communities. Contemporary scholars must be much more cautious about making facile generalizations about "primitive peoples" than were those of a generation ago. Since 1900 the ethnologists have described primitive peoples of great variety in social organization. M. Mead has illustrated three types of primitive communities on the basis of the individual's opportunities for expressing opinion.[4] In the first, illustrated by the

[1] There are no satisfactory classifications of large publics. Such data as exist are presented in Chap. XVI.

[2] This is a central thesis in Allport, F. H., *Institutional Behavior*, 1933.

[3] Dicey, A. V., *Law and Public Opinion in England*, p. 3, 1905.

[4] Mead, M., "Public Opinion Mechanisms among Primitive Peoples," *Pub. Opin. Quar.*, 1: 3: 5–16.

Arapesh, the Andamanese, the Ojibway and the Eskimo, there is the maximum opportunity for the formation of individual opinion upon the issues of daily life. Personal opinion achieves expression in these groups, but Dr. Mead errs in identifying this type of personal opinion with the "public opinion" of the great societies. In these primitive groups there is no opinion process, no interaction with the resultant group opinion, comparable to the process in modern publics. In the second type, illustrated by the Iatmul people of New Guinea, there are clan, age and moiety groups within the tribe. Group attitudes are developed within these subdivisions, and these attitudes are applied to conflict situations. The attitudes which the individual acquires in one group may differ from those which are maintained by another group, and confusion ensues. But there is no public opinion in the sense of discussion on a controversial point. In the third type, illustrated by the Balinese, the rule of the general mores is relatively complete and all issues are decided by customary principles. There is no public-opinion situation. There are distinctions as between various primitive peoples in the range of personal-opinion expression. In whatever system exists, the individual is held within the limits of traditional expression. Among the Dionysiac Plains Indians, the individual could swagger, aggrandize his own accomplishments, tell unusual dream experiences and emphasize certain individual variations. Among the Apollonian cultures of the Southwest, the individual was expected to efface himself and proceed ceremoniously in most situations.[1] In any case, he was bound by the traditional values, and variation therefrom made him subject to the taunts, jeers and recriminations of his fellows. The deliberative judgment of groups, whether swayed by rational or irrational factors, but admitting new and alien values and arguments, is rare in the primitive and folk communities. They are swayed by custom and lack the comparative and relative habits of mind. They are static and tradition-bound cultures.

In the ancient civilizations, public opinion played some part, but the publics were limited in number and size, the mechanisms for expression of opinion were rudimentary and communication was limited. Among the early Hebrews, the institution of the prophets, who made direct appeals to crowds, canalized popular attitudes.[2] But there was little opportunity for popular discussion, and the role of the individual was that of a recipient of the supposedly revealed truth that the prophets trumpeted. However, among the Greeks, public opinion developed to an extent unequaled until modern times. By the sixth century B.C., "in their various struggles against aristocracy and tyranny as well as in their

---

[1] Benedict, R., *Patterns of Culture*, 1935.
[2] Read the fascinatingly vivid historical novel on Jeremiah, Werfel, F., *Hearken unto the Voice*, 1937.

reaction against the mystical otherworldliness of such cults as Orphism the aggressive citizenry of the towns, particularly Athens, developed an atmosphere of individualism conducive to the unhampered competition of opinions and ideas."[1] Publicity was emphasized and there were popular appeals to the masses. Of course, the masses did not include all people, but were composed of all citizens. In the fourth century B.C., there were approximately 120,000 adults, of whom 40,000 were free citizens, 25,000 unenfranchised free foreigners and 55,000 slaves. In the communal assemblies of the city states, the citizenry deliberated and reached joint decisions. There were also public speeches and the theater. "A new sort of people, these people of leisure and independent means, were asking questions, exchanging knowledge and views, developing ideas. So beneath the march of armies and the policies of monarchs, and above the common lives of illiterate and incurious men, we note the beginnings of what is becoming at last nowadays a dominant power in human affairs, the free intelligence of mankind."[2] There were terms with which to refer to opinion and the opinion process. "The Greek concepts *ossa, pheme,* or *nomos* were familiar in Athens and were even accorded on occasion a niche in the Hellenic pantheon."[3] Argumentative conversation developed. Rules of the game emerged for intellectual conversation and debate, consisting of assertions and questions and the taking of contrary positions. The art of dialectics was codified. Political and philosophical argument became fashionable. Public opinion emerged on controversial issues. But the size of the publics was small, and there was no belief in general equality—only a democracy of the elite.

The urban culture of the later Roman Empire gave scope for the opinion process. And the Romans came to speak of the *vox populi.* The wide-ranging conquests of Rome provided information about many peoples with their values, religions, economic and political systems. The size of the empire resulted in emphasis upon news. Hence the professional newsmongers, and in the later periods, the publications of the *Acta Diurna.* There was much to discuss, the culture was dynamic and the opinion process was stimulated.

Through the Middle Ages, with the diverse, scattered, small groups and agrarian communities and with cultures blanketed under a common religious ideology oriented toward revelation and the supernatural, there could be little of dynamic popular opinion. Rather, there were consensus and traditional mores. Ultimately, there was popular acquiescence in the forms of government and the religious hierarchy—not the support of popular opinion. Opinion emerges from the controversial. As Lord

---

[1] Bauer, W., "Public Opinion," *Ency. Soc. Sci.*, 12: 671.
[2] Beard, M., *On Understanding Women*, p. 102, 1933.
[3] Bauer, *op. cit.*, p. 669.

Bryce wrote, "In the earlier or simpler forms of political society public opinion is passive. It acquiesces in, rather than supports, the authority which exists, whatever its faults, because it knows of nothing better, because it sees no way of improvement, probably also because it is over-awed by some kind of religious sanction."[1]

The opinion process was vivified when, in the fifteenth century, printing was invented in Europe, the Reformation questioned clerical authority and emphasized the individual and arts, letters and science began to cast off the bonds of authoritarian revelation. Public opinion developed as larger groups became concerned with religious issues, political systems, relative values and with ideologies in general. And the new means of communication, printing, coupled with a slowly growing literacy, distributed the ideas. We must distinguish between the opinion process and the theorist's preoccupation with the opinion phenomena. The opinion process begins to ferment in the fifteenth century, although it was not until the eighteenth century that the term "public opinion" was created and the social theorists centered attention on the molding of this power for decision. The Enlightenment of the seventeenth and eighteenth centuries was the turning from the authority of divine revelation to the authority of reason and human understanding. When "natural reason" was posited, then individual opinions became important, and the theorists turned to an examination of the opinion process.

The rise of modern publics during the past four centuries is based upon certain material innovations and upon changes in social organization. The invention of printing, and later of the telegraph, telephone, photography, motion pictures and radio, provided systems of communication whereby the great societies could be woven together. In this sense, the printing press of necessity preceded democracy, popular education and the diffusion and animation of communication. Communication is the fundamental human institution in that it sets the limits of community size and by its nature affects all types of human association. Speech confined association to the limits of human migration and the voice; writing and printing freed man for association in larger and more diverse societies.[2] The increased organization of craft production and later of manufacturing, as well as of trading, brought about a growth of cities from the fifteenth century onward. As had been true in Greece and Rome,

---

[1] Bryce, J., *The American Commonwealth*, vol. II, p. 271, 1891.

[2] Some of the relations between communication and the opinion process are considered in Chap. III (Communication), Chap. IV (Psychological Processes and Opinion), Chap. V (Language), Chap. XIX (The Radio), Chap. XX (Motion Pictures), Chap. XXI (The Newspaper) and Chap. XXII (The Graphic Arts and Public Opinion).

the animation of the opinion process followed the urban massing of populations.[1]　Membership in street crowds, mobs, audiences and other urban groupings provided more numerous opportunities for interchange of information and news.　Varied discussion was physically possible. Impressions were multiplied, the city became a center of cultural diversity and mental flexibility was engendered.　But, fundamentally, the city provided the arena and through the physical propinquity of large masses of people the stage was set for gossip, rumor, discussion, speech making, the reading of posters and, in general, the animation of the opinion process. The trading, manufacturing and commercial activities of the city changed the class structure of society also.　And the emerging middle class was most influential in rejecting the ancient authoritarianism, in breaking down the medieval consensus and in providing a forum for the doctrines of the Enlightenment.

　　Of the nonmaterial factors that were most decisive in the beginnings of modern publics, the most important were the spread of literacy, the rise of a philosophy of rationalism and the assumption of man's natural reason, and the democratic ideal.　That the individual can listen and understand may suffice in the folk community, but that he can read the newspapers, periodicals, captions, directions, posters, bulletins, and the like, is requisite in the great society.　Widespread literacy is a modern phenomenon.　Protestantism, with its emphasis on the personal relationship between the individual and his God through Bible reading, gave the first great impetus to popular literacy.　The doctrine of natural rights, as it was propounded in the eighteenth century, gave the second great impulse to the teaching of the common people.　The nationalism of the nineteenth century, with the concomitant emphasis on welding together the culture of a nation, was the basis of the third great drive for mass literacy.[2]　In the seventeenth century few persons could read.　In the 1920's the percentage of illiteracy in the United States was 4.3 per cent; Mexico, 62.2; Brazil, 71.2; Argentina, 24.0.　At the same time in Europe, the rate for England, Switzerland, Sweden and Denmark was under 1 per cent; France, 8.0; Italy, 28.0; Spain, 42.9; the U.S.S.R., 42.3 per cent.　Most of these figures are for the population of ten years of age and over.[3]　Millions of people have gone from a life based on personal experiences to the larger world of vicarious experience through reading.

　　Faith in the possibility of an enlightened popular opinion developed with eighteenth-century rationalism.　Already in the seventeenth century we find Descartes declaring that "good sense" is the most widespread thing in the world.　Middle-class man had learned to exercise foresight

---

[1] The relation between spatial position and opinion is discussed in Chap. IX (The Geographic Distribution of Group Opinion).

[2] Poole, DeW. C., *Princeton Alumni Lectures*, 1936.

[3] Sullivan, H., "Literacy and Illiteracy," *Ency. Soc. Sci.*, 9: 522.

and to organize life rationally, and he projected this capacity upon all men.   Unrealistic theorizing about the rational man dominated the larger sector of eighteenth century thought.   Naturally the opinions of man in the mass were dignified and his capacity to achieve rational solutions cooperatively with his fellows became an article of faith.   The opinion process, if freely operative among masses of mankind, would produce truth and would arrive at rational decisions.   During the past century, the psychological depreciation of the common man's capacity for rational decisions, the emphasis on the fact that man's thinking on public issues is not a formal intellectual game but is conditioned by his cultural values, his group allegiances and prejudices, and an increasing emphasis on the limitations of the data that the general public usually has as a basis for decision have undermined the rationalistic assumptions.

The importance of the opinion process in large publics was further emphasized in the tenets of liberal democracy.   Freedom of opinion was made a preeminent value.   The great proponents of democratic government did not declare that public opinion was always right, but they did place faith in the ultimate soundness of popular judgments.[1]   That the masses, under democracy, have cultivated values of a low order has been declared with increasing frequency of late years, not only by dictators but also by philosophers and psychologists.[2]

Granting the inadequacy of popular decisions under modern democracy, an important school of political theorists has declared that the failure is due to a lack of an adequate supply of truthful news, in the absence of which no rational decisions are possible.   Walter Lippmann once wrote, "It may be bad to suppress a particular opinion, but the really deadly thing is to suppress the news."[3]   But as Mr. Lippmann matured, he expressed increasing doubts of the capacity of the common man, narrowed the fields in which he thought the general public could effectively function and stressed the importance of the selection, canalizing and interpretation of the news by well-intentioned individuals.   As he himself has been labeled the "Great Elucidator" on the basis of his explanations in his newspaper columns, we can assume that he considers his type of interpretation as a reputable sample of such mediated communication.[4]

[1] For statements on the role of public opinion in democracy, read: Cooley, C. H., *Social Organization,* Chaps. 11–18, 1909; Lowell, A. L., *Public Opinion and Popular Government,* 1913.

[2] See Ortega y Gasset, J., *The Revolt of the Masses* (English trans.), 1932; Martin, E. D., *The Conflict of the Individual and the Mass,* 1932.   For a summary of criticisms of public opinion in democracy, read Wilson, F. G., *Elements of Modern Politics,* Chap. 11, 1936.

[3] Lippmann, W., *Liberty and the News,* p. 64, 1920.

[4] Trace the evolution of W. Lippmann's ideas through *Liberty and the News,* 1920; *Public Opinion,* 1922; *The Phantom Public,* 1925; *The Good Society,* 1937.

But the achieving of an adequate supply of truthful news depends in large part upon men being equally interested in the results that news has on opinion. And they are not equally interested. As special interest groups increased during the nineteenth century, types of special pleading, one form of which has latterly been labeled "propaganda," became more common. The control of opinion became the objective of various religious, political, economic and reform groups. The propaganda of the modern authoritarian state is based upon the absolute control of formal news channels, upon censorship and upon the selection of news. In such a situation there is no possibility of truthful news. But within the liberal democracies various interest groups partially distort the news and the distribution of information. As the scramble for the markets for consumers' goods became increasingly intense from the late nineteenth century onward, economic groups called in the aid of advertising, publicity and propaganda. There are no equally interested organizations to provide the consumer with more impartial information. As reform groups increased in number during the past fifty years and became vigorous and effective in the peddling of their particularistic moral, economic or political panaceas, they leaned heavily upon modern publicity methods. There are usually no equally interested opposing groups to correct their statements and implement the public with opposing arguments.[1] But the answer is not less but more organization—the organization of publics now diffuse, chaotic and amorphous. The organization of opposing groups and preferably, where possible, the dissemination of more impartial information are the only answer within the framework of democracy. In many cases, a few tentative opposing statements of fact or argument would elicit such a response that the heart of the distortion would be laid bare. Calvin said, "I know by their roaring I have hit them right." Latterly there have been some roars from advertisers and other special pleaders. In the case of many types of special pleading, it is not necessary for the opposition to have so large a publicity budget nor to make so extended an appeal as the special pleaders. There are many questions that, if once asked, are difficult to overcome. They spread by all sorts of informal means of communication.

It is evident that popular opinion has been considered increasingly important during the past century. All types of governments attempt to manipulate the opinions of their citizens and those of other countries. Economic groups depend upon the convincing of large publics as to the quality of the goods that are purveyed and upon the creation of good will. Many types of special interest groups strive for a following. Through

---

[1] Material on Special Interest Groups is presented in Chap. XVI, on Censorship in Chaps. XIV and XV and on Propaganda and The Art of Propaganda in Chaps. XVII and XVIII.

their hired publicity agents, societal leaders and notorious personages attempt to create their legends or to explain their behavior, attitudes and purposes to those sectors of the great society which they consider important for their purposes. None of these leaders would publicly subscribe to the Marquis de Sade's cynical statement that "it is a danger to love men, a crime to enlighten them," but, in the pursuit of personal and group objectives, true popular enlightenment would be inconvenient. However, much of the confusion is unintended. As the late Prof. Cooley stated, "Most of the harm in society is done with the elbows, not with the fists."

The problem becomes one of values. Is the objective the unity of mass opinion for the furtherance of some societal institution, from the state on down to a minor interest group? Or is the preeminent value the development of the individual's psychological experience through his having access to a rich and stimulating diversity of fare? Is it possible to achieve a sufficient unity for the successful organization of the economic and political activities of the modern great society without regimentation of popular opinion? Modern communication provides the means for either course.

CHAPTER III

COMMUNICATION

"It is the nature of art to build languages, of which the verbal is but one. In sound, color, form and motion we beget evolving incarnations in which the human spirit can live and grow."[1]

"Many shall run to and fro, and knowledge shall be increased."[2]

Underlying all social process and all societal forms is the transfer of meaning between individuals. Social life can exist only when meaningful symbols are transferred from individual to individual. Group activities of any sort are impossible without a means of sharing experiences. In the terminology of the social studies, the process of transmitting meaningful symbols between individuals is designated "communication."[3] As Cooley has stated, "By communication is meant the mechanism through which human relations exist and develop—all the symbols of the mind, together with the means of conveying them through space and preserving them in time. It includes the expression of the face, attitude and gesture, the tones of the voice, words, writing, printing, railways, telegraphs, telephones and whatever else may be the latest achievement in the conquest of space and time."[4] Communication is the fundamental social process in that the way in which meanings are transmitted must inevitably affect all other social processes and the resultant forms, folkways, mores and institutions. Public opinion, among other social processes, is affected by the communication methods in many ways, but most fundamentally in the size of the groups that may be involved and the distribution of these groups in space. Because of their face-to-face speech and gesture methods of transmitting symbols, the simpler primitive people can focus attention, discuss, and carry on other aspects of the opinion process only within small groups and in limited geographic areas. Owing to the invention of new forms of communication, the radio, telegraph, telephone and television, the attention area[5] of a contemporary

[1] Cooley, C. H., *Life and the Student*, p. 137.
[2] Daniel, 12: 4.
[3] Willey, M. M., and Rice, S. A., *Communication Agencies and Social Life*, p. 6, 1933.
[4] Cooley, C. H., *Social Organization*, p. 51, 1909. Quoted by permission of Charles Scribner's Sons.
[5] Term used by Lasswell, H. D., *World Politics and Personal Insecurity*, p. 186, 1935.

radio-listening urbanite may be practically world-wide and, at least for special interests, some of his discussion groups may be international if not world-wide in area. The attention area of the newspaper reader, at least for certain types of news such as the particularly atrocious murder, an unusual incident in the romantic quest, trade news or believe-it-or-not curiosities of behavior, is almost world-wide in scope.

The methods of communication include all the ways whereby meaning may be transferred from individual to individual. These range from the most rudimentary of gestures, ill-defined and vague, to the most elaborate deaf-mute codes; from the crudest pictograph to the most precise notations of mathematical symbolism; from the most spontaneous cry to which meaning is attached to the most elaborately defined scientific terminology. These meanings may be understood within groups of varying size from the two schoolgirls whose special meanings for particular words give a uniqueness to their association, to those versed in the universal codes of mathematics, a special science or a world language. The methods of communication may be classified in terms of primary processes, those fundamental techniques which are universal, and secondary techniques, which facilitate the process of communication.[1] Gesture and language are primary and universal in this sense. Writing facilitates the transfer of language and other symbol forms. The developing physical means whereby symbols may be transported—messenger, domesticated animals, boats and mechanical transportation—make it possible to disseminate the copies of the writing or pictured symbols. Later, printing vastly multiplies the units to be distributed. The telegraph, telephone and radio transmit code and speech, and the motion picture preserves and disseminates pictured forms. These methods of mediated communication have vastly increased the swiftness of transfer and the diffusion of symbols.

Face-to-face communication is subject to many errors of meaning and interpretation. One individual expresses by gesture or speech; another, or others, interprets. Many psychological and cultural factors prevent a perfect transfer of meaning. Errors of perception, predispositions, the emotional state of the individuals and other factors distort the process of communication. However, in the direct contacts, when several sensory processes augment one another, the transfer of meaning may be less subject to error and distortion than in the mediated communication. The pictured representation of the cinema is not exactly that seen in face-to-face contact; the radio voice is not the voice of the public speaker or the conversationalist; writing notoriously formalizes speech. The transmitters have somewhat modified the content while conveying it. This distortion results from the nature of the transmitting agencies, but

[1] Sapir, E., "Communication," *Ency. Soc. Sci.*, 4: 78.

it may also be augmented with conscious intent. When a propagandist mistranslates "Deutschland über Alles," when a scholar wrenches a phrase of his enemy from its context and ridicules it, when a photographer with a candid camera catches a political executive with cigarette smoke in his eyes making him look pained, they are consciously distorting in ways made possible by the media in which they operate.

All communication is based upon symbolic forms that are acquired from the cultures with which the individual has contact or are learned in personal experience. When a child learns a word and then experiences an idea, when it sees a gesture such as kneeling and learns its religious significance, when it sees symbolic pictured obscenity and learns to interpret, it is abstracting forms from the general culture. When the boys in a gang select a password and give it a special meaning, they are learning from personal experience. Both forms are transmissible. The symbols may be learned, and in this process man is clearly distinguishable from other species.

Individuals differ greatly in their ability to communicate and in their opportunities to do so. / Differences in innate ability and in training and knowledge prevent the equal sharing of the culture of a period. Variations in skill of expression are also a differential. In gesture, for example, the trained actor is more superior to the average adult than the adult is to the small child. In speech forms there is a range from the vocabulary of the incoherent, loutish dolt to the skilled manipulations of language by a subtle poet. Expressiveness in writing varies from the average business letter to the nuances of a novel by Marcel Proust. Differences in ability to communicate may also be based upon structural variations from the normal. Sensory differences in sight, hearing, and the like, may partially isolate the individual, rendering him incapable of communication through the usual channels. Also, cultural differences between groups make communication difficult because of language differences, meanings, concepts, variable response to emotionally charged words and other symbols. Attention areas may be expanded without increase in the range of understanding of the diversity of culture. Thus, although the attention area of the urban newspaper reader of our time includes something of French politics, he usually has little understanding of the French political institution, the position of parties and their maneuverings. Recently, a Japanese general in commenting on the Manchurian situation said, "The Japanese never retreat, but sometimes they advance in a rearward formation." Or so it was translated for the newspapers. Perhaps the general meant that psychologically they did not falter, although sometimes they were forced to give way a little in physical terms. Or perhaps not. But to the average newspaper reader, this was a play on words, nonsense, "legpulling" or just another instance of the bland chicancery and psychological duplicity of the Japanese military. There can be little understanding through such distorting media. Isolation may also be due to separations in space, which thus prevent communication. Individuals, long-separated more than the average from their fellows, deteriorate in their capacities for communication. Prisoners, herders, long-exiled explorers, traders at isolated ports illustrate this variation. It is an intriguing theme for the writer, and there are many literary descriptions of the result. There are some autobiographical sketches of psychological change in isolation.[1] However, under conditions of modern transportation and communication, isolation usually need not be prolonged except through choice. Recently some of the hermits of Colorado formed a club. Partial isolation, either psychological or spatial, with the resultant variations in the communicative processes, limits the fields of discussion and the group memberships of those who are thus isolated. Isolation, quite obviously, modifies the opinion process.

The primary means of communication, gesture and language, have been extensively discussed in the literature of the social studies.[2] We will not consider them at great length at this point, especially as language forms have been related to the opinion process elsewhere in this volume.[3]

GESTURE

All physical movements or postures to which meaning is ascribed comprise the form of communication known as "gesture." These forms of expression range from the interpretation of an involuntary movement in indicating attitude to the conscious use of an elaborate code of signals, as in the occupational codes of railwaymen, surveyors or structural workers, the wigwag of Boy Scouts, the deaf-mute sign language. Certain gestures, such as a small baby's smiles and grimaces, are unlearned, as are the involuntary movements of the eyes and hands of a witness. These are socially significant because they are interpreted, even though the fond mother may usually misinterpret. Most gestures, however, do not have such specialized and individual interpretation but are a part of the common culture groups where they are learned and used as an auxiliary and supplementary form of communication. Even the simplest of such gestures must be understood in terms of its associated

[1] A brilliant recent item is: Kuncz, A., *Black Monastery*, 1934.
[2] Prof. C. H. Cooley elaborated the relationship between communication and social life in his *Social Organization*, Chaps. 6–10, 1909, thus drawing the attention of American sociologists to this fundamental process. Since then all textbooks discuss communication. The most elaborate and adequate treatment may be found in Hiller, E. T., *Principles of Sociology*, Chaps. 6–9, 1933.
[3] See Chap. V.

meaning in the particular culture. Indicating, for example, is not invariably done by pointing arm or finger; some American Indian tribes indicate by pointing the lips in various directions while conversing. The play of features, the variety of facial expression must, with the exception of a few involuntary movements, be interpreted in terms of the conventional gestures. Likewise, many bodily movements convey meanings in accordance with a predetermined code. Symbolic gestures may have the same, varied or exactly opposite meanings in different cultures.

Gestures are related to the group opinion process in many ways. All transfer of meanings is of potential significance here. Especially, however, in the face-to-face contacts of leaders and groups the significant role of gesture in indicating attitude may be noted. The orator or demagogue develops individually unique and meaningful movements. The confident toss of the head, the clenched and bared teeth, the wide, grimly closed mouth, the flailing arms have characterized significant American leaders. Determination as exhibited by Mussolini's chin has become a symbol, not only in Italy, but to the entire newspaper-reading and cinema-attending world. During the most controversial periods in political opinion process, gestures may be significant symbols. The upraised arm, the Fascist salute, the threatening contortions of a war leader at a tribal dance when a primitive group is attempting to decide upon the desirability of a raid, the wildly gesturing leader demanding attention, the heroic pose of the dictator defying the world are phenomena of crisis conditions. Within group situations, crowds, mobs and audiences and other face-to-face groups, the membership is affected not only by the gestures of leaders, but by the physical poses, facial expressions and other gestures of their fellows. Such gestures may be profoundly indicative of attitude.

LANGUAGE

Language is superior to gesture because of its range, specific meanings, nuances and variety of expression and infinite capability for abstraction. At best, gestures are, in comparison, a rudimentary and auxiliary form of communication. However, unless they are written, language forms cannot be exactly preserved, as the changes in folk tale, the growth of verbal legends or the parlor game of gossip illustrate.

Languages are a part of the culture of all peoples. The child, after its early experimental sounds and cries, begins to take over the language forms, as it acquires other elements of the culture. Thus the child is restricted to the limits of meaning and idea that exist within its language. Our language limits in a very real fashion the range of our thoughts. We acquire words and then learn meanings, ideas and concepts. As

Cooley writes, "The word usually goes before, leading and kindling the idea—we should not have the latter if we did not have the word first. 'This way,' says the word, 'is an interesting thought: come and find it.' And so we are led to rediscover old knowledge. Such words, for instance, as good, right, truth, love, home, justice, beauty, freedom; are powerful makers of what they stand for."[1] The same process operates in various groups within a culture. Terminology may direct and limit the operation of thought. Within a Communist group, an oft-repeated Marxian terminology high-lights certain economic processes but hides others in shadows. So does the language of every other particularistic philosophy. Words directing and limiting the individual's field of inquiry thus determine what the subjects of opinion may and may not be. The thought of the members of every group, national, occupational, class, religious or philosophical, is subtly guided by its language forms. Of this, the members are, for the most part, unaware.

Not only does language as communication limit the range of thought within which the opinion process may operate, but the content of language also in part directs the methods of controversy. The use of vague phrases and words, devoid of exact and absolute meaning, is a commonplace of controversial discussion. By the use of these catchwords and phrases, which are usually associated with general attitudes of emotional response, leaders in controversy attempt to build on existing attitudes in creating the new opinion. The pattern of controversy is also determined by the content of the existing language forms for name calling and epithet hurling at opponents. In this process, for the want of a differentiating language, opponents of quite divergent types may be categorized in common as "damn radicals," and the like. A solution of opinion controversy is sometimes achieved in the selection or coining of a popular phrase or word. In many a political and economic controversy, peace has been restored through the surrender of a word, phrase, title, party label, tax name or other significant language symbol. The way in which a thing is said may largely account for its controversial importance.

Not only is the individual limited in his thought and opinion problems by the range of language forms within particular interest groups, but he is also limited in the larger scene by the language or languages with which he is familiar. Amidst the growing extralingual contacts of the modern world there is a slowly growing demand for a type of communication that crosses the existing language boundaries. Simplification of existing languages such as basic English do not provide an adequate range of expression for international discourse. Various artificial languages such as Esperanto have been developed, but existing language loyalties are so powerful that these invented forms have not acquired many adherents.

[1] Cooley, *op. cit.*, p. 69.

However, newly invented languages are tentatively put forward from time to time.[1]

Although the quantity and complexity of a language is not always an index of the complexity of a culture in other respects, these characteristics do, in general, indicate the possible range of thought. Languages have differentiated and grown at various rates, but all the languages of the Western world have grown rapidly during the past few centuries. One method of indicating that growth is by the number of citations in dictionaries. In English, for example, after the rapid growth through culture borrowings of the sixteenth century, there were listed about 16,000 terms in Thomas Blount's dictionary of 1656. In 1755 Samuel Johnson produced a two-volume dictionary in which were about 50,000 words. Noah Webster's two-volume dictionary of 1828 listed 70,000 words. *A New English Dictionary* published in ten volumes between 1884 and 1928 included 414,825 words. *Webster's New International* and the *New Standard Dictionary* have about 600,000 entries each. It is estimated by language scholars that there are probably from 1 million to $1\frac{1}{4}$ million English words at the present time.[2] The growth of language indicates the expansion of thought. It makes possible a wider range of opinion phenomena and in part illustrates opinion change in the past.

Writing and Printing

Writing gives permanence to communication, preserves the record and makes it accessible. Speech is transitory and distorted in remembrance. Oral tradition is faulty, perverted by human psychological factors and limited in amount by the capacity of memory. Without writing there can be little organization and permanence of knowledge. Religious, political and philosophical thought could develop complexity only after the accumulations of successive generations could be adequately recorded. Record sticks, cords, marks, tallies, pictorial representations of various kinds and on many media have been developed by many primitive peoples to give permanence to a part of their records. Obviously, these permitted but limited communication, however, and it was not until pictorial and phonetic writing developed that complete records of incidents, of history, folk wisdom and sayings, of legal forms, thought and opinion could be made. People were then freed from the immediate and the local. But these records were limited in number and accessible only to the elite. With printing came the diffusion of knowledge, but not immediately. At first, printing was viewed as a way of avoiding error, for even the most careful scribes made mistakes. Block printing was first developed in China in the sixth century, and movable type made

[1] Jespersen, O., *An International Language*, 1928.
[2] Kennedy, A. G., *Current English*, pp. 389 *ff.*, 1935.

of earthenware was invented in China between 1041 and 1049. The casting of tin type followed shortly, and by 1314 a typesetting machine using wooden type was employed.[1] Alphabetical type and the printing press were European inventions. In the second quarter of the fifteenth century, Gutenberg produced the printing press in Germany. Printing spread quickly, especially to Italy and France where scores of cities established presses and began to print the classics. The Renaissance was based in part upon printing.[2]

Printing could develop only in conjunction with satisfactory paper and inks. But these, too, had been invented by the Chinese in the early centuries of our era. Although the date A.D. 105, to which the invention of paper is ascribed in the Dynastic Records, may have been arbitrarily chosen, it is certain that by the third century the Chinese were using paper of rags, hemp and various plant fibers. Paper of various colors was used not only for writing but as wrapping paper, decoration and for other uses.[3] An oily ink, suitable for use with stencils, stamps, seals and type had likewise been developed by that time. Although type printing was independently invented in Germany in the fifteenth century, the arts of paper making and of ink manufacture had, long before, been diffused from China throughout Europe.

The first significant use of printing to popularize knowledge, making appeals beyond the ranks of the elite, occurred when the leaders of the Reformation attempted to extend the influence of their doctrines and to arouse groups previously apathetic to the abuses of the church. They printed cheap books and pamphlets as propaganda. Indeed, proselyting zeal, especially for Christianity, has been responsible for the printing of scores of native languages since that time. In China, the earliest printed materials were Buddhist pictures and texts. Of religious influence in the development of printing, Carter states, "It can be said with equal truth that every advance into new territory made by printing has had its motive in expanding religion. In the whole long history of the advance of printing from its beginning in China down to the twentieth century, there is scarcely a language or a country where the first printing done has not been either from the sacred scriptures or from the sacred art of one of the world's three great missionary religions."[4] The disruptive effect upon existing institutions of the popularization of knowledge was recognized at once, and in 1501 Pope Alexander VI issued his edict against unlicensed printing. A decade before that, the German universities had established censorship boards. Printing made possible

[1] Carter, T. F., *The Invention of Printing in China*, Chap. 5, 1925.
[2] Duffus, R. L., "Printing," *Ency. Soc. Sci.*, 12: 480.
[3] See Carter, *op. cit.*, Chap. 3.
[4] Carter, *op. cit.*, p. 17.

popular education and political democracy; it energized thought and stimulated agitation, enlarged publics and brought forth a new type of leadership.

Diffusion of Communication

The factors contributing to the efficiency of communication have been characterized as "expressiveness, or the range of ideas and feelings it is competent to carry; permanence of record, or the overcoming of time; swiftness, or the overcoming of space; diffusion, or access to all classes of men."[1] Some gains have been made in expressiveness during the past century. The increased number of words, the rapid growth of which we have noted, has provided a more flexible language tool. Combinations of sensory stimuli in the talking picture or in television when popularized provide a somewhat different but not more expressive medium than actual face-to-face contacts. In the various art forms, experimental techniques of manipulation of line, color or words persistently attempt to make communication more expressive. Thus far these innovations have had little popular success. Some increase in permanence of the record has been achieved through pictorial libraries (of still and moving and talking pictures), improved materials in books and papers (one New York newspaper prints a special rag edition for libraries) and the variety of sources from which information may be obtained, thus giving a better chance for survival. Yet much material from the far-distant past has been found in an adequate state of preservation. For example, in 1900, a mendicant Taoist priest discovered in a walled-up chamber in the Caves of the Thousand Buddhas in the province of Kansu, China, a collection of 1,130 bundles of manuscript written between the fifth and the tenth centuries. Most of the 15,000 books in the bundles were in as good condition as if recently written, so perfected was paper and ink manufacture among the Chinese by that time. Nonetheless, owing to climatic factors as well as to the quality of materials, most records have been lost. Preservation of records, thus ensuring cultural continuity through historical description, is now assured.

However, it is in swiftness and diffusion of the various media of communication that the great changes of the modern period have occurred. Before considering something of the social significance of this increased swiftness and diffusion, some quantitative materials, illustrative of the speed of transfer and of the distribution of books, newspapers, periodicals, motion pictures and radio, will be listed. The earliest known printed book, a Chinese block print, was discovered in China in 1900. It is a volume of six sheets of text about 2½ feet long by 1 foot wide. According to the preface it was printed on May 11, A.D. 868 by

[1] Cooley, *op. cit.*, p. 80.

Wang Chieh for "free general distribution, in order in deep reverence to perpetuate the memory of his parents." A few thousand volumes had been printed by the Chinese before the invention of the printing press by Gutenberg. By the end of the fifteenth century there were, perhaps, 30,000 items in all Europe. After that they multiplied rapidly. "The world's total book production to date has been estimated at 17,000,000 volumes. The present annual output is about 283,000; while the total number published during the entire sixteenth, seventeenth, eighteenth and nineteenth centuries was, respectively 520,000; 1,250,000; 2,000,000; and 8,250,000. The Bibliothèque Nationale of Paris occupies first place among the libraries of the world, with its more than 4,000,000 volumes. The Library of Congress at Washington is second, with 3,556,765 volumes. In 1930 there were over forty-four million volumes in the libraries of American universities and colleges."[1] In the United States in 1929, there were 6429 libraries of more than 3000 volumes each, with 154,-310,000 volumes.[2] The number of copies of books and pamphlets issued in the United States by years is reported by the *Census of Manufactures*. In round numbers, there were 160 million in 1907, 470 million in the peak year of 1927, and 268 million in 1933. Certain types of books increased but little or in terms of population increase have even decreased per capita. For example, contrary to popular belief, there were 46 million copies of fiction books produced in 1909, 34 million in 1927, and 11 million in 1933. Of course this does not necessarily mean less reading of fiction, as there are now large numbers of lending libraries and fewer individuals buy books of fiction. Other types have increased rapidly; children's books, for example, have quadrupled production.

The development of various kinds of communication in the United States from 1900 to 1935, as compared to the growth of population, has been indicated on Fig. 1. The rate of increase is indicated thereon.

In 1810 there were 359 periodicals and newspapers published in the United States; in 1932 there were 16,706.[3] We have apparently become insatiable readers of monthly periodicals, for their circulation in 1933 was 103 million and in 1929, 133 million, whereas in 1899 there were but 37 million copies distributed. The household magazines, the farm journals, the "pulps," the "slicks" and the weeklies have all gained enormously. The wide circulation of some of these journals may be indicated by the fact that of the household magazines, *The Ladies Home Journal, Woman's Home Companion, Pictorial Review, Good Housekeeping* and *McCall's*, all have well over 2 million per month distribution. Certain

---

[1] Hiller, *op. cit.*, p. 134. Reprinted by permission of Harper & Brothers.
[2] Willey and Rice, *op. cit.*, p. 211.
[3] *Census of Manufactures*, 1905, Bulletin 79, p. 240, and *Ayer's Directory of Newspapers and Periodicals*.

journals meeting a definite popular demand reach an amazing circulation very quickly. *True Story*, providing vicarious experience, chiefly amorous, for its readers, topped 2 million less than six years after first publication. Of the weekly magazines, *The Saturday Evening Post*, *Collier's* and *Liberty* are each well over 2 million circulation. Diverse in content, policy and the reading publics to whom they appeal, these monthly and weekly periodicals are potent factors in influencing popular opinion. The circulations of the monthly and quarterly periodicals, as

POPULATION GROWTH AND COMMUNICATION IN THE UNITED STATES

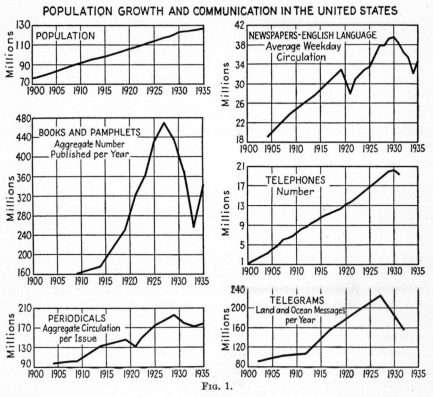

Fig. 1.

compiled from the various issues of the *Census of Manufactures*, are presented in Table I.

With the development of popular journalism in the 1890's, in the period of the "yellow" journalism of Hearst and Pulitzer, newspaper circulations began to mount rapidly as larger publics became newspaper readers. To the newspaper's essential function of reporting important news with comments thereon, there were added the purveying of organized gossip, vicarious experience in the personal doings of great and of representative individuals, and numerous feature sections. The newspaper was circulated among new millions. Although accurate information

TABLE I.—CIRCULATION OF MONTHLY AND QUARTERLY PERIODICALS

Year	Monthly	Quarterly
1850	740,651	25,875
1860	3,411,959	101,000
1870	5,650,843	211,670
1880	8,139,881	1,964,049
1890	18,632,723	8,124,500
1900	37,869,897	11,067,422
1909	63,280,535	16,058,099
1919	91,681,807	18,920,544
1925	111,875,957	22,840,186
1929	133,048,488	20,605,002
1933	103,192,794	23,237,557
1935	102,193,740	23,277,089

on newspaper circulations, based upon publishers' sworn statements, exists for only the past few years, what figures there are have been incorporated in Table II.

Letters, pamphlets, periodicals, newspapers, books and the other media of communication could reach only those points to which there was some means of transportation and could arrive there only at the speed of the transport. Runners and domestic animals, rowboats and sailboats could proceed but slowly. A century ago, in 1834, Sir Robert Peel was summoned from Italy to England on secret affairs of state. Traveling posthaste he made the journey in no shorter time than would an old Roman emperor. But mechanical transportation means were being invented. First, in the nineteenth century, came the steamships, then the railroads. By the middle of the eighties Butler in England and Daimler in France had developed automobiles. Electric railways had also been invented. Then in 1905 Farman and the Wrights began to fly biplanes. The speeds of these various means of transportation increased rapidly during the past 50 years. Hornell Hart has recorded this increase with the following figures.[1] The world's record for a mile run is at the rate of 14.6 miles per hour; for a 100-yard sprint it is 24.5 miles per hour. At these rates, man has practically reached his limits. The running record for a horse is 37.8 miles per hour, which can be raised but very little by breeding and training. Locomotives in 1825 attained a speed of 15 miles per hour, in 1829 of 44, in 1848 of 68, and in 1901 of 120. Automobiles developed from 14.7 miles per hour in 1895 to 301 in 1935. Airplanes in 1905 had started with a speed of 33 miles per hour; in 1935 F. Angello flew 423 miles per hour. The shrinkage of the world in terms

[1] Hart, H., *Technique of Social Progress*, pp. 76–79, 1931. The author has added the figures for 1935.

TABLE II.—NUMBER OF BOOKS AND THE CIRCULATIONS OF PERIODICALS AND NEWS-PAPERS, 1904–1935

Year	Books and pamphlets, number of copies	Periodicals, aggregate circulation per issue	English language newspaper circulation, aggregate circulation per issue		
			Morning	Evening	Sunday
1904		96,312,570	19,632,603	(Morning and evening totaled)	12,022,341
1909	161,361,844	103,309,138	9,605,694	14,606,283	13,347,282
1914	175,166,698	135,453,780	11,692,368	17,085,086	16,479,943
1919	252,068,816	146,831,438	33,028,630	(Morning and evening totaled)	19,368,913
1921	325,950,602	134,795,803	10,144,000	18,279,000	19,041,000
1922			10,809,619	18,898,322	19,676,725
1923	359,391,018	150,819,366	11,475,071	19,978,632	21,463,289
1924			12,365,215	20,634,222	22,219,646
1925	433,211,253	176,314,991	12,440,387	21,298,982	23,354,622
1926			13,335,796	22,666,007	24,435,192
1927	470,374,947	187,003,338	14,145,823	23,820,933	25,469,037
1928			13,995,104	23,977,488	25,771,383
1929	435,199,433	197,316,747	14,448,878	24,976,737	26,879,536
1930			14,434,257	25,154,915	26,413,047
1931	370,515,790	183,518,736	14,342,790	24,418,397	25,701,798
1932			13,711,382	22,696,297	24,859,888
1933	258,948,413	174,759,493	13,711,382	21,968,533	24,040,630
1934			13,223,958	19,031,915	25,366,000
1935	345,822,762	178,613,672	13,447,719	20,852,911	25,969,106

SOURCES FOR TABLE II

Year	Books and pamphlets	Year	Periodicals	Year	Newspapers
1935	*Census of Manufactures,* 1935, pamphlet, Table 8, p. 19	1935	*Census of Manufactures,* 1935, pamphlet, Table 7, p. 18	1935	*Editor and Publisher International Year Book,* 1936, p. 146
1933 ⎫ 1931 ⎭	*Census of Manufactures,* 1933, pamphlet, Table 7, p. 12	1933 ⎫ 1931 ⎭	*Census of Manufactures,* 1933, pamphlet, Table 6, p. 12	1934	*Editor and Publisher International Year Book,* 1935, p. 133
1929 ⎫ 1927 ⎭	*Census of Manufactures,* 1929, Table 5, p. 386	1929 ⎫ 1927 ⎭	*Census of Manufactures,* 1929, Table 22, p. 594	1922 ⎫ 1933 ⎭	*Editor and Publisher International Year Book,* 1934, p. 109
1925	*Census of Manufactures,* 1925, Table 6, p. 662	1925 ⎫ 1923 ⎪ 1921 ⎭	*Census of Manufactures,* 1925, Table 23, p. 676	1919 ⎫ 1914 ⎪ 1909 ⎭	*Census of Manufactures,* 1919, Table 109, p. 152
1923 ⎫ 1921 ⎪ 1919 ⎪ 1914 ⎬ 1909 ⎭	*Census of Manufactures,* 1923, Table 8, p. 607 *Census of Manufactures,* 1919, Table 111, p. 154	1919 ⎫ 1914 ⎭	*Census of Manufactures,* 1921, Tables 530, p. 635; 535, p. 638; 536, 537, p. 639	1914 ⎫ 1909 ⎭	Morning and evening figures from *Census of Manufactures,* 1914, Table 41, p. 651
		1909 ⎫ 1904 ⎭	*Census of Manufactures,* 1914, Tables 51, p. 658; 57, 58 and 59, p. 661	1904	*Census of Manufactures,* 1914, vol. II, Table 39, p. 649

of transportation speeds has often been commented upon. This may be illustrated by the record of the number of days required to circle the globe. The time was decreased from the 1090 days needed by Magellan's crew in 1522 to the time of Henry Frederick, who made the trip in 1903 in 54 days; to that of Evans and Wells, who encircled the globe in 29 days in 1926; to that of the "Graf Zeppelin," whose record was 21 days in 1929; to that of Post and Gatty, who in 1931 flew around the world in 9 days; to that of Hughes and his associates, who circled the globe in 3 days, 19 hours, in 1938. These are records; average transportation is, of course, much slower.

All means of transportation are used to carry the mails. From the time when Cyrus the Elder, 2500 years ago, had conquered the Persian Empire and organized mail routes for political messages, until the coming of the railroads, there was no speedier method of transporting mail than the man on horseback.[1] In Colonial America the mail service was a haphazard affair. After 1753 when Benjamin Franklin was made Deputy Postmaster General for the Colonies, a more orderly system was developed, but it frequently was weeks before a letter posted in Philadelphia was delivered in Boston. Mail was first delivered by railroad in the 1830's. As the railroad mileage was extended, reaching 193,346 miles by 1900 and 249,052 miles in 1930, more and more towns received mail direct by rail without the use of auxiliary carriers. Transportation by water rapidly increased in speed through the nineteenth century, and the speediest vessels were used for mail delivery. In 1918, Congress made a first appropriation for an air-mail system, the first route being from New York to Washington.[2] In the meantime, various means of intraurban mail transportation such as the pneumatic-tube systems were developed. The communication needs of our economic systems, the rise of special interest groups with scattered memberships, the speedy development of printed forms and the mobility of populations, which created a larger need for correspondence, brought about a rapid increase in the quantity of mail. In the United States the pieces of mail carried were four billion in 1890, eight billion in 1900, fourteen billion in 1910, twenty-five billion in 1925, and twenty-eight billion in 1930.[3]

Other means of increasing the swiftness of communication likewise developed. Throughout human history, shouts, calls, signals, drum language and other means of transferring limited meanings have been used. With the invention of gunpowder, sound signals were used, especially in warfare or for special events. When the Erie Canal was

[1] Woodbury, D. O., *Communication*, p. 179, 1931.
[2] See the Rand McNally *Commercial Atlas* for the present network of railroads, motor roads and airlines over which mail is transported.
[3] *Statistical Abstract of the United States*, 1931.

opened, the inrush of waters was heralded in a few minutes by cannon fire from Erie to New York. Rapid communication of complete and elaborate messages, however, was possible only after the invention of electrical transmission in the nineteenth century. Mechanical extension of the range of the human voice had been slightly developed before that time. In 1670, Sir Samuel Moreland is said to have talked with the king by means of a *tuba stentorophonica* at a distance of 1½ miles.[1] The great step in the transmission of messages was made when Samuel Morse produced his first working model of a telegraph in 1837. Other telegraphic systems were in use in England and in France, but these were quickly superseded by Morse's simple device. With money appropriated by Congress he built a line from Washington to Baltimore and successfully transmitted messages in 1844. From then on, the growth of telegraph systems was rapid. In 1902 there were 237,990 miles of line, and in 1927 this had been increased to 256,809 miles.[2] But the capacity of these lines had increased many times, owing to inventions making possible the transmission of as many as eight messages simultaneously.[3] Transoceanic telegraphy by means of cables was accomplished in 1858 after numerous unsuccessful attempts. The cable functioned, but, owing to faults in insulation, it failed a few months afterward. It was not until 1866 that a successful North Atlantic cable was completed. By 1931 there were twenty-one North Atlantic cables. The Pacific had been spanned in 1903 and world service inaugurated. The number of messages transmitted by oceanic cables increased from 820 per day in 1902 to 13,987 in 1927. Land telegraphic messages during the same period increased from 90,835 to 215,595.[4] In terms of increasing populations this was a per capita increase of 60 per cent.

By the summer of 1876, after several years of experiment, Alexander Graham Bell not only had developed the central idea of telephonic communication but with the assistance of T. A. Watson had created a working model. At first viewed as a novelty exhibited at the Philadelphia Centennial and in Bell's lectures throughout the country, it was commercially established in 1877. Various lines were rapidly established, later for the most part joined together in the Bell System, a federation of independent units. The growth in the number of telephones in the United States is from 1,355,911 in 1900 to 19,690,187 in 1931. The per capita calls per year have increased from 64 in 1902 to 246 in 1927.[5]

[1] Woodbury, *op. cit.*, p. 8.
[2] Willey and Rice, *op. cit.*, p. 123.
[3] Popular descriptions of the development of telegraph may be found in Kaempffert, W., *Modern Wonder Workers*, pp. 289 *ff.*, 1924, and Woodbury, D. O., *op. cit.*, Chap. 5.
[4] Willey and Rice, *op. cit.*, Table 39, p. 126.
[5] *Ibid.*, Table 42, p. 138.

The theoretical background for the production of the radio had been developed before 1895 by the work of the physicists Faraday, Oersted, Maxwell and Heinrich Hertz, the discoverer of Hertzian waves. The inventor of wireless telegraphy, however, was not a professional scientist but an Italian boy, twenty years of age, Guglielmo Marconi. He obtained the first patent in 1896. Communication between ships at sea, between ships and land stations and from point to point without wire connections became possible. Remote areas were brought within the orbit of communication centers. This new agency was rapidly incorporated into the communication system so that by 1927 there were 3,777,538 messages transmitted.[1] By 1906, wireless telephony had been achieved, but it was not until 1920 that popular programs were broadcast. In that year, the Westinghouse Electric and Manufacturing Company began to broadcast programs to near-by amateurs. Meeting with an enthusiastic popular response, radio spread rapidly. Within two years, there were 382 broadcasting stations scattered throughout the country, and by 1930 there were 612. In 1922 there were 190,000 receiving sets in use; the Bureau of the Census in 1930 enumerated 16,026,620 sets; the *Census of Manufactures* shows 2,896,964 new sets constructed during 1933. Of course, some of these were replacements. Radio receiving sets in the United States are distributed very unevenly. In New Jersey, 63.3 per cent of all families own sets, whereas in Mississippi only 5.4 per cent of the families have acquired sets. Elsewhere in the world, distribution varies from areas such as Canada, Argentina, Denmark, France, Germany, Sweden, Australia and the United Kingdom (where the distribution of sets, although lower than in the United States, is highest of the rest of the world) to vast populous areas of China, India, Africa, where the number of sets is negligible.[2]

The motion pictures, a most vivid pictorial portrayal, later augmented by sound, started in the United States in 1902. By 1931 there were 22,731 motion-picture houses with a seating capacity of 11,300,000 and an estimated weekly attendance of about 100,000,000. The effects of the motion-picture presentation upon popular opinion, although obviously far-reaching, are not known in any exact fashion.

With the successive introductions of these various means of communication, there have been prophecies of the rapid decrease or disappearance of any widespread use of other forms. Thus the telephone was to oust the telegraph, the radio seriously to damage the newspaper and wireless telegraphy to eliminate the submarine cable. Naturally they have greatly affected one another, but, in a world of rapidly growing

---

[1] *Ibid.*, p. 130.
[2] For a more elaborate quantitative account of radio facilities, see Chap. XIX; of motion pictures, see Chap. XX.

needs for communication, new uses and a secure place for each of them have been made.   Preoccupied with the invention and development of all these forms and with the content of the materials communicated, our understanding of the social significance and of the effects upon the individual of this rapidly diversified world of contacts has not kept pace with the inventions themselves.

THE CONTENT OF COMMUNICATION[1]

The content of various media of communication has been studied by various types of measurement and analysis.   Of the many organized but nonquantitative studies of the content of media of communication there are the following: the various services summarizing news; résumés of particular sections of the newspaper; historical studies of the newspaper for a special content, such as Irene C. Willis' *England's Holy War;* surveys of the content of different classifications of books, such as reviews of family folkways and mores as portrayed in contemporary novels; surveys of the content of textbooks, as in the works of D. R. Taft and Bessie L. Pierce or in C. J. H. Hayes' volume on France;[2] the study of the language forms in sections of the newspaper or the radio and many other types of analysis.   But we may limit our interest here to the quantitative studies of content.

1. The most extensive list of such studies deals with the subject matter of the newspapers.   The larger question is, of course, the influence of the newspaper content on the readers and the way in which known reader attitudes affect the presentation of news.   However, until very recently there had been no experimental attempt to measure such influences. Some of the problems of a program of research in this field have recently been indicated by J. L. Woodward.[3]   On the other hand, content studies of the newspaper have been numerous.   In 1900, D. F. Willcox measured, by the column-inch method, and classified the contents of a single issue of each of 240 newspapers.   Since then, samples of urban and country newspapers have been measured in this way, with an increasing refinement of classification and adequacy of sampling.   Latterly, M. M. Willey and his students have been most active.[4]   In the measurement of the amount of

[1] This section is an excerpt from the author's article, "The Content of Radio Programs, 1925–1935," *Soc. Forces,* 16: 338–349.

[2] Taft, D. R., "History Textbooks and International Differences," *Publs. Am. Sociol. Soc.,* 19: 180–183 (1924); Pierce, B. L., *Civic Attitudes in American School Textbooks,* 1930; the chapter on textbooks and the appendix of Hayes, C. J. H., *France, A Nation of Patriots,* 1930.

[3] Woodward, J. L., "Quantitative Newspaper Analysis as a Technique of Opinion Research," *Soc. Forces,* 12: 526–537.

[4] Willey, M. M., *The Country Newspaper,* 1926.
    Walker, G., "A Yardstick for the Measurement of County Weekly Service,"

space devoted to special subjects in the papers, the students of crime have been most solicitous as to whether criminals were corrupted by the press. This has led to an assiduous measuring of space and counting of citations, from the study of Francis Fenton in 1911 to that of Virginia Cole in 1927 to Frank Harris in 1932.[1] There is no convincing evidence of the influence of the newspaper on crime. There have been other studies of a special content, such as Simpson's study of Negro news in white newspapers, Woodward's measurement of the amount of foreign news in American newspapers and Hornell Hart's scale for rating newspapers by their content.[2]

With the exception of a sample taken twenty-five years after the Willcox study for comparison with that early effort and of Taubner's Minnesota record, these content measurements have been neither comparative studies nor, because of differences in classifications, usually comparable. And yet this comparison over time intervals may well be their chief value. For the factors that they do not measure, such as position or relative effectiveness and quality of writing may be assumed not to vary greatly, at least in relatively short time comparisons, or to cancel one another, while at the same time significant changes may be exposed by the series of comparisons by quantitative column-inch measurements.

2. The content of the commercial motion pictures had not been studied in an organized fashion until the recent Payne Fund Studies,[3] although a very extensive discussion of that content has appeared in periodicals since 1910. However, the articles dealt in controversial opinions both as to the

---

Jour. Quar., 7: 293–302.

Taubner, I. B., "Changes in Content and Presentation of Reading Material in Minnesota Weekly Newspapers, 1860–1929," *Jour. Quar.*, 9: 281–289.

[1] Fenton, F., *The Influence of Newspaper Presentation upon Crime*, 1911.

Cole, V. L., *The Newspaper and Crime*, University of Mo., Bulletin 28, 4, 1927.

Harris, F., *Presentation of Crime in Newspapers: A Study of Methods in Newspaper Research*, 1932.

[2] Simpson, G., "Negro News in White Newspapers," *Publs. Am. Sociol. Soc.*, 25: 157–159 (1930).

Woodward, J. L., *Foreign News in American Morning Papers*, Columbia University Press, 1930.

Hart, H., and Kingsbury, S. M., "Measuring the Ethics of American Newspapers," *Jour. Quar.*, 10: 93–108, 10: 181–201 (1933).

Hart, H., and Kingsbury, S. M., "Newspaper Bias on Congressional Controversies," *Jour. Quar.*, 10: 323–342.

[3] There had been studies of particular pictures used for educational purposes. Also, certain special interest groups had made general surveys. For example, the question of internationalism as treated by the motion pictures has been discussed in several brief surveys summarized in articles in that curiously titled periodical of a League of Nations subcommittee, the *International Rev. Educational Cinematography*.

content of the motion pictures and their effects on various age groups. Certain aspects of the content of a sizable sample of motion pictures have recently been classified and enumerated in Edgar Dale's report.[1] After attempting, without much success, to weight for frequency of attendance, he selected 115 pictures, 45 made in 1929, 46 in 1930 and 24 in 1931. These pictures were viewed and certain items of content recorded on schedule sheets, with sections dealing with locales of pictures, economic status of leading characters, occupations of leading characters, types of residences, number of crimes per picture, murder techniques, types of crime attempted and other classifications. Of these 115 pictures, 40 were selected for more intensive analysis, such items as the following being considered: age of leading characters; nationalities; types of clothing worn by characters; techniques, circumstances and frequency of love-making; marital status of characters; recreation; frequency of use of liquor and tobacco; apparent objectives in life of leading characters; other items of behavior and attitude. In addition, Dale classified the titles of 500 pictures for each of the years 1920, 1925 and 1930. He also analyzed the content of two newsreels, one for a period of 59 weeks and the other for 44 weeks. Certain ethical aspects of the content of the feature pictures were classified in greater detail by C. C. Peters, who wrote brief accounts of incidents of ethical significance in the pictures and submitted these to several small groups. The members of these groups judged whether or not the behavior of the motion-picture characters, as described in the written account submitted to them, was in agreement with the prevailing mores in their experience.[2] The validity of thus abstracting single items and incidents from their context and also of transferring from one medium of communication (the movies) to another (the written account) is open to grave questioning as to method. The judge's response as to whether Miriam's amorous escapade with Robert is in accord with the mores may be quite different when that behavior is described in written form and when it appears as a culminating experience after an hour's sympathetic response by the judge, not only to Miriam's enchanting loveliness and zest for life, but also to her particular human problems. By that time he may well believe that most people could see that there are extenuating circumstances.

3. A few years ago F. M. Vreeland classified the content of the articles of the *American Birth Control Review*. Two judges classified and counted the articles as having a predominantly emotional appeal, propagandistic content, essentially scientific viewpoint, and the like. The purpose was to show the changing emphasis of the *Birth Control Review* in the various periods of development of the organized movement in the United States.

[1] Dale, E., *The Content of Motion Pictures*, 1935.
[2] Peters, C. C., *Motion Pictures and Standards of Mortality*, 1934.

This was, so far as is known to the author, a pioneer study in periodical content.[1] Hornell Hart's recent extensive survey of the titles of articles cited in the *Reader's Guide to Periodical Literature* is the most elaborate study of the magazines. The titles dealing with the various items were counted in the yearly editions of the *Reader's Guide* from 1900, and the increase and decline of frequency of discussion was assumed to reflect in a general way changing social attitudes and interests.[2]

4. The popularization of the radio during the past fifteen years has been accompanied by a wealth of prophetic writing as to its potentialities, the future content of its programs and its important political and social destiny. Glenn Frank, among many others, proclaimed that America had found its acropolis. Organized gathering of information, however, has been largely dominated by the research divisions of commercial broadcasting companies, interested in listener response. And much of their data has not been published. Most of the published material, and it is voluminous,[3] deals with listeners' choices of programs, the various methods of eliciting information about these choices and correlated buying habits or other responses.

Published studies of the content of programs are not numerous. And the content has been recorded in different ways. In 1927, G. A. Lundberg, using the published schedule of programs and time of all the stations of New York City for the month of February, classified the percentage of time spent on various programs as follows: educational, 9.3; religious, 5.3; dance music, 26.2; other music, 48.0; children's programs, 1.1; drama and readings, 2.6; information, 2.8; sports, 1.8; miscellaneous, 2.6.[4]

Another type of record is illustrated by C. Kirkpatrick's study of radio broadcasting in Minneapolis.[5] Although the bulk of his report is devoted to the attitudes and habits of radio listeners, he has included a brief section on program content. Students sampled the programs of the Twin Cities for a week, classifying them according to an elaborate schedule. The sampling was obtained by listening in to the various programs and noting on a schedule card the amount of time devoted to different types. A check of listener agreement shows an average of 80.2 per cent agreement by classifiers.

[1] Vreeland, F. M., *The Process of Reform with Especial Reference to Reform Groups in the Field of Population*, thesis, University of Michigan, 1929.

[2] Hart, H., in *Recent Social Trends*, pp. 382–442, 1933; "Changing Opinions about Business Prosperity," *Am. Jour. Sociol.*, 38: 665–687.

[3] Examine the bibliography of 732 items appended to Lumley, F. H., *Measurement in Radio*, Ohio State University Press, 1934.

[4] Lundberg, G. A., "Content of Radio Programs," *Soc. Forces*, 7: 58–60.

[5] Kirkpatrick, C., *Report of a Research into the Attitudes and Habits of Radio Listeners*, Webb Book Co., St. Paul, Minn., 1933.

A more extensive, but methodologically inadequate, record of a sample of one day's programs of 206 commercial stations was made by the *Ventura Free Press* in California.[1] The sampling was done by tuning in at 15-minute intervals. Apparently there was no comparison of the listeners' reliability of classification. H. S. Hettinger, using a rather arbitrary classification schedule, presents the percentages of program content for key stations of the national networks during the second weeks of November, 1931 and 1932, and the last week of January, 1934. The sample is small.[2] H. Cantril and G. W. Allport, in their recent volume on the radio, report on a classification of program content for one month of a single station (WBZ, Boston, for October, 1933). They used a schedule of thirty-two items. The reliability of the classifiers is not reported.[3] The data for the analysis were obtained from the records of the broadcasting station.

These are the principal types of study of content. Diverse in methods, sources and schedule forms, they provide us with little that is comparable, adequate or inadequate though the individual studies may be, and, with the exception of the sample from the two years 1931 and 1932 taken by Hettinger, there is nothing on trends of content. The author has reported elsewhere the results of an extensive study of content of radio programs.[4]

COMMUNICATION AND SOCIAL RELATIONS

The effects upon social structures and processes, including the opinion process, of increased speed and diffusion of communication are discussed or implicit in the various sections of this volume. There is no attempt at this point to give a recapitulation of details. However, there are certain general effects that may profitably be summarized. Among these are the following: the creation of large political units; individual opinion and international relations; the expansion of interest groups; effects upon individual and small-group uniqueness; the organization of the opinion processes; the spread of culture forms; the creation of new fields of vicarious experience; the bulk of communicated materials as compared with the individual's capacity to absorb them.

When Plato defined the limits of the size of a city as the number of people who could hear the voice of a single orator, he was illustrating the

[1] "American Broadcasting: An Analytical Study of One Day's Output of 206 Commercial Radio Stations," *Ventura Free Press*, 1933.

[2] Hettinger, H. S., "Broadcasting in the U. S.," *Ann. Am. Acad. Pol. Soc. Sci.*, 177: 1–14, table, p. 13.

[3] Cantril, H., and Allport, G. W., *The Psychology of Radio*, p. 76, 1935.

[4] See Chap. XIX, and Albig, W., "The Content of Radio Programs, 1925–1935," *Soc. Forces*, 16: 338–349.

limits that communication places upon community. The integration of any social unit is dependent upon the capacity to transfer ideas, to transmit administrative orders and to prevent disintegration at outlying points. It is a truism that the size of political units is limited by the methods of communication and transportation. By means of horse travel, messengers and signals, the early empires governed sizable territories, but always with a precarious foothold in those areas far distant from the center of government. Effective coordination of even the then known world was impossible. It is often stated that the modern national and territorial states were brought into existence by the development of adequate means of communication. Indeed, "the central fact of history, from a psychological point of view, may be said to be the gradual enlargement of social consciousness and rational cooperation."[1] The organized sway of public opinion in the great society was possible only when opinion could be formed and expressed by large groups within relatively short time periods. Thus, the printing press preceded democracy, for large states could be based only upon common knowledge. In the maintenance of political integration the influence of the newspaper and periodical, the telegraph and telephone, and the recent influence of the radio is obvious.

The present means of communication have made possible an integration far beyond the present political boundaries. But even though physical space has been annihilated, the psychological differences among people of different countries remain. And these are often maintained or enhanced to ensure national unity in the struggle for some objective. For example, in recent years Norwegian politicians and leaders have, as a matter of deliberate policy, changed certain Norwegian words in order to differentiate their language from that of the Danes. Awareness of the opinions of other peoples is obscured by censorship, by a controlled press and by propaganda. Communication does not invariably bring either understanding or amity. On the contrary, clashes of interest are thereby frequently made more apparent not only to leaders but to whole peoples. Newspaper accounts, even when true, may inflame hatreds. Motion pictures, internationally distributed, may cause peoples to dislike each other rather than bring about mutual understanding. European colonial officers in Africa often bitterly complain that certain motion pictures, as interpreted by the natives, make the whites ridiculous. For ten years the radio has been a source of dissension in Europe; in the radio-armament race, powerful nuisance transmitters have been erected near national boundaries.

Of late years, especially in England and the United States, the technique of solving international controversy by popular understanding

---

[1] Cooley, *op. cit.*, p. 113.

of the issues has been enthusiastically endorsed by a host of international amity organizations. A method of round-table discussion of conflict situations on race, labor relations and economic problems, at times used successfully in face-to-face relations, is to be applied to larger groups. Place the cards on the table; frankly tell all the facts; explain attitudes; publicly verbalize the essential differences. Admirable and successful though this procedure often is in certain conflict situations, can it be doubted that with the present cultural diversity of national groups, a naïve application of this principle could disastrously antagonize the opposing peoples where real differences of interests are involved? As Sorokin has stated, "There is another doubtful point, namely, the belief that the more truth men obtain in their information about human affairs, the more beneficial will be its role. In spite of the popularity of such a rationalist opinion, one may doubt it. If every man or group knew exactly what other men really have in mind and what is really happening in the world, the animosity, hatred, war, and conflicts would scarcely be decreased. If many present conflicts due to imaginary animosity would have disappeared in this case, other ones, due to a knowledge of the hidden animosity unknown now, would have taken their place."[1] Nonetheless, in spite of the intensified conflicts that sometimes ensue from widened popular communication, it is likewise true that understanding on an international scale has resulted at other points. There the numerous and growing international organizations have real scope, as, for example on questions of slavery, child welfare, the relief of suffering resulting from catastrophe, and the like. Interchange of thought in universalizing certain principles made this possible. The methods of communication have so developed that any kind of international organization is possible in so far as the attitudes of divergent-culture peoples permit.

Interests and loyalties were once local, regional and based upon isolated units. The stranger, the outsider, the alien-culture element were viewed askance. Incorporation in the local group was a slow and tedious process. In a New England churchyard is a headstone put there by the neighbors of a dead man. On it is inscribed "He lived among us sixty years, and, though a stranger, we loved him well." Increased communication makes possible many types of association reaching beyond the local community. From the development of printing onward, man was partly released from the local and the immediate, for printing was not long monopolized by special classes. Innumerable organizations based upon a common interest were created, crossing local, regional and finally,

[1] Sorokin, P., *Contemporary Sociological Theories*, p. 709, 1928. Reprinted by permission of Harper & Brothers. See also Clark, C. N., *Unifying the World*, pp. 46 *ff.*, 1920.

national boundaries. These interest groups vary from international organizations of a political, economic or class interest to an association of stamp collectors. Not only have special interests been organized, but attention areas of the newspaper reader or radio listener are constantly widened. The materials he selects from his attention areas, however, are largely determined by his interests and attitudes which to a considerable extent are still the product of community or local cultures. Hence, he may be primarily concerned with the incidental, ephemeral, anecdotal, personal and human interest items that these attitudes dictate. And in the newspaper, radio and newsreels the supply meets the demand.[1] And the very multiplicity of these contacts may weaken reflective thought. As Lewis Mumford has written:

The lapse of time between expression and reception had something of the effect that the arrest of action produced in making thought itself possible . . . a series of inventions began to bridge the gap in time. . . . What will be the outcome? Obviously, a widened range of intercourse; more numerous contacts; more numerous demands on attention and time. But unfortunately, the possibility of this type of immediate intercourse on a worldwide basis does not necessarily mean a less trivial or less parochial personality. For over against the convenience of instantaneous communication is the fact that the great economical abstractions of writing, reading and drawing, the media of reflective thought and deliberate action, will be weakened.[2]

Interest groups and attention areas have expanded beyond the local scene, but the interests and items attended to are still largely dominated by the values of the community. And the very plethora of such fare inhibits development of other attitudes in the individual.

It is frequently charged that local variations, not only in elements of material culture, but in ideas, attitudes and expressed opinion, have been greatly decreased by general communication. Implicit in this assertion is the idea that a dead level of mediocrity tends to supplant desirable local variations. It is apparent that standardization of elements of material culture, clothing, housing, food and the innumerable "gadgets," gewgaws and knickknacks of our civilization, has gone on apace. Elements of nonmaterial culture, language, anecdotes, legends and innumerable other elements, are likewise more uniform over large areas. And what of opinions? These, too, it is said, have rapidly become much more alike, molded by the mass agencies of communication, chains of newspapers, periodicals with circulation in the millions and national

[1] Lasswell, *op. cit.*, Chap. 9.
    Chapin, F. S., *Contemporary American Institutions*, Chap. 1, 1935.
[2] Mumford, L., *Technics and Civilization*, pp. 239, 240, 1934. Quoted by permission of Harcourt, Brace & Company.

broadcasting chains. Variations based upon local isolation are being rapidly effaced.

Several points are frequently lost sight of in such discussions. These are: (1) the use of variations of opinion based upon membership in interest groups transcending the local scene, which groups, as we have seen, have proliferated enormously; (2) the interaction in the larger scene, permitting the injection of more varied elements in the opinion process; (3) the question of how much real diversity in local opinion existed (for was it not largely based upon similar small community experience?); (4) the fact that opinion is affected, not only by the mass agencies of communication, but also by interests and attitudes based upon political, economic, and religious variations which often have a regional, if not local, variation. For example, how effective were the newspapers and Democratic mass propaganda when they ran counter to the religious prejudices of the South in the Smith-Hoover election? Variation remains, but it is based much more upon choice and interest than upon the chance of local position. If such variations are decreasing and a pervasive uniformity appearing, the change is due, not to the methods of communication, but to a lack of organization of interest groups. To be sure, in large political areas of the world today, such groups are forcibly restrained from organizing.

The growth of mass communication was accompanied by the rise of organized groups bent upon affecting the opinions of the larger publics. First, organized religion, threatened with growing dissent, censored and propagandized. Then states, whose governing groups felt endangered, increasingly controlled the newspapers and pamphleteering in the seventeenth and eighteenth centuries. Today, the press and other media of communication are absolutely controlled in Japan, Italy, Germany and elsewhere. In the nineteenth century, economic groups developed advertising and sometimes acquired policy control of newspapers and periodicals. Then interest groups, more and more dependent upon the support of large publics, entered publicity, advertising and propagandistic activities. Toward the close of the nineteenth century, various cliques, blocs, reform groups and special pleaders of many kinds began highly organized attempts to manipulate communication. Of course, interest groups have always sought to influence the opinion of larger publics, but a truly revolutionary change has come in the development of organized methods.

In tribal society, the individual was limited to his personal experiences, the oral tradition and wisdom of his fellows and the local culture. With the development of pictorial forms, he could enter somewhat more vividly into certain experiences of his kind. Writing and printing provided the thought of men long dead, never seen or far distant in space.

Limited at first to folk material and institutional pronouncement, printing rapidly became more diversified in content. Individual memoirs, introspective analysis, unusual experiences were recounted. There were always limitations; the informal censorship of the mores was operative, when more formal restrictions did not exist. But a more varied collection of materials gradually developed. The individual, through vicarious experience, could now range far in time and in the varieties of human experience. Children shrill and squirm with emotional excitement at the action portrayed on screen or radio hour to an extent not usually accompanying reading. The psychologist records the emotional excitement of an adolescent boy solemnly viewing the screen version of *The Feast of Ishtar*. The shop girl carries her copy of *True Stories* to her hall bedroom. Vicarious experience is also more vivid in many of those fields in which large publics express opinions. No one really knows the effects of war pictures upon popular attitudes; of the partly fictional *March of Time* upon opinions; of a cowboy picture upon the Samoans; of Mussolini's air fleet in review upon an English cinema audience. But vicarious experience has been popularized and made vivid. Where once the imaginative and highly literate were selectively affected, great masses of people now experience a buzzing confusion of newspaper, motion-picture and radio stimuli, which provide vicarious experience that sometimes satisfyingly titillates, thrills and emotionalizes but again frightens and makes uneasy.

The rapid transfer of culture forms, both material and nonmaterial, from one group or class to another and from one culture to another has been made possible by easy communication and transportation. Change was accelerated; fashion, style and fad increased their tempo. Static societies were in large part static because of the absence of easy mass communication. The individual attitudes and psychological factors encouraging rapid fashion change are themselves a product of the cultural situation that permits it. Communication is responsible for the enlargement of the area over which a fashion may spread and for the accelerated tempo of fashion change. Kroeber has quantitatively shown the increased speed of change in women's styles from 1844 to 1919.[1] The invention of new forms is likewise stimulated. Communication between inventors informs, accelerates, lessens duplication of effort and increases the probability of quickly bringing together the elements necessary for a new creation. Elements of nonmaterial culture, language forms, songs, literature, dances, games, as well as theories of all kinds, have likewise spread more rapidly over wider areas. Anthropologists have maintained that, in general, material elements are diffused more readily

[1] Kroeber, A. L., "On the Principle of Order in Civilization as Exemplified by Change in Fashion," *Am. Anthro.*, 21: 235–263.

than nonmaterial elements.   At many points of contact of modern cultures this would be a questionable thesis.   Ideas, programs, types of organization and opinions now spread very rapidly indeed.   Leaders more rapidly acquire popular prestige, symbols are more quickly learned, interaction is stimulated, the opinion process accelerated.

Owing to modern communication, as we have seen, the individual's attention areas have widened, his membership in interest groups involving certain opinions have increased, most elements of his culture change at a more rapid tempo and the blatant stimuli demanding his attention have enormously multiplied.   To what extent can he intelligently deal with such multiplicity and complexity?   In many discussions of this point, it is apparently assumed that there is a widespread popular attempt to arrange these thronging stimuli into neat and logically coherent patterns. The intellectual demands such patterns and constantly projects his wishes.   But man in the mass, although intermittently confused, baffled and frustrated, can usually project his own provincial attitudes upon this wider world of discourse and find no incongruity.   Capacity to compartmentalize experience is apparently quite elastic.   And a hurried, touch-and-go and incomplete contact with some fragment of information, some superficially experienced emotional response or some hasty action based upon rapidly changed symbols is not necessarily alien to the man on the street.   His education and culture have trained him to respond thus to the flood of urgent suggestions.   His experience and training have made him essentially anti-intellectualistic.   He is not persistently harried by the need for consistency, logical patterns or rational relations.

CHAPTER IV

PSYCHOLOGICAL PROCESSES AND OPINION

The discreet and effective showing up of revered prejudices, including the sacred dogmas of all the frantic simplifiers of human riddles, should be at least one of the main precautions to be taken in our efforts to make a good man out of a college boy.[1]

A great deal of the newer learning in the social sciences, especially of psychological knowledge as interpreted to large student groups, has tended to remove much of the dignity and significance of human life. The better social scientists have the dignity of the quest for knowledge. But the expositors and teachers of their findings, in providing popular guides to knowledge, have interpreted in such a way as constantly to lessen man's significance. The intellectual has revolted wildly from nineteenth-century intellectualism. Depreciation of our physical world in terms of a widening universe, the contrasting of nineteenth-century rationalism with man's persistent irrationality, the elevation of the instinctive life, the lauding of physical force and a flight from reason, and the purveying of a pseudoscientific psychological and psychoanalytic jargon are characteristic of our time. At the beginning of this century, psychological reality demanded the combating of the nineteenth-century intellectualistic assumption that human behavior resulted from a logical intellectual process. This clearing away of an intellectual myth was accomplished with a vigor that, by the second decade of the century, had become a questionably spirited attack and, apparently, in some cases evidenced an irresponsible intellectual abandon. The content of this chapter must inevitably emphasize many forms of irrational thinking. However, we should not gather the impression that all popular opinion is based upon illogical thinking. The common man as a member of large publics may often be motivated by irrational impulses; he may respond to slogans and symbols; on public occasions he often experiences emotional "thrill" to his own betrayal; he persistently follows the personal leader while losing sight of the issue. As a member of a large public or group he may often be silly and absurd, but sometimes he desires not to be.

Although generalizations about the processes of thought may be abstracted in psychological theory, thinking about thinking is usually most fruitful when the thought processes and the subject matter of

[1] Robinson, J. H., *The Human Comedy*, p. 334, 1937.

53

thought are considered concomitantly. Much of the psychological process may not be generalized into universal verities. The materials of a particular culture determine the content of the mind and also, to some extent, the ways of the mind. The cultural anthropologist and the sociologist are peculiarly aware of this fact. The psychologist, in his preoccupation with the organism, has often been neglectful of the ways in which it is conditioned by culture. As yet there is no highly developed science of comparative psychology. Yet psychological study in divergent cultures has given insights on some relations between culture content and psychological processes. This has been most dramatically indicated in the ill-developed field of the psychology of primitive peoples.[1] Perception is determined in part by what is to be perceived. There are characteristic directions of attention: an Apache of the original culture and a contemporary Chicago Y.M.C.A. dweller would attend to quite different elements in an Arizona landscape. Social factors modify the processes of memory as well as the materials remembered. This may be illustrated by primitive practices in remembering numbers, as compared with the memory practices of one equipped with the Arabic numeral system; by the memory of design as illustrated by interpretation of design sketches;[2] by the voluminous experimental psychology of memory in witnesses; and in many other fields. Yet only a small minority of psychologists have ever considered these important conditionings of mental processes. Indeed, one psychologist recently wrote, "Nowhere in the literature of psychology is memory action treated as an intimate mode of response to very specific features of the person's actual surroundings (persons, events and conditions)."[3] Ways of thinking have latterly been ascribed somewhat more to cultural influences. For example, it has long been noted that primitive peoples usually think in terms of objects, situations and specific events rather than in terms of abstractions. The ability to recognize uniformities among apparent diversities is more characteristic of some groups of modern man. This difference was once ascribed to differences in quality of mentality. But in those areas of thought where abstract thinking prevails, modern man is guided, not only by the tradition of abstract thinking, but also by the accumulated abstractions of past generations. It now appears that the direction of attention and various aspects of the cultural life are primarily involved in determining thought processes.[4]

[1] See Sherif, M., *The Psychology of Social Norms*, 1936; Bartlett, F. C., *Remembering*, 1933.

[2] A contemporary London dweller interprets a sketch of a hand pointing upward as an antiaircraft gun; Bartlett, *op. cit.*, p. 244.

[3] Kantor, J. R., *Principles of Psychology*, vol. II, p. 116, 1926.

[4] *Cf.* Thomas, W. I., *Primitive Behavior*, pp. 772 *ff.*, 1937; Klineberg, O., *Race Differences*, 1935; with Lévy-Bruhl, L., *Primitive Mentality*, 1923.

The ways in which individuals perceive, remember and think are determined in part by characteristics common to organisms, in part by individual differences and in part by cultural factors. Among the cultural factors are the traditional elements acquired in folk and group experience and those acquired from the professional thinker. Both types are involved in popular opinion. Let us illustrate. Thinking in American publics is in part conditioned by the background of American folk experience, as in the relation between man and nature in the conquest of the continent. Many of our dominant attitudes were developed in relation to this struggle. The pioneer, struggling with an adverse physical environment, must devote himself to the solution of his problems of adjustment to that environment.[1] He cannot preoccupy himself with psychological nuances, introspective analyses, aesthetic values, and the like. The frontiersman was not intellectual, not glibly skeptical, not a controversialist on aesthetic values. Characteristically, he was not flexible, he did not adjust well with human beings. In America today, as human action deals more with human beings and less with physical environment, we are undergoing a necessary modification of cultural values and individual attitudes. The individual's capacity for flexible adjustment must be increased. The influence of the frontier is but one of numerous uniquely American experiences that have determined, not only a part of American traditional thought, but also the ways of perceiving, remembering and thinking.[2] But, of course, both the content and processes of thought are modified, not only by experiences within the immediate culture and its recent history, but also by the general history of thought.[3] The results of the American experience are incorporated into a larger framework of the history of popular thought of western civilization. In the last four centuries the powerful currents of secularism, Protestantism, rationalism, liberalism and democracy have stirred the common man. Professional thinkers develop techniques of thinking. These, in garbled form, are incorporated in popular thought. Prof. G. Boas notes that our new ways of thinking may be contrasted with the ways of the past in: (1) the shift from Aristotelian logic to an acceptance

[1] See, notably, Turner, F. J., *The Frontier in American History*, 1920.

[2] The ways in which concepts are formed and also the problems of abstraction usually have received philosophic, rather than psychological, treatment. The limited experimental approach of the psychologists is illustrated by: Fisher, S. C., "The Process of Generalizing Abstraction and Its Product, The General Concept," *Psychol. Mon.*, 21: 2 (1916); Hull, C. L., "Quantitative Aspects of the Evolution of Concepts," *Psychol. Mon.*, 28: 1 (1920); Kuo, Z. Y., "A Behavioristic Experiment in Inductive Inference," *Jour. Ed. Psychol.*, 6: 247–293 (1923); Smoke, K. L., "An Objective Study of Concept Formation," *Psychol. Mon.* 42: 4 (1931).

[3] On American thought as influenced by literary history, see, notably, Parrington, V. L., *Main Currents in American Thought*, 3 vols., 1927–1930.

of statistics as explaining the facts of the world, (2) the substitution of a
living principle of growth for mechanical impact, as a cause of change,
(3) the present conception of the world as unified and stabilized by means
of the instruments and techniques of observation.[1] When popular
thought follows parts of the techniques of the professional thinker, it is
usually betrayed by its own oversimplifications of these processes.
This is well illustrated in popular pseudoscience.

If the differences between cultures condition the individual members
and modify ways of thinking, class and group differences may partially
isolate their members from one another. If the class or group has
developed an ideology, its members may be partly insulated from representatives of other classes, not only by their interests, but also by their
ways of thinking. Communication is made difficult. Their divergent
use of words and other symbols, differences in emotional conditionings,
and the like, make impossible the creation of a common opinion. They
may differ, not only in the use of symbols and in information and knowledge, but also, and more fundamentally, in ways of thinking.

We shall consider certain processes characteristic of the development
of opinion in the larger groups and publics. Stereotyping, the relations
between emotions and opinions, personification, rationalization, opinion
and the unconscious, conditioning and memory, in the members of large
publics, are the more important psychological processes relating to
opinion formation in such groups. In a sense, it is much easier to isolate
the principal psychological processes common to individuals as members
of groups than it is to organize the more varied and diverse psychological
processes of an individual in his total experience. Social psychology
should be making rapid strides in collecting data and generalizing.

STEREOTYPES

There is a persistent tendency of the human mind to provide concrete
illustrations of abstractions and to confer a greater reality than is
warranted upon its own conceptions and perceptions. Although present
in many types of thinking, it is especially characteristic of popular
thought, that is, of the subject matter of thinking characteristic of
individuals as members of large publics. This tendency has sometimes
been called "reification."[2] Instances of reification common to the members of large publics often become so psychologically "real" as to be developed into rigid preconceptions or patterns of perception. Woodard has

---

[1] Boas, G., *Our New Ways of Thinking*, 1930.
[2] From Plato onward this tendency has been known to philosophers. It has
recently been given sociological orientation in: Woodard, J. W., *Reification and
Supernaturalism as Factors in Social Rigidity and Social Change*, The Sociological
Press, Hanover, N. H., 1935.

indicated four types of reification.   (1) The conceptual is taken as the perceptual.   "Examples of it are the reality and power given to names by primitive peoples and young children; conceptual realism in science; philosophic idealism; the failure to remember the fictional character of methodological fictions in science and philosophy."[1]   (2) The relational is taken as if it had an existence. This may be illustrated by the conceptions of mana among primitives; by children's conceptions of relationships as absolutes; by the adult's acceptance of ethical statements of good and evil as absolutes, rather than as relative to cultural needs and situations.[2]   (3) The quite nonexistent is given existence.   "The hallucinations, emotionalized projections, and delusions of insanity, with relation to which the individual lacks insight"[3]; the personification of gods and demons; the personification of abstractions, and the like, are illustrations of this tendency.   (4) The subjective is taken as the objective.   What is subjectively very real may be taken as if it were objectively real.   Primitive magic is a case in point.   Popular legends about living persons cause large publics to respond in this way.   Although the individual develops his own reifications, we are here concerned with those which he acquires in the principal groups of his culture.   Thus, in public opinion, the symbols of the flag, cross, altar, elephant and donkey, the projecting of corporations as personalities and hundreds of other concretions reify the fundamental institutions.

Another fundamental tendency of the thinking of the members of large publics is "simplification."   Perhaps this is too common and well known to require illustration.   On public issues the "pictures in our heads" are simplifications of reality.   Indeed, it could not be otherwise. "For the attempt to see all things freshly and in detail, rather than as types and generalities, is exhausting, and among busy affairs practically out of the question."[4]   Moreover, as the attention areas of modern man widen, he acquires more and more of these simplifications.   These are the psychological basis of popular action.   They may diverge very far from objective reality.   In a society where the facts of interaction are comparatively uncomplicated, these simplifications may be essentially accurate.   When the facts of human society were simple, it was possible to simplify them still further without disastrous consequences.   Proverbs, simple images and folk wisdom were adequate guides to behavior. But in a society of increasing complexity in fundamental social relations,

[1] *Ibid.*, p. 9.

[2] *Ibid.*, p. 10.   This tendency to make codes of morals rigid has caused many responses that are functionally destructive.   Prof. G. Boas, *op. cit.*, p. 31, has written, "The only reason why the race has survived morality is, I imagine, that few have done more than attempt to make others practice it."

[3] *Ibid.*, p. 10.

[4] Lippmann, W., *Public Opinion*, p. 88, 1922.

the gap between simple popular conceptions and objective reality widens. Yet the demand for simplicity persists as publics increase in size and the items attended to multiply. Large publics cherish the simple definition, the summarized conception, the simple melodrama of human relations, a phrase, a personified conception, and the like.

The popular stereotype is based upon these two basic psychological tendencies to reification and simplification. "Stereotypes" are preconceptions acquired from the culture; those reifications and simplifications which are current in large groups.[1] The individual also develops his own simplifications. For example, a literary critic heads the chapters of a volume: G. B. Shaw, "The Naughty God"; Sinclair Lewis, "The Anti-Elk"; Rex Beach, "Open at The Neck"; G. K. Chesterton, "A Paradoxical Blimp"; and the like.[2] These are personal characterizations. However, if Sinclair Lewis came to be generally referred to by literate Americans as the "Anti-Elk," that would be a stereotype.

If the individual's reifications and simplifications often diverge widely from objective reality, those collective representations and stereotypes which are bandied about in large publics may be even more erroneous. If sense perceptions are often so little determined by objective fact (as has been established by an extensive experimental psychological literature), the representations or stereotypes acquired from the cultural definitions are often even greater distortions of objective reality. And, obviously, conscious distortion and manipulation of these channels are widely practiced today. Publicity, propaganda, advertising and all kinds of special pleading are sometimes avowed, often concealed.

The stereotypes are conventional labels. These labels consist of words, phrases and language forms, of images and pictorial symbols. They are acquired from the language itself and from all means of communication. As Lippmann has stated, "For the most part we do not first see, and then define, we define first and then see. . . . We are told about the world before we see it. We imagine most things before we experience them. And these preconceptions, unless education has made us acutely aware, govern deeply the whole process of perception."[3] But true statements about complicated issues, about groups of people or races or nationalities or about organizations and social classes cannot be summed up in a few words or a simple picture. The theory of relativity popularly

---

[1] The term "stereotype" was brought into use among American writers by Mr. Walter Lippmann, in his *Public Opinion*. This concept had long been common to philosophical thought. The English sometimes write of "tabloid thinking" (see Thouless, R. H., *Straight and Crooked Thinking*, Chap. 7, 1932).

[2] Hamilton, C., *People Worth Talking About*, 1933.

[3] Lippmann, *op. cit.*, pp. 81, 90. By permission of The Macmillan Company, publishers.

expressed as "everything is relative"; the complicated ideology of evolution appearing as "the monkey theory"; war guilt glibly ascribed to the "Hun"; and either verbal or pictorial representations about capitalists, Nazis, Bolsheviks, Jews, labor, nationalities, the clergy and the gangster, distort the objective reality as it is preconceived in the mind. The stereotypes also motivate behavior toward the proponents of these theories and toward groups and classes. Stereotypes may be counterfeits of reality.

Of course, stereotyping is psychologically inevitable in thinking and in memory. The stereotypes provide the symbols of discourse. They are the postulates of popular discussion. And "the popular controversialist has indeed a serious complaint against those who do not accept the tabloids of thought ordinarily current, because these are the agreed postulates for popular discussion."[1] They provide consistent practical attitudes motivating action toward ideas, objects and people. Especially in times of popular emotional excitement, anyone who blurs the stereotypes is suspect. The enemy must be simply defined; and the stereotypes of the cause, party, class or group may be emotionally defended. It is difficult to grasp even the essentials of a complex situation, and members of large publics have not the psychological equipment with which to do so. In addition, there is widespread lack of the mental vigor and activity required to deal with a multifarious reality. Further, these simplifications may be easily remembered and transmitted. The individual acquires thousands of stereotypes from many sources in his culture. Some of these constantly motivate, others are definitions infrequently called upon. If he discards one set of stereotypes, he acquires another.

Some of the more effective stereotypes are images of persons who stand for classes and types. These have been experimentally tested in several simple studies. Rice presented nine photographs to 141 students, who were informed that they were photographs of a premier, a labor leader, an ambassador, a governor, a bootlegger, and the like. The appearance of each of the men in the photographs was striking, and they differed greatly from one another. The students indicated a definite stereotyped conception of what the appearance of a labor leader, Bolshevik or banker would be.[2] It is surprising that social psychology has not presented an extensive experimental literature on this subject, but, so far, Rice's suggestive study has not been elaborated. We shall discuss the problem of language stereotypes in a following chapter on Language and Public Opinion.

---

[1] Thouless, *op. cit.*, p. 131.

[2] Rice, S. A., *Quantitative Methods in Politics*, Chap. 5, 1928. Another study of stereotypes was conducted by Litterer, O. F., "Stereotypes," *Jour. Soc. Psychol.*, 4: 129.

Personification

There may be some innate basis for sociability, association and psychological preoccupation with persons. Whether this is true or not, it is obvious that the individual experiences people from the earliest days of life. That the human mind, therefore, should come to think persistently in personal terms, whenever it is not trained to think abstractly, is not surprising. Very early in life we evidence this personification in thought. The common experience of "imaginary conversation" in the psychological process of early childhood indicates the need to think in dialogue.[1] This early tendency of thought is later modified by the acquiring of other ways of thinking, but a large residue of personifications exists in every human mind. Of course, "people differ much in the vividness of their imaginative sociability. The more simple, concrete, dramatic, their habit of mind is, the more their thinking is carried on in terms of actual conversation with a visible and audible interlocutor."[2] The common man of large publics, either lacking in adequate data on which to form opinions or intellectually incapable of doing so, nonetheless develops opinions on these issues. These opinions are often based upon his personifications of the issues, his assumption of the personal symbols. It is precisely on some of the most complex issues of human association, issues puzzling to the abstract thinker of every age, that the common man provides the greatest wealth of personifications. These he dogmatically and stubbornly defends.

As large publics have successively turned their attention to a consideration of religious, political and economic phenomena, simplifications and personifications have proliferated in those fields. Personifications of the supernatural appeared in the conceptions of anthropomorphic gods and devils. The history of the devil is an interesting study of the successive personifications of evil. Ethical concepts have been presented in legendary figures, allegories, morality plays, and the like. Nature was early personified. Justice, liberty, law and a hundred abstractions are personified in folk art. Political power has been notoriously personified. The economic process is largely translated into personified terms by the common man, with his beliefs as to what Morgan, Rockefeller, Ford, John L. Lewis and others "could do" to solve the economic problems. Groups are also personified. As Prof. Cooley noted, "The sentiment by which one's family, club, college, state or country is realized in his mind is stimulated by vague images, largely personal . . . the impulse which we feel to personify country, or anything

[1] For an incisive discussion of this tendency see Cooley, C. H., *Human Nature and the Social Order*, Chap. 3, 1902.

[2] *Ibid.*, p. 95.

else which awakens strong emotion in us, shows our imaginations to be so profoundly personal that deep feeling almost inevitably connects itself with a personal image."[1] In personification, publics name and provide personal symbols for abstractions, concepts, sentiments, and the like.[2] The orator, popular artist, cartoonist and other special pleaders become experts in manipulating these personified symbols. Of course, general publics do objectify and depersonalize certain sectors of the subject

TABLE III.—SOURCES OF IDEALS CHOSEN BY URBAN CHILDREN FROM THREE CITIES*

		All ages	6–8	9	10	11	12	13	14	15	16	17–20
						Age in years						
Numbers												
	Boys	4199	320	349	390	438	466	575	542	516	323	280
	Girls	4614	343	387	382	424	551	673	693	556	362	243
Percentages:												
Characters from immediate environment	Boys	19.9	43.4	32.0	27.3	26.1	16.3	13.9	13.2	13.3	11.9	11.0
	Girls	46.5	72.1	56.0	48.7	44.3	42.1	43.4	40.3	40.7	45.7	47.0
Historic and public characters	Boys	70.5	43.4	56.5	62.1	62.3	76.4	76.6	78.6	79.4	79.7	77.2
	Girls	45.1	21.7	34.4	44.0	47.1	48.6	48.2	53.5	50.1	43.4	42.3
Characters from fiction	Boys	3.1	2.8	3.6	4.9	5.6	1.5	4.0	2.4	2.0	1.6	2.8
	Girls	2.5	1.7	3.8	2.1	2.4	3.7	2.7	.7	3.1	3.3	2.9
Characters from religion	Boys	1.8	2.8	1.9	2.2	2.1	1.8	1.7	.6	1.0	2.4	2.1
	Girls	2.1	3.2	3.6	1.0	1.4	3.1	2.1	1.7	1.4	1.3	2.8
Miscellany	Boys	4.8	7.0	6.0	4.5	5.8	4.6	3.8	4.6	4.0	5.3	6.4
	Girls	3.8	1.7	3.0	2.0	4.7	4.4	3.5	2.4	4.5	6.3	7.4

* Hill, D. S., "Personification of Ideals by Urban Children," *Jour. Soc. Psychol.*, 1: 382. Permission to reproduce granted.

matter to which they attend, but the resultant objectifications and abstractions never arouse the same group loyalties and warm emotional responses that accompany the personified symbol. Auguste Comte advised his disciples to create a visual image of Humanity in the form of the remembered figure of some known or loved woman. Personification is psychologically inevitable. It provides concrete, direct and simple mental content.

Some personifications are individually unique or are provided within the primary group, but the majority are provided from the general culture. There has been little systematic study of the personifications common to large groups, although the process is frequently noted. From a recent questionnaire study of 8813 school children, a social psychologist

[1] *Ibid.*, pp. 113, 114. Quoted by permission of Charles Scribner's Sons.
[2] Pareto, V., *The Mind and Society* (English trans.), vol. II, pp. 636 *ff.*, 1935.

has adduced some generalizations.[1] He found that the largest number of personifications of ideals were selected from historic and public characters and that each year from eight to fifteen years of age these are increasingly important to the individual. These characters from remote environment are more important in the choices of the boys than of the girls. Personifications from the immediate environment (relatives, acquaintances, teachers, and the like) account for 34 per cent of the choices and decrease steadily in importance as the child grows older. Table III summarizes the results. This is an interesting though simple and fragmentary study.

Personification is a fundamental type of folk thinking. The tendency to desire simple explanations and descriptions is a universal human trait exhibited by large publics. In every period, man has exhibited the tendency to ascribe complex social processes to simple causes and explanations. If these simplifications can be cast in personal terms, they are even more readily acceptable to large publics. Therefore, masses are conditioned to respond to these personal symbols. We shall discuss the process in greater detail in later chapters on The Leader and Personal Symbolism and on Legends and Myths.

Although the process of personification in thinking is very simple and the ways in which folk personifications are acquired are quite obvious, it is by no means easy to substitute one personification for another, as many a leader has discovered to his cost. The prevailing personifications are emotionally defended, inasmuch as they provide the illusions of certainty and security for the common man. They may be changed, but they usually change slowly. Personifications once widely used in any large groups are usually not quickly supplanted by other symbols in the same field, though there are some notable exceptions. Nor do they suddenly disappear from general use. They are gradually outgrown and forgotten by a public with new and changing needs for simplification in other fields.

EMOTION AND PUBLIC OPINION

The simple, clear-cut dichotomies of mind and matter and of reason and emotion are no longer satisfactory to the psychologist. The mind is viewed as part and parcel of the body, and bodily changes are considered as they affect mental processes. The ways of thinking characterized as reason and emotion are not distinct entities motivating particular instances of behavior but exist in varying proportions in the different situations. Man is never exclusively, and usually not even essentially, a reasoning being. Feelings and emotions, likes and dislikes,

[1] Hill, D. S., "Personification of Ideals by Urban Children," *Jour. Soc. Psychol.*, 1: 379–392.

in varying degrees are component parts of every human situation. It is only for descriptive purposes that one may use the terms "reason" and "emotion."

Emotions have been quite variously defined and catalogued. Some groups of psychologists have described emotions primarily in terms of changes within the organism. Emotions are sometimes described in behavioristic terms of stimulus-response. The extended arguments of this dispute are not of concern here.[1] Watson distinguished fear, rage and love as the essential emotions. These are elsewhere amplified as anger, rage, fear, terror, sexual love, maternal love, laughter emotions, grief, disgust, jealousy, delight, agony and many others. However designated, it is evident that visceral disturbances relating to each caption have not been isolated. They are not entities.

Emotions, however they may be described and designated, are enormously significant in relation to the opinion process, in the fields of economics, politics, religion, education, and the like. Appeals, primarily to arouse emotional response, are made by the demagogue, public speaker, preacher, advertising man, and, indeed, by all those who reach large publics. People fear want, isolation, disease, death, unpopularity; and to the dread of these, as to many other fears, the public pleader frequently addresses himself. Theoretically the educator has faith in logic and avoids the emotional appeal. The propagandist, advertising man or demagogue has no such qualms.

The stimulus to emotional response may be language, action, gesture or, indeed, any form of communication. A philosopher has recently differentiated between the permissible and (to him) not permissible use of communication to achieve such response. Poetry, romantic prose and emotional oratory are legitimate fields for emotional appeal; political or economic speeches should avoid emotionally tinged terms. He illustrates emotional appeal in poetry.

The use of emotionally toned words is not, of course, always to be condemned. They are always harmful when we are trying to think clearly on a disputable point of fact. In poetry, on the other hand, they have a perfectly proper place, because in poetry (as in some kinds of prose) the arousing of suitable emotions is an important part of the purpose for which the words are used.

In the Eve of St. Agnes, Keats has written:

> "Full on this casement shone the wintry moon,
> And threw warm gules on Madeline's fair breast."

These are beautiful lines. Let us notice how much of their beauty follows from the proper choice of emotionally colored words and how completely it is lost

---

[1] For summary discussions see Young, P. T., *Motivation of Behavior*, Chap. 9. 1936; Young, K., *Social Psychology*, Chap. 8, 1930.

if these words are replaced by neutral ones. The words with strikingly emotional meanings are *casement, gules, Madeline, fair*, and *breast*. *Casement* means simply a kind of window with emotional and romantic associations. *Gules* is the heraldic name for red, with the suggestion of romance which accompanies all heraldry. *Madeline* is simply a girl's name, but one calling out favorable emotions absent from a relatively plain and straight-forward name. *Fair* simply means, in objective fact, that her skin was white or uncolored—a necessary condition for the colors of the window to show—but also *fair* implies warm emotional preference for an uncolored skin rather than one which is yellow, purple, black or any of the other colors which skin might be. *Breast* has also similar emotional meanings, and the aim of scientific description might have been equally well attained if it had been replaced by such a neutral word as chest.

Let us now try the experiment of keeping these two lines in a metrical form, but replacing all the emotionally colored words by neutral ones, while making as few other changes as possible. We may write:

"Full on this window shone the wintry moon,
  Making red marks on Jane's uncolored chest."[1]

Regardless of what, in the abstract values of the philosopher, may be considered permissible, emotional appeals have played the major role in popular thought and opinion. Nor can the relation of emotion to mass opinion be adequately described by considering original tendencies, even if these could be adequately isolated. Regardless of the innate character of emotional responses in the young child, the attitudes of adults with their emotional components have been conditioned by a variety of human experiences. When large American publics harbor attitudes and express opinions indicative of desire for security, love of money, resentment at class privileges, pacifist sentiment, race prejudice, or a yearning for isolation, the cultural history provides the more adequate description of the development of their opinions.

It is difficult to evaluate the relative importance of emotional responses and of other factors on major public issues.[2] Emotional elements usually bulk large, for as Prof. Cooley has said, "the originality of the masses is to be found not so much in formulated idea as in sentiment. . . . The common people, as a rule, live more in the central current of human experience than men of wealth and distinction . . . some tendency to isolation and spiritual impoverishment is likely to go with any sort of distinction or privilege . . . the sentiment of people is most readily and

---

[1] Thouless, *op. cit.*, pp. 16–18. Quoted by permission of Simon & Schuster, Inc.

[2] For an excellent, though popularized, statement of emotion in mass movements, see Fülöp-Miller, R., *Leaders, Dreamers and Rebels*, 1935; contrast this with a shallow and unscholarly treatment in Denison, J. H., *Emotional Currents in American History*, 1932.

successfully exercised in their judgment of persons."[1] Sentiment and emotional response are frequently related to the major stimulus, the symbol of the person, word, slogan, place, object, ceremony, and the like. And the number and proportion of emotional appeals are multiplied as the publics increase in size. The popularization of a political program, economic doctrine or theological creed necessitates broad emotional appeals. Of American Methodism, an observer writes, "The advance of Methodism with its passionate propaganda, broadened and coarsened religious thought. The Methodists addressed themselves to the masses, and attempted to control their way of life. They may not have possessed the cultural traditions of New England, but they had the faculty of gripping the souls of the masses."[2] Excitement and emotional thrill, even of fear, if not too violent, is a pleasurable experience. Of course, popular emotional responses are of short duration, and successively stronger stimuli must be applied to retain the state. Hence, in wartime, in racial conflict or class struggles, increasingly crude and violent appeals usually appear as the struggle progresses.

Various emotional feeling tones operate in the isolated individual stimulated by his own mental processes. Indeed, "the emotion following an ideational process may possibly be far more turbulent than one preceded by a perceptual activity."[3] However, emotional responses are extraordinarily contagious and are much in evidence in group situations. Individuals, as members of crowds and large publics, are notoriously susceptible to emotional appeals. People are said to "lose their heads" in crowds. And as modern communication has increased the number and size of publics, the field of emotional appeals has widened.

We may illustrate this in the widening areas of appeals to fear. Fear has always been important in modifying and developing fundamental attitudes and opinions. In the simpler societies, fear is pervasive. "The great and primal dream, common to all the peoples of the earth, one which has troubled the mind of man since the dawn of his first beginnings, is an anxiety dream; for apprehension dominates the earliest and deepest strata of human thought and feeling; dread inspired by the vastness of the universe and by man's loneliness therein; dread of the mysterious, incalculable, capricious powers with which his imagination peoples the realms of space."[4] In Western societies the Christian religion made its lurid appeals to fear. Jonathan Edwards said, "The bow of God's wrath is bent, and the arrow made ready on the string, and justice

[1] Cooley, C. H., *Social Organization*, pp. 135, 136, 138, 142, 1909. Quoted by permission of Charles Scribner's Sons.

[2] Bonn, M. J., *The American Adventure*, p. 249, 1930.

[3] Kantor, *op. cit.*, vol. II, p. 7.

[4] Fülöp-Miller, *op. cit.*, p. 8. Quoted by permission of The Viking Press, Inc.

bends the arrow at your heart, and strains the bow, and it is nothing but the mere pleasure of God, and that of an angry God, without any promise or obligation at all, that keeps the arrow one moment from being drunk with your blood."[1] However, fears of the supernatural abated with increasingly naturalistic descriptions of the universe. Through the late nineteenth century to the present, Western man, relieved somewhat of fear of the supernatural has assumed a host of new and intensified fears, insecurities and apprehensions. Decreasing fear of the universe has been accompanied by increasing fear of other men, of social classes and groups, of insecurity of status and, indeed, of the functioning of one's own organism. And the conscious manipulation of these fears is very much in evidence. That the advertising man has increasingly used fear appeals since 1920 is not merely a fashion in advertising. He fishes in troubled waters. "Scare copy" manipulates opinion as to insurance of one's possessions or economic future, as to the choice of dentifrices, antiseptics, tobacco, the best talcum powder for baby, an adequate mausoleum for relatives, as to matters of social prestige and as to falling hair and a score of obscure and pseudoscientifically labeled ailments. Playing upon the fears and insecurities of large publics, modern demagogic dictators have aroused compensating aggressions against minority groups. Of the Nazis' tide of emotion, a correspondent has written, "It is a triumph of baiting, communist-baiting, Jew-baiting, free-thought-baiting, newspaper-baiting, sex-baiting (Let's clean up Germany), and superior-person-baiting (that above all)."[2] In the democracies, appeals to fear are more frequent as crises multiply. Fear is contagious, and popular action dominated by fear may be entirely illogical. Public opinion is profoundly affected by conscious appeals to fear.

RATIONALIZATION

Human reason and logical thinking are constantly diverted into non-logical mental processes. "One recalls the argument of the German who insisted that stupid children make invincible soldiers, inasmuch as the gods themselves fight in vain against stupidity—*Gegen die Dummheit, streben die Götter selbst umsonst.* Human reason Luther compared to a drunken man on horseback: 'set it up on one side and it bumbles over on the other.'"[3] One of the ways in which individuals and groups frequently stray from logical thinking is by providing socially acceptable

---

[1] Quoted by Graves, W. B. (ed.), *Readings in Public Opinion*, p. 264, 1928.

[2] Bagnold, Enid, "Nazis Swept Along on Tide of Emotion," *New York Times*, June 18, 1933.

[3] Wallis, W. D., "Some Phases of the Psychology of Prejudice," *Jour. Abn. Soc. Psychol.*, 24: 4: 424.

rather than real reasons for behavior. "Rationalization" is an ideal reconstruction of past behavior or thought. A belief or action is justified rather than explained. We search for the ostensibly good reason, a socially acceptable one. My pet dog is notoriously tame. If he bit the child, he did so because—because—because—because. As rationalization is an unconscious process, it is difficult conclusively to designate rationalizations, as such, either by introspective analysis of one's own thinking or by assumptions with regard to the reasons provided by others. The term "rationalization" was applied to this kind of thinking by Dr. E. Jones, who, in 1908, defined it as "unconsciously fictitious justification for behavior."[1] A considerable proportion of discussion consists of explaining actions and intentions. And many of the explanations are rationalizations. "The result is that most of our so-called reasoning consists in finding arguments for going on believing as we already do."[2] We have "good" reasons and "real" reasons.

The process of rationalization is by no means limited to those capable of only the elementary forms of thought. Great thinkers have propounded rationalizations which were afterward established and standardized in popular thought. The philosopher's defense of slavery among the Greeks was a rationalization. Interest on capital as a reward for abstinence is a rationalization when applied to interest on 100 million dollars. In male-dominated cultures, the incapacities of the female and her psychological inferiorities are proclaimed by the best minds. The Bohemian has used Freudian psychology as a rationalization for relatively unbridled licentiousness. "Freud says inhibitions are dangerous; let us be very careful to get rid of our inhibitions." Pareto says that professional thinkers long underestimated the amount of nonlogical conduct in society, for if that were admitted it would be much more difficult for them to construct systematic theories of social interaction.[3] The Russian judge does not say that Soviet justice is social expediency. He says that it is real justice as distinguished from the false justice of the *bourgeoisie*. Indeed, quite generally, legal thinking includes numerous rationalizations. "It becomes more plain why the practice of law is often referred to as an 'art,' an art which cannot be taught rationally but must be grasped intuitively. Indeed the practice of law as now practiced is one of the major arts of rationalization."[4] It is clear that rationalization is pervasive in the thinking of the expert and professional thinker as well as in that of the common man.

[1] Taylor, W. S., "Rationalization and Its Social Significance," *Jour. Abn. Soc. Psychol.*, 17: 410.
[2] Robinson, J. H., *Mind in the Making*, p. 41, 1921.
[3] Pareto, V., *op. cit.*, vol. I, p. 178.
[4] Frank, J., *Law and the Modern Mind*, p. 31, 1930.

The real motives of large groups are frequently disguised. The bulk of man's rationalizations of the social scene are acquired in the general culture. His opinions about other national groups, his foods, racial prejudices and class prejudices are enveloped in rationalizations. His extravagance becomes generosity, his party membership becomes loyalty, his lack of skepticisms becomes firm and noble conviction, and the like. One of the functions of successful leadership in large publics is the providing of many good, acceptable, and plausible rationalizations for the behavior of followers who are primarily motivated by other "reasons." Hitler has provided a wealth of rationalizations for middle-class followers who had strong racial prejudices, in part based upon envious and avid self-seeking. Modern wars are notoriously fought for other than avowed economic reasons; civilize the brutal and barbaric Ethiopians; prevent the inroads of communism in China. Strong self-feeling, associated with beliefs and rationalizations, defends the self. "Passion and self interest may be our chief motives but we hate to admit the fact even to ourselves. We are not happy unless our acts of passion can be made to look as though they were dictated by reason, unless self-interest be explained and embellished so as to seem to be idealistic."[1]

The process is inevitable, persistent, and at many points rationalization is psychologically useful. It provides a defense against the exposure of socially undesirable motives and therefore maintains individual and group morale. Persistently to see oneself in the worst possible light is disintegrating. Groups, stripped of certain rationalizations, often look yearningly at the masquerades of their past. The reformer who would strip a society of some cherished rationalization should have something to offer in its stead. Society must be balanced, not chaotic. At best, a group can reconsider but a small sector of its beliefs at any one time.

CONDITIONING PUBLIC OPINION

As each generation, or at least each intellectual age, must rewrite history in its own image, so, too, many psychological processes, long known to the thinker, must be renamed and labeled. Although the process now called "conditioning" has been experimentally described by Pavlov and the behaviorists, the association of two stimuli in evoking response in social behavior has long been a commonplace to the philosopher. Most readers are acquainted with the psychological experiments on conditioning. If two stimuli act simultaneously or successively on the nervous system and one stimulus evokes a definite response, that response will likewise come to be associated with the second stimulus. To be sure, the term "conditioning" has come to be widely used to describe

---

[1] Huxley, A., *The Olive Tree*, p. 16, 1937.

types of associated stimuli and response when there is complete ignorance of the factors involved.

In dealing with public opinion, orators and public speakers, editors and pamphleteers, preachers and revivalists and special pleaders of all sorts have been aware of such associations. They have conditioned emotional responses to words, proverbs, slogans and to stereotypes and symbols of many kinds by relating these items to known attitudes. Is mother love widespread? Relate its expression to "Say It With Flowers." Is prolonged and detailed intellectual effort abhorrent to the common man? Relate this dislike to a simple formula of economic utopia. Is popularity widely desired? Relate this to a hundred advertised ways by which it may be enhanced. Is the professor widely thought of as a doddering ineffectual? Relate this to the popular physical stereotype of the doddering ineffectual in the cartoon, and the professor may be attacked. Does grinning, as an evidence of vitality and ebullient health, have a high evaluation in our culture? Chew chewing gum, and perhaps you will be as radiant as the gorgeous creature on the billboards. Such suggested associations condition modern man in many fields.

Erroneous beliefs and opinions through untrue associations of stimuli have always motivated much of man's behavior. Today, in many quarters, we find much more conscious organization of these conditionings than has previously been true. Totalitarian states, the advertising man, the demagogue, the popular editor, a great many motion-picture producers have every reason consciously to cultivate the irrational. In terms of many of their objectives, they have a real grievance against any group that interferes with their conditionings.

Conditioning is a most significant process in social behavior and the building up of related attitudes and opinions. But it must not be supposed that the propagandist or advertising man can manipulate these stimuli at random. Quite the contrary. He has to deal at all times with the already existing attitudes. He may relate his flowers to mother love, but if he attempts to relate them to a gangster with a cauliflower ear (except at his funeral) the result will be a subject of humor. Emotional conditioning, however, permits of innumerable associations, even if there are some that cannot readily be made. "While thousands of reflexes are associated in a general way, those which are linked up through the emotions are the most persistent and dominant in the personality. This fact will be illustrated in our treatment of images, ideas, and attitudes, in patriotic and crowd behavior, in prejudice, in leadership, in fads and fashions, and in public opinion."[1] In conclusion, it may be noted that in many instances of apparent emotional conditioning the responses to the two stimuli, although related, are by no means the same.

[1] Young, K., *op. cit.*, p. 88.

The responses to the girl of the cigarette advertisement are not the same as the responses to the cigarette. "The propagandist is interested in arousing certain pre-existing attitudes, not because their affective tone will be transferred to the desired integration, but because they will induce many individuals to perceive his stimulus situation."[1] These are not true conditionings in the original meaning of that term.

THE COLLECTIVE UNCONSCIOUS

Although the concepts "conscious" and "unconscious," just as "rational" and "irrational," have at times been placed in naively simple dichotomies, it is evident that there are certain aspects of the mental field that are more or less in immediate awareness. A great many physical actions, based on long-established habits, are carried on without the individual's immediate awareness of them. Gestures, walking from place to place, and the like, may be performed while conscious attention is otherwise cccupied. In Charles Reade's *Cloister and the Hearth*, one of the male characters, disguised as a woman, is in the public room of an inn. A guest, suspicious of the sex of this character, tosses a coin into "her" lap. From the spontaneous closing of the knees, he adduces that here is a man in disguise. There is a wide variety of such "unconscious" behavior. It is also evident that in the mental field there are relatively more or less conscious attitudinal sets. The term "conscious" may be applied to immediate awareness; "foreconscious" to the field from which the desired material may readily be summoned to the conscious (facts, names, dates, ideas, etc.); "unconscious" to the field from which material cannot readily be recalled at will. The unconscious cannot be directly probed introspectively.

Violent controversy has developed between the psychoanalysts and other schools of psychology over the concept of the unconscious. A résumé of this controversy would lead us into a discussion of the following: the relative proportions of the mental field existing in the conscious and unconscious; the quarrel over the chance versus directly motivated transference of materials from the conscious to the unconscious; the dispute over whether or not the existence of materials in the unconscious may be adduced from indirect evidence obtained by the psychoanalyst; the accuracy of the interpretation of symbols by the psychoanalyst; other problems which, for lack of space, we may not discuss here.

Our concern is with the part played by unconscious motivations in the public-opinion process. There are strong general attitudes which are relatively latent in the individual unconscious. That judgments on public issues and expressions of opinion are affected by these attitudes is a matter of common comment. Opinions in racial conflict may be modified by

[1] Doob, L. W., *Propaganda*, p. 122, 1935.

prejudices of which the individual is not commonly aware, opinion responses to personality types are largely determined by attitudinal sets of which the individual is not conscious, and so on, in thousands of opinion situations. "Unconscious stimulation and the loss to consciousness of earlier stimulations must be reckoned with in describing and interpreting the social behavior of individuals. Especially are the emotional feeling-tones and attitudes carried through life in this nonconscious stream of activity. However we react to the theories of Freud, Jung, Prince, or others, the facts of dissociated unconscious attitudes and acts are at hand."[1] We may disagree with the assumption of the psychoanalyst that the unconscious primarily contains repressed material ("repressed" as contrary to prevailing "good" values) and still admit the profound significance of the unconscious in group life, including public opinion.

What is the basis of selection of the material existing in the unconscious? According to the psychoanalysts much of it is the product of what they, especially Jung and his followers, describe as the "collective unconscious." As the individually unique unconscious is conceived as the repository of the individual's forgotten experiences, so the collective or racial unconscious contains the early experiences of humanity incorporated in the unconscious of the person. They maintain that the great bulk of the materials of the unconscious has never been conscious so far as the given individual is concerned as he has inherited most of these materials. The psychoanalyst maintains that specific images, formulae, symbols and principles are thus inherited. These products of social-group experience are conceived of as hereditary. The psychoanalyst uses this theory to explain the content of myths and the persistence of symbolism, and at many other points. With this viewpoint we vigorously disagree. Such a hypothesis has not been demonstrated by the evidence. It has not been demonstrated that the individual harbors elements in the unconscious that he has not at some point consciously considered or absorbed unconsciously from his specific environment.[2] Moreover, the dominant theories of psychological inheritance would refute the psychoanalysts' hypothesis. Psychoanalytic interpretation of the popularity of the film *The Three Little Pigs* and the song "The Big Bad Wolf" assumes an unconscious identification of the little pigs' situation with the world crisis.[3] These are symbols of devouring danger and helpless insecurity identified by masses of people because there exists such symbolism in their "collective unconscious." This is absurd. This story was not unknown to the majority of people today. If, to some extent, these

---

[1] Young, K., *op. cit.*, p. 173. Quoted by permission of F. S. Crofts & Co., Inc.
[2] Bartlett, *op. cit.*, p. 281.
  Klineberg, O., *Race Differences*, 1935.
[3] Analysis in *Intercine*, January, 1935, p. 34.

animals did become symbols of a social situation, we do not need a hypothesis of a racially inherited collective unconscious to explain this very simple association. We reject the notion of a collective unconscious as inherited images, formulae, symbols, and the like.

However, socially conditioned response systems based on the existing standards and values are developed in the individual. Within a culture, these are common to large numbers of persons. Incorporated in the individual's attitudinal sets, they determine opinions on many issues without a conscious consideration by that individual of the values involved.

SYMBOLS AND COLLECTIVE REPRESENTATIONS

To arrange the variety and complexity of human experience in intelligible terms, capable of classification and remembrance, the mind must create symbols. These symbols are a simplification and a concretion of a complex and sometimes abstract reality. Prof. Whitehead has defined symbolism as follows: "The human mind is functioning symbolically when some components of its experience elicit consciousness, belief, emotions, and usages, respecting other components of its experience."[1] Language, figures, images and other concretions provide classificatory systems of referential symbols. Thinking in symbols is an inevitable basis for thought in common. When groups of phenomena are thus simplified into the symbol, we have artificially eliminated the variations in the world of experience. It is then possible to communicate readily as between individuals.

STREAMLINED CROSSES
THE DEGRADATION OF A SYMBOL
FIG. 2.

A group symbol may be venerated and emotionally defended. Flags, historic spots, shrines and other symbols must be generally respected or their prestige is lowered. The cross is such a venerated symbol. Yet, recently, the fashions have decreed the wearing by young women of "streamlined crosses." This fashion is illustrated by the advertisement reproduced in Fig. 2. Crosses as religious symbols and the crosses as simple designs for the adornment of the young female have a quite different functional significance.

Not all symbols are common to groups. All individuals develop some individually unique symbols. The mentally aberrant person

[1] Whitehead, A. N., *Symbolism*, p. 7, 1927.

creates symbols that are frequently unintelligible to those about him. Yet the legally sane individual may develop an unusual wealth of unique symbols. Examine the writings of John Cowper Powys. The psychoanalysts have constantly reiterated the importance of an understanding of the symbolic tendency of the mind.[1] However, the problems of individual symbolism do not concern us at this point.

The stereotypes, personifications and other concretions of abstractions and of groups are the symbols widely used in the popular-opinion process. Key words, phrases, slogans, songs, images, pictures, statues, flags become symbols common to large publics. All groups create and maintain a number of such symbols. In large groups, images are even more effective than words. "It is no doubt possible completely to supplant images as vehicles of thought by words or other conventional signs. Yet, when the major burden of significance is carried by symbols other than images, the latter usually arise in the process. In most minds significant imagery is never wholly absent."[2] The member of a large public or group usually understands but little of the theoretic and conceptual position of that group in social organization and process, but he can readily be conditioned to respond to its significant symbols. The symbolic objectification of abstractions in church and state are obvious. It is precisely at the points of greatest complexity and abstraction that the simplest and most concrete symbols are provided for popular consumption.

A generation ago these symbols common to large groups were referred to by Lévy-Bruhl, Durkheim and others as "collective representations." These were thought of as "common to the members of a given social group," as "transmitted from one generation to another," as "impressing themselves upon its individual members and awakening in them sentiments of respect, fear, adoration, and so on."[3] These collective representations or symbols provide a system of reference and condense the diffuse and complex. Since these symbols so neatly and simply organize the thinking of those who use them, it is inevitable that they should be emotionally defended. And such is usually the case. As Clemenceau wrote, "Nothing is so contagious as a symbol, and, moreover, no one ever adopts one without attaching to it something of the virtue of a talis-

[1] The psychoanalysts' insistence on the frequency of the symbolic use of common objects of the environment may be illustrated by the items classified under symbolism in *Inter. Jour. Psychoanalysis*, index, vol. I–X. Under Symbolism we find listed: of clothes, of a camera, cigar, of an apparatus, of a pancake, of appendicitis, of a syringe, of baseball, of black gowns, of cigarettes, of fire, of graves, of Medusa, of passing through a window, of stairs, of an automobile, of the button, of the cat, of the collar, of the house, of the nose, of the tree, etc.

[2] Eaton, R. M., *Symbolism and Truth*, p. 11, 1925.

[3] Myerson, A., *Social Psychology*, p. 251, 1934.

man."[1] The symbols are related to favorable and unfavorable attitudes, and the manipulation of the symbols or collective representations often evokes powerful emotional responses in large publics.

The use of symbols is common to organized social groups in all ages and in all types of culture development. Certain simple symbols of man, woman, serpent, moon, sun, earth, and the like, are so widespread among primitive groups and in preliterate mythology that some anthropologists, notably W. H. R. Rivers, have argued for a universal system of symbolization based on the psychic unity of mankind.[2] With this viewpoint we would disagree.

In the more complex cultures there is a great difference in the quantity of symbols popularly used in various periods. "The slightest survey of different epochs of civilization discloses great differences in their attitude toward symbolism. For example, during the mediaeval period in Europe symbolism seemed to dominate men's imaginations. Architecture was symbolical, ceremony was symbolical, heraldry was symbolical. With the Reformation a reaction set in. Men tried to dispense with symbols as fond things vainly invented, and concentrated on their direct apprehension of the ultimate facts."[3] In the democratic and Protestant nations of the West, there has undoubtedly been a decrease in the number of popular symbols in religion and government during the past century. Symbols of respect for rank, ceremonials, and the like, have been simplified. The relation between the use of symbols and authoritarian control is clearly illustrated by the wealth of symbolism already created by the Fascist, Nazi and Communist states. We may note certain other relationships between the amount of symbolism and other aspects of the social process. (1) Symbolism flourishes in periods of well-integrated society, with an agreed underlying ideology.[4] (2) When the culture is complex, transitional and characterized by diverse definitions of the situation by various groups, symbolism develops in these groups, but the bulk of the symbols is not popularly diffused. (3) The development of symbolism, like other aspects of culture, arrives at a point where it proliferates and spreads over various human institutions.

There is a vast amount of conscious organization and manipulation of symbols in Western culture today. There is little of the veneration of persistent symbols, such as existed in the Middle Ages, but there is a vast to-do about conditioning the members of large publics to respond to symbols of various groups. The blue eagle goes "from egg to earth."

[1] Clemenceau, G., *In the Evening of My Thought*, p. 321, 1929.
[2] See discussion in Bartlett, *op. cit.*, pp. 288 *ff.*
[3] Whitehead, *op. cit.*, p. 1. By permission of The Macmillan Company, publishers.
[4] On symbolism in medieval thought, see: Dunbar, H. F., *Symbolism in Mediaeval Thought*, 1929; Sorokin, P., *Social and Cultural Dynamics*, vol. 1, pp. 343 *ff.*, 614 *ff.*, 1937; Silberer, H., *Problems of Mysticism and Its Symbolism*, 1917.

The general staff members of Hitler's storm troops are given poly-phonous sirens for their automobiles. Others are forbidden to use them. Nazi political leaders have consciously propagated a wealth of symbolism. We think at once of the swastika, the salute, forms of address, the personal symbols of legend-evoking national heroes, the flags, the seals, anthems, uniforms, and the like. Other types of consciously propagated modern symbolism are to be found in advertising: its slogans, trade-marks, and pictorial symbols of various kinds; in consciously developed legends about living persons; in the conscious and organized manipula-tion of symbols by the leaders of clubs, lodges, luncheon clubs and a host of other groups. Leadership also cultivates the manipulation of a variety of pictorial symbols in the cartoon and poster and in motion pictures. With a wider knowledge of mass psychology, with new media of communication and with the size of publics increasing, modern leader-ship has become more conscious of the processes of symbol manipulation and better organized to create and distribute these symbols. A folk people could gradually evolve a symbol of the "Little Father" of all the Russias, but, in our time, publicity men create a "Coolidge legend." Millions must be impressed, and that right quickly.[1] The conscious build-up of modern symbols is indirectly illustrated by some humorous suggestions of a *Chicago Tribune* editorial in which, following a statement that the Commissioner of Fisheries was to have a new flag, the writer suggested flags for other departments, such as: Works Progress Adminis-tration—a golden rake above three tattered and well-worn leaves; Tennessee Valley Authority—a large dynamo, connected with a single electric curling iron; Interstate Commerce Commission—a locomotive, bound in red tape; for Mr. Jones of the Reconstruction Finance Corpora-tion—a large bottle of red ink on a field of blue, signifying hope.

Though modern leadership is so prolific in creating symbols and so active in promulgating them, most men in large publics develop no such allegiance to these transient symbols as did the crusader with his cross. The very plethora of modern symbols diffuses attention. A folk people evolve as many symbols as they need. A modern propagandist may become too enamored of his own handiwork. He may create too many symbols. General Goering has already designed too many uniforms and has become a subject of ridicule. The cohesive force of symbols created by modern authoritarian states remains to be tested by crisis conditions.

In the preceding discussions we would appear to have been preoccu-pied with the essentially nonlogical forms of mental functioning. That is true, but the inconsistencies and illogicalities of thinking in large publics are evident on every hand. "Neither the existence nor the positive

[1] See Merriam, C. E., *Political Power*, pp. 37 *ff.*, 105 *ff.*, 1934.

value of the irrational in man is to be glossed over. All the instincts, impulses and emotions which push man into action outside the treadmill of use and wont are irrational. The depths, the mysteries of nature are non-rational."[1] However, the nonlogical and nonrational processes of large publics do not always result in irrational behavior. Large publics often do the right things—those which may be supported by logical analysis—for the wrong reasons. Socially desirable causes are supported more often than not because of the personal characteristics of their leaders, the rationalizations that the leaders supply, the emotional responses that they stimulate, and so forth. Large publics have persistently survived, and often quite happily, a vast amount of bumbling, emotional, personalized, simplified mentation. But the simplification has not been all on their side. When the logician would remedy such a situation with large doses of logical thinking among the masses, he shows a limited understanding of recent psychology. How could large opposing groups be trained to think logically about a specific issue, when they have been conditioned differently, respond to various symbols and perhaps embrace quite divergent ideologies?

However, the results of nonrational psychological processes among masses of people have not always been socially desirable, and in the immediate future they may be very unhappy indeed. For there is a terrifyingly intentional and deliberate cultivation of the irrational in modern life. The rise of a wide variety of interest groups has been accompanied by the conscious cultivation of popular irrationality, for the achievement of the purposes of these political and economic groups. We cannot hope to achieve quickly, "A really educated democracy, distrustful of emotional phraseology and all the rest of the stock-in-trade of the exploiters of crooked thinking, devoid of reverence for ancient institutions and ancient ways of thinking, which could take conscious control of our social development."[2] The majority of men cannot now rapidly be trained to heroic doses of logical thinking. Fortunately, they do not need to be so trained. The rise of a skillful and socially well-intentioned leadership, with realistic definitions, logically achieved, may yet control and direct toward objectives that will make possible the good life for the common man. He may support these with his sentiments. It is to be hoped that this may be achieved within a politically democratic framework.

In our introductory chapter, we have already discussed divergent viewpoints on this problem among contemporary educators, publicists and politicians. We shall consider them at some length in a later chapter on Propaganda.

[1] Dewey, J., *Characters and Events*, vol. II, p. 587, 1929.
[2] Thouless, *op. cit.*, p. 226.

CHAPTER V

LANGUAGE AND PUBLIC OPINION

It is difficult to see adequately the functions of language because it is so deeply rooted in the whole of human behavior that it may be suspected that there is little in the functional side of our conscious behavior in which language does not play a part.[1]

Most students of linguistics are preoccupied with a series of problems that do not concern the sociologist or social psychologist. The descriptions of the structures, roots and meanings of particular words and phrases; the historical development, tracing origins and growth of language; the comparative study of language forms and their diffusion; the grammatical classifications on the basis of etymology are of but limited interest to the social psychologist. Few linguists have dealt in a more than incidental fashion with the relations of language to the social processes or with the relations of thought and language.[2]

Although, from Hobbes to Max Müller, students have insisted on the intimate connection of language and thought, it is only recently that this basic problem has received intensive consideration by psychologists, social psychologists and philosophers.[3] To a considerable extent the behaviorists have stimulated the recent discussions, but "the weakness of the behavioristic theory of meaning is that it affords no criterion by which acts of understanding can be distinguished from other habitual acts."[4] A stimulus-response description is an oversimplification. Nor is there any conclusive proof that thinking is always consciousness of language forms. Obviously there is much verbalization that is merely response to stimuli. A person, incapable of understanding, may babble words in a learned sequence. There is much divorce of language and thought, but this does not adequately describe all of language behavior. Language has been described as having four main functions: (1) the direct instigation of determinate actions; (2) the provoking of revelations as to the character and range of experience of others; (3) the control of affective states; (4) the communication of knowledge.[5]

[1] Sapir, E., *Ency. Soc. Sci.*, 9: 159.
[2] There are exceptions. See, notably, Jespersen, O., *Language*, 1921; Bloomfield, L., *Language*, 1933; Sapir, E., *Language*, 1921.
[3] Perry, C. M., "Language and Thought," *Monist*, 38: 211–230.
[4] Eaton, R. M., *Symbolism and Truth*, p. 26, 1925.
[5] Brown, H. C., "The Use and Abuse of Language," *Jour. Phil.*, 26: 553–41.

A language is the product of a particular culture. It is composed of those words and expressions which label the material objects, relationships, ideas, concepts and values with which that culture is or has been concerned. The individual, in learning that portion of his language which he acquires, is guided in his thought to a considerable extent by the labels which he learns. In a very basic way, language largely determines the content of thought. This is quite obvious either to an ethnologist attempting to explain the concept of romantic love to an individual in a primitive culture or to a missionary struggling with the communication of the idea of the Trinity. Moreover, within a language group, the individual knows but a portion of the existing words. His vocabulary is a measure of his participation in his culture. Various estimates of the language of the contemporary common man have indicated a vocabulary of a few thousand terms.[1] Such limited language tools do not permit of a wide range of knowledge and of thinking. Further, one's thinking is canalized by the language used in the groups from which the individual has obtained his fundamental ideologies. The language forms of an ideology are made up of preconceived ideas. These thwart thought. Opinion process, as other mental processes, is carried on within a particular language, of which the individual has learned only a part. Moreover, he is limited by his ideological preconceptions.

A generation ago it was maintained that languages differed in their grammar and content of words because peoples thought differently. Contemporary social psychology would be more likely to maintain that peoples think differently because their language forms differ. The individual speaks the language of his culture group and thinks as that group thinks or has thought. In ethnological studies, since Wundt, language has been extensively analyzed as reflecting the social processes, values and standards of primitive life. Modes of behavior and life ways, the cultural framework and social processes, are reflected in language forms. Hundreds of such processes and relationships, strange to modern Western thought, have been revealed by such studies. Degrees of relationship, often more complicated among primitives than in our society, are indicated by special words. Enumeration systems, sex classifications of objects, descriptive adjectives, the curiously involved tabooed language forms of various primitives, magic and words and many other topics can be studied, in part, in language forms.[2]

[1] These estimates have been thought to be too low by a few writers. J. M. Gillette devised a test whereby he found that he had a vocabulary of 127,800 words, and two of his students, 65,800 and 52,489. Admittedly these are highly selected subjects, however. Gillette, J. M., "Extent of Personal Vocabularies," *Sci. Mon.*, 29: 451–457.

[2] The relations between words and magical properties, not only in primitive and

Language has implicit in it a mass of social relations. In the relatively static and, in some respects, simpler primitive cultures these may be seen more clearly than in the language forms of the great cultures. Therefore, the ethnologist has used such analysis much more extensively than has the sociologist. But some sociological studies have utilized certain simple forms of language analysis. Let us illustrate, at random, a few such uses. L. von Wiese's students, following earlier studies, attempted a classification of social processes as designated by German words. He notes, "The idea of deriving sociologically usable materials through intensive analysis of words denoting relations, etc., has already been advanced by Waxweiler, Michels, and in more recent years by Eubank."[1] The students in von Wiese's seminar classified dictionary words that indicated social relationships. In the Lynds' studies of *Middletown*, the authors informally refer to words and phrases, catchwords and slogans as indicative of culture values in this Midwestern town from 1890 to 1935.[2] There are a number of compilations of the slang of special groups, such as soldiers, sailors, tramps, stage folk, school boys, and a few other groups. However, there has been little sociological analysis of these sources.[3] Volumes on principles of sociology sometimes refer more or less casually to language analysis.[4]

In the chapter on Communication we have considered some relationships between the various processes of communication and popular opinion. In this chapter we shall discuss certain relationships between language, as communication, and the opinion process. There are certain language forms that play an especially significant role in popular discussion. Proverbs and opinion; slogans; name calling; changes in reference terms; emotion, words and opinion; literature as propaganda will be considered briefly. Today, there is an increasingly conscious manipulation of language forms in economic and political controversy by a more

---

contemporary magic but also in mental aberrations, are especially intriguing problems. See Thomas, W. I., *Primitive Behavior*, pp. 92–97, 214–217, 1937; Young, K., *Social Attitudes*, pp. 111–118, 1931; Murchison, C. (ed.), *Handbook of Social Psychology* Chap. 12, 1935.

[1] von Wiese, L., and Becker, H., *Systematic Sociology*, p. 129, 1932. See pp. 128–132.

[2] This is especially true in the second volume, *Middletown in Transition*, 1937.

[3] A few such language forms have been discussed sociologically. See Anderson, N., *The Hobo*, 1923; Marshall, R., "Contributions to the Life History of the Northwestern Lumberjack," *Soc. Forces*, 8: 270–275; Wood, W. G., *Personal Names*, unpublished Master's thesis, University of Illinois, 1933.

[4] In Hiller, E. T., *Principles of Sociology*, 1933, there is an unusually extended discussion, noting language as consensus, as social ritual, as a bond of unity, as transmitting culture and as isolating by excluding from participation. In Lumley, F. E., *Means of Social Control*, 1925, there are sections on the language of praise, flattery, persuasion, slogans, gossip, name calling, commands and threats.

psychologically sophisticated leadership. Even so, the selection, coining and popularization of language forms is still more of an art than a science.

PROVERBS AND PUBLIC OPINION

We have defined opinion as expression on a controversial point. In primitive society and in the relatively static folk cultures the range of opinion material is usually very narrow. There is more individually divergent behavior in primitive societies than the ethnologists of a generation ago recognized. The writings of Malinowski, Benedict, Mead, Radin and many other contemporary anthropologists have described such divergence. However, in general, preliterate groups are relatively static, and the cultural definitions are incorporated in individual attitudes to an extent that precludes much range to the controversially discussible. The group beliefs and values are incorporated in myths and legends, stories and songs, sayings and proverbs. Personal relations and intergroup relationships are fairly simple and usually clearly defined. The language form that most clearly reflects primitive values is the proverb. Proverbs preserve practical wisdom and can be quoted to quell individual expressions of divergent opinion. Likewise, among folk peoples, the proverb is an important agent in controlling opinion and behavior.

The proverb is a language form that has largely passed out of use in contemporary American culture.[1] Current speech and literature provide but few quotations or allusions to the proverb. There are isolated areas and surviving cultures, notably first-generation foreign-language groups of peasant origin, where the proverb retains some of its former vigor as an educational and controlling agent. Every popular proverb has seemed good to a multitude of men, but, in a culture that has largely dispensed with them, even a single quotation may call forth the wondering ridicule directed toward a cultural variation. Many a contemporary audience considers a proverb as somehow vaguely humorous. The proverb is a social definition of a situation. When that situation appears to the literary and political leaders, who coin such phrases, less simple, less personal and less subject to dogmatic solution, the supply is cut off and the old forms fall into disuse. Other forms of stereotyped phrases take their place. The proverb is a cultural invention. It is not inevitable.

---

[1] There is no absolute agreement as to the definition of a proverb, but the sense of the definitions appears to be that it is a sentence or short statement indicating some supposedly profound reflection on human or, at times, cosmic and supernatural relationships. Lord John Russell called it, "the wisdom of many and the wit of one"; Lord Bacon indicated that it was the "genius, wit and spirit of a nation"; Cervantes declared the proverb to be, "a short sentence drawn from long experience."

The proverb frequently has characteristics of structure that give it a high memory value. Like the slogan, the motto, the rallying cry and other condensed language forms, its success is in part dependent upon just such details. Furthermore, in periods during which a high degree of unanimity in social judgments exists, the proverb appears to masses of people as the expression of profound wisdom, a sort of well-rounded, easily communicable truth. It may happen that, "they interfere between husband and wife, parents and children, and teach all of them manners with unsparing frankness. They play with the children, counsel their parents, and dream dreams with the old."[1] The specific types of proverbs in daily use are indicative of the conflict tensions in the social process.

The proverb does not appear to be characteristic of a complex culture under conditions of rapid change in beliefs dealing with social and supernatural relationships. The forms in existence fall into disuse, and the literary, political and economic leaders provide no new forms. More transient word forms provide the current phrases. The variety of conflicting social judgments assumes a different language form, no less dogmatic probably, but much less permanent. Sentences from popular songs, slang phrases, "wise cracks," items from the cinema, slogans of economic advertising, phrases from the radio, and the like, become the coin current in the process of communication.[2]

SLOGANS

Words and brief, easily remembered phrases label and stereotype social objectives and definitions. Publics persistently become attached to certain language forms. Social reform movements flourish on rallying cries. One of the early popular reform movements in the economic field was led by John Ball in England in the fourteenth century. His mass meetings began and ended with the chant, "When Adam delved and Eve span, who was then the gentleman?" But long before that, popular movements had been symbolized by mottoes, catchwords and slogans. Gibbon recounts that in Alexandria one religious faction chanted, "Glory be to the Father, and to the Son, and to the Holy Ghost," to which the other replied, "Glory be to the Father, in the Son, and by the Holy Ghost." Thereby street crowds were led to a fury that ended in head cracking. Effective conditioning to phrases is an ancient art. The modern process is merely characterized by more organization, a more

[1] Elmslie, W., *Studies in Life from Jewish Proverbs*, p. 24, 1917.
[2] The preceding discussion is largely drawn from Albig, W., "Proverbs and Social Control," *Sociol. Soc. Res.*, 15: 527–535. See Hertzler, J. O., *Social Thought of the Ancient Civilizations*, pp. 373–388, 1936.

sophisticated psychological analysis of language and a more conscious use of language by societal leaders. In *Middletown in Transition*, the Lynds report a marked tendency to define the major political and economic problems in terms of a few phrases and language forms, such as "harmony," "boost," "we will reduce taxes," "economy," "civic unity," "radicalism is un-American," and the like. These are bandied about by speakers, the newspapers and the men's civic clubs.

The effective slogan has a few well-known, simple characteristics of structure. An advertising man writes, "The slogan should be simple to understand, easy to remember, and pleasant to repeat. Since the success of a slogan depends largely on its repetition, the qualities of brevity, aptness, and original approach are imperative. Seven short words would seem the maximum to use in a slogan, six just few enough to be within the margin of safety, and less than that even more desirable."[1] "Back to Normalcy" was an almost perfect political slogan, as it appeared to mean almost all things to all men and was inherently meaningless. Lumley describes the most effective slogans as brief; rhythmical; alliterative; repetitive; affirmative; appealing to curiosity, the sentiments, class and authority; punning; appearing to summarize a profound idea.[2] Select your own illustrations of slogans that have some of these characteristics. There is certainly plenty of material in the language of contemporary politics and business. The effective slogan becomes a stimulus situation to arouse known attitudes.

The political and religious fields are the ancient stamping ground of the slogans. Their use in advertising, by causes, movements and various organizations, is a recent development appearing during the last fifty years. In the political field, slogans have been especially associated with popular mass movements. Those related to the prevailing attitudes such as the famous "Liberty, Equality and Fraternity" are strong, effective and persistent. Those applied from above which do not tap such attitudes are transient and relatively ineffective. Certain slogans are officially adopted by nations, parties, groups and organizations. "In God We Trust" is printed on American money. During the depression a waggish banker suggested that there should be stamped on the other side, "I hope that my Redeemer liveth." National objectives may be stated, as in "Make the World Safe for Democracy." Group declarations are incorporated in slogans, as in the case of the Japanese feminists who rally around the phrase "The Sun Is Female." Crisis and conflict situations are the breeding ground of slogans. All the wars and group conflicts of recent centuries have called forth many phrases. Emotional campaigns necessitate catchwords.

[1] Kleppner, O., *Advertising Procedure*, p. 112, 1934.
[2] Lumley, *op. cit.*, Chap. 7.

Many slogans are associated with particular personalities. General Pershing is credited with "Lafayette, we are here," Marshall Petain with "They shall not pass," and the Kaiser was the object of the phrase "The War Lord." William Jennings Bryan was long known by "You shall not press down upon the brow of labor this crown of thorns; you shall not crucify mankind upon a cross of gold." Vanderbilt never outlived "The public be damned." Personality stereotyping is sometimes accomplished in phrases.

There is a fashion element in the coining of phrases. In the early nineties a Kodak company and a hook-and-eye company advertised with "You Press a Button; We Do the Rest" and "See That Hump," respectively. These were given wide publicity and were paraphrased and parodied on the stage, in the newspaper and in conversation.[1] For the next decade, advertising largely consisted of slogan making. This word jugglery often was crude, inept and ineffective. But many advertising men of that day appeared to believe that if they could only discover the proper phrase success was assured. Today, hundreds of phrases are retained in the advertising of various products, but such slogans have become a relatively minor part of advertising technique. Popular contests in the coining of slogans are primarily used today to preoccupy thousands of people with the advertised product rather than for the discovery of a telling phrase. When the playing with words is popular, sheer verbal exuberance leads to crude excess. The groceterias, morticians, shellubrications, and the like, are characteristic of the more flamboyant phases of American business life. Slogan making by the publicity men spread from commercial advertising to the campaigns of athletic groups, education, religious organizations, communities, reform groups and civic clubs.

The mind of modern man is stimulated by an increasing variety of impressions. Condensation of appeals is inevitable, as is evidenced by forms of stereotyping, newspaper headlines, and the like. Slogans are peculiarly adapted to this need. They may distort, but they satisfy. Social psychology is not adequately developed to provide very exact answers as to their effectiveness. If the phrase happens to be adapted to existing attitudes, it is successful. But the special pleader cannot manipulate at will. Advertising men are frequently too sanguine as to the effect of slogans. But catchwords are persistent and inevitable.

NAME CALLING

Among the simpler peoples, the relationships between language forms and the objects they designate are often mystically conceived. The name is thought of as an intrinsic part of that which it designates.

[1] Presbrey, F., *The History and Development of Advertising*, p. 369, 1929.

Therefore, primitives' magical conceptions frequently lead them to the use or avoidance of names as a way of manipulating that which is named. You may kill or injure a person by the proper spells or incantations in which you incorporate his name. Likewise, you may influence the spirits or objects in nature by naming them. The language of magical reference and the tabooed language forms of various preliterates provide a baffling and intricate problem for the ethnologist. When primitive peoples indulge in derisive name calling and in opprobrious epithets in face-to-face ridicule, there is an especially potent invasion of personality. One is not only socially depreciated but also magically attacked. Hence, many primitive peoples find name calling and ridicule an effective method of social control. Formal name-calling ceremonies were a widespread method of conflict among North American Indians and Eskimos.[1]

Children's language, the verbalizations of the mentally aberrant and the naming by opprobrious epithets indulged in by large publics, evidence something of the same tendencies. Honorific and humilific terms exist in every language. There are more of the latter. Both types are widely used in social conflict, not only to designate those referred to, but also to laud or depreciate them. When the conflict develops between large popular groups, the process is inevitable. Of course, there may be more or less of it. Like other elements in a changing culture, there are fashions in name calling. The practice waxes and wanes, depending upon the rise and imitation of expert name callers and upon changes in the social structure that present new tensions and conflict groups. A Theodore Roosevelt greatly increases name calling for a political generation. Protestantism provided ever new sects to hurl opprobrious epithets at one another, since they had diverse interpretations of the ways of the gentle Christ.

As increasingly divergent definitions of religious, economic and political phenomena have developed during the past four centuries; as special interest groups of many kinds have arisen; as populations have become more mobile and have come in contact with more diverse types of people; as the attention areas of modern man have widened, providing him with more things to be prejudiced against, the practice of name calling has increased. Name calling is rife wherever there are major divisions in society between which conflict intermittently occurs. Names are hurled back and forth between political groups, between churches, economic groups in conflict, town and country, between the sexes, at the physically different, at foreigners and, indeed, wherever conflict is occurring between the standards and ideas of two or more groups. Political functioning in American democracy has persistently been conducted amidst more or less name calling, taunts and crude buffoonery.   J. G.

[1] Thomas, W. I., *Primitive Behavior*, pp. 544 *ff.*, 1937.

Blaine's railroad deals were referred to when crowds chanted, "Blaine, Blaine, J. G. Blaine, The continental liar from the state of Maine. Burn this letter." Cleveland's supposed illegitimate son gave rise to the campaign jingle, "Ma, Ma, where's my pa? Gone to the White House. Ha, ha, ha!" In Chicago's brawling primaries of the Thompson period, the candidates outdid one another in hurling back and forth such names as "chimpanzee," "nut," baboon," "looney," and the like. Senator Brookhart was an able name hurler. In his last senatorial campaign such terms as "cockroach," "bologna fiddler," "pay-roll racketeer," "bunk shooters," and "hee-haw Chautauqua weight lifter" were coined. The late Senator Huey Long and Father Coughlin were experts. General Johnson is an astute manipulator of lurid epithets.

In the struggles between Protestant denominations during the last half of the nineteenth century, a choice variety of names were created and mutually exchanged. These names are not so much in evidence now, which is perhaps an indication that the rank and file of their memberships are not now so much interested in the fine points of doctrinal difference. The conflict has shifted to religionists versus nonreligionists. The late Billy Sunday convulsed large audiences with his vivid name calling. He once said, "Our country is filled with a socialistic, I.W.W., Communistic, radical, lawless anti-American, antichurch, anti-God, antimarriage gang, and they are laying the eggs of rebellion and unrest in labor and capital and home; and we have some of them in our universities. I could take you through the universities and pick out a lot of black-hearted, Communistic fellows who are teaching that to the boys and sending them out to undermine America."[1]

Changing relationships increase or decrease name calling. One does not hear or read of the variety of names directed at the "city slicker" by the country folk or toward the "rube," "hayseed" or any of the other names thrown countryward by the city dweller of thirty years ago, probably because the more obvious and discernible differences of dress, speech and manners have diminished.

Prof. Lumley has characterized the meaning of this name-calling practice as a "protest against social change and thus as a means of social control."[2] It is a warning to innovators, but usually not a socially conscious process. Name calling may be most profitably described in terms of its influence on popular opinion in conflict situations. The Puritans were referred to by the Cavaliers as "Roundheads," because most of them had their hair cut short. Such names designate and depreciate the outsider and by implication elevate the name caller. In the community, groups call names at foreigners or at alien cultural or

[1] Quoted by Huse, H. R., *Illiteracy of the Literate*, p. 175, 1933.
[2] Lumley, *op. cit.*, p. 300.

racial groups. "Bohunk," "wop," "dago," "chink," "greaser," "nigger" are all belittling names. They denote the outsider, the stranger, the alien person who must be battered down. This name calling is a form of fighting; it is a protest against invasion and an attempt to assign an inferior position to the stranger. Other types of opprobrious epithets perform a similar function. The names usually apply to the most obvious differences, such things as personal appearance, manners, **food** preferences, variant religious exercises, speech, and the like.

CHANGE IN REFERENCE TERMS

The meanings of words may be gradually changed by folk practice or through redefinitions by language experts. In English, "to haul" means to move by force and violence, but, in America, the meaning is "to transport"; "to heft" in English means "to lift up," but, in America, the meaning gradually came to be "to weigh by lifting."[1] In other cases the word is the same and its objective definition is the same, but popular responses to it have changed. Recently, a young woman of New York was being beautified by a French hairdresser who was a recent immigrant. He noticed a blue pin that she was wearing and inquired its meaning. "That," explained the young woman, "means that I am a Daughter of the American Revolution." "Oh, this is most terrible," said the Frenchman, throwing up his hands in horror. "I always thought Mademoiselle such a nice, sweet girl, and now you tell me you are a revolutionist." In still other cases, the word is changed to another, while the objective reality remains the same. Popular speech of the Victorian period changed "legs" into "limbs," a wine cooler into a "sarcophagus," "breast" into "bosom," and a young girl was informed that "only animals sweat, men perspire but young ladies merely glow." In many cases, changes in language forms reflect changing popular values and opinions. Many euphemistic terms result from popular aversion to certain words. Hence, the references to the "deceased" and the "departed" and to "misconduct" and girls "in trouble", the variety of terms for "drunken" and scores of other softened words.[2]

On the other hand, language changes may be brought about by individuals and groups who manipulate language in the interests of a cause, a viewpoint or some other special bias. When a Chicago paper refers to the unemployment insurance bill, it persistently headlines it as the "idleness" insurance bill. When the break in sterling took the English pound to its lowest level, newspaper readers were not told that sterling was down but that "gold leaps up again." Groups change language in their own interests. "The concrete realities of politics are

[1] Mencken, H. L., *The American Language*, pp. 121–124, 1936.
[2] Huse, H. R., *op. cit.*, pp. 32 *ff.*, for further illustrations of euphemistic terms.

individual human beings, living together in national groups.   Politicians
—and to some extent we are all politicians—substitute abstractions for
these concrete realities, and having done this, proceed to invest each
abstraction with an appearance of concreteness by personifying it."[1]
When a military writer likes to speak of "sabers" and "rifles" instead
of "cavalrymen" or "foot soldiers," he has abstracted in this fashion.
In a recent Associated Press report, one reads, "The Japanese troops
accepted the challenge.   Japanese reinforcements are being rushed in
consideration of casualties expected."   Troops have been personified in
the idea that they as individuals had accepted a "challenge" and, on
the other hand, have been tragically abstracted when referred to as
"casualties."   The astute political leader substitutes new words for those
which have become unpopular.   LeBon noted that "when crowds have
come, as the result of political upheavals or changes of belief, to acquire
a profound antipathy for the images evoked by certain words, the first
duty of the true statesman is to change the words without, of course,
laying hands on the things themselves."[2]   The work of the Consulate
and the Empire in France, according to De Tocqueville, consisted, in
part, in clothing the old practices and institutions with new words,
replacing the words in disrepute.

The manipulation of language by the advertising man is obvious.
Corsets and underwear are far too unromantic and harshly descriptive for
an advertising vocabulary, which is enriched by the following: (1932),
Freeflex, Youthlastic, Chalkettes; (1933), Snugflex, Scamp Bra, Teds;
(1934), Joylastiques, Sheathlynes, Lasteze; (1935), Scandalettes, Silk-
skin, Slim-a-Hip; (1936), Super-Control, Adaptolette, Flexees and
Stryps.   As I walked to my office today, a blaring radio informed me
that "Van Raalte is unsurpassed in modifying the rear profile."

All of this is not mere legerdemain of the word, so to speak.   Members
of large publics do not understand words as mere labels.   Ogden and
Richards indicate that words become our masters because the nature of
language fosters a belief in the independent reality of what are merely
verbal contrivances.   We are emotionally conditioned to certain words.
That is why interest groups manipulate language.

EMOTIONS, WORDS AND OPINION

It is reported that a professor of economics recently delivered to a
popular audience a scholarly address on economic problems and foreign
affairs.   Respectful applause followed the lecture.   But when the following speaker said, "Prof. *X* has given us a learned address, but I
think he missed the essential point—what the world wants is more

[1] Huxley, A., *The Olive Tree*, p. 96, 1937.
[2] LeBon, G., *The Crowd*, p. 121, 1896.

brotherly love," the applause was deafening.[1] The second speaker had mentioned an emotionally tinged word. "Love" has been much mouthed in the Christian tradition and has acquired still more emotional conno tations in the romantic tradition. We remember that in *Of Thee I Sing* the presidential candidate was successful on the one-word platform—love.

That, as members of large publics, we are conditioned to respond with various emotions to certain words is an obvious fact. An American electorate, congregation, audience, reader of class periodicals or adver tising public is, at times, the victim of a leadership manipulating emo tionally tinged words. Emotional responses play a large part in the popular-opinion process. Leaders and special pleaders, advertising men and publicity experts use various appeals to the emotions. In the art of propaganda, the attempt is made to use catchwords that will arouse emotion and thwart reflection. However emotion may be described in psychological terms, the individual is aware of behavior during disturbed states of bodily and mental functions that differs from behavior in the absence of such disturbance. One of the uses of language is to stimulate such disturbances and the resulting behavior. Fear, anger, resentment, insecurity, avid self-seeking and many other emotional ele ments are related to certain words. Only the intellectually mature person, and he only under exceptionally favorable conditions of training and of the immediate situation, may partly escape from this bondage to words. His escape is only intermittent.

Appeals to traditional emotional attitudes may be made when the simplest logical analysis would indicate a quite different state of affairs. In the battle against votes for women, especially in England, women were appealed to as "ministering angels," "gentler natures" and "civi lizing influences." In the name of "noble maternity," they were asked to abjure political functioning.

Escape from the emotive words is sometimes achieved by inventing new words or changing the designative terms. For example, certain human relationships and social processes have common names in popular parlance. A "science of society," however, develops an esoteric verbiage in sociology or ethnology or law. This is necessary in order not only to designate concepts and provide for the niceties of distinctions but also to create a certain popular respect and to avoid the connotations of the popularly used emotive words. A part of the Marxist appeal has been a complex language with the resultant appearance of objectivity. The two volumes on Middletown have achieved a large number of readers. These books are excellently written and, in comparison with the com munity surveys that preceded them, relatively thorough studies. How ever, one factor in their popularity among diverse reading publics has

[1] Garrett, J., "America Laughs at Herself," *The New Statesman and Nation*, Sept. 29, 1934, p. 394.

been that an ethnological terminology has largely concealed whatever bias their authors may harbor. When, in the middle of the last century, a few bold professors concluded that sex was neither an obscene mystery nor a dirty joke, they invented a polysyllabic Latin vocabulary with which to discuss it. Using terms that were devoid of popular emotional associations, they were able to discuss sexual functioning with the minimum of disturbance to large publics and to themselves.

Among masses of people, emotional attitudes are related to particular words by training, inculcation, formal and informal education. In earliest language experience there are words rich in emotional, rather than conceptual, connotation. "Bugaboo, hobgoblin, bugbear, hoo-doo, have no clear conceptual content, but they do stand for something to be feared. And in maturity we have a long list of terms whose real significance is as much emotional as it is conceptual. Such, for example, are the terms mother, home, country, traitor, and the like."[1] In the American community there are emotional responses to such words and phrases as "honesty," "kindness," "booster," "knocker," "success," "average man," "practical," "snob," "common sense," "steady," "progress," "radical," "conservative," "atheist," "community spirit," "the happy child," "red-blooded," "the American way," "expert" and scores of other terms.[2] Lists of words with obvious emotional connotations may be developed for different cultures, ages, groups and classes, and the like. Prof. Friedrich notes a greater emotional response to the words and phrases of nation and country among rural dwellers than among urban proletarians.[3] In a recent study a series of sixteen statements on social issues was presented to 742 subjects, who were asked to indicate "yes" or "no" to each of them. Some time later, these statements were presented once more, having been divided into equal groups of two statements each, with each group headed by the comment that the statements in it were typical of conservatism, fascism, patriotism, pacifism, liberalism, radicalism, socialism or communism. The subjects once more indicated "yes" or "no" to each statement. No reliable shifts in response were noted for conservatism, patriotism, pacifism, liberalism or socialism. But opposition to fascism was indicated by shifts of from -11.8 to -70.0 per cent in the various groups, radicalism brought about a negative change of -32.1 per cent, and communism caused -19.0 to -62.2 per cent of the subjects to change their answers.[4] Societal leaders, in public utterances, constantly make use of their knowledge of the effects

---

[1] Britan, H. H., "The Function of Emotions," *Psychol. Rev.*, 33: 37.

[2] Lynd, R., and Lynd, H. M., *Middletown in Transition*, pp. 403–419, 1937.

[3] Friedrich, C. J., "The Agrarian Basis of Emotional Nationalism," *Pub. Opin. Quar.*, 1: 2: 50–61.

[4] Menafee, S. C., "The Effect of Stereotyped Words on Political Judgments," *Am. Sociol. Rev.*, 1: 614–621.

of certain words upon their hearers or readers. Of course, the process is as old as human speech. When attacked by a mob in the Temple at Jerusalem, Paul started to discuss resurrection. This immediately divided the crowd into warring factions, and he was momentarily forgotten. Today, leadership is not necessarily more astute, but its knowledge of language is systematized and more consciously applied.

The relations between language and communication, between symbol and meaning, between words and understanding limit and, also, direct the opinion process, as well as other social processes.[1] But the study of these relations, being peculiarly baffling, has been relatively neglected in social psychology. What are the prevailing attitudes toward certain words and phrases in cultures, classes or groups? The words used in popular controversy and opinion have shifting, variable meanings. How widespread are such attitudes; who is involved; how were such attitudes developed; when and how were emotional conditionings accomplished; how may they be changed? To what extent are meanings involved? Is there a relatively clear-cut concept or understanding of the definitive limits of meaning within which the word may be used? Have certain words, contemporaneously used as catchalls or as vague and hazy reference terms, always been so vague when they have been used by large publics in the past? What is the history of their popular definition? For example, congregations contentedly sing popular hymns without the slightest understanding of many of the phrases therein. These phrases had meaning in the theological controversies of a century or two ago. In a sense, language makes possible the preservation of the emotions of bygone periods, because the anxiety dreams, the fears and the hopes of past ages may be described. But if such emotional experiences of earlier publics are to be understood by contemporaries, they must be described in the language of contemporaries. Phrases, slogans and words about which were woven the warmest emotional loyalties or which aroused fear and antagonism a century ago may leave the modern reader undisturbed. To recapture in any adequate way the significance of any symbols of a people of a bygone age is always difficult. And language symbols are usually more difficult to understand adequately in retrospect than are concretizations in stone, design, pictures and images. How may sentiments be countered by other sentiments? What are the limits of language manipulation on any given topic? What is the record of the language of popular rationalizations in American experience? The members of a businessmen's luncheon club of a decade

[1] For further discussion of language, thought and opinion, see Arnold, T. W., *The Folklore of Capitalism*, 1937, especially Chaps. 5, 7, 8; Chase, S., *The Tyranny of Words*, 1938.

ago achieved an emotional glow over "service" and thereby often rationalized group acquisitiveness. When have publics learned formal definitions, but have not understood, or have misunderstood, the essence? These and many other questions about language, opinion and social behavior cannot be exactly answered. There is an art, but not a science, of these language forms.

CHAPTER VI

THE LEADER AND PERSONAL SYMBOLISM

How many turn back toward dreams and magic, how many children
Run home to Mother Church, Father State,
To find in their arms the delicious warmth and folding of souls.
The age weakens and settles home toward old ways.
An age of renascent faith: Christ said, Marx wrote, Hitler says,
And though it seems absurd we believe.
Sad children, yes. It is lonely to be an adult, you need a father.[1]

The problems of authority and individual freedom and of impersonal
and personal authority are persistent. Such problems are also as old
as the higher civilizations. Institutional authority of impersonal types
is exhibited in the control exercised by laws, constitutions, creeds, symbols, and the like. For the past four centuries, the Western world has
been the arena of intermittent revolts against the authority of church
and state, and against standards in art and science and economic life.[2]
Personal authority is exhibited in the activities of the leader as headman
and symbol, as well as in his organizing, directorial, functional capacities.
Such personal leadership may gain in authority in institutional crises.
At such points, large publics exhibit their persistent fondness for
the understandable personal symbol and follow the dramatic leader. The
recent charismatic tendencies of Germans and Italians illustrate the
flight of harried masses to the personal leader.

But leadership functions not only at world crises but to some extent
in every social situation. The roles and functions of the leader, the
characteristics of the leader and the techniques of leadership vary with
the situation. Various groups, differing in size, the nature of their
constituents and the group purposes and functions, require different
types of leadership. The characteristics of the leader and the leadership
process are obviously dissimilar in a board meeting, a theater fire, and a
Southern political gathering. Moreover, types of leadership and of
preferred personalities vary greatly in different cultures and at different
periods of culture history.[3] There are no universal principles of leader-

[1] Jeffers, Robinson, *Such Counsels You Gave to Me*, p. 105, 1937. Reprinted by
courtesy of Random House, Inc.

[2] Dewey, J., "Authority and Social Change," in *Authority and The Individual*,
Harvard Tercentenary Publications, 1937.

[3] Prof. P. A. Sorokin has presented an ingenious analysis in his *Social and Cultural
Dynamics*, vol. III, Chap. 15, 1937.

ship, but there are processes of leadership and patterns of relationship between leader and follower that are characteristic of types of groups.

The Bases of Personal Authority

The sociologist Georg Simmel declared that submission may be exhibited toward a person, a group or an impersonal principle.[1] But in large groups, personal authority is the kind most frequently and dramatically exercised. The leader is the most vital authority to the common man. However, in special groups, also, thinking and discussion are frequently carried on by appeal to personal authority. This volume is strewn with references, quotations and footnotes, because those quoted have explained or defined with greater clarity than I and because the academic tradition decrees the allocation of intellectual credit. I have greater security and you are more readily convinced by such references.

Large groups persistently ascribe social change, political innovation and mechanical invention to personal leaders. Folk tales and legends reflect the doings of heroes, anthropomorphized gods and devils. The personal stereotype is pervasive. This tendency in the individual mental process we have described as a form of stereotyping. The popularization of abstractions and processes is achieved by personalization. The social philosopher has long understood this process. Milton stated, "Delineate so, by likening spiritual to corporal forms, as may express them best." Today, the terse slogan of *Time* magazine is "Names Make News." The names of significant personalities become tags for processes. The idea of mass production is referred to in Europe as "fordisme." The medieval churchman associated wanton destruction with the sack of Rome in 455 by the Vandals, hence "vandalism." Personal leaders provide many symbols of discourse.

Members of large publics understand the functioning of personality and personal relationships better than they do the statement of abstractions, principles or ideologies. Concern with the personal characteristics of oneself and of others is a daily preoccupation. During the past year, the American literate public has bought over 600,000 copies of *How to Win Friends and Influence People;* over 200,000 copies of *Life Begins at Forty;* over 100,000 copies of *Wake Up and Live.* Interpersonal influences and values are a popular interest. The desired personal characteristics provide one basis for the choice of popular leaders and are also, in part, molded by the attributes of those leaders. Although there is a growing tendency toward impersonal thinking, principles and theories are often abandoned in crises, and the old, personal, leader-follower relationship is embraced once more. The struggle between the

[1] Spykman, N., *The Social Theory of Georg Simmel*, p. 100, 1925.

emphasis on the great man, the leader principle reincarnated in Der Führer, Il Duce and Stalin, and the historical materialism of a socialist movement, rising through the nineteenth century, has found no solution in the popular mind. Analysis of movements, parties and other large-group phenomena in the nonpersonal terms of general social process was achieving some increased popular understanding during the past century. The successive state and economic convulsions of the past twenty years made attractive once more the dramatic personal symbolism of the great man. Large publics have retrogressed to the values with which they were acquainted.

The quest for personal leadership is based in part upon fear and uncertainty. In projecting the father image onto the leaders of the great society, millions of followers seek for the security and personal response of an intimate primary group. There is more belief in authority than in fact and experimentation, because the members of large publics have more confidence in their ability to discern personal qualities than in their capacity to winnow out the pertinent facts. And uncertainty is terrifying to the average man. Publics seek for charismatic leaders.

The guide most favored by mankind has been the medicine man, or priest, reputed to have direct access to divine wisdom; and in his wake came along presently the philosopher who, sinking a shaft into his own mighty mind, and prospecting and introspecting through its darksome galleries, emerged with Absolutes infallible to the good life; Truth, Beauty, Duty, Faith, Loyalty. The philosopher has never seriously crowded his predecessor in popularity, because he could never tell people, in a few plain, loud words what to do. Besides, philosophers talked a mysterious jargon and each has contradicted the other. When the old-time priest rumbled out of his beard, "Thus saith the Lord: Fetch a goat!" that was something any clod could understand and carry in mind. He hurried off to get the goat.[1]

Today, the quest for certainty, the quest for simple, understandable, comprehensible plans in a world of complex social relationships, has intensified the quest for trustworthy personal authority. Authoritarian political leaders are not merely officials, directors, organizers and guides. They are spiritual chiefs. Reliance upon them may be misplaced confidence, but it is psychologically understandable.

But the demand for personal leadership in our time is, in a sense, a mystic quest. It is the search for a magic formula, as if someone had the big secrets and the problem of the masses were simply to find the right person. Fundamentally, however, the derangements of our social order are faults of balance, proportion, organization and the

---

[1] Keller, A. G., *Man's Rough Road*, p. 4, 1932. Quoted by permission of Yale University Press and Frederick A. Stokes Company.

absence of a fundamental logic of life. If there existed an adequate description of the flaws of our order—whereby masses of people are thwarted, frustrated and, hence, enraged—very ordinary leaders could explain it simply. The dogmatic prophet can only confuse.

Social philosophers have often maintained that the basis for personal authority resides in the instinctive attitudes of masses of men. A generation ago, Gustave LeBon wrote of the instinctive need of all beings forming a crowd to obey a leader.[1] Roberto Michels recently wrote that the basis for leadership "may be the instinctive, natural submission of the weak or conventional man who yields to any government, autocratic or democratic, national or alien, because he accepts without question the traditional values or existing configurations of the rapidly shifting social forces."[2] It is not necessary to posit an instinct for such response. Indeed, Prof. Michels himself indicates a basis in the second half of his sentence. Habituation to leader-follower patterns is developed from our traditional values in human relations.

INSTITUTIONAL AUTHORITY

Although the authority of institutions is expressed in part through personal representatives, there is a vast difference between institutional authority and personal leadership. Institutional authority resides in the traditions, creeds, constitutions, laws and principles of a church, state, legal system, system of knowledge or traditional order. Although leaders of successful mass movements attempt to institutionalize their positions, so that they may be perpetuated, the power process is quite different in institutional administration from that of personal domination.[3] Intermittent revolts against institutional authority are the dominant trend of the past four centuries, but there are some minor trends in the opposite direction. For example, one might cite the small but growing group of intellectuals, conscious of a need for order in the modern scene, who have joined the Roman Catholic church, thus reversing the intellectuals' centuries-old criticism of ecclesiastical authority.

TYPES OF LEADERSHIP

Many classifications of types of leadership appear in the literature of social psychology. No type classification has thus far proved convincing or adequate. There is a bewildering variety of human associations within which the leader functions. Classifiers, with their various

[1] LeBon, G., *The Crowd*, Chap. 3, 1896.
[2] Michels, R., "Authority," *Ency. Soc. Sci.*, 2: 319.
[3] Read the discussion of the development and mortality of power in Merriam, C. E., *Political Power*, 1934.

objectives, have been preoccupied with some one facet of society. However, there is one useful distinction that may be posited as a starting point for classification of authority types. Leadership may be distinguished from domination,[1] the leader from the headman[2]; leadership may be distinguished from coercion,[3] power with from power over.[4] Such a distinction is implicit in our preceding discussion. "Leadership is a process of mutual stimulation which, by the successful interplay of relevant individual differences, controls human energy in the pursuit of a common cause."[5] But authority may also result from societal position, from office holding, from membership in any dominant group or institution. Such position permits the individual to exert domination, to be a headman, to coerce. Integrative leadership functions through personal qualities.

Personal leadership, as distinguished from other forms of authority, may be usefully differentiated into representative, or symbolic, and dynamic, or creative, leadership.[6] The representative leader serves as a symbol for a group without changing its direction or purposes. Dynamic or creative leadership exists when the personal leader directs or modifies the objectives of the group. Obviously, the same individual frequently functions in both capacities. Nevertheless, this is a useful theoretical dichotomy. It is also true that institutional authority and personal leadership are exhibited frequently by the same individual. The Popes of the Roman Catholic church have often been notable examples of this truth.

Classifications of types of authority, other than these fundamental dichotomies, have depended upon the purposes of the writers. Let us illustrate from a few studies, in order to indicate the range and diversity of classification:

Sanderson:[7]	Bogardus:[8]
1. static	1. direct or indirect
2. executive	2. partisan or scientific
3. professional	3. social, executive, mental
4. group leaders	4. autocratic, paternalistic, democratic
	5. specialists in leadership

[1] Pigors, P., *Leadership and Domination*, 1935.

[2] Cowley, W. H., "Three Distinctions in the Study of Leaders," *Jour. Abn. Soc. Psychol.*, 23: 144–157.

[3] Schmidt, R., "Leadership," *Ency. Soc. Sci.*, 9: 282.

[4] Follett, M. P., *Creative Experience*, p. 189, 1924.

[5] Pigors, *op. cit.*, p. 16.

[6] Schmidt, *op. cit.*, 9: 282–286.

[7] Sanderson, D., and Nafe, R. W., "Studies in Rural Leadership," *Pub. Am. Sociol. Soc.*, 23: 163–175.

[8] Bogardus, E. W., *Leaders and Leadership*, Chap. 2, 1934.

Nafe:[1]		Munro:[2]
1. volunteer	5. temporary	1. reformers
2. drafted	6. conscious	2. bosses
3. general	7. professional	3. leaders
4. specialized	8. paid	

There are many other classifications. For the most part, the psychologist has attempted to classify types in terms of personality types, and the sociologist, in terms of selection for group needs.

As we have indicated, it is not profitable to attempt to classify types of leaders on the basis of personal qualities alone. These must be considered in conjunction with the situation in which leadership was exhibited. Psychological studies have often been unconvincing because the personal qualities of the leaders were not adequately related to situation. From a study of forty-one psychological biographies of leaders, F. Fearing concludes that the factors most frequently stressed by the authors are: (1) childhood experiences as conditioning factors, (2) the unconscious motivation of adult action, (3) the compensatory component in much individual activity and (4) rationalization.[3] Such studies represent a particularistic approach. On the other hand, the collection of data about leaders, their parentage, place of birth, occupational status, economic status, educational status, group affiliation, and the like, is inadequate.[4] Useful though such data may be, they do not explain the leadership process. We need now a large number of studies of institutional growth and the types of leaders who have emerged at different stages of that growth.[5] Such data should be correlated, whenever possible, with personality studies of the particular leaders as they develop. Accurate portrayal will not atomize the process but will show a functional relationship between personal qualities and situational needs.

THE CHARACTERISTICS OF LEADERSHIP IN LARGE PUBLICS

All dynamic or creative leadership influences the opinions of followers. Institutional authority may simply reflect the mores. But dynamic

---

[1] Nafe, R. W., "A Psychological Description of Leadership," *Jour. Soc. Psychol.*, 1: 249.

[2] Munro, W. B., *Personality in Politics*, 1924.

[3] Fearing, F., "Psychological Studies of Historical Personalities," *Psychol. Bull.*, 24: 521–539.

[4] Sorokin, P. A., "Leaders of Labor and Radical Movements in the United States and Foreign Countries," *Am. Jour. Sociol.*, 33: 382–411; "Leadership and Geographical Mobility," *Sociol. Soc. Res.*, 12: 21–23.

Taussig, F. W., and Joslyn, C. S., *American Business Leaders*, 1932.

Visher, S. S., "Ecology of American Notables," *Human Biol.*, 1: 544–554.

[5] A vigorous discussion of the relation of the leader to "field structure" is presented in Brown, J. F., *Psychology and the Social Order*, Chap. 17, 1936.

leadership also functions in guiding choices at levels below those at which opinions could be said to exist. Goldfish, placed in a bowl with a fish that has been successfully conditioned to a simple aquarium maze, learn at a faster rate than do those in a group without a leader.[1] In human groups, leaders provide many patterns of behavior which are copied by followers who have not considered the alternatives. However, from the smallest to the largest groups the opinion process is influenced by leaders in varying degrees.

The characteristics of successful leaders and the processes of leadership in influencing opinion differ with the size and type of groups and with the situation or "field structure." There do not appear to be general characteristics of leadership that are everywhere effective in influencing the opinions of followers. The psychologist's quest for general leadership "traits" has been futile. The characteristics of leaders of small discussion groups—committees, gangs, families, clans, neighborhoods and other small groups—differ from leadership qualities in large publics consisting of thousands and hundreds of thousands of members. There is some experimental literature on leadership in small groups.[2] Certainly, opinions are influenced in all such groups, but we shall not discuss the studies of face-to-face relations. In the large groups and publics, there are diverse preferences for leadership qualities, depending upon the group's size, organization, purposes, relation to other groups, the prevailing attitudes and values and, in general, upon its field structure. The situation must always ultimately determine the preferred qualities. Leadership qualities vary under democracy, fascism, communism; in different ages, periods, cultures; under national ascendency or degradation; in an expanding or contracting economy.

The psychologist rarely considers the situation in his search for leadership traits. But long before the social psychologist attempted his more detailed classifications, the social philosopher had much to say about the characteristics of leaders in large publics. Certain generalizations are essentially valid for whole groups of cultures and over long time periods. For example, the advantage of positive statements in comparison with negations has been realized in Western cultures for many centuries.

[1] Allee, W. C., "Relatively Simple Animal Aggregations," in *Handbook for Social Psychology* (Murchison, C., ed.), p. 944, 1935.

[2] Examine the publications of *The Inquiry*, especially: Sheffield, A. D., *Creative Discussion, A Statement of Method for Leaders and Members of Discussion Groups*, 1926; Elliott, H. S., *The Process of Group Thinking*, 1932.

Hollingworth, H. L., *The Psychology of the Audience*, 1935, has summarized the studies on audience situations.

Murphy, G., Murphy, L. B., and Newcomb, T. M., *Experimental Social Psychology*, pp. 522–528, 1937, summarize the studies of leadership in children's groups.

Regardless of the situation, large publics cherish the positive statement. Their own requirements may be vague, but the leader of opinion in any large public states a positive program most of the time, although his program may be an attack on the existing order. The individual thinker or small esoteric groups may maintain a negative or pessimistic viewpoint in philosophy, political ideas or economic doctrine. But not the large publics in the Western world of the last few centuries. Grim predestination never won the mass converts as did Methodism. And the village atheist of the last half of the nineteenth century trod his lonely way amidst the bounding folk life of America. The agnostic or atheistic attitude is disparaged. Political nihilism was never a mass doctrine. In such a "climate of opinion," the confident leader with a positive statement is at an advantage. The power of J. L. Lewis and the Congress of Industrial Organizations has been primarily in their positive, if vague, program. The Fascist leaders state positive programs embellished as a great spiritual message. Mussolini mouths grandiose generalities about the rebuilding of the glory that was Rome. A depressed and bewildered nation welcomed the positive and confident assertions of Roosevelt. Contemporary insecurities have intensified the quest for leaders with positive programs. In the democracies, this has made ever more true the old political maxim "You can't whip somebody with nobody."

Although leadership qualities cannot be considered abstractly but must be related to the type of situation and the specific situation, we may generalize somewhat about leadership qualities under nineteenth-century political democracy. Men were leaders in democracies without possessing all the qualities we shall note, but not without evidencing many of them. Viscount Bryce said that leaders in democracy must possess initiative, comprehension of the forces that affect the needs of the people, eloquence of voice and writing, self-confidence and the ability to inspire confidence, attract capable lieutenants and achieve personal publicity.[1] These he considered the minimum general requirements.

Political leaders must arouse faith in themselves. In the rapidly changing social order of the Western world, faith is accorded to the leaders who exhibit speed of decision. Decisiveness, especially at crises, injects something clear-cut into the vagueness and confusion of the situation. In a battery of tests given to a number of leaders, W. H. Cowley included three on speed of decision. The leaders made unquestionably high scores on these tests.[2] The most popular American presidents have all exhibited at least apparent speed of decision.

[1] Bryce, Viscount, *Modern Democracies*, Bk. II, Chap. 76, 1921.
[2] Cowley, W. H., "The Traits of Face-to-face Leaders," *Jour. Abn. Soc. Psychol.*, 26: 304–313.

"The prime condition of ascendency is the presence of undirected energy in the person over whom it is to be exercised; it is not so much forced upon us from without as demanded from within."[1] Leaders survive and grow in power who reflect the vague feelings and general aspirations of large groups. Hitler hurls defiance at what many followers consider international persecution. President Roosevelt has retained numerous followers who oppose almost every specific measure his administration has put forward. But they agree with a general attitude that he seems to express clearly and with obvious justice, portraying existing convictions in a vivid manner. It is in this sense that it has long been declared of leaders in democracy that they are "the common mind to an uncommon degree."

The popular leader must have or build up some elements of personal uniqueness. The most popular American leaders have been colorful figures. Dramatic situations for exhibiting uniqueness must exist or be created. He is a character. A distinctive carriage and style of dress, unusual phrases, gestures and dramatic utterances have been his usual stock in trade. A political commentator has written, . . . "probably the most important single accomplishment for the politically ambitious, the most effective asset they can possibly acquire, is the fine art of seeming to say something without doing so."[2] The leader has a marginal uniqueness and magnetism.[3] If he does not have these qualities and attains high office, his publicity men ascribe them to him.

Breadth of sympathy is requisite for successful leadership. Contemporary insecurity increases the importance of friendliness in the leader. In crisis situations the great humane figure becomes legendary. Lincoln is our most notable example. Firm in public, he was kindly and sympathetic in personal relations. It is difficult to feign sympathy. Crude though the expressions of sympathy of the urban precinct leader may be, they are more often than not a product of genuine human interest, as well as of political tradition. Indeed, some of the most corrupt of political bosses have been men of genuine and strong sympathies. And constituents understand and appreciate such responses, though they may be vague as to the allocation of city funds. Smiles, greetings, participation in simple human incidents, kindliness, a measure of conviviality are necessary to the politician who must come in contact with his public.

The leader appears as master of the situation. He is dominant and assured. In face-to-face situations he may be blatantly assured, as witness the techniques of the demagogue or revivalist. On coming

[1] Cooley, C. H., *Human Nature and the Social Order*, p. 319, 1902.
[2] Kent, F. R., *Political Behavior*, p. 73, 1928.
[3] Bogardus, *op. cit.*, Chap. 16.

upon the platform the demagogue commands, "Let's try that applause again," or, "I ought to get a better hand on that one," if one of his epigrams fails. Of Aimée Semple McPherson, it is said, "As a director she is incomparable. While others are performing, she never for an instant permits interest to flag; at the first sign of restlessness she steps forward. 'All join in with him now! Sail on!' If a young singer's voice proves weak and, therefore, uninspiring, Sister snatches her own tambourine and drives home the rhythm. Let a recitation be dull, she will advance beaming to inquire if it isn't grand."[1] However, browbeating is an unsubtle, though often an effective form of command. Mastery and personal ascendency depend upon a myriad of factors. Physical characteristics are important in the more visually dramatic types of situations. The oft-criticized studies of E. B. Gowin on the size and weight of executives indicated that the more important executives were heavier and taller than the less important.[2] Though part of the differences in weight may be explained in terms of age and sedentary life, the differences in height are not so readily explained. There are fashions in preferred physical types, but these characteristics cannot be considered in isolation.

A certain reserve and a modicum of mystery and inscrutability are characteristic of popular political leadership.[3] Mystery may be crudely presented, as in Hitler's assurance to mass audiences that he had the plans for the economic regeneration of the German Reich in the drawers of his desk in the Brown House in Munich. The imagination of followers is stimulated. Even the most frank and apparently confiding of leaders retains areas of reserve. The creation of mystery may be heightened by an inscrutable countenance, silence (von Moltke was said to be silent in seven languages), mysterious phrases, journeys, meetings, and the like. The primitive leader and folk leaders made much of mystery. Doctors, lawyers and religious leaders are often titillatingly inscrutable. Certain professors and lecturers lead their audiences on and on by the method of the "big secrets." The modern political leader cannot forgo this effective technique of power.

The leader of large publics must be an organizer and also make astute use of existing organizations. Under the party system in democracies, the leader must have ability to function within party organizations. Indeed, Frank R. Kent insists that nothing will compensate for the lack of ability to deal with party organization.[4] Leaders of mass movements must competently organize their contacts with lieutenants and select

---

[1] Nafe, *op. cit.*, 1: 250. Permission to quote granted.
[2] Gowin, E. B., *The Executive and His Control of Men*, 1915.
[3] Cooley, *op. cit.* The chapter on leadership is the most brilliant essay in English on leadership and personal ascendency.
[4] Kent, *op. cit.*, pp. 68 *ff.*

subordinates who will organize the channels of communication and of administration out to the most distant followers. Of course, this is all carried on within the values of a particular culture. When Hitler speaks, the German people are told that there can be no excuse for not having listened to every word spoken by their beloved leader. But the American political leader, not only of groups in power but of those striving for power, must be capable of organizing or of selecting lieutenants to organize rituals, ceremonies, public relations, subgroups, committees, divisions, the efficient direction of energies of followers, the briefing of records and a host of other directorial duties. He organizes and integrates.

We have indicated some of the general characteristics of leaders in large democratic publics. In conclusion, we shall list the requisite qualities, as described in the writings of a number of commentators. None of these lists is complete or adequate, but they illustrate the existing generalizations.

THE QUALITIES OF LEADERS

Bernard:[1]

Trained experience	Humanitarianism	Soundness of judgment
Size	Honesty to cause	Mental flexibility
Good looks	Good faith	Forethought
Appearance of strength of body	Insight	Moral vision
	Courage	Positive idealism
Appearance of strength of character	Persistence	Inhibition
	Good natural ability	Self-discipline
Self-confidence	Originality	Even temper
Sympathy	Initiative	
Sense of justice	Good intellectual training	

Allport:[2]

Trait of ascendence	Reinforcement of energy	Keenly susceptible to social stimulation
Physical power	Restraint	
High motility	Inscrutability	Tact
Tonus	Expansiveness in field of action	Zeal
Erect, aggressive carriage		Social participation
Tenacity	High intelligence	Character
Face-to-face mode of address	Understanding	Drive

Bogardus:[3]

Superiority complex	Mental energy and its focalization	Achievement
Marginal uniqueness		Organizing ability
Fine physique	Confidence	Mental flexibility
size	Painstaking forethought	Versatility
height	Inhibition	Enthusiasm

[1] Bernard, L. L., *Introduction to Social Psychology*, Chap. 34, 1926.
[2] Allport, F. H., *Social Psychology*, pp. 419 *ff.*, 1924.
[3] Borgardus, E. S., *Social Psychology*, Chaps. 36–39, 1917.

Bogardus: (*Continued*)

Physical energy and endurance	Emanatory	Prestige
		Sociality

LeBon:[1]

Keen foresight	Tyranny	Energy
Conviction	Will	Prestige
Perseverance	intermittent	Dominance
	permanent	

Miller:[2]

Simplicity	Judgment	Courage
Earnestness	Justice	Faith
Self-control	Enthusiasm	Loyalty
Assiduity	Perseverance	Acumen
Common sense	Tact	Truthfulness
		Honor

TRAITS

The psychological discussion of the characteristics of personality, including leadership and subordination, has been carried on primarily in terms of "traits." Consideration of characteristic dispositions or traits as a "certain kind of response manifested in a particular kind of situation"[3] and of the listing and classifications of such traits for various human groupings has been hindered by the conflict between biologically minded psychologists and culturally minded sociologists. There are great individual differences, and there are great diversities of the social situation. To assume characteristic dispositions in particular situations means ignoring neither the basis of the disposition in the organism nor the diversity of expression of the disposition in various situations. Considered thus, the concept of trait is usable, just as the sociologist's concept of attitude is permissible. No single trait or any combination of traits determines behavior; the conditions of the moment are also decisive. Traits are discovered through inference from the individual functioning. The psychologist properly considers traits as the most reasonable units for use in the study of personality. But he must guard against any assumption of their existence as unvarying units.

It is assumed, then, that there are characteristic dispositions or traits underlying the conduct of a person. The psychologist does not usually assume that the traits correspond exactly to the neuropsychic dispositions of individuals. Nor are traits assumed to be innate, although innate factors are related to some of them. In large measure, traits are acquired in the social experience of the individual, being determined by the pre-

[1] LeBon, *op. cit.*, Bk. II, Chap. 3.
[2] Miller, Major A. H., *Leadership*, Chap. 2, 1920.
[3] Murphy, G., *et al.*, *op. cit.*, p. 779, 1937.

vailing values of the society. Is the businessman brusque? The social definition of adequate business functioning has been largely responsible. Is he ambitious? This characteristic, as well as the objects of his ambition, are socially defined. Though some traits are peculiar to the individual, others are common to classes and groups.

And what are the traits of leadership and domination? We have already noted that the characteristics of leadership depend upon the situation. Hence, almost any items from the complete lexicon of traits may apply to the leader under some conditions. How many traits are there? The common man as well as the psychologist uses trait names to designate the characteristics of personality. A large vocabulary of trait names has been accumulated. Allport has listed about 18,000 such terms among the 400,000 words in *Webster's New International Dictionary*.[1]

Dispositions are inferred from behavior. And the significant behavior is differently designated in various cultures and periods. Allport states, "There is, however, a second influence determining our lexicon of trait names, namely, the tendency of each social epoch to characterize human qualities in the light of standards and interests peculiar to the times. Historically, the introduction of trait names can be seen to follow this principle of cultural (not psychological) determination to a striking degree."[2] The current cultural interests determine them. Allport relates Galenian medicine to "sanguine," "choleric," "phlegmatic," "good-humored"; the Protestant Reformation to "sincere," "pious," "bigoted," "fanatic"; eighteenth-century subjectivity to "depression," "daydream," "apathy," "diffidence," "embarrassment"; the present preoccupations are reflected in "booster," "hoodlum," "yes man," "climber," "chiseler," "Babbitt," etc.

The characterization of the most important traits is often difficult. The traits are not wholly independent of one another. The task of designating them by adequate systems of terms is surrounded by many pitfalls. Common and individual traits require almost endless enumeration. However, the task is not always so intricate, for the significant traits do appear in clusters of general dispositions. The central traits can be identified. Those related to leadership will depend upon the situation, the type of group and the leadership process to be considered. One cannot say that Mr. Jones has 80 per cent aggressiveness and will be a good leader. Eighty per cent aggressiveness on a scale of 100 per cent may be too much aggressiveness for some situations and too little for others. Moreover, Mr. Jones will display varying amounts of

[1] Allport, G. W., and Odbert, H. S., "Trait Names, A Psycholexical Study," *Psychol. Mon.*, No. 211, 1936.

[2] Allport, G. W., *Personality*, p. 304, 1937.

aggressiveness in different situations and may select the wrong situations in which to be overaggressive. And, further, the desirable amount of aggressiveness is also dependent upon a large number of other characteristics possessed by Mr. Jones. Abnegation is important in leaders of mass movements, who must not appear to be selfish and self-seeking. Prof. Merriam has pointed out that Gandhi, Tolstoy, Masaryk, the Franciscans and many others achieved power through apparent sacrifice.[1] But among a group of artistic creators, sacrifice has often been depreciated. All this being true, the enumeration of traits, while permissible, has thus far been largely unenlightening in the sociopsychological description of leadership.[2]

The Leader as Symbol

A symbol is a representative simplicity substituted for some complexity. As we noted when discussing psychological processes and opinion, the process of symbolizing is inevitable. The leader not only organizes a wide variety of symbols for his followers, but in many cases he himself becomes a personal symbol of paramount importance. The dynamic or creative leader may intermittently serve as a symbol, but the representative of an institution is almost wholly a group symbol.

The principal reasons for personal representations are psychological. We discussed the need for personal imagery in commenting on the basis of stereotypes. These tags for groups and types are innumerable. There are popular symbols of the male and the female, the ignorant and the learned, the aristocrat and the boor, the rich man and the poor man, and so on, in the infinity of human classifications. Human variety is too complex for popular thinking. And so there are representative personal symbols. Many such figures are provided in the graphic arts. The cartoonist and the artist implement mass thinking by providing personal stereotypes. Distorted legendary figures provide many more. But living leaders also serve as representative figures. Roosevelt, Hitler, Mussolini, Stalin, Gandhi and King George, Einstein and Dewey, Lindberg and Byrd, Shaw and Wells, Pope Pius XI and Buchman, Ford and Morgan, Chaplin and Frohman and scores of others are dynamic leaders who are likewise symbols. They have caught the imagination of mankind. Not, in all cases, the most important leaders in their fields, they are none the less the representative figures. To such figures are related the warm emotional attachments and loyalties of masses of men. Questioning of the symbols is resented. But, if once they are

---

[1] Merriam, *op. cit.*, pp. 239 *ff.*

[2] Discussions of the trait problem will be found in: Allport, G. W., *op. cit.*, Chaps. 11, 12; LaPiere, R. T., and Farnsworth, P. R., *Social Psychology*, pp. 290–311, 1936; Murphy *et al.*, *op. cit.*, pp. 274–277, 330–336.

questioned or generally discussed as symbols, they lose a part of their value. The popular discussion of the meaning of Britain's kingship during the crisis of 1937 may have done inestimable damage to the prestige of the British Crown.

The average man quests for the ideal personal figure. "The reason is that the function of the great and famous man is to be a symbol, and the real question in other minds is not so much, What are you? as, What can I believe you are? What can you help me to feel and be? How far can I use you as a symbol in the development of my instinctive tendency?"[1] Personal symbols are first obtained from the immediate environment, the father and mother, relatives and friends, but later the processes of communication provide a wealth of symbols from the general culture.

The Growth of Legends

Which leaders become symbols will be determined by the paramount values of the culture. The heroes of the past have been representative personages who have achieved dominance through strength, war, sainthood, the championship of ideal values, dignified age, courageous exploration, learning, invention, industry, and the like. In primitive life the wise, the aged and the courageous; in the Middle Ages the knight, the scholar and the Saint; in Chinese culture the formal scholar; in recent Western civilization the captains of industry have been representative men. The modern authoritarian state has reemphasized the leader principle, with its Führer and Duce.

In the creation of contemporary symbols, modern publicity plays a dominant role. The process is speeded up. In the great society, ideas about leaders are acquired primarily from press, radio and motion picture. The leader symbol of the past could not emerge so suddenly for large publics. Moreover, although gossip, legend and rumor could distort the popular image of the great man, there could not be so much conscious propaganda of his legend. In Nazi propaganda, the build-up of Hitler, Goering, Goebbels, von Hindenburg, Horst Wessel and Schlageter has been blatant. The way in which personalities are presented to the public will depend in large part upon the interests controlling particular sectors of the means of communication. In the following chapter we shall discuss the processes of legend making.

We may illustrate the difficulty of acquiring accurate information about disputed figures in political life today by referring to the biographical accounts about one young political leader in the present administration. A number of secondary leaders have been the successive targets of attack by opponents of the administration. Moley, Tugwell and

[1] Cooley, C. H., *op. cit.*, p. 341. Quoted by permission of Charles Scribner's Sons.

Secretary Ickes have been followed by two young lawyers, Thomas Corcoran and Benjamin Cohen. In the following table we have presented in parallel columns statements about Thomas Corcoran that appeared during the last six months of 1937 in five periodicals and one newspaper column.[1] These illustrate the various ways in which approximately the same information may be used to create quite different impressions. Such diverse results are achieved chiefly by implication.

[1] In the following excerpts, the italics are the author's.

Washington Merry-Go-Round[1]	Saturday Evening Post[2]	Literary Digest[3]	American Magazine[4]	Nation's Business[5]	New Republic[6]
Parentage					
Tom Corcoran was born in Pawtucket, R. I., of a mother who was the daughter of a sea captain, a very strong-willed woman. Tom goes home to visit her frequently. *His father is a small town lawyer, and sometimes comes down to visit his son in the nation's capital.*	....	... his conservative family	Both come of typical American middle-class families. Corcoran was born in Pawtucket, R. I., on December 29, 1900. *His father is a lawyer, who has among his clients a number of utility companies.*	....	....
Anonymity					
Tom Corcoran has a "passion for anonymity." In fact, he is the man who devised that phrase, once used by the President in describing the quality of a good White House secretary. *Keeping in the background to him has become almost a religion.* He has a disorderly little office in a corner of the reconstruction finance corporation, and although he now devotes all his time to the White House, he holds no rank or official position. *"The others all want the*	Because of the missteps which he made when he entered the harsh world of practical politics, Tommy lost the anonymity which was so precious to him. *Both Corcoran and Cohen decided early in their Washington careers that their importance depended on their keeping out of the public prints.* Tommy and Benny have never written an article or made a public speech. In order to avoid having his in-	Zoologists say some land tortoises live 200 years because they don't stick out their necks when in danger. Perhaps similar discretion has something to do with the prolonged political life of the singular team of Corcoran and Cohen, Presidential aids, amateur musicians, and professional intellectuals. Alternately regaling innocent neighbors with	Yet their names are little known outside the higher officialdom of Washington and the taller skyscrapers of Wall Street. *They have chosen to remain in the background. Let others strut the stage. They prefer to prompt and direct from the wings.* Occasionally they have been pushed into the spotlight by their opponents, but always they have scurried back into the protecting	If ever two young men in public service possessed that "passion" for anonymity which the reorganization committee would require of those who would be super-secretaries to the President, it is these two brilliant young lawyers. *They seem destined by nature to become two of the "Selfless Six."* . . . If they possess any one of the required qualities of a presidential assistant	There are one or two facts about these two men worth keeping in mind. One is that of all the New Dealers *they have been content to work without reward—even without the reward of glowing publicity.* All or at least most of the former aids of the President have been busy feathering their nests, hunting up prosperous connections for themselves, some of them with the very enemy itself. Tom Cor-

coran and Ben Cohen have stuck on.

epaulets," says Corcoran, referring to the more spectacular brain trusters. "But since I have no epaulets, they can't take them away from me." This is true, even today, when Corcoran has lost his anonymity—despite his passion for it—and become a very much limelighted young man.

cognito destroyed by the sharp-shooting columnists of Washington, Tommy made an alliance with them; his "kiddies" became a dragnet of news and gossip for the columnists, in return for which no mention was made of Tommy or Benny. *Corcoran drilled his little chicks to "keep their heads down," to work in secret, to avoid publicity like small-pox.*

weird musical selections and supplying Pres. Roosevelt with refreshing legislative ideas, *these ancient Brain Trusters have survived since 1933 because they haven't stuck out their necks.* Moley, Tugwell, Berle and others had their brief days in the sun. Cohen and Corcoran linger on in the shadows. . . .

shadows.
When Mr. Roosevelt presented his plan for reorganizing the executive departments, he said he wanted six personal presidential assistants, sir men "with a passion for anonymity." Corcoran and Cohen were assumed to be two of the men foremost in Roosevelt's mind, because these two have long been very close to the President, have enjoyed his deep confidence, have kept their mouths shut, and have fled publicity like a pair of bishops on a bender. . . . Their reasons for this differ . . . *Corcoran, the roving contact man, wants privacy for reasons of policy.* Most of his work, confidential and strategic, can be done more effectively without benefit of trumpeters and outriders.

to a greater degree than another, *it is the passion for anonymity.* Consistent adherence to this policy explains their political longevity in Washington. . . . *They come by the trait naturally.*

[1] Pearson, D., and Allen R., *Daily Washington Merry-Go-Round,* July 31, 1937.   Quoted by permission of the authors and United Feature Syndicate.
[2] Johnston, A., "White House Tommy," *Sat. Eve. Post,* July 31, 1937, pp. 5 ff.   Quoted by permission of The Editor.
[3] "Today's Rooseveltian Brain Trust, Team of Corcoran and Cohen," *Literary Digest,* 123: 7–8, May 22, 1937.   Quoted by permission of *Time.*
[4] Smith, B., "Corcoran and Cohen," *Am. Mag.,* August, 1937, pp. 22 ff.   Permission to quote granted.
[5] Belair, F., Jr., "Two of the 'Selfless Six,'" *Nation's Business,* 25: 25–6, July, 1937.   Permission to quote granted.
[6] Flynn, J. T., "Punches for Corcoran and Cohen," *New Republic,* 92: 46, Aug. 18, 1937.   Permission to quote granted.

Washington Merry-Go-Round[1]	Saturday Evening Post[2]	Literary Digest[3]	American Magazine[4]	Nation's Business[5]	New Republic[6]
			Scholastic Training and Accomplishments		
Tom has studied under three remarkable teachers. At *Harvard law school he was a disciple of Felix Frankfurter.* After graduation, he became the secretary to Oliver Wendell Holmes, beginning a friendship which lasted until the Justice's death. Simultaneously he also became the friend of Justice Brandeis, for whom he has done a great deal of research.	*He was a glutton for scholarships and medals in school at Pawtucket, Rhode Island,* where he was born. He was the valedictorian of his class at Brown University. He was beaten by an eyelash for a Rhodes Scholarship—one of the few academic defeats he ever suffered. . . . *It may explain something to state that at the Harvard Law School he was a favorite pupil of Prof. Felix Frankfurter,* probably the greatest living teacher and molder of young men. He came under the influence of one of the other great minds of the period,	*He had returned to Harvard for special study under Felix Frankfurter, doing research in corporation, international and labor law.*	Corcoran went to Brown University, which has nurtured other such noted "communists" as Comrade John D. Rockefeller, Jr., and Comrade Chief Justice Charles Evans Hughes. Corcoran took a lot of punishment playing center on the scrubs, graduated at the head of his class, *won all the prizes in sight for English composition and debating,* was the leading actor of the college in Sock and Buskin, won honors in mathematics, and was chosen to make the Commencement Day address. . . .	Product of a New England textile town, Corcoran spent his undergraduate days at Brown University and went on to Harvard for law, *remaining there at the suggestion of Felix Frankfurter for an extra year of study to obtain a doctorate in juridical science.* With the idea of going into teaching, Tom worked for a year as Secretary to Justice Oliver Wendell Holmes but abandoned the idea when the venerable Justice one day said to him: *"My boy, don't play marbles for fun; play for keeps."*	....

that of the late Justice Oliver Wendell Holmes, who employed Tommy as a secretary. . . . He graduated from Harvard Law School first in his class.	*Corcoran went to the Harvard Law School, graduated with high honors, took a year of graduate work,* and was chosen for the enviable job of serving for a year as secretary to Mr. Justice Holmes of the Supreme Court. Tom's good humor and high spirits made him one of the favorite companions of the old justice. Until Holmes's death seven years later, Corcoran visited him every week to read aloud to him. Corcoran read Holmes the whole of the Old Testament, of Montaigne, and of Dante.

[1] Pearson, D., and Allen R., *Daily Washington Merry-Go-Round*, July 31, 1937. Quoted by permission of the authors and United Feature Syndicate.
[2] Johnston, A., "White House Tommy," *Sat. Eve. Post*, July 31, 1937, pp. 5 ff. Quoted by permission of The Editor.
[3] "Today's Rooseveltian Brain Trust, Team of Corcoran and Cohen," *Literary Digest*, 123: 7–8, May 22, 1937. Quoted by permission of *Time*.
[4] Smith, B., "Corcoran and Cohen," *Am. Mag.*, August, 1937, pp. 22 ff. Permission to quote granted.
[5] Belair, F., Jr., "Two of the 'Selfless Six,'" *Nation's Business*, 25: 25–6, July, 1937. Permission to quote granted.
[6] Flynn, J. T., "Punches for Corcoran and Cohen," *New Republic*, 92: 46, Aug. 18, 1937. Permission to quote granted.

Washington Merry-Go-Round[1]	*Saturday Evening Post*[2]	*Literary Digest*[3]	*American Magazine*[4]	*Nation's Business*[5]	*New Republic*[6]
		Wall Street Experiences			
After leaving Holmes Corcoran joined the law firm of Cotton and Franklin, where he worked with Joseph P. Cotton, later under secretary of state, *and got to know all the tricks of Wall Street.* When chided on his past as a Wall Street lawyer, Corcoran replies: "Of course. Where did you think I got wise to the stock market—at a tea party?"	In 1925, Tommy, after graduating from Harvard Law School, served his year as secretary to Justice Holmes. *He then went to New York and became a corporation lawyer and a stock-market speculator.* Employed by the Wall Street law firm of Cotton, Franklin, Wright & Gordon, he did legal work in connection with the reorganization of companies and with the issuance of boom stocks. *Tommy testified before a congressional committee several years later that he had taken a trimming in the stock market.* He traded through a Boston brokerage house and ran up a shoestring to more than $100,000, but he did not get out in time. *A margin speculator, he wound up heavily in debt for a young man.*		Corcoran, when he had finished his service with Justice Holmes, went to New York for four years *with a noted corporation law firm.* Much of his work dealt with the complicated structure of large corporations, and he saw Wall Street from the inside. *He, too, got into the market—deep.* At one time he was believed to have a paper fortune of half a million dollars. *When the crash came he was burnt badly.* Cohen lost money in the crash, and *Corcoran was cleaned. To infer that they have both been busy ever since taking revenge makes a neat story, but seems to me rather naive.* Tom is too buoyant, Ben too philosophical, to cherish such a grudge. *They know that "Wall Street" is not a person, but an aggregation of thousands of people, good and bad, most of whom lost as much in the crash as they did*	Determined to play for keeps, young Corcoran applied for a job with the New York law firm of John W. Davis and mentioned casually that he topped his class at Harvard in 1925, two years earlier. They didn't believe him and sent him away, only to send after him when they found it was true. *But by that time Tom had located with the equally prominent New York firm of Cotton and Franklin.* . . . He was carried along on a rising market by the people for whom he worked as counsel and *at one time was worth plenty on paper.* But he was also carried along by the same people when the market dropped. *He did as they did and ended about even.* But from some of the stories that once circulated one would think he had lost an inherited fortune. *According to some accounts he was driven out of his mind by his losses and attempted*	

themselves. *They want to reform the system, not take revenge on it.*

suicide by jumping from his Wall Street office, his life being spared by the alertness of an associate who grabbed his coattail in the nick of time. Another story has it that he was driven to the same distraction *when the same heavy losses forced him to part with his watch.* When it became known that he had worked on the Securities Act, it was bruited about that he was only trying to get back at those responsible for his market losses. Attempts to run down all such stories lead up the same blind alley and only bring ridicule upon the credulous inquirer. *Whatever happened, Tom Corcoran does not look like a man who would attempt suicide. He gets too much fun out of life.*

[1] Pearson, D., and Allen R., *Daily Washington Merry-Go-Round*, July 31, 1937. Quoted by permission on of the authors and United Feature Syndicate.

[2] Johnston, A., "White House Tommy," *Sat. Eve. Post*, July 31, 1937, pp. 5 ff. Quoted by permission of The Editor.

[3] "Today's Rooseveltian Brain Trust, Team of Corcoran and Cohen," *Literary Digest*, 123: 7-8, May 22, 1937. Quoted by permission of *Time*.

[4] Smith, B., "Corcoran and Cohen," *Am. Mag.*, August, 1937, pp. 22 ff. Permission to quote granted.

[5] Belair, F., Jr., "Two of the 'Selfless Six,'" *Nation's Business*, 25: 25-6, July, 1937. Permission to quote granted.

[6] Flynn, J. T., "Punches for Corcoran and Cohen," *New Republic*, 92: 46, Aug. 18, 1937. Permission to quote granted.

Radicalism

Washington Merry-Go-Round[1]	Saturday Evening Post[2]	Literary Digest[3]	American Magazine[4]	Nation's Business[5]	New Republic[6]
To anyone who did not know Tom Corcoran, the recitation of his achievements would make him out to be a scheming, vindictive radical, bent upon revenge against the interests with which he once worked. But he is just the opposite.	When radicalism became the order of the day in Washington, Tommy became a shouting radical and was soon in a front seat on the New Deal band wagon.	In Washington, Thomas Gardiner Corcoran and Benjamin Victor Cohen are known as "hot-dogs." They are protégés of Prof. Felix Frankfurter. That qualifies them for the gustatory sobriquet. They do not resent it—are proud of it.	Opponents have nick-named them "Professor Frankfurter's two chief Hot Dogs." They have been called radicals and Communists. One choleric old gentleman in Washington told me, in somewhat mixed metaphor, that they were "Bolsheviks and beard-less Rasputins." Friends have said that they are selfless idealists, slaving away their youth for a principle. . . Both are believers in democracy and the American system, but believe the machinery requires constant regulation to keep it in order. Cohen prefers the small,	Neither Corcoran nor Cohen are economic planners in the sense that Moley and Tugwell were. Neither believes it possible to concoct an economic theory for eliminating booms and depressions that can be applied universally. To them, such attempts overlook the human equation. Without figuring that in, the most finely drawn economic plans are not worth a hoot. Both believe firmly that, after abusive practices have been outlawed, the most that business and Government can do is to supply themselves with the "man power" to	....

independent business-man of the old American type to the financial managers of vast corporate aggregations of capital. This view is just the opposite of that of the Socialist, who approves of huge corporations as a step toward the Socialistic state, in which the whole country would be one great corporation owned and operated by the government. As for Communism, as one of Tom's friends expressed it, "*Ben and Tom would be two of the first people the Communists would shoot, as they shot the Mensheviks in Russia.*"

meet economic disturbances as they arise.

¹ Pearson, D., and Allen R., *Daily Washington Merry-Go-Round*, July 31, 1937. Quoted by permission of the authors and United Feature Syndicate.

² Johnston, A., "White House Tommy," *Sat. Eve. Post*, July 31, 1937, pp. 5 ff. Quoted by permission of The Editor.

³ "Today's Rooseveltian Brain Trust, Team of Corcoran and Cohen," *Literary Digest*, 123: 7–8, May 22, 1937. Quoted by permission of *Time*.

⁴ Smith, B., "Corcoran and Cohen," *Am. Mag.*, August, 1937, pp. 22 ff. Permission to quote granted.

⁵ Belair, F., Jr., "Two of the 'Selfless Six,'" *Nation's Business*, 25: 25–6, July, 1937. Permission to quote granted.

⁶ Flynn, J. T., "Punches for Corcoran and Cohen," *New Republic*, 92: 46, Aug. 18, 1937. Permission to quote granted.

Business' Attitude

Washington Merry-Go-Round[1]	Saturday Evening Post[2]	Literary Digest[3]	American Magazine[4]	Nation's Business[5]	New Republic[6]
All of which explains why, next to the President himself, he is the man most hated by big business and most unpopular with conservative senators of any man in the Roosevelt administration.	Some of the industrialists, bankers and public-utility chiefs who have had battles with the team of Cohen and Corcoran like to think that they are out to revenge themselves for their failure to get rich during the boom. This is shallow reasoning, however, as neither Corcoran nor Cohen is a man to mourn over the past.	Bankers, brokers, manufacturers and plain and assorted business men manifest scant interest in the team's symphonic endeavors, but they'd give a lot to know what Corcoran & Cohen produced in their bill-drafting labors. But they can't find out. Corcoran & Cohen don't talk. They pull in their necks.	The public utilities, representing ten billion dollars of assets, lined up solidly against the bill and urged their stockholders to write to their congressmen. Wall Street said the bill was "vindictive," whispered that Corcoran and Cohen had themselves lost their shirts in stock speculation, and were now out for revenge.	....	And it is also a singular fact that the measures they have managed have come in for the least denunciation by the angry conservative groups that fight the President. Also, and this is the most significant of all, the largest amount of venom spat out in Washington at these two men comes, not from the hard-shelled tories, but from those former New Deal favorites who have lost their place in the first circle and blame Tom Corcoran for their expulsion. Indeed I have every reason to believe that the Saturday Evening Post article was inspired, not by some staunch American trembling over the fate of his country at the hands of the "hot dogs," but by some erstwhile collaborator in the work of ruining the country.

Securities Legislation

. . . . .	He helped put through the securities act regulating the sale of stocks and bonds to the public. He helped draft the stock exchange act which attempted to protect the public from the raiders of Wall Street. He was the brains behind the holding company act, is helping to plug up the holes in the income tax law, and now is waging a campaign for passage of the wages and hours act.	. . . . .	Tommy's career received a great impetus when he was selected by Brain Truster Moley, on recommendation of Professor Frankfurter, to work on legislation for the regulation of stock exchanges. Corcoran and Cohen were thrown together on this job, and they became the greatest legislation-drafting team in history. The regulation of stock exchanges and the issuance of securities are usually placed among the New Deal's foremost achievements, and a considerable part of the glory goes to Corcoran and Cohen.	As Wall Street lawyers and government attorneys studied the Securities Act they realized that it had been drafted by a master hand. This law was not thrown together slap-dash, like some other New Deal legislation, for example, the NRA, loosely and with many a Constitutional crevice. This law was like the farmer's ideal fence: "horse-high, bull-strong, and hog-tight." For this credit was given partly to the ingenuity of Corcoran but even more to the thoroughness and brooding craftsmanship of Ben Cohen.	Results of their collaboration are found in the Securities Act of 1933, the Securities and Exchange Act of 1934, the Public Utility Holding Company Act of 1936 and, more recently, the judiciary reorganization and wage and hours legislation.	. . . . .

[1] Pearson, D., and Allen R., *Daily Washington Merry-Go-Round*, July 31, 1937. Quoted by permission of the authors and United Feature Syndicate.

[2] Johnston, A., "White House Tommy," *Sat. Eve. Post*, July 31, 1937, pp. 5 ff. Quoted by permission of The Editor.

[3] "Today's Rooseveltian Brain Trust, Team of Corcoran and Cohen," *Literary Digest*, 123: 7–8, May 22, 1937. Quoted by permission of *Time*.

[4] Smith, B., "Corcoran and Cohen," *Am. Mag.*, August, 1937, pp. 22 ff. Permission to quote granted.

[5] Belair, F., Jr., "Two of the 'Selfless Six,'" *Nation's Business*, 25: 25–6, July, 1937. Permission to quote granted.

[6] Flynn, J. T., "Punches for Corcoran and Cohen," *New Republic*, 92: 46, Aug. 18, 1937. Permission to quote granted.

CHAPTER VII

LEGENDS AND MYTHS

We may say that legends are modified accounts of the past events and of historic personages, whereas myths are imaginative accounts of the meaning of life. . . .

Myths and legends come down to us from the past as a part of our cultural heritage. . . .

The ordinary man today is as unaware of the myths and legends about him as myths and legends, as is the primitive person. . . .

The myth and legend are adult extensions of the infantile world of fantasy and make believe. . . .

The process is really inevitable. If we did not have our present legends to hand on, we would unconsciously create others. . . .

As we become more and more skilled in advertising and conscious propaganda, legend making has become more deliberate. . . .

Whether legends are deliberate or not, the fact remains that masses of mankind live in these images. . . . [1]

During the last half of the nineteenth century, various social theorists became increasingly preoccupied with the problem of myths and legends. Students of religious ideas and institutions, taking up the cudgels for rationalism, discussed the mythology of the various religious systems. The evolutionists studied myths and legends as an early development in culture history. Etymologists considered the development of myths as related to changes in language. Ethnologists found in the mythology of primitive peoples an inexhaustible source for the building up of theories about the past values and concepts of primitive peoples. Psychologists and psychoanalysts have examined mythology and found, to their satisfaction, evidence of persistent psychological drives. The historian pieced out the historic record with mythological evidence. And finally, by the close of the century and in the opening decades of this century, certain modern beliefs were discussed in terms of mythology and legendry by Sorel, Pareto, Delaisi and others.[2] During the past year Prof. T. W. Arnold has enraged his opponents and delighted his adherents by discussing certain aspects of the ideas about private property, corporations

[1] Young, K., *Social Psychology*, Chap. 17, 1930. Quoted by permission of F. S. Crofts & Co.

[2] Sorel, G., *Reflections on Violence*, 1906.

Pareto, V., *The Mind and Society* (English trans.), vol. 1, Section 650 *ff*., 1935.

Delaisi, F., *Political Myths and Economic Realities*, 1928.

118

and government as mythology.[1]   The folklore of 1937 is a vastly more intriguing, but also more controversial, subject than the mythology of the ancient Greeks, the medieval supernaturalist or the Australian Arunta, the Indian Bellacoolas, the Southern Negro or the African Gandas.

A part of the beliefs and ideas of all peoples are the stories that of late years have been called "myths" and "legends." Among primitive peoples and in folk cultures the myths and legends are a part of the folk-lore of the people.   These stories satisfy some psychological need and maintain cultural values.   In the great society such stories are increasingly imposed by a self-conscious leadership which aims at the promulgation of some doctrine or the elevation of some individual.   The terms "myth" and "legend" are often used synonymously.   However, the anthropologists have come to designate as myths those stories which deal with the world of the supernatural.   "Myths are tales of the supernatural world and share also, therefore, the characteristics of the religious complex."[2]   Such tales have no factual origin.   But the legend is a greatly exaggerated or untrue account, of some person or incident, that may have had some basis in fact but has been distorted in the telling.   The legend recounts material about a person or incident; the myth relates to a general concept of supernatural relations or central folk value.   All sacred books begin with myths of gods, demons, personalized animals and various animistic conceptions.   There are the great social myths of God-ordained rulers, economic processes, utopias, and the like.   In every society there is also a wealth of legendary material about founders or early leaders; the legends of Roland, King Arthur, Robin Hood, Virgil, Washington and many others.   There are also numerous legends of incidents in a people's history.   Man evidences a persistent tendency toward what Henri Bergson called the "fabulatory function," that is, the creation and maintenance of exaggerated and fabulous legends.   And these myths and legends obviously influence popular opinion when their subject matter deals with topics that have become controversial. The legends about other peoples are a basis for opinion formation in international crises; legends about economic processes influence boards of directors; legends about racial groups complicate race relations; legends about personality types affect everyday judgments; legends about national heroes and villains influence popular conceptions of history. Masses of people are not aware of such stories as legends, although the professional thinker has been aware of some of the popular stories as myths and legends since the time when Aristotle began the verificatory process.

[1] Arnold, T. W., *The Folklore of Capitalism*, 1937.
[2] Benedict, R., *Ency. Soc. Sci.*, 11: 179.

The Psychological and Cultural Bases for Myths and Legends

Cultural values become incorporated in the psychological functioning of the individual. There are also drives, impulses and instincts which, although modified and conditioned by human social experience, are characteristic of the original structure of man. In describing the bases of cultural products it is common to contrast the cultural and the psychological bases. We thus set up a false dichotomy, for they are often inextricably intertwined. At the present moment we often belabor the obvious in discussing psychological and cultural factors. But it seems necessary for a contemporary writer to do so, inasmuch as individualistic psychology has been so diffused in popular thought. Social systems control the expressions of human drives, but human drives are also in part responsible for certain expressions in social systems.

The content of those accounts which we label myths and legends is primarily determined by the social situation and societal values, but it is also to some extent the product of the original nature of man. The individual has food hungers. When he is inadequately satisfied, he may create legends of bountiful fare. Paul Bunyan was a legendary figure created by American lumbermen. In the cycle of stories dealing with Bunyan's exploits, one whole group recounts in descriptive detail the types and amounts of food that he provided for his lumbermen. This "wishful thinking" of the raconteur is in sharp contrast to the actually scanty fare in American lumber camps in the last century.

The physical and psychological conditions of the upper-class Southerner "after the war" were wretched. It was in this period that legends of life "before the war" arose. Today, national stereotypes are still influenced by this picture—the white-columned houses, the boxwood hedges, the charming women, the gallant men, the numerous and contented slaves. A whole class, wounded in spirit, inflated the realities of Southern life into a legendary mélange. Sectional groups and the various families therein fostered the legends of their past importance.

After the Russian Revolution, a rationalistically minded leadership attempted to supplant the folk preoccupation with the supernatural by providing naturalistic explanations. The folk resisted with a flood of popular stories purporting to give accounts of supernatural intervention in the affairs of men. For example, there was the widely told story of a little girl of about twelve years of age who called upon a doctor and asked him to come and see her mother who was desperately ill. The doctor said that he would call upon the mother in an hour or so. He did so, found the woman critically ill but thought he could save her life. However, he said that she should have a nurse, as her daughter was too small to care for her properly. "Daughter?" said the woman. "I have

no daughter; my daughter died two days ago.   She is behind that screen."
The doctor looked behind the screen, and there was the little girl, who
quite obviously had been a corpse for days.   Such legendary stories
were widely disseminated.[1]

Legends develop about historic figures.   Some of these legends are
literary creations; others are folk products.   Clusters of anecdotal stories
are attached to the name of a folk hero.   The stories are created or fall
into disuse largely in terms of the prevailing values of any age.   The
"debunking" biographies of the past fifteen years have primarily
"debunked" those items in biographical accounts that are not now in
good repute.   Legends about historic figures have utility in supporting
the prevailing social norms and as an agency of social control.   The
legendary figure becomes a type.   He personifies useful values.   The
legendary stories are developed from experiences wrongly interpreted;
from false inferences from actual occurrences; from incidents that might
have happened to such a person; from incidents that actually happened,
but not to the person to whom they are ascribed (Parson Weems, first
biographer of Washington, told the cherry-tree story about Washington;
this incident actually happened to Parson Weems, with the exception
that he did tell a lie and did receive a whipping).   Those things which
augment his legend are ascribed to the legendary figure.   For example,
Virgil is a historical character, but there is also a Virgil legend.   There
were numerous legends of Virgil's birth, the most widespread of which is
that when Virgil was born the whole city of Rome shook from end to
end.   (This satisfied the persistent folk belief that supernatural powers
are especially concerned with superior persons.   Similar legends of the
cataclysms of nature accompanying their births have been created about
practically all outstanding popular leaders.   The Lincoln legend contains
many such stories.)   Virgil's amorous experiences became the basis of
legend.   The folk are persistently interested in this fundamental avocation.   Virgil was credited with magical powers.   The folk ascribe such
power to most legendary personages.   The Virgil of legend heroically
defied the emperor of Rome.   The more popular folk heroes usually
illustrate the wishful thinking of the masses to defy constituted
authority.[2]

Although folk values are preeminent in determining the content of
myths and legends, the mental processes of the originators are also
involved.   The distortion of an incident, having some basis in fact, into
the popular legendary account is due in part to individual psychological
processes.   K. Young lists the principal psychological factors as:

---

[1] Duranty, W., "Off the Russian Record," *Esquire*, July, 1935.   In this article, Mr.
Duranty cites numerous stories of this type.

[2] Pareto, *op. cit.*, Section 668.

(1) The emotional state of the observers. This is usually increased at the time of observation, if the situation is dramatic.

(2) Errors of perception at the time of observation. If the event is spectacular or unfamiliar, it is more difficult to perceive it accurately. Attention will be limited to a few details.

(3) Errors in recall. These are especially evident when the event is later being described to others.

(4) Predispositions, the apperceptive mass of the observers. These predispositions are made of old stereotypes, prejudices and legends still persisting in the observers.

(5) False interpretations by the observers. As far as they imagine the characteristics of the observed individuals, the observers will err in interpreting their acts.

(6) The time elapsing between perception and recall. After a very brief interval, the event as recalled differs from the actual event. As the time elapsing between the event and its recall increases, observers begin to add or change or forget innumerable details.[1]

The content of a great many myths and legends is based upon desires and wishes of the narrators. These desires may have been culturally instilled or may be relatively innate, as in the case of hunger and sex drives. Among the psychologists, the psychoanalysts have been especially active in interpreting myths as symbolic expressions of suppressed wishes, or as frankly avowed expressions of conscious wishes of a general character. Desires for a glorious hereafter, for social achievement and prestige, for physical power and for other values are expressed in the mythology of various peoples. Such values are the product of cultures. But wish fulfillment in myths providing expression of the Oedipus complex, or of simple sexual adventure, or of the Madonna cult is more universal. Freud maintains that our psyche has the tendency to work over the world picture so that it corresponds to such wishes. Fairy tales, myths and legends are among the most popular expressions of such wish structures. For the psychoanalyst, myths represent the unconscious processes of whole groups and races. These stories have been adapted to the common needs of countless generations. The individually unique elements have been eliminated, and there remain the general themes that are common to all the individuals of the groups. Further, one may analyze myth content in terms of fundamental emotions. Obviously, many a story is related to fear. In many Southern towns there are few Roman Catholics. Yet the South is a breeding ground for legendary stories about the church leaders, especially the Pope. Bandying about many such stories, Senator "Tom-Tom" Heflin split the Democratic party in Alabama in 1928. Popular legends based upon fear have had persistent utility for societal leaders.[2]

---

[1] Young, *op. cit.*, p. 440. Quoted by permission of F. S. Crofts & Co.

[2] Of course, there are other aspects of myth construction in addition to those we

The legends and myths which persist in a culture are those which fulfill some popular wish or maintain some generally accepted social value. Therefore, they can best be understood in terms of particular cultures. The legends of a people preoccupied with struggle, action and competition reflect that interest. The legendary figures who impassively contemplate life are primarily a product of Oriental cultures. Legendary figures among the Plains Indians had splendid "visions." The dominant values are reflected.

LEGENDS AND MYTHS IN PRIMITIVE SOCIETY

The cultural basis of the content of myths and legends can be seen most clearly in primitive cultures. Scholars now understand that primitive legends and myths are not the product of psychological play and fantasy. They are the accounts and explanations of the world and its inhabitants and of the realm of the supernatural. As such, they have social utility, as they impress and systematize the fundamental notions of life. One of the stock pastimes of primitives is storytelling. This is the fundamental educational process. These myths and legends strengthen the traditional values by relating them to past events and to supernatural authority. "Behavior and attitudes become more articulate in folklore than in any other cultural trait, and folklore then tends to crystallize and perpetuate the forms of culture that it has made articulate."[1] However the stories originate, those which persist are the accounts which reinforce some important existing value. Legends and myths are created to account for those aspects of the world and the supernatural which appear important to a primitive group at any period of its development. There are stories of the creator of the group, gods, cosmology and cosmogony; animal life and characteristics; taboo, magic, the dead, ghosts; heaven, hell and other-world journeys; marvels, tests; wise, foolish and clever persons; luck and the aleatory element; rewards and punishment; sex, personality traits and many others.[2] A fighting people cherishes legends of powerful heroes; a secure people high-lights other values, such as wealth, cleverness or vision capacity; whereas a slave people compensates with stories of the shortcomings and limitations of their masters. Sometimes such stories may be introduced by a self-conscious leadership intent upon manipulating the attitudes of the followers, but in primitive society they are characteristically a folk product. In contrast to this, contemporary leadership in modern

have mentioned. In interpreting the content of primitive mythology, Paul Radin makes much of the technical literary traditions of the mythmaker. See Radin, P., *Social Anthropology*, Chap. 23, 1932; *Method and Theory of Ethnology*, pp. 238 *ff.*, 1937.

[1] Benedict, R., "Folklore," *Ency. Soc. Sci.*, 6: 291.

[2] See classification of primitive myths in Thompson, S., *Motif Index of Folk Literature*, 1932–1936.

Western society intentionally promulgates myths and legends for various purposes. A book about the adventures of Mickey Mouse and Donald Duck has been adopted for use in the second grade of the New York City schools. It is anticipated that pupils will be more interested in their reading lessons if these are couched in the familiar world of movie mythology. The political utility of a Coolidge legend is obvious.

In the absence of naturalistic explanations, primitive man turns to mythological description somewhat more frequently than does contemporary man. But only in certain fields. And the common man today reverts easily. In 1914, M. Jean Jaurès, the great pre-War French Socialist, was assassinated by Raoul Villain. In 1938, a plane dropped bombs on a Spanish island where the assassin was living. Raoul Villain was killed. The Spanish Loyalist plane that dropped the bomb was named "Jean Jaurès." This event may be discussed in terms of chance elements. There are not many Loyalist planes and, of course, one of them was labeled "Jean Jaurès." However, some millions of contemporary Europeans have not chosen this explanation.

In primitive societies, those topics which did become controversial and the subject of popular opinion were usually referred to the authority of the traditional myths and legends. Folk peoples also depend upon myth and legend for many of their social definitions. And the content of these stories is primarily a social product. The folk legends have too often been explained in terms of more or less uniform individual tendencies and inadequately analyzed in terms of folk values. The myths of the future, of heaven, hell, Valhalla, and the like, have been ascribed to individual longings and fears. But, although those beliefs are incorporated in individual psychological responses, they are originally a folk invention to meet needs for social control. The content of various folk legends cannot be adequately described in terms of a few deep-seated individual needs.

The Legends of Primary Groups

Legends and myths have a functional role in society. Opinions are influenced by the prevailing tales. The standards of primary groups, as well as those of the larger associations, are buttressed by such stories. Families, clubs, neighborhoods, gangs and numerous other primary groups create legends that are functionally useful in supporting dominant values. Most families develop legends that are used to influence the children and to maintain family pride and prestige in various ways.

The role of such stories is obvious. The preciousness of the individual to the family and the importance of his position in the universe may be emphasized in family legend. Theodore Dreiser reports, "In connection with my own birth, I have heard both of my parents and my eldest sister tell of having seen, at the time my mother was laboring with the birth of me, three maidens (graces, shall we say) garbed in brightly colored costumes, come up the brick walk that led from the street gate to our front door, into the room in which my mother lay, pass about the foot of the bed and finally through a rear door into a small, exitless back yard, from which they could have escaped only by vanishing into thin air."[1] How profoundly such a story would influence a small child regarding his own significance! The late Corra Harris recounted a delightful story of the enhancement of her own feeling of importance as a child by the oft-recounted tale of her birth.

When I was very small and negligible I derived my first sense of importance from the story mother told of my birth. I was born in the company room of my grandfather's house, she said, and I did not miss the distinction of having arrived hot-footed in this chamber set aside for hospitality, on a March morning, at daybreak. The wind was roaring outside so fiercely the very house rocked in the gale. And there was great excitement inside, everybody running to and fro, because they were expecting me—my grandparents, my father, the doctor, and all the servants. I seemed to know by instinct that mother was also present, and did not ask her about that. There were two candles burning on the mantelpiece, and their flames were bending with the wind that rattled the windows. If she forgot to mention the other candle, I interrupted her at this point in the narrative to know if one was also lighted on her candle stand, because, as far back as I can remember, mother had her own candle blooming softly on a small table by her side, and on this great occasion so personal to me, I could not bear to be cheated of this familiar illumination.

"And at last you came!" she would say. Whereupon I would rise up and clap my hands with pride and joy. The look she gave me then, the half smile of a witty benediction, may have been the reason I so often entreated her to tell this tale again.

"Was I very good?" I always wanted to know at once. This was really a touching question, because during the whole of my life I have never been praised much for goodness, except that which I confer upon myself by implication or frankly, from time to time.

"Yes, you were good."

"And beautiful?" I urged.

"You were perfectly beautiful. Everyone said you were a wonderful baby."

"And what did father say?" I must know.

"He was speechless with admiration." As often as she assured me on that point I never missed the thrill of having produced this effect upon my father, who was rarely made speechless by anything.[2]

Certainly the theme of the intervention of Providence at one's birth is common enough in popular legend. But perhaps the most widespread

[1] Dreiser, T., *Dawn*, p. 6, 1931.

[2] Harris, Corra, "The Old Penitentiary School of Childhood," *Sat. Eve. Post*, Feb. 21, 1931, p. 30. Permission to quote granted.

type of family legends has to do with the superior wealth of an ancestor or with his clever economic dealings.   This is inevitable in a society oriented, as is ours, to prestige from wealth.   We are referring here to the legends that are created within a family group.   And the dimmer these stories become with age, the more they can be varied in the telling. Increasing distortion makes possible their use for illustration of ever more varied values.   In addition to the legends unique in a particular family, each family draws upon the varied store of popular folk legend.

MODERN LEGENDRY

The legends of primary groups relate to a relatively narrow range of values, whereas the scope of the subject matter of legends in the great society is much broader.   New legends are created in connection with every social movement, and as the attention areas of modern man have widened the number of his legends has increased.   The political legendry of primitive and folk peoples was relatively limited, dealing with a few folk heroes and leaders, past and present.   Political legendry of man in the great society provides a galaxy of hundreds of legendary figures, taken from many national groups and from various historic periods.

These legends are now formally transmitted in textbooks, popular literature, political speeches and the motion pictures.   In textbooks in use in the American public schools there are innumerable distortions at variance with the best contemporary scholarship concerning prominent American leaders.   Washington, Franklin, Adams, Hamilton, Benedict Arnold, Andrew Jackson, Lincoln, Andrew Johnson, and many others are still frequently presented in accounts that are more in accord with popular legendry than with historic fact.   There is no need to tear down our national idols.   But the present simplicity of presentation reflects the limited interests of the common man, rather than historic knowledge concerning these figures or our functional needs for more complex symbols.

Moreover, as societal leadership has become more skilled in manipulating popular impressions, legend making has become more deliberate. In building the legend of Mr. Harold Ickes, the opposition press has recently been associating him with Donald Duck.   Every major political figure is concerned, as are numbers of his skilled lieutenants, with the development of his legend.   Sometimes such legends are created in an incredibly short time, as, for example, the Calvin Coolidge legend. And not only in the political field has the manufacture of legends become a highly skilled and conscious art.   Businessmen and financiers, society women and movie stars, religious leaders and reformers, and, indeed, all persons who achieve a high visibility are in quest of a legend.   In the field of entertainment, Hollywood has developed a whole industry devoted to legendry and gossip in the screen magazines and newspaper stories. The story of the stars follows the general pattern of the national fairy tale, of rise to fame, of material wealth and opulence, of sex and beauty. "The nation has turned to the worship of these picture gods, real and yet unreal, common as life and yet larger than life, known in minuter detail than the next door neighbor and yet shiningly remote, because they have come to represent certain national ideals reduced to the lowest common denominator."[1]

The particular structure of society and its pyramid of values has determined the legendary figures of every age. Today the process of legend making is accelerated and the number of legends vastly increased. A folk people creates as many legends as it needs in the functional activities of its life and thought. But today, societal leadership provides a plethora of legendry, often more adapted and suited to the needs of the creators of the legends than to those of the masses who are asked to believe them.

We shall briefly sketch three legends: the myth of the devil, which was primarily a folk product, although partly limned by the leaders of the church; the Lincoln legend, which contains many elements of folk invention and others produced by a self-conscious leadership; and the legend of Calvin Coolidge, which is almost entirely the product of astute publicity men.

THE MYTH OF THE DEVIL

The mythologies of various peoples contain anthropomorphic devils. Personification of evil pervades folk thinking, and man has persistently imagined epic struggles between good and evil demons. Vritra, Ahriman, the Egyptian Set and the Christian devil, or Satan, are major evil spirits, but there are also a host of others. There is an evolution of the devil in Old Testament records. He was a fallen angel, the original tempter of man, the envious rival of Yahweh, and he was often conveniently identified with the enemy's gods.[2] Under early Christianity he assumed gigantic spiritual proportions, as all the greatness of the gods of the pagan world were centered in him. He was everything the Christian abhorred. But it was in the Middle Ages that the Satan mythology became most elaborate and specific. In that gloomy period Satan loomed increasingly large in the consciousness of the folk. Terror dominated the Middle Ages, and mass preoccupation with the devil became most evident in the frenzied harassing of his earthly colleagues, the witch and the sorcerer. The theological concept of the devil changed rapidly through that period,

---

[1] Suckow, R., "Hollywood Gods and Goddesses," *Harper's*, July, 1936.
[2] Rudwin, M., "Diabolism," *Ency. Soc. Sci.*, 5: 119.

but the folk interpreted in their own values those ideas of Satan which the professional churchmen gave to them. "In a very great number of popular beliefs and folk tales, we see before us a devil profoundly different from the Devil of the theologians and of the ascetic legends; a devil who has the form and nature of a man, has a house such as men have, and occupations and cares such as a farmer or an artisan might have; a devil who eats, drinks, and wears garments; who sometimes runs into debt, sometimes falls ill; and who retains nothing, or but very little of his diabolic character."[1] The folk spun rapidly changing descriptions of the devil's nature, works, ways, appearance.

Of the many phases of the devil's evolution and of the various aspects of his nature, we may choose a few illustrations to indicate the popular basis of this myth. The person of the devil changed with the changing antipathies of the mass. In the early Christian period his form was often that of pagan divinities, as the Christians' struggle was primarily with competing religions. The devil also appeared as various animals in accordance with the social reputation of those animals from age to age. The Trinitarian dispute is reflected in the three persons or three faces of the devil. In the Middle Ages, he is portrayed as a man of physical distinction and beauty, and later, as the masses came to despise the foppishness and dandyism of the upper classes, the devil becomes a dandy in the refinements of his dress, beard and behavior. In the sixteenth and seventeenth centuries the devout masses became ever more alienated from the frills, finery and fashion of their masters, and they ascribed these attributes to the devil.

The popular devil was a sexual adventurer. His inhuman sexual prowess was attested to by thousands of hysterical women who claimed intimate knowledge of his ways. The witches' Sabbath was in part a sexual orgy. The devil also made use of beautiful and seductive women to tempt the faithful. If the ascetic church leaders were bedeviled with such imaginings, masses of people also were not loath to concern themselves with these aspects of the devil's activity. And the variety of the mythological record rapidly increased.

The devil was a shrewd bargainer. The notion of compacts with the devil developed from the tenth century onward to the Faust motif. People thought in terms of simple, personal bargains. Various cults of devil worshippers made their formal bargains with Satan.

In the absence of naturalistic descriptions of physiological processes, it is understandable that the folk should ascribe much illness to the personal activities of the devil. Through the Middle Ages, people attributed obscure diseases, indefinite pains, piercing sensations in the region of the heart, kidney pains, paralysis, impotence and many other disorders to the

---

[1] Graf, A., *The Story of the Devil* (English trans.), p. 231, 1931.

devil's invasion of their persons.[1] Unusual psychological experiences and various mental diseases were ascribed to demoniacal possession. The physical tribulations of the churchmen were often even greater than were those of the common man. One abbot declared that the devil, "afflicted him with bloating of the stomach and with diarrhoea, with nausea and giddiness; so benumbed his hands that he could no longer make the sign of the cross—made him cough, forced him to expectorate, hid in his bed and stopped his nostrils and mouth so that he could not breathe, compelled him to urinate, and bit him like a flea."[2]

As the conflicts of the religious ideology with rationalism increased, the devil was associated with reason, argument, dissension and questioning. "Satan was regarded as the incarnation of human reason in contrast to the Savior, who represented faith. To the dominion of the devil the church handed over all sciences and arts."[3] Folk suspicion of learning ascribed a splendid intellectuality to Satan.

Although church leaders used the myth of the personal devil as a potent means of social control and although theologians in part guided the developing concept of the devil, the essential outlines of the devil myth through the Middle Ages were the simple ruminations of the folk. Later, the record of the devil's works, ways and person were essentially the product of the great writers, especially Dante and Milton.[4] But in the heyday of his earthly power, Satan was a folk myth.

THE LINCOLN OF POPULAR LEGEND

The Lincoln legends illustrate, not only the development of legends as a folk product, but also the increasingly conscious manipulation of legendary material by societal leaders, by churchmen, prohibitionists and politicians. The Lincoln who lives in the minds of masses of Americans is not the Lincoln of the biographers (eulogistic, realistic or debunking), but a legendary Lincoln of gossipy folk tale and of legendary stories promulgated by interested leaders.

There is a plethora of folk legend. The accounts of the poverty of the Lincoln family have been grossly exaggerated, because the folk required a hero who had run the entire gamut from dire poverty to greatest eminence. He was born in a rude frontier community in a log cabin. But material wealth is relative, and in comparison with those round about Lincoln was not an underprivileged child.

Hero legends usually ascribe certain elements of mystery to the birth of the hero. The male progenitor is often assumed to be someone

[1] Garçon, M., and Vinchon, J., *The Devil*, p. 82, 1930.
[2] Graf, *op. cit.*, p. 98.
[3] Rudwin, *op. cit.*, p. 120.
[4] Tsanoff, R. A., *The Nature of Evil*, pp. 176–184, 1931.

other and greater than the legal father.   Such was the case in the Lincoln legend.   "It was natural to wonder how so unpromising a backwoodsman as Thomas Lincoln could have begot so superhuman a son as Abraham. . . . Soon there was a feeling abroad that the hero must have had some author more plausible than 'Tom,' who was reputed to have been shiftless and dull.   Inevitably there grew the myth that Lincoln's real father had been some greater man."[1]   The willingness of masses of people to believe such stories made possible the organized "whispering campaigns" of the 1860 and 1864 elections.   This was a natural folk legend, but it was spread about by political opponents.   In an earlier age such a legend would have persisted, but with the means of communication in America of the nineteenth century the bastardy tale was finally scotched, but not until a half century after Lincoln's death.

Folk legend made of Lincoln a model boy, never late to school, cleanly, quiet, honest and kind to animals.   But these stories were created after Lincoln was prominent, great and martyred.   And so, the boy had to be great.   Undoubtedly most of the later witnesses must have been unreliable.   But true or false, these legends provided models for harassed mothers to hold before their sons.

Lincoln's gentleness and kindness were cherished by the folk.   There are some true stories to illustrate these qualities, which the adult Lincoln undoubtedly possessed.   But there are scores of untrue stories.   If they were all true, Lincoln would have spent all his time interviewing distracted mothers, comforting the widows and orphans, solving the personal problems of soldiers and issuing pardons.   Historians and biographers have proved most of the folk legends to be untrue.   But the folk cherished the story of the kindly ruler and embroidered ever new accounts.

A heroic saga was created.   The stalwart railsplitter, the adventurous bargeman, the heroic fighter in the Black Hawk War became legends long after the facts.   The frontier provided a harsh life, and human endurance was tested.   The popular record of frontier life required its hero symbols, and such a symbol was created from a man already great in political life.   "What there is of the frontier hero in the great Lincoln of poetry and fiction, and the religious legend which they preserve, is spiritualized and hallowed by the simple process of omission, emphasis, and invention, which has so largely biased even the biographical accounts."[2]

The death of Abraham Lincoln inevitably gave rise to numerous legends of unusual, unnatural and supernatural occurrences.   It was

[1] Lewis, L., *Myths after Lincoln*, pp. 368 *ff.*, 1929.
[2] Basler, R. P., *The Lincoln Legend*, p. 147, 1935.

said in Illinois that the brown thrush was not heard singing for a year after Lincoln's death. There are many such stories.

Organized manipulation of Lincoln legends occurred in many fields. The most notable instance deals with the question of his religious faith. In the struggle between agnostics and churchmen in the closing years of the nineteenth century, each side collected and used stories that purported to align him with each. The Methodists, Quakers, and other sects claimed him. Their opponents gained solace from the stories told by Lincoln's law partner, Herndon. In the Prohibition struggle, Lincoln was claimed by both the wets and the drys. Lincoln was no friend of intoxicating drink, but there is considerable doubt as to his views on prohibition. The wets claimed that Lincoln had been a saloonkeeper in his storekeeping days.[1] Practically every social movement since Lincoln's day has attempted to link this magic name to its cause and in doing so has assiduously collected legends.

The human and historic greatness of Abraham Lincoln has been distorted by legends that high-lighted those qualities which the common man or the special pleader has found it convenient to emphasize.

THE LEGEND OF CALVIN COOLIDGE

The Coolidge legend was constructed very rapidly in the months immediately succeeding his elevation to the presidency. Organized publicity by the Republican National Committee and the less organized legend making of the Washington correspondents, soon limned the outlines of a silent, unintellectual, honest, cautious, shrewd, average man. The newspaper-reading public accepted and embellished the legend. It is now agreed that President Coolidge had the "best press" of any American president. Yet here was a man who, a few years earlier, had been considered by many party leaders as too weak and nondescript for the vice-presidential nomination. "Here is a sensible and normal man who until a few years ago was accustomed to taking political orders and being treated more or less indifferently, at times even contemptuously, by the party leaders in his state."[2] But shortly after Calvin Coolidge became president, an eminent newspaper man stated, "The indisputable fact is that Coolidge has to some degree been 'sold' to the nation, as the advertising men say, and by advertising men's methods."[3] There were more avenues of publicity than ever before: the radio was developing, the country was entering into a prosperous period, legend making by publicity was becoming more astute, the nation required a

[1] Odegard, P., *Pressure Politics*, p. 61, 1928.
[2] Sharp, W., "President and Press," *Atlantic*, 140: 239.
[3] Bliven, B., "The Great Coolidge Mystery," *Harper's*, 52: 45.

symbol of cautious conservatism, and the new President fitted, or could be made to fit, the need. And so, from that August morning in 1923 when the American people saw the lean face of their new President in the light of his father's kerosene lamp in a Vermont farmhouse, the legend grew.

From the beginning, the Washington correspondents praised and protected him. Why? F. R. Kent declares that reporters inflate important public figures, magnifying their good qualities and minimizing defects for two reasons. "The first is a more or less psychological one—a tendency, springing from the inferiority complex of the reporter and born of his poor pay and precarious position, to permit the public official to assume the superior or dominant attitude. . . . The second reason is a simple and practical one. The reporter's business is to get news. The more news he gets the more secure his job and the greater his value to the paper. The public official has what the reporter has to have, to wit, news."[1] He further states, "Not in the memory of anyone now living has there been a President who leaned so heavily on this newspaper tendency to praise and protect, who profited by it so much, who would shrivel so quickly if he lost it, as Calvin Coolidge." The newspaper men built the legend, but they built it for a receptive and acquiescent public.

What were the outlines of the legend? One of the principal strands in the tradition of this President was built of the innumerable stories of his silence. Historically, silence has often been noted in leaders and attributed to a sphinxlike wisdom. In personal relations President Coolidge was undoubtedly taciturn. Bruce Bliven says that this characteristic was magnified by newspaper men because it was in such startling contrast to their own volubility. "The trait is particularly puzzling to the newspaper men who come in closest contact with him and who write what the public reads about him, they being invariably expert and incessant conversationalists."[2] And certainly the President was not given to small talk. The American public hesitated for a moment in its chatter and was filled with wonder. A man must be profound to so control his speech. And then the flood of anecdotes began. It was said that when Coolidge was four years of age he was sitting quietly with his father and his grandfather. The grandfather spoke. "John," he said, "Cal don't say much." "No," said John, "Calvin, he ain't gabby." They smiled at each other. Neither were they.[3] Certainly in public life, Mr. Coolidge was not a silent man. He spoke for hours on end, he wrote lengthy addresses to Congress, he wrote extensively. "We can begin with the fact that Mr. Coolidge not only talks in public fre-

---

[1] Kent, F. R., "Mr. Coolidge," *Am. Mercury*, 2: 386.

[2] Bliven, *op. cit.*, p. 48.

[3] Rogers, C., *The Legend of Calvin Coolidge*, p. 11, 1928.

quently (265 times a year), but talks at length. His formal addresses are not snapped off short. They average something more than thirty-seven hundred words apiece."[1] But there was no glib loquaciousness in this man. And the bulk of the general public cherished the legend.

Another strand of the legend was the account of his lack of flexible intellectuality. This was well received by a public who were in general suspicious of flashing intellects and among whom a too high order of intelligence was suspect. Emphasis was placed on good intentions, conservative thinking, character and solidity.

Again, inaction was counted a virtue, and many stories were told to indicate that the President was not given to waste motion or a thrusting aggressiveness aimed at any new solution of economic and political problems. In a prosperous period the maintenance of the *status quo* was at a great premium. The President was portrayed as nursing prosperity by encouraging thrift and balancing the nation's books. Experimentalism was not considered a virtue in the 1920's. There was little popular demand for constructive solutions.

Much was made of the fact that the President was an "average man." Stories of his simple tastes in housing, food and daily living were spread abroad. His ethical standards and values were portrayed as simple and traditional. Here was no theorist ranting of the "new morality." "The average American saw in Coolidge just the virtues that were supposed to constitute the American ideal and supposed to have made America. Coolidge incarnated thrift, self-denial, plain and simple living, straightforward, hard-headed honesty. The average American had heard that his fathers had these virtues and had made a great nation by means of them."[2]

The President was portrayed as honest, cautious and shrewd. Honesty was especially stressed in comparison with the notorious scandals of the preceding administration. Stories were told of his meticulous and sometimes picayunish honesty. Cautiousness was prized in a period when there was a high level of national income. Shrewdness may be a limited virtue at best, but it is highly valued in a nation that developed this emphasis in the trading, haggling, small-bargaining, horse-trading, tricking days of nineteenth-century expansion.

The stage was set for the Coolidge legend. It was easy to star President Coolidge because he had to a considerable extent many of the characteristics ascribed to him. Lack of color helped rather than hindered the rapid growth of the legend. "In the absence of a national crisis and in a time of prosperity his lack of strength is an asset rather than a liability, provided he has sufficiently powerful press support and

[1] Mertz, C., "The Silent Mr. Coolidge," *New Republic*, 47: 51.
[2] Bradford, G., "The Genius of the Average," *Atlantic*, 145: 6.

the approval of the great business interests—and no President of our time has had both to the same extent."[1] President Coolidge permitted the growth of his legend. The press agents and the correspondents painted a distorted picture of him, but, in fairness, it must be noted that he did not actively pretend to qualities he did not possess.

Every age has myths and legends which are defended and propagated by the believers. Transmitted into simple myth and personal legendry these stories are symbols for masses of mankind. They are types of simplification. As such these popular stereotypes are constantly utilized in the opinion process. They are psychologically inevitable in the thinking of the common man about leaders and heroes, enemies and friends, and religious, political, philosophical and psychological ideas. They are a part of family, group and national traditions.

These myths and legends may or may not partly correspond to objective reality. In his *Political Myths and Economic Realities*, F. Delaisi contrasts the Christian myth, the feudal myth, the papal myth, the monarchical myth and the democratic myth with the economic realities. But systems of ideas have their own reality. In retrospect, the expert may discuss the utility that a system of ideas had for a particular culture. He may consider these as relative and transitory. But to an individual enmeshed in a particular ideology it has an absolute value and is considered immortal. A part of the ideology is the accompanying myths and legends. Sorel discussed the "myth" of the general strike, but he considered this idea to have a central function in the whole Socialist movement. The adherents of that movement did not discuss this idea as "myth."

Today, leaders promulgate myths and legends in a more conscious, organized and orderly fashion. New means of communication have aided the unification of large publics under common ideologies with their accompanying myths and legends. An increasing proliferation of myths and legends may be anticipated. Many people vaguely sense the sterility for life processes of much of objective science. They are thrusting strongly for a more satisfying ideology as a basis for human social relations. Scientific leaders of the nineteenth century pursued objectivity with a vigorous enthusiasm that was in itself not objective but was humanly satisfying. They infected large publics with their faiths and hopes. But now there is a demand for a renewal of satisfying belief. And man begins once more the ancient task of spinning his subjective ideologies, more and more divorced from objective realities. Dramas become internal. Stereotyped heroes and legendary villains, personalized symbols of the perturbing, conflicting elements, are provided

---

[1] Kent, F. R., "In Weakness There Is Strength," *The Nation*, 124: 167.

by interest groups for the general publics. The satisfactions that so many people cannot find in human relations are to be vicariously enjoyed in the world of imagination. The function of legends is not only to provide a basis for objective actions but also to satisfy psychological needs. And the tempo of changing needs and changing myths and legends is increasing.

CHAPTER VIII

VIOLENCE AND PUBLIC OPINION

You can do anything with bayonets save to sit on them.[1]

Societies restrain, threaten and discipline their members and minority groups with varying proportions of psychological and physical compulsion. Cultures differ greatly in their relative use of physical coercion and violence. The individual has been subjected to beatings, injury with weapons, many forms of torture, crucifixion, starving, stoning, suffocation, burnings, breakings on the wheel and rack, hanging, electrocution, assassination and many other forms of physical coercion. The individual's attitudes and opinions regarding these procedures reflect the standards and values of his groups and culture in his time and place. Torturings and public burnings conducted by representatives of the religion of the gentle Christ may not appear inconsistent to a populace daily accustomed to other forms of violence. In both the simpler and more complex cultures, physical force and violence have been prevalent but not universal.

There have been many attempts to generalize about the uses of physical coercion in the social process. Observing the ways of life and reviewing the historic record, the social theorists, philosophers and psychologists of the Western world in the nineteenth century quite generally ascribed the prevalent physical coercion to inherent drives. Man was viewed as a fighting animal motivated by an instinct of pugnacity. Social Darwinism ascribed a high survival value to those generously equipped with this drive. The social philosophers, impressed by the pervasive "struggle for existence," frequently overestimated, though they deplored, prevalence of conflict and of physical force in society.[2] From another frame of reference, conflict was minimized

---

[1] Talleyrand.

[2] This emphasis on the pervasiveness of conflict and force in society had preceded Darwinian evolution. As Hiller, E. T., *Principles of Sociology*, p. 271, 1933, has noted, "These beliefs were given systematic expression by Machiavelli, Bodin, Hobbes and others, who helped to justify the imperialism of aristocracies and thus contributed to the later popularity of a distorted application of Darwinian theories to human society." However, the later theorists were somewhat more systematic, namely: Gumplowicz, L., *Der Rassenkampf*, 1883; Ratzenhofer, G., *Die Sociologische Erkenntnis*, 1898; Schäffle, A. E. F., *Bau und Leben des Socialen Körpers*, vol. I, pp. 391–527, 1875–1878. Many scores of commentators may be listed in the history

and general cooperation, sympathetic responses and humanitarianism were assumed to be based on a more dominant innate drive.[1] Kropotkin, Tolstoy and others maintained that fighting, violence and physical coercion were perversions from man's original pacific tendencies. On both sides of this controversy, which raged at the close of the last century, books were produced filled with selected illustrations from the behavior of other species and of man in the simpler cultures. And on both sides there was exhibited the philosopher's tendency to project his understanding of his own nature into the realm of universal generalizations. The majority of the intellectuals of the nineteenth century preferred types of conflict other than physical coercion. As Wyndham Lewis has noted:

> The philosopher at all times is opposed to violence; at least it is very seldom that he is not, Sorel and Nietzsche being exceptions. The philosophic man inveighs against violence ostensibly on other peoples' behalf. Really he is speaking for himself; not only has he no mandate, but he would be found on careful investigation not to have the sanction of life for his humane intentions. . . . The philosopher is apt to regard life as precious and full of mysterious power and sanctity, because his own is full of interest and vitality. That is probably not the general view; most people cannot develop any such flattering conception of their personal existence.[2]

The psychologists were usually much more specific than the philosophers regarding the nature of this "innate drive." Although many psychologists differentiate between biologically defined instincts and culturally conditioned drives, the majority have usually emphasized the physiological bases of antagonisms and the use of physical force in conflict situations. The sociologist would most often agree with W. I. Thomas that "while there are in fact no 'instincts' in the sense of specific internal entities or prompters of the release of specific forms of activity, the unlearned behavior reactions may be referred to as 'instinctive' or 'instinctual.'"[3] Although the various social scientists disagree as to the relative importance of the organic mechanism in explaining complex conflict behavior in adults, they would agree that the unconditioned reactions of the organism provide some basis for the use of physical force.[4] Anger, fear and other emotional responses including that which recently

---

of conflict theory. A critical analysis of their positions appears in Sorokin, P., *Contemporary Sociological Theories*, Chap. 6, 1928.

[1] Kropotkin, P., *Mutual Aid*, 1903.

[2] Lewis, W., *The Art of Being Ruled*, p. 65, 1926. Reprinted by permission of Harper & Brothers.

[3] Thomas, W. I., *Primitive Behavior*, p. 23, 1937.

[4] McDougall, W., *Introduction to Social Psychology*, 1909; *cf.* Hiller, *op. cit.*, Chap. 17.

has been so loosely termed "sadism" are involved. "Sadism is a term identified with the hurting of, or injury of the person who is the object of an individual's amatory desires."[1] But sadism is now often popularly used as a blanket term for motivation not only of all kinds of violent physical aggression on children, adults, members of the opposite sex, animals, but also of enjoyment of prize fights, and the like. There are individual responses that emanate from innate psychological bases for appreciation of the use of violent physical aggressions. But no single term will cover this complex. Intrinsic determination is increasingly seen as less exact and specific.

The cultural standards determine the extent and ways in which these tendencies are expressed, inhibited or sublimated. Moreover, the standards will be differentiated for age, sex, class and other societal positions. Children tease and torture pets in ways that would be considered inexcusable in adults. Males use violence at times when it would be deprecated in the female. The military man may be expected to use violence. "When the commanding officer of one of the Guards Regiments which made the palace revolution and set Empress Catherine on the throne of all the Russias called upon his men to give three cheers for their new mistress they shouted 'We won't serve a baba—a female.' The colonel thereupon nearly felled the man nearest him with a formidable clout on the ear. The cheers were then heartily given, for as the men said, the thing had been properly explained to them."[2]

Violence may be consciously cultivated.[3] Gang members, swaggering officers, labor leaders, managers of prisoners and many others may develop "hard-boiledness," thereby gaining prestige in the opinions of their fellows. Ability to give and to take punishment may be esteemed.

Violence is very evident in some cultures and almost nonexistent in others. Although it is functionally related to other types of behavior and standards in a culture, it is not directly related to the complexity or state of development of a culture. No valid generalizations have been adduced to indicate such relationship. Some quite simple peoples are quite violent, but so are members of complex cultures.

Force may be used on members of the out-groups (wars, raids, slavery, etc.), on in-group members (discipline, personal conflict, etc.), on both or on neither. Space does not permit a summary of ethnological literature on this point, but we shall select a few illustrations . War

---

[1] Dorcus, R. M., and Shaffer, G. W., *Abnormal Psychology*, p. 144, 1934.

[2] Broderick, A. H., *World Digest*, March, 1937. Permission to quote granted.

[3] The term "violence" is sometimes distinguished from other forms of physical coercion, as being an illegal use of force (see *Ency. Soc. Sci.*). However, this distinction is not consistently used in the literature of the social sciences, and the author is here using the terms interchangeably.

plays a prominent part in the lives of some primitive peoples, notably the African Negro tribes; North American Indians, especially Plains Indians, South American Indians and many groups of Pacific Islanders. There are a number of notable cases where war does not exist. Prof. Boas reported in his early studies of the Eskimo that real wars or fights between settlements did not occur. The Todas of India, the Kubas of Sumatra, most Australian groups and a number of other tribes have no pattern of forceful conflict with those round about.[1] Although warfare is often conducted for the means of subsistence, for religious motives and for women and slaves, it is also frequently carried on for glory and prestige. Historically, national groups have likewise fought wars for various objectives. At one era of world history there is the dream of universal dominion, at another the conquest of lands; again the religious struggles dominate, and trade wars have characterized the modern period.[2] Whatever the motives for conflict, they are incorporated in individual attitudes and expressed in popular opinion.

The frequency of violence within a culture usually reflects the amount of force used on outside groups. Peoples become accustomed to forcible coercion and utilize it on women, children, inferiors and enemies. Margaret Mead has recently contrasted the way of life in several New Guinea tribes.[3] The Arapesh, living on infertile hills, are isolated. Free from aggression from outside, without need of sturdy defenders, the personality types prized among them are characterized by passivity, responsiveness, physical sympathy and cooperativeness. Both men and women develop these traits. Sensuous physical responsiveness to living things is characteristic of both men and women. Children are fondled by the hour. Violent individuals are depreciated and restrained when they occasionally develop such divergent behavior. Anger is played down. The fear and discomfort resulting from any expression of anger is worked into a pattern of sorcery to frighten and restrain the angered person. The general policy of Arapesh society is to punish those who are indiscreet enough to become involved in any kind of violent scene. Popular opinion opposes physical coercion. On the other hand, the Mundugumor of the Sepik River emphasize violence and daily conflict. They inhabit a fertile land which they have had to defend. They train both sexes with a Spartan vigor. Children are beaten, blows are exchanged between men and women. Brothers speak only under ceremonial conditions. Fighting the out-groups and head-hunting traditional enemies are a

[1] Davie, M., *Evolution of War*, Chap. 4, 1929.
Sumner, W. G., and Keller, A. G., *Science of Society*, vol. II, 1927.
[2] Johnson, A., "The International House of Cards," *Yale Rev.*, 25: 433–442.
[3] Mead, M., *Sex and Temperament in Primitive Society*, pp. 433–442, 1936. See also *Conflict and Cooperation in Primitive Society* (Mead, M., ed.), 1937.

seasonal occurrence. Within the group, social organization is based on
mutual hostility. Individuals value personal liberty and fight interference. The sympathetic individual is considered to be weak. Popular
opinion supports these violent practices. Admittedly, these are extreme
illustrations, but it is evident that wide differences exist between cultures
in their patterns of violence.

Physical violence may prevail in the daily life of a people. Life in
the medieval barony was a rough, roistering existence. The fighting
men had reckless brawls and then quickly came to agreement. The
knight would not hesitate to kick or pummel a servitor. Torture was
frequently inflicted on enemies and captives. Cooks and chiefs of
sections would chase varlets from the kitchen. Ladies, on occasion,
would smite their maids. And it is reported that, "many a noble
lady can answer her husband's fist with a rousing box on the ear, and if
he is not a courageous man, make him quail and surrender before her."[1]
In a culture thus suffused with physical coercion, the use of force is
naturally supported by attitudes and popular opinion.

NONVIOLENT COERCION

As in some cultures force and violence may be used to dramatize an
issue and otherwise affect the more general public opinion, so, elsewhere,
when the values of the culture depreciate physical force, forms of passive
resistance may be used to coerce an opponent and arouse a public opinion.
Oriental peoples have quite generally used passive resistance. To the
West it is alien and has been used only sporadically by a few minority
groups, usually with indifferent success. Conscientious objectors,
Quakers, female hunger strikers in the woman's movement, and some
minor religious sects have eschewed force.

The peoples of the West are best acquainted with passive resistance
and noncooperation as used in the Orient through Gandhi's campaigns
in India. Mass passive resistance was widely used in the Indian independence movement. There, violence by authority was frequently met
by mass demonstrations of passive resistance, when thousands of people,
bent on demonstrating at a forbidden place, would march to that place,
preceded by their own ambulances, and stand calmly and with disciplined dignity until knocked over by the police. Such stoical composure
aroused widespread admiration among their fellows. But American and
English audiences, seeing in the newsreels flashes of brutal violence used
by the police to disperse Indian crowds, no doubt usually responded with
mixed feelings of physical sympathy for the injured and rather disdainful
irritation at them for permitting themselves to be hurt. In general,
passive resistance has been rather ineffective in arousing more than

[1] Davis, W. S., *Life on a Mediaeval Barony*, p. 76, 1923.

temporary sympathetic response from American publics. Humanitarian responses are largely canceled by the tradition of self-reliant use of violence as a weapon. There is little popular understanding of the significance of passive resistance used as tactics in social conflict. The effectiveness of Gandhi's campaign in India has not as yet been adequately evaluated by those acquainted with the situation; therefore we cannot generalize about its use in the Orient.[1] However, even widespread passive resistance by some minority group in the United States would probably not win popular support here. Even in the Orient, H. N. Brailsford concludes that it is "in theory irresistible, in practice very difficult," as a political technique, because of the rare degree of solidarity required for its successful use.[2] In cases of individual conflict it is indubitably successful at times. In Japan and India, fasting on the doorstep of an enemy or of one who has injured the faster has been common. Popular opinion humiliates the object of such attentions.

One form of nonviolent coercion used somewhat of late years in Western nations is the hunger strike. From 1909 onward, hundreds of Englishwomen endured the hunger strike when they were sent to prison for their activities in the suffrage movement. The Irish have used this technique extensively in their political struggles. In the United States there have been but relatively few cases of such protest. It was used somewhat in the suffragette and birth-control reform movements. Forcible feeding aroused considerable public outcry. The objective of the hunger strike is publicity and appeal to popular opinion. The intensity of the convictions of the strikers is dramatically evidenced by their willingness to die for crimes not deserving of death. However, as it becomes less of a novelty the publicity value is partly lost.

The sit-down strike is a technique of nonviolent coercion recently developed for American labor by the CIO. It is claimed that it reduces the amount of violence, as strike-breaking thugs are not imported. First widely publicized in the General Motors-CIO controversy of 1937, the sit-down strike spread rapidly to many industries. Under existing laws it is clearly an illegal trespass on private property and the threat of union seizure by means of the sit-down strike could easily be met by the injunction and arrest. However, during the early months of such strikes, it was usually considered inexpedient to attempt to eject strikers, as the state of popular opinion was not definitely known. Employers were hesitant. Many labor leaders also were fearful of this new technique. They could see how a too widespread wave of sit-down strikes (some of which might be staged by *agents provocateurs*) could discredit the unions.

[1] *Ency. Soc. Sci.*, 12: 13.
[2] The most extensive discussion in English is Gregg, R. B., *The Power of Non-Violence*, 1934.

A too rapidly successful labor movement may arouse popular opposition. English labor overplayed its hand in the general strike of 1926 and has never recovered from the unfavorable popular reaction. The general public was confused by the new technique of sit-down strikes. The implications, in terms of labor dominance or defeat, upon the general price levels and many other issues were not clearly seen. A dominant public opinion had not emerged.

On the basis of theory, many have been intrigued by the possibilities of various forms of passive resistance and nonviolent coercion. It has been espoused both in the humanitarian flight from physical force and through the recognition that force does not achieve permanent solutions. Moreover, nonviolent coercion and passive resistance are possible methods for masses ill-equipped for the refinements of violence. Its advocates laud the essential justice of such procedure. It is less often pointed out that, if successful, nonviolent coercion could be directed to unjust ends. Indeed, all other successful techniques of social conflict at times have been unjustly used. The enthusiasts for nonviolence neglect this aspect. However, there is no immediate danger of such abuse; for nonviolent means require a discipline, an integrity, endurance and a group solidarity that are but little developed and practiced in American life. The aim of nonviolent tactics is to convert or defeat the opponent by changing the conflict from one plane to another and by appealing to him and to the general public. There is the attempt to arouse sympathy and admiration for suffering bravely endured under disciplined conditions. But the technique must be appreciated by the general public if the opponent is to be successfully coerced. And how alien to the Western mind is a real belief in nonviolence! A case in point is the ethical confusion of children confronted with the idea that if smitten on one cheek they should turn the other. Conscientious objectors, hunger strikers and various types of passive resisters have not aroused widespread admiration and sympathy in the United States.[1]

VIOLENCE AND THE LABOR MOVEMENT

Organized social revolt has often been accompanied by violence. Frequently social changes have been thus dramatically introduced. Many times when violence was not used, the threat of force was a potent factor in the background. Where large publics are concerned and masses are aroused, violence has been the almost invariable concomitant of social reform and revolution. In this way, organized movements have usually acquired their legendary leaders, their personal martyr symbols and an excitingly dramatic context.

[1] For a summary of techniques with historic illustrations, see Case, C. M., *Non Violent Coercion*, 1923; a recent discussion is in Gregg, *op. cit.*

The labor movement has not varied from this general pattern. Minorities, with a philosophic and theoretical tradition that violence is the only way to bring about social change, have usually been present at the major clashes between labor and employers or authority and have often precipitated conflict. In the United States there have been many violent incidents during strikes, especially in the clothing and textile industries, the building trades, coal mining and the steel industry. The bloody wars at the Colorado mines, the Pullman strike, the Herrin massacre, the Homestead strike and many others are tragic pages in the history of labor conflict. Force has been used upon strikebreakers or scabs, upon strikers, upon police, both public and private, and infrequently upon employers. Both or all sides usually repudiate any intent to use violence, maintaining that they were driven to it by circumstances or as a defense measure. Even that organization which the general public associates most often with violent methods and intent formally repudiates force in its public statements. The Industrial Workers of the World in 1920 stated that the organization did not then and never had believed in or advocated either destruction or violence as a means of accomplishing industrial reform.[1] The Socialist movement in England waged a long struggle against the use of violence by its members even in the face of organized violence by governments and the private armies of opponents.[2] On the tactical basis it was early recognized that violence and terroristic acts brought popular revulsion when used in England or the United States. Socialism has more and more diverged from the principle of violence and espoused passive resistance, moral resistance, strikes, economic penalties, education and propaganda.

Although physical force has usually been repudiated by organized labor groups and by responsible leaders, in practice violence has often been used by labor to control strikebreakers, as a gesture in strategy, during the conflicts of picketing, because of emotional hatred of the enemy, to dramatize the issue and to affect general public opinion. Often strikebreakers or scabs may be intimidated by threats of violence or by use of physical force when persuasion has proved ineffective. Physical injury and pain may be understood when argument fails. At first such violence may be quite tentative, threatened blows and imitation of acts of violence, until the cumulative intensity of emotional stresses causes certain individuals, meeting with resistance, to begin the fight, although it was originally intended that physical force would be merely threatened.[3] Indeed, if large groups are involved it is very difficult to

---

[1] Gambs, J. S., *The Decline of the I.W.W.*, Appendix II, 1932.
[2] The history of this struggle has been ably recounted in Hunter, R., *Violence and the Labor Movement*, 1914.
[3] Hiller, E. T., *The Strike*, pp. 108–111, 1928.

use threatened violence as a gesture in strategy. In conflict situations the individual may sometimes do so, if schooled in the control of his emotional responses. However, in large crowds there are always impulsive persons who are difficult to control. Entirely aside from the ethical problem of violence, the technique of strategy necessitates caution in the use of tentative violence as a gesture. Many bloody fights have resulted from the leaders' loss of control while attempting this tactic. Picketing, especially in the early days of labor disputes, was often successful because of the intimidation of the strikebreakers by threats of violence. Many court decisions now define the rights of the strikebreaker to freedom not only from intimidation but also from annoying importunity.[1]

Among the objectives of violence in the labor movement are the control of scabs, intimidation, the defense of picketers, revenge on the police and publicity. Employers utilize violence in order to continue operations, to intimidate, to remove the leaders of the strike, and to prevent communication. Publicizing of their violent deeds may promote solidarity within the striking group, raise up new popular leaders from the rank and file, and above all draw attention to the struggle so that the larger public may become involved, especially through the creation of a favorable and sympathetic popular opinion.

The opinion of the immediate community and of the larger national public is often the deciding factor in an industrial dispute. Each side, intent upon discrediting the other, appeals to the fears and prejudices of the larger publics. To convict the other side of unprovoked and ruthless violence often causes a wave of indignation and revulsion against them. Of the famous steel strike of 1919 it has been reported:

Preceding and during the strike both sides in the hostilities employed all sorts of devices—all of them well known in industrial struggle—to influence public opinion and to break the power of their opponents. . . . The Corporation attempted to discredit the movement by alleging . . . that its real objects were the overthrow of established leaders and established institutions of organized labor and perhaps the overthrow of the established government of the country. . . . The hue and cry raised in every district where the strike was in effect; the parading of strike breakers through the streets; the mobilizing of Federal troops in Gary, Indiana district; the occupation of troubled areas by state militia and in Western Pennsylvania by State Constabulary; the spreading of subversive reports of "bloody riots" and "red revolution"; the breaking-up of picket lines and peaceful gatherings of strikers; the holding of huge anti-strike mass meetings in the open air; and raids upon union halls, the homes of some of the strikers, and certain offices of the labor press, were designed to impress the public and terrorize the strikers. . . . Charges were made against the strikers that they were guilty of intimidating non-striking workmen and inciting to riot.[2]

[1] *Ibid.*, p. 118.
[2] Adapted from Dawson, C. A., and Gettys, W. E., *Introduction to Sociology*, pp. 526–528, 1935. Quoted by permission of the Ronald Press Company.

Despite the general American tradition of violence, the larger publics are frequently repelled by its use in labor controversies. This often results from the way in which the occasions of violence are reported by the newspapers.[1] Yet, as we have noted, violence has other uses than that of influencing popular opinion one way or the other. And violence has been widely used in the American labor movement.[2]

Religious Opinions and Physical Force

Coercion by physical violence has been practiced at times by organized religious institutions, as well as by the fanatically faithful, in curbing the free expression of alien religious beliefs and in maintaining or inculcating the one true faith. This is evidenced in religious wars, crusades and jehads against alien religions; in the forcible conversion of individuals of other culture groups, of which the history of European contact with native peoples in the sixteenth and seventeenth centuries gives ample illustration; in the discipline or annihilation of the variant from the faith. The most organized example of this last is the Inquisition.

Deviation from accepted religious teachings through the holding of and defense of opinions contrary thereto was called heresy by the medieval church. The Inquisition was an elaborate institution for the punishment of and suppression of heresy. Physical force came to be extensively used in repressing heresies, such as the Albigensian movement (Catharism in the south of France) and the Waldensians in Italy. In addition there was the persistent struggle with the devious ways and practices of the witch and the wizard. The witch was usually considered far more dangerous than the wizard, and there were a great many more of them. The popular conceptions of the witch were molded and colored by the findings of the church inquisitors during the fifteenth century. The evil heresies of the witches increasingly were supposed to include sexual aberrations, the orgy of the witches' Sabbath and congress with the devil. Thus, in part, the particular psychological fears and phobias of their judges were projected upon the witches, who in turn accepted the suggestions and unfolded more and more lurid detail.[3] Increasingly, force was used to extort confessions. The rack, the thumbscrew and the various ingenious tortures of the period were used to extract the so-called "voluntary" confessions. Burnings became more frequent. By the middle of the fifteenth century an aroused public, angry and desperately fearful, began that popular madness of witchhunting which was to last two centuries. The total number of victims, during those centuries, has

---

[1] See Seldes, G., *The Freedom of the Press*, 1935.

[2] The historic record of violence in the labor movement is developed in Hunter, *op. cit.*, and especially in Adamic, L., *Dynamite* (revised ed.), 1934.

[3] For an excellent literary description of the witches' Sabbath, see Merejkowski, D., *Leonardo da Vinci*, Bk. IV.

been variously estimated from one hundred thousand to several hundred thousand. Attempts at forcible suppression, far from decreasing the heresy of witchcraft, made of it a mass delusion on a large scale and drew into the ranks of the eventual victims hordes of mentally aberrant and deranged women whose vivid hallucinations were made of the stuff of popular beliefs and the ghostly world of their questioners. And the excesses of physical violence further distorted the psychological processes.

However, violence was used by the church in dealing with heresy long before the persecution of the witches. The eleventh and twelfth centuries were characterized by a revival of learning and with that learning the emergence of various heresies. The problem of eliminating them became ever more difficult. Physical force was used informally by the orthodox and by heretics, by civil rulers and by mob violence, but not formally by ecclesiastical authority. During this period, church authorities frequently incited the mob to acts of violence; it was therefore not necessary for the religious institution to develop more formal techniques.[1] But by the thirteenth century the scene changed. The more cultured people of western Europe were losing faith; in some sections heresy was endemic. And heresy was becoming organized. The Waldensians were founded about 1179. They renewed the popular preaching of sermons that the church had permitted to fall into disuse and attempted many reforms including poverty and renunciation of authority. The Albigensian heresy developed in the early eleventh century, its leaders asserting the existence of good and evil deities; their contempt for the church, its sacraments, the doctrine of transubstantiation; in general, their abhorrence of all forms of symbolism. The Albigenses were the first of the heretics to be burned at the stake.[2] They denied the individual's right to take life, human or animal. They also deprecated sexual experience. Hence, a suspect, in his defense before a tribunal, logically declared, "Hear me, my lords! I am no heretic, for I have a wife, and cohabit with her, and have children; and I eat flesh and lie and swear and am a faithful Christian."[3] Other sects multiplied, and civil authorities became more lenient toward them. For the most part the feudal rulers who knew the heretics well did not object to them as subjects, although violence was sometimes resorted to by the lords in order to gain favor with the local clergy. In the south of France, the sects became so powerful that they organized meetings and public debates, and large classes of society felt free to question the fundamental tenets of the church. Finally many French noblemen were converted to the Catharist sects. Some used this as an excuse to seize the property of the

---

[1] Coulton, G. G., *The Inquisition*, p. 32, 1929.
[2] Maycock, A. L., *The Inquisition*, pp. 37 *ff.*, 1927.
[3] Quoted by Coulton, *op. cit.*, p. 46.

Roman Catholic church.   In the closing years of the twelfth century numerous church missions were sent out to combat heresy by preaching and persuasion, by clerical competition in goodness and austerity, by debate and excommunication.   These measures had but partial success; therefore, a Papal Bull of Nov. 17, 1207, called upon the peoples of northern France forcibly to repress the Albigenses, granting to all who would take part in such a crusade all the indulgences of crusaders to the Holy Land.   After varying fortunes the nobles and Albigensians of the South were finally defeated in 1229.   When, on the basis of persuasive competition, the church was losing ground, it turned to violence.   It could be ruthless with physical beings when souls were to be saved.   A campaign to repress and exterminate the heretics was begun, and the sects became secret organizations.

And so, the Inquisition began.   Confiscation, the stake and torture were its effective forces.   According to Coulton, the principal characteristics of the Inquisition were: (1) Guilt was assumed unless innocence could be proved, (2) the judges were ecclesiastical, (3) procedures were secret, (4) names of witnesses were concealed, (5) infamous persons and children could testify, (6) it was made a punishable crime to appear in defense of a guilty person, (7) defense witnesses also were suspected of heresy, (8) torture could be used not only on suspects but also on witnesses, (9) torture had no legal limits, (10) the smallest of nonconformities could be made punishable by death.[1]   Suspects, heretics, and concealers and defenders of these were denounced, pursued, tried, tortured and killed by the thousands in the thirteenth and fourteenth centuries.   As the inquisitors gained in ability to extort confessions, they felt it their duty to record their ingenuities for posterity; therefore, a number of inquisitors' manuals for plying tortured victims with questions were written for younger and less seasoned colleagues.   And, of course, individual inquisitors soon went to extremes.   Torquemada is reported on good authority to have burned 2000 heretics.   And he had many emulators.   But the field of the Inquisition, although very extensive, did not comprise the whole of the Christian world.   The Scandinavian kingdoms escaped it almost entirely, England experienced it only once in the case of the Templars and Portugal knew nothing of it before the reign of Ferdinand and Isabella.[2]   It raged with especial violence in the south of France.

Violent coercion of the individual's beliefs and opinions was carried to ever greater lengths.   Here is one of the bloodiest pages of the history of man's inhumanity to man.   Religious excesses and psychological aberrations leading to physical cruelty have frequently gone hand in

---

[1] Coulton, *op. cit.*, pp. 67 *ff.*
[2] Vacandard, E., *The Inquisition*, pp. 182 *ff.*, 1908.

hand when not checked by institutional authority. Masochistic and sadistic motives are evident in the excesses of fugitive sects at times, the Russian "scourgers," flagellants, Penitentes and other cruel sects. Personal satisfaction as well as zeal for souls may have motivated some of the inquisitors, but most were no doubt preoccupied with the religious problem of the heresies. And of course fair play and physical humanitarianism are of lesser importance to persons obsessed with immortal souls. Apparently some of the inquisitors used relatively little torture, relying upon ingenious cross-questioning. However, whatever the method of carrying on the trial, the end was almost certain condemnation. Indeed, at certain periods of the Inquisition, representatives of the inquisitors would begin confiscating the property of the accused before the trial had begun, so certain was the judgment, especially in the case of the wealthy who had fallen from grace.

Threatened institutions ultimately resort to force. The church has been no exception. No institution can be permanently maintained by force alone. On the other hand, in societies where violence is prevalent, no institution can, in crises, dispense with it altogether and survive. The intrusion of such violence upon a society that had otherwise largely dispensed with physical coercion would develop popular revulsion and adverse opinion. However, in the period of the Inquisition, force was the order of the day in many aspects of society. In the opinions of both faithful and heretic, physical coercion was a normal pattern of action. It was expedient and expected.

The State and Violence

States have varied greatly in their violent coercion of their various minorities. However, physical coercion or the threat of physical coercion is in the nature of any kind of state rule, although states differ markedly in the occasion and degree of its use. In the states of the authoritarian tradition, autocratic governments utilize crude, brutal physical force at many points both within and without. The Hegelian philosophy of the state theoretically justifies the subjection of the individual and minority groups to autocratic and powerful central governments. Once the sovereignty of such a government is granted, its use of physical force for coercive purposes becomes a problem not in ethics but in expediency. In recent times such governments achieved greatest control in the German states of the nineteenth century, in Czarist Russia, and latterly in Soviet Russia, in Fascist Italy and in Nazi Germany. But historically there have been many brutal governments utilizing physical force and terror with varying degrees of skill. As C. E. Merriam has stated, "Restraint, the lash, torture in many forms, mutilation, humiliation, isolation, exile, and finally death are items in the thick catalogue of force.

The rack, the boot, branding, the dungeon, the 'hell hole,' boiling water and molten metal, crucifixion, burnings, sawings and pullings asunder. These are only a few of the devices from time to time employed in the service of the states."[1] With the development of the modern democratic and liberal state the scope of violence was lessened. Only those individuals and groups who were the object of popular aversion were ordinarily subjected to physical violence. Various aspects of the treatment of the criminal, although gradually modified under a developing humanitarian tradition, continue as one field in which recourse to violence is frequent. In race and labor relations there remains some use of physical coercion under democracy. However, the state has been progressively restrained from using violence on minorities. Pity and sympathy and physical humanitarianism are a late development in social relations and are unstable even now. Respect for power and for physical force rigorously administered has been the more usual response of masses of mankind and is the dominant attitude in large sections of the world today. How unstable the aversion to violence is may be illustrated by the amazing recrudescence of a faith in force among masses of people in the Western world today under the difficulties of the past decade. There has been a flight from reason, logic, humanitarianism, the techniques of peaceful adjudication, the rights of minorities, free speech. There have been a rise of faith in violence; the deliberate cultivation of the irrational, sentimentality and emotionalism; an increased reliance on supposed instinct, the "voice of the blood," and the like. These changing popular attitudes are evidenced, not only in changing state forms, but in literature and other aspects of culture. The systematic cult of the irrational and of faith in violence is indeed sinister.

The most extensive as well as most influential justifications and defense of the use of physical force and violence by the state, in suppressing minorities at home, as well as in relation to other states, appear in the writings of the Russian Pobiedonostsev, of the German Trietschke and of the Italian Pareto.[2] Administrators, Pobiedonostsev declared, should not be limited and hence weakened by rules and doubts. The persons whose duty it is to act should act in an unrestricted fashion, using violence as freely as expediency decrees. All agencies of public administration, as well as the press, education and the judiciary, should be in the hands of these administrators. To Pobiedonostsev, free education was dangerous; the press was venal, gossipy and scandalous

[1] Merriam, C. E., *Political Power*, p. 135, 1934.
[2] Pobiedonostsev, K. P., *Reflections of a Russian Statesman*, 1898. Trietschke, H., *Politics*, original ed., 1898. English trans., 1916. Pareto, V., *The Mind and Society* (English trans.), Sections 1826–1875, 2054–2059, 1935.

and should be repressed. Authority ultimately was holy, justified in whatever acts of violence were necessary to maintain the organic functioning of existing government in an uninterrupted fashion. Such was the political philosophy of the most influential man in Russia in the closing years of the nineteenth century. In Germany, Trietschke was writing in the 1870's those essays which were to be so influential in the next half century. He justified the *Machtpolitik* of the Prussian military monarchy. For him, power is the most distinctive attribute of the state, and the state is justified in applying this power in any way. Individual aims and interests are of no concern. Physical force should be used to whatever extent is necessary for achieving unity and stability of the state. Normally the state should rely upon force to ensure obedience and should neither attempt to appeal to its subjects upon the basis of reason nor court popular approval. Such was the theory so widely quoted in Germany prior to 1914. Pareto advocated the use of vigorous force and physical coercion upon divergent groups within a state. Thus would the elite maintain themselves and prolong their existence. An elite preserves its ascendancy by manipulating symbols, controlling supplies and applying violence.[1] Pareto would intensify the violence. He maintains that only thus may a strong, orderly state exist, and that, contrary to beliefs propagated in the Western world during the humanitarian movement of the nineteenth century, cruel aristocracies last longer than meek, humanitarian aristocracies. Aristocracies do not last, they decay and disappear, but they will last longer and exhibit a desirable vigor in proportion as they wisely and expediently use force for coercion. Many other nineteenth-century theorists overemphasized both the amount of violence required and the necessity for physical coercion in society.

The church used force when threatened by the heresies. The state used violence, threatened violence and developed philosophies of force in the intensified state competitions and expansions of the nineteenth century. In colonizing and empire building there were natives and other states to be subjugated. As Hilaire Belloc said,

> Whatever happens, we have got
> The Maxim gun, and they have not.

Also the expansion of other states and the competition for prestige were increased. There was intensified recourse to violence. Within the state, divergent political minorities were springing up. And the killing of critics has often been the simplest and most efficacious way of disposing of opposition.

[1] Lasswell, H. D., *World Politics and Personal Insecurity*, p. 3, 1935.

The ultimate pattern of force is international war. Although the average length of wars decreased during the nineteenth century,[1] the preparation for war, its cost and the number of men under arms increased sharply.[2] Attempts to curb these preparations have failed. By their actions, nations stand committed to violence. However, popular opinion has been increasingly preoccupied with this problem during the breathing spell since the World War. But there is a growing desire, not only for peace, but also for security and welfare. If there is a passing of force as the supreme factor in the relation between states, there must be an adjustment of the economic problems of states (which seems inconceivable at the moment); the development of a trusted machinery to settle disputes; the conditioning of the attitudes of vast populations toward expression of opinion for peace.

On the other hand, the Fascist movement has emphasized force and violence. The official motto of the Fascist educational system is "The textbook and the musket make the perfect Fascist." Violence is threatened without and applied within the state. The extent to which whole populations have been indoctrinated with a philosophy of violence remains to be seen. Within the Fascist state (in Italy, but more especially in Germany) violence served to discharge long-accumulated aversions to opponents; it provided symbols of ruthlessness (dress-suited executioner with ax); it destroyed and intimidated foes. Mussolini has vigorously advocated violence and has developed various rules for its use. He has stated,

> Was there ever a government in history that was based exclusively on the consent of the people and renounced any and every use of force? A government so constituted there never will be. Consent is as changeable as the formations in the sands of the seashore. We cannot have it always. Nor can it ever be total. No government has ever existed that made all its subjects happy. Whatever solution you happen to give to any problem whatsoever, even though you share the Divine wisdom, you would inevitably create a class of malcontents.
> . . . How are you going to avoid that this discontent spread and constitute a danger for the solidarity of the State? You avoid it with force: by bringing a maximum force to bear; by employing this force inexorably whenever it is rendered necessary. Rob any government of force and leave it with only its immortal principles, and that government will be at the mercy of the first group that is organized and intent on overthrowing it. Now fascism throws these lifeless theories on the dump heap. When a group or a party is in power it has the obligation of fortifying itself and defending itself against all.[3]

[1] Lasswell, H. D., *Politics*, p. 53, 1936.

[2] Hodges, C., *The Background of International Relations*, tables, pp. 576, 579, 583 *ff.*, 1931.

[3] Finer, H., *Mussolini's Italy*, p. 223, 1935. Quoted by permission of Henry Holt & Company.

Individuals and minority groups have been terrorized and intimidated through threat of violence by those in power.   There is a technique of terror or subjugation through fright, which utilizes secret police, spies, special courts, *agents provocateurs*, arrest on suspicion, hostages, concentration camps, the bludgeon, the knife, the firing squad and other forms of violence.   To the individual who has a profound faith in a political creed, these means may not seem unreal or indefensible for securing the acceptance of his viewpoint.

The systematic application of violence may also be used by minority groups to terrorize and intimidate representatives of governments.[1] Planned assassination has been utilized by dissident groups to terrorize their opponents and to give publicity to their cause.   In Russia there was organized in June, 1879, a professed terrorist party.[2]   From then until the revolution, organized but sporadic violence occurred.   Bakunin was the theorist of Russian terrorism.   An extensive philosophy in defense of such acts was produced by the revolutionary parties.   This romantic "propaganda of the deed" spread to other political systems but was nowhere so widely utilized as in Russia.   Masaryk notes that the personal characteristics of the Russian terrorist were youth, fine enthusiasm, desire for publicity and martyrdom, mysticism and a nervous, restless temperament.   Such a person often achieved an enthusiastic and admiring following among the women of the movement and became increasingly indifferent and reckless.[3]   "But it now appears reasonable to conclude that selective assassination fails of its purpose as revolutionary propaganda. . . . The peasants did not rise; hence terroristic tactics passed into disrepute."[4]

CONCLUSION

It has often been noted that most successful movements of social revolt have used violence at some point in the acquisition of power. In general this has been true in the Western world.   However, the amount and types of violence vary with the prevailing cultural values.

Liberalism has denied the validity of violence in the political field, and the associated humanitarianism has sought to lessen the use of physical coercion on all forms of sentient life.   On the other hand, modern dictatorship has declared the necessity of violence to solve otherwise irreconcilable principles.   Modern humanitarianism has its origins in the nineteenth century.   It has been related to the rise of a middle class trained for peace, a numerous middle class conscious of the value of human

[1] "Terrorism," "Intimidation," *Ency. Soc. Sci.*

[2] Masaryk, T. G., *The Spirit of Russia*, vol. II, p. 95, 1919.

[3] *Ibid.*, pp. 107–113.

[4] Lasswell, *op. cit.*, p. 66. Quoted by permission of the McGraw-Hill Book Company, Inc.

life, a middle class accepting science and rationalism and recoiling from cruelty.[1] Liberal humanitarianism provides the ideological basis for antislavery; for reform movements to improve the treatment of prisoners, women, children and animals; for social work and welfare movements. Popular conceptions and opinions in the Western world were oriented toward pity and sympathy. But these responses are quite unstable, and there is much inconsistency. In a sense, humanitarianism is a luxury associated with secure societal organization. Within contemporary cultures there are great inconsistencies between violent coercion in some fields and tender humanitarianism in others. Nazi leaders, though bent on toughening German sensibilities, have at the same time passed stringent rules restricting vivisection and attempted to prohibit it altogether.

The confusion in popular opinion is very evident in America. Our history has made it so. Ideological humanitarian sentiment and Christian tenderness were widespread. But the harsh realities of frontier life, the clashes between quite different cultural groups in our population, the unsettled race problem, the fierce violence of numerous industrial disputes have made the majority of Americans profess one viewpoint and frequently practice another code. The terrible record of race violence evidences one unresolved conflict.[2] Perhaps the lack of immediately threatening external enemies has accentuated violence within the land.

The individual may be conditioned in quite various ways in response to violence. If normal man is endowed by nature with a portion of cruelty, this may certainly be greatly accentuated or minimized. Under the humanitarian tradition it was depreciated. But at other times the taste may be cultivated until wildly enthusiastic throngs flock to the arena, the burning, quartering, whipping or hanging. There can be no doubt that in America today there is an increasing cultivation of vicarious violence in comparison with, say 1900. This is due to the cult of violence elsewhere in the world and to the intellectual flight from reason. But it is more especially due to the common man's awareness of existing violences as purveyed to him by the newspapers, periodicals, radio and other means of communication. There is considerable confused acceptance by the newspaper reader of the fact of fights, murders, gangs, lynchings, rapes and terrorism. An individual taste for such material may be cultivated. The world of contemporary vicarious appreciation of violence is exhibited in the action of much of our popular fiction: in mystery fiction; in those hard, staccato phrases descriptive of action

[1] Brinton, C., "Humanitarianism," *Ency. Soc. Sci.*, 7: 544–548.
[2] Cutler, J. E., *Lynch Law*, 1905.
White, W. F., *Rope and Faggot*, 1929.
Raper, A. F., *The Tragedy of Lynching*, 1933.

in a Dashiell Hammett mystery; in those writhing, tortured females who sprawl over the front covers of scores of pulp magazines; in that fierce interest in violent action in the true mystery and crime magazines. This is not to say that these serve as models for behavior, but they certainly do indicate the conscious cultivation of violence in thought. Personal violence in many fields may come to be taken for granted.

Violence by majorities aims to subjugate, eliminate or terrorize opposition. Minorities may also attempt to intimidate. In both situations there is an attempt to win the sympathies of an even larger public. In this process certain instances of violence become symbols for the groups. As Lasswell notes, . . . "the cult of violence is a kind of symbolism to which the tactics of the early Fascist squadrons have been reduced. This cult expresses itself in the growls and threats which pervade Fascist oratory and manifestoes."[1] The issue may be symbolized in a personally dramatic fashion, as in the personal violence of a John Brown or Carrie Nation. During the early years of the depression, the Communists staged dramatic hunger demonstrations and marches in many large American cities. As these were usually the occasions for violence and bloody riots, they became front-page news.[2] Violent incidents may also provide symbols around which the loyalties of the in-group may be organized. Sympathetic response to the physical trials and agonies of the members of the in-group may be treasured in the traditions of a family, gang, party, sect or nation and recalled at appropriate occasions. Thus the memories of the agonies of the Christian martyrs, the execution of Sacco and Vanzetti, the psychological trial of William Tell, the last gasps of the defenders of the Alamo or the writhings in the Black Hole of Calcutta become treasured possessions of a group.

There are many limitations to the effective use of violence in large groups. Violence brutalizes those who apply it; usually, physical coercion cannot be stopped until it devours its own offspring; violence in the modern world alienates some of the most sensitive but useful persons from the group and cause that espouse it;[3] it breeds fraud and evasion; it is often wasteful and inefficient; it readily develops antagonistic responses from those on whom it is used, causing counter movements. However, violence has often been successfully used for a time, especially in periods of cultural transition. Popular opinion has permitted and endorsed it. And obviously, physical coercion cannot be wholly abolished in contemporary social systems.

[1] Lasswell, H. D., *Propaganda and Dictatorship* (H. L. Childs, ed.), p. 46, 1936. Quoted by permission of Princeton University Press.

[2] Adamic, *op. cit.*, Postscript on Violence, pp. 458–480.

[3] MacIver, R. M., *Society, Its Structure and Changes*, pp. 36–42, 1931.

CHAPTER IX

THE GEOGRAPHIC DISTRIBUTION OF GROUP OPINION

The record of man's beliefs and opinions as well as his behavior may be and has been developed from a number of different viewpoints and frames of reference. For example, historical studies have been written primarily in terms of personalities, of peoples and races, of cultures, of economic motivations, of political ideologies, of psychological and of geographic factors. Personal factors are the perennial preoccupation of the common man and, indeed, until very recently have been the center of attention for social philosophers and scientists. That innate racial characteristics are responsible for differences in behavior and belief has been the thesis of an enormous literature. The cultural divisions of mankind have been increasingly described and differentiated during the past century. Economic motivations have been especially emphasized since Karl Marx. Political ideologies have been a distinguishing classification since the rise of great states. And the spatial distribution of both material and nonmaterial culture elements has latterly proved a fruitful approach to the study of human life. Interrelations resulting from spatial positions have been explored in the literature of human ecology. We shall consider briefly the significance of position in space as this affects public opinion.

The influence of geographic factors in affecting man's beliefs, opinions and ideologies has been discussed ever since there has been an organized body of social theory. Hundreds of social theorists have dealt with such relationships. "There is scarcely any physical or psychical trait in man, any characteristic in the social organization of a group, any social process or historical event, which has not been accounted for through geographical factors by this or that partisan of this school."[1] That the thought life of man in both content and quantity has been considerably affected by either direct or indirect geographic influences is obvious. However, this type of causal relaionship has been carried to absurd extremes by many a geographic determinist.[2]

The influence of the natural environment has often been an important factor in the formation of beliefs and in the opinion process in changing those beliefs in the simpler primitive cultures and folk cultures. Hence,

[1] Sorokin, P. A., *Contemporary Sociological Theories*, p. 100, 1928.
[2] For a criticism of the most extreme examples, see *idem.*, Chaps. 3 and 7.

the relationship between physical environment and the content of myths, the conceptions of gods and their nature, the afterlife, the stories and folk tales, the language symbols, and other items. Many figures of speech are taken from items common in the region. In the teachings of Christ the frequent references to vines, trees, sheep, the good shepherd, and the like, illustrate this point. The proverbs of folk peoples also reflect their surroundings.[1] These elements have been colored by development in a given geographic area but have not been determined thereby, as is evidenced by the presence of similar elements elsewhere in the world and also by the existence of similar geographic areas in which no such culture elements have developed. The cultural anthropologists have been extremely critical of the excesses of geographic determinism; they have maintained that geographic factors are a limiting, but not a determining, factor. For example, climatic conditions may serve as a limiting factor in decreasing the quantity of mentation and the alertness of a people. The debilitating effect of the tropics on the mental life of the white man, the paucity of imaginative legendary elements in Eskimo cultures are extreme examples of such influences. However, although in the simpler cultures geographic influences place some limits upon the quantity and quality of man's thought, the possible range of the products of thought outside of these limits is almost infinite. And as one proceeds from the simpler to the more complex and mobile societies, the influence of geographic factors dwindles and other elements bulk larger.

Not only climate and topography, but also the distribution of various items in space, are considered as geographic phenomena. During the past two decades the social sciences have increasingly considered spatial and territorial distribution of their phenomena. The concept "human ecology" refers to the way in which human beings and their institutions assume characteristic distribution in space. This is a significant frame of reference only in those cases where the spatial distribution assumes a meaningful pattern. "The term pattern is here used to mean any property of a whole which is characteristic only of the whole and not of parts into which the whole may be divided. Pattern properties seem to depend upon the totality of parts rather than upon their simple addition."[2] Are there significant spatial distributions of opinion groups within communities, regions and areas? H. D. Lasswell states, "Attention groups, sentiment groups, crowds and publics have their geographical aspects. We may properly speak of attention areas, sentiment areas, crowd areas and public areas, and we may profitably explore their interrelationships."[3] In an extensive study of race attitudes, E. S. Bogardus

[1] Albig, W., "Proverbs and Social Control," *Sociol. Soc. Res.*, 15: 527–535.

[2] George, W. H., *The Scientist in Action*, p. 128. Williams and Norgate, 1936.

[3] Lasswell, H. D., "The Measurement of Public Opinion," *Am. Pol. Sci. Rev.*, 25: 2: 316.

notes the distribution of opinions within the community and concludes that "racial opinion occurs in high-pressure areas with low-pressure regions between. The first express either antipathy or friendliness. The antipathetic areas possess a higher emotional pressure than the friendliness-pressure areas. In between are the low-pressure or neutral districts in which high pressures are likely to be manifested at any time."[1] In this case a meaningful pattern may exist. The presence of such a pattern would have to be tested. As with other phenomena, significant relationship must be proven. P. Sorokin has noted:

One of the main ways of bringing order out of chaos of the whole universe as well as of the cultural world is furnished by the causal-functional formulae of integration. They give us the patterns of uniformity that are to be found in the relationships of a vast number of individual components of this infinite chaos. . . . When the formula shows that the variables A and B, depression and the birth rate, modes of production and ideological forms, psycho-social isolation and suicide, urbanization and crime, are more or less uniformly associated with one another in the sense that B normally follows A or changes with A, this uniformity builds the variables together, introduces a readily understood causal order into disorder.[2]

In mapping opinions on race we must therefore have more than one map. Changing opinion must be shown to be associated with location, if spatial position is to be proved a significant factor.

The decision as to whether or not opinion and position are possibly related to one another is made by the researcher. Here, as elsewhere in research, he does not test all possible relationships. He first decides as to whether there is a logical coalescence between these items. Sometimes spatial position is obviously the basic factor in determining opinions. This is the case when the immediate group is practically inescapable and is the sole source of information, as is usually true of the primitive community. In the folk society, also, the local community provides most of the data from which opinion decisions are made. The limited gossip and discussion areas of the individual are for the most part the limits of his world. As the great societies have emerged, increasingly equipped with new and more effective agencies of mass communication, the attention areas of the individual have widened. The impress of the local geographical community and of the neighborhood are of lesser importance for most opinions. An investigator may find birth-control clinics, supported by local opinion, widely distributed in Wisconsin. However, he may know that this is due to agitational activities directed from

[1] Bogardus, E. S., *Immigration and Race Attitudes*, p. 237, 1928; *The New Social Research*, Chap. 12, 1926.

[2] Sorokin, P., "Forms and Problems of Culture Integration," *Rural Sociology*, 1: 346. Permission to quote granted.

New York and would therefore not attempt to show a regional diffusion. Membership in interest groups, contact with media of communication

FIG. 3.—Map drawn from data on the distribution and size of broadcasting stations as listed in the *International Radio Index* (1936).

and other factors may be much more important than place of residence. However, certain opinions are clearly a local product.

In the larger areas an uneven spatial distribution of ideas and opinions may be seen. "There is no doubt that ideas experienced by individuals and groups differ quantitatively as well as qualitatively. These ideas

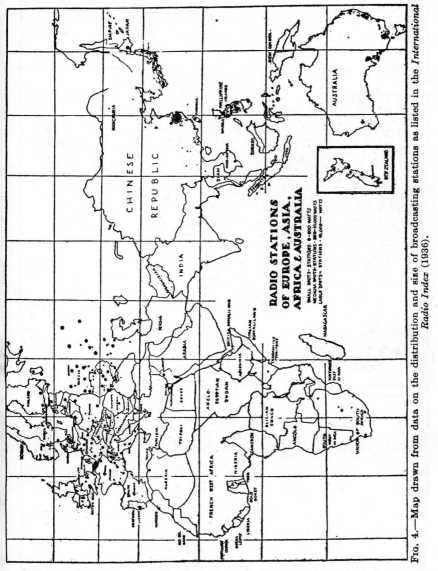

Fig. 4.—Map drawn from data on the distribution and size of broadcasting stations as listed in the *International Radio Index* (1936).

depend on contact."[1]   Satisfactory criteria for mapping such psychological areas have not been evolved.   Whether they should be mapped or not will depend upon the investigator's conception of how they have

[1] Taft, D. R., *Human Migration*, p. 557, 1936.

been diffused.   Certainly the sources of stimulation may be significantly distributed.   Printing, the telegraph, telephone, motion pictures and radio are unevenly distributed within areas and over the entire world. They have shortened physical and psychological distances, not only integrating peoples through increased understanding, but also making conflict tensions more acute.   In this sense it is today a commonplace to refer to the world as shrinking.   To portray graphically the distribu-

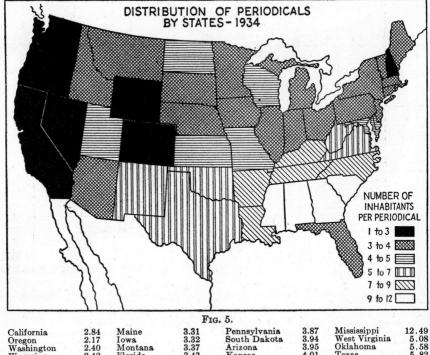

DISTRIBUTION OF PERIODICALS
BY STATES – 1934

NUMBER OF
INHABITANTS
PER PERIODICAL

1 to 3
3 to 4
4 to 5
5 to 7
7 to 9
9 to 12

FIG. 5.

California	2.84	Maine	3.31	Pennsylvania	3.87	Mississippi	12.49
Oregon	2.17	Iowa	3.32	South Dakota	3.94	West Virginia	5.08
Washington	2.40	Montana	3.37	Arizona	3.95	Oklahoma	5.58
Wyoming	2.42	Florida	3.43	Kansas	4.01	Texas	5.82
Nevada	2.79	Nebraska	3.45	Utah	4.03	New Mexico	6.18
Colorado	2.92	New York	3.51	Wisconsin	4.03	Virginia	6.52
New Hampshire	2.96	New Jersey	3.54	Delaware	4.16	Kentucky	7.68
Massachusetts	3.02	Minnesota	3.60	Missouri	4.20	Tennessee	7.89
Connecticut	3.07	Illinois	3.61	Maryland	4.65	Louisiana	7.94
Michigan	3.07	Idaho	3.65	North Dakota	4.80	North Carolina	8.77
Ohio	3.09	Indiana	3.70	Alabama	10.72	Arkansas	9.07
Vermont	3.14	Rhode Island	3.70	South Carolina	10.51	Georgia	10.28

tion of these various stimuli would require a separate monograph.   On this point we may insert only a single exhibit, the distribution of radio stations throughout the world.   In Figs. 3 and 4, the concentration of radio stations at certain points, as well as the vast blank spaces, may be noted.   The size of the dots indicates the class of power of the stations.

Data on means of communication have usually been collected in terms of political rather than natural areas.   For the United States, most such materials are summarized by states.   This is often unsatisfactory. However, some types of data appear in significant distribution by states. Sources of information from periodicals, class periodicals and the radio are indicated by the distribution of these media as portrayed in Figs. 5, 6 and 7.

Of course, the average number of individuals using each copy of a periodical or listening to each radio should also be known. Perhaps when these are less well distributed, as in the southern states, the average

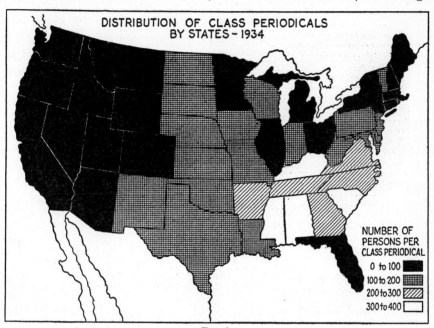

FIG. 6.

California	39.92	Maine	86.46	Pennsylvania	102.85	Mississippi	411.63
Oregon	48.96	Iowa	117.53	South Dakota	125.37	South Carolina	397.04
Washington	54.04	Montana	74.06	Arizona	74.30	Texas	142.66
Wyoming	58.16	Florida	75.93	Kansas	129.36	New Mexico	142.88
Nevada	56.41	Nebraska	111.37	Utah	83.17	Virginia	220.91
Colorado	81.48	New York	80.81	Wisconsin	116.40	Kentucky	317.72
New Hampshire	91.33	New Jersey	103.44	Delaware	132.34	Tennessee	244.31
Massachusetts	86.89	Minnesota	98.28	Missouri	124.91	Louisiana	192.41
Connecticut	80.46	Illinois	88.34	Maryland	128.16	North Carolina	244.00
Michigan	74.09	Idaho	81.85	North Dakota	148.12	Arkansas	258.89
Ohio	84.71	Indiana	106.93	West Virginia	130.87	Georgia	280.08
Vermont	105.04	Rhode Island	115.29	Oklahoma	136.63	Alabama	322.28

number of users per item is larger. The per capita distribution of forty-seven leading magazines, of newspaper circulation, of families owning radio sets and of library circulations is presented in Table IV. The rankings of the states indicate a high correlation between items in the groups of states at the top and bottom of the list. There is a greater diversity and scattering among those in the middle of that list. Contact with the extracommunity world is least in the group of southeastern and south-central states. Of course this is well known. These data support the generalization.

TABLE IV.—DISTRIBUTION, BY STATES, OF MAGAZINES, NEWSPAPERS, RADIO SETS AND LIBRARY CIRCULATIONS

State	Population (1930), thousands	47 leading magazines per 1000 population[1]	Rank	Newspaper circulation per 1000 population[2]	Rank	Percentage of families owning radio sets[3]	Rank	Circulation of library books per capita[4]	Rank
Alabama	2,646	132	47	227	39	9.5	46	0.88	45
Arizona	435	377	14	369	26	18.1	39	2.41	31
Arkansas	1,854	161	43	170	42	9.2	47	0.39	48
California	5,677	497	4	692	8	51.9	8	9.14	1
Colorado	1,035	406	11	672	9	37.8	28	3.84	23
Connecticut	1,606	414	10	435	20	54.9	6	6.68	7
Delaware	238	346	22	303	31	45.8	16	4.33	18a
District of Columbia	486	626	1	1582	1	53.9	7	5.39	11a
Florida	1,468	366	19	423	21	15.5	40	1.64	36
Georgia	2,908	149	46	347	29	9.9	45	0.94	44
Idaho	445	400	12	291	34	30.3	33	2.73	28
Illinois	7,630	345	23b	746	6	55.6	5	4.12	21
Indiana	3,238	343	26	469	19	41.6	23	6.43	8
Iowa	2,470	370	17	474	18	48.6	11	4.60	16
Kansas	1,880	327	27	360	27	38.8	27	2.55	30
Kentucky	2,614	174	42	289	35	18.3	37	1.04	41
Louisiana	2,101	150	44b	359	28	11.2	43a	0.98	43
Maine	797	396	13	299	33	39.2	26	4.76	15
Maryland	1,631	255	35	633	10	42.9	21	2.10	34
Massachusetts	4,249	373	16	910	3	57.6	3	7.77	2
Michigan	4,842	369	18	575	11b	50.6	10	4.37	17
Minnesota	2,563	357	20	530	14	47.3	15	4.04	22
Mississippi	2,009	114	49	87	49	5.4	49	0.36	49
Missouri	3,629	284	33	759	5	37.4	29	2.76	27
Montana	537	451	7	333	30	32.0	31	3.13	26
Nebraska	1,377	347	21	486	15a	47.8	13	3.31	25
Nevada	91	492	5	300	32	30.6	32	3.61	24
New Hampshire	465	418	9	141	48	44.4	18	7.21	3
New Jersey	4,041	315	31	266	36	63.3	1	5.39	11b
New Mexico	423	227	39	144	47	11.5	42	1.05	40
New York	12,588	345	23a	1013	2	57.8	2	4.33	18b
North Carolina	3,170	150	44a	194	41	11.2	43b	1.03	42
North Dakota	680	279	34	168	43a	40.8	25	1.51	37
Ohio	6,646	374	15	575	11a	47.7	14	4.99	13
Oklahoma	2,396	247	36	422	22	21.6	35	2.29	32
Oregon	953	520	2	776	4	43.4	20	6.82	6
Pennsylvania	9,631	321	28	556	13	48.1	12	2.27	33
Rhode Island	687	317	30	478	17	57.0	4	4.94	14
South Carolina	1,738	120	48	160	45	7.6	48	0.63	47
South Dakota	692	320	29	205	40	44.2	19	2.68	29
Tennessee	2,616	184	41	406	23	14.3	41	1.70	35
Texas	5,824	235	38	385	25	18.6	36	1.45	38
Utah	507	344	25	486	15b	41.1	24	4.23	20
Vermont	359	429	8	168	43b	44.6	17	6.25	9
Virginia	2,421	213	40	253	37	18.2	38	1.15	39
Washington	1,563	502	3	717	7	42.3	22	6.83	5
West Virginia	1,729	238	37	243	38	23.3	34	0.65	46
Wisconsin	2,939	310	32	402	24	51.1	9	5.89	10
Wyoming	225	458	6	151	46	34.0	30	6.97	4

[1] Adapted from Allen, E. W., "Circulation Density," *Jour. Quar.*, 12: 2: 122.

[2] Compiled from circulation figures in *Editor and Publisher*, 63: 37 (1931), International Year Book, Sec. 2, p. 125.

[3] Adapted from Willey, M. M., and Rice, S. A., *Communication Agencies and Social Life*, Table 53, pp. 188–189.

[4] Compiled from *Bull. Am. Lib. Asso.*, May, 1935, 29: 5: 252–253.

Another way in which significant spatial distribution of opinion is indicated is in the records of voting.   Patterns may be noted by mapping the results of various elections.   Voting records opinion at a given moment.   Although often unsatisfactory for the purpose of predicting behavior inasmuch as it forces the variety of attitudes into two opposing camps, voting does show the practical popular decision.   There are

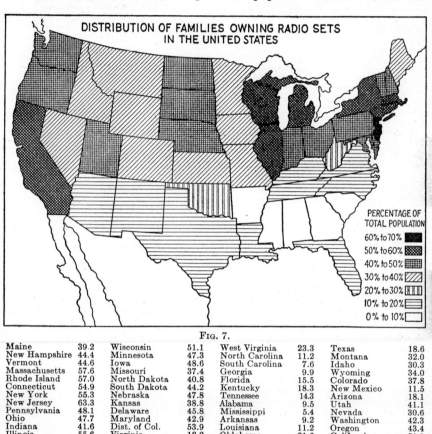

DISTRIBUTION OF FAMILIES OWNING RADIO SETS
IN THE UNITED STATES

PERCENTAGE OF
TOTAL POPULATION

60% to 70%
50% to 60%
40% to 50%
30% to 40%
20% to 30%
10% to 20%
0% to 10%

FIG. 7.

Maine	39.2	Wisconsin	51.1	West Virginia	23.3	Texas	18.6
New Hampshire	44.4	Minnesota	47.3	North Carolina	11.2	Montana	32.0
Vermont	44.6	Iowa	48.6	South Carolina	7.6	Idaho	30.3
Massachusetts	57.6	Missouri	37.4	Georgia	9.9	Wyoming	34.0
Rhode Island	57.0	North Dakota	40.8	Florida	15.5	Colorado	37.8
Connecticut	54.9	South Dakota	44.2	Kentucky	18.3	New Mexico	11.5
New York	55.3	Nebraska	47.8	Tennessee	14.3	Arizona	18.1
New Jersey	63.3	Kansas	38.8	Alabama	9.5	Utah	41.1
Pennsylvania	48.1	Delaware	45.8	Mississippi	5.4	Nevada	30.6
Ohio	47.7	Maryland	42.9	Arkansas	9.2	Washington	42.3
Indiana	41.6	Dist. of Col.	53.9	Louisiana	11.2	Oregon	43.4
Illinois	55.6	Virginia	18.2	Oklahoma	21.6	California	51.9

hundreds of studies of voting records by states and other political units, but the most elaborate graphic portrayal of voting by states in American history is presented in the *Atlas of the Historical Geography*.[1]   This monumental work is the product of two decades of effort by a research staff. Selected and adapted maps from this source dealing with two major issues are given in Fig. 8.   The political results of social reform conducted over many years are portrayed.

[1] Paullin, C. O., *Atlas of the Historical Geography of the United States*, 1932.

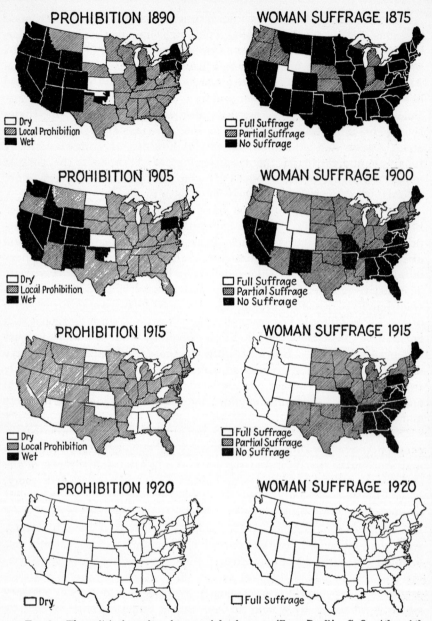

Fig. 8.—The political results of two social reforms. (*From Paullin, C. O., Atlas of the Historical Geography of the United States. Reproduced by permission of Carnegie Institution of Washington and the American Geographical Society of New York.*)

On some issues, fewer now than during the nineteenth century, state divisions are useful in mapping opinion. Organization of attitudes, loyalties and opinions about state symbols, such as flags, mottoes, seals, songs, birds, flowers, popular names, and the like, has been common in American history. Within state borders, individuals were united in like response to these common stimuli. Economic interests are sometimes coincident with state borders, although this is rarely so. Under the guidance of economists and various specialists preoccupied with areas, regions and other nonpolitical subdivisions, the scholar is likely today to underestimate the vitality of state concepts in the popular mind, especially in the South. In successive voting periods, state records, when mapped, frequently show pattern.

Numerous social phenomena have been studied in terms of areas, sections and regions. The distribution of opinions may sometimes profitably be considered in such terms. The contrast of urban-rural attitudes and opinions is presented in many recent books.[1] The sources of information of the two groups have been surveyed exhaustively. The usually greater indirect experience of the urban dweller has been traditionally stressed in comparison with rural folk experience. Certain of the mores differ. For example, "adultery in a rural setting is still generally a tragic theme, while in metropolitan life it is a stock subject for social comedy."[2] However, both the mores and opinions are today diffused more similarly through rural and urban areas than was previously true. Exceptions to this will be found chiefly in divergent political and economic attitudes and opinions, due to more conscious class interests and organization.

Sectional divisions were of paramount importance in nineteenth-century America. Differences of life ways and opinion between the South and the North, the West and the East, the frontier and the rest of the country, as portrayed in Professor Turner's fruitful historical dichotomy, were authentic divisions.[3] But the region is now the more valid unit of analysis. What is a region? "Region" has different meanings in the various social sciences. The political scientist, although latterly somewhat influenced by the concept of economic regions, usually has in mind the various political areas. "The geographer is likely to conceive of regions as entities that are set off from one another by physiographic barriers, while the sociologist views as a region that territory which is inhabited by a more or less unified human group—unified by

---

[1] See, notably, Williams, J. M., *Our Rural Heritage*, 1925; Sorokin, P., and Zimmerman, C. C., *Systematic Source Book in Rural Sociology*, vol. III, pp. 251 *ff.*, 1930.

[2] Fergusson, H., *Modern Man*, p. 224, 1936.

[3] Odum, H., *Southern Regions*, pp. 245–261, 1936. Prof. Odum has clearly compared the sectional and regional approach.

forces of commerce and communication—such as the people of a great city and its environs or 'trade territory.'"[1] Regional classifications have been developed in great numbers. Prof. Odum notes that over 100 administrative regions have been mapped out for functional use in banking, commerce, military strategy, power and relief. Retail shopping zones and trading centers have been delimited. General cultural regions have been assumed by the novelist and sociologist. Are any of these divisions useful for the student of public opinion? Certainly, they are of but limited usefulness at the moment. Most mores, attitudes and opinions have not been recorded in a definite form that permits of mapping. But there are certain related phenomena that may be treated regionally. For example, one may map the distribution of radio audiences of particular stations. Or the potential coverage of stations may be graphically shown. Newspaper circulations may be used to map areas of diffusion and influence. One such map, taken from Prof. McKenzie's study *The Metropolitan Community*, is presented in Fig. 9. Harold Geisert mapped the newspaper circulation of Illinois towns and indicated the way in which the means of transportation determined the shape of the area.[2] Communication, and with it the opinion process, is fundamental to the existence of every form of society. The limits of newspaper circulation of a metropolitan area may therefore be assumed to outline a natural area.

The boundaries of an area or a region are determined by the phenomena under consideration. If the data can be shown to be distributed in a number of significant geographic patterns, then we have regions. We have seen that such regions exist with regard to those stimuli which influence opinion, the newspapers, radio and other means of communication. What evidence is there of the existence of opinion regions? Such regional mapping is limited by the relatively few items of opinion that have been formally recorded by areas. Obviously the principal sources of data, therefore, must be voting records. Some years ago, S. A. Rice attempted to delimit some such regions.[3] Unfortunately the political scientists have been very slow in checking his conclusions or furthering this work. They have lagged in the application of experimental and quantitative techniques even in cases such as this where these methods were indicated. Rice instituted a remarkable series of studies. Certain changes in economic situation and in attitudes were correlated. Both the diffusion and social density of political attitudes, as indicated by

[1] House, F. N., *Development of Sociology*, p. 139, 1936.

[2] Geisert, H., *Newspaper Circulation in Illinois*, unpublished Master's thesis, University of Illinois, 1929. See, also, Park, R. E., "Urbanization as Measured by Newspaper Circulation," *Am. Jour. Sociol.*, 35: 60–79.

[3] Rice, S. A., *Quantitative Methods in Politics*, especially Chaps. 10 and 11, 1928.

votes for candidates, were traced in studies of voting in Wisconsin, Michigan and Philadelphia. The patterning of votes within states was tested. In Minnesota, "concentrations of the radical and conservative vote along geographical lines, with their correlated areas of crop speciali-

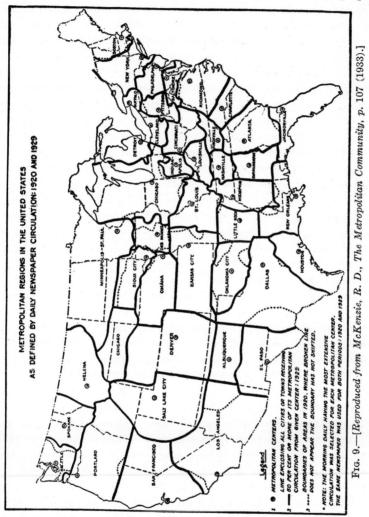

FIG. 9.—[*Reproduced from McKenzie, R. D., The Metropolitan Community, p. 107 (1933).*]

zation were noted."[1] In North Dakota the conservative eastern counties differed markedly from the radical western counties. Rural prosperity was greatest in the eastern part of the state. Regional groupings within the state associated with crop-producing areas appeared evident. In the Brookhart (Radical) and Cummins (Conservative) campaign in

[1] *Idem.*, p. 126.

Iowa in 1920, cleavages of a regional nature rather than primarily on occupational or class lines appeared. In those counties in which the average farm values were highest, the largest vote for Cummins occurred. Similar evidence was collected from regions in Nebraska. If this is a true regional rather than political unit phenomenon, the similarities of vote should cross state lines. And Rice finds evidence to support this thesis. The Missouri River valley contains counties in Iowa, Nebraska and South Dakota. The Red River valley is in Minnesota and North Dakota. In each case there is a homogeneous geographical and economic area. Testing the hypothesis that the votes should show this economic uniformity, Rice concludes, "The hypothesis of culture areas of political attitudes has strong *a priori* support, and is consistent with the data assembled, but has not yet been established empirically."[1] He found, however, that state boundaries interposed real barriers to similarity of the vote. These boundaries became less influential when shopping areas crossed state lines. In another study he finds changes in political opinion unevenly distributed over the state of Washington. In this case the underlying factors were economic conditions based, not upon geographic conditions (upon land value), but upon the distribution of the labor vote throughout the state. In this case we have an occupational rather than a regional pattern.

Another study attempting to relate conservative and radical voting to the more obvious geographic and economic conditions was made by G. A. Lundberg.[2] Ten radical and ten conservative voting counties in North Dakota and Minnesota were compared, as to composition of population, improved acres per farm, average value of property per farm, value of crops, assessed valuation, mortgages and other economic phenomena. Radicalism in voting was found to be associated with adverse geographic conditions (western Dakota), undeveloped communities and economic insecurity. The author concludes that the attitudes of the community and the physical and social character of the community tend to be mutually selective and formative. These studies support the thesis that certain voting habits may be identified with geographic factors and economic regions. It may well be so. However, the distribution of most opinions will not be found to follow the patterns of economic regions of the United States, even when there is a spatial distribution. Economic class consciousness has not achieved so definite a distribution. On most public issues, the symbols and other stimuli in the formation of opinion are largely common to various economic classes. Business class symbols are used by the industrial worker, and the symbols of rural aims and objectives may be mouthed by the

[1] *Idem.*, p. 155.
[2] Lundberg, G. A., "The Demographic and Economic Basis of Political Radicalism and Conservatism," *Am. Jour. Sociol.*, 32: 719–732.

farmer with a thousand fertile acres and the scrabbling "hillbilly." Considering the vast *terra incognita* of opinion phenomena and the lack of research funds, it would be very unwise at the moment for the sociologist to attempt to test the thesis of identical economic and opinion areas.

To locate opinions spatially may be helpful in getting at the fundamental patterns, even if the individual's opinion is not primarily due to his position. We may anticipate many studies of this kind. Despite the ballyhoo and overextravagant claims, certain of the commercial polls (Gallup, Crossley, etc.) have been doing fruitful experimentation in sampling techniques. Adequate but not too extensive or expensive sampling, as well as perfected methods of recording the individuals' opinions, should make possible successive polls on various issues. These may be recorded in terms of areas, not because location was primarily responsible for the creation of their opinions, but because the density of opinion at a given place may be an important factor in the future trends of opinion in that area. To locate the members of an interest group according to residence does not mean that one necessarily assumes that their place of residence had anything to do with their membership in that group. If, however, it is a proselyting, agitational group, the location of its members at any given time is of obvious significance to its future growth.

In dealing with the record of past popular opinions, the mapping of opinion is of even more importance than for contemporary mass opinions. Owing to the limited means of communication, there was then a greater tendency for opinion to diffuse in concentric circles.[1] As has often been noted, the popular mass communication of the present century is destroying the neat patterns of diffusion of ideas and opinions that largely prevailed when opinion was based on face-to-face discussion.

The study of the spatial distribution of opinion in contemporary large publics is by no means futile. There often is a pattern. But probably more often this is not the significant frame of reference. In the United States there is greater diversity of beliefs and opinions than of the elements of material culture. There is an increasingly pervasive uniformity in most material things. Opinions and beliefs have been more resistant to regimentation. The local and regional cultural elements are inculcated in the family and primary group. But gradually in many fields locality and regional groups are superseded by interest groups in providing stimuli for individual opinions. Apparently this is not occurring so rapidly as many social theorists anticipated. Man does not move rapidly into the great society.

[1] In his recent *Environment and Nature*, 1936, Griffith Taylor has published several hundred maps, many of which would illustrate this point. For example, there are those dealing with the spread of Christianity, language diffusion, the Renaissance, the spread of universities and architecture.

CHAPTER X

ATTITUDE AND OPINION

It is well for changes to come slowly but it would seem that sociologists have been over-slow to grasp the liberating significance of this concept of social attitudes which has so much of value for their work. The concept of the mores with the emphasis on their mutability and their power has influenced other fields. But the stubborn individual yet remained, and the fluid character of social life congealed against the absolutes of his inborn equipment. Yet social attitudes, once they are grasped in their full significance, become the counterpart, in individual equipment, of the richly varied customs of the peoples of the world—differing as customs differ from land to land, and changing as the mores change, from age to age. For the social attitudes of individuals are but the specific instances in individuals of the collective phenomena which the sociologists have labored for a century to bring to the consciousness of their colleagues in social science.[1]

Preoccupation with the innate factors motivating behavior has existed among the experimental psychologists, since the early studies of Lange, Wundt, Külpe and others on the factors of preparation for action; among the theoretical psychologists, philosophers and theologians in the many varieties of instinct theory; and among the social psychologists and sociologists, since about 1920, in the study of attitudes. Of course, this organic basis of behavior is a fundamental problem of all those branches of learning concerned with the behavior of living forms, but our interest lies in those disciplines concerned with the psychological and social life of man.

In 1888, Lange propounded the theory that the process of perception was largely in consequence of muscular "set." Then, following Wundt and Külpe, the study of the preparation of the subject for action was experimentally described in the laboratory results of the Wurzburg school which appeared in the writings of N. Ach, A. Messer, K. Bühler and others.[2] This experimental work was often very simple, consisting of introspective accounts of the process of judgment in differentiating weights, of tests with stimulus words and the subjects' responses, and the like. States in the preparatory process were described. Although the

[1] Faris, E., in *Social Attitudes* (Young, K., ed.), p. 5, 1931. Quoted by permission of Henry Holt & Company.

[2] See Fearing, F., "Experimental Study of Attitude," in *Methods in Social Science* (Rice, S., ed.), pp. 715–728, 1931; Allport, G. W., "Attitudes," in *Handbook of Social Psychology* (Murchison, C., ed.), pp. 798–844, 1935.

German experimentalists of that period used a variety of words to express the set of the organism, the concept of "attitude" and later the term came to be widely accepted by psychologists. These "tendencies to act" were not, however, always conceived of as irreducible elements.

INSTINCT

Among the theoreticians, also, the idea of an organic set for behavior likewise developed. It appeared in the most definite form in the concept of instincts. Although some conception of the innate drives called "instincts" appeared in the works of the Greek philosophers, in the theological literature of the Middle Ages and in the beliefs concerning innate sentiments, especially moral sentiments, during the seventeenth and eighteenth centuries, it was not until the middle of the nineteenth century that classifications of instincts were developed. The method was theoretical and speculative. Although the term was very loosely used, the instincts were usually thought of as specific and definite inherited or unlearned responses, universal in nature. Lists of such instincts, varying from a half-dozen innate drives to more than a hundred, were presented by scores of writers with the developing interest in social phenomena from the 1890's onward.[1] As the lists of instincts lengthened, it appeared that their authors' method was the observation of quite widespread similarities of behavior which were then assumed to be based upon an instinct. Social philosophers, seeking a prime mover of human social behavior, likewise posited some innate, original tendency. In the ferment of social theory of the closing nineteenth century, stirred by biologic interpretations and Darwinian evolution, a renewed emphasis upon innate factors appeared. Pervasive conflict was ascribed to the instinct of pugnacity by Gumplowicz, Ratzenhofer, James and many others, and sympathy and associative tendencies, long asserted by the Christian church fathers as based on human innate tendencies, were formally linked with instinct by Kropotkin, Hans Blührer and others. But these general terms could not account for the infinitely rich variation of the phenomena in patterns of social behavior. Nor could the relationships between the behavior and the assumed instinct be proved.

The lists of instincts that were prepared by the psychologists were applied to many fields: advertising, salesmanship, education, personality, group control and many others. Carleton Parker even ascribed the more radical labor movements of the Northwest to thwarted sex instincts. In the meantime, the developing study of culture forms during the first twenty years of this century made less and less necessary the assumption of pervasive similar innate drives to account for similarities of behavior. Revolt against such interpretations grew, and by 1920 the battle was

[1] See Bernard, L. L., "Instinct," *Ency. Soc. Sci.*, 8: 81–83.

joined.   As an academic battle it was a short, sharp engagement.   Lack of ability to agree on a list of instincts to defend; a scurrying and undignified word jugglery in the attempt to get a more definitive term for "innate drives"; the fact that "instinct" was used in such varied ways that it had come to be considered the last refuge of the psychologically destitute rapidly weakened the defense, and it was soon generally agreed that most of the so-called "instincts" were not inherited mechanisms, but acquired ways of behavior, similar in many individuals because of cultural diffusion.   The concept and the term are still used by popular authors, novelists, poets and literary folk but are usually eschewed by the psychologist.

The sociologist is primarily occupied with the analysis of forms and patterns in the processes of interaction of human beings and with the residual results of that interaction, culture.   Intermittently he becomes aware of the inadequacy, inaccuracy and unreality of his analysis unless he attempts to consider the motivating power behind human behavior. Indeed, this is the dilemma of all the social studies dealing with culture forms.   To what extent are these forms the result of, or related to, psychological factors of desires, wishes, interests, instincts, sentiments, emotion or attitudes in the individual?   To what extent are culture forms and human social behavior the product of the operation of objective realities?[1]   This is a very old problem.   Every age answers it differently. However, psychological factors do not determine culture forms, nor may psychological entities be adduced from culture forms or types of human behavior in the social process.   The great differences of culture and of human behavior indicate that the same desires may be accompanied by a wide variety of forms of overt activity, whereas similar activity may be motivated in part by widely divergent desires.   Yet psychological factors are involved, and the sociologist must attempt to deal with them in some terms.   His primary field is the analysis of forms, patterns and processes of human interaction.   But social experience, as well as the philosopher, constantly warns of the sterility of analysis of forms of action and behavior, of the overt and visible, divorced from their source in the set of the organisms that gives rise to them.   The unity of the life processes is thus violated.   Psychological factors are involved.   In daily life some assumptions about the set of the functioning organisms of those with whom we come in contact, about intent and consciousness, are made in a wide variety of human-contact situations.   These range from the simplest of involuntary physical gestures to complex symbolic systems of behavior; from involuntary sounds and cries to the most illusive, allusive circumlocutions of academic discourse or the formal language of international politics; from the simplest and least voluntary to the most conscious and

---

[1] Sorokin, P., *Contemporary Sociological Theories*, pp. 636–659, 1928, gives an analytical and illustrated discussion of this fundamental problem.

complex behavior. By 1920, sociologists, intermittently attempting to relate tendencies to act to the action and behavior, found the instinct psychology, with its emphasis on the inheritance of specific innate behavior patterns, no longer tenable. They were too much aware of the variety of human behavior in various cultures. Some concept of tendency to act was required, differing from instinct in that the tendency was, at least in part, acquired. The term "attitude" appeared, and it has become perhaps the most widely used and indispensable concept in social psychology and but little less widely used in sociology.

ATTITUDE

"Attitude" originally meant a position of the body suited to a certain action, a physical preparation by position for action. Its meaning was much broadened to cover all preparation and tendency to act, either overt or inner and psychic. The term has been quite variously defined in the sociological literature of the past twenty years, but there is an underlying unanimity on general "set of the organism" and "tendency to act."

It is the set of the organism toward the object or situation to which an adjustment is called for. When the adjustment is made the attitude disappears, except in so far as it is retained in memory or in the habitual set of the organism.[1]

By attitude we understand a process of individual consciousness which determines real or possible activity of the individual counterpart of the social value; activity, in whatever form, is the bond between them.[2]

An attitude is a tendency to act. The term designates a certain proclivity, or bent, a bias or predisposition, an aptitude or inclination to a certain type of activity.[3]

An attitude is a pronounced tendency to a certain way of reacting.[4]

An attitude, roughly, is a residuum of experience, by which further activity is conditioned and controlled. An inner mental organization takes place which predisposes the person to a certain type of activity toward objects, persons and situations.[5]

An attitude is a mental and neural state of readiness, organized through experience, exerting a directive or dynamic influence upon the individual's response to all objects and situations with which it is related.[6]

W. I. Thomas first emphasized the concept of attitude as basic in social psychology.[7] His students have recently noted their obligation

[1] Bernard, L. L., *Introduction to Social Psychology*, p. 246, 1926.

[2] Thomas, W. I., and Znaniecki, F., *The Polish Peasant in Europe and America*, vol. I, p. 27, 1918.

[3] Faris, E., "Attitudes and Behavior," *Am. Jour. Sociol.*, 34: 2: 277 (1928).

[4] Williams, J. M., *Our Rural Heritage*, p. 9, 1925.

[5] Krueger, E. T., and Reckless, W. C., *Social Psychology*, p. 238, 1935.

[6] Allport, *op. cit.*, p. 810.

[7] The first section of *The Polish Peasant in Europe and America*, 1918, is devoted to an analysis of the concepts of value in society and attitude in the individual.

to him for this fruitful viewpoint.[1] Cooley, Faris, Williams, and Dewey were also prominently associated with the early development of the movement to interpret action ways in terms of the underlying attitudes.[2]

INDIVIDUAL AND GROUP ATTITUDES

"Attitude" as used in contemporary sociology and social psychology has a wide variety of meanings. These range from the temporary set of the organism, or *Aufgabe*, to relatively permanent and complex tendencies to act, such as one's attitude toward war. The term is used in reference to the preparation of the organism for overt physical behavior and to tendency to act in mental processes, such as the individual's response to the idea of adultery, patriotism or alma mater. Further, attitude is used for tendencies to act that are individually unique and also for those group attitudes, either cultural or collective, that the individual abstracts from culture or from group experiences. The cultural attitudes are those which are incorporated in individual attitude through the acceptance of the cultural values. The citizen's response to the national anthem, the Northwest Indian's pride in the ceremonial of the potlatch, the modesty of the naked Indian female of the Amazonian basin—outraged by a missing ear ornament—are attitudes that the individual has developed from cultural values. The individual's response to the mass of stereotypes and collective representations, the symbols, ceremonials and all formal patterns of his culture, is based upon attitudes that have been developed through earlier contact with these culture forms. Some of these attitudes have been developed through formal indoctrination in the organized institutions; others have resulted from formal inculcation of favorable and unfavorable responses due to usage. Attitudes of color preference or odor preference are largely due to culturally determined tastes. Different people respond variably in their choices and preferences and revulsions and disgusts. These are cultural attitudes. The "group-mind" controversy is resolved for the sociologist in the existence of many common attitudes in the members of a culture group based on their learned cultural heritage.

Collective attitudes are those which are developed in the individual by experience in groups, crowds and publics—the more spontaneous

[1] Young, K., ed., *Social Attitudes*, 1931.

[2] Cooley, C. H., *Social Organization*, Chaps. 4 and 5, 1918.

Faris, E., "The Concept of Social Attitudes," *Jour. App. Sociol.*, 9: 404–409 (1925); "Attitudes and Behavior," *Am. Jour. Sociol.*, 34: 2: 271–281 (1928).

Young, K., ed., *Social Attitudes*, pp. 3–16, 1931.

Williams, J. M., *Our Rural Heritage*, 1925.

Dewey, J., *Human Nature and Conduct*, 1922. Prof. Dewey does not use the term "attitude," but deals with the essential problem of the relation of culture forms to the "tendency to act" in the individual, substituting "habit" for "attitudes."

and, in a sense, elementary forms of association.[1] The attitudes engendered in the individual by participation in a crowd or a mob, the emotional anger, hatred, exultation, feeling of unity with one's fellows and the like, are collective in the sense that they would not exist without participation in crowd or mob activity. They are related to the cultural attitudes, inasmuch as the objects of that group activity are culturally determined and the individual has attitudes on these; but the additional elements could not exist without group participation. The Southerner who becomes involved in a lynching mob already has a wide variety of somewhat contradictory and inconsistent attitudes with regard to the Negro; but that frenzied response to the sight of the victim is the especial product of the mob situation. He does not experience that group of attitudes when he is alone or when he judicially interviews the prisoner. Collective attitudes are experienced in a tribal war dance; in those responses to the god which are experienced only when a thousand suppliants are simultaneously prostrate; in that irrepressible titter at the socially gauche person at a formal reception; in the *esprit de corps* of troops; in all situations where the mere presence or awareness of a group is responsible for attitudes in the individual that would not otherwise exist. The members of such groups need not always be in physical proximity, although the most emotional of collective attitudes are usually developed in face-to-face situations. However, collective attitudes are likewise experienced by the individual as a member of secondary group associations. As one of several million American stamp collectors, he develops an attitude with regard to the importance and social maturity of his avocation. It is not puerile, it is popular. As a member of the Wild Life Protective Association, an attitude of authoritative knowledge tempers his discourse on birds. As a member of a fraternal order, he clasps that German brother whom as a national he might have shot.

SPECIFIC AND GENERAL ATTITUDES

Are attitudes specific in the sense of tendencies to respond in a definite way to a particular situation, or may attitudes develop into general dispositions to respond to a whole class of phenomena? This is a highly controversial point in psychology.[2] It has recently been disputed once more owing to the conclusions of Hartshorne and May in their character education studies. They found that in children's

[1] Park, R. E., and Burgess, E. W., *Introduction to the Science of Sociology*, Chap. 13, 1921.

[2] Cantril, H., "General and Specific Attitudes," *Psychol. Mon.*, 1932, 42, No. 192. Hartshorne, H., and May, M., *Studies in the Nature of Character*, 3 vol., 1928. Allport, *op. cit.*

school experiences readiness to cheat varied with the type of situation and was not a general attitude. However, it has been argued that the children were too young to have developed generalizations from their experiences. Cantril, on the other hand, concluded in his study of general and specific attitudes that "general determining tendencies are more constant and enduring than specific content." That there are general attitudes would be the contention of almost all sociologists, although they have no experimental literature to present in evidence. However, they have long maintained the idea of general attitudes in discussions of race relations, of attitude toward nationalities[1] and of the specific attitudinal base of stereotypes of groups, classes, types, associations and institutions. Apparently, both kinds of attitudes do exist. There are quite evidently specific attitudes developed by the individual toward particular objects, people and ideas. Attitudes as tendencies to act are developed in relation to material objects, animate beings and psychological processes. As a small boy, the author was given an air rifle. With it he happily prowled the hillsides for several summers, pursuing sparrows with more or less skill. Twenty-five years later, in an introspective moment, he realized that to this day sparrows are targets to him. When a sparrow is sighted, he frequently notes its position, the intervening obstacles, the best angle for a shot, and has a vague sense of the plump of the bullet as it will enter through the breast feathers. He has an attitude toward sparrows.

There are also general attitudes toward classes of objects, people and ideas. Moreover, these general attitudes are sometimes the result of generalizing from a few experiences of a particular sort, and others are inculcated from the general culture. Clearly, two individuals differ very greatly in the proportions in which specific or general attitudes dominate their behavior. These differences are as yet ill-understood, and classifications of personality types on this basis have not been made. This is a basic problem for the student of public opinion, determining the viewpoints that he may take on the stereotyping processes, on specific propaganda material versus the inculcation of principles and on many other problems.

CONSCIOUS AND UNCONSCIOUS ATTITUDES

Of many of his attitudes the individual is aware. He is conscious of, and perhaps discusses, his attitude toward the "damyankee," the "dago," fascism or mother's cooking. Of other attitudes he is not conscious, or at least only intermittently conscious. Most of the values incorporated from the general culture into individual attitudes come to appear as indisputable mores and are applied as the only cultural

[1] Bogardus, E. S., *Immigration and Race Attitudes*, 1928.

reality. The responses of students in introductory cultural anthropology indicate a wide range of attitudes of which they are only slowly and sometimes painfully becoming aware. The concept of unconscious attitudes has been central to psychoanalytic theory. The Freudian "censor" is a general attitude on sex behavior, on religion, or what not, that will not permit the conscious consideration of certain materials and viewpoints. This necessitates the circuitous and labored emergence of the forbidden materials through symbolic forms of language, dream and imagery. The psychoanalysts have also stressed the emotional elements in most attitudes.

An individual's attitude pattern about any subject may consist of some conscious and many unconscious or subconscious elements. A professed liberal may be secretly relieved when the strike is broken, when the tabooed subject is repressed, when the too radical colleague is suppressed. That behavior is so frequently widely at variance with certain attitudes of the individual is not surprising, for on a given point he has many other attitudes in his attitude pattern. He may be inconsistent, especially superficially inconsistent. Enjoyment of innuendo, of the joke of double entendre, may be only superficially inconsistent for the deacon. Moreover, inasmuch as that section of attitudes which we have designated as group, cultural or common attitudes are but the incorporation of culture into individual attitudes, the inconsistency of the cultural elements to each other will be reflected in individual attitude. General consistency is never achieved. Because the attitude pattern is often so very complex, knowledge of a few attitudes of which the individual is conscious never provides, with absolute certainty, a basis of prediction of what that person will do in a crisis. The very fact of crisis may call forth attitudes of which he has not been conscious, or he may acquire new attitudes from the changed situation that has caused the crisis. Actually, behavior and known attitude are, of course, not so chaotic as that. In social interaction we do successfully predict behavior from assumed attitudes. In crisis experiences or in unusual situations to which adjustment must be made, such prediction is most unsuccessful because there emerge both attitudes that have been latent and new attitudes that are produced as a result of the new situation. Not only individuals but members of large publics become more unpredictable in a crisis.

CLASSIFICATION OF ATTITUDES

The infinite variety of human attitudes and attitude change is obvious. Classifications have at times been attempted. Bernard, although he recognizes that attitudes are as numerous as relationships between people, attempts a classification according to several general criteria, the most significant of which are: the collective relationships that standardize and stereotype attitudes through interconditioning (urban, rural, sectarian, racial, nationalistic, political, occupational, etc.); the objective or aim of the behaving person (humanitarian, exploiting, protective); the valuation placed upon the objective or the technique utilized (approving, discouraging, etc.); the object calling forth the attitudinal response (attitudes toward money, radicals, sex, etc.); the time reference of the attitude (traditional, progressive, temporary, permanent, etc.).[1] But any classification must be limited to those common attitudes which are assumed to be widely distributed. Nor has any classification yet propounded included any large proportion of all the common attitudes. For the organization of lists of attitude is dependent upon the frame of reference and the classifier's purpose in making it. The *individual* attitudes to which we have already referred are obviously so diverse, varied and unique as to make classification impossible. Moreover, it is at once apparent that when we attempt to classify any section of those common attitudes which many people may be assumed to share, we are dealing, not with ultimate units, but with combinations in varying proportions of other attitudes. This confusion is evidenced in language forms, of which every novelist, but not every psychologist or sociologist, is aware. There do not exist adequate and mutually exclusive terms for such a classification. Consider a common attitude, such as the preparation for action of the type of holding fast, of resisting intrusion, of immobility, of unyieldingness, which we designate as "firmness." This term lacks scientific precision, but not more so than most terms for attitudes. It not only has different meanings in conjunction with various words, but there is a different favorable or unfavorable response to it in connection with different social situations. In general, in our culture, firmness is approved. Assumed attitudes of unyieldingness of which we do not approve are otherwise designated. It has been said, "I am firm, thou art obstinate, he is pigheaded." It is quite evident that, among other difficulties, there does not exist a terminology for an extensive classification of common attitudes. This difficulty is not insoluble, but it has not been solved. However, any classifier may, if he will, carefully define his terms and attempt to have them more widely used with his meanings.

The classification of all attitudes is clearly impossible. But lists of common attitudes are developed depending upon the author's purpose and viewpoints. Even these classifications are by no means satisfactory, because:

1. Attitudes are not units but complexes of other attitudes. As such they are general tendencies to modes of response, not to particular

---

[1] Bernard, L. L., "Social Attitude," *Ency. Soc. Sci.*, 2: 305.

responses. And, as MacIver has stated, "When we attribute an attitude to a person, such as love or fear or pity, we do not completely express the state of consciousness so described. . . . the integral attitude is too complex for such summary description. All that we mean is that the attitude factor so named is dominant or at least recognizable in the subject. Our pity, for example, may contain love and fear as well."[1] Attitudes are not independent entities.

2. The existing language forms are totally inadequate to distinguish even common attitudes.

3. Attitudes shade into one another, and arbitrary classifications may distort reality.

4. Even if idealized classifications are developed, the comparison of individuals *A* and *B*, who are said to have that common attitude, is only approximate, because the ingredients of the attitude in each may be in different proportions. However, fruitful results have been obtained by acting "as if" they were comparable.

ATTITUDE AND OPINION

When an overt expression on a controversial point appears, we have an opinion. Although usually expressed in language forms, it may be indicated by gestures, signs or symbols. "Thumbs down" decided a dramatically controversial point in the Roman amphitheatre; the nod of the judge, examining *in camera* during the political conflicts of the Middle Ages, might mean the prisoner's release or his extermination depending upon the system of signals. Any expression of opinion, therefore, involves attitudes. As a form of action it involves, first, a number of physical and muscular attitudes. Psychologists still use the term "attitude" to refer to motor preparedness. After behaviorism, there was a futile attempt to describe opinion in such terms. But "laryngeal behavior," has never proved helpful to those attempting to account for the opinions of the citizens of Kentucky on the World Court. Then there are the various predispositions that have found expression in the stated opinion. And these may be many and varied; predispositions toward the questioner if the situation is face to face; toward his voice, tones, facial expression, and the like; toward his attitudes on the subject under discussion; toward the attitudes on that subject of the persons who are thought to be associated with the questioner; the attitude pattern of the person interviewed with regard to the problem itself; perhaps scores of other predispositions. Is it any wonder that the early naïve tests, questionnaires, interviews and other modes of attempting to bring the "real attitude" into overt opinion behavior, based as they were on so simple a concept of the nature of attitudes and their interaction,

[1] MacIver, R. M., *Society*, p. 44, 1937.

proved so discouraging? To be sure, opinions always express attitudes, but which attitudes? The attempts to distinguish attitudes and to isolate the ones related to an expressed opinion have been a special interest of the social scientists for the past fifteen years.

One of the sociologist's fundamental dilemmas is the problem of the extent to which he, as a student of the forms and structures of social life and of processes of interaction, may profitably concern himself with the phenomena of attitudes. The cultural and collective attitudes, as we have seen, are abstracted from the general culture and from group experience and incorporated in the individual tendency to act. In addition, individual social attitudes are developed from direct experience with persons and situations. And, finally, personal experience may be generalized in the stereotypes, categories and classifications which the individual develops, as well as those which he receives from the common culture. All these social attitudes, cultural, collective and individual, motivate behavior in human interaction.

The attitudes and attitude patterns cannot be ignored by the sociologist. He must assume their existence if he would make certain aspects of human relations and the social processes of any culture intelligible. Without such assumptions, descriptive systems cannot be completely and logically organized. On the other hand, he cannot occupy himself with the welter of individual attitudes. This is the chaotic field of a number of special disciplines, and there is no apparent limit to the ramifications involved. The sociologist's interest is in the common social attitudes, the cultural and collective attitudes. But these he has not adequately listed and described, because, as we have seen, they are not distinct units, they shade into one another; and no adequate terminology has been developed for even the general "tendencies." So he is pursued by a conceptual Frankenstein which he can neither ignore nor escape. Lacking a solution and often lacking a clear-cut statement of the problem, he has usually been forced to round out his descriptions of behavior with vague and ill-defined terms for the attitudes to which such behavior was assumed to be related. It is not that the sociologist wanted to base his descriptions of the social order upon these subjective states. Of this particularistic fallacy the work of the American sociologist has been singularly free, perhaps because of his general preoccupation with description of specific social situations rather than the building of systems of sociology. But there remained the need of relating the culture forms to individual attitudes, and this has never been satisfactorily done.

CHAPTER XI

THE MEASUREMENT OF OPINION

> I conclude, therefore, that the imaginations which people have of one another are the solid facts of society, and that to observe and interpret these must be a chief aim of sociology.[1]

The persistent interest in attitudes has developed, not only from the need to complete a theoretical schema, but also from the observed relationship between certain attitudes and successful life adjustment within our culture. Personnel workers, psychiatrists, educators, social workers and others have attempted to study, through various simple measurements and tests, certain social attitudes of the individual. For example, one type of attitude that has been extensively investigated with experimental techniques is that of interests. It is maintained that interests and aversions are closely related to successful adjustment. Therefore, general interest inventories have been developed and standardized by personnel workers and educators. Clusters of interests, characteristic of variously classified groups, social and mechanical, introverted and extroverted, professional groups, student groups, and the like, have been isolated.[2] The direction of activity and the quality and quantity of accomplishment are correlated with interests. Therefore, tests and questionnaires designed to disclose interests have been constructed.

Bent on the recording and measuring of attitudes, the corporals of research have marched from many quarters armed with an odd assortment of tools. Before reviewing their approach, attacks, defeats and results, we shall briefly consider the problem of measurement.

MEASUREMENT

Measurement, the quantifying of data, has been introduced as method into ever new fields of social relations and of psychological phenomena. Tests of intelligence, interests, personality traits, ethical judgment, leadership and scores of other types of tests are the commonplace of contemporary educational and psychological practice. But measurement as description may be more erroneous and perverted than word description. As Chapin states, "There is nothing about measure-

[1] Cooley, C. H., *Human Nature and the Social Order*, p. 121.

[2] Fryer, D., *The Measurement of Interests*, 1931. Fryer has critically summarized this field of psychological investigation.

ment as a form of scientific description which makes it intrinsically and absolutely superior. . . . The great advantage of measurement as quantitative scientific description is that it is more susceptible of accurate recording, independent verification and transmission than are other methods such, for instance, as the case method."[1] These advantages can be achieved, however, only if the fundamental principles of measurement are followed. These are a standard unit of measurement and a scale on which to measure. Counting may be distinguished from measurement. In counting there is an enumeration of units, but these are not stated in terms of some scale and, hence, are not measured. To measure, the units must be set off against some scale of numerical values. A great deal of so-called "measurement" in the social studies violates one or the other of these criteria. In much of the quantitative material the units are not standardized, and in very little is there actual measurement of units against a scale. The sociologist deals for the most part with phenomena that have been referred to in general verbal terms but have not been expressed in terms of numerical symbols and reduced to verifiable units. Of those which have been dealt with quantitatively there has been more counting than measurement. Chapin notes, "When we count the number of potatoes in a pile on the floor, this act does not measure the potatoes. It is only when we place all the potatoes in a container which is by convention called a bushel basket that we measure the number of potatoes. The bushel is an arbitrary unit of volume. . . . Voting behavior, or votes, are something to be measured against an arbitrary scale. To count the number of votes and to call this act measurement is like counting the number of potatoes in the pile. To measure votes we must set them off against some arbitrary scale of numerical values. Perhaps an attitude scale."[2]

However, the problem of recording attitudes by measurement allows of only approximate accuracy in the isolation of units. For, as we have already stated, an attitude is a complex "tendency to act" and not a unit. It may be modified in many ways, as it has been created in many ways. Therefore, although the increasing variety of categories, according to which the attitudes of a group of people toward anything may be recorded, makes for a narrowing of the distinctions and, hence, for a nearer approximation of units of measurement, it must be admitted that these mental units of measurement are not units in the same sense as physical entities are units. This holds true not only for the attempted measurement of attitudes, but for that of interests and other subjective phenomena. It is clear that of ten people expressing a dislike for Orientals, the general attitude may be held for many different reasons, physical distaste,

---

[1] Chapin, F. S., *Contemporary American Institutions*, p. 353, 1935.

[2] Chapin, *op. cit.*, pp. 356, 357. Reprinted by permission of Harper & Brothers.

economic competition, childhood conditioning, and the like. Indeed, to make the person's attitude intelligible, it is necessary to know something of the background of experience out of which it developed. And that would determine in part his behavior as related to that attitude and the conditions under which it would be changed. As we isolate more and more the clusters of individuals who approximate one another's position, we approach the isolation of units. However, we can never do so except in an approximate sense, which is true of other subjective "units of measurement" also. It has proved very profitable to act "as if" these were units. Indeed, in almost all psychological measurement, the probability of relations is the basis for measurement. Thus, if a scale of opinions is developed, it is necessary to proceed "as if" two people whose opinions have placed them on the same point on the scale had identical attitudes. Otherwise there can be no units of measurement.

Moreover, in the development of a scale it must be assumed that the points on a scale from, say, one to ten are qualitatively the same, but quantitatively more or less. Actually in dealing with social phenomena this is seldom true. In terms of social interaction a group of 100 people is not ten times ten people, but qualitatively something different, and a family of ten is not two times a family of five. This same problem is met in the measuring of material phenomena also, but not so generally as in social and psychological measurement. As F. Znaniecki has stated:

Quantitative variations as directly experienced in the social field are still essentially variations in degrees of irreducible qualities and a degree which is quantitatively higher or lower than another is also qualitatively different. Strictly speaking, the latter is also true of many quantitative variations in the domain of nature; thus, various degrees of heat are experienced as not only quantitatively, but also qualitatively different. Quantification of natural phenomena has become possible only because for each non-measurable gradation a measurable parallel or equivalent has been found, which allowed us to ignore as irrelevant for certain scientific purposes the variations of quality which in concrete experience are inseparable from quantitative variations. Thus, in measuring temperature the gradual expansion of certain bodies was substituted as a purely quantitative equivalent for the experiences of gradation of heat and cold as empirical characteristics of reality.[1]

Although such assumptions as to both units and scale must be made in opinion measurement, we should critically examine the studies in this field to ensure that the assumptions, once made, have been consistently maintained.

If attitudes as subjective phenomena can be measured, it may be done only indirectly through a record of speech and other behavior.

[1] From Znaniecki, F., *The Method of Sociology*, p. 310, 1934. Reprinted by permission of the publishers, Farrar & Rinehart, Inc.

When behavior, verbal or otherwise, displays any consistency, it is assumed to be related to stable human attitudes. But the determination of consistency may require a long-time record of behavior, and, moreover, a type of record that does not lend itself readily to quantitative treatment. And this is a fundamental problem on which the attitude testers and those who do not believe in the quantitative record disagree. Both agree that you get to know and observe attitudes and other subjective states in actions and behavior, but those who oppose testing maintain that, in attempting to apply mechanical quantitative techniques to attitude records, the testers betray their lack of understanding of the nature of attitudes, of the complexity and changeableness of attitude. The testers retort that of course no single numerical index will describe everything about an attitude but that, in testing, certain well-defined aspects of the general attitude may be thus recorded. The non-testers reply that an attitude is more than the sum of its parts. Which, of course, it is. But, on the other hand, valuable insights into the nature of attitudes may be gained if the changes in certain aspects of an attitude may be quantitatively recorded, for these changes may then be correlated with the individual's experience, behavior and other attitudes in the interim. Attitudes are not static, and the tester must not act as if they were. The ultimate object is to learn how and why they change. But the "how" and "why" of changed attitudes are not unrelated to "how much." And here the tester may render a service. If he can set the time limits within which change in some aspect of an attitude has occurred and if he can report how great the change has been, he may then relate this change to the intervening experiences of the individual, in so far as is possible. And if the tester cannot adequately describe an attitude in all its aspects, he can certainly provide data for the non-tester in his inductive approach. The fundamental difference between them remains. The non-tester will not act "as if" the units were invariable units and the opinion scale a quantitative scale. However, knowledge has frequently been advanced by such assumptions.

THE MEASUREMENT OF OPINION

There have been so many studies of attitudes during the past fifteen years that a summary or review of all of them would not be profitable. In the reference list for this section many of the more important contributions to this field are classified. Comprehensive bibliographies of attitude studies have been compiled during the past few years so that the materials, though widely scattered, are now accessible.[1] Moreover,

[1] Lasswell, H. D., Casey, R. D., and Smith, B. L., *Propaganda and Promotional Activities* (An Annotated Bibliography), pp. 344–372 (1935).

Childs, H. L., *A Reference Guide to the Study of Public Opinion*, pp. 81–90, Prince-the attitude studies have already been summarized by a number of writers who have provided varied classificatory systems of types of studies.[1] Their classifications have been either of types of attitudes or of methods of attempting to measure attitudes. An analysis and comparison of these systems of classification would not further our understanding of attitude measurement, until we had described at some length a basis of classification with which others could be compared. The following simple basis of classification in terms of types of measurement is proposed: (1) yes-or-no, true-or-false and cross-out tests; (2) essay type or case method; (3) multiple-choice tests; (4) rating tests; (5) ranking tests; (6) an attitude scale; (7) the Thurstone scale; (8) tests in which there is an attempt to compare opinion and behavior as indicating attitude. Some of these types have appeared in other classifications. We shall describe one or two studies that illustrate the use of each method and then consider some of the uses and limitations of each type. Further examples will be found in the appropriate classifications in the reference list. The studies described are not necessarily definitive studies that have made the utmost use of their methods and critically sought out the weaknesses thereof. They are merely illustrative. However, the works of Watson, Bogardus, Allport and Hartman, and Thurstone have led in their turn to widespread discussion and critical examination.

YES-OR-NO, TRUE-OR-FALSE AND CROSS-OUT TESTS

Some years ago it was usual to seek solutions of educational and social problems by tabulating from questionnaires the responses of the subjects on statements of fact or of opinion on some controversial point. Indeed, the questionnaire, still widely used, has many legitimate functions, provided that it is used in accordance with the principles which have been

---

ton University Press, 1934.

Murphy, G., and Murphy, L. B., *Experimental Social Psychology*, pp. 690–694, 1931.

Bain, R., "Theory and Measurement of Attitudes and Opinions," *Psychol. Bulln.*, 27: 357–379 (1930).

[1] Droba, D. D., "Methods for Measuring Attitudes," *Psychol. Bulln.*, 29: 309–323; "Methods Used for Measuring Public Opinion," *Am. Jour. of Sociol.*, 37: 410–423.

Albig, W., "The Quantitative Measurement of Social Attitudes," *Publ. Mich. Acad. Sci.*, 10: 103–115.

Symonds, P. M., *Diagnosing Personality and Conduct*, 1931.

Bain, *op. cit.*

Katz, D., and Allport, F. H., *Students' Attitudes*, Chap. 20, 1931.

Murphy and Murphy, *op. cit.*, Chap. 11.

Lundberg, G., *Social Research*, Chap. 9, 1929.

Thurstone, L. L., "The Measurement of Social Attitudes," *Jour. Abn. Soc. Psychol.*, 26: 249–269.

established through extensive use.   Questionnaires may be classified as:
(1) those asking for facts which the reporter has observed; (2) those
asking for facts to be found in records; (3) those asking for reactions of
the individual, such as beliefs, preferences, likes and dislikes, wishes,
judgments and choices.[1]   It is to the third type that attitude questionnaires belong.   For some years, until about 1930, they were very extensively circulated, asking thousands of questions to be answered "yes"
or "no" about the attitude of the individual members of many scores
of groups.   The attempt to collect opinions in this fashion developed,
in part, from: (1) the wide gaps in information about prevalent social
attitudes of which the social scientists were becoming acutely aware,
(2) a lack of clear concepts of the nature of attitudes, (3) the growth of
quantifying in other fields of social knowledge, (4) the ease with which
these questionnaires could be constructed and answered, (5) a general
belief that a majority is likely to be right, and (6) the ease with which
the results could be compiled, a process of simple counting.   Although
the simple questionnaire serves a useful purpose, at times, in recording
factual information, it is needless to emphasize that this method has
been used with laborious futility when the questions have been direct
requests to indicate an attitude "yes" or "no" by statements of opinion
on controversial issues.   For example, a social-attitudes questionnaire
contained such questions as:

Should a city hold community pageants or celebrations?
Should mosquitoes be killed at public expense?
Should a city provide parks liberally?
Should a man be required by his employers to work regularly over eight hours
a day?
Should America follow a policy of isolation?[2]

And again:

Is God a person?
Is God an impersonal Force?
Does God interfere in the world by providences, miracles, etc.?
Was Jesus Very God?
Was the Bible verbally inspired by God?[3]

[1] Rugg, H. O., *Statistical Methods Applied to Education*, 1917; quoted by Symonds,
op. cit., p. 123.
[2] Symonds, P. M., "A Social Attitudes Questionnaire," *Jour. Ed. Psychol.*, 16:
316–322 (1925).   There were over 100 questions in this test to be answered "yes"
or "no."   The liberal or conservative nature of the replies was then determined by
the voting of five judges as to whether the question should have been answered "yes"
or "no."   The affirmative or negative votes of three of the five judges determined
some of the answers.
[3] Bain, R., "Religious Attitudes of College Students," *Am. Jour. Sociol.*, 32:

Sometimes instead of having the questions answered "yes" or "no," the wording was "true" or "false"; and in other studies the subject merely checked in one column or another, indicated plus or minus or crossed out one or the other of the terms used.

On the basis of our earlier discussion of the nature of attitudes, some of the limitations on the value of the use of such questionnaires are apparent.

1. An attitude is not an entity, but a complex of other attitudes in varying proportions. Moreover, an attitude of one individual may differ, in fine shadings, from that of another. In answers of "yes" or "no," these variations are ignored, quite different elements being thus forced into a single classification of opinion. This limited response provides a highly inaccurate opinion representative of the essential attitudes. Ten persons may respond "yes" to a statement indicating dislike of the Japanese. However, the essential components of their attitudes may be very dissimilar, being based on personal experience with Japanese, on newspaper reading, on economic competition and on scores of other items. For most purposes, this limited opinion is worthless for any understanding of human attitudes.

2. The language difficulty leads to more serious error in the simple questionnaire than in any other form of measurement. In a response with a greater variety of possible positions, the words used may be misinterpreted, but that may cause a variation of one position on a scale of five or ten places, whereas in the "yes" or "no" categories there may be a complete change of position from positive to negative due to language misunderstanding. The language meanings to the individual are a partly uncontrolled variable, as every tester knows.

3. If, instead of simply counting the responses, there is an attempt to measure, that is, to indicate the relation of the answers to some standard (as in Symonds' assumption of liberalism or conservatism in terms of the "yes" or "no" answers); then the standard is constructed by the experimenter or by a limited group of judges. These judges, however, do not provide a valid scale for the group tested, since they themselves come from another group, often with varied attitudes. We shall consider this problem in greater detail in discussing the Thurstone test.

ESSAY TYPE OR CASE METHOD

Attitudes may be assumed from opinions expressed in written essays and in letters, case-history descriptions, autobiographies, diaries or

---

762–770 (1927). An attitude test of sixteen questions was presented to 200 students.
As already indicated, these selections are simply illustrative. The authors would use quite different methods today. Indeed, Prof. Bain has violently repudiated the attempt to record attitudes directly from opinions.

oral or written interviews. These permit of an extensive range of
expression, avoid the measurement limitations of the "yes-no" categories but offer methodological problems in any attempt to classify and
quantitatively to manipulate the results. In social practice, expressions
of opinion in such forms have always been ascribed to the individual's
attitudes, and in the case of representative writers, autobiographers
and diarists, the common social attitudes of groups and of historic
periods have been described. Not only these individual statements,
but also group products, folk songs, folklore, proverbs and, indeed,
most culture forms, are translated into the social attitudes that have
motivated them. However, it is only in recent years that organized
study of such sources as attitude records has been carried on by the social
scientists.

It has frequently been maintained by sociologists that life histories,
letters, autobiographies, diaries, and the like, are superior to any form
of attitude test, as the informal record is more likely to show the origins
and development of attitudes. They are also less likely to be perverted
by social pressures due to the presence of the questioner, interviewer
or test giver. However, the writers of such personal expressions are
subject to the social values of their culture incorporated in their attitudes;
therefore, certain attitudes will be modified in their expression by other
attitudes, and certain motivations may be elaborately rationalized or
otherwise perverted. For example, descriptions of sex behavior and
attitudes, in autobiographical literature from Rousseau to the recent
queer psychological jumble of John Cowper Powys's *Autobiography,*
indicate the shortcomings of purported confessional autobiography.
And, indeed, Tolstoy and many others have complained of the pervasive
informal popular censorship that modified their output in spite of
intended frankness.

Letters, diaries and other types of statement not intended for general
public perusal have been used by sociologists as indicating attitudes,
especially since the monumental work twenty years ago of Thomas and
Znaniecki on the Polish peasant.[1] Thousands of letters from Polish
peasants in the homeland to immigrants in Chicago and from America
to Poland provided one basis for the discussion of attitudes. Diaries
have also been used somewhat by European and American sociologists
and psychologists, especially psychoanalysts. These have been used
for the study, not only of attitudes, but of other psychological phenomena.[2] One small study of attitudes as indicated by the subject matter
of conversations was made by C. Landis, who generalizes on national

---

[1] Thomas, W. I., and Znaniecki, F., *The Polish Peasant in Europe and America,*
2 vol., 1918.

[2] Murphy and Murphy, *op. cit.,* pp. 570–574.

differences from fragments of conversation overheard in New York and Columbus, Ohio, as compared with similar snatches overheard in the London streets.[1] He found differences in attitudes between the sexes implied in the tendency of the Englishman to adapt his conversation to the woman's interests, whereas the American woman more often adapts her conversation to the interests of her masculine companion. Also, English women talk more frequently of other women, while American women talk of clothes and men. In all such studies, the problem of the adequacy of the sample must be kept constantly in mind. Does the sample afford a cross section of the phenomena considered? Usually the sample has not been adequate. All fragmentary materials must be carefully related to the group that is represented, and generalizations beyond that group cannot be made. For example, W. F. Vaughan studied the content of 762 letters written to a Boston newspaper in which the writers attempted to state why they were going to vote for Hoover or Smith.[2] He concludes that the liquor question was the most important, that there were deep-seated emotional attitudes on both sides, that there was allegiance to groups and not to principles and that the religious issue was important. The source of his data was an ingeniously chosen sample, but it is a sample only of those who write letters to newspapers, not of the general public.

Of late years, all of these spontaneous expressions have tended to be superseded more and more by partially controlled forms, as the desire for comparable quantitative materials has developed. To quantify, it is necessary that there be some uniformity in content, arrangement of content, types of statements, and the like. An increasing number of studies based upon oral or written statements prepared at the behest of the questioner have appeared. About twenty years ago, J. H. Leuba studied brief essays written by 1000 men of science and college students on immortality and belief in a personal God.[3] B. Lasker has used this procedure in studying children's attitudes on race.[4]

In this type of brief essay the judgment as to meaning and assortment of answers rests with the investigator; it is therefore unstandardized and subject to error. S. A. Stouffer attempted to overcome this difficulty by employing four judges.[5] His subjects, 238 students who had taken

[1] Landis, C., "National Differences in Conversation," *Jour. Abn. Soc. Psychol.*, 4: 354–357 (1927).

[2] Vaughan, W. F., "An Experimental Study of Political Prejudice," *Jour. Abn. Soc. Psychol.*, 25: 268–274.

[3] Leuba, J. H., "The Belief in God and Immortality," *Jour. Abn. Soc. Psychol.*, 25: 268–274 (1930).

[4] Lasker, B., *Race Attitudes in Children*, 1929.

[5] Stouffer, S. A., *An Experimental Comparison of Statistical and Case History Methods of Attitude Research*, abstract of thesis, University of Chicago, 1929–1930. Also reported by Murphy and Murphy, *op. cit.*, p. 622.

a Thurstone test on prohibition, wrote accounts of their opinions on prohibition. These essays were about 1000 words in length. Four judges read the essays and rated the attitudes of their writers on a scale of favorable to unfavorable to prohibition. The judges had a remarkably high agreement: the intercorrelations of ratings of each judge with the ratings of each other judge was $+.87$, the range being from $+.83$ to $+.89$.

The oral interview, either following a definite outline or as apparently casual conversation, with the answers either transcribed at the time of the interview or written up later, presents special methodological problems in addition to those of the brief essay. Its superiority over written forms lies in the spontaneity of response; if the interview is made too formal, this advantage is lost. Further, the personal qualities of the questioner are introduced into the situation to a greater extent than in essay answers. Altogether, oral interviews are a much more difficult medium to arrange in any fashion permitting quantification. They are obviously useful for the collecting of informal, unstandardized accounts whereby some insight into the individual attitude process may be gained. Sometimes they have been transferred into simple quantitative terms by counting the answers common to a number of interviews.

This procedure was used some years ago as a part of a study of opinions about Mexican immigrants in Flint, Mich.[1] A number of ranking tests were constructed from statements made by junior-college and high-school students about the thousand Mexicans who had recently migrated to that city. The tests were then given to 600 students throughout the city. In addition, the statements made during interviews with several hundred neighbors, businessmen, school children, teachers, police, social workers and professional men were recorded. In these interviews the author informally worked into the conversations a brief list of questions but strove to keep the discussion as spontaneous as possible. From these records it was possible to count similarities in statement, and the quantitative results were appended to each chapter dealing with the interviews with the various groups. For example, in forty interviews with neighbors the following general assertions were made:

1. The Mexicans of the neighborhood are:
   - clean and neat...................................... 3
   - slovenly and dirty................................... 31
   - not stated.. 6
2. The Mexican children are:
   - neighborhood nuisances............................ 5
   - well behaved....................................... 25
   - not stated... 10

[1] Albig, W., *Group Opinion and the Mexican*, thesis, University of Michigan Library, 1929.

3. The Mexicans are very:
   shiftless and careless.................................. 34
   not stated.. 6
4. They move too often, are not a solid element:
   true... 34
   not stated.. 6
5. The effects of the Mexican immigration on work are:
   bad, keeps wages down.............................. 17
   does not affect.. 5
   don't know.. 18
6. Prices of houses in the neighborhood are:
   lowered.. 15
   not affected... 8
   don't know.. 17
7. The Mexican is accustomed to:
   go to church.. 16
   not to go to church................................... 4
   not stated... 20
8. The Mexican people:
   drink and are quarrelsome........................... 13
   are quiet.. 19
   not stated... 8

A sample of the interview records may be noted.

Mr. B., student, age 19.

These Mexicans are crowded all over the place. Next door to us they're so crowded they come out in the yard to eat. In the summer they eat out in the back yard, just walk around and eat, and then throw melon rinds and stuff all over the place. They're dirty as hogs. Sometimes they kinda dress up a little, the younger ones, but I don't think they're very clean. You know there's so many of them in that house next to us that I don't know how many there are. They seem to move around a good bit and new ones come in and out.

I don't know how they get along. I used to work in an A and P store. They always bought good food, what they did buy, when they had money. The women are pretty dumb, they never do learn to talk. I delivered a box of peas one day which weren't what the woman wanted, and she was too dumb to tell me.

The worst thing about these Mexicans is that they're stubborn and bull-headed. They fight, too. I work in a theater now, usher. I've had trouble with four or five Mexicans. They annoy women and I got to report them to the manager. There's lots of them go to this theater and they're the most stubborn and bull-headed people we got to handle. They're more particular than white people about sitting beside a nigger. They think the usher is just trying to put them there and they won't go.

The desirability of the extended types of individual statement and of brief essays appears in the insight that may be gained into the individual attitude process, the origins and development of attitudes. However, they do not readily permit of quantitative analysis, because: (1) the providing of any formal outline of what to write about largely eliminates spontaneity and hence defeats the investigator's purpose; (2) the treatment of the results is dependent upon the judge or judges who read the essays or documents, and the standard or scale that he or they set up is a standard valid only for the judges or persons of similar attitudes (this applies both to the attitudes that they ascribe to the writers and also to their interpretation of language); (3) the essential problem still remains, the relation between this form of opinion and other types of behavior. Clearly preferable to simple tests, however, these sources have provided more understanding of the attitude process in the individual than has been obtained elsewhere by the social sciences. The methods of quantifying them should be experimented with extensively. They do not have quantitative validity.

MULTIPLE CHOICE AND CROSS-OUT TESTS

As the range of response in the yes-or-no tests is too limited and as the essay, oral interview and other forms of extended response are so difficult to classify and score, some experimenters attempted a wider range of expression of opinion by providing a list of statements or words to be checked by the subjects. The situation might be presented in a paragraph or brief essay description, followed by a number of phrases or words, of which the subject was to check the one that most nearly agreed with his attitude. For example, in the Van Wagenen American History Scales, there are such tests as the following:

Two American soldiers, Jasper and Newton, returning from scouting duty, were told that a man who had left the King's cause had been captured by the British. Eight guards were now taking him to Savannah, where he was to be hanged the next day. They hastened toward a spring a few miles from Savannah, where the guards would be likely to stop to get a drink. When the British came to the spring, they stopped to get a drink. Two of the guards were left to watch the prisoner. The rest stacked their guns against a tree. Leaping from their hiding place, Jasper and Newton each snatched a gun, shot the two guards and seized the rest of the muskets. The six unarmed guards surrendered and were marched along back to the American camp with the rescued prisoner.

Draw a line under the three of the following words which you think best describe this action of Jasper and Newton:

selfish   treacherous   daring   cruel   spiteful   timid
fearful   brave   bold   cowardly.[1]

[1] Van Wagenen, M. J., *Historical Information and Judgment in Pupils of the Elementary Schools*, 1919. Quoted by permission of Bureau of Publications, Teachers College, Columbia University.

Another form of this type of test may be illustrated from the Allports' Ascendance-Submission Study.[1] A portion of their questions deal with behavior, but some of them attempt to elicit statements of attitude. Of the forty-one items of the test, there are a number like the following:

Are you embarrassed if you have greeted a stranger whom you have mistaken for an acquaintance?
_____ very much
_____ somewhat
_____ not at all

Another variation is the word cross-out test. In an attempt to record fair-mindedness as an attitude, G. B. Watson used as the first part of the test fifty-one words such as bolshevist, mystic, Sunday blue laws, dancing, Unitarian, Holy Communion, and the like. The subject was instructed to cross out all those which he found annoying or distasteful. A tendency to cross out an unusually large number of words was taken as an indication of some sort of emotional set or conditioning.[2]

Although tests of these types may be indicative of some sort of emotional set, there are a number of difficulties involved in their use. There are obvious advantages in providing a concrete situation as the stimulus as Van Wagenen does, but how are the results to be classified? The language difficulty is very apparent here. The terms are not mutually exclusive. They are not terms that have clear, definite meanings to the subjects. Nor are the categories scaled to clear-cut stages or steps of attitude difference. Just what is the line between "very much" and "somewhat"? Moreover, the descriptive words have been provided by the tester; perhaps the students tested would have developed a quite different list as significantly descriptive of that situation. The tester has, in part, projected his own attitudes by his selection of words. Moreover, the order and arrangement of the words may be significant factors. It has recently been pointed out that position may be so important in tests with alternate responses as to invalidate all the rest of the test. A response word when printed above its alternative was marked 33.8 per cent more often than when it was printed below its alternative. A response word when printed to the left of its alternative was marked 3.2 per cent more often than when printed at the right of its alternative. This source of perverting statements is likewise applicable to other types of tests. In spite of the limitations of the multiple-choice tests, we find some advance here as the range of response has been widened. But there is no adequate basis for measurement.

[1] Allport, G. W., and Allport, F. H., *A-S Reaction Study*, 1928.
[2] Watson, G. B., *The Measurement of Fair-mindedness*, 1925.

RATING

Another common form of attitude test is a rating device whereby a choice may be made of one of various degrees of opinion about a given question. In different tests the degrees of opinion have been presented in three, five, to as many as twenty-one categories. For example, a statement of opinion may be preceded by: "certainly right," "probably right," "doubtful," "probably wrong," "certainly wrong"; or by +2, +1, 0, −1, −2; or by some other arrangement, one item of which is to be checked by the subject. Lund used a rating system in which there were twenty-one positions ranging from "belief allowing for no doubt" at +10 to "disbelief allowing for no doubt" at −10.[1] The difficulty of attempting introspectively to divide any attitude into twenty hypothetical divisions must have been a considerable strain upon the imaginations of those taking the test. How large a number of positions may be used in a rating device to deal with subjective phenomena? This can only be determined experimentally with specific material, but it is doubtful if more than five or seven positions could be successfully coped with by even a trained and serious student. Moreover, this is a rating device of abstract positions that are not objectified by indicating some concomitant behavior. In general, especially for tests to be widely administered, those rating tests are better which indicate a specific type of behavior as indicative of attitude. A more objective approach of this sort is made by Bogardus in his social distance tests.[2] In these, the subject was asked to indicate his attitudes toward various nationality and racial groups by responses to questions as to his willingness to admit members of those groups to seven degrees of relationship. For example, the responses of 1725 Americans to forty different races were recorded by percentages.

Table V shows the first four, the middle four, and the last four of the nationalities in the results of one of the Bogardus social-distance tests.[3] These tests represent a distinct advance over the preceding ones. Concrete potential behavior situations are substituted for abstract degrees of relationship. This makes for greater standardization in the understanding and response of the subjects to the steps. For example, the distinction between admitting to a club or to marriage is a difference in intimacy of relationships understood by the subject in a way that +5 and +3 on an abstract scale of attitudes is not differentiated. As the subjects' responses lie on a more common base, these tests have

---

[1] Lund, F. H., "The Psychology of Belief," *Jour. Abn. Soc. Psychol.*, 20: 63–81.

[2] Bogardus, E. S., *Immigration and Race Attitudes*, 1928. Also numerous articles in *Sociology and Social Research*.

[3] Bogardus, *op. cit.*, p. 25.

uses for comparative purposes. On the other hand, several points are apparent. (1) We do not have a scale in which the steps are of equal size, in that the intervals are similar. That is, we have no basis for judging the relative importance in decreasing intimacy between admission to kinship by marriage and to club membership and between admission to club membership and to the street as neighbor. Although there is apparently a general scale of stages of decreasing intimacy, it is not a measured scale. The steps are unknown. (2) The list of nationalities

TABLE V.—REACTIONS OF 1725 AMERICANS TO DIFFERENT RACES BY PERCENTAGES

Regarding races	1 To close kinship by marriage	2 To my club as personal chums	3 To my street as neighbors	4 To employment in my occupation	5 To citizenship in my country	6 As visitors only to my country	7 Would exclude from my country
English......................	93.7	96.7	97.3	95.4	95.9	1.7	0.
Americans....................	90.1	92.4	92.6	92.4	90.5	1.2	0.
Canadians....................	86.9	93.4	96.1	95.6	96.1	1.7	0.3
Scotch.......................	78.1	89.1	91.3	92.3	93.3	1.7	0.
Portuguese...................	11.	22.	28.3	47.8	57.7	19.	3.3
Poles........................	11.	11.6	28.3	44.3	58.3	19.7	4.7
Rumanians....................	8.8	19.3	23.8	38.3	51.6	22.	4.6
Czechoslovaks................	8.2	16.4	21.1	36.	47.4	26.	9.5
Chinese......................	1.1	11.8	15.9	27.	27.3	45.2	22.4
Mulattoes....................	1.1	9.6	10.6	32.	47.4	22.7	16.8
Koreans......................	1.1	10.8	11.8	20.1	27.5	34.3	13.8
Hindus.......................	1.1	6.8	13.	21.4	23.7	47.1	19.1

was chosen by the investigator. These are not necessarily nationalities on which even a majority of the subjects have stereotypes and attitudes. (3) In such an extensive list of nationalities the subject may be unable to imagine the possibility of personal situations involving such choices with all of those on the list and yet be unwilling to acknowledge, even under the cloak of anonymity, lack of information or experience with regard to any one of the groups. (4) In this, as in other rating scales, the points on the scale are developed by the investigator on the basis of a logical arrangement, rather than from the attitudes of those tested. Related to this logical assumption of steps is the belief that the acceptance of each degree of intimacy implies a willingness to accept the succeeding ones. This is not necessarily true.

Ranking

The order-of-merit method is a simple type of measurement that the psychologist constantly uses. It has frequently been used in tests of judgment of weights, measures, sizes, colors, and the like. The materials of the test vary with the subject under consideration, but the principle is that of arrangement of units into scaled order by the person tested. This ranking of items does not make any assumptions with regard to the size of the intervals between the steps. That is, if there are eight objects to be placed in order of increasing weight, the differences in weight between that in the first position and that in the second position and between the second and third are not equal. One may be many times the other. Likewise, in the application of this method to the ranking of subjective states, there is no assumption of a scale with known steps. A study of statistical ethics, largely based upon this principle of ranking, was carried on for many years by A. P. Brogan.[1] After a series of questionnaires, in which students were asked to list the most reprehensible practices that they knew, he selected the sixteen that were most frequently mentioned. These were presented to class after class for ranking according to order of merit. This procedure illustrates one sound principle. The materials of which the test was constructed were taken from the same group as those later tested, or from a group similar to theirs. The students could therefore be expected to have attitudes toward the practices about which they were asked. The projecting of materials from the experimenter upon his group has been a serious shortcoming of all the tests we have so far considered. The ranking method, however, in addition to not being a measured scale, has one other basic limitation. How many items may be utilized in a ranking of attitudes? If the list is long, will there be an increase of inaccuracy toward the end of the list? For example, if a student is asked to list sixteen unethical practices or to enumerate twenty-five national groups in the order of their social distance from the subject, is there not the probability that the first named will be the most obnoxious practices or nationalities, that those toward the middle of the list will be the least obnoxious, and that the ones at the end will represent practices or nationalities which the student utilizes merely to fill in the requisite number? When the ranking of size or weight of units is used in a psychological test, the units are at least present to each subject. In the classification of opinions the units are not all necessarily of significance to each subject. The subject may have no attitude on which to base an opinion of a Korean, let us say, or of some unethical practice. He is asked, however, to rank in

---

[1] Brogan, A. P., "Problems and Methods in Statistical Ethics," *Pub. Am. Sociol. Soc.*, 21: 174–177.

order of merit twenty-five nationalities or sixteen ethical practices. He has attitudes on fifteen and ten, respectively. Yet he must complete the requisite number. The test is not analogous to one in which twenty physical units are placed before the subject for discrimination. The number of items that may be used in a ranking of attitudes can be determined only in relation to the particular subject matter. This has not been done in attitude measurement. However, it is possible to discriminate between a limited number of items, and we may illustrate from the author's study in race relationship, referred to earlier in this chapter. From statements made by junior-college students in Flint, the statements most frequently appearing on the Mexican's physical

TABLE VI.—PERCENTAGES OF THOSE ASCRIBING RANK POSITIONS TO REASONS FOR DENYING CITIZENSHIP TO MEXICANS

Rank	Reason number					Rank	Reason	Per cent
	1	2	3	4	5			
1	32.0	11.1	16.7	12.5	27.8	1	1	32.0
2	16.7	23.6	23.6	15.3	20.8	2	2, 3	23.6
3	16.7	23.6	19.4	20.4	19.4	3	2	23.6
4	12.5	19.8	25.0	15.3	15.3	4	3	25.0
5	6.9	11.1	1.4	18.1	4.2	5	4	18.1
N	15.3	9.7	13.9	18.1	12.5	N	4	18.1

characteristics, health, results of miscegenation, mental ability, temperament, political capability and economic capability were developed into a series of ranking tests. Those taking the test were asked to rank in the order of their validity five statements on each subject. A sample of statements and of the results obtained from one group may be cited as an illustration of ranking-test procedure.

FLINT JUNIOR COLLEGE

DATA ON POLITICAL CAPABILITY OF MEXICAN[1]

(Number in Group—100)

I would deny citizenship to a Mexican, because:

Reason
number

1. Domination and superstition have made him incapable of understanding democratic principles.
2. Although he may ultimately be politically capable, he is not now capable.
3. The average of intelligence of the Mexican has been shown to be so low that he is unfit for citizenship.

[1] Albig, *op. cit.*, p. 109.

4. Some Mexican immigrants might be good citizens, but the majority would not be; therefore, the only practical procedure is exclusion of all on the basis of nationality.

5. The Mexican laborer is an economic peril, and to deny citizenship is one step in exclusion from immigration.

Percentage of males denying citizenship.................................. 64
Percentage of females denying citizenship............................... 80
Percentage of both denying citizenship.................................. 72

In Table VI one may note that 32 per cent of the subjects state that reason 1 is the most important reason for denying citizenship to Mexicans; 23.6 per cent maintain that reasons 2 and 3 are second in importance, and so on.

CHAPTER XII

OPINION MEASUREMENT: THE ATTITUDE SCALES

An early study by Allport and Hartman had a considerable influence in stimulating later studies of attitude.[1] Thurstone, who has worked extensively in this field, credits this study with arousing his interest. It was the first study that attempted to create a scale on which attitudes could be measured. The purposes of the study were (1) to develop a scale technique for measuring the distribution of opinion upon public questions and (2) to inquire into the psychological characteristics of those who adopt certain attitudes upon such questions. It is the first of these two objectives that interests us at this point. Seven issues of political interest, selected by the testers, were given to sixty upper-class students, who were asked to write their views on them. The resulting essays were read by six judges, who abstracted the principal statements of opinion from them and arranged these opinions in order from one logical extreme to the other. On each of the seven issues these statements were then mixed, so as not to be in order as arranged by the judges, and presented to 367 students. On each issue the student was to check one statement that most nearly expressed his opinion. For example, on the League of Nations question he could choose from twelve statements; on the qualifications of President Coolidge, from ten statements; on the distribution of wealth he could choose from five positions, and the like. The results were then arranged along the original scale as developed by the judges and the percentages of the persons taking the test who chose each statement as representing their opinions were distributed along this line. The results were graphed. For example, on the qualifications of Mr. Coolidge, the percentages of the students selecting each of the 10 statements as most important are:

14.9 Coolidge is perfectly fitted for the office of President of the U. S.
22.0 Coolidge is the best man we could find for the office today.
20.3 Although Coolidge has been a very good President, he cannot be compared to our strongest Presidents.
12.5 Coolidge is better than the men nominated by the other parties.
18.5 Coolidge may be the right man, but he has not yet had sufficient chance to prove it.
3.8 Coolidge is a little too conservative.

[1] Allport, F. H., and Hartman, D. A., "The Measurement and Motivation of Atypical Opinion in a Certain Group," *Am. Pol. Sci. Rev.*, 19: 735–760 (1925).

199

4.6   Mediocre is the word that sums up Coolidge's qualifications for President.

1.4   Coolidge favors the financial interests too much.

1.6   Coolidge is controlled by a band of corrupt politicians.

0   A man such as Coolidge is bound to bring with him a corrupt government.

Charted, the results appear as indicated:

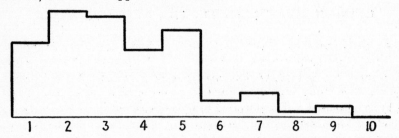

The steps are indicated along a base line, which has been developed from the decisions of the six judges as to the importance of the reasons. The vote of those taking the tests may then be figured in terms of percentages of those checking each of the statements. These results are then allocated to the proper division on the base line.

Certain advances in recording were scored by this test: (1) The statements were originally taken from students when students were to take the test. This eliminated positions suggested from outside the tested group. (2) A greater variety of possible positions was presented on each issue than in the simpler tests. (3) As a base line was developed from the decisions of the six judges and the results located on this line, we have actual measurement rather than merely counting.

The principal limitations of this test were that: (1) the statements were not mutually exclusive; (2) the determination of the base line was based upon the judgments of a group quite dissimilar in attitudes from those taking the test; (3) the points on this base line were not equidistant from one another; that is, in quantitative terms one statement might be many times as important as another. Hence, it would occupy many times the space on the base line. Therefore, we may not be dealing with steps that are even approximately equal. We are provided with no way of determining their relative size. It was to these problems that Thurstone turned his attention.

THE THURSTONE SCALE

L. L. Thurstone emphasized that the ranking of opinions may show the relative importance of one or the other opinion in the group tested but that ranking does not measure, in that it does not show the quantitative relationship between the opinion types as measured on some scale. He, more than any other, has influenced opinion measurement since 1930 and has provided a score or more of attitude scales that have been widely utilized. Thurstone extended the psychophysical techniques to the measurement of attitudes that Cattell had first used for social phenomena. The development and application of Thurstone's methods have been extensively described in a monograph on measurement of attitude toward the church, in which study he collaborated with E. J. Chave. From that source we shall briefly describe his procedures.

Many individuals were asked to write their opinions about the church, and from these a list of statements was prepared. The list of 130 statements remained after the collection of statements had been edited, it having been kept in mind that:

(1) The statements should be as brief as possible so as not to fatigue the subjects who are asked to read the whole list; (2) The statements should be such that they can be indorsed or rejected in accordance with their agreement or disagreement with the attitude of the reader. Some statements in a random sample will be so phrased that the reader can express no definite indorsement or rejection of them; (3) Every statement should be such that acceptance or rejection of the statement does indicate something regarding the reader's attitude about the issue in question; (4) Double-barreled statements should be avoided except possibly as examples of neutrality when better neutral statements do not seem to be readily available. Double-barreled statements tend to have a high ambiguity; (5) One must insure that at least a fair majority of the statements really belong on the attitude variable that is to be measured. If a small number of irrelevant statements should be either intentionally or unintentionally left in the series, they will be automatically eliminated by an objective criterion, but the criterion will not be successful unless the majority of the statements are clearly a part of the stipulated variable.[1]

The collection of the materials of the test from opinions expressed by individuals of the same or a similar group satisfies the objection that we raised regarding the projection of attitudes of the experimenters upon those tested. The language difficulty still remains, as indeed it does to some extent in all tests, but the statements have been carefully culled to remove those containing words that would be likely to be misunderstood.

The next step was the sorting procedure, in which a group of judges were asked to sort into eleven piles the 130 statements, which had been mimeographed. At one end were to be placed those statements favoring the church, at the other those opposed, and in pile 6 the neutral statements. In the intervening spaces were to be placed those statements which the judges decided were less and less or more and more favorable to the church. The objective here was to develop a scale from the judgments of those who were to take the test or were similar in background

[1] Thurstone, L. L., and Chave, E. J., *The Measurement of Attitude*, 1929. Quoted by permission of University of Chicago Press.

and opinion statements to those who would take it. It was thought thus to eliminate the artificial scales developed when those of different background do the judging, as in the Allport-Hartman test. Many judges supplant few judges (there were 300 in this test); judges of similar opinions supplant possibly alien judges. The results were then counted and worked out in a table of percentages in accumulative proportions.

Statement	A	B	C	D	E	F	G	H	I	J	K
1	0.00	0.00	0.00	0.00	0.00	0.08	0.17	0.23	0.33	0.52	1.00
2	0.02	0.13	0.35	0.72	0.93	0.97	0.98	0.99	1.00	1.00	1.00
3	0.00	0.00	0.01	0.01	0.01	0.09	0.33	0.60	0.84	0.98	1.00
39	0.16	0.57	0.85	0.95	0.99	0.99	0.99	1.00	1.00	1.00	1.00
40	0.00	0.00	0.00	0.01	0.05	0.08	0.21	0.43	0.71	0.93	1.00
100	0.40	0.85	0.95	0.98	1.00	1.00	1.00	1.00	1.00	1.00	1.00

We now have a table (the above is a sample of 6 statements out of the 130) in which the cumulative percentages of the judges' decisions on each of the 130 statements appears. That is, statement 39 was placed in classification *A* (most favorable to church) by 16 per cent of the judges, in classification *B* by 41 per cent, etc., but in this table the percentages are accumulative, that is, each classification includes all the preceding ones.

The next problem is the determination of the scale value (based upon the judges' decisions) of each statement. These scale values were determined graphically for each statement. The graphs are plotted from the accumulative proportions as shown in the above table. For example, statement 39 reads, "I believe the church is absolutely needed to overcome the tendency to individualism and selfishness. It practices the golden rule fairly well." In the judges' sorting, 16 per cent considered this statement as expressing highest appreciation of the value of the church; 57 per cent considered that it was either highest or next highest; etc. In Fig. 10 we have a graph showing the cumulative percentages.

On this graph the curve crosses the 50 per cent level at 1.8, and this is assigned as the scale value of this statement. Half of the judges classified this statement as more favorable toward the church than 1.8, half as less favorable.

The objective is to obtain a basis for selection of statements about which the judges have been in greatest agreement and of statements which are evenly distributed along a scale from 0 to 11, thus providing a test that covers the gamut of expressions of opinion from most to least favorable toward the church. The graphs for all the 130 statements will show curves of many shapes. In the case of statement 39, the quartile points for the curve are located at scale values 1.3 and 2.6 respectively. Thurstone labels the distance between these two points 1.3, the *Q* value, or the measure of ambiguity of the statement. If the Q value is low, there is a high degree of agreement among the judges; if the Q value is high, the statement is very ambiguous, the different readers having scattered their judgments. Such statements would be discarded.[1]

Having discarded ambiguous and irrelevant statements, those remaining of the 130 statements are distributed at their scale-value points along the scale from 0 to 11. The selection of the questions for the test is now made by deciding approximately how many statements are desired and

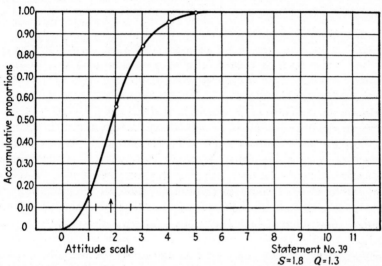

Fig. 10.—Attitude scale graph. (*From Thurstone, L. L., and Chave, E. J., The Measurement of Attitude, p. 37. Reproduced by permission of the University of Chicago Press.*)

then selecting statements that are distributed by more or less uniform intervals along the scale. That is, if 22 statements are to be used, select, in so far as possible, statements whose scale values are separated from one another by one-half a point on the scale. Such an ideal distribution will not be possible, but it is to be approximated. In the Thurstone-Chave scale, 45 statements were retained.

The 45 statements are then shuffled and presented as a test, in which the subject is to check every statement that expresses his sentiment toward the church. For scoring the results the procedure is as follows: The scale value of each of the 45 statements is known. Add the scale values of each of the statements endorsed by the subject, and calculate their arithmetic mean. The result is the subject's position on the scale.

[1] Thurstone determines the reliability of the scale values, develops an objective criterion of ambiguity and of irrelevance. These procedures are described on pp. 44–58 of the monograph cited.

The authors felt justified in using this mean scale value of the opinions endorsed by the subject as his position on the scale, as there were approximately the same number of opinions available for him to check in each class interval. The reliability of scoring thus was tested. If a group of 100 subjects take such a test, the results will appear as 100 points on a scale line from 0 to 11. In conclusion, it may be noted that the selection of eleven divisions in sorting and on the scale was an arbitrary choice. This number might have been smaller; it probably could not profitably have been larger. The sorting judges would have been confused. However, this is a matter for experimental determination in each test.

The basic problem in this, as in the other tests, is whether attitudes, as expressed in opinions, are units that may profitably be handled quantitatively. Aside from this, there are certain technical objections to the construction of the tests; the source of materials; the range of those materials; the determination of a scale. The Thurstone test largely overcomes these problems. However, certain criticisms have been made. (1) The tendency of the judges to place a statement more frequently in the end piles than in the intermediate piles has been called the "end effect." This end effect tends to shorten the distances between the end statements and the adjacent statements so that in the final scale values the middle statements are further apart than the end statements, although the quantitative scale values may indicate an even distribution. It has been suggested that the division of all the statements into those "for" and "against" and then further sorting of each category would eliminate this skewing.[1] (2) Whether or not a scale developed by using one group of judges is applicable to quite different groups of subjects has been questioned. To what extent will the judges' attitudes affect the scale?[2] Some differences were found in calculating three independent sets of scale values for certain statements of opinion about the Negro: the first by Southern white subjects, the second by Northern subjects prejudiced in favor of the Negro, and the third by Negroes.[3] Although Thurstone and his students maintain that this factor is of little importance, it remains to be investigated. (3) The time and labor involved in the construction of.a Thurstone scale has been discouraging to many. The sorting procedure is especially laborious and time-consuming, so that none but selected judges has been effectively used. Instead of the sorting procedure, a method of rating on an eleven- or nine-point scale, printed in the left-hand margin of a mimeographed list of opinions, has been suggested. It

[1] Droba, D. D., "Methods for Measuring Attitudes," *Psychol. Bull.*, 29: 309–323. Katz, D., and Allport, F. H., *Students' Attitudes*, p. 366, 1931.

[2] Rice, S., *Statistics in the Social Studies*, Chap. 11 and commentary, 1930.

[3] Hinkley, E. D., "The Influence of Individual Opinion on Construction of an Attitude Scale," *Jour. Soc. Psychol.*, 3: 284–292.

is maintained that a saving of over 50 per cent in time is achieved.[1]   (4) We have noted the superiority of the Bogardus test to some of the other simple nonscaled tests because Bogardus used concrete situations rather than abstract formulations.   Katz and Allport have suggested the development of a scale, using the Thurstone techniques, on which the scale continuum is one of behavior other than opinion.[2]   This brings us to the problem of opinion versus other forms of behavior as an accurate index of attitudes.

Attitude, Opinion and Behavior

Expressions of opinion, no matter how recorded, have frequently been objected to as indexes of attitude.   It is urged that forms of behavior other than opinion will more reliably reveal attitudes.   Considerable controversy has ensued from this division of opinion on verbalizations versus other forms of behavior as indicators of attitude.   Like so many such controversies, it has arisen in part from a willful misinterpretation of the opponents' viewpoints and terms.   Even the most enthusiastic investigator does not assume that all attitudes are amenable to measurement by language tests.   That conventional answers, rather than opinion expressions of all attitudes involved, will usually be given to questions dealing with sex relations, miscegenation, religion or any other issue on which there have been strict mores is quite clear.   The subject's rationalization, rather than conscious deception of the investigator, will usually be indicated.   So basic is this tendency to give the conventional answer that even anonymity may not modify the subject's response. Most investigators have assumed that the individual's hidden attitude, rather than the conventional response given in such situations, is the real attitude.   If by "real" is meant that which is more likely to result in action, it by no means follows that the individual's hidden attitude is more real than the conventional response.   Although usually more willing to disclose the conventional attitude and thus avoid antagonistic responses, the individual may also be much more willing to *act* in accordance with that conventional attitude.   Thus action as well as opinion is a fallible indication of all the attitudes involved in a situation.   As Thurstone has maintained:

There comes to mind the uncertainty of using an opinion as an index of attitude.   The man may be a liar.   If he is not intentionally misrepresenting his real attitude on a disputed question, he may nevertheless modify the expression

[1] Seashore, R., and Hevner, K., "A Time-saving Device for the Construction of Attitude Scales," *Jour. Soc. Psychol.*, 3: 366–374. See also Likert, R., Roslow, S., and Murphy, G., "A Simple and Reliable Method of Scoring the Thurstone Attitude Scales," *Jour. Soc. Psychol.*, 5: 228–238.

[2] Katz and Allport, *op. cit.*, pp. 368–371.

of it for reasons of courtesy, especially in those situations in which frank expression of attitude may not be well received. This has led to the suggestion that a man's action is a safer index of his attitude than what he says. But his actions may also be distortions of his attitude. A politician extends friendship and hospitality in overt action while hiding an attitude that he expresses more truthfully to an intimate friend. Neither his opinions nor his overt acts constitute in any sense an infallible guide to the subjective inclinations and preferences that constitute his attitude. Therefore we must remain content to use opinions or other forms of action merely as indices of attitude. It must be recognized that there is a discrepancy, some error of measurement, as it were, between the opinion or overt action that we use as an index and the attitude that we infer from such an index.[1]

In everyday life the individual's expressions of opinion are considered a significant part of his behavior. We use these as well as other types of behavior as indications of his attitudes. They are; although we may misinterpret the attitudes involved or have an incomplete understanding of them. When expressions of opinion are made the subject of organized analysis in opinion testing, they remain significant indicators. And this would be admitted by those who favor stressing other forms of behavior in a research program on attitudes, although in the controversial process they sometimes incautiously write as if verbalizations were of little significance. For example, in discussing racial attitudes, La Piere writes:

For the conventional method of measuring social attitudes is to ask questions (usually in writing) which demand a verbal adjustment to an entirely symbolic situation. Because it is easy, cheap, and mechanical, the attitudinal questionnaire is rapidly becoming a major method of sociological and socio-psychological investigation. The technique is simple. Thus from a hundred or a thousand responses to the question "Would you get up to give an Armenian woman your seat in a street-car?" the investigator derives the "attitude" of non-Armenian males toward Armenian females. Now the question may be constructed with elaborate skill and hidden with consummate cunning in a maze of supplementary or even irrelevant questions, yet all that has been obtained is a symbolic response to a symbolic situation. The words "Armenian woman" do not constitute an Armenian woman of flesh and blood who might be tall or squat, fat or thin, old or young, well or poorly dressed—who might, in fact, be a goddess or just another old and dirty hag. And "yes" or "no" is but a verbal reaction, and this does not involve rising from the seat or stolidly avoiding the hurt eyes of the hypothetical woman and the derogatory stares of other street-car occupants.[2]

While one may have sympathy for indignation at the absurd oversimplification of the early attitude testers, it must be evident that in the

---

[1] Thurstone and Chave, *op. cit.*, p. 7. Quoted by permission of University of Chicago Press.

[2] La Piere, R. T., "Attitudes vs. Actions," *Soc. Forces*, 13: 230–237. Permission to quote granted.

later and more complex tests such a question would not be asked or, if it were, it would not stand as an isolated response on which generalizations about Armenian females and American males would be developed.   On the other hand, the behavior response to the particular, let us say beautiful, Armenian woman on the streetcar is not a record of attitudes toward Armenians.   The subject may not know that she is Armenian, may grant her as an exception, and the like.   His stereotype of "Armenian" may not be modified by such an encounter.   The problem is that of the extent to which various attitudes are involved in different types of situations.   In the attitude complex of the individual about race relations and in his attitude complex about Armenians, there are attitudes that would motivate one kind of action in the case of the beautiful young Armenian woman and others that would be at the basis of action on a political decision, and the like.   It would be quite as erroneous to base generalizations about attitudes toward Armenians upon such an action incident as it would be to assume that a test described all attitudes which could be involved in American-Armenian relations.

Whenever possible, comparison and correlation of action and opinion as indicating attitudes are clearly desirable.   Unfortunately, social psychology has not, as yet, provided any large number of formal studies that attempt to show this relation.   Several years ago F. M. Vreeland noted the geographic distribution of the *Birth Control Review* as indicating the areas in which attitudes most favorable to birth control were to be found.[1]   R. R. Willowby studied the distribution of the *Nation* as significant in the spread of liberalism, and there have been a few other fragmentary studies of various media of communication.   However, such results are of little value unless compared with other indicators; the attitudes involved in subscription to any periodical may be quite varied. P. A. Sorokin asked several sociology classes to (1) buy materials for departmental use, (2) help three brilliant but needy students, (3) help Chinese and Russian students.   The statement as to what contributions would be given showed that, in numbers contributing and in amounts given, the students would aid their own work first and Russian students last, although on an attitudes test they subscribed to the statement that we should be equally ready to help all.[2]   In such a situation the students subscribed to the conventional phrase and gave money on another basis, but the conventional response is a socially significant type of behavior also.   There has been some attempt to relate voting behavior to attitudes in studies by S. A. Rice, C. E. Merriam, H. F. Gosnell, G. Lundberg,

---

[1] Vreeland, F. M., *The Process of Reform with Special Reference to Reform Groups in the Field of Population*, thesis, University of Michigan, 1929.

[2] Discussed by Murphy, G., and Murphy, L. B., *Experimental Social Psychology*, p. 625.

C. E. Robinson and many others. In the obviously significant but difficult problem of research on opinion versus action as indicators of attitudes there have been few helpful contributions. Adequate methodology has not emerged.

The Measurement of Group Opinion

Any number of people interacting in any kind of social relations, out of which grow common interests, constitute a social group. In even the simplest societies, groups are very numerous; in contemporary complex societies they are of almost infinite number and variety. The growth of communication has made possible the rapid increase in variety of association. Groups involve the interests and attitudes of their individual members in widely varying degrees, from the myriads of attitudes that are acquired from and used in the primary group of the family or the school play group, to the relatively few attitudes associated with membership in the Philatelists of America. Various-sized segments of the individual's behavior and also of his attitudes are not only determined by but are involved in these various group memberships. Moreover, as the number and variety of the individual's group memberships increase, the attitudes associated with different groups are more likely to be in conflict or in partial disharmony with one another. This is necessarily so; for, if the values of the social order are not consistent, the individual's attitudes which reflect them must be inconsistent. Although we are not ordinarily aware of these disharmonies, having accepted without question the prevailing viewpoints of our various group associations, intermittently the conflicts of attitudes receive conscious consideration. The individual attempts to deal with these inconsistencies and then to verbalize his conclusions. Without overemphasizing the rational and logical processes or the demand for consistency of the average person, it is evident that individual opinion process is frequently stimulated by the diversity of attitudes thus acquired. Moreover, new groups and alignments result at times from the awareness of these inconsistencies by a number of group members. Thus the multiplication of groups, this proliferating tendency toward new associations, is in part dependent upon the inconsistencies of the values engendered in the already existing groups. For example, a new alliance for the farmer results from the failure of the Republican party, the Methodist church, his fraternal orders, and many other groups of which he is a member, to satisfy attitudes toward consumption that the farmer has developed from contacts with salesmen, advertising media, and the like. New attitudes in the individual and new group values, expressed in aims, programs, promises, and the like, develop.

In neither the new nor the old groups, however, is the opinion process a mere summation of individual judgments, nor is it a mean or an average of those individual opinions. It is an interactive process in which many factors are involved. The results are something that would not have been individually achieved. In this sense we have a group or public opinion. The groups range in size from a few persons, who discuss in order to achieve some common statement of position, to the largest number that can possibly be involved by the use of all the modern media of communication. They do not become a group in so far as opinion is concerned until interaction has occurred. Imagine a hundred people met together to discuss the Townsend Plan. The individual members already have attitudes which they are willing to express as opinions. A Thurstone test scaled from 1 to 10 would show a distribution of individuals all the way from "favorable" to "unfavorable." You now know the position of the individual members. Could it be predicted that the group opinion will be the sum, the mean, the average, or, indeed, any mathematical formula applied to those individual scores? Quite obviously, if the scores were all you knew about the hundred people, you would prove a sorry prophet. In the process of interaction hundreds of attitudes will be involved; those related to the present economic position of the individuals of the group, past attitudes toward the speakers and those involved in discussion, personality interaction, the skillful or unskillful manipulation of symbols, emotional response to particular words, various attitudes among individuals in their wishes for security, order of presentation and many others. Test again. The distribution of individuals may be almost the same or may have swung markedly to one or the other end of the scale. This transient experience may have produced little or very marked results, which may be quite different a few hours or a few days hence. Like the attitudes developed in a religious revival they may often be quite evanescent. But suppose this same group met fifty times. By the twentieth meeting a certain stability of scores and positions would be achieved and rather consistently maintained. This would be no casual popular impression but a relatively stable statement of position, consistently maintained until new factors are introduced. The entire process and the results are the group opinion or public opinion. In this case, to be sure, a much more formal process of interaction has occurred than is possible in large secondary-contact publics as the people of New York, the readers of the *Chicago Tribune*, a self-conscious proletariat or the Indian untouchables. But interaction is characteristic of groups or publics. The measurement of group opinion is therefore the record of opinions of individuals who have been selected on the basis of membership in that group or public within which interaction on that subject has occurred. There is no mystical group opinion or group mind, but simply the attitudes of individuals developed from association therein. The individual opinions resulting therefrom may then be separated into majorities and minorities, blocs, clusters or any other form of classification.

But will the results approximate an average of the individual positions? C. H. Cooley concludes that:

The average theory applied to public consciousness is wholly out of place. The public mind may be on a lower plane than that of individual thinking in separation, or it may be higher, but it is almost sure to be on a different plane; and no inkling of its probable character can be had by taking a mean. . . . A little common sense and observation will show that the expression of a group is nearly always superior, for the purpose in hand, to the average capacity of its members. . . . There is a widespread, but as I believe a fallacious idea that the public thought or action must in some way express the working of the average or commonplace mind, must be some kind of mean between the higher and lower intelligences making up the group. It would be more correct to say that it is representative, meaning by this that the preponderant feeling of the group seeks definite and effectual expression through individuals competent to give it such expression.[1]

As applied to large publics these conclusions are fundamentally a matter of faith. Prof. Cooley's scale on which he was locating the average was a rational or an ethical scale. Whether the preponderant result will be above or below the median or the average will vary with the size of the group, its composition, the subject under discussion and many factors that could only be known by a complete history of the controversy under consideration in that group.

Discussion of the group and social mind, of communal spirit, folk soul, and the like, has been extensive in recent political and social theory. Sometimes it has become perfervid controversy between psychologists and sociologists. Often the conflict has been based primarily upon misinterpretation of terms, but it has likewise developed, in its present form, because of the divergent frames of reference of the individual psychologist and the cultural sociologist. However, man has long reflected profoundly on the nature of interaction in social groups. Whenever man has developed an organized social theory, this problem has arisen. It appears in Aristotle's *Politics*, in Plato's *Republic* and in the legal ideologies of the Romans, but the modern controversy had its inception in the revolt against the excessively individual and rational political philosophies of the eighteenth century. The problem of individual and public opinion is part of this larger conceptual framework.

From the foregoing discussion it should be evident that we consider opinion as an individual expression. It is a group or public opinion when it has been affected by interaction in a group situation. The

---

[1] Cooley, C. H., *Social Organization*, p. 124, 1909. Quoted by permission of Charles Scribner's Sons.

individual's opinion has been modified by (1) those cultural elements affecting the issue which are unique to that group and (2) his experiences with interaction within that group and the development of consensus. The group and interaction of members within it are social reality; attitude and opinion are individual phenomena. These individual opinions are recorded and measured. Group-opinion phenomena are inferred from changes in individual opinions as shown by successive measurements as well as directly observed from the record of the group in action.

The interest in and expenditure of effort on the problem of attitude measurement are evidenced by the variety of methods that we have surveyed in the preceding discussion. But vigor of attack does not always assure solution of the problem. Can attitudes be measured? If not, how are they to be recorded? The social scientist must deal with them in some fashion. They are essential entities to which the sciences of social forms and processes must relate their materials. Certainly the student of public opinion must assume attitudes in the individual as motivating expressions of opinion. An attitude as general "tendency to act" is obviously a complex phenomenon that may be infinitely variant in individuals. It is evident, therefore, that the social psychologist as well as the psychologist must be cognizant of individual differences. However, many types of attitude are not so variant. There are common social attitudes, a very great number of them. They are acquired from common sources in similar fashion, and they motivate common types of behavior. It is with these that we are primarily concerned in the study of public opinion. Mr. Jones may have an attitude of dislike for and vote against a political candidate some of whose mannerisms he finds distasteful. Because of Mr. Jones's unique composition of attitudes on this point he is motivated to behave in a manner socially significant, that is, to vote against the candidate. Obviously, however, there can be no attempt to measure Mr. Jones' aversion if it is a unique phenomenon. Nor are the social studies preoccupied with such individual attitudes and behavior. Eighty-five per cent of those voting in the same election vote against that candidate. They do so for many reasons. Noting what a sample of these voters state as their principal reasons, you may classify these and count the numbers of those who state one reason or the other for voting against the candidate. There is a scattered 5 per cent with divergent reasons, but the remaining 80 per cent of the total voters defeat the candidate because of party affiliations, his stand on prohibition and the recent scandal in which his supposed seduction of his secretary's sister was made public. We are now dealing, not with unique phenomena, but at least with statements of opinion common to sizable groups.   We still have Mr. Jones with us, however, for he told the investigator that he voted against the candidate because of the prohibition issue. Actually, Jones, a fastidious man, has for many years found the candidate distasteful because of his mannerism of flopping a drooping, half-chewed cigar from side to side of his mouth, because of his gold tooth and his habit of meditatively scratching the back of his head.   Jones may rationalize or, conscious of his real reasons, may simply choose a more politically acceptable reason to disclose to the investigator.   For the moment, he is listed with those who voted on the basis of the prohibition issue; perhaps he will be eliminated from this group later.

It is very clear that the attitude of opposition and hostility to the candidate is a complex phenomenon incapable of being adequately described by any simple numerical index or, indeed, by any other simple statement.   There appear to be at least three common social attitudes involved here as determining factors in this voting behavior.   Perhaps an attitude scale on party affiliation, one on prohibition and one on seduction will provide additional knowledge as to the distribution of attitudes of the voters, at least within the limitations of the validity of scales, which we have already discussed.   In the process of testing Mr. Jones, we discarded him from the category of those opposing the candidate on the prohibition issue, because of the quality of his answers.   His rationalization might very well have been convincing, however, whereupon he would have remained thus classified.   Our procedure, then, would not have been adequate to disclose all the attitudes involved in this situation.   This is a shortcoming common in varying degrees to all behavior records of subjective states.

We have, then, isolated the few common social attitudes involved in this situation, have indicated their range and have noted the position of a large number of the voters on these scales.   We have limited ourselves to the common social attitudes and those on which methods existed for a quantitative record.   Preferable at some points as the statistical record may be, we must remember that we have by no means adequately or completely described the attitudes involved in this situation.   Especially must this be recalled because testing engenders an illusory sense of completeness.   The desire to proceed quantitatively sometimes leads to a formulation of concepts and problems thus incomplete, but with the illusion of completeness.

What other procedures may be used to disclose attitudes?   Introspective accounts and the use of forms of behavior other than verbal may be used in addition to or in place of tests.   The introspective account, subject as all self-revelation is to rationalization, autistic thinking and other deviations from the real motivations, usually achieves even partially adequate exposition only in the reports of trained subjects.   "It is difficult to see how a technique which involves the indication of one's position on an attitude scale is scientifically more satisfactory than a technique which involves the reporting of highly trained subjects of their attitudes which appear in consciousness under conditions of careful experimental control."[1] Certainly these introspective techniques are desirable if they are reported by trained subjects and presented in such a fashion that they may be quantified if the attitudes are assumed to be common. Significant insights have been gained in this fashion. We need not choose one or the other method; they may be made supplementary. Our record of attitude, acquired by means of tests, lacks depth. It does not provide insights into typical ways in which such attitudes were developed. From introspective accounts and from case studies these processes may be learned. "It is certain, at least, that every man's opinion becomes more intelligible if we know the particular circumstances under which it was conceived; particularly if we know also the circumstances that have reaffirmed and intensified it. It is for this reason that, in studying opinions, we seek to go back to the point of genesis, seek to define the concrete circumstances under which opinions took form, and the motives which inspired them."[2] For the observer to enter imaginatively into the experiences of the subject, so that he may come to understand the inception and development of certain attitudes, he must be provided with these longer accounts of experience, and not only of the objective experience, but also of the mental processes of his subjects. He cannot dodge the mental and emotional processes; and for understanding these the introspective accounts of typical subjectives are invaluable. Their typicality can only be determined by gathering an adequate sample. Moreover, all forms of behavior indicative of attitude should be used, when possible, for supplementary and comparative purposes. These methods can be correlated for the development of as full a record as possible.[3]

Finally, there has been no orderly approach, even with such methods as are available, to the recording of opinion phenomena in various groups. The subject matter of those studies which have been made has been determined either by what appeared as most profitable to an investigator interested primarily in method or by the interests of the investigator, his special problems, who was subsidizing him, and the like. Preoccupation with method has largely precluded formal classifications, in the literature of social psychology, of the groups and publics in which attitudes are outstandingly affected. The approach thus far has been primarily individual and psychological rather than sociological.

[1] Fearing, F., "Relationship among Controlled Factors," in *Methods in Social Science* (Rice, S. A., ed.), p. 727, 1931.

[2] Park, R. E., "Experience and Race Relations," *Am. Jour. Sociol.*, 9: 20.

[3] See Murphy, G., Murphy, L. B., and Newcomb, T. M., *Experimental Social Psychology*, Chap. 13, 1937.

CHAPTER XIII

OPINION CHANGE

Individuals express opinion about controversial issues. In relatively static societies the number of such issues at any time is small; elsewhere the scope of the controversial widens. Change in any aspect of culture involves the opinion process in groups. Many issues involve large groups. In a sense, therefore, all culture change is a record of opinion change. Anything may become controversial, and, considering all human cultures, almost everything has at some time been the subject of conflict. In the simpler societies, at those periods which are highly static, any innovation is attended by vigorous disagreement. Changing forms evidence the momentarily victorious position. For example, simple art forms are dependent upon the structure of the human organism which permits of almost infinite variety, upon the qualities of the materials and upon the tribal patterns. Although changes may occur but intermittently, individuals do become innovators and for various reasons change the patterns. The earliest known drawings are those sketches of other species which appear on the walls of caves of what is now southern France. When innovations appeared in the methods of portraying these various animals, one can imagine the indignation of a tribal elder, ruefully viewing this sacrilege to his magical beliefs about the potency of an arrow placed here or there on the drawing and the animated discussion that ensued.

There are certain basic processes developed out of the common human experience of the simpler primary groups that are less often questioned, but even these are controversial in some groups. There is also the residue of that which at any given time is not controversial. Especially in mathematics and the physical sciences there are certain materials, much fewer than is popularly supposed, which may be verified and established to the satisfaction of the expert group. This is scientific fact, and it is cumulative, serving as the basis for new developments. Yet all these fields have changed at times with amazing speed, so that, as a seventeenth-century man of learning said, "what was conjuring in the last age is Mathematiques in this." Opinion thereon is formed in the expert group. Popular opinion enters more immediately and more often into the statement of positions on the subject matter of the social studies. Large publics are always involved in some type of controversy in religion, economics and politics. The experts are less often in agreement, and their lack of agreement is more generally exposed. Because their propositions are less irrefutably proved, they more persistently turn to popular support for some hypothesis or cause. It is in the field of the social studies, therefore, that there has been the greatest eagerness to devise methods of discovering what opinions are held by the members of large publics. When large numbers of issues are popularly controversial, the need for such techniques for taking a record is more apparent. This, in large measure, accounts for the present preoccupation of psychology and the social sciences with the methods of opinion study.

It is evident that the purpose of opinion measurement is prediction and control. But even the most sophisticated of the present methods of measurement merely breaks down the statements of general position into a scale of statements running the gamut of possible positions in that group. But this is not adequate for prophecy, for the resulting statements to which an individual may accede may still be based upon quite variable attitudes. It is apparent, therefore, that whatever merit these tests possess exists in their usefulness as instruments for discovering what lies behind the statements of opinion. This may best be done by attempting to use them to chart opinion change. Thus, it may be possible to infer the process. Difficulties are at once apparent. A Thurstone test, for example, if given at intervals may not in each case cover the entire range of what opinions have then become in the group. If new tests are given each time, the results are then not comparable. Further, language changes may have occurred in the meantime so that certain words of the test have changed meaning somewhat. For example, in testing opinions about the present Democratic administration some statement on "boondoggling" might be included. This term has had somewhat varied connotations during the past two years, however, and the responses would vary with the time of testing. By careful construction and continued analysis of test content, these shortcomings may be in part overcome, and the tests may be useful tools for recording opinion change. But it must be recognized that they are but relatively accurate instruments for making observations about opinion change and the attitudes upon which it is based.

There are several ways by which changes in opinion may be studied: (1) Observers may present generalizations about the process, based upon their experiences, upon participant observation or upon a nonquantitative examination of records, newspapers, documents, and the like. (2) Tests may be given at time intervals and quantitatively treated. (3) Tests may be given with partly controlled stimuli, such as a speech, movie or other item, intervening. (4) Quantitative studies of opinions other than those expressed in tests may be made, such as studies of voting records, changing content of various media of communication, buying habits and other behavior records. Without making any attempt to provide a critical summary of the literature, we may illustrate these procedures. Cataloguing of authors and titles of studies will be found in the reference list. The mere listing of bibliographical material at this point would be of no service to the reader.

GENERALIZATIONS ABOUT OPINION CHANGE

In those sections of political and social philosophy in which the opinion processes of large publics are considered, thinkers have long pondered over the problem of opinion change. Numerous generalizations may be found in the writings from Plato to the latest treatise on political science. Let us sample a few, taken at random.

There are certain generalizations, based upon common experience and similar observations, which are repeated time and again. Robert Owens' famous tactic "Never argue, repeat your assertion" has been otherwise expressed many times. Recognition of the force of repetition existed among political leaders, tacticians and philosophers long before the advertiser, under the tutelage of the psychologist, made himself almost insufferable to the sensitive.

Another long recognized procedure for bringing about a change of popular opinion is the so-called "red-herring technique," the diversion of public attention from one subject to another. In this connection Lecky remarked that "people do not disprove miracles, they outgrow them." In large publics, few opinions are changed by being disproved. Much more often, attention is simply diverted to something else. The effectiveness of positive statements in contrast to indirect or indecisive statements is likewise a generalization learned from experience and frequently stated. The effective political leader of large publics has a program, not a policy of negation. Change in opinion is brought about by specific positive appeals. Two hundred dollars a month to everyone above a certain age, share our wealth with ten thousand dollars capital for every man, woman and child—such proposals are specific enough. The demagogue knows this. The positive religious program has a permanent popular advantage over agnosticism. The positive statement is appealing. William James once referred to Wilhelm Wundt as a perfect professor, because he had an opinion on every subject and, having an excellent memory, he seldom forgot what his opinions were. Recognition of this principle will be found scattered throughout the literature of group processes. These positive statements, moreover, should more often be hope-bringing and optimistic rather than pessimistic appeals, if they are effectively to modify mass opinion. Sorel said that there was a popular aversion to every pessimistic idea. This is usually held to be true, except for short-time periods in crises. Or we may consider generalizations such as those of the economic determinists of the nineteenth century. They maintained that shifts in opinion were brought about, primarily, by modifications of the economic order, not by ideas. The politician who, following a sweeping defeat, said that "we couldn't expect to beat fifteen million unemployed" was momentarily of this school of thought. These and many other generalizations have been repeated so often that they are the principles assumed in most discussions of the process of opinion change.

Changes of opinion, according to Plato, are forced when they occur under the "violence of some pain or grief"; "the enchanted are those who change their minds either under the softer influence of pleasure or the sterner influence of fear." Cooley notes, "A group makes up its mind in very much the same manner that the individual makes up his. The latter must give time and attention to the question, search his consciousness for pertinent ideas and sentiments, and work them together into a whole, before he knows what his real thought about it is. In the case of a nation the same thing must take place, only on a larger scale." Such a description of popular opinion process is based upon a faith in the rationality of the process and the ultimate triumph of logic. That the shifts in opinion are based upon sound judgment was also stated by Locke who, depreciatory of the demagogue, wrote, "Nor let anyone say that mischief can arise from hence as often as it shall please a busy head or turbulent spirit to desire the alteration of government. It is true, such men may stir whenever they please, but it will be only to their own just ruin and perdition." Distinguishing between two types of subjects on which opinions may be changed, some by reasonable arguments, others by emotional appeals, E. A. Ross notes, "In areas where, after all, feeling or instinct, not reason decides, discussion can do little to accelerate the issue." Alexis de Tocqueville, commenting on changing public opinion in a democracy, notes an increase in the depreciation of the elite in proportion to the decrease in class differences, saying, "The hatred which men bear to privilege increases in proportion as privileges become fewer and less considerable, so that democratic passions would seem to burn most fiercely just when they have least fuel." The principal processes of opinion change, according to A. L. Lowell, are that "opinions change by making exceptions to general rules until the rule itself is broken down" and "opinions have this in common with intrenchments that they offer an obstinate resistance to a frontal attack, but not to a turning movement." Lord Bryce concluded that opinion changes were instigated in America by a limited group, principally politicians, a "set of men, who are to be counted by hundreds rather than by thousands; it is the chiefs of great parties who have the main share in starting opinion, the journalists in propagating it." In his *Public Opinion and Lord Beaconsfield* G. C. Thompson summarizes the changes in public opinion during a generation in England. One illustration of rapidly changing popular opinion occurred during the Turkish war when atrocity stories were circulated. Thompson thus describes the steps in the process: "At first there had been doubt, then astonishment, then a great emotion of pity and indignation, a desire that the persons who had suffered should be helped and the persons who had done wrong should be punished, then came the perception that things of this kind were not strange and unheard of exceptions, but only a capital example of the incidents of Turkish rule, and finally the conviction indelibly branded into the public mind that Turks were not fit to be trusted with sovereignty over Christian populations." We have here an instance of generalization based upon a specific situation.

In the preceding quotations we have only fragments, snatched from the writings of these eminent commentators. Let us summarize one other source in which there is a more complete discussion of the bases for sudden changes in group opinion.[1] According to E. H. Paget, sudden opinion change in large publics occurs under the following conditions: (1) A group opinion that is neither founded on a thorough comprehension of the points at issue nor supported by strong associations with some enduring prejudice may easily disintegrate. (2) Many expressions of opinion are but empty formalism. Changes in opinion may seem to occur suddenly, but actually the attitudes behind the opinion have been changing for a long time. (3) Group opinion may shift quickly because of unwise and overaggressive action of those who attempt to direct opinion. Leaders may become too confident of public backing and attempt to go too far. (4) There is a general willingness of members of large publics to respond positively (voting "yes") to propositions when they still retain doubts. Therefore, a majority may change very quickly. This has been experimentally verified. (5) As a rule, people oppose situations, not principles. Sudden shifts in opinion may occur if the situation is modified. (6) The introduction of a new personal force, vividly dramatizing an issue, may bring about a sudden change in opinion. Facts, reasons and evidence have rarely gained a secure hold on the minds of most men.

We have strung together this rather chaotic list of quotations, which could readily be amplified, in order to indicate something of the variety of comment on opinion change. Such wise and experienced thinkers as Bryce, de Tocqueville, Thompson, Lowell and many others, on the basis of their observations and logical analysis of the mass opinion process, have formulated many valid generalizations. It is questionable whether contemporary social science can, at least for some time, improve upon the sympathetic insight of the political theorist and the social philosopher.

[1] Paget, E. H., "Sudden Changes in Group Opinion," *Soc. Forces*, 7: 438–442.

However, a more exact science of social relations may provide certain information that they could not supply. For example, it might be very illuminating to analyze and note the frequency with which opinion changes are induced by the red-herring technique, by reiteration, diversion, positive assertions, and the like. Public information is canalized through well-known agencies. Examine their output. Assess, in terms of frequency of use, the devices that the publicity agents of the U.S. Department of Agriculture call into use between July 1 and Jan. 1. Surely a more exact science of society would provide information, not only on what the techniques were, but upon the frequency of their use by different agencies as well as exact descriptive accounts of the specific case.

Opinion Change with Controlled Stimuli

During the past few years there have been a number of attempts to record the effects of certain oral, printed and pictorial materials upon the opinions of those subjected to them. It has been demonstrated that shifts of opinion may occur after but very limited contact with spoken, written or pictorial stimuli. More and more detailed analysis of the process of changing attitudes is being attempted, although the experimental methods are necessarily very crude and the stimuli but partly controlled. From the limited body of experimental literature that has been produced in the past five years we may select a few items for brief discussion. Other references will be found in the selected reference list. Most of the studies thus far have used students as subjects since they were an available and a fairly homogeneous group. The shortcomings of many of the experimental techniques are fairly obvious and must be criticized, but at the same time the difficulties of this pioneering research should be well understood. Let us first consider studies of oral, then of written and then of pictorial, stimuli affecting opinion.

W. H. Wilke conducted an interesting comparison of the relative effects of speech, radio and printed page, by giving speeches on war, on the distribution of wealth, on birth control and on the existence of God, to classes in New York University.[1] These speeches were transmitted by microphone to other classes and were given in printed form to a third group. There were 341 subjects in all. Opinion scales were given two weeks before and after the speech, radio or reading, dealing with the subjects discussed therein. These attitude tests were the rating-scale type containing five steps, of which position 3 was neutral, position 1 in agreement with the speaker and position 5 in greatest disagreement. Of all the neutral or undecided scores on the original test, that is, those

[1] Wilke, W. H., "An Experimental Comparison of the Speech, the Radio and the Printed Page as Propaganda Devices," *Arch. Psychol.*, No. 169, 1934.

checking position 3 on the scale, the greatest number were brought nearer to agreement with the special pleading by the speaker, the loud-speaker being next most effective and the printed material least effective. Attitudes that in the first test were opposed to the views expressed by the propaganda material were more likely to change to a position of agreement than to swing merely to a neutral position. Further, those who in the original test espoused the more extreme positions tended to retain these positions much more than any other group. The average of all changes on all topics brought about by the speaker was 9.5 per cent of the total possible changes; by the loud-speaker, 7.9 per cent; by the printed materials, 6.3 per cent. These differences, though not large, are significant. Obviously, such fragmentary data, collected from a limited number of subjects on a few topics by means of an inadequate testing method, do not provide a basis for generalization about the effectiveness of different stimuli. But this is the type of study, with the stimuli at least partially controlled, which may in time provide an accretion of materials from which such generalizations may be adduced.

W. K. Chen studied the influence of oral propaganda material on student attitudes.[1] An opinion test of forty-five statements selected from speeches, articles and interviews on the Manchurian problem was developed and made up as a five-point rating scale. These statements favored both the Chinese and the Japanese viewpoints. They were presented to nine university classes in various schools from Stanford to Columbia, to be checked on the "absolutely true" (A.T.), "partly true" (P.T.) undecided (U), "partly false" (P.F.) and "absolutely false" (A.F.) scale. If a statement favoring the Chinese viewpoint is endorsed A.T. it is in position 1, and if A.F., in position 5, undecided being 3. The positions of the students before hearing propaganda material were recorded. Then two articles, one favoring the Chinese position and another the Japanese position, were developed, and a neutral article was taken from a publication of the Foreign Policy Association. These were given to instructors of classes, who, after memorizing the arguments in them, gave talks to their classes on one or the other position. The students were tested once more a few days thereafter. Each group was found to shift its position in the direction toward which the particular propaganda, to which it had been subjected, impels. Apparently a few minutes of oral propaganda produces large and measurable results. In each case more than half of the members of the class shifted from the original undecided position to one of the others. When, instead of propaganda for the Chinese or Japanese positions, neutral material was presented, a tendency to reduce the originally more popular opinion was noted. The author further con-

[1] Chen, W. K., "The Influence of Oral Propaganda Material upon Students' Attitudes," *Arch. Psychol.*, No. 150, 1933.

cludes that propaganda material does not need to cover a large number of issues to bring about a shift in general attitude. It does need to create a vivid general impression. And, moreover, the author suggests that information did not play a determining role in shaping attitudes toward the Manchurian problem. A definite attitude was possible in the absence of any specific information. Although the materials are too limited for such generalizations, the author has here posed some basic problems of opinion change. The stimuli were quite variable in this test and the conditions not carefully controlled (it was given during a period of wide-spread popular discussion of this problem so that the effectiveness of the single class speech could hardly be isolated). Among the greatest variables are the personal characteristics of the speakers, including methods of presentation. These are not equated in this study. With all its limitations, this experiment nonetheless poses some basic questions on the effectiveness of speech forms in changing opinions. It is to be hoped that numerous studies in this field will soon appear.

Of late years there have been increasingly exact methods for testing information acquired through reading materials on the social studies. The latest and most comprehensive review of achievements in this field has recently been published by the American Historical Society.[1] Tests of opinion change, however, have appeared only during the last decade, and as yet there are only a few of them. A. D. Annis and N. C. Meier studied the influence of editorial material on students at the University of Iowa.[2] Using the regular daily editions of the newspaper, they "planted" thirty editorials, fifteen of them favorable and fifteen unfavorable to a Mr. Hughes, Prime Minister of Australia from 1915 to 1923. Previous to the tests they ascertained that none of their 203 subjects knew anything about Mr. Hughes. The editorials were from 150 to 300 words in length and resembled the usual editorials in style. They purported to give information and opinions about Mr. Hughes who was supposed to be traveling on a lecture tour through the Middle West. One group read the editorials favoring Mr. Hughes, the other, those opposed to him. This reading was done during the regular psychology laboratory meetings, two a week, over a period of two months. The objective was to attempt to record the influence upon opinion of such limited contacts with editorial writing about an individual. This problem of editorial influence has long been disputed in conferences on journalism and social psychology. Of course, this test varied from the usual conditions of editorial reading, as the moot point usually is whether the editorials are or are not read, whereas here the reading was assured. At the con-

---

[1] Kelley, T. L., and Krey, A. C., *Tests and Measurements in the Social Sciences*, 1934.

[2] Annis, A. D., and Meier, N. C., "The Induction of Opinion through Suggestion by Means of Planted Content," *Jour. Soc. Psychol.*, 5: 65–81.

clusion of the two-month period tests were given. Ninety-eight per cent of the subjects reading the favorable editorials became favorably biased toward Mr. Hughes, and 86 per cent of those reading the unfavorable editorials became adversely biased. Moreover, the attitude toward Mr. Hughes was recalled four months later when another test disclosed approximately the same expressions of opinion as were made immediately after reading. Further, seven editorials were found to be as effective as fifteen in developing the opinions one way or the other. The authors conclude that by means of a very few editorials, presenting but little factual information and largely through indirect suggestion, it is possible to build up definite attitudes toward individuals. Limited though the materials of this study may be, the authors have made a definite contribution to method in using a medium to which the subject is accustomed, and modifying but one section of it. The conditions are thus more nearly normal. One of the most difficult problems in opinion testing is the need of duplicating, in so far as possible, actual life situations. Indeed, this is a problem of all psychological experimentation. Theoretical abstractions may go far astray from the humanly possible. It is reported of Catherine the Great that when her friend and teacher Diderot urged upon her the voluntary renunciation of autocracy, saying that despotism was criminal even if benevolent, the Czarina replied with amiable sarcasm, "These fine-sounding principles of yours may be all very well in the world of books, but they do not suit the world of affairs. You do your work on patient paper. I, who am only an empress, have to work on human skins, and they are ticklish."[1] In opinion testing, the closer the approximation to life situations, the better the test.

On the effects of pictorial forms in changing opinion, our discussion will be limited to the motion-picture studies of L. L. Thurstone. Indeed, but little other experimental work has been done in this field. For several years after 1929, in connection with the Payne Fund Studies of Motion Pictures and Youth, Prof. Thurstone gave attitudes tests to high-school students in Illinois communities and to children at the Mooseheart Home, before and after showing them selected motion pictures.[2] The problems of opinion change that were dealt with were the effects of single pictures, the cumulative effect of pictures and the persistence of effect. The tests used were attitude scales and paired-comparisons tests. The procedures and results follow:

1. An attitude scale on the Germans and on war was given to 133 high-school children of Genoa, Ill. Twelve days later the motion picture

---

[1] Quoted by Fülöp-Miller, R., *Leaders, Dreamers and Rebels*, p. 130, 1935.

[2] Peterson, R. C., and Thurstone, L. L., *Motion Pictures and the Social Attitudes of Children*, 1933; Thurstone, L. L., "The Measurement of Change in Social Attitude," *Jour. Soc. Psychol.*, 2: 230–241; "Influence of Motion Pictures on Children's Attitudes," *Jour. Soc. Psychol.*, 1: 291–304.

Four Sons, a picture sympathetic to the personal problems of a German family, was shown. The following day the students were retested. On a scale of 11 points the average attitude of the group before seeing the picture was 5.66, afterward 5.28, a change of opinion favorable to Germans in the amount of the difference, which is not large. The tests on war indicated a change from an average attitude of 5.19 to 5.10, a small change toward disapproval of war.

2. A number of pictures on gambling and on prohibition shown in several communities brought about practically no change in opinion; in one case the average on the scale was 6.96 before and 6.97 after seeing the picture. Likewise a picture on capital punishment, *The Valiant*, was shown without appreciable effect. A picture *The Criminal Code* shown to 276 students in Watseka and 246 in Galesburg brought about considerable change in attitude toward the punishment of criminals. Greater leniency was espoused with changes from 5.30 to 4.80, and from 5.13 to 4.64 in Galesburg.

3. Marked changes in expressions of opinion about racial groups were brought about by the showing of pictures. Two pictures, *Son of the Gods*, a romantic melodrama with a Chinese hero, and *Welcome Danger*, a picture so alien to Chinese interests that the Chinese ambassador had lodged a complaint against it, were shown, the first in Geneva, the other in West Chicago, Ill. The picture with the Chinese hero made the high-school students more favorable toward the Chinese on the average of 6.72 on the scale to 5.50, a very great change. The other brought about a slight (5.71 to 5.88) increase in antipathy. Although it is probably true that in general there is a greater willingness to make favorable rather than unfavorable changes, these results could not be cited in proof of that contention, as the pictures are in no way equated.

The most pronounced change in opinion on the race question was brought about by the picture *The Birth of a Nation*, which in its 1931 edition with sound accompaniment was exhibited to 434 high-school students in Crystal Lake, Ill. The change to attitudes unfavorable to Negroes was very pronounced, from an average on the scale of 7.41 to 5.93. The distribution of the results is indicated in Fig. 11.

4. The cumulative effect of pictures was tested at Mooseheart, where the pictorial experiences of the subjects could be controlled. About 750 children were divided into five groups, to which pictures were exhibited in various combinations. Some slight cumulative effect on opposition to war was noted when *All Quiet on the Western Front* and *Journey's End* were combined. These pictures differed greatly from one another in the potency of their appeal to children of these age groups, and the conclusions are not very satisfactory.

5. The persistence of effect was studied by retesting at intervals from 10 weeks to 19 months. The effects of the motion pictures were claimed to persist, although there was a general tendency to return part way to the position held before the picture was presented. The adequacy of this retesting might be questioned. Would not a number of other factors, including the subject's memory of how the previous test had been answered, be involved in a series of retests, in addition to the effect of the single picture?

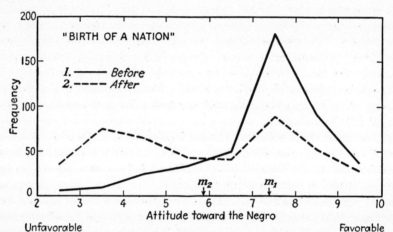

Fig. 11.—Crystal Lake High School, Crystal Lake, Ill. 434 children of grades 6–12 inclusive. (*From R. C. Peterson and L. L. Thurstone, Motion Pictures and Social Attitudes of Children, p. 37, 1933. Reproduced by permission of The Macmillan Company, publishers.*)

Mean$_1$ (before) = 7.41 P.E.M.$_1$ = .046 σ_1 = 1.4 r_{12} = .55
Mean$_2$ (after) = 5.93 P.E.M.$_2$ = .070 σ_2 = 2.2
$D_{M_1-M_2}$ = 1.48 P.E.$_D$ = .058 D/P.E.$_D$ = 25.5

INDIRECT EVIDENCE OF OPINION CHANGE

A number of quantitative studies of opinion change as reflected in statements of opinion in periodicals, in citizens' voting records, in straw votes as compared with elections, in the voting records of legislative bodies, in changing buying habits and in other behavior records have been made in the past few years. These sources have long been used as indicators of opinion, but only recently has there been any quantitative treatment. For some purposes such indirect evidence is superior to testing; but, as we have previously shown, forms of behavior other than that recorded on tests are by no means invariably superior indexes of attitude. Further, it must be very certain that the samples are adequate if they are to be used as a basis for generalization. This is very difficult to determine in any exact fashion. For example, in the most ambitious study of changing attitudes attempted by an American student, Hornell Hart counted the titles of the *Reader's Guide to Periodical Literature* from 1905 to 1932. The titles were classified by subjects, and the increase and decrease of discussion were thus noted. This was a most ingenious utilization of sources. But if, on this basis, one presumes to report on the changing social attitudes and interests for America during those years, one may well be questioned on the adequacy of the sample, as the author himself recognizes.[1] In addition, to what extent does magazine opinion express general social attitudes? What sections of the population are not thus represented? What geographic areas produce and read few periodicals? Printed opinion is but one kind of expression of opinion; others will be found in movies, books, speeches, radio, and other media. Do articles express the attitudes of readers? Even after classifying periodicals according to general circulation, does a mere counting of titles of articles therein provide an adequate sample? Do titles adequately reflect subject matter? Does the amount of discussion in periodical literature necessarily introduce or even herald change? Would not the proportion of articles pro and con be indicative of probable change in mass opinion? There is often a great deal of discussion about some spectacular issue which is not seriously defended by many people and upon which there is little likelihood of popular opinion change. Is it adequate to consider only the number of articles, when one article, because of the prestige of its author, the way it is written, and the like, may have ten times the readers and a hundred times the effectiveness of another article with the same title? These and other questions evidence the caution that must be exercised in generalizing from these results. The amount of discussion on the twoscore of topics classified in this study was expressed in terms of articles per thousand indexed by years. If we agree with the author's premise that discussion is most intense at two periods in the life of a social institution, when it is under construction and when it is being remodeled or demolished, we have here a rough sort of measure of opinion change from indirect evidence.

Some elaboration of this procedure appears in a later contribution of Prof. Hart.[2] In this study of opinion change about business prosperity, there was not only a mere counting of the number of articles dealing with this and allied topics, but also some qualitative analysis of statements made in the articles and of types of words used. For example, in support of the proposition "Economic conditions are good or sound," there were found in the huge-circulation magazines during 1929, 283 affirmative attitude indicators and only 63 negative, whereas during the first three

[1] Hart, H., "Changing Social Attitudes and Interests," in *Recent Social Trends*, Chap. 8, 1933.

[2] Hart, H., "Changing Opinions about Business Prosperity," *Am. Jour. Sociol.*, 38: 665–687.

months of 1932 there were 89 affirmative and 266 negative statements. This is not exact measurement, but it is counting, which gives a rough approximation of trends. There was also some counting of the optimistic and pessimistic words used in titles and headlines. Another comparison was made in contrasting the magazines of large circulation with the *Survey, New Republic, Nation* and *Christian Century* in the number of articles dealing with the "buy now," "anti-hoarding" and similar campaigns. There were fifteen times as many articles in the journals of mass circulation. The entire study covered the years 1929 through 1932, and, in addition to the mere counting of titles in the *Readers' Guide*, some analysis of content was attempted by the counting of statements made in the articles on some twenty-five propositions and topics. Throughout, there is a comparison of journals of mass circulation (a million or more) with the *Survey, Nation, New Republic* and *Christian Century*. The problems of size, of sample, the definition of units and the question of the extent to which the media of communication express the opinions of their readers must be carefully considered in studies of this type. However, with all the limitations, some gains result from supplanting impressionistic accounts with quantitative data. In many fields, quantitative analysis of certain aspects of the changing content of various media might be profitably attempted. For example, the journals, papers and other records of reform movements might be studied in this way; the changing content of certain sections of the newspaper might profitably be quantified; the output of various special interest groups might be dealt with in a more detailed and significant fashion with a closer definition of units than was possible with these journals of huge circulation. We have elsewhere indicated some of the possible uses of successive studies of content for recording opinion change.[1]

Voting registers expressions of opinion within the limited categories of "yes" and "no." Some quantitative studies of opinion change by analysis of votes have been made by political scientists during recent years. Of these, we may illustrate two types, (1) the comparison of voting records and (2) straw votes in comparison with voting records. Of the first, the votes compared on various issues may be those of a special group or of a general electorate. H. C. Beyle compared the votes of legislators for the 1927 session of the Minnesota State Senate, showing not only the changing expressions of opinion by individuals but also the various blocs with different degrees of similarity in voting record.[2] With his ingenious methods of analysis, the voting record of any small group may be examined to find significant cohesions of subgroups as indicated

[1] See Chap. XIX.
[2] Beyle, H. C., *Identification and Analysis of Attribute-Cluster-Blocs*, University of Chicago Press, 1931.

by the successive votes. C. H. Wooddy and S. A. Stouffer examined the evidence of some 14,000 elections in attempting to answer the question whether or not the opportunity for a community to decide a public issue by vote tends to stabilize public opinion on that issue.[1] Does changing opinion tend to change just so far and then become fixed, if public expression through voting must be given from time to time? Their data were taken from the election returns of Massachusetts communities, where for 40 years each town was required to vote annually on saloon licensing, and from counties in Arkansas and Michigan. Although the findings were inconclusive in some details, in general it appeared that there was a marked tendency to vote more decidedly wet or dry after some local option experience. Some crystallization of opinion apparently occurs when an issue must be met time after time. Although the conclusions of this single study are obviously inadequate for generalizations about the process of opinion change, it is this type of study that will lay the foundations for sound generalization.

Prophecies of voting and of opinion change have of late years increasingly been made on the basis of samples and straw votes. The statistician, taking samples at successive periods, noting the rate of change, making assumptions with regard to continued change and projecting his trends may prophesy the voting record.[2] W. F. Willcox, inspecting the records of the various states, concluded that there were sixteen in 1922 and thirty-seven in 1930 which were above the 50 per cent line and so would have probably cast a majority of wet votes. Projecting the changing sentiment of the other states, he concluded that the voters would be ready to vote for repeal in Iowa in March, 1931, Nebraska in October, 1931, and the like, to North Carolina, which would be ready in July, 1968. However, the dangers of simply projecting trends for any phenomenon that may be as swiftly changed as popular opinion must be apparent. There has not been much quantitative prophecy of this type.

Not only the data of successive voting records, but also samples such as the straw vote may be compared with the election returns in studying opinion change. C. E. Robinson has summarized American experience with straw votes.[3] Although popular interest in straw votes (and hence their significance in changing the very thing they are sampling in order to predict) has been aroused only during the past decade, there have been polls of this sort for forty years. First started by the newspapers,

[1] Wooddy, C. H., and Stouffer, S. A., "Local Option and Public Opinion," *Am. Jour. Sociol.*, 36: 175–205.

[2] Willcox, W. F., "An Attempt to Measure Public Opinion about Repealing the 18th Amendment," *Jour. Am. Stat. Assoc.*, 26: 243–261.

[3] Robinson, C. E., *Straw Votes*, Columbia University Press, 1932.

they have been taken up by commercial organizations (the Rexall drug store presidential poll of 1920) and have been most significantly and extensively developed by periodicals, especially the *Literary Digest.* The sponsors gain in publicity, advertising, circulation and reader interest. The voting may be on ballots in the paper or periodical, by personal canvass or by mailed ballots. The mailing lists of the *Literary Digest* were compiled from telephone directories and automobile-registration files. Its circularization list contained over twenty million names. In the polls on candidates for the years 1916, 1920, 1924 and 1928, the *Literary Digest* polls showed an average plurality error of 20, 21, 12 and 12 per cent.[1] Other straw votes have erred from that of the Hearst newspapers in 1928 with 5 per cent of average plurality error for states to that of the *Farm Journal* with 17 per cent error in the same election. The principal causes of straw-poll error, according to Robinson, are (1) manipulation, dishonest count for popular effect on voting, (2) stuffing the ballot box, (3) geographical bias, (4) class bias, disproportionate representation of one economic or social class, (5) voting in straw poll but failure to vote in official election, (6) an insufficient number of straw ballots, (7) change of opinion during time between straw ballot and election.[2]

Not only changing opinion on candidates but also popular opinion on issues has been tested by straw votes. Of these, the *Literary Digest* polls of 1922, 1930 and 1932 on prohibition are the most extensive, and the Gallup polls have dealt with the larger number of issues. In 1922, ballots were mailed to eight million telephone owners, in 1930 to twenty million automobile and telephone owners (five million votes returned) and in 1932 to about the same number. Numerous as were the ballots of these *Literary Digest* polls, certain errors in sampling have frequently been charged. They are: (1) that the rural sample is inadequate (charge probably unfounded); (2) class bias, that the mailing list based on telephones and automobiles does not reach certain sections of the working class (true); (3) that the poll did not adequately reach women, who vote drier than the men (contention sound); (4) that the returns were distorted because the dry leaders counseled their following not to vote (in part true).[3] The difficulties of management and the problems of adequate sampling persistently distort these straw votes for measuring opinion change. They can be fairly accurate, but it is questionable whether it would pay any sponsor to exercise the care in management necessary to assure reliability.

The preelection polls of 1936 provide the most extensive data on the possible accuracy and the relative reliability of present methods used in

---

[1] *Ibid.,* p. 72.
[2] *Ibid.,* p. 78.
[3] *Ibid.,* pp. 147 *ff.*

straw votes. The week before the election the predictions of the most widely publicized polls were:

Polls	Percentage of major party vote[1]	
	Roosevelt	Landon
Literary Digest............................	42.6	57.4
American Institute of Public Opinion.........	54	46
Fortune....................................	74	26
Crossley Survey............................	52	48
Baltimore Sun..............................	64	36
Farm Journal..............................	43	57
"Grass roots"...............................	39.5	60.5

[1] Cantril, H., "Straw Votes This Year Show Contrary Minds," *New York Times*, Oct. 25, 1936.

In the election the Roosevelt vote was 60.2 per cent of the major party vote. When the predictions of electoral, rather than popular, vote are considered, the polls are seen to have diverged even further from the election results. The *Literary Digest* prophesied a Landon victory with 370 electoral votes. In the election Roosevelt won 523 out of a possible 531 votes.

Why were the polls so inaccurate? Why did they differ so greatly from one another? The election indicated that there is still much to be learned about sampling techniques. In the preelection controversy over method, one group relied on a large sample, other groups on selected samples. All the polls were conducted by mailed ballots, personal interviews or combinations of the two. The *Literary Digest* mailed 10,000,-000 ballots; had 2,158,789 returned. The American Institute of Public Opinion (Gallup) uses a combination of mailed ballots and interviews with a sample never exceeding 300,000, and usually much less than that. The *Fortune* poll was based on about 3000 interviews, and the relative accuracy of their prediction must have been based on chance, as such a small sample could not possibly include the various groups in the United States. The Crossley Survey, published by Hearst, used about 30,000 interviews. The *Baltimore Sun* circularized the registered voters of Maryland, sending out 771,000 ballots and having less than 300,000 returned. The *Farm Journal* made a house-to-house canvass of farmers in thirty states. The "grass-roots" poll was conducted by ballots printed in country newspapers. None of the results were so accurate as their sponsors had hoped and predicted. However, the relatively greater accuracy of the Gallup and Crossley polls indicates the superiority of selective sampling over mass ballots by mail. But the various methods and sampling techniques would differ in their accuracy on different elections, as the voting public is of different composition in each election. Of the 75,000,000 potential voters in the United States, about 60 per cent voted in the fiercely contested 1936 election. And the same 60 per cent would not vote in the next election. Therefore, a poll is a sample of a sample, and the methods of collecting the poll sample will be determined somewhat by the composition of the general election sample. A. M. Crossley concludes as to the sample that:

1. It must be flexible. Its basis must not be an outdated mailing list. It must be so designed that it can be adjusted readily if new information, such as registration figures, becomes available during its course. As a part of its flexibility, it must reveal enough about the individual voter and about individual cities and towns, economic groups, etc., to permit adjustment where needed.

2. A fairly small sample will work properly in all but close states.

3. The distribution of the sample is of paramount importance.

4. It should be not cumulative, but repeated in similar cross sections at intervals to show trends.

On all these counts the *Literary Digest* method is outmoded.[1]

Since the election the polls have been denounced in many editorials and articles and in the comments of public officials. Some oppose the polls as useless and inaccurate. Others consider the revelation of public opinion at frequent intervals and on many topics as dangerous to our form of government, claiming that legislators, if convinced of the accuracy of polls, would be all too apt to heed the results from week to week. Again, straw votes are condemned by those who are convinced that publication of results draws voters to the winning side in "bandwagon" fashion. The polls have also been viewed with suspicion as potential agencies of conscious propaganda. The nature of the polling procedure is such that either simple issues or greatly simplified issues provide the best subject matter. It is charged that sustained popular interest in the polls would result in directing attention toward the simple but not necessarily the most important issues. If we grant the possibility of a much more accurate sampling technique so that the polls more adequately reflect popular impressions, the attitude of various types of societal leaders toward frequent polling will be based upon their special interests and more fundamentally upon the attitudes of various groups of leaders toward a larger or lesser incorporation of popular opinions in legislative and executive decision.

Even though an accurate sample were taken by straw ballot about any issue or candidate, the position of the voting public might change before election. With the popularity of these polls and the widespread

[1] See Crossley, A. M., "Straw Polls in 1936," *Pub. Opin. Quar.*, 1: 27.

publicity given to the results, such polls themselves become a factor in opinion change. The shift of opinion to majority opinion has been experimentally demonstrated in a few attitude studies of student subjects. It is probably a general principle wherever majority opinion is known. The possibilities of the use of successive straw polls on the same subject to indicate changing opinion have not been explored. In this case, with identical methods, the polls could be made fairly nearly alike and the results then compared. However, successive voting records become meaningful and useful for prediction, only in so far as there is some understanding of the changing attitudes behind these shifts in opinion. And these are not apprehended by a mere examination of the counted results of yes-no polls. If one is to be a prophet, the intervening stimuli that have affected an opinion change must be known as well as the composition of the attitudes of those who have not as yet shifted opinion, at least not so far as to reverse their votes. And straw polls limited to yes-no responses will not provide this information.

Politicians, reporters, publicity men and commentators on world affairs work out informal, usually nonquantitative devices for testing opinion change. Prognostication based thereon may be far from an exact science, but it is often amazingly accurate. Walter Lippmann recently states:

Newspaper men develop devices of various sorts by which they test opinion. Many of them sound absurd when described in cold print. For example, a political writer once told me that he used to take the pulse of Woodrow Wilson's emotional attitude by watching how often the word "very" appeared in a speech of Mr. Wilson's. He had found that when Mr. Wilson was least sure of himself, he put a very in front of all his adjectives and generally doubled his adjectives as well; that, said my friend, was Mr. Wilson's way of whistling when he had to pass a cemetery at night. Another Washington observer used to look to see how long Mr. Hoover's sentences were and particularly how many dependent clauses were hanging onto their coat-tails. On days when Mr. Hoover was unusually complicated, this newspaper man would shake his head and say: "The President has certainly been worrying over that." My own particular method of guessing at the state of confidence among those who in the chief centers of population strike the key-notes of feeling among business men is a gadget that I am almost ashamed to acknowledge. It is the stock market average of industrial securities.[1]

The experimental study of opinion record and opinion change has just begun. Most of its fundamental problems are as yet unsolved. To what extent may the results of present opinion tests be trusted? Under what conditions will the subject sincerely express his real opinion?

[1] Lippmann, W., syndicated article in *Today and Tomorrow* column, May 5, 1935. Quoted by permission of New York Tribune, Inc.

How is it possible to differentiate between such opinions and conventional responses? On what subjects will conventional responses be most likely in various kinds of publics? Will there be a consistency between opinion expression and other forms of overt behavior? Has the subject had an opinion before the test, or was his response induced by the test? Has he been conscious of the attitudes underlying his opinions? Will the same opinion be expressed at another time under similar circumstances? May the processes of opinion change be considered with any measure of detachment as processes, or will the variation with different subject matter be so great as to prevent the development of social science in this field? There are many fundamental problems of method here.

Limited attempts to answer a few of these questions have been made. T. F. Lentz retested with the same set of questions one month after giving his test and recorded the changes in statement of opinion.[1] Two hundred statements were given to fifty-seven students in each case. Changes in opinion occurred in 19.6 per cent of possible cases; 44 per cent of these changes were from agreement to disagreement, 50 per cent from disagreement to agreement. However, considering the entire group, 81 per cent of the changes neutralized one another, leaving only 19 per cent of the total number of changes as the difference between the first and second test. This resulted in a correlation of .94 between the total results of the first and the second test. Of course, as this second test was given a month after the first, it cannot be assumed that the changes which did occur were due to momentary impulse and lack of opinion on the questions. A certain amount of change of opinion due to the intervening influences may have occurred. The results of this test are by no means conclusive, the number of subjects was small and variability in response would certainly vary with subject matter. However, the author has raised a very important question which should be intensively investigated.

The tendency to answer affirmatively rather than negatively should also be studied. M. F. Fritz conducted an investigation that indirectly bears upon this problem.[2] In nineteen true-false examinations in which 211 statements were true and 209 were false a total of 3065 errors were made of which 64 per cent were "true" answers (incorrect) and 36 per cent were "false" answers. The margin of 28 per cent between the two indicated an unmistakable tendency to give "true" reactions rather than "false." Further, this tendency to give "true" responses was about the same, regardless of whether class materials on which the students had been instructed or statements on which they had not been informed, were used. This seems to indicate a tendency to answer affirmatively. Other

[1] Lentz, T. F., "Reliability of Opinionaire Technique Studied Intensively by Retest Method," *Jour. Soc. Psychol.*, 5: 338–364.

[2] Fritz, M. F., "Guessing in a True-false Test," *Jour. Ed. Psychol.*, 18: 558.

evidence likewise verifies these results. It is likely that opinion tests would show a similar tendency.

To what extent does the knowledge of majority opinion influence responses to tests? D. Wheeler and H. Jordan gave a questionnaire of fifty questions on campus affairs and political and economic issues.[1] A week later the same questionnaire was given once more to get chance changes in opinion. Then the answers to both tests were tabulated, and those which showed a two-thirds majority of either yes or no answers were selected to be given once more. Twenty-seven questions had such a majority. Given the statements the third time, the subjects were informed indirectly of the previous results, but were not given the impression that they were expected to let this influence their opinions. The results of the third test showed that group opinion facilitates the agreeing of individual opinions to an extent of about three times chance when the majority answers to the statements are "yes," and about one-half chance when the majority answers are "no." There did not appear to be any significant differences according to subject matter of the questions. These data likewise augment the evidence on the problem considered in M. F. Fritz's study.

Evidence on these problems could be gleaned not only from test material but also from case studies of opinion change, especially if the cases were handled quantitatively in so far as possible. A recent volume on race attitudes in children contains materials that might be thus treated.[2] The case studies provide more detailed responses which make possible a more sympathetic understanding of the processes of opinion change.

Experimental literature has touched on but few points and has dealt with limited subject matter. Its reliability and validity are often questionable. The tests have frequently created wholly abnormal and unusual conditions. The subjects tested have been a limited group, most often those in educational institutions. Faulty though the procedures are, they must be refined and increasingly used in the future. The variety of human interactivity and of the opinion process has become too great for adequate synthesis and generalization otherwise. The results of experimental procedures must provide suggestions for the synthesizer and interpreter. From these studies of behavior he must assume human attitudes and be able to enter into sympathetic observation of individuals as members of groups. These processes cannot be disjointed. There is no choice. All of the process must be comprehended.

[1] Wheeler, D., and Jordan, H., "Changes of Individual Opinion to Accord with Group Opinion," *Jour. Abn. Soc. Psychol.*, 24: 203–215. See also Jennes, A., "Social Influences in the Change of Opinion," *Jour. Abn. Soc. Psychol.*, 27: 29–34.

[2] Lasker, B., *Race Attitudes in Children*, pp. 261–385, 1931.

CHAPTER XIV

CENSORSHIP

"Faith must be persuaded to men, and not imposed upon them."[1]
"Yet it would be better that they were coerced by the sword of that
magistrate that beareth not the sword in vain than that they should be
suffered to bring many others into their own error."[1]

Not only the churchman quoted above but innumerable men of good
will during the past several centuries have found themselves torn between
a liberal disposition and the urgency of propagandizing a special cause.
In the art of persuasion it is especially difficult to realize that the end
does not justify the sacrifice of an abstractly liberal stand. Yet freedom
from censorship has become increasingly important during the past two
centuries as the agencies of mass communication have increased and
diffused. The struggle for the control of these media assumed epic
proportions. In heroic deeds and nobly liberal utterances, outstanding
leaders have defied authoritarian restriction. Today a liberal, freedom-
granting, democratic way of life stands in stark contrast to a now widely
diffused authoritarian, censoring, propagandizing rule. These modern
authoritarian states are not new in principle. They are historically the
rule. They are newly equipped with elaborate techniques of mass
impression and restriction. But it is not simply a struggle of ideological
contrasts. Few social processes are so simply particularistic. The
complex of ideas, psychological attitudes, culture forms and economic
and objective patterns are, as usual, in intricate interrelation. However,
the history of the ideas is a basic element, and we cannot proceed to a
discussion of the conflict between censorship and freedom of communication until we have briefly traced the rise of the ideas of liberty and
liberalism in modern thought.

The essential idea of that concept which, since the eighteenth century,
has been designated as "liberalism" is the free play of intelligence out of
which man may by rational consent subscribe to the organization and
institutions of society. The idea had appeared in the ancient philosophies, but it was not until the excessive autocracies of the seventeenth
century had awakened in many groups a popular demand for liberty that
the social philosophy of liberalism emerged. Laski relates its appearance
to the overthrow of the medieval papacy and the resulting widespread

[1] St. Bernard.

spirit of inquiry; to the development of a secular temper replacing spiritual with social values; to the widening of the physical world by geographic discovery and the accompanying enlarged data on primitive cultures; to the growth of scientific knowledge which challenged the accepted religious verities; to the accompanying philosophical systems which incorporated the experimental method.[1] In the field of political and economic power a large middle class was arising, increasingly cramped by the authoritarian concepts of church and state. Beliefs and the social realities were in rapid transition. Philosophers with new frameworks of definitions were awaited. The essential concepts came from England, where peaceful conditions and political history were more favorable to the development of liberal philosophy than in the war-torn and centralized states of the Continent. Locke (1632–1704) pronounced the basis of government to be in the consent of the people. Political organization existed for the individual good. Man has natural rights to life, liberty and property. The social contract of free men provides the area within which political institutions may operate. Moreover, theocratic government can claim no political validity. Reason was enthroned as innately characteristic of man. Locke's liberalism also defended the individual's right to property, safe from the confiscatory aggressions of the state.[2] His influence was enormous. The liberal temper of Locke's generation was canalized by his concepts. He became the "gospel of the Protestants," the progenitor of Rousseau, and in his insistence on the consent of the governed was significant in the American and French Revolutions.

This early liberalism, preoccupied essentially with political processes, was modified by the course of the economic history of the eighteenth century to relate primarily to freedom in production and exchange. Industrial and commercial expansion centered attention upon the role of the state in these fields. In England, Adam Smith (1723–1790) pronounced the economic activities of man an outgrowth of natural law and state interference an invasion of individual liberty. In France, the Physiocrats, surveying an agrarian society, likewise protested governmental interference. The economists propounded a laissez-faire liberalism. Jeremy Bentham (1748–1832) denounced the existing legal restrictions upon industrial expansion as an unwarranted interference with individual happiness and the sum of happiness to be enjoyed by the greatest possible number. A growing and powerful class of industrial leaders espoused this economic liberalism which coincided with their interests. Bentham brushed aside the earlier concepts of natural rights and substituted a liberalism based upon the rights of individual welfare.

[1] Laski, H. J., "The Rise of Liberalism," *Ency. Soc. Sci.*, 1: 104–106.
[2] Dewey, J., *Liberalism and Social Action*, pp. 6 *ff.*, 1935.

However, as applied in the economic field such liberalism led increasingly to widespread misery. The economic disadvantage of increasing numbers in the population became apparent. During the nineteenth century the humanitarians, religionists and romanticists modified laissez-faire liberalism by advocating state interference through welfare legislation in the interest of the dispossessed, the exploited and the depressed workers. Liberalism was given a new definition, but it was also diluted into schools. Although modern liberals are in general committed to state interference in the interests of individual liberty, they never agree on the extent of state activity. Liberals have therefore had to undergo the snubs of the conservatives, the execrations of socialists and communists and the taunts of dictators.[1] Liberals have usually been at a disadvantage in periods of crisis. Those who cherish freedom of opinion fear the excesses of heated controversy and hesitate to assume either of the extreme positions on great and complicated issues.

The development of various types of modern liberalism has given rise to the extended and thorough philosophic discussion of the nature of individual freedom and liberty and of authority and restraint. Although the Stoics had emphasized self-realization, and under early Christianity the disinherited were appealed to in terms of the dignity of the individual personality, the development of the organized church provided an institutional rather than individual concept of liberty for many centuries. Liberty was interpreted as freedom of the church institution from state control.[2] After the Reformation, from the sixteenth century onward the various aspects of individual liberty became a preoccupation of the theorist. By the eighteenth century, freedom and liberty conceived as "natural rights" had become emotionally charged words to arouse masses of revolutionaries, and in the nineteenth century they were applied to ever increasing fields of human relationships. "Freedom is a new religion, the religion of our time," said Heine, and Byron wrote, "I desire men to be free, as much from mobs as kings, from you as me."

It is apparent from the foregoing discussion that liberty and freedom have been variously conceived at different times during the past four centuries. Liberty in the abstract is of concern only to the metaphysician; but for liberty in the realm of politics, religion, the other institutional structures and the media of communication, speech and the press, large groups of men have been willing to sacrifice and to fight. But the particular content of liberty will always be changing with the conditions of time and place. The sphere of action in which freedom is demanded will depend upon the area of behavior in which men feel momentarily

---

[1] European liberalism has had a thorough and incisive historian in De Ruggiero, G., *The History of European Liberalism*, 1927.

[2] Laski, H. J., "Liberty," *Ency. Soc. Sci.*, 9: 444.

most fettered. Cooley has noted, "Every person at every stage of his growth is free or unfree in proportion as he does or does not find himself in the midst of conditions conducive to full and harmonious personal development."[1] Thwarted at various points, masses of men have redefined freedom and partially achieved it, often by means of violence. The history of liberty is the record of changing objectives. Once achieved, a particular form of liberty may then be partly restricted by laws, by judicial procedure, by the encroachments of administrative authority and by popular apathy. It has often been noted that freedom degenerates unless it has to struggle in its own defense. In the modern authoritarian states, political freedom has been sacrificed in part in the hope of enhanced economic security. It is said in defense of the Fascist state that the people are "enjoying the liberty of feeling themselves members, part and parcel, of a powerful, organic state, which is ruled for the welfare of everybody and not in the interests of a chosen few, a state which has social justice within and international prestige without its borders."[2] Such a conception is entirely alien to the tradition of political liberty as freedom of thought and expression, of education, of worship, of work, of association and assembly and of the right to change the party in power by means of elections. Although freedom may have many aspects, showing first one facet and then another, such authoritarian organization violates its very essence.

Like all popular concepts, liberty and freedom have been stereotyped in phrases, slogans and popular catchwords. These do not keep pace with the changing concept, and the slogans of an earlier day may be used to confound the advocate of the essence of freedom. When Locke pronounced the right of private property relatively free from state aggression as the basis of freedom, he did so in terms of the economic and political organization of the seventeenth century. The property aspect was emphasized more and more until Blackstone could declare, "So great is the regard of the law for private property, that it will not authorize the least violation of it; no, not even for the general good of the whole community."[3] But, to treat property ownership as sacred in an economic order of progressively limited ownership is a restriction upon other liberties, in so far as it limits the life activities of many people. In reference to the "have-nots," Justice Holmes' remark that "the necessitous man is not free" is often quoted. But rights of property are expressed not only in the web of legal definitions but also in popular phrases accumulated during the past two centuries. Thus great corporations cry for protection from the "tyranny" of governments, and chains

---

[1] Cooley, C. H., *Human Nature and the Social Order*, p. 424, 1902.
[2] Pei, M. A., "Freedom under Fascism," *Ann. Am. Acad. Pol. Soc. Sci.*, 180: 13.
[3] Quoted by Smith, T. V., *The Promise of American Politics*, p. 51, 1935.

of newspapers—the content of which could by no stretch of the imagination be said to be determined by those who actually write them—cry for "freedom of the press."[1] Psychological obfuscation not only of publics but also frequently of the experts permits such perversion.

The achievement of individual liberty in any field is dependent upon freedom of thought and discussion. Freedom of assembly, speech, writing and all the forms of communication underlies individual liberty. Censorship is the restriction of the content of any means of communication. Such restriction defends some special interest usually incapable of defending itself under free discussion. Freedom of expression is never completely won. The beginnings of general public discussion in the Reformation were not immediately followed by the development of a principle of free discussion. The early Protestant church leaders eagerly censored their opponents when the opportunity to do so was presented. The passion for freedom of thought and discussion increased through the sixteenth and seventeenth centuries, being gradually extended among the theologians, philosophers, literary leaders, artists and scientists. Reason was increasingly taken as a guide of life. Leaders issued finesounding pronouncements on the principle of freedom of expression. Voltaire wrote, "Though I disagree with every word you say, I will defend with my life your right to say it." With the coming of the eighteenth century, the principle of free discussion permeated the upper and middle classes, although it was by no means universally accepted. At the close of the century, Thomas Jefferson wrote, "I have sworn upon the altar of the living God eternal hostility against every form of tyranny over the mind of man." But along with this powerful current of advocacy of free thought and free expression there were and are many forms of censorship, both informal and formal. There are the projections of popular prejudices and mass standards and the organized censorship of church and state, legally imposed. The battle has been fought successively about each of the forms of communication from speech to the latest outbursts of popular censorship of motion pictures. To the nature of censorship, its forms, its history, its advocates and its applications we will now turn our attention.

CENSORSHIP

Censorship is the process of deleting or limiting the content of any of the media of communication. Although the process has become more organized and consciously applied during the past four centuries, it has existed as an informal control in all societies. The term "censorship"

[1] Liberty defined primarily as freedom to manage property without interference is discussed in Hoover, H., *The Challenge to Liberty*, 1935, and Lippmann, W., *The Method of Freedom*, 1935.

comes from the Romans. In the fifth century B.C., the Roman Senate appointed two magistrates called "censors." Among the duties of the censors were the recording of a census of persons and the overseeing of their morals and manners, clothing, food and public and private behavior. The censors could, within limits, set standards in these fields and enforce their decrees by fines and other punishments. Modern censorship is preoccupied with the regulation of the transfer of ideas. This censorship policy arose with the popularization of the means of communication, especially the development of printing in the fifteenth century. Established power then faced new problems and sought protection by attempting to limit the spread of ideas. Authority, desiring unanimity of thought as well as of action within the province of its special interests, limits the "bad" ideas, apparently believing with the poet, that

> Vice is a monster of so frightful mien
> As to be hated needs but to be seen;
> Yet seen too oft, familiar with her face,
> We first endure, then pity, then embrace.

And so, from the first church regulation of printing in 1501 to the latest regulation by an authoritarian state, there are centuries of intermittent but often intensive censorship. In an Associated Press report from Germany during 1934, one read, "Five persons were sentenced to prison today for listening to Soviet broadcasts from the Moscow radio station. Sentences of one to two years were imposed because they tuned in while news about Germany was being broadcast by communists. . . . " Authority assumes the correctness of its position. As John Fiske declared, "The persecuting spirit has its origin morally in the disposition of man to domineer over his fellow creatures, intellectually, in the assumption that one's own opinions are infallibly correct."

Assumptions of infallibility in the institutional definitions of church and state provided the defense of early censorship. And classic liberalism, in opposition to these assumptions, took its stand against censorship and defined freedom as "freedom from" these restrictions. The concept of "freedom for" individual and group development did not develop until the nineteenth century. Such freedom may require restriction in the individual or group interest. Defense of censorship on that basis has not yet been definitively stated by English and American scholars.

Censorship of communication and also of mental content is applied, not only by authoritarian restrictions, but also in the individual's mental processes. Of late years this has been described in psychologically sophisticated terms, especially by the psychoanalyst. Freud developed the idea of a censorship of thought whereby the dominant consciousness limited the admission of certain materials to conscious attention. In individual development, standards and values are learned from the general culture and also developed in ways that are individually unique. These standards, existing in the conscious mind, reject alien and dangerous subjects. This process may be so complete that the dominant conscious does not recognize the entrance of these alien words, impressions, and ideas. But they exist in the preconscious or unconscious. In psychoanalytic literature, this material is assumed to lie in wait for a favorable opportunity to emerge, usually in symbolical form in slips of the tongue, puns, jokes, humor, mispronunciations, daydreams and dreams. The psychoanalyst sleuths through these symbols. He overemphasizes the frequency and amount of such materials. However, this limitation of the mental life may be verified by introspective analysis. It has never been adequately explained in neurological terms.

In everyday experience such censorship is important. A newspaper reporter, having absorbed the standards of his employer and editor, limits his observation to what he should see, writes what he should write and after a time may be quite unaware of his limitations of observation and record.[1] The materials that are contrary to the individual's values may be labeled, whereupon refusal to attend to them is even more simply canalized. "Labelling ideas, images and attitudes as evil, as immoral, as unpatriotic, is usually an effective method of stopping the development of such notions and attitudes. All forms of social taboos are designed to do just this. They furnish the individual with guide posts in his associative thinking which keep him within the boundaries set by the moral codes. The ideas, images or attitudes with which the new ideas conflict are sacred. They are right. They are proper. Therefore, persons having the same social and cultural heritage may develop a consensus of opinion that the divergent ideas or attitudes ought to be stopped."[2] Informal censorship is applied in the individual mental process, both in the case of restrictions of which he is not conscious and of limitations consciously applied.

The values, standards and ideas that are incorporated in the individual's attitudes are, for the most part, products of the culture in which he is involved. Shifting values determine the objects of censorship. When man's attention is turned to religion, heterodoxy and blasphemy are censored; the state represses treason; an ascendant industrial order attempts to restrict radical utterances; puritanical publics forbid verbalization of sexual processes; the Jones family does not mention the disgraced Uncle John. Folk values are imposed on discourse. V. Randolph writes of the Ozark hillman:

[1] Seldes, G., *Freedom of the Press*, p. 350, 1935.

[2] Young, K., *Social Psychology*, p. 636, 1930. Quoted by permission of F. S. Crofts & Co., Inc.

Sex is rarely mentioned save in ribaldry and is therefore excluded from all polite conversation between men and women. . . . In general it may be said that the names of male animals must not be mentioned when women are present. . . . Such words as bull, boar, buck, ram, jack and stallion are absolutely taboo. . . . The Ozarkers usually say male, cow-critter or cow-brute, . . . It was only a few years ago that two women in Scott County, Arkansas, raised a great clamor for the arrest of a man who mentioned a bull-calf in their presence. . . . A preacher recently told his flock that Pharaoh's daughter found the infant Moses in the flags, the poor man didn't like to say bull-rushes.[1]

This informal censorship in the interests of the folk values is pervasive and insidious. It is usually far more effective than the formal censorship of a ruler or hierarchy. Their tyranny is seldom crushingly effective or persistent. But the mores may restrict the areas of discussion during long periods.

Censorship is a conflict process. Any particular censorship is rapidly incorporated in the emotional responses of the individual combatants. Although ostensibly in the public interest, the actual objectives of the censor are all too often a punitive retribution upon stubborn minorities, and resistance to censorship becomes a holy cause. The tactics frequently become more and more extreme as the conflict progresses, for, as Heywood Broun said of Anthony Comstock, "a man who fights for the safety of his immortal soul can hardly be expected to live up to the best Queensberry traditions in the clinches."[2]

The avowed objectives of censorship are the protection of incapable and incompetent groups from the harmful stimulus. The church members, the citizens, the newspaper readers, the females, the immature youth, the alien and other groups should, according to authority, be shielded from the sacrilegious, the seditious, the immoral or the unaesthetic. Authority propounds the political, the economic or the ethical equivalent of the theological notion of the weakness and depravity of man from which he must be saved by stern ordering and forbidding. We shall consider briefly the application of censorship to various media of communication.

THE CHURCH AND CENSORSHIP

Any institutional structure is erected upon certain fundamental premises which must be unquestionably accepted by most of its adherents. Otherwise the institutional forms, structure or very existence is threatened. This is obviously true of formal church organizations. Fundamental premises, if undiscussed and undiscussible, may thus be the more

[1] Randolph, V., *The Ozarks*, p. 78, 1931. Quoted by permission of Vanguard Press, Inc.

[2] Broun, H., and Leech, M., *Anthony Comstock*, p. 265, 1927.

impregnably ensconced in an enveloping blanket of silence than behind a barricade of reasons and rationalizations. In the authoritarian tradition this has usually been thought to be true. The High-churchman censors and is silent, the dictator does not permit comparative discussion, the autocratic boss pocket-vetoes the underling's suggestion without comment. Whereas the insurgent sect, the outsider, the rebel and the liberal desire discussion during the period of the insurgency, perhaps believing with Tertullian that "when a thing is hidden away with so much pains, merely to reveal it is to destroy it."

Many religious groups have attempted informal and formal censorship but the church of Rome in its long experience has instituted the most formal restrictive measures. The *Index Librorum Prohibitorum*, developed since the invention of printing, is the modern expression of authoritarian selection of the limits of reading and comparative thought. It is a list of books that communicants must not read. Exceptions are readily made in the case of scholars, theologians and other trained students who, in good faith, desire to examine the prohibited works. The local bishop may grant such exceptions. Although there has been less formal organization of restriction of communication among other religious groups, the spirit of the censor is ever abroad. In America, the Christian Scientists have organized an extensive and sometimes effective censorship. Whenever Protestant groups have developed very extensive organization with central authority, the clamor for censorship has arisen intermittently. A century ago a Protestant writer in England, opposing the rising demand for censorship, declared, "Let Protestants be consistent, let them be Protestants indeed; let them revere in act as well as in word the sufficiency of the Holy Scripture; let there be no Protestant Index of prohibited books; let there be no shackles and cramps for the human mind."[1] Recently a Baptist leader drew loud cheers and applause from his audience by asserting that the Baptists have never persecuted those who differed with them or attempted to limit their freedom of expression. When the cheers had subsided, he drily added that they had never had a chance. Early Protestant churchmen zealously applied themselves to censorship and to the burning of books, although they lacked the system and organization of the Roman Catholic church. Savonarola enveloped Florence in a system of espionage. His child police visited homes, confiscating prohibited books and pictures as well as personal adornments which they carried off to the burnings. A few decades later Calvin, with even greater distrust of the capacities of man to resist the snares of the devil, organized in Geneva a rigid discipline by secular legislation. Catholic books of worship and song were confiscated and burned. Houses and shops were searched for all heretical books.

[1] "Index Librorum Prohibitorum," *British Quar.*, 14: 133–156 (1851).

In 1539 the magistrates decreed that all books must be examined and licensed before they could be printed. Considerable organization of censorship developed. Calvin's organization for suppression was carefully studied by representatives from England and Scotland, and similar restrictions were later applied in Great Britain. In the revulsion against Rome, art objects, images, pictures, monuments and books were burned and their production censored.[1] It is difficult today to appreciate the fear and horror of the Roman Catholic church that came to prevail in England and Scotland.

The longest and most consistent record of censorship is that of the Roman Catholic church. Isolated historical incidents, such as the burning of the works of the Greek philosopher Anaxagoras (450 B.C.) because of their impious implications, or the destruction of works on magic during the later Roman Empire, preceded organized censorship by the church. The church early forbade the reading of pagan and heretical books and, from the first centuries of the Christian church through the Middle Ages, condemned, burned and censored the production of many works. In the fifteenth century the invention of printing revolutionized the processes of communication.[2] At first the rulers of the church welcomed printing as a valuable instrument for the spread of sound doctrine and supported a number of the early presses. The use of the presses in the pamphleteering activities of the leaders of the Reformation aroused the churchmen to the potential perils of printing to the authority of the church and the uncorrupted purity of the minds of communicants. If the incapables were to be protected against the new heresies, some system would have to be devised whereby the printing press could be supervised and controlled. Before the end of the fifteenth century, the University of Cologne was examining and censoring every book before printing.[3] Pope Sextus IV congratulated the university. In 1501 Alexander VI extended this practice by forbidding printers, under pain of excommunication, to print any book without permission of their bishops. General prohibition of books by title was started in 1520 when Leo X condemned all the writings of Martin Luther. Lists of prohibited books were then published by bishops, by the universities and by inquisitors. In this chaotic situation, Paul IV ordered the Congregation of the Holy Office to make a catalogue of prohibited books. In 1559 the first *Index Librorum* appeared. Its lists of condemned books were divided into three categories: (1) heretical works, (2) works on magic and immo-

[1] Gillett, C. R., *Burned Books*, 2 vols., 1932.
[2] See Chap. III.
[3] Putnam, G. H., *The Censorship of the Church of Rome*, 2 vols., 1906, is the most extensive and available work in English on church censorship; see also Bondinhon, A., "Index," *Ency. Religion and Ethics*, vol. XVII, pp. 207–209.

rality, (3) books generally unwholesome in doctrine, usually anonymous. In 1588 a Congregation of Cardinals and consultants was established, and this organization has continued to the present day and has been responsible for the successive *Indexes* in their various editions.[1] Preoccupation with the struggle with Protestantism determined the content of the early *Indexes*. Although the editions of the past century have increasingly stressed moral rather than theological problems and thousands of the earlier prohibited items have been eliminated, it has been estimated that 90 per cent of the condemned works in the 1930 edition deal with theology, dogma, ritual or history of the church. The eleven classes of works on the *Index* are:

1. All books which propound or defend heresy or schism, or which of set purpose attack religion or morality, or endeavour to destroy the foundations of religion or morality.

2. Books which impugn or ridicule Catholic dogma or Catholic worship, the hierarchy, the clerical or religious state, or which tend to undermine ecclesiastical discipline, or which defend errors rejected by the Apostolic See.

3. Books which declare duelling, suicide, divorce lawful, or which represent Freemasonry and similar organizations as useful and not dangerous to the Church and to Civil society.

4. Books which teach or recommend superstition, fortune-telling, sorcery, spiritism, or other like practices (*e.g.*, Christian Science).

5. Books which professedly treat of, narrate, or teach, lewdness and obscenity.

6. Editions of the liturgical books of the Church which do not agree in all details with the authentic editions.

7. Books and booklets which publish new apparitions, revelations, visions, prophecies, miracles, etc., concerning which the canonical regulations have not been observed. (This practically means that such books and booklets are forbidden if they appear without the bishop's approbation. . . . Newspapers, weeklies, etc., are not prevented by this rule from relating uncommon happenings. They should, however, be careful not to make such events appear as undoubtedly supernatural, before the Church has taken a stand.)

8. All editions of the Bible or parts of it, as well as all biblical commentaries, in any language, which do not show the approbation of the bishop or some higher ecclesiastical authority.

9. Translations which retain the objectionable character of the forbidden original.

10. Pictures of Our Lord, the Blessed Virgin, and angels and saints and other servants of God, which deviate from the customs and the directions of the church.

11. The term "books" includes also newspapers and periodicals which come under the foregoing classes, not, indeed, if they publish one or two articles

[1] G. H. Putnam lists 53 *Indexes* that were issued under the authority of the church from 1526 to 1900.

contrary to faith and morals, but if their chief tendency and purpose is to impugn Catholic doctrine or defend unCatholic teachings and practices.[1]

The present *Index* is a volume of 563 pages, prohibiting a total of some 8000 works. The modern *Index* forbids, in general, the reading of books prejudicial to the faith, and no attempt has been made to examine and list all books that might be condemned. It is notable for its exceptions, as well as being an interesting historical document because of its selections. This is likewise true of the books prohibited on moral grounds. For example, no American writer is included. As far as the *Index* is concerned, Ingersoll, Paine, Walt Whitman and scores of moderns never existed. Nor did Rabelais. A few examples of philosophers and reformers on the *Index* are: Comte, Diderot, Descartes, Grotius, Rousseau, Renan, Savonarola, Taine, Spinoza, Locke, Voltaire and John Stuart Mill. Names in literature, such as Addison, Steele, Gibbon, Goldsmith, D'Annunzio, Flaubert, France, Maeterlinck, Sand, Sue and Zola, are indexed.[2] The service of the *Index* in suppressing or discouraging books *contra bonos mores* has been characterized as unimportant.[3] The *Index* is not intended as a complete bibliography of prohibited books. It provides samples and notorious illustrations of types of condemned writings.

The *Index*, although variously applied, and with punishments of unequal severity at different times, has been one of the important instruments with which the church has attempted to guide and to restrict access of its members to the various means of communication. Sometimes it has merely advertised the prohibited writings; sometimes it has proved ineffectual in stemming a tide of communication, as in sex expression in literature; but the extent to which it has inhibited the expression of writers and lecturers can never be known. This is especially true of the sixteenth and seventeenth centuries. Today the variety of means of communication outside the authority of the church largely circumvents the effectiveness of an index. In its defense Cardinal Merry del Val wrote in the preface to the present edition:

Hell is now stirring against the Church a more terrible battle than those of earlier centuries . . . for the evil press is a more perilous weapon than the sword. St. Paul, as we know, set the example for censorship, he caused evil books to be burned. St. Peter's successors have always followed the example; nor could they have done otherwise, for their Church, infallible mistress and sure guide of the faithful, is bound in conscience to keep the press pure . . . those who wish to feed the Holy Scriptures to people without any safeguards are also upholders of free thinking, than which there is nothing more absurd or harmful. . . . only

[1] Quoted in Seldes, G., *The Vatican*, p. 168, 1934.
[2] See article in *New York Times*, Nov. 10, 1930.
[3] Putnam, *op. cit.*, p. 33.

those infected by that moral pestilence known as liberalism can see in a check placed on unlawful power and profligacy a wound inflicted on freedom.[1]

FREEDOM OF SPEECH

The successive battles over freedom of speech have raged about freedom of assembly and public speech; the products of the press, newspapers, books, dramas and novels; pictures and pictorial art and, latterly, the radio. The center of conflict has shifted as authority has thought itself imperiled by one or the other medium of communication. Decrease of restriction and pressure in any field does not necessarily indicate an increased tolerance. It may mean that that form of expression is no longer thought to constitute a danger to authority, to social unity, and to traditional beliefs. A more conscious and intelligent leadership may permit soap-box oratory in the local scene, relatively unharried even by informal pressures, but may desire a considerable degree of control of motion picture, press and radio. Authority constantly encounters new problems in attempting to regulate communication.

Agitation may be carried on through gossip and discussion, but is usually most effectively achieved in assemblies and mass audiences. Such groups give publicity to the issues. Thus freedom of speech is balked, if freedom of association is denied. Such freedom has never been universally admitted as a legal right. Even when, in recent times under democratic governments, freedom of assembly has been granted in principle, it has been hedged about by various restrictions. In Great Britain there is no direct legal barrier, but activity in many fields may bring one in conflict with the sedition laws. In the United States, most states have laws forbidding the promotion of syndicalist and Communist viewpoints, public discussion of birth control, a meeting assembled to plan crime (that is, violation of existing laws), the gathering of a group intending to commit a breach of the peace and a meeting assembled to use force or the threat of force (three or more persons creating a disturbance to terrify others constitute a riot). It is clear that no state charged with the maintenance of social order can admit unlimited right of association. In a democracy, bodies advocating the use of violence rather than persuasion to bring about social change threaten, not only an existing government, but the basic concept of majority rule. But at just what points should restrictions be applied and with regard to which issues? Which opinions should be prohibited? In which media of communication? Should one rule apply in normal times and another in crises? When will attempted interference with freedom of assembly simply exacerbate the temper of those interfered with and bring about a more vigorous opposition? These and many other questions of tactics

[1] Quoted by Seldes, *op. cit.*, p. 195. Reprinted by permission of Harper & Brothers.

must be answered by authority. And frequently they are not answered wisely from the point of view of self-interest of that authority. In the conflict situation the emotional responses of the representatives of authority are also a factor in the situation. H. J. Laski has questioned whether restriction on association is ever effective in the long run. "It is difficult in the light of history to see that anything has been gained in the long run by multiplying prohibitions upon the right of association. Where men feel passionately upon some object they will combine to promote it; and any prohibition upon their effort to do so only serves to drive their activities into secret channels."[1]

The record of restrictions in the United States shows many inconsistencies in attempted regulation in the interest of religious, state and special interests, especially economic interests. Until well toward the middle of the nineteenth century there were prosecutions for blasphemy based on the old strict Colonial statutes. Expressions considered dangerous to morals are still restricted under the Comstock Act of 1873. National restrictions on speech in assembly range from the Sedition Act of 1798, in which the Federalists induced Congress to make seditious libel a crime, to the Sedition Act of 1918 passed under the conditions of world war. The provisions of this act prohibited: (1) conveying false reports with intent to interfere with military or naval forces; (2) attempting to cause disloyalty, insubordination or mutiny; (3) obstructing recruiting or enlistment; (4) obstructing the sale of United States bonds; (5) uttering abusive or disloyal language intended to cause contempt or disrepute as regards the form of government of the United States, the constitution, the flag or the uniform of the Army or Navy, or any language intended to incite resistance to the United States; (6) urging any curtailment of production of any things necessary to war; (7) advocating, teaching, defending or suggesting doing any of these acts; (8) words supporting or favoring the cause of any country at war with us.[2] The states, likewise, have passed a great many laws dealing with the conditions of freedom of assembly and freedom of speech. As each major issue in American history has come to the fore, there have been frequent denials of the freedom of assembly and speech to minority groups.

Legal restrictions and the police power of the state have often been augmented by the informal but effective restraints extralegally imposed by interested groups. Informal groups have dispersed the meetings of religious groups, abolitionists, feminists, race groups, birth-control advocates, strikers and many other minorities. From the Civil War onward,

---

[1] Laski, H. J., "Freedom of Association," *Ency. Soc. Sci.*, 6: 449.

[2] An extended description of procedure under this act will be found in Chafee, Z., *Freedom of Speech*, 1920.

as economic groups became better organized, there were frequent struggles for freedom of assembly and expression and innumerable violations of these rights. In each of the great depressions, freedom of speech has become a hard-fought issue. With the increased organization of labor in the nineties, the battles became very bitter. From then until the World War, free-speech fights were constantly organized. The more extreme groups developed techniques especially annoying to authority. The IWW sometimes invited arrest, imported all members available into the disturbed community, started speeches by the score, were dragged off to jail in large numbers, until their nuisance techniques at times brought concessions from city councils and the rescinding of local ordinances on street speeches. In labor conflicts, freedom of assembly is denied in many a town and city to the present day. This is often achieved by indirection through city ordinances ostensibly aimed at some other objective and enforced by the local police power.

Whoever has power usually has freedom of assembly and speech. Such freedom has frequently been denied, in practice, to minorities in the United States. As an increasing number of public officials have come to recognize the "safety-valve" function of such freedom, there has been somewhat less tampering with assembly, talk and discussion. However, in crises, old restrictions are invoked. But the center of conflict has shifted to what have become the more significant media of communication, the press, motion pictures and radio.

CHAPTER XV

CENSORSHIP.—(*Concluded*)

"Modern society will be destroyed by ink" is a saying attributed to Napoleon. At the beginning of the nineteenth century, authority was already well aware of the power of the newspaper. Napoleon is said to have feared a powerful German newspaper more than an army corps. The European press was at that time fettered by libel laws and systems of licensing, and the newspaper in the United States was just obtaining protection from political interference under the First Amendment to the Constitution. The legal restrictions, however, are meaningful only in terms of their administration. Nominal freedom may be accompanied by large numbers of prosecutions under those laws which do exist, whereas laws may be ignored elsewhere. Yet legal limitations are not the only restrictions on freedom of expression. An absolutely free press exists nowhere except in the theoretical suppositions of extreme libertarians. There is always the restraint of social conventions, the popular standards, prejudices and beliefs of the society in which publication occurs. There is always the restraint imposed by the policy and interests of the owners or managers of the press. Their commercial objectives place obvious limitations on its content.

The defense of formal censorship by authority is usually quite simple. The newspaper readers are to be protected from subversive minorities; from alien influences; from their own fears in wartime; from morally debasing accounts, and from such materials as are forbidden by the obscenity laws; from a too intrusive interest in the personal experiences of others; and, in general, from their own fallible thinking in whatever field authority decrees them to be peculiarly subject to error. Authority assumes a greater wisdom.

The application of censorship during the past century has shown no consistent trends. In the United States, freedom from governmental restriction, except in wartime, has been accompanied by a growing restriction in the financial interest of owners and advertisers. In England, until recently there was a growing freedom from political control but strict application of libel laws. There has been an increasing commercial interest. Vacillation in the theory and practice of censorship of newspapers in France has produced many swift reversals of policy. France has debated this issue more than any of the great

249

nations, as evidenced by an enormous literature on freedom of the press. Other European powers have likewise fluctuated in censorship policy.

After the World War, under the authoritarian governments that arose, countries theretofore permitting some measure of freedom instituted repressive measures. The postwar dictatorships limited freedom of speech both in theory and practice. The newspaper and the radio, as the most potent channels of communication, are now especially manipulated and controlled. The absolute right of the state to supervise the formation of public opinion is proclaimed. We shall consider briefly the censorship practices of Japan, Germany, France and the United States.

Until the coming of the European dictators the control of the press in Japan was more complete than that existing anywhere in the world. Nothing may be printed in Japan that is considered by the Home Ministry "subversive of public morals or provocative of disorder." Although of late years the trend has been toward relaxation of legal restrictions, commentators report that little actual liberty has been gained. H. E. Wildes states, "The more legal freedom is accorded the press the less real liberty exists. The journals of Japan are far from free. Experience has taught them that their liberation is illusory and that extra-legal controls are even more effective than the printed law."[1] However, the editors are usually in complete accord with the government on all foreign policy. They are thus governed by an inner loyalty and do not find the censorship irksome. If they should in any way be indiscreet in commenting on foreign relations, their papers may be censored or suspended by the Home Ministry, and by the War, Navy, and Foreign ministries. On home policies there is a certain latitude, always excepting anything affecting the emperor. If the news is not too disturbing, mild criticism of governmental policy is permitted. But "errors in diplomacy, distasteful truth, too aggressive activity, and scandals in the administration of the armed services" are to be kept, at all costs, from the eyes of foreigners. However, the Japanese editors are not accustomed to the tradition or ideology of free speech and press and feel little rancor at such restriction. On the other hand, in dealing with persons, personal characteristics and behavior there is no such restriction as exists under the libel laws of England or even the very much less strict laws of the United States. The chief objectives of authority in Japan are to control the press in the interest of national welfare and to suppress radicalism, not to censor accounts of personal morality. Indeed, the Japanese papers constantly print accounts of the sex experiences of individuals prominent in public life. This reporting is often so detailed and frequently so personally libelous that it could be printed nowhere else in the world. The newspapers of Japan are censored and filled with propaganda. Their objective is the development of public

[1] Wildes, H. E., *Japan in Crisis*, p. 191, 1934.

opinion to further what authority conceives to be the national interest. On international affairs the content of the newspapers reflects the position of the government.   In the purveying of personal gossip, the editor is free.

Effective censorship of the newspapers has usually been dependent upon secrecy and unobtrusive administration.   At least this has been true wherever the principles of liberty and freedom have permeated the general population.   Germany has been no exception to this principle. During the World War the German newspapers did not appear with blank spaces where the censor had at the last moment deleted a story, as was frequently true in France.   The newspapers were by no means free, but the censorship was moderately subtle.   Today, under the Nazis, having rejected the liberalistic civilization of the Western world, the censorship is not only probably the strictest in all Europe but it is also obvious.   It has been estimated that the drop in circulation of newspapers since Hitler's advent to power is at least 30 per cent.[1]   Censorship and propaganda are open and avowed.   Walter Funk of the Propaganda Ministry has stated the government position in declaring that the German press is "no longer a barrel organ out of which everybody is permitted to squeeze whatever melodies he likes, but a highly sensitive and far-sounding instrument or orchestra on which and with which only those shall play who know how, and in whose hands the Führer himself has placed the conductor's baton."[2]   In pursuing this objective the opposition press was abolished and there were left only the National Socialist papers, supported by the party and now part of the government, and the so-called "coordinated" press, which, although under private ownership, is subject to such rigid state control that its content on essential subjects is the same as that of the party papers.   In either case both the editors and editorial writers must be licensed by the state.   A law passed in October, 1933, provides, among other qualifications, that the men who serve the press must be "morally mature and nationally minded."   Their conduct outside as well as during working hours is subject to state supervision. "Not every one has the right to write for the public," Dr. Goebbels explained, "that right has to be earned through moral and patriotic qualifications."[3]   He states further that freedom of thought and opinion must be curbed at the point where these conflict with the interests of the nation as a whole.   As a result of the many and ever changing restrictions the newspapers soon became too uniform and dull.   The Ministry of Propaganda has persistently criticized this tendency, apparently desiring editors who would wholeheartedly support the party program but do so with versatility.   But pervasive fear, kept alive by the examples

[1] Riegel, O. W., *Mobilizing for Chaos*, p. 148, 1934.
[2] *New York Times Mag.*, July 14, 1935, p. 8.
[3] *New York Times*, Oct. 8, 1933.

of colleagues in concentration camps who had had the temerity to criticize even mildly, has made for a cautiousness that breeds dullness. Governmental censorship, by forbidding mention of many dramatic issues and incidents occurring both at home and abroad, drastically limits the editors' choice of interesting news. The vital conflict between the religious groups and the Nazis has not been described in the German press. Of course, the German press had never been fundamentally a news press in the sense in which American newspapers collect and make news and emphasize the reporter. It was an opinion press—the agent of some party or group, a special-pleader and propagandist press. But, during the years of the Democracy, the many factions all achieved some expression in their newspapers. The totalitarian state continues the tradition of a propagandist press but eliminates all competitors. In dealing with foreign correspondents, censorship has not been official, but it has been effective. Dr. Goebbels lectures to the correspondents periodically on the rights and limitations of a correspondent who is the guest of another country. Sources of news are made inaccessible at crucial times. Press dispatches not favorable to the government may be delayed or garbled. In various ways the life of a critical correspondent may be made very uncomfortable, a technique perfected in Italy a decade earlier. German administration has not been subtle in dealing with the foreign press. Within the Nazi state, newspaper content is now almost completely controlled. Absolute freedom of the press never existed there, and that it has a right to exist is now denied.

As we have seen, press freedom in Japan is limited to the discussion of persons but has wide latitude in such discussion because of the absence of strict libel laws, whereas in Germany the entire newspaper content is censored in the interests of the state. During the past year, even those newspaper critics dealing with the stage, literature, motion pictures, music and art have been gagged by the propaganda ministry. In France, there is in normal times very little interference by the state with newspaper content. However, as most papers are edited in the interests of a particular group, party, politician, economic organization or other special interest, there is an effective censorship by those who own or subsidize the particular paper. Although these refracting media provide a wealth of conflicting opinion, it is sometimes difficult to get reliable information on crucial news events. With the exception of the five years of strict governmental censorship during the World War, this freedom for conflicting propagandas has been permitted since the press law of 1881. This law provided that:

Every journal must have a director who is a French citizen in full enjoyment of his civil rights. Every publication must bear the name and address of the printer. It is not necessary that articles be signed, as they usually are; but at the time of publication of each issue, two copies signed by the director must be delivered to a court of the first instance. As to individual responsibility the director of a paper is obliged to print a reply of any person whom he has named or designated in his paper. Furthermore, if a libelous statement is printed, both the director and the author of the article can be brought before a correctional court. Journals published in foreign countries and those printed in France in a foreign language are subject to police control.[1]

French papers have great liberty to attack the government, parties and persons. This freedom is cherished. On the other hand, there is little sense of responsibility for a complete and thorough presentation of the news. The French press with its avowed special pleading probably reinforces the prejudices of its readers. Just how influential it is in modifying opinions is a subject of debate among journalists. But there exists a wide range of freedom. Minorities are often permitted expression under conditions that would be permitted nowhere else in the world. This freedom is usually carried over into dealings with foreign correspondents, although an incidental and not very effective censorship of outgoing telegraph messages is applied occasionally by the Ministry of the Interior when the national interest is thought to be at stake. Sometimes particular prejudices against individuals find expression, as in forbidding entry to France to W. R. Hearst during several years. And officious individual bureaucrats do sometimes play with foreign correspondents, deleting and delaying telegrams and annoying them in various ways.

Of the great powers, Japan, Germany, Italy and Russia have an avowed censorship of the press, England and France a limited, indirect government censorship; but the United States has so far resisted such limitation. This freedom is a product not only of our history, of the development and defense of the idea from the first constitutional amendment onward, but also of our form of government. Under parliamentary governments, the heads of state have the greater reason to desire restriction of press comment since they are subject to recall, but our elected officials have time, within the limits of their terms in office, to justify and explain their positions.[2] Hence, in normal times the newspaper in the United States is restricted only by the laws of libel and obscenity and various associated legal limitations. The courts have consistently maintained this press freedom from legal censorship in the many cases of attempted invasion of that right. One of the most recent attempts, that of the late Senator Long to tax the opposition papers of Louisiana into submission, was stopped by the Supreme Court. American press history

---

[1] Buell, R. L., *Contemporary French Politics*, p. 291, 1920. Quoted by permission of D. Appleton-Century Company, Inc.

[2] Krock, A., "The Press and Government," *Ann. Am. Acad. Pol. Soc. Sci.*, 180: 163.

contains many incidents of attempted restriction in the various states. The first case from which the struggle for press freedom in the United States is usually traced is the famous Zenger trial, which occurred in New York in 1733, two generations before the revolution. After the infamous restrictive episode of the Federalists' rule and the passage of the First Amendment, the principle of press freedom was established. Thomas Jefferson, ardent champion of the newspaper, declared that "our liberty depends on the freedom of the press and that cannot be limited without being lost." Thus far, that freedom has been legally invaded only in time of war. Informally, however, such freedom has been denied to various groups on many occasions. In the period of agitation during the 30 years preceding the Civil War the printing establishments of Abolitionists were in many instances destroyed by mobs. In the later years of this period the Postmaster General was forbidding Abolitionists the use of the mails, although he had no legal basis on which to do so. During the Civil War, many printing establishments were destroyed by mobs, sometimes by soldiers. Over thirty newspapers were suspended under temporary legislation. During the World War, the restrictions were used to decimate the ranks of the foreign language and immigrant press.[1] Censorship of the press under special legislation was also instituted in the interests of the conduct of the war. Military censorship is usually justified on the basis that it prevents the transmission of important information to the enemy and that such press censorship prevents discouragement at home and at the front. Under the conditions of modern communication such assertions are of doubtful truth. In a brilliant discussion of the limitations of military censorship, L. M. Salmon[2] has noted the following points: (1) The lack of consistent policy as to standards of censorship caused the Allies to censor so variously that almost everything got through—accounts of defeats deleted by some were reported by others. (2) The means of communication are now so many and their content so enormous that the organization of censorship will be cumbersome and leaks will be inevitable. (3) An ordinarily free press will soon be at odds with the censors and will attempt in every way to circumvent them. (4) Censorship arouses suspicion among the troops and adversely affects the general morale at home. (5) Deceit, concealment and evasion have deleterious effects on the morale of the censors and administrative officers themselves. (6) Censorship is essentially negative and unproductive, and the deletions are in part supplanted by crops of wild rumors. News vendors grasp at straws. (7) Suppression of news prevents desirable criticism of official incompetency, inefficiency

[1] See Park, R. E., *The Immigrant Press and Its Control*, 1922.
[2] Salmon, L. M., *The Newspaper and Authority*, 1923. These statements are a summary of Chap. 5.

and stupidity. (8) Censorship will inevitably be prolonged after the end of hostilities. In France, censorship, in spite of numerous government promises, was continued until after the Peace Conference. (9) The ability in circumventing censorship that the press developed during the World War indicates the futility of such suppression in the modern world. (10) Censorship will inevitably be linked with propaganda which becomes more and more irresponsible as it is protected. (11) An intelligent public opinion cannot be created under such conditions. Censorship is ineffective in preventing the transmission of military information, its ostensible purpose, but it does permit political manipulation which is undesirable from the viewpoint of the general national interest. And although usually defended in general theory, military censorship in its application in the modern state inevitably arouses opposition because these discrepancies become obvious.

Denial of freedom of printing has been informally applied, by mobs destroying the output, wrecking the establishments and intimidating the editors of various papers and journals published by reform groups, racial groups, labor groups, suffragettes, municipal factions and others. Large publics do not display tolerance when they feel endangered or outraged. It requires a mature, liberal wisdom to understand that an obnoxious opinion is less dangerous to public welfare than its arbitrary suppression. The chief extralegal limitation on the newspaper has been the policy of its owners and advertisers. The general or specific interests of these have led to the most usual American types of suppression and distortion of news. The record of most of the American newspapers is especially bad in the censoring of news of labor conflicts, strikes and attendant private and governmental violence, and the like.[1]

During the past three years the question of the relation of the national government to press freedom has arisen once more. This issue has appeared owing to the attempt to develop a newspaper code under the National Recovery Administration, to the propaganda efforts of government bureaus, resulting occasionally in clashes with Washington correspondents, and to presidential criticism of the political columnists and commentators. In the early days of the NRA most newspapers urged the acceptance of codes by the various businesses. When their own newspaper code was taken to Washington, it was found to be so written as to permit the newspaper publishers to escape most of the obligations they were so actively recommending to other businesses. A code written by government representatives was not acceptable to the newspapers. It was at that time that a large part of the press suddenly discovered

---

[1] The newspaper treatment of a Pittsburgh strike is described in *The Steel Strike of* 1919, Interchurch World Movement, Commission of Inquiry, 1920. See also Seldes, G., *Freedom of the Press*, Chaps. 4, 5, 6, 1935.

that freedom of the press was endangered. Distinguished publishers hastened to a ceremonial laudation of the heroic Peter Zenger who, 200 years before, had defied the Tories. A minority of publishers repudiated this outcry as hypocrisy. They were unable to see how the wage, age and hour requirements of the NRA code menaced press freedom. The reply was that an unreasonable increase of the cost of production menaced the existence of many papers, just as excessive taxation would ruinously hamper them. A compromise code was finally accepted which contained a section declaring that the publishers did not waive any constitutional rights to freedom of the press. President Roosevelt in accepting the code wrote, "The recitation of the freedom of the press clause in the code has no more place here than would the recitation of the whole Constitution or of the Ten Commandments."[1]

With the accession to power of the Democratic administration in 1932 the press relations of government bureaus were reorganized. Scores of new publicity agents were appointed to the various departments. These appointees, usually former newspaper men, prepared handouts, decided what departmental people should be interviewed and often were the only direct contact between the press and the department.[2] The very nature of this system of organization with the increased canalization of news made inevitable the charge of informal censorship and of the perversion, distortion and fabrication of news.

The censorship issue is arising in another quarter. In the relationship between presidents and correspondents the chief executive has sometimes attempted to silence a particular correspondent by protesting to the publishers. This has been done throughout our national history. President Theodore Roosevelt was a notoriously violent protestor. In most cases the publisher has resisted the request, although sometimes, on proof of bad motives or false statement, a correspondent is removed. Of late years new types of correspondents, the commentator on public affairs, the interpreter and the columnist play an increasingly important role in winnowing out the important issues, explaining and interpreting political news. Some have a large following. Naturally the interpretations of these columnists are not free of their own particular prejudices, likes and dislikes. And they come in conflict with administrators. A political commentator recently reported, "The President has often indicated that, if he could have his way, these columnists would be barred from the press. His view is that they air their motives and prejudices, likes and dislikes and give the public a false view of what is going on. His objection covers the widest possible field from the writers of gossip

[1] Quoted, Seldes, *op. cit.*, p. 303.
[2] See discussion of governmental propaganda in Chap. XVII.

columns to the most pedestrian of commentators."[1] No doubt this issue will soon receive public discussion.

The press in the United States is free, more free than any other, from governmental control. It has enjoyed liberties without parallel. Informally, however, it has been censored many times and in many ways. The principal restrictions have been the interests of newspaper publishers and advertisers. We shall discuss those limitations elsewhere in commenting on the history of the development of the American newspaper.

CENSORSHIP OF BOOKS

An informal, extralegal censorship of books is always operative. As a rule the prevailing standards of a culture limit the expression of an author in so far as they are incorporated in his own standards, in his hopes for large sale and wide circulation and in the standards set up by his publisher. The publisher usually desires to avoid court action and knows the standards of his clientele. Through the nineteenth century the publisher was even more influential than he is today in determining the content of books. Not only were popular standards more integrated and uniform, but the publisher could, with especial clarity, discern the standards of the middle class which provided the bulk of readers. In England, the publishers, in conjunction with the managers of the great circulating libraries, were especially responsive to the public opinion of their readers. Inasmuch as most of the readers obtained their copies of books from the circulating libraries, the managers of these exercised an effective informal censorship for several generations. They lost their dominant position in this field during the first decade of this century.[2] In America, the public libraries exercised a similar but much less effective censorship. The contemporary circulating libraries are likewise guided by the tastes of their readers, but, as tastes have become extremely varied, there is little informal censorship by these organizations. They are limited only by the applications of existing laws. And these have not been vigorously enforced during the past fifteen years in the United States. Our authors have publicly explored the varieties of amorous experience and the deviations of sexual and psychological behavior. Their work has been purveyed in the crudest of cheap pulp magazines and in the most expensive privately printed erotica. With the exception of the inhabitants of limited geographic areas we are largely free from the censor's ban at the present time.

[1] Krock, A., *New York Times*, Apr. 26, 1936.
[2] Ernst, M. L., and Seagle, W., *To the Pure*, Chap. 5, 1929.

After the development of printing and the pamphleteering activities of the Reformation, formal censorship was developed by the church which organized its list of prohibited books. The states of the Western world likewise condemned, burned and forbade the publication of books thought to be deleterious to their interests. Gradually through the eighteenth and nineteenth centuries greater freedom of expression was achieved; first on religious, then on political and finally on moral subjects. After the World War the authoritarian states, Communist, Fascist and Nazi, reversed the trend within their borders and rigorously censored political and ethical utterances. The Nazi state has been especially assiduous in publicly burning books on communism, books favorable to or written by Jews and books, not only of erotic but also of scientific vintage, dealing with sexual behavior, as well as in controlling the projected publication of such books. Laws limiting freedom of expression are now very strict in Germany.

Censorship in the United States has been primarily concerned with moral questions. Formal censorship has been applied by local ordinances, state laws and some Federal legislation. Boston has been most notorious in local regulation of bookselling. Most of the states have laws on obscenity and blasphemy which have been used from time to time in prosecuting book publishers and sellers. As the principle of freedom of the press is recognized in the Federal Constitution, as well as in the constitutions of the various states, most censorship of books has been indirect. There was no legal basis for such censorship in the eighteenth and early nineteenth century. The short-lived Alien and Sedition Act of 1798 passed by the Federalists, ostensibly to check French propaganda in the United States but actually to serve as a weapon against the Republicans, was used to censor a number of newspapers, periodicals and books. Jefferson, when he became president, pardoned all those punished or prosecuted under this law. The earliest statutes on obscene publication were passed in Vermont, 1821; Connecticut, 1834, and Massachusetts, 1835.[1] The Postmaster General may exercise a censorship by his power to exclude materials from the mails. For two decades before the Civil War it was customary to exclude Abolitionist propaganda from the mails to the South. During the Civil War, exclusion of various materials from the mails was justified as an emergency measure. Afterward, Congress granted authority for such censorship by a series of acts in 1865. Adequate legal basis for prosecution and the suppression of publications by the Post Office was finally provided by the so-called "Comstock Law" of 1873. It declared, in part, that "every obscene, lewd, or lascivious, and every filthy book, painting,

---

[1] Lasswell, H. D., "Censorship," *Ency. Soc. Sci.*, 3: 290–294.

picture, paper, letter, writing or print, or other publication of an indecent character . . . and every article or thing designed for . . . preventing conception or producing abortion . . . or the giving of information directly or indirectly, where or how or from whom or by what means any of these articles can be obtained, is a crime."[1] Under this law, Anthony Comstock, as a special officer of the Post Office department from 1873 to 1915, was instrumental in "bringing 3,648 prosecutions and he obtained 2,682 convictions. He secured the destruction of 50 tons of books, over 28,000 pounds of stereotype plates, almost 17,000 photographic negatives, and 3,984,063 photographs."[2] The Supreme Court declared this act to be, not an invasion of the principle of freedom of the press, but a necessary regulation in the interest of public morals. In interpreting this act, the lower courts have shown an amazing variety of definitions of the "obscene, lewd and lascivious." Of late years, the number of prosecutions has been very small.

The national censorship of books has also been accomplished through forbidding entrance and importation of books considered obscene. There has been some regulation since the Tariff Act of 1842. Customs agents have, until recently, acted as judges of the obscene, under standards set up by numerous court decisions. Under the Tariff Act of 1930, such literary censorship was taken away from the customs agents and put in the hands of the United States district courts. It was believed that this change would liberalize the administration of the law, as the Customs Division had built up a bibliography of almost 800 forbidden books. It was thought that customs officers would be somewhat more hesitant to censor if their rejections had to be defended in court.

Of late years, as even the more extreme reformers now realize, the principal result of attempted censorship of books has been widespread publicity and the calling of popular attention to the forbidden book. Hence, some decidedly third-rate books have been widely read. It is often maintained that censorship of books, however administered, is dangerous as an opening wedge for invasion of the general principle of free speech. Further, there are great differences of opinion as to the effects of reading even avowed pornography. Heywood Broun, maintaining that sheer nastiness is feeble stuff and that "indecency is a tiny kingdom and one tour covers it," declares that one road to purity lies in making the not particularly grand tour and being done with it.[3] Jimmy Walker, as state senator, in objecting to a proposed censorship law once asked his associates, "Did you ever know a woman who was ruined by a book?"

[1] Whipple, L., *The Story of Civil Liberty in the United States*, p. 285, 1927.
[2] Odegard, P., *The American Public Mind*, p. 263, 1930.
[3] Broun, H., and Leech, M., *Anthony Comstock*, p. 269, 1927.

The question also arises whether or not censorship should be determined by the standards desirable for the guidance of children, even if there existed an adequate psychological understanding of the influences of each of the media of communication upon thought and behavior.

CENSORSHIP OF THE MOTION PICTURES

As the organized church, preoccupied with doctrine and faith, sought to censor the heretic and a threatened state burned the treasonable books and repressed the traitor, so modern democracies turned to the restriction of what the good citizens considered their principal dangers. These were of a personal rather than an institutional character. Above all, a common denominator of personal fears in modern democracies has furnished stimuli to sexual imagery or behavior. In America, the confusion resulting from an allegiance to abstract liberty in the political sphere and a widespread desire to censor personal morality has become chronic. Books, plays, pictures, statuary and various art works have from time to time been subjected to the formal and legal as well as informal censorship by organized minorities supported by sizable publics. Minorities have frequently demanded increased legal censorship. The larger publics have fluctuated between dislike of the censorship process and an intermittent angry resentment at certain of the products of communication which have come to the local community from the extracommunity world of book publishers, playwrights, artists and motion-picture producers.

This confusion is most clearly illustrated in the history of the censorship of motion pictures in the United States. The motion pictures have appealed to the masses of people, children and adults, male and female, the ignorant and the learned. Although the occasional picture has been sophisticated, artistic or seriously propagandistic in the political and economic fields, the content of the vast majority have been largely dramatic action, individual conflict, the purveying of feminine nudity to the provinces, popular musical entertainment and the personal characteristics of stars. Such a content has from time to time provided a field day for organized censorship groups, recruited from reform organizations, worried parents and religious orders. Such censorship has been primarily concerned with sexual behavior, the nudity of females and certain types of criminal behavior. On these subjects, motion-picture content has been determined by a kind of tentative regulation, advancing and retreating before popular opinion. Every few years since the beginning of the motion picture there have been periods of cleansing induced by the organized attacks of censors. In this process, state censorship has been of relatively little importance, but informal pressures have been enormously significant. Naturally the widespread motion-picture business has responded very quickly to any popular criticism.

A brief sketch of the periods of agitation for motion-picture censor-ship would begin with the incident in 1907 when, after the showing of a melodramatic film called *The Great Automobile Robbery* an actual auto-mobile theft occurred which was associated with the picture.[1] Numerous articles on the relation between the pictures and crime appeared, and discussion groups demanded state censorship. In 1909, the mayor closed the motion-picture theatres of New York City. A citizens' committee was formed to inspect films before they were released. This organi-zation, the National Board of Censorship, was supported by the voluntary contributions of various organizations until 1914.[2] It was then decided to accept fees from the motion-picture producers for reviewing the films, and the name was changed to the National Board of Review. It placed at the disposal of women's clubs and other organizations advance infor-mation about the pictures and evaluated and classified film content in a weekly bulletin. The National Board of Review has frequently been charged with creating a popular impression that it is a governmental body with official status, whereas it is actually a citizens' organization subsidized by the producers. In 1915, the way was cleared for legal censorship when the Supreme Court decided that the motion pictures differed from all other forms of communication. The films could be censored in advance of public showing, for they were viewed in this decision not as an art form communicating ideas but as an industry. The products of that industry, like foods or drugs or other products for general consumption, might therefore be inspected before being offered to the public, whereas means of communication such as the press, art forms and drama must, under constitutional amendment, be regulated only by prosecution after violation of the laws. In seven states, New York, Kansas, Maryland, Ohio, Pennsylvania, Virginia and Florida, censorship systems were established within a few years after this decision. But official state-censorship legislation has never been successfully advo-cated since that time. Although, by 1921, censorship bills had been presented in thirty-six additional states, none of them has ever passed. Strong and well-organized minorities have persistently agitated for

[1] Material on the incidents in the history of motion-picture censorship in the United States will be found in: *Ann. Am. Acad. Pol. Soc. Sci.*, November, 1926; Lewis, H. T., *The Motion Picture Industry*, Chap. 12, 1933; Beman, L. T., *Censorship of the Theatre and Moving Pictures*, 1931; Seabury, W. M., *Public and the Motion Picture Industry*, pp. 143–159, 1926.

[2] The Peoples' Institute of New York, a citizens' bureau for social research, was the principal contributor. When the financial burden on this organization became too heavy, fees were accepted from producers at the rate of $3.50 per reel until 1920 and $6.50 per reel from 1920 to the present.

municipal, state and national censorship, but majority opinion has apparently been reluctant to permit governmental regulation of this favorite form of commercial recreation.

Widespread popular support has been given to reform and religious groups, when, during four periods since 1912, these organizations have exercised a powerful informal censorship of movie themes by agitation and the threat of legislative action. Municipal censorship boards have been created in more than thirty cities since 1915.[1] For the most part these city boards have operated with inconsistent and ill-defined rules, untrained personnel and inadequate budgets. They have been relatively ineffective in achieving any results other than deleting incidental items of obscenity, profanity and nudity. Agitation for national censorship legislation has welled up from time to time. Certain restrictions already exist under national laws, such as the prohibitions on the transportation of obscene or lascivious books or pictures in interstate commerce. These regulations have sometimes been applied. During the agitation by reformers in 1913 when prize-fight pictures were especially opposed, such films were forbidden interstate transportation. Congress has passed no general censorship legislation, although at three periods there has been extensive agitation for Federal laws. From 1913 to 1915 there was a growing resentment among reform organizations, directed at the motion pictures featuring crime, violence and the prize-fight pictures. These groups sponsored the Hughes Bill of 1915, which provided for a Federal motion-picture commission of five members who should direct the censoring and licensing of all films before they were admitted to interstate commerce. This bill was debated at some length but finally defeated. However, the protests, agitation and discussion resulted in the voluntary deletion of the more objectionable themes by the producers. By 1921 the protests of reform groups, who were this time primarily objecting to the "vamp," had once more become vociferous. The larger motion-picture producers organized the Motion Picture Producers and Distributors of America and in 1922 elected Mr. Will Hays as the much publicized "movie czar." A lull in hostilities ensued, especially due to the fact that Mr. Hays appointed a committee composed of most of the prominent opponents of the movies to serve as an advisory board on motion-picture content. But most of these shortly withdrew in disgust at their futility, although in the meantime the producers had voluntarily eliminated most of the objectionable features. Then the reform groups, clamoring for national legislation, supported the Upshaw Bill which provided for a commission of seven members with broad powers to (1) preview and license films, (2) examine and censor scenarios and (3) supervise production. In 1925, the idea of Federal censorship was given the most thor-

[1] *Ann. Am. Acad. Pol. Soc. Sci., op. cit.,* p. 172.

ough political and public discussion it has ever received. The bill was defeated. When, in 1934, the church-organized Legion of Decency claiming twelve million members was giving the worried producers the worst fright of their harried lives, there was less unanimity among the reformers as to the desirability of national censorship. Not only were most of the church and reform groups impressed with the ineffectiveness of state censorship as it had been applied during the preceding twenty years, but some of them, existing in the midst of the political and economic turmoil of that year, had glimpsed something of the political implications of a national censorship board. The chastened producers mended their ways, and the reform organizations, impressed with the effectiveness of informal censorship and boycott, subsided from their agitation.

No governmental censorship body in America ever achieved anything other than the deletion of a few items. It could not effectively censor the underlying theme. All such bodies were governed by laws, most sections of which were so general as to leave the standards of censorship in the hands of the board or commission which, in the long run, usually succeeded in pleasing no one. For example, the Kansas law of 1917 on which the laws of most other states were based, cited the following standards for the censorship board of that time:

A. Pictures should be clean and wholesome and all features that tend to debase morals or influence the mind to improper conduct should be eliminated.

B. Ridicule of any religious sect or peculiar characteristics or any race of people will not be approved.

C. Evil suggestions in the dress of comedy characters will be eliminated.

D. Infidelity of marriage ties will be eliminated.

E. Loose conduct between men and women, cigarette smoking by women will be eliminated and wherever possible, bar-room scenes and social drinking.

F. A display of nude human figures eliminated.

G. Crimes and criminal methods such as give instruction in crime through suggestion omitted or abbreviated.

H. Prolonged and passionate love scenes when suggestive of immorality shall be eliminated.

I. Scenes of houses of ill fame, road houses, and immoral dance halls.

J. The theme of white slavery or allurement or betrayal of innocence will be condemned.

The difficulty of determining satisfactory standards for censorship was rather generally admitted after a few years' experience with such laws. In January, 1925, the National Committee for Better Films stated, "It [censorship] has failed to recognize and dare not recognize, because it is based on the theory that there are final, unchanging, universal standards of good and evil and of good and evil influences, that fundamental in the whole question of the motion picture is a legitimate and inevitable difference of opinion between sections, communities, groups and individuals." Moreover, the limited field of censored topics is quite apparent when one examines the records of state censorship boards. The Division of Motion Pictures of the New York Department of Education (the censorship board in that state) examined 903 feature films and 1394 shorts during the period Jan. 1, 1932, to Mar. 31, 1933. Of the feature films they passed 61.5 per cent, deleted something from 35.9 per cent and rejected 2.6 per cent. The rejections were almost all foreign films. Of the deletions the general categories were sex (44 per cent), crime (16 per cent), violence (29 per cent), government (5 per cent) and religion (3 per cent). The following table provides some details of the deletions made by this board.

TABLE VII.—CATEGORICAL DESCRIPTION OF DELETIONS ENFORCED BY THE DIVISION OF MOTION PICTURES OF THE NEW YORK DEPARTMENT OF EDUCATION FOR THE 15-MONTH PERIOD BEGINNING JAN. 1, 1932, AND ENDING MAR. 31, 1933[1]

Censorship categories	Applied in connection with "feature" films		Applied in connection with "shorts"		Totals
	Dialogue	Scene	Dialogue	Scene	
Sex:					
Sex, general................	667	308	11	24	1010
Nudity....................	0	134	0	75	209
Slang.....................	19	0	1	0	20
Language.................	15	9	0	3	27
Crime:					
Technique................	96	123	1	28	248
Reward...................	42	80	7	8	137
References...............	13	0	1	0	14
Poison...................	0	24	0	17	41
Violence:					
Human...................	139	94	22	46	701
Animals..................	0	65	0	0	65
Government:					
United States.............	72	50	1	0	123
Foreign...................	19	0	0	0	19
Religion....................	25	1	0	0	26
Unclassified.................	15	4	10	0	29
Totals.................	1122	1292	54	201	2669

[1] *Report of the National Council on Freedom from Censorship*, Introduction, 1933. Quoted by permission of the National Council on Freedom from Censorship.

The failure of state censorship is implicit in this record of deletions. Not only is it entirely negative, but such censorship can be applied only to the more obvious, simple and unsubtle elements of a picture. To be sure, the bulk of motion pictures deals with the simpler human dramas, situations and appetites. Mr. Will Hays has estimated that only 3 per cent of the audiences go to the theater for originality, ideas and literature. However, the censor deals only with the most obvious of the simpler elements of the film and not with underlying themes, motives and the entire scale of values involved in the picture. Recently, the more rabid reform groups are beginning to understand that even when judged by their scale of values the rejections and deletions of the state censor are scarcely worth taking out, in comparison with what remains in the picture.

For thirty years the problem of control of the motion pictures has been debated. Minority groups have demanded censorship for the protection of those whom they judged incapable, especially the children and youth. The themes especially decried have been crime, violence and sex. Until recently there were no factual surveys of the content of the films.[1] A decade ago it was stated that:

Evil in the movie plots is typified usually by sex. If you will keep track of the scenes you are shown in the movie plays you will find that two-thirds of them are theoretically lewd. Were the heroine involved a human being whose emotions and attitudes were not dictated by a moralistic plot, these scenes would be downright "obscene." The movies concerning themselves almost entirely with the triumph of morality have revealed to the world an orgie of kissings, huggings and attempted rapes, the like of which has never been known in any art or semi-art of any other civilization. The movie producers observe only one law. This is the law of the Virtuous Finish. The average movie plot is based on the vicissitudes of Virginity. The public discussion of female virginity, which preoccupies the moralist, is an intensely more sexual stimulus than the public discussion of prostitution or sexual promiscuity. Write your own psychological caption. If I were to draw a cartoon of the movie heroine, I would draw a picture of a pretty girl with her head buried in the ground offering the rest of her person as the battlefield of drama.[2]

Although this was disdainfully written by a cynical novelist, it is apparent that stern moralists were also convinced of the truth of such assertions. Violence and crime were found objectionably present in cycles of Western, comedy, terror, war and gangster films. In the desire to censor and limit such a content, several fundamental questions were seldom adequately considered. (1) To what extent does motion-picture content differ from the prevailing folkways and mores of our culture at the present time? (2) Wherein does motion-picture content

---

[1] See Dale, E., *The Content of Motion Pictures*, 1934, and additional discussion and references in Chap. XX.

[2] Written by Ben Hecht, quoted by Merriam, Mrs. C. E., *Ed. Screen*, 3: 190. Permission to quote granted.

differ from that of other media of communication and from objective life situations to which the individual ordinarily has access? (3) Are the fields of behavior to which objection is raised the most vital in contemporary life? May not the perversions of economic reality and, indeed, of the scales of values in general, as portrayed by the motion pictures, have as profound an effect as incidents of violence or sexual behavior? (4) Is it possible to define the meanings of immorality, indecency and obscenity in a way sufficiently objective to provide a legal basis for censorship? (5) To what extent do the patterns of behavior provided in the motion picture motivate similar behavior on the part of those who view them? It is quite obvious that these questions could be but partly answered by using whatever methods and techniques of investigation social psychology and the various sciences of behavior have developed. We shall consider elsewhere the existing studies on motion-picture content and effect.[1] The censor has usually not even posed these questions. He has assumed the answers.

Though legal censorship is neither effective nor desirable, certain types of control of the motion-picture industry in the public interest would appear to be indicated. Legal censorship creates more problems than it solves, imposes the standards of a group upon the community and state and nation and may stifle presentation of divergent economic and political ideas. However, there are some types of regulation that would free rather than restrain the expression of opinion of the community and organized publics. Prohibition of block booking and blind booking would make possible a range of choice on what pictures were exhibited in the community. In the development of the industry the producers found it profitable to compel exhibitors to contract for large blocks of pictures. These were rented by exhibitors who not only had never seen the films but had often contracted for them long before they were made. Although the Motion Picture Code permitted a return of 10 per cent of the features, the exhibitor was so restricted that this quota was largely meaningless. A bill was introduced into the House of Representatives in 1935 to forbid block booking. Such legislation is bitterly opposed by the motion-picture industry.

The regulation of the attendance of various age groups at motion-picture performances has frequently been urged. As the pictures are a major leisure-time activity of all age groups, the various parts of their diversified content are not equally suitable for all groups. Certain adults may be hardened to observation of sexual or violent behavior that would shock the adolescent, even if it did not lead to attempts at similar behavior. Such materials might provide a stimulating or compensatory vicarious experience for a large portion of the adult group and be a desirably integrating factor in their life experiences. The same

[1] Chapter XX.

materials might be distasteful to, or ignored or not understood by small children. In the case of the adolescent they might be an addition to the stress and strain of a period of sexual adjustment. Furthermore, an adult's impression is obtained from an understanding of the picture as a whole with its underlying theme, and a quite different impression is gained from the parts of the picture that the small child understands. A solution for this difference of response has been thought by many to lie in providing certain regular times each week for the showing of pictures suitable for small children, for family audiences of adults and children or for adults. Such regulation of attendance, if administered on the basis of a limited and narrowly prejudiced scale of values of what would be "good for" the child, might be more undesirable than subjecting him to unsuitable impressions. However, wisely administered in terms of the best social psychological knowledge of our time, such regulation of attendance could be in the public interest. Such regulation, likewise, is bitterly opposed by the motion-picture industry.

Another method of control is the boycott and the informal pressures upon producers. This has been used, not only on a national scale by the Legion of Decency in 1934, but in limited areas and against local theaters from time to time. Although the programs of such pressure groups will inevitably be narrowly conceived, they do at least inform the producers of points at which large publics have been outraged. However, such organization is possible only with disciplined groups and homogeneous communities.

If, as it is usually conceived in the United States, the control of the motion picture is to be fundamentally in the interests of children and youth, a constructive program will utilize all the existing agencies of instruction to inculcate standards and scales of values on the basis of which youth may judge the picture. The ultimately effective censor is in the individual and not in legal restrictions. Additional interest on the part of parents in the selection and classification of pictures has led to the establishment, during the past few years, of eleven bureaus maintaining offices at Hollywood for this purpose. Most of these are maintained by women's organizations. To be sure, these organizations serve a selected and limited clientele of middle-class parents at the present time, but the principle might be extended. The schools could increasingly advise and select. And the community may regulate the attendance of various age groups. The motion pictures are an important part of our national life and culture. They are a fundamental means of communication. They may become an important art form. Expression in this medium of communication should not be limited by any type of legal censorship or the standards of any special group or class; but access to the products of this industry might wisely be limited in the public interest.

We have traced some of the essential elements in the authoritarian position and in that of the classic liberal and have noted fields in which the conflict between them was especially bitter. Classic liberalism, narrowly conceived in terms of "freedom from," inevitably rejected the principle of censorship, whereas authority embraced it, both for punitive and restrictive purposes. We have noted the pervasiveness of an informal censorship based upon individual psychological processes and the standards of the mores. We have sketched the formal applications of censorship in several fields. Both the censors and the opponents of censorship have frequently been motivated by deep convictions, stubbornly maintained and emotionally defended. However, social psychological knowledge as to the actual effects of the various media of communication upon individuals of various age, sex and knowledge groups is very imperfect. The same stimulus may have very different effects upon the mental life and behavior at different times and under various conditions. A recent autobiographical account of the experiences of internees in France during the World War reports on the growing vividness of amorous imagery as stimulated by reading books, which ordinarily had not been so exciting but after prolonged imprisonment were almost unendurably vivid.[1] Censorship has been based upon folk beliefs rather than upon data provided by social science.

In conclusion we may note one further problem. Latterly, it has been argued that a liberalism, conceived in terms of "freedom for" the development of individuals and groups toward the limits of their capacities, might require restrictions on communication in the public interest. An increasing minority advocates extended governmental censorship in the public interest, since it is more aware of the psychological limitations of the individual, his inability adequately to classify and evaluate the thronging stimuli of modern communication and the distortion and fabrication of news at its source through controlled channels of press and radio and motion picture. At the same time, this minority rejects the contemporary applications of censorship in the authoritarian states of Europe. And it is unable to agree on definitions of the public interest. But it usually agrees on repudiating the intrusions of business interests into the media of communication, the activities of the ubiquitous advertiser and of the business pressure groups. They demand that these be controlled by government but at the same time contend that freedom from any special political censorship should be maintained. But the principle of liberty of communication is not readily divisible into sectors. Restriction has a way of growing, and regulations proliferate. These modern liberals espouse a dangerous course.

[1] Kuncz, A., *Black Monastery*, pp. 183 *ff.*, 1934.

CHAPTER XVI

SPECIAL INTEREST GROUPS

In modern complex societies there is a large and growing number of organized associations and interest groups. These groups are developed about a wide variety of special interests. In the simpler societies there are fewer associations, with each association performing a much wider range of functions. In the folk society there are the family, clan, age and sex groups, but not the variety of political, economic, vocational and avocational interest groups. In the simpler organization of the folk societies a large proportion of the individual's interests, time and personal functioning was involved in each of the great associations. In the highly diversified interest groups of contemporary society only a small proportion of the individual's interests and time is involved in each of the numerous groups of which he is a member.[1] Another fundamental distinction may be made on the basis of the processes of association in the various groups. In the associations of the simpler societies interaction occurs primarily in face-to-face relations. Hence, opinion is formed on the basis of discussion, gossip, personal influences and the variety of stimuli provided in such contact. Most of the activities of the interest groups of the great society are carried on through the indirect contacts of writing, publications, pictures, radio and the other methods of secondary communication. Publics of various types emerge.

In the social sciences, preoccupation with groups is a central interest. Any number of individuals, from two to scores of millions, compose a group, and the nature of the group association varies infinitely. Any number of people having social relationships compose a group. Groups have been classified in terms of numbers of members, the way in which they are united, the purpose of the group, and the like. Types of classification are innumerable, as they depend upon the aspect of association that the classifier wishes to emphasize. Sociologists have discussed primary and secondary groups, in- and out-groups, horizontal and vertical, voluntary and involuntary, institutional, permanent and impermanent, kinship, ideological, conflict and cooperative, open and closed, class and caste, instinctive and rational, interest and locality groups, and

---

[1] Prof. F. H. Allport, in his volume *Institutional Behavior*, has used the terms "total inclusion" groups and "partial inclusion" groups, so as to distinguish the proportion of the personality involved in each. He concludes that modern society undesirably dissociates personality.

many others. Groups have been classified from the most intimate family, play and neighborhood groups to the least intimate international, race, age and sex groups.[1] Today there is more organization of groups at all levels than has been true in the past. New bases of interest emerge, as in the case of the organization of families with children versus childless families. Organizations of each type are often somewhat opposed on issues of taxation, regulation of amusement, community order, and the like.[2] Although the opinion process obviously operates in all groups, we will concern ourselves with the classifications of the major interest groups of the great society.

In a sense, all groups are interest groups. But the interest may be transient and the association fleeting. In a narrower sense, interest groups are those organized round about some enduring interest. "When a number of men unite for the defense, maintenance, or enhancement of any more or less enduring position or advantage which they possess alike or in common, the term interest is applied both to the group so united and the cause which unites them."[3] Thus, in the fundamental divisions of society there are sex groups, age groups, political groups, economic groups, class groups, race groups, and the like. These may be considered interest groups when they organize to provide some effective means for the attainment of aims held in common by their memberships. Interest groups arise when women organize associations, when the aged join a Townsend movement, when a political party organizes, when employers and employees, bondholders or the unemployed form associations, when a class organization appears with a more or less developed ideology or when a racial group develops an organization to face its foes or advance its status. Within such interest groups there are habitual and similar modes of behavior on the part of their individual members. They have their organizations and means of communication. The passengers on a streetcar are a group. They become an interest group when they express a grievance to the conductor or to the company. When such an association is formed, the attention of both the membership and the outsiders is increasingly turned upon the common interests.

As societies became larger, as their memberships were more widely distributed in space and as their cultures became more complex, the number of interest groups increased. As the modern state has assumed more functions in the lives of individuals, the number of organizations of sectors of its citizenship have increased. In modern political theory

[1] See classification in Bernard, L. L., *Introduction to Social Psychology*, pp. 418 *ff.*, 1926.

[2] See Seldes, G., "The War Between the Parents and the Childless," *Scribner's*, November, 1935.

[3] MacIver, R. M., "Interests," *Ency. Soc. Sci.*, 8: 144.

there is a persistent dispute over the extent to which the state should be based on group interests or on general community interests.   Meanwhile, the state has had to adjudicate conflicting interests.   "With the increase in organization the conflict of interests takes new forms, and the problem of establishing harmony between them thrusts new tasks upon the state."[1]   Since the emergence of Protestantism, ever new religious interest groups have been formed.   In the economic field, thousands of new interest groups have been organized since the beginning of the nineteenth century.   As divergent ideologies and values in the fields of ethics and in social relationships in general have been formulated, their proponents have organized many thousands of additional associations.   Interest groups slowly increased in number in the fifteenth century and rapidly in the nineteenth century and have proliferated enormously during the past fifty years.

All such groups influence opinion outside their own memberships. But it is often difficult to determine the importance of an interest group. Membership number is an inadequate criterion.   Membership distribution, composition and intensity of interest are factors in ascribing weight.   And all such groups have their spokesmen.   In the welter of conflicting testimony today, it is often difficult to determine who really represents whom.   The general public is frequently baffled.   Perhaps they can distinguish between a statement by a soapbox economist and a statement by President Roosevelt; but they cannot always distinguish between two spokesmen, each of whom claims to represent a million followers.   The failure to stress adequately the weight and extensiveness of influence makes possible the quoting of all kinds of statements as expressions of public opinion.   But—which publics?

Types of Interest Groups

Interest groups and pressure groups are sometimes distinguished. "A pressure group is defined by its techniques, an interest group by its objectives."[2]   However, this distinction is not consistently maintained in the literature of political and social science, and, as interest groups are also pressure groups, we shall use the terms interchangeably.   There are many types of such groups, and they may be variously classified. The geographic and political area within which they operate may be used as one basis of classification.   Groups operate internationally, nationally or within states, counties, regions, communities or other political subdivisions.   For example, the League of Nations has listed

[1] MacIver, *op. cit.*, p. 147.
[2] MacIver, R. M., "Social Pressures," *Ency. Soc. Sci.*, 12: 347.

the international organizations.[1] Counting those listed in the various divisions according to interests, we find that the number of international organizations devoted to pacifism is 16; law and administration, 4; labor, 63; education, 35; feminism, 9; sport and tourism, 32; humanitarianism, religion and morals, 89; economics and finance, 12; agriculture, 21; trade and industry, 32; communication and transit, 39; arts and sciences, 93; medicine and hygiene, 45; miscellaneous, international languages, protection of nature, politics, library, etc., 48. Among these are such organizations as the International Christian Peace Fellowship, Women's International League for Peace and Freedom, International Federation of Civil Servants, and so on, through the list of 574 internationally organized groups. These are formally organized. But there are interest groups, bound together by some common medium of communication, that are not formally organized. In Ayers's *Directory of American Newspapers and Magazines*, there are listed over 200 such groups that are not formally organized but that are served by one or more specialized publications. A bibliography on propaganda and promotional activities devotes sections to party groups, professional, labor, agrarian, ecclesiastical, age and sex groups.[2] The classification will depend upon the purposes of the writer.

We shall be concerned with interest groups that are most active in attempting to influence opinion outside their own memberships. Most interest groups perform many other functions. The technical societies and trade associations of the United States, without exception, are involved in publicity to influence various publics, but they engage in many other activities. In 1933, 301 such organizations, from the Abrasive Paper and Cloth Manufacturers Exchange to the World Calendar Association, engaged in some form of standardizing their products or activities.[3] Unfortunately, there is no comprehensive directory of interest groups in the United States, but we shall select data from a number of specialized directories and other sources. Such interest groups attempt to influence opinions of general publics, to reform or proselyte or to exert pressure on the opinions of legislators, administrators and political executives.

No one can say how many interest groups there are, nor do there exist exact data on their memberships. Fragments of information may be obtained from various sources. The *World Almanac* (1937 edition) lists 614 such groups. Of these, 166 have from 1 to 500 members; 51,

[1] *Handbook of International Organizations*, League of Nations, 1929; Supplement, 1931.

[2] Lasswell, H. D., Casey, R. D., and Smith, B. L., *Propaganda and Promotional Activities*, 1935.

[3] *Standards Yearbook*, 1933, Bureau of Standards Miscellaneous Publication, No. 139.

from 500 to 1000; 177, from 1000 to 5000; 61, from 5000 to 10,000; 41, from 10,000 to 20,000; 30, from 20,000 to 50,000; 24, from 50,000 to 100,000; 16, from 100,000 to 200,000; 23, from 200,000 to 500,000; 10, from 500,000 to 1,000,000; 17, from 1,000,000 to 5,000,000; 5 groups have memberships over 5 million.[1] There are hundreds of other groups not listed in this compilation. Most of these interest groups are represented by part- or full-time publicity agents or propagandists, devoted to influencing public opinion. These agents have various titles. Among the simpler and most innocuous-appearing titles are those used in the various bureaus of the Federal government, where publicity men are listed as principal specialists in information, senior experts in information, junior experts in information, head specialists in information, directors of information, special writers, and the like.

Prof. Beard has classified the chief interest groups as economic, reform, professional and religious organizations.[2] In the first group are the numerous industrial, trade, farm and labor associations. The reform groups are quite varied in their interests. There are patriotic societies, women's reform groups, governmental reform groups, prohibition organizations, and the like. Scores of professional groups scan the horizons of political action and of popular opinion to discover and change actions and beliefs inimical to their interests. Most of the Protestant churches maintain national organizations, some of which are powerful, such as the Board of Temperance, Prohibition, and Public Morals, or the Federal Council of Churches of Christ in America. And also there is the National Catholic Welfare Council. In addition to activities aimed at the influencing of opinion in general publics, many of these groups maintain representatives at Washington to influence the opinions of and exert pressure upon governmental officials. E. P. Herring lists 462 interest groups represented in Washington.[3] Of these, some of the larger and more important organizations are the Chamber of Commerce of the United States, National Association of Manufacturers, National Education Association, National League of Women Voters, American Legion, Board of Temperance, Prohibition, and Public Morals of the Methodist Church, National Grange, Federal Council of Churches, Anti-Saloon League, and the larger trade associations. The interest groups are represented by executives of quite varied backgrounds, training and abilities. A recently published volume gives brief biographical sketches of some 2700 executives, secretaries, managing directors and publicity men who represent 1372 organizations maintaining national offices.[4]

[1] Compiled from *World Almanac*, 1937, pp. 393–405.

[2] Beard, C. A., *The American Leviathan*, pp. 212 *ff.*, 1932.

[3] Herring, E. P., *Group Representation before Congress*, pp. 277–283, 1929.

[4] *Who's Who among Association Executives*, 1935. Published by the Institute for Research in Biography, Inc., New York.

The influence of pressure groups upon public opinion is obviously dependent upon the opposing organizations or the general attitudes that are encountered. Some groups that encounter little opposition have a significant influence without exerting much effort. Their effectiveness is also dependent upon the quality of their leadership, the size, character and distribution of their memberships and upon their material and psychological resources.[1]

THE ECONOMIC INTEREST GROUPS

The Census of 1930 listed the occupational distribution of workers as: manufacturing and mechanical, 14,110,652; agriculture, 10,471,998; trade, 6,081,467; domestic and personal, 4,952,451; clerical, 4,025,324; transportation and communication, 3,843,147; professional, 3,253,-884; extractive and minerals, 984,323; public service, 856,205; forestry and fishing, 250,469. Less than 15 per cent of the workers of various kinds are affiliated with organizations of the labor, business or professional types. But, of course, the organized interest groups exercise power far out of proportion to their numerical strength as compared with the total number of workers.

Of the business groups, the Chamber of Commerce of the United States has been by far the most important. As an exponent of business interests this organization, with a membership of something less than a million, maintains lobbies, exerts pressure on legislative and executive officers, maintains a speakers' bureau and engages in various publicity activities.[2] Its slogan is "What's good for business is good for the country." The Chamber of Commerce as an institution representing a cross section of American business has come to be recognized as the mouthpiece of business interests. It maintains an elaborate fact-finding bureau which collects data on various industries and businesses. It discovers and marshals the opinion of its membership on controversial issues. There are referendums on issues of national importance dealing with underlying principles. There are speakers who constantly tour the associated chambers and present such results and other material to the members. About 300,000 members subscribe to the official publication *Nation's Business*. Its press bureau is powerful and effective. The Chamber of Commerce maintains that it does not engage in lobbying or bringing pressure to bear on legislators or administrators. But officials are not unaware of its weight.

[1] See Childs, H. L., "Pressure Groups and Propaganda," Chap. 6, in *The American Political Scene* (Logan, E. B., ed.), 1936.
[2] See the discussion of the activities of the Chamber of Commerce in Herring, *op. cit.*, Chap. 5.

There are many commercial and industrial organizations. The Department of Commerce listed, in 1931, over 19,000 organizations that had for their purpose the advancement of industry or trade, the promotion of commerce and industry. Of these, there were 2634 interstate, national and international organizations, 3050 state and territorial groups and 13,625 local organizations.[1]

Among these organizations, the trade associations have become increasingly important. These are associations of producers or distributors of commodities. The earliest groups were formed shortly after the Civil War. During the past twenty years, hundreds of new associations have been formed. The NRA stimulated a great deal of organization of this type. There are now at least 1500 trade associations of various kinds. All major fields of economic activity are organized. These groups collect and distribute information about their industries, standardize practices, develop policies for their affiliated members, organize and maintain national and state lobbies and conduct publicity campaigns for the industry as a whole, both in the advertising of products and distributing publicity on policies. Over 200 of the trade associations maintain lobbies with permanent spokesmen in Washington. In addition there are many temporary lobbies to advocate or oppose specific measures. The trade groups also engage in special pleading. In a following chapter on propaganda, we shall discuss several illustrations of their publicity activities of a propagandistic nature. They also engage in publicity for the advertising of their various products. National campaigns have been conducted on the qualities of fruits, nuts and other agricultural products, on the superiority of electricity to other forms of light and heat, on why copper is the "Metal of the Ages," on why one should "Say It With Flowers," on the qualities of cypress (the "Wood Eternal") and about scores of other products.

Among the economic interest groups, the various labor organizations have the largest memberships. The American Federation of Labor has a membership of approximately three and a half millions, the CIO claims a million two hundred thousand and there are numerous small unaffiliated unions. The larger groups maintain publicity bureaus, publicize the studies and surveys that they make, organize demonstrations and "propaganda of the deed" and have become more or less skilled in appealing to popular opinion.

REFORM ORGANIZATIONS

The urge to improve the world is persistent and especially endemic in America. It is based upon a dominant value in our culture, that of the

---

[1] *Commercial and Industrial Organizations of the United States*, U. S. Department of Commerce Publication, 1931.

possibility of progress. Under democracy, like-minded individuals gather together in reform organizations. There have been hundreds of such groups in American history, ranging from transient and sporadic organizations, advocating a position on an immediate issue, to powerful organizations that have continued their agitation for decades. Such groups are preoccupied with some aspect of what they consider the general welfare and, presumably, not with the furthering of self-interests. They would better the conditions of some group or class (the elimination of slavery, the obtaining of votes for women, the protection of child life, the prevention of cruelty to animals, etc.), prohibit or not prohibit alcoholic beverages, introduce more or less violence in international relations, or improve public administration, and the like. There are several hundred such organizations of national scope at the present time. In addition, many of the other interest groups become reform organizations from time to time. Representatives of reform groups often exhibit great self-confidence in their ability to order and arrange desirably the lives of others.

One of the most effective reform groups in American life has been the Anti-Saloon League. Fifty years of temperance and prohibition agitation preceded the organization of the Anti-Saloon League in 1893. It developed a paid staff of professional workers and an extensive speakers' bureau, made use of a number of existing church organizations, created lobbies in each of the states and in Washington, exerted pressure on Congress and the assemblies and maintained an elaborate organization for publicity to influence public opinion and voting. The astute leadership of the league recognized the tactical value of emotional appeals, dramatized the saloon as the enemy of the child and corrupter of youth, personalized their inanimate enemy in cartoon and symbol, and related the saloon to vice, crime and evil in general.[1] They were early users of fear propaganda and drew vivid pictures of alcohol as the great destroyer and inciter to violence. In addition to their numerous speeches, the league tacticians broadcast their appeals and viewpoints in an enormous literature.

By 1912, its eight presses were printing more than forty tons of temperance literature each month, including thirty-one state editions of the American Issue, with an aggregate monthly circulation of more than 500,000. . . . By 1916, the Westerville plant was printing six different temperance journals, including four monthlies with an aggregate circulation of about 420,000, one weekly with a circulation of over 130,000 each week, and a daily with a circulation of approximately 15,000. . . . One might almost say that the liquor business was drowned in a flood of temperance literature. From October, 1909 to January, 1923, the American Issue Company turned out 157,314,642 copies of temperance papers.

[1] Odegard, P., *Pressure Politics*, 1928.

The periodical literature so far discussed comprised only a part of the League propaganda. The record of the job department at Westerville follows. The figures cover the period from 1909 to 1923.

Books	1,925,463	Other cards, tickets, etc.	18,522,471
Pamphlets	5,271,715	Miscellaneous	21,553,032
Leaflets	104,675,431	General printing	80,512,132
Window cards	2,322,053	Total	244,782,296*

* Reprinted from Odegard, *op. cit.*, pp. 74, 15. By permission of Columbia University Press.

The league worked extensively in the public schools. Talks, leaflets, poems, prose, motion pictures, essay contests and songs declared their message.[1]

WOMEN'S ORGANIZATIONS

Many reform groups, some occupational groups and a few economic interest groups have been composed primarily of women. By the middle of the nineteenth century, women in America were becoming increasingly group conscious and articulate. Women's colleges had been founded, women had been active in the antislavery movement, and in 1848 the first woman's rights convention was held. From then on, women added rapidly to the number and variety of their organizations. In the 1860's, two suffrage associations were formed, the National Woman Suffrage Association and the American Woman Suffrage Association. The General Federation of Women's Clubs was launched in 1890, and at the first biennial convention in 1892 there were 185 clubs represented.[2] By 1896 over 100,000 women were represented. According to Prof. Breckenridge, the principal features of the organization of women from that time onward were first federation, then cooperation between groups and then specialization of function.

We shall list briefly the principal women's groups as they appeared from 1900 to the present.[3] In 1903 the National Woman's Trade Union League heralded women's organizations in the labor movement. Women in medicine were organized in 1904, women in home economics in 1908. In that year the Council of Women for Home Missions was founded. From 1900 to 1910 the General Federation was extending its activities into the fields of civil service reform, education, forestry, household economics, pure food, industrial and child legislation and library extension. By 1910 the federation claimed a membership of 800,000.

[1] Pierce, B. L., *Citizens' Organizations and the Civic Training of Youth*, Chap. 27, 1933.

[2] Breckenridge, S. P., *Women in the Twentieth Century*, pp. 17 ff., 1933.

[3] This list is based upon Prof. Breckenridge's excellent historical sketch, *ibid.*, Chaps. 3–6.

In 1912 the Junior Leagues were organized on a national scale with six associations. In 1916 the Federation of Teachers was formed. The Woman's Peace Party was organized in 1915. The sporadic organization of business women had been occurring for some time, and in 1919 the National Federation of Business and Professional Women's Clubs was founded with delegates from 105 clubs. Meanwhile, the increase in variety of interests characterizing existing organizations was proceeding apace.

Women's organizations based on war activity and patriotism next appeared. The Service Star Legion, organized in 1919, rapidly developed a membership of 50,000 but has since lost all but 10,000 of its members. The Legion Auxiliary had a membership of 412,063 in 1931. The Daughters of the American Revolution held its first congress in 1892, and in 1932 there were 2463 chapters with a total membership of 169,626.

The National Council of Catholic Women, founded in 1920, had 1700 local societies by 1930. And the various parents' organizations were growing. A Mothers' Congress met in 1897, which by 1931 had become the Parent Teachers Association, with a national enrollment of 1,511,203 in 22,000 clubs. These follow, with more or less care, the organization, personnel and educational practices of the schools. The Young Women's Christian Association had 603,876 members in 1930. Over 50,000 paid and volunteer workers engage in activities with the girls of various age groups.

Meanwhile, the vocational organizations had grown. In 1930 the American Home Economics Association had over 10,000 members; in the American Nurses' Association over 76,000 registered nurses are enrolled; the Federation of Teachers has over 40,000 members; the Medical Woman's National Association has about 600; and there are about 56,000 individuals enrolled in the 1100 local clubs of the National Federation of Business and Professional Women. The farm women had organized into associations too numerous to be discussed here.

Most of the women's organizations have had some direct or indirect interest in political functioning, in influencing legislators and in attempting to mold general popular opinion. E. P. Herring reports that the following groups maintained Washington offices and were involved in politics: American Home Economics Association, American Nurses' Association, Daughters of the American Revolution, General Federation of Women's Clubs, International Association of Police Women, National League of American Pen Women, National League of Women Voters, National Woman's Party, Women's International League.[1]

The political activities of the National League of Women Voters surpass those of other women's groups and are, in general, more effective.

[1] Herring, *op. cit.*, p. 280.

This organization was formed in 1920. It now maintains a national office staffed by seventeen executives and twenty clerks. The league has unquestionably contributed greatly to the political education of its members and their husbands and friends. Study groups, forums, round tables, the quizzing of embarrassed political candidates and their own internal group politics have engaged the activities of these busy and serious women. Although its membership has remained relatively small, perhaps in part owing to the care and meticulous detail with which legislative proposals are assessed and to the nonpartisan nature of the league's appeal, this is the most promising organization for political education in America. There is no parallel group of equally serious male voters.

There are many other types of interest groups. Space forbids further elaboration. Table VIII indicates national organizations by fields of activity. This table is based upon the lists appearing in *A Directory of Organizations in the Field of Public Administration.*[1] This directory listed 1744 organizations in 1932, 1900 in 1934 and 1932 in 1936. Of these, the groups by areas were:

Organizations	1932	1934	1936
National	466	484	546
State	1131	1243	1220
Regional	65	85	79
Canadian	82	89	87

The increase in the number of interest groups results from the emergence of new interests and from the schisms within existing groups, which occur as the memberships disagree about interests and policies. This trend will no doubt continue for some time. And in so far as these groups represent real interests of their memberships and are really effective in molding the attitudes and opinions of their members, a certain isolation from the general public results. "Some tendency to isolation and spiritual impoverishment is likely to go with any sort of distinction or privilege. . . . These foster special tastes, and these in turn give rise to special ways of living and thinking which imperceptibly separate one from common sympathy and put him in a special class."[2] Moreover, as these groups become fixed and their organizations develop effectiveness in publicity and pressure, they put an ever increasing strain upon political government. Compromise and adjudication become more difficult. At

[1] Paige, R. M., ed., *A Directory of Organizations in the Field of Public Administration*, Public Administration Clearing House, Chicago, 1936.

[2] Cooley, C. H., *Social Organization*, p. 138, 1909.

TABLE VIII.—CLASSIFICATION OF NATIONAL ORGANIZATIONS BY FIELDS OF ACTIVITY

Adult education	20	Negro welfare	9
Agriculture, promotion of	26	Noise abatement	1
Aviation, regulation and promotion of	2	Oil conservation	3
Banking, regulation of	6	Parks	11
Blind, welfare of the	5	Pensions	1
Building, inspection and building codes	14	Physical education	6
Business and economic life, regulation of	24	Planning	16
Child health	13	Police	9
Child welfare	16	Ports and waterways	3
Childhood education	11	Prisons, administration of correctional institutions and	11
Consumers, protection of interests of	7	Professional training and registration	13
Crime prevention	9	Public administration—country and rural	7
Cruelty to animals, prevention of	1	Public administration—Federal	7
Deaf or hard of hearing, welfare of the	7	Public administration—general	15
Education	34	Public administration—municipal	9
Education for citizenship	7	Public administration—state	8
Education for public service	4	Public health	41
Fire protection	7	Public personnel administration	11
Fiscal control	10	Public personnel administration, postal service	8
Foreign born, welfare of	8		
Forestry	6	Public utilities, operation and regulation of	17
Game and fish protection	10	Public welfare	44
Gasoline taxation	2	Public works	15
Handicapped, welfare of	10	Purchasing	4
Highway construction and highway safety	29	Racing, regulation of	1
		Radio education	3
Hospital administration	12	Recreation	13
Housing	8	Refuse disposal	2
Indians, welfare of	6	Safety	10
Insurance, regulation of	3	School buildings	6
Justice, administration of	17	Securities, regulation of	2
Labor, regulation of conditions of	10	Sewerage and sewage disposal	6
Law, public	3	Social security	5
Legislation	5	Taxation	17
Library administration	9	Universities and colleges	14
Liquor control	1	Veterans, welfare of war	4
Mental hygiene	5	Vocational guidance, adjustment and placement	13
Milk and food inspection	5	Water supply	4
Motion pictures, regulation and supervision of	1	Weights and measures regulation	5
Museums	3		

times they are effective aids to formal government, but the more powerful groups have often made serious inroads on genuinely democratic government.[1]

[1] Friedrich, C. J., *Constitutional Government and Politics*, Chap. 24, 1937.

But what do they presage for popular opinion? In the United States, interest groups have been permitted a maximum of freedom to compete for opinion control. They use all the means of communication and all the methods of publicity. There is relatively little official control of such groups. The result has been a clarification of some issues but a confusion of counsel on many others. Much of the information distributed by pressure groups is distorted, incomplete and fragmentary, and sometimes untrue.

The development of these interest groups and their use of publicity and propaganda are inevitable results of the growth of modern society. Several schools of thought now advocate divergent policies in dealing with existing groups. There are advocates of various plans based on some variation of the European practice of incorporating them into the governmental framework of the state. Others would achieve unity by increasing the activities of the Federal government in opinion leadership and the formulation of policy.[1] Others would increase the number of opinion groups, encourage the creation of groups to counter those now existing, give additional publicity to the activities of all of them and struggle for some regulation of their activities and statements by legal restrictions. We shall consider some of the specific proposals in the following chapters on propaganda. H. L. Childs writes, "It is within the competence of the state, democratically motivated, to prescribe the 'rules of the game,' and so far as possible to raise the standards of pressure-group competition, thereby giving to the concept of 'survival of the fittest,' a more rational rather than a non-rational emphasis. By so doing, the ruinous consequences of ruthless pressure group competition may be avoided without abandoning the concept of freedom and accepting the fatal consequences of dictatorial state pressure in matters of opinion."[2] This objective is logical in principle but difficult to achieve. The unhappy liberal realizes the difficulties of governmental and legal control to assure veracity of interest-group propaganda and fair competition between groups. However, in principle he espouses such objectives.

[1] Herring, E. P., *Public Administration and the Public Interest*, 1936.
[2] Childs, H. L., *op. cit.*, p. 242. Reprinted by permission of Harper & Brothers.

CHAPTER XVII

PROPAGANDA

"Slogans about the 'menace of propaganda' contribute to the confusion and intensify the insecurities which threaten democratic government. . . . Propaganda against propaganda is just another propaganda."[1]
"The propagandist is a man who canalizes an already existing stream. In a land where there is no water, he digs in vain."[2]

Popular opinion becomes increasingly important in the modern world. Under diverse political systems—fascistic, communistic, monarchical, representative democratic and popular democratic—leadership is increasingly dependent upon popular approval. Under Protestantism, religious ideas and practices were democratized. Today, ethical codes very often reflect the folkways and are not developed into an integrated, consistent and logical ethical order. Economic groups search for the popular desires in consumers' goods. Large publics are increasingly consulted. Government, perhaps authoritarian rule most of all, must ascertain the wishes of the governed. Modern authoritarian rulers are not despots, they are mass creations. However, leadership in diverse fields does not merely reflect the popular values; it also attempts to mold them. Hence, there is special pleading of many kinds. Governments develop varieties of propaganda bureaus, special interest groups retain specialists in public relations and individuals hire publicity agents. The public-relations counsel is a significant symbol. In class relations, such interpreters create popular stereotypes of their employers. The families dominant in economic status in America during the nineteenth century often did not think it necessary to placate popular opinion. By 1911, the late Mr. Rockefeller had hired a publicity agent. The number of groups and individuals attempting to create a certain impression or to distribute interested information constantly increases. Truths as well as falsehoods and misinformation are disseminated.

Of late years, there is some popular understanding of the prevalence of special pleading. "We live among more people than ever who are puzzled, uneasy, or vexed at the unknown cunning which seems to have duped and degraded them, . . . these people probe the mysteries of propaganda with that compound of admiration and chagrin with which

[1] H. D. Lasswell.
[2] A. Huxley.

the victims of a new gambling trick demand to have the thing explained."[1]
Exposés of governmental propaganda in the World War, of the publicity
of utility companies, and the like, have stimulated an emotional
quest for the villain in the piece. Like the barber of Dayton, Tenn.,
who, during the evolution trial, bit the ear of a customer who
expressed an opposing viewpoint, there are many who wish to snap at
the illusive special pleader. However, students of human relations must
eschew personal praise and blame, except in so far as these are functionally
useful, cease haranguing on the propaganda menace and first attempt to
understand special pleading in terms of the general social process. It is
an inevitable concomitant of the growth and organization of society
during the past century.

The attempt to disseminate interested information and to win adherents to special viewpoints is as old as human society. The maneuverings
of the primitive chieftain and the circumlocutions of Mary Jones, in her
attempt to persuade her brother to do her household chores, illustrate
special pleading. Such personal relationships are persistent. There is
always competition for control of behavior and opinion. But in recent
times there is far more organization of the process, special pleading is
more consciously attempted and more individuals and publics are
engaged in the process. The competition for popular support has been
intensified.

The phenomenal increase in special pleading is based upon a number
of general factors. We have discussed at some length the development
of communication. Technological changes produced printing, pictorial
representations and finally the radio. With increased means of communication came literacy and the ability to use these agencies. On this
was based the development of political democracy and popular suffrage.
Popular education emerged and resulted in the diffusing of all sorts of
information and viewpoints. Society rapidly became more complex.
Diverse interests became apparent. And these interests led, as we have
noted in the preceding chapter, to a widespread proliferation of interest
groups. Representatives of these groups proselyted for their particular
viewpoints. Competitive special pleading for the control of publics outside these groups has been constantly intensified. But with the emergence of diverse interests and viewpoints there was also a heightened
popular awareness of the variety of possible positions. This has resulted
in psychological insecurity. Insecurity begets a quest for definitive
statements. New special pleaders emerge to meet this popular need.
These special pleaders, in turn, have expanding needs for communication. Hence, the intensified struggles for the control of newspapers,
cables, motion pictures and radio stations that have characterized the

[1] Lasswell, H. D., *Propaganda Technique in the World War*, p. 2, 1927.

past fifty years. And, as the publics enlarged, the methods of appeal and the various techniques of transmitting information reached lower common denominators. More means of communication, more organization, more groups, more special interests and causes, more competition for opinion control and the inevitable lowering of types of appeal. Then, too, the process is accelerated as communication becomes swifter. Added to this are the psychological insights that a science of human relations has placed in the hands of special pleaders. Partisan appeal by means of misinformation, emotional pleading and the short-circuiting of thought is no new thing. It has been the familiar accompaniment of special pleading. But the power of modern publicity is that it is directed by individuals who have greater understanding of the effective manipulation of motives, impulses and attitudes. Hence, with all its limitations, the effectiveness of modern publicity is unprecedented in history. All these trends have been developing for many years. They were not intended; they were certainly not planned. However, there has recently developed an increased popular awareness of the process, and certain aspects have become controversial. In addition, latterly, the social scientist has purveyed his sometimes more impartial insights.

Modern special pleading has been relabeled, and we now use the terms "publicity," "advertising" and, since the World War, "propaganda."

THE MEANING OF PROPAGANDA

If communication is to be accurate and meaningful, the definitions of many of the words used in the social sciences must be construed with some consideration of the meanings current in popular speech, as well as the specialized meanings created by the social scientists. In its original meanings, "propaganda" was any form of proselyting, publicity or education directed toward the changing of opinions. During the World War, it acquired the sinister connotation of special pleading that, from concealed sources, distributed untrue or only partly true information by devious routes. Popular emotional revulsion to the idea of such propaganda was pronounced. Today, governmental special pleaders sometimes label their bureaus as "counterpropaganda agencies." Thus they imply that their opponents distribute falsehoods which the bureau is attempting to correct with accurate information. Certainly the term "propaganda" is now in popular disrepute in the English-speaking world.

In the social sciences a working definition of propaganda is slowly emerging, but, owing to the emotional aura that the word has acquired in popular usage, it would probably be wiser to abandon it altogether and select other terms to designate the processes. However, as publicity men, political scientists, psychologists and sociologists are still using this word, let us examine some of their meanings. It would be futile and largely repetitious to quote several scores of definitions; we may therefore limit ourselves to a few significant descriptions of the concept.

We may first delimit the field of our concept by noting that propaganda is developed within the processes of communication, in contrast to the control of opinion by violent coercion or other types of behavior. "Propaganda may be defined as a technique of social control, or as a species of social movement. As technique, it is the manipulation of collective attitudes by the use of significant symbols (words, pictures, tunes) rather than violence, bribery, boycott."[1] Propaganda is disseminated through all the channels of communication.

We may further delimit by noting that propaganda is material that is consciously disseminated. There is intent on the part of the propagandist. "Propaganda refers to the conscious attempt to manage the minds of other and usually more numerous publics."[2] Doob has written of unintentional as well as intentional propaganda, noting that many of the social consequences of the propagandist's activity are unforeseen and unintended.[3] This is true regarding particular items, but the propagandist may be assumed to have a general objective. In any field, classifications based on motives are difficult, as motives must be assumed from indirect evidence. And the objective of the propagandist may not be evident from one particular statement. However, from a mass of evidence one may usually glean some knowledge of his intent. So we shall here limit propaganda to intentional special pleading.

The communication of information intended to influence opinions occurs in various types of special pleading, in advertising and publicity as well as in propaganda. A common distinction is to limit propaganda to special pleading in which there is an attempt to conceal the source.[4] After rejecting numerous definitions of propaganda as too general, F. E. Lumley concludes that, "Propaganda is promotion which is veiled in one way or another as to (1) its origin or sources, (2) the interests involved, (3) the methods employed, (4) the content spread, and (5) the results accruing to the victims—any one, any two, any three, any four, or all five."[5] We have then, a form of intended communication in which there is an attempt to conceal the source. It is the effort, without avowing the aim or revealing the motivation, to induce others to adopt beliefs.

Further, propaganda is usually characterized by the selection of materials favorable to the interest of the propagandist and the suppression

[1] Lasswell, H. D., "The Person: Subject and Object of Propaganda," *Ann. Am. Acad. Pol. Soc. Sci.*, 179: 89.

[2] Childs, H. L., in *The American Political Scene* (E. B. Logan, ed.), p. 226, 1936.

[3] Doob, L. W., *Propaganda*, pp. 76, 77, 1935.

[4] Biddle, W. W., "A Psychological Definition of Propaganda," *Jour. Abn. Soc. Psychol.*, 26: 285.

[5] Lumley, F. E., *The Propaganda Menace*, p. 44, 1933.

of unfavorable information. There is no attempt to present the facts objectively. There is deliberate distortion by selection. There are "partial and deliberately misleading statements."[1] We have, then, "a partisan, one-sided, self-serving communication to the public from an irresponsible and concealed source, calculated to influence public thought, either for or against a public cause or policy."[2] The objective of the propagandist is to achieve public acceptance of conclusions, not to stimulate the logical analysis of the merits of the case. In this he differs from the avowed objective of the educator under democracy. Obviously, the educator does not consistently maintain an objective presentation, but such is his ideal. But "it is obvious that propaganda has little respect for human personality. Propaganda is not education, it strives for the closed mind rather than the open mind. It is not concerned about the development of mature individuals. Its aim is immediate action. The propagandist merely wishes you to think as he does. The educator is more modest; he is so delighted if you think at all that he is willing to let you do so in your own way."[3]

Further, not only does the propagandist distort by partial and misleading statements, but he usually, by preference, appeals to the emotions of his subjects rather than attempting to stimulate a logical and rational analysis of his material. "Propaganda, as I understand it, means the process whereby public opinion is formed and controlled by appeal to the irrational side of man's nature in such a way that it is usually favorable to the interests of those directing the propaganda."[4] With all this intentional distortion and selection of materials to be disseminated as conclusions by emotional appeals, it is little wonder that to the common man propaganda has come to mean deliberate lying.

Of course, one is not unaware of the distorting effect of the accepted standards, values and viewpoints of any culture and its subgroups upon the opinions of its members. Such distortion is inevitable. Members of large groups cannot understand any controversial issue with entire objectivity. They begin with traditional biases. But such general distortions are not propagandistic. Propaganda is a special term referring to the intentional dissemination of conclusions from concealed sources by interested individuals and groups.

HISTORICAL SKETCH

The history of propaganda may be discussed in terms of the development of theories about special pleading, its defense and condemnation

[1] Steed, W., *The Causes of War* (A. Porritt, ed.), p. 172, 1932.

[2] Pew, M. E., "Propaganda," *Teachers College Record*, 31: 37.

[3] Martin, E. D., *The Conflict of the Individual and the Mass*, p. 29, 1932.

[4] Beaglehole, E., "Some Aspects of Propaganda," *Australian Jour. Psychol. Phil.*, 6: 96.

or in terms of the analysis of social structures and situations in which propaganda has been functionally significant. The theoretical justification of propaganda stems from Plato, who, in the *Republic*, advocated the suppression of the poets as special pleaders whose influence was disruptive. However, an official state poet was to be permitted to express the governmental position. The Platonic myth was to be inculcated. From Plato to the latest official justifications of propaganda emanating from Dr. Goebbel's Propaganda Ministry, there have been a host of theoretical defenses of propaganda, especially as administered by state and church. Distortion and lying, by leadership, for the public good has frequently been justified. The sociologist is primarily interested, not in the history of ideas about propaganda, but in the actual use of propaganda in social situations as a means of social control. Propaganda has ever been a concomitant of group conflict situations when it was necessary to plead with large publics. Propaganda has appeared whenever a leadership has attempted to weld the opinions of a people, from the political propaganda of a Julius Caesar, the propaganda of the Roman Catholic church, the propagation of the Napoleonic legend, Potemkin's propagandizing for Catherine the Great, Sam Adams' pamphleteering propaganda for the American Revolution, the propaganda of both North and South in the Civil War, to the proliferating propagandas of all sides in the World War. That propaganda is rife today on so many fronts merely reflects the variety of viewpoints and interests. That there is so much discussion of propaganda in Western publics reflects a more widespread consciousness of the importance of the springs of information. But the process is not new, although the extensive cultivation of it by so many groups is a modern phenomenon.

A few fragmentary historical references will illustrate the earlier use of propaganda.

According to Bertrand Russell, Herodotus, the father of history, was a hired propagandist of the Athenian State. He employed his literary talents as a historian to glorify his employer. In the war of the Guelphs and the Ghibellines, the Pope, Mr. Russell insists, won because he outdid the emperor in the organization of propaganda. At the time of the Armada, both Philip and Elizabeth indulged in energetic propaganda campaigns. Philip accused Elizabeth of every imaginable crime, while the friends of Elizabeth made all England shudder at the horrors of the Inquisition. Even Shakespeare was a propagandist, if we accept Mr. Russell's opinion. *King Henry VIII* was propaganda for Elizabeth and *Macbeth* for James I, who is shown as the descendant of Banquo, wearing a triple crown.[1]

[1] Viereck, G. S., *Spreading Germs of Hate*, p. 7, 1930. Quoted by permission of Liveright Publishing Corporation.

The simplicity of language of Caesar's *Commentaries*, which has made it a favored introductory exercise for Latin scholars, has been ascribed to Caesar's political appeals to the Roman masses. Such appeal was necessarily couched in simple language. Octavian and Antony are reported to have engaged in every then-known trick of political propaganda, and Cicero is portrayed as an accomplished propagandist.[1]

Sporadic appearances of propaganda are to be noted through the Middle Ages, especially in connection with the Crusades. The atrocity stories at the time of the Crusades are remarkably similar to those distributed during the World War. The witchcraft delusions and the Reformation were accompanied by some propaganda from official sources. All mass movements have their legends, rumors, stories and distorted and untrue information. Some such material is an inevitable result of human psychological processes under the strains of crises. Today, the fleeing Chinese are reported to be spreading atrocity stories about the Japanese. Only a small proportion of these probably are true. Propaganda is the organized dissemination of interested information. Though some organized propaganda existed in the ancient civilizations, in the Middle Ages and in the succeeding centuries, it was not until the seventeenth century that an organization devoted to the systematic development of special pleading appeared. In 1622, Pope Gregory XV inaugurated the *congregatio de propaganda fide*. This organization was charged with the supervision of liturgical books, the reports of bishops and other officials abroad and the carrying on of political, as well as religious, propaganda. Working through the thirty-seven large brotherhoods and special missions, this body strove for the strengthening of the political power of the Pope.[2]

Through the eighteenth and nineteenth centuries the stream of organized propaganda increased. "William Cobbett, about 1800, would use a lesson in grammar as a means of propaganda. Ostensibly illustrating the use of the verb "to be" he would write, To say that 'all Kings and priests is liars and oppressors of the poor' is not correct, but it is correct to say 'all Kings and priests are liars and oppressors of the poor.'"[3] At the close of the eighteenth century, Catherine had a master press agent and propagandist in her erstwhile lover Potemkin.[4] Napoleon was a propagandist who used all the then existing channels of communication, but he lacked a great propaganda director. He could suppress, limit and control (indeed, he suppressed sixty of the seventy-

[1] Lumley, *op. cit.*, pp. 58, 59.

[2] Stern-Rubarth, E., *Public Opinion and World Politics* (Wright, Q., ed.), p. 98, 1933.

[3] Desmond, R. W., *The Press and World Affairs*, p. 156, 1937. Quoted by permission of D. Appleton-Century Company, Inc.

[4] Dreifuss, J., *Catherine and Potemkin*, 1936.

three Parisian newspapers), but he did not effectively influence public opinion by indirection. "The press bureau under him was not a success; he could suppress, censor, crush, and intimidate the press; he could secure its adulation and its homage, but he evidently could not force his opinions on it."[1] Later in the nineteenth century, the organization of propaganda became more effective, the plans more astute and the methods more carefully worked out. Bismarck was a master propagandist. Through the press bureau, Bismarck suggested and dictated articles, indicated where and how they should appear, used fabricated letters to the papers purporting to come from France or Rome, started rumors and organized foreign propaganda.[2] The need for influencing popular opinion was becoming more evident, and the methods of distortion were being created.

In America, propaganda has accompanied each great mass movement. In the agitation preceding the Revolutionary War, a number of propagandists, notably Sam Adams, were effective inciters to revolution. Sam Adams organized town meetings, pamphleteered, manipulated newspapers and became expert in spreading rumors and creating legends. He has been designated a pioneer in propaganda.[3] This Puritan Machiavelli was a fomenter of revolt, a manipulator of mass emotions. In the Civil War, propaganda was more organized. "Supplementing their formal diplomatic negotiations, Lincoln and Davis both paid court to the art of propaganda. The extent to which the federal government engaged in frank and covert efforts to influence foreign opinion is not easy to discover because all the official papers are not available. . . . As to the propaganda of the Confederacy in foreign fields, more is actually known because its archives, seized after the war, were thrown open by the national government, revealing to the public the official efforts of President Davis to win support by the circulation of prepared ideas."[4] The Spanish-American War was conducted amid a welter of propaganda resulting in part from the search for spectacular stories conducted by the correspondents of the burgeoning press of the late nineties.[5] Theodore Roosevelt was one of the first public officials to perceive the importance of shaping public opinion by modern methods. Economic groups increasingly engaged in propaganda.

Competent individuals have long understood the uses and the principal methods of propaganda. But propaganda has lately increased enormously because of increasing group conflicts and diversity. The

[1] Salmon, L. M., *The Newspaper and Authority*, p. 323, 1923.
[2] *Ibid.*, p. 326.
[3] Miller, J. C., *Sam Adams*, 1936.
[4] Beard, C. A., *The Rise of American Civilization*, pp. 85, 86, 1927.
[5] Read Millis, W., *The Martial Spirit*, 1931.

stream of ideas in western Europe for centuries was obtained from the Bible and from the Greek and Latin classics. Political ideologies were not so varied as they have become. The underlying myths were more nearly alike. Today there is political diversity (the followers of Hitler have bought some millions of copies of *Mein Kampf*, and Lenin's followers have bought over four million sets of his collected works), numerous economic doctrines compete for a hearing and there is a phantasmagoria of conflicting values in various fields. The special pleader fishes in the troubled waters of contemporary cultural and group diversity. Propaganda in the modern sense begins approximately at the middle of the nineteenth century. "The Anti-Corn Law League, founded by Cobden and Bright in England in the year 1839, inaugurated the first highly organized persuasion peculiar to our times."[1] The crumbling of values and the processes of disorganization were accelerated by the World War. It was then that the harried governments indulged in the extremes of blatant propaganda. The flight from reason was accelerated. It was from the close of the war onward that the average newspaper reader observed more and more frequently this alien Latin word—propaganda.

Propaganda and the World War

In the World War, there was great diversity, on each side, in the cultural backgrounds of the peoples engaged in the struggle. It was necessary for the Allies and also the Central Powers to weld together the ideas and opinions of their peoples. This diversity also offered each side a fertile field for special pleading among the enemy, who might be divided and their morale disrupted. Therefore, propaganda was more extensively used than in any preceding conflict. "The definite purposes of war-time propaganda in every belligerent country were to maintain the morale of the armed forces of the state, create a favorable state of mind at home, diminish the morale of the enemy, influence favorably neutral opinion concerning the reason, justice, and necessity of the conflict, and, if possible, induce friendly action."[2] However, propaganda on a large scale did not begin with the World War, as numerous writers have asserted, but it was more widely disseminated and more highly organized than it had ever been before. Societal leadership became increasingly conscious of the uses and methods of propaganda. And since the war, propaganda has become a subject for public discussion. Numerous popular exposés of the war propaganda; the widely read autobiographical accounts of its chief practitioners, who, during the twenties,

---

[1] Biddle, W. W., *Propaganda and Education*, p. 20, 1932.
[2] Lutz, R. H., "Studies of World War Propaganda," *Jour. Mod. Hist.*, 5: 496–516.

half ruefully displayed their derelictions from the paths of truth;[1] the debunking accounts of popular historians in the decade after the war provided the more literate with an astounding record. But, essentially, propaganda was an inevitable product of modern special interests and the growth of communication. The World War simply intensified greatly the use of nationalistic propaganda and high-lighted the process. Opinion was mobilized as never before, and, after the war, the intellectuals and then masses of people became aware that such had been the case.

The widespread use of propaganda in the World War was inevitable. Long before the war, the stage was being set. The rise of modern publics, the development of means of communication, the need for general public approval in order to carry on modern warfare which necessitated the mobilization of civilians as well as soldiers, the existence of trained publicity men who had learned their art while advertising economic goods, the rise of a scientific psychology that made available to leadership the principles of mass suggestion, the knowledge of the cultures of alien peoples that had been accumulating rapidly during the preceding century—all these were factors. The channels of communication were mobilized in part before the war. Channels for the collection and distribution of foreign news were in large part nationally controlled. The diplomats of France with its Havas Agency, Great Britain with Reuter's, Germany with Wolff had already learned to use these national news bureaus to slant, distort and create news.[2] Foreign offices had plans for systematic propaganda at home and abroad.

Before the war, various German scholars had been employed in making meticulous studies of foreign psychologies. Although masses of information had been accumulated, it was rarely adequately coordinated, as the various departments and ministries that had sponsored these studies were relatively autonomous. After the war started, each department went ahead in its own way. There is general agreement among students of World War propaganda that a fatal flaw of the German system was the lack of coordination among the propagandists of the War Ministry, the Navy Department, the Colonial Office, the Foreign Office and other governmental divisions.[3] Within Germany, the principal

---

[1] Blankenhorn, H., *Adventures in Propaganda*, 1919.
   Charteris, G. J., *At G.H.Q.*, 1931.
   Creel, G., *How We Advertised America*, 1920.
   Crozier, J., *In the Enemy's Country*, 1931.
   Stuart, Sir C., *Secrets of Crewe House*, 1920.
   Viereck, *op. cit.*
   Bernstorff, Count von, *My Three Years in America*, 1920.
   Gibbs, Sir P., *Now It Can Be Told*, 1920.
[2] Irwin, W., *Propaganda and the News*, p. 122, 1936.
[3] Lasswell, *op. cit.*, p. 22.

themes of the propagandist were hatred and disparagement of the enemy, the war as self-defense against encirclement, the historic mission and high culture of the Germans and the inevitableness of victory.[1] But, because of the lack of agreement between departments, no effective national campaigns carried these appeals to all the German people. This is usually ascribed to the obstinacy of the War Office and the General Staff, which remained unconvinced as to the necessity of propaganda within Germany. In a brilliant analysis of German propaganda, Dr. Friedrich Thimme points to this failure as a radical fault.[2] Moreover, German propaganda abroad is credited with few real victories. Special pleading in Turkey was an exception. In a well-worked-out plan of bribery of a corruptible press, of specially written news reports and of pressures on officials, the German propagandists influenced the Turkish mind so that Turkey was brought into the war on the side of the Central Powers. Another exception was the skillful management of news sent from the Nauen wireless station. These news reports are credited with considerable success in influencing neutral opinion in Mexico and in most of South America.[3] However, most German propaganda abroad failed through ineptitude. As German leadership was unconvinced as to the importance of this work, the best minds were not directed to the problem. German propaganda had some successes. Russian morale was weakened by the flood of German printed newspapers and pamphlets. Holland and the Norwegian countries were influenced considerably. But at the crucial points, in the United States and among the Allied armies, it was relatively unsuccessful in comparison with the propaganda of the Allies among the Central Powers. G. S. Viereck, one of the German propagandists in the United States during the early years of the war, although he overstates the effectiveness of his own work, finally concludes that "the Germans were amateurs compared to the British. Nevertheless, German propaganda in the United States cannot be pronounced as a failure if its object was to keep America out of the war from August, 1914 to April, 1917."[4] It is true, however, that the German propagandists operated under great handicaps. Their armies had gone through Belgium and were invading France. In any invading army there will be incidents of brutality and violence which may be dramatized by the opponents and which are difficult to refute. German submarine warfare angered Americans and could not be explained away. The affinities between England and America could not be broken down.

---

[1] Lutz, *op. cit.*, p. 500.

    Salmon, *op. cit.*, p. 336.

[2] Thimme, H., *Weltkrieg ohne Waffen*, 1932.

[3] Irwin, *op. cit.*, pp. 129 *ff*.

[4] Viereck, *op. cit.*, p. 118.

The failures of German propaganda have been extensively reported, both by their own writers and by foreign observers.[1]

The lack of capable organization among the Allied propagandists during the first year of the war is generally admitted, but they had several great advantages over the Germans. As the English controlled the cables and cut most of the cables between Germany and the rest of the world, the Allies could spread stories about the German invaders; a language common to England and America was of inestimable advantage; the Allies had many organizations in the United States that were proponents of their cause. By the end of the first year of the war the main outlines of the English and French propaganda organizations for influencing the opinions of their own peoples and those of the neutrals had emerged. Intensive propaganda among the enemy came later. The importance of the work of maintaining civilian morale in England was made dramatically evident in 1915 when a series of exposés of military inefficiency confused and angered the English people, thus causing the formation of a new cabinet.[2] Steps were then taken to bring about a closer control of English news and communications. The importance of propaganda among neutrals, especially in the United States, was recognized from the beginning of the war. "Mitchell divides the subject matter of this propaganda into five parts. First, the militarist ideal in German life with its contempt for arbitration and its malice aforethought toward neutral Belgium. Second, the war policies of imperial Germany and a comparison of these 'damnable practices' (atrocities, deportations of workers, submarine warfare, etc.) with Allied methods. Third, a comparison of British colonial methods with German methods. Fourth, the idealistic war aims of the Allies in contrast with the German motives for opposing the new world order. Fifth, Great Britain's friendship for the United States described in the phrase 'Hands Across the Sea.'"[3] Historians differ as to the importance that they ascribe to English propaganda as a cause of America's entrance into the war. But they agree that most of the English propaganda campaigns in the United States were well organized, adequately subtle and for the most part quite successful in influencing opinion here.

[1] Thimme, *op. cit.*

Gerlach, H. von, *Die Grosse Zeit der Luge*, Charlottenburg, Verlag der Weltbuhne, 1926.

Mitchell, P. C., *Report on the Propaganda Library*, 3 vols., London, H. M. Stationery Office, 1917.

Lechartier, G., *Intrigues et diplomaties à Washington*, Paris, Plon-Nourrit, 1919.

For further bibliographical material on this point, see Lutz, *op. cit.*

[2] Irwin, *op. cit.*, p. 150.

Willis, I. C., *England's Holy War*, 1928.

[3] Lutz, *op. cit.*, p. 511. Quoted by permission of University of Chicago Press.

When the United States entered the war, government publicity and propaganda were quickly organized under the guidance of the Committee on Public Information. The committee was formed by executive order on Apr. 14, 1917. It consisted of the Secretaries of State, War and Navy, with Mr. George Creel as civilian chairman. Numerous publicity and newspaper men were available, men trained in advertising, the publicity of pressure groups, and in American journalism where the fine art of slanting news was a commonplace. The committee created subdivisions which dealt with (1) distribution of releases from civil and military departments, (2) a daily official bulletin, (3) civic and educational cooperation through the preparation and circulation of the *Red, White, and Blue* and the *War Information* pamphlets, (4) speaking in motion-picture theatres by four-minute men, (5) major public speaking campaigns, (6) syndicate features, (7) films, (8) pictures, (9) foreign-language papers, (10) distribution, (11) women's war work, (12) reference, (13) art, (14) advertising, (15) foreign educational work and (16) business management. On one point President Wilson was adamant. The funds of the committee were not to be used for bribery of officials in charge of channels of communication abroad. Fortunately for the maintenance of this high moral tone we were not under great pressure to influence neutrals. In general, governmental publicity and propaganda were quite successful in the United States.[1] The war ended too soon for our special pleaders of the Division on Foreign Educational Work to develop extensively the channels for veiled propaganda abroad. They did give wide publicity to the statements of the war aims of the United States, especially through quotations from President Wilson.

In 1918, the Allies conducted an extensive propaganda campaign within Germany by means of leaflets, books, news sheets and pamphlets which were distributed by planes and balloons and in various ways smuggled into Germany. These aimed to shatter the faith of Germans in their own leaders and ideas and thus disrupt morale. Dr. Thimme credits the United States with providing the fundamental thesis of this drive through President Wilson's utterances for freedom and democracy against militarism and autocracy. Though it cannot be denied that Allied propaganda was an important factor in disrupting German morale in 1918, it is possible that its influence in bringing about the German downfall has been overestimated. Most of the Allied propagandists who have written about this campaign have perhaps overestimated the effectiveness of their own work, and German commentators, likewise, have had patriotic reasons to overestimate the results of this drive.

[1] Creel, G., *op. cit.* A laudatory estimate of the activities of American propagandists.

Civilian morale appears to have followed closely the trends of German military position and success and failure. G. G. Bruntz, using the original charts of the United States War Department, has developed a simple chart indicating military position and the percentages of civilian morale.

We have presented only a few general statements about war propaganda.[1] This is not the place to summarize at great length the numerous descriptive accounts of national propaganda in wartime. A sizable literature of descriptive and analytic accounts on this subject has appeared

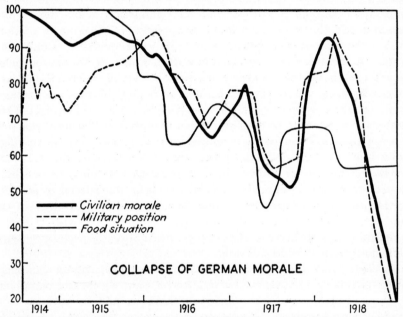

Civilian morale
Military position
Food situation

COLLAPSE OF GERMAN MORALE

FIG. 12.—(*From Bruntz, G. G., "Allied Propaganda and the Collapse of German Morale in 1918," Pub. Opin. Quar., January, 1938, pp. 64, 65. Permission to reproduce granted.*)

during the past twenty years. The student of war propaganda must turn to these for extensive records. The methods and processes of propaganda are not essentially different for propaganda in wartime and national propaganda in peacetime, except in so far as war increases governmental control and gives the propagandist a freer hand. He may thereupon be more blatant and use cruder tactics. In the following chapter we shall refer to the methods of the wartime propagandist, as well as those of the peacetime special pleader, under the caption The Art of Propaganda.

[1] The best two books on the processes of war propaganda are the volumes by Lasswell and Thimme to which we have referred in preceding footnotes.

THE STATE AND PROPAGANDA

It is possible today to generalize about the methods of propaganda. These are common to the propaganda disseminated by states, economic groups and institutional special interest groups in all Western cultures. We shall essay such generalization in the following chapter. However, no single student is adequately conversant with the different languages and the special cultural and political conditions of various contemporary European states to present an adequate descriptive and analytical account of the diverse and rapidly changing propaganda agencies of those states. We shall content ourselves at this point with a few fragmentary statements about national propagandas.

Political leaders have always used propaganda to further their causes. But, as we have noted, contemporary propaganda is quite different from that of earlier periods, in extent and amount, in conscious and highly skilled direction, in the variety of channels through which it is disseminated and in the diverse causes that it serves. Modern state propaganda, though similar in essence, is as functionally different from that of the Athenians as is the modern daily newspaper cartoon from the few scrawls of similar nature that were produced by the ancient Hindus. Propaganda is essential to the development of unanimity in modern states. It was incidental to the development of tribes or simple folk peoples.

Contemporary governments increasingly engage in special pleading and organized propaganda. "Fifty-seven or more countries are seeking in one way or another to obtain public acceptance of their objectives. Germany, Italy and Russia have incorporated in their governmental structures special departments and agencies for utilizing modern techniques of opinion management."[1] There is the propaganda conducted by national states, and that carried on in the interests of the state by private organizations. The extent of such propaganda cannot be known now. It cannot be calculated in terms of amount or cost. The propaganda budgets for activities within and without a state are hidden in many a departmental budget. The admitted activities are a small part of the total. In 1933, when demanding and obtaining an increased appropriation of 33 million francs for French propaganda abroad, Foreign Minister Paul-Boncour declared that during the preceding year the admitted expenditures of Germany for the same purpose were 256 million francs (before Hitler); of Italy, 119 million francs; of France, 71 million francs; of Great Britain, 69 million francs; of Poland, 26 million francs; and of Hungary, 23 million francs.[2] These figures have meaning

[1] Childs, H. L., article in *Seventh Yearbook, National Council for the Social Studies*, p. 1, 1937.
[2] *Time*, Apr. 17, 1933.

simply as indicators of the large sums involved. They are neither accurate nor complete. Most expenditures of this type are hidden in budgets. Since 1933, expenditures for propaganda have increased. In Germany, during 1937, Dr. Goebbels' Propaganda Ministry was allotted 48½ million dollars, and an additional 21 million dollars for propaganda abroad.[1] It is impossible to distinguish between governmental expenditures on informational service and its propaganda activities.[2] There are no accurate figures on the cost of governmental propaganda at home and abroad for any major nation.

The expansion of state propaganda activities developed during the World War and has been continued since then. Under authoritarian governments the individual citizen has been the object of special propaganda efforts, and the world outside has been deluged with special pleading. But the governments in power in democracies have also increasingly engaged in propaganda at home and abroad. The effectiveness of these efforts varies with the special conditions in each case. For example, existing attitudes and prejudices make ineffective much of the propaganda activity between France and Germany. But Mussolini's propaganda among tribesmen of Africa and the Near East has been notably successful. The United States has not spent large sums on state propaganda abroad, but the largely incidental propaganda of certain motion pictures has been notably influential in many parts of the world. The influence of a state's propaganda abroad can be measured neither by the money nor the effort expended thereon. Moreover, in the prevalent opinions of the citizens of any two nations about one another, the influence of unofficial special pleading may be far more effective than official propaganda. And the objectives of unofficial special pleaders may likewise be hidden. Dr. Lin Yutang maintains that the average citizen in the United States has been influenced far more by missionaries' accounts of the Chinese people than by any other reports.[3] And the

---

[1] Editorial, *St. Louis Globe-Democrat*, Jan. 16, 1938.

[2] See: Kent, F. R., "Washington's Ballyhoo Racket," *Am. Mag.*, September, 1937; Carroll, G., "Dr. Roosevelt's Propaganda Trust," *Am. Mercury*, September, 1937; Michael, G., *Handout*, 1935. The last item is a perfervid pamphleteering attack on the present administration and no doubt contains many inaccuracies.

Opponents of the present Democratic administration have maintained that governmental informational services, a large part of which they label "propaganda," cost over 200 million dollars a year—over 100 million in lost postal revenues, 25 million for paper and 75 million for printing—all this in addition to the salaries paid to publicity men in various departments.

See also: Herring, E. P., "Official Publicity under the New Deal," *Ann. Am. Acad. Pol. Soc. Sci.*, 179: 167–175; Hanson, E., "Official Propaganda and the New Deal," *Ann. Am. Acad. Pol. Soc. Sci.*, 179: 176–186.

[3] Yutang, L., "A Chinese Gives Us Light on His Nation," *New York Times Mag.*, Nov. 22, 1936.

ideas that the missionary has disseminated about the Chinese are those spectacular and dramatic items about Chinese folkways which will be most likely to influence Kansas audiences to give more funds to missionaries. International propaganda activities are pervasive in the modern world because of the variety of interests involved. Of these, the state is but one, unless, as in the case of authoritarian states, it assumes a monopoly of export propaganda.

The distortion and suppression of facts and other aspects of special propaganda pleading are defended and assumed as a justifiable activity of governments under dictatorships. In Russia, Italy, Germany and under a host of minor authoritarian governments, the notion of a completely informed public opinion is rejected. Substituted for this idea is the doctrine of the paramount necessity of prevailing upon people at home and abroad to accept the "proper beliefs," that is, the beliefs revealed or developed by their leadership. Public opinion process, in the sense of controversial discussion, is repudiated. For them, political truth is something, not that the individual seeks for himself, but that exists or is revealed in party programs with which the individual must be brought into harmony. Political truth is a monopoly of the Communist doctrine or of fascism or of Nazi principles. The writings of Marx, or Pareto or Sorel are used to bolster the leaders' contentions.

In Germany, Nazi propaganda was organized long before Hitler came into power. It was related to attitudes that already existed among masses of Germans. Many people wanted the Jews persecuted, the trade unions dissolved, national sovereignty asserted, reparations stopped, political parties suppressed and a more unified national culture created. The Nazis provided a general program and defended it as an inspired cause. Der Führer enunciated a program and became a prophet. After coming to power, the Nazis organized at once their plan of censorship and restriction and of propaganda of the cause. Intimidation was inadequate; the vacillating must be convinced. "The organization of a National Ministry of Propaganda and Popular Enlightenment immediately after the hour of triumph had struck for the Brown Shirt forces, is in itself a remarkable comment on Hitler's reluctance to rely primarily on the fists of his followers or the display of governmental authority."[1] Supporters were to be enrolled, not only by actually changing some objective realities, but also by ideological conscription. Symbols were widely used, emotional loyalties aroused and the sources of information controlled. Dr. Goebbels of the Propaganda Ministry organized seven divisions to which were entrusted all channels of communication.

[1] Marx, F. M., "State Propaganda in Germany," in *Propaganda and Dictatorship* (Childs, H. L., ed.), p. 13, 1936. Quoted by permission of Princeton University Press.

Division I: Legislation and Legal Problems; Budget, Finances, and Accounting; Personnel Administration; Ministerial Library; National Chamber of Culture; Council of Commercial Advertising (*Werberat der Deutschen Wirtschaft*); Fairs and Expositions.

Division II: Coordination of Popular Enlightenment and Propaganda (*Positive Weltanschauungspropaganda*); Regional Agencies of the Ministry; German Academy of Politics (*Deutsche Hochschule für Politik*); Official Ceremonies and Demonstrations; National Emblems; Racial Questions; Treaty of Versailles; National Literature and Publishing; Opposing Ideologies; Youth Organization; Business and Social Politics; Public Health and Athletics; Eastern and Border Questions; National Travel Committee (*Reichsausschuss für Fremdenverkehr*).

Division III: Radio; National Broadcasting Company (*Reichsrundfunk-Gesellschaft m. b. H.*).

Division IV: National and Foreign Press; Journalism; Press Archives, News Service; National Association of the German Press (*Reichsverband der Deutschen Presse*).

Division V: Cinema; Moving Picture Industry; Cinema Censorship; Youth Literature Censorship.

Division VI: Theater, Music, and Art; Theater Management; Stage Direction; Design; Folk Art.

Division VII: Protection against Counter-Propaganda at Home and Abroad.[1]

Newspapers were controlled, journalists certified, literature scanned and certified and radio and motion-picture productions administered by Nazi officials, in the interests of the party. The Japanese call their combination of censorship and propaganda "thought control." German propaganda under Dr. Goebbels has often been subtle thought control. It is true that the propagandist in the authoritarian state may readily be credited with more cleverness than he has really exhibited, owing to the fact that he is likewise a censor. None the less, it is generally admitted that the Propaganda Ministry has exhibited an astute knowledge of the desires of the German people. German propaganda abroad has been less successful. In the United States, it has been carried on through many organizations favorable to Germany, by distributing literature and by promoting tourism.[2] This propaganda has been largely unsuccessful because the actual and reported events in Germany alienated large sections of the American population, which were intolerant of violence, persecution and undemocratic political procedures.[3]

Any authoritarian government seeks to substitute political uniformity for party strife. Modern dictatorial governmental control has its longest

[1] Marx, *op. cit.*, p. 20. Quoted by permission of Princeton University Press.

[2] Riegel, O. W., *Mobilizing for Chaos*, p. 205, 1934. German propaganda activities in the United States were the subject of a Congressional Investigating Committee report entitled *Investigations of Nazi Propaganda Activities, 73rd Congress, Second Session, Hearings No. 73-DC-4; 73-NY-7; 73-NY-12; and 73-NY-18*.

[3] Read Doob, *op. cit.*, pp. 290–301.

history in Soviet Russia. Opinion management has been the objective of Communist leaders since 1917. If they have not exhibited the virtuosity in opinion control that has been evidenced in Germany, this is due to the lack of development of Russia's means of communication and to the diverse, varied and backward populations with which they have had to deal. On Nov. 12, 1920, a decree was issued for the creation of the Main Political Education Committee of the Republic.[1] This committee has charge of the entire work of political propaganda and education. Its objective has been to inform masses as to what the party stands for. The first section of the committee has charge of the school system and has supervised the content of school subjects, especially in the social studies. The second section, the *Politprosvet*, has charge of the general work of political education and propaganda. The fundamental unit of this section is that which develops the peasant reading huts and the town clubs. The reading huts and clubs have been consistently increased in number, until in 1933 there were 54,623 such organizations.[2] These clubs have striven for the liquidation of illiteracy, especially among adults.[3] Reading lists, general histories, geographies and outlines of political economy have been prepared and distributed among the clubs, as well as in the formal schools. Lectures, motion pictures, radio broadcasts, and excursions are organized for the club members. One must remember the vast number of illiterates still existing in Russia, despite the intensive endeavors of the party. In 1928 there were over eighteen million illiterates in European Russia and more than that number in Asiatic Russia, and over 40 per cent of the children of school age were still without access to schools.[4] Large appropriations have been made for libraries into which have been placed selected lists of books. In 1934 there were 32,456 such libraries. Amusements, plays and motion pictures are also supervised; indeed, nowhere else have the stage and screen been so completely organized in the interests of political propaganda.[5] The huge army, with its changing personnel, has been a fertile center for political education in Russia. The soldiers receive a thorough course in indoctrination in party principles as a part of their training. During two full years they receive political education as well as military training. Newspapers, periodical publications and, indeed, all printed materials are vigorously supervised. The press is propa-

[1] Maxwell, B. W., "Political Propaganda in Soviet Russia," in *Propaganda and Dictatorship* (Childs, H. L., ed.), p. 62.

[2] Maxwell, *op. cit.*, p. 66.

[3] Harper, S. N., *Civic Training in Soviet Russia*, Chap. 13, 1929.

[4] Maxwell, *op. cit.*, p. 70.

[5] Propagandistic motion pictures have not always been popular. Indeed, the recent increase in importation of foreign motion pictures has resulted from popular demand.

gandist, and some papers (such as the *Workman's and Peasant's News-paper*) have enormous circulations. In spite of all this intensive cultivation of the "right" political attitudes, political education constantly lags behind the expectations of party leaders, and the Central Committee of the party is persistently occupied with this problem.

Regimented opinion is the objective of authoritarian states. Dictators maintain that social discipline can be achieved in no other way. From this viewpoint, effective state action is declared to depend upon doctrinal unity. Moreover, the doctrines are flexible and are changed in terms of immediate objectives. Dictatorial propaganda, with varying degrees of skill, strives to align people with state programs. The methods used and the success achieved vary with the situation. Descriptive accounts of such propagandas are available in a growing literature.[1]

In a world of competing political doctrines, the partisans of democratic government cannot depend solely upon appeal to reason or abstract liberalism. But the propaganda for democracy cannot be disseminated by the government in power nor by the state schools without violating the basic principle of such states, that of toleration of heterodox opinions. Of course, in practice, the content of education under democratic rule contains special pleading for democracy. That is inevitable. It is the "climate of opinion." But beyond this there must be organized special pleading for democracies. The deliberate cultivation of private agencies with this objective is the only practice consistent with democratic principles. Such activities may be conducted by political parties, voters' leagues, endowed agencies and a host of various existing organizations. The political parties may be especially effective. As Prof. G. E. G. Catlin concludes, "The position is then that a democratic government, without forfeiting its own title to allegiance, is not entitled to use propaganda in the sense defined. It is, however, free and under an obligation to encourage voluntary agencies, and primarily party agencies, to put forward the views upon which its own authority rests. There is an entirely legitimate field of governmental party propaganda, as distinct from state propaganda. How to make that propaganda effective is the most important issue of current practical politics."[2]

ECONOMIC GROUPS AND PROPAGANDA

By definition, propaganda is the dissemination of conclusions, from concealed sources or with concealed motives, by interested individuals or groups. The number of interest groups that have occasion to distribute

---

[1] In this discussion we cannot attempt to summarize even one particular case. That is a subject to be dealt with in volumes. But every student should read *Propaganda and Dictatorship* (Childs, H. L., ed.), Princeton University Press, 1936.

[2] *Propaganda and Dictatorship* (H. L. Childs, ed.), p. 138.

propaganda has increased rapidly during the past century. We have noted this development in the preceding chapter. Among these interest groups, the business organizations have been notable in their extensive use of advertising, publicity and propaganda. When a National Dairy Association has a health clown going about in the elementary schools, amusing the pupils with his clown stunts but interspersing these with doggerel and songs about the beneficial effects of milk and dairy products —that is propaganda.[1] Thousands of business organizations, from the national organizations of trade associations to the local business group spreading rumors about its competitors, are engaged in propaganda. This propaganda, as well as advertising and publicity, was inevitable, as the business process came to depend more and more on popular opinion.

The most notable, the most highly organized and, finally, owing to a Federal Trade Commission investigation, the most notorious of the propaganda attempts by business groups have been the propaganda campaigns of the utility companies. The revealing of the propaganda activities of the utility companies came about as incidental to a Federal Trade Commission investigation of the control and financing practices of these companies. In 1927, Senator Walsh had proposed a Congressional investigation of the financial activities of utility holding companies. This investigation was likely to be popular and politically meaningful. After all, there were twenty-five million users of electricity, fifteen million users of gas and many disgruntled investors. However, this proposed investigation was sidetracked, and a Federal Trade Commission investigation was substituted for it in 1928. This investigation was carried on during three years and resulted in a voluminous report of some 14,293 pages. In the intent of the investigators, publicity and propaganda activities were of minor interest. However, these proved so spectacular that attention was centered more and more upon this phase of the activity of the utility companies. The results of this investigation were not widely publicized in the newspapers but have been extensively discussed in periodical literature and in books.[2]

The propaganda activities of the National Electric Light Association (national association of utility companies), as exhibited in the report of the Trade Commission, have been violently attacked as contrary to the public interest. For the most part the charge is undoubtedly true. But the activities of many other business groups that have not been

---

[1] A "stunt" of the early 1920's.
[2] Gruening, E., *The Public Pays*, 1931.
   Levin, J., *Power Ethics*, 1931.
   Raushenbush, H. S., *High Power Propaganda*, New Republic, Inc., 1928.
   Thompson, C. D., *Confessions of the Power Trust*, 1932.

subjected to an equally searching investigation are similar in intent if not in extent. There is nothing gained by centering attack upon one group. Such propaganda activities are part of a process of special pleading made inevitable by modern conflicts of interest and the creation of the means by which popular appeals may be made. However, the utilities propaganda has been the most extensive and the most discussed of the special pleadings of the business groups· so we shall briefly sketch the essence of their propaganda activities.

In the United States, during the past two decades there has been a growing debate over public or private ownership of utilities. The great and inexhaustible source of power is water power. Should hydroelectric plants be state-owned and -directed? Should there be municipal owner-ship of the local systems? As the groups interested in municipal or state ownership increased their activities during the 1920's, the utilities responded with extensive campaigns of publicity and propaganda for private ownership. The cost of these campaigns could be charged to the public. Publicity directors were advised not to be sparing in their expenditures. In the heyday of the N.E.L.A., over thirty million dollars was spent annually on these campaigns for private ownership. In 1919, Mr. Samuel Insull called together the executives of his companies for a discussion of public relations. They were told to do something. Two years later, Mr. B. J. Mullaney, one of the vice-presidents, reported:

"When the committee celebrated its second anniversary last April, it had passed the five million mark in pieces of literature distributed. Those five million pieces of literature, all helpful to the utility industry, were not merely scattered broadcast, but were definitely placed; with newspaper editors for themselves and their readers; with customers of public utilities; with business men, bankers, lawyers, employers (for their employees), teachers, preachers, librarians, students in colleges and high schools, mayors, members of city councils and village boards, public officials of all kinds, and candidates for public office. Members of the legislature, for example, received informative matter on public utility questions, not after they were elected, but before they were even nominated."

Mr. Mullaney summarized the other activities as follows: "A news service goes regularly to the 900 newspapers in the state, about 150 of them dailies.

"Speakers' bulletins are issued. . . . The bulletins furnish ample material to any intelligent person for sound talks on each subject and they have been widely used.

"A bureau is operated to find engagements before clubs, civic associations and so on, for dependable speakers. . . .

"Pertinent addresses and articles by important men, resolutions or other expressions by chambers of commerce and other bodies, exceptional editorials and the like, and special matters for customers, investors and employees have been printed and circulated among special classes by hundreds of thousands.

"More than 800 Illinois high schools are regularly furnished informative literature for classroom theme work, and debating-society use."[1]

By the end of 1922, the N.E.L.A. had organized committees on public relations in the majority of the states and had divided the country into twelve general zones for publicity campaigns. Mr. G. B. Cortelyou, chairman of the advisory committee of the N.E.L.A. stated that the objective was "to demonstrate that the entry of Government whether national, state or local into this field is constitutionally unsafe, politically unwise, economically unsound, and competitively unfair."[2] In 1933, after the publication of the report of the Federal Trade Commission investigation of the utilities, the N.E.L.A. voluntarily disbanded on the decision of the fifty board members present at the meeting. The Edison Electric Institute was formed, and Mr. G. B. Cortelyou, who had been president of the N.E.L.A., became president of the Edison Electric Institute. However, the constitution of the institute specifically declares that it will not engage in propaganda, that its publicity statements will be accurate and will clearly indicate their source.

The ramifying activities of the N.E.L.A.—the influencing of officials, editors and college professors; the distortion, slanting and fabrication of news and information for textbook writers, for the country editor, for the press associations; the partial information distributed by radio and screen, by speakers and all means of communication; the work of utilities representatives upon various organizations, the church, civic organizations, labor organizations, farm groups, women's clubs and others—are reported in the exhibits presented in the many volumes of the report of the Federal Trade Commission. There is the record of the most extensive campaign of propaganda ever conducted by a private organization. Falsehoods and purposeful distortion of fact are very evident in this campaign. At this point we shall not consider the methods of the private-utility propagandists. These will be sketched in the following chapter.

There exist the objective realities of public-utility service, rates and charges, stock values, watered stock, plundering holding companies and the various misfortunes of the utility companies of late years. These have become known somewhat to the general public, although the newspapers, owing either to principle or to a desire to secure utility advertisements, have been reticent on adverse utility news. Then there are the special pleadings of the utility propagandist, his assurances about the justice of the rates and the skill of private management and assertions that public ownership would be very wasteful. But the record and the

[1] Quoted by Gruening, *op. cit.*, p. 19. Quoted by permission of Vanguard Press, Inc.

[2] Quoted by Raushenbush, H. S., and Laidler, H. W., *Power Control*, p. 24, 1928.

assertions do not agree. And so, if the private-utility propagandist encounters increasing popular opposition to his pleas, the explanation may be found, not in his lack of skill as a propagandist, but in the experience that so large a proportion of the general public has had of the charges made upon it for service and in the anger engendered by widespread losses in the common stocks of the utility companies. The propagandist can intensify existing attitudes, but he cannot reverse the attitudes of large publics when they believe that their own interests are at stake.

ADVERTISING AND PUBLIC OPINION

Advertising may be distinguished from propaganda in that the sources of the advertisement are stated and the motives of the advertiser may be readily assumed (when the sources are concealed, as in the case of a food-products company publicizing its claims over the name of a supposed scientific research organization, we have commercial propaganda). There is a perennial debate over the effectiveness of advertising as a creator of markets, but it is quite obvious that advertising has been enormously influential in causing people to buy particular products. At many points commercial advertising has been far more successful in swaying opinions than has propaganda for causes. Aldous Huxley has reasonably maintained that the commercial advertisers have modified opinions more extensively than the political or ethical propagandists, not because their techniques are superior but because advertising is concerned with matters of no importance. When the political propagandist begins a campaign, he does so because there exist some real differences of opinion among the members of a general public. He deals with issues. But when an advertiser urges one to buy one soap or another of equal merit or worthlessness, or one kind of cigarette among a number of cheap cigarettes, and the like, there is no real issue for the consumer.[1]

As a means of spreading of information, rather than as high-pressure persuasion, advertising has existed from earliest times. Modern persuasive advertising is a product of modern methods of communication, of the historically recent orientation of industry toward the production of masses of consumers' goods and of the development of the advertising business itself which further stimulates its own activity. Advertising of the high-pressure, persuasive type has developed in the period since 1890. American publicity men have been the most effective high priests of commercial publicity.

It is quite obvious that advertising has been very effective in swaying popular opinion as to the qualities of consumers' goods and in influencing the choice of those goods. It was primarily the advertising man who lifted the product of the cigarette manufacturers from its status of lowly

[1] Huxley, A., "Notes on Propaganda," *Harper's*, 174: 32.

"coffin nail" to that of a national necessity.   Folkways with regard to gum chewing were created by publicity.   The citizen's preoccupation with the cleanliness of his teeth and skin surfaces was developed largely from the information provided in the advertisements he read.   The hunt for germs in the various orifices and on the surfaces of the body was stimulated by the manufacturers of germicides.   Information and mis-information about food values have led to fashions in foods.   Cereals used for the American breakfast have been pounded, exploded, inflated, sieved and woven as the "scientific" facts propounded by the advertising man have convinced consumers that their foods should be so treated. And so on.   Opinions and behavior have been rapidly changed as the advertiser has presented his phantasmagoria of changing information.

It is only during the past decade that the advertising process has been extensively discussed and attacked.   A number of intellectuals, evidencing that they felt the appeals and wiles of the advertising man to be a personal insult, have indicated their revulsion in no uncertain terms.[1]   The principal types of discussion have been as follows.

First, the expenditures on advertising have been attacked as econom-ically wasteful.   Since 1920, advertising in the United States has cost from one billion to two billion dollars annually.   The opponents of modern advertising maintain that the effort and materials utilized in advertising might have been expended on the creation of more goods. The defenders of the process declare that, inasmuch as advertising informs potential consumers of the existence of goods and stimulates purchase, advertising has been responsible for a part of the consumption of goods.   They declare that national income, as measured in dollars, is, therefore, increased by much more than the two billion dollars spent on advertising.   No reputable economist has essayed the difficult, if not impossible, task of calculating just what the advertising expenditure should be to achieve the maximum distribution of goods without waste in the advertising process itself.   On this point, pronouncements by high authority are few.   And, of course, the critics would not desist even if they were convinced that in terms of counters (dollars) the total national income had been increased.   They would turn at once to the problem of the relative quality of goods, as

Second, the critics of advertising say that the appeals of the advertis-ing man have led to the consumption of inferior and ill-selected types of consumers' goods.   Instances of adulteration, misrepresentation and quackery are stressed.   The advertising man declares, "This, then, is the gist of the matter; somebody must determine what goods are to be produced.   The decision must rest either with the Government or with

[1] Chase, S., *The Tragedy of Waste*, Chap. 7, 1926.
Rorty, J., *Our Master's Voice*, 1934.

consumers. As society is now organized, consumers decide. The only way they can make their decisions effective is through exercising their freedom of choice in the ordinary course of marketing. This freedom of choice constitutes the chief risk of business and gives rise inevitably to profits and losses."[1] "Little by little it seems to be recognized that this demand factor is not a spineless effect but a restless and irresistible cause."[2] But the advertising man does not stress that the psychologically bound consumer—harried, frightened, cajoled, and misinformed—is not free. And it is to the methods of appeal that the critic most violently objects, stating that,

Third, only a small proportion of advertising is based on logical appeals or argumentative procedures (long-circuit appeals); the bulk of advertising is based upon appeals to the emotions, upon unworthy motives or upon direct suggestion (short-circuit appeals). Indeed, a large proportion of the textbooks and articles on the "psychology of advertising" are devoted to the analysis of the relative strength of various appeals in relation to particular types of products. D. Starch notes the basic desires as those for food, comfort, mating, power and approbation.[3] A. T. Poffenberger inventories the fundamental desires as those for drink, food, sex experience, ease, escape from danger, dominance, conformity, parenthood, play, cleanliness, beauty and economy.[4] It is assumed, not that these desires are all innate, but simply that they are dominant in our culture. There are scores of such classifications in psychological literature dealing with advertising. Certainly the advertising man knows that however limited the capacity of the common man for sustained logical analysis, his responsiveness to appeals to fundamental desires is almost limitless. The consumer responds to suggested short cuts ("learn French in ten lessons"); to the titillation of sex interests; to the prestige of individuals; to fear (the whole gamut of scare copy of the advertising of germicides, insurance and scores of products); to pseudo science; to numerous other widely distributed appeals. Certainly the advertiser has investigated desires in greater detail than has any other type of special pleader. And he persistently exploits the limited capacity of most of us for logical thinking. To his critics, the defender of persuasive advertising simply replies that he is not responsible for popular dispositions, nor is he the creator of psychological values. He is simply utilizing those which he discovers extant in the general public, so that he may distribute the maximum quantity

[1] Cherington, P. T., *The Consumer Looks at Advertising*, p. 63, 1928.

[2] *Ibid.*, p. 38.

[3] Starch, D., *Controlling Human Behavior*, p. 32, 1937.

[4] Poffenberger, A. T., *Psychology in Advertising*, Chap. 3, 1925. For a criticism of the earlier desire inventories, see Link, H. C., *New Psychology of Selling and Advertising*, 1932.

of goods.   And many of these goods—though, he sometimes admits, not all of them—add to the general standard of living.   Moreover, the advertiser sometimes defiantly asks his critics to answer his contention that the advertising of many products creates values other than those of the immediate utility of the product.   (A girl buying a beauty product may not be made beautiful thereby, but the advertiser helps to kindle hope.) The general issue is fairly clear.   The advertising man is not responsible for societal values.   But he does at times accentuate values that the moralist deplores.   However, it is a waste of time to attack the advertisers personally.   Certain of their more extreme activities, especially direct falsehoods, may be regulated in the public interest.   Exaggeration, misleading implications, unfounded scientific claims, the use of questionable testimonials, and the like, may be somewhat more carefully regulated in the near future.   That is all.   Either that, or a dictatorship of consumption.   But any interested minority may attempt to educate the general public in values in consumption.

Fourth, the critic also accuses the advertising man of vulgarity, defacing the landscape, a low level of aesthetic appeals and a number of other misdemeanors of which advertising is obviously guilty.   But so are all the media of communication in a culture that stresses a low common denominator of popular appeal.   The advertising man is likewise accused of furthering standardization of goods and abetting the creation of a dull uniformity of material things.   This uniformity is peculiarly grueling to the aesthetically sensitive.   But it is obviously an inevitable concomitant of mass production and distribution.

Those who have attacked advertising, in a number of volumes rather widely read during the past decade, have generally left the impression of advertisers as low, unethical fellows involved in chicanery and deceit and having nefarious designs on the welfare of the general public.   Obviously, this is sometimes an accurate description.   There is much untrue, insincere and misinformative advertising.   There is much more of advertising that disseminates false impressions indirectly.   Advertising is special pleading, and a highly competitive special pleading at that, so that in many an advertising campaign each side stimulates the other to more and more extreme statements.   If advertising is really effective, it leads consumers to make purchases they would not have made without having seen the advertisement.   In the quest for these purchasers the advertising man has used every type of appeal that he found to be effective.   He is limited only by the attitudes of the general public, by very fragmentary legal restrictions and by the rudimentary ethics of his profession.   By experience and by knowledge of the general culture values he learns what will be believed.   The recent attempt to place greater legal restrictions upon his claims has not yet been successful.   To some extent, business has regulated the content of advertising. Many of the more blatant untruths have been eliminated from some types of advertising, owing to the activities of business groups with a "Truth in Advertising" slogan.[1] But, of course, distortions of the truth in the special pleading of contemporary advertising is a part of the very fabric of our modern competitive economy. As long as goods compete for markets, the art of "puffing" will play an important part. And granted the wide variety of economic goods for modern consumers, informative advertising would exist under any economy or any political system.

But, just as we have done in the preceding discussion, the critic of advertising stresses the more obvious and dramatically antisocial activities of the advertising man. Many of the large advertisers make and sell products of dubious or little value. But, of course, the bulk of advertising consists of special pleading for articles that have raised the standard of living of modern populations. If there is great waste in the competitive clamor about wares, it is also true that this clamor has been in part responsible for the swift acceleration of the production of consumers' goods. Certainly, advertising has influenced popular opinions about these goods. It has forced the national economy into the present mold. The selection of which goods shall be produced is in part determined by existing popular wants and, in part, by wants that are to some extent created by the advertiser. But in any case, either when the advertiser verbalizes existing wants or when he tells a public what it should want, the new importance of popular opinion is indicated by the assiduous cultivation of large publics since the closing decades of the nineteenth century.

Propaganda is pervasive in our time. There has always been some propaganda, but in the modern age it is organized, intentional and relatively more effective. Moreover, modern propaganda emphasizes distortion and derationalizes the popular opinion process. It usually does not help the individual to come to a rational understanding of public issues but rather attempts to induce him to follow nonrational emotional drives. All fields of human activity in which special interest groups exist, and there are constantly more of them, are the areas in which the propagandist operates. Obfuscation is somewhat more a science than in preceding ages. Students of government, of economic groups and of many varieties of societal organization are giving increased attention to the problems of propaganda. And certainly the student has reason to scrutinize many of his sources of information with a jaundiced eye. Suspicion is rife. Likewise, the general public has had some inkling of

[1] See the discussion of the growth of this movement as reported in the lectures *Ethical Problems of Modern Advertising,* Ronald Press Company, 1931.

the varieties of special pleading. In the zeal to brand opponents as "propagandists" publicity has been given to the process by many groups. Newspapers write of "foreign propaganda," and economic groups decry the "propaganda" of their opponents. There has been a great deal of propaganda against propaganda. And with reason. But there is some necessity for students to be cautious not to overemphasize the issue of propaganda and not to develop the illusion that we live entirely in a world of propaganda myths. Suspicion is a mushroom growth. It is possible to get in the state of mind of the two extremely canny business rivals who met on a Continental railway train. After some chatter in which each attempted to learn the destination of the other, one volunteered the information that he was going to Vienna. The other eyed him suspiciously. "Now why do you not tell me the truth?" he asked. "You know you tell me you are going to Vienna so that I will think you are going to Cracow, when you know very well you are really going to Vienna. Why do you lie to me?"

CHAPTER XVIII

THE ART OF PROPAGANDA

A considerable body of information has been accumulated about the psychology of advertising economic goods. In a partial sense there is a science of advertising. There is much verifiable psychological knowledge in this field. Many problems of attention, as related to advertising, have been investigated; categories of appeals and the relative strength of human desires have been inventoried for advertising purposes; the psychologist can tell us much about problems relating to the magnitude, position, color, illustration, line and form, preferable type and the functioning of association in advertisements. Also, he knows something of the manipulation of language in advertising and selling. An expert in sales appeals advises his clients on preferred words and phrases in their advertisements and sales talks. Don't ask "if"; ask "which." Don't ask whether the purchaser wants a large or small Coca Cola. Ask "Large one?" Don't ask "Check your oil," but question "Is your oil at the proper driving level?"[1] On the basis of verifiable experiment, there have been a great many generalizations developed by the psychologist in advertising. The propaganda process has not been so exactly described. There is no literature on the techniques of propaganda comparable with that on advertising. As yet there are practically no experimental data on the methods and the results of propaganda activity. Everyone is at times a propagandist in his daily life experience. And, although we understand a great deal about such person-to-person relationships, there is no compact handbook of generalizations about effective manipulative activities. Propaganda campaigns for groups and organizations are conducted by professional special pleaders, recruited principally from former newspaper and publicity men. Many of these have a vast experience in attempting to manipulate popular attitudes. But they have not been successful in providing generalizations about the process. The reason is quite apparent. The propagandist attempts to manipulate attitudes about political, economic and other controversial issues. The situation in which each issue occurs is individually unique. There are infinite nuances of situation and group attitudes, whereas a great deal of advertising deals with oft-repeated situations. Therefore,

[1] Littell, R., "When Every Clerk Uses the Right Word," *Readers' Digest*, February, 1938, pp. 40–43.

at least a portion of advertising may be conducted according to rules. But there is an art and not a science of propaganda. When the students and practitioners of propaganda attempt generalizations, the unsatisfactory nature of the results is evident. The generalizations are too general, the exceptions too apparent.[1] Nevertheless, we shall essay a discussion of the generalizations that do exist.

THE TECHNIQUE OF PROPAGANDA

In the confusion of contemporary ideas and amidst the prevailing mental insecurities, propagandas perform the dual functions of catharsis and readjustment.[2] Tensions may be partially relieved by mass preoccupation with the symbols that the propagandist provides. There may be little or no change in the objective reality, and yet a partial catharsis results from adherence to a particular propaganda. Thus, propaganda for many causes cannot reasonably be expected to result in the changes that are demanded, but the emotional zeal of the adherents may prove an end in itself. The Townsend movement and the late Senator Long's "share the wealth" agitation could not be expected to be economically practicable in the form in which they were presented, but they could and have resulted in release of tensions through "wishful thinking." And, incidentally, a leadership achieved prestige. On the other hand, propaganda may be directed toward definite and explicitly stated readjustment. The utility propaganda had such an aim, the minimizing of the demand for government ownership. The techniques of propaganda will vary, depending upon whether that propaganda may reasonably expect merely a psychological or an objective response. Unfortunately, we do not now possess a descriptive and analytical literature of specific propaganda campaigns that is extensive or detailed enough to permit of logical classifications of types of propaganda and their respective techniques. Therefore, we must content ourselves with generalizations sufficiently inclusive to apply to all types.

One such generalization is that the most effective propaganda is conducted by those who are likewise in an authoritarian position that simultaneously permits of censorship. Competition is eliminated. Propaganda fills the gaps left by the censor. Hence the success of propaganda during the World War. Our foreign correspondents have persistently depreciated what they consider as the overlauded astuteness

[1] Doob, L. W., *Propaganda*, 1935.

Lasswell, H. D., *Propaganda Technique in the World War*, 1927.

Lumley, F. E., *The Propaganda Menace*, 1933.

Monthly letters, Institute for Propaganda Analysis, 132 Morningside Drive, New York City.

[2] This useful characterization is suggested by Lasswell, H. D., in *Propaganda and Dictatorship* (Childs, H. L., ed.), p. 111, 1936.

of the propaganda ministries of modern authoritarian states, declaring that without censorship powers these propagandists would be relatively ineffectual. Despite the friendliness of most of the newspapers, the utilities propagandists of the late 1920's were largely unsuccessful because they could not control all the channels of communication.

Another generalization is that propagandists persistently appeal to the emotions of their subjects. Argument and discussion openly carried on is one thing; veiled propaganda appealing to hate, fear, pride, selfishness, greed, and the like, is a quite different process, short-circuiting discussion of the issue. The propagandist mobilizes hatred of the enemy, appeals to the fear that economic chaos would result from the opponent's plans, taps the popular allegiances to some loved symbol, and the like. The propagandist does not respect the human mind. He holds man's reason cheap, and he attempts to deprive man of the opportunity to display logical processes. He is not unique in this attempt. Various other types of special pleaders likewise predominantly use emotional appeals. An intelligent minority which recognizes propaganda as such can sometimes discount a part of the emotional appeals, attempt to obtain additional information, partially identify themselves with the opponents, read the literature of the other side and attempt to become intelligent partisans. If he has not hopelessly alienated this group, the propagandist must then prepare appeals calculated to persuade its members. For example, he may utilize the authority of economists, historians and other social theorists to distribute appealing rationalizations; he may prepare subtle, but partial, arguments; he may confuse with statistics, and so forth. But most of his subjects respond to direct emotional appeals, if these are linked with existing attitudes.

Almost inevitably, the propagandist becomes a liar. He not only distorts, he also fabricates. He is usually driven by the logic of events to more and more extreme falsehoods. He creates stories about the opposing leaders, falsifies statistics, creates news stories, starts rumors and in many ways falsifies the process of discussion. Of course, such falsification is most effective if it cannot be contradicted because the means of communication are controlled. This is obviously true of much national propaganda in wartime. "When war is declared, Truth is the first casualty." "Falsehood is a recognized and extremely useful weapon in warfare, and every country uses it quite deliberately to deceive its own people, to attract neutrals, and to mislead the enemy."[1] Of course, lying is proportional to mass credulity. Sir Arthur Ponsonby has collected a number of the official and unofficial falsehoods of the

[1] Ponsonby, A., *Falsehood in Wartime*, p. 13, 1928.
See also: Irwin, W., *Propaganda and the News*, Chaps. 11–13, 1936.
Viereck, G. S., *Spreading Germs of Hate*, 1930.

English in the World War. Among these were the atrocity stories, so numerous that they have not to this day been completely classified by historians. They were circulated by word of mouth, leaflets, speeches and newspapers. Stories of assaults, torturings, rapes, attacks on children, and the like, were widely circulated. The German army as invaders were at a disadvantage in the dissemination of such stories. Their propagandists could not reply in kind. Of course, amidst the brutalities of war, such things do happen. But the majority of the atrocity stories were outright fabrications. Some of these stories were officially created; few were denied. Such stories have been created in most wars throughout history, but those of the World War were impressive in bulk. The contemporary student is so well acquainted with official lying in wartime that we need not stop at this point to relate specific stories. Faked photographs, the doctoring of official papers, the false-hoods about the enemy's strength and morale, the ascribing of satanic motives were commonplace techniques of propaganda bureaus in modern warfare. The crop of propagandists' lies in wartime can be large because the means of communication are controlled, the general population has developed a maximum will to believe and no substantial opposition exists. The peacetime propagandist must be more careful. The propagandist who falsifies must make peace with himself. The difficulty experienced by some of the World War propagandists is evidenced by the rueful way in which they confessed their falsehoods after the conclusion of the War.

Just as individuals in face-to-face conversation exaggerate the stories, rumors and information that they transmit so that they may gain effectiveness, the propagandist exaggerates in the interest of his cause. The publicity men of political parties exaggerate the derelictions of their opponents, the propagandists for grain manipulators exaggerate the news reports of crop shortages, the military propagandist exaggerates victories, the actress's publicity man exaggerates the value of her stolen jewels— indeed, all special pleaders exaggerate at times. In this activity they are aided by the popular tendency to embellish an account. In the copying of newspaper stories the account is sometimes garbled into an exaggerated form. This is often intentional. The processes of exaggeration are inevitable, but the propagandist consciously distorts in this way, thereby adding to existing confusions.

The propagandist further distorts by selection. He is not concerned with providing impartial data. He has a cause to plead. His problem consists principally in selecting such information and such social suggestions as are best calculated to evoke the desired responses. A propagandist for the Federation of Utility Investors (renamed American Federation of Investors) cannot be expected to disseminate impartial information about the TVA.   Selection and particular emphasis become so much a commonplace in the propagandist's experience that after a time he is not consciously aware of his choices.   Just as a veteran newspaper correspondent "slants" the news in the direction of his employer's or readers' attitudes, so the propagandist plays up materials favorable to his cause and underemphasizes the rest.   The propagandist's selection of his comments upon any controversial issue will be determined by what he can successfully work into any medium of communication.   In the total situation in which he operates there may be very little that he can inject into communication.   When St. Thomas' Church in New York was built, a waggish young architect worked in a dollar sign over the bride's door and three moneybags initialed J. P. M. over the choir stalls. Anything more obvious would have been discovered even sooner than were these items.   In extreme instances the propagandist may work painstakingly to introduce one item favorable to his cause.   Twenty years ago, the late Ivy Lee inspired the writing of an article about the Cathedral of St. John the Divine for the *New York Times* Magazine, so that he could incorporate therein a single phrase.   This phrase declared that the metal work of the cathedral was made of copper, "The Metal of the Ages."   At that time, Mr. Lee was a propagandist for the copper producers.   These are unusual illustrations.   However, in his more normal activities, the propagandist persistently selects items, slants the news and omits data favorable to the opposition.   He is the foe of even a relative degree of impartiality.

One of the oldest devices of the manipulator of public opinion is the distraction of attention by the use, among others, of the "red-herring" technique.   The propagandist finds it invaluable.   In face-to-face argument, a simple device for confuting an opponent is to lead him off the track of the principal issue into the discussion of some trivial point or to divert him into the discussion of something quite beside the point at issue.   State other propositions, inject irrelevant objections and change the issues.   Just so, in dealing with publics, the propagandist frequently attempts to distract attention from items dangerous to his cause.   The methods of popular diversion are of infinite variety.   Inject humor and satire, call names, divert attention to personalities, change the issue, center attention upon unimportant and harmless matters or distract the group's attention to points favorable to one's own position.   The hard-pressed employer in labor disputes may divert attention to welfare activities; publics are distracted from political issues by "bread and circuses"; the opponents of woman suffrage turn attention upon the role of woman as mother and homemaker; the political boss diverts attention from political issues to his party's beneficences; the special pleader questions the honesty and motives of his opponents.   Of course, not only the hidden propagandist, but all special pleaders, use this device at times.

The propagandist eternally repeats his assertions. The value of repetition has been experimentally tested by advertisers, as any volume on the psychology of advertising will attest. "If you have an idea to put over, keep presenting it incessantly. Keep talking (or printing) systematically and persistently."[1] In *Mein Kampf*, Hitler states, "The intelligence of the masses is small, their forgetfulness is great. Effective propaganda must be confined to merely a few issues which can be easily assimilated. Since the masses are slow to comprehend, they must be told the same thing a thousand times." One need not be a cynical commentator on the mental limitations of the common man functioning in large groups to realize the psychological effectiveness of repetition.

It is a propagandist's rule to avoid argument. Dr. Goebbels, major propaganda chief of Germany, has this to say. "The ordinary man hates nothing more than two-sidedness, to be called upon to consider this as well as that. The masses think simply and primitively. They love to generalize complicated situations and from their generalizations to draw clear and uncompromising conclusions."[2] In this rule he has the blessing of the psychologist. Prof. Dunlap writes, "Avoid argument as a general thing. Do not admit there is any 'other side' and in all statements scrupulously avoid arousing reflection or associated ideas, except those which are favorable. Reserve argument for the small class of people who depend on logical processes, or as a means of attracting the attention of those with whom you are arguing."[3]

The contemporary propagandist can and does tap all the accumulated lore and science regarding the most efficacious methods of attracting attention. The principles of attention are too many and varied for discussion at this point. Startling statements, sudden appeals, color, size and position of published items, novelty, appeals to interests, an infinite variety of direct sensory stimuli, the spectacular, the creation of conflicts, and the like, are standard methods of attracting attention.

However, such generalizations as we have been enunciating are of but limited usefulness to the propagandist or to those who would understand the propaganda process, because they must be applied with infinite variation to the particular situations. As Dr. Goebbels has said, "Propaganda in itself has no fundamental method. It has only purpose —the conquest of the masses. Every means that serves this end is good." The propagandist must adapt his methods and the content of his appeals to the common social attitudes of his subjects. For example,

[1] Rule number one of propaganda, in Dunlap, K., *Social Psychology*, p. 256, 1925.
[2] Quoted in *New York Times Mag.*, p. 27, Feb. 14, 1937.
[3] Dunlap, *op. cit.*, p. 256.

when dealing with large publics in the United States, he ordinarily should not appeal to avowed self-interest on the part of his subjects. Such publics have long been nurtured in an atmosphere of professed unselfishness. Hence, the development of special pleading or of a program of action based upon consciously selfish interests, the pursuit of individual or group self-interest, is repugnant in a culture that, at least verbally, subscribes to the larger group interests. Therefore, any programs of self-interest must usually be camouflaged with a protective coating of rationalizations which interpret them in terms of the values of the prevailing mores. This is necessary, not only for the popular acceptance of the propagandist's statements, but also for the comfort of really self-interested minorities. For, incorporated in the attitudes of these, too, are the altruistic catchwords and democratic pretensions.

The propagandist must know the prevailing attitudes of his subjects. And he must, in every possible way, connect with their dominant attitudes the idea that he wishes to promulgate. Many a propaganda item has failed of acceptance because of the ineptitude of the propagandist who has failed to inform himself of some deep-seated prejudice. Communist propaganda in the United States has often failed to consider the widespread aversion of masses of Americans to the identification of themselves as "the proletariat." Class appeals have often been futile in the development of the American labor movement. Lasswell recounts the failure of German propaganda to arouse the desired response with its account of Belgian Roman Catholic priests' having urged their parishioners to bushwack the invading German troops; the failure was due to the prejudice of Roman Catholics both abroad and in Germany against believing that priests would give such advice. The propagandist must use traditional prejudices to which he may relate his cause and be careful not to run afoul of deeply imbedded adverse prejudices. B. Russell maintains that successful propaganda essentially makes people hold more emotionally to their opinions and beliefs, rather than develop new opinions. L. W. Doob states, "The propagandist employs attitudes that are already dominant as related attitudes or he arouses related attitudes that remain dominant over a period of time," and, "The propagandist varies the content of his stimulus situation, in order to arouse related attitudes in different people, and, by changing their stereotypes, to construct new attitudes in others through positive suggestion."[1] For example, the propagandist knows, as does the advertising man, the value of relating his cause to popular figures having prestige. Attitudes favorable to these prominent personages already exist. And so, such personages are urged to say a few words, be four-minute speakers, endorse a cause, sign a proclamation, enunciate the desired

[1] Doob, *op. cit.*, p. 414.

rationalizations.　We have referred to propaganda as an art and not a science, because there can be no hard-and-fast rules that may be experimentally verified about such procedures.　The propagandist must study existing popular beliefs and opinions, so that he may know which ideas, words, symbols, persons and organizations the majorities of a population are for and against.　Then he relates his cause to the favorable attitudes, usually stating the relationship in very general and non-specific ways.　Thus he hopes to stimulate decision and not debate.

What are the dominant attitudes?　In an earlier discussion we have considered the difficulties of classifying attitudes.　No two social scientists have agreed on a list of dominant social attitudes.　The social theorist in his descriptions of American culture persistently turns to the enumeration of popular attitudes.　But no list is even approximately complete.　The Lynds, in their latest volume on Middletown, have courageously attempted a classification of the things that this mid-west industrial community is for and against.[1]　By and large Middletown believes in kindness, honesty, friendliness, good fellowship, success, character, unpretentiousness, common sense, steadiness, progress, slow change, good will, optimism, enterprise, hard work, community spirit, loyalty, small business, economic conditions as a natural order, initiative, saving, the monogamous family, philanthropy and that women are purer than men, that childhood is a happy time, that a man who is still able to work should not retire, that America is the freest country on earth, and so on, through a list some fifteen pages in length.　This list is based upon observation, and shrewd observation at that, but of course we do not know what proportion of the total population holds each of these general attitudes or the intensity of conviction in each case.　But the contemporary propagandist cannot await more exact description. He uses such classifications as he may create or obtain and attempts to suggest the relationship of his cause to such dominant attitudes as he may reasonably expect to tap.　But, clearly, the propagandist must be intimately acquainted with the cultural values and the general individual attitudes, with popular beliefs and majority opinions.　He desires integration with these attitudes and then, as a next step, action favorable to his cause.

As the technique of propaganda is the manipulation of symbols, the propagandist must have a thorough knowledge of the symbols whereby attitudes are expressed.　Incomplete knowledge of some of the nuances of symbol meaning and popular emotional linkages to these symbols has led to fatal errors in appeal.　This problem is especially acute when the propagandist is dealing with people of a culture alien to his own.　He must then rely upon the advice of those intimately acquainted with the

[1] Lynd, R. S., and Lynd, H. M., *Middletown in Transition*, pp. 403–419, 1937.

meanings of words (the dictionary is inadequate for popular meanings), with the popular responses to pictorial representation and with all other types of symbols.

The propagandist must be simple, clear and precise. He may attempt to provide a spurious but convincing clarity to the workings of his program by giving opportunity for first-hand contacts with his program. Hence, the propaganda tours through Soviet Russia, Nazi Germany or Fascist Italy. He may simplify with exhibits, personalizations, simple statistics, oversimplified definitions, slogans, concretions of abstractions, catechisms of questions and answers, dramatizations, stories and illustrations, pictures, specific instances, demonstrations, familiar terms, and the like.[1] Most of these procedures for simplification appear in any well-organized propaganda campaign. Quantifications are increasingly used, as general publics are even less competent in analyzing statistics than in winnowing out significant facts from verbal presentations. Yet there is a widespread faith that figures do not lie. In the national campaign of 1936, the Republican party used appeals by figures more extensively than had been true in the publicity of any preceding campaign.[2] Such simplifications are frequently fatal to impartial consideration but are usually useful in the dissemination of conclusions.

But, as we stated at the beginning of this discussion of propaganda techniques, we cannot satisfactorily generalize about the propaganda processes. The propagandist exercises his ingenuity upon a particular situation, and, if he is a successful propagandist, his methods are infinitely adaptable to situations. He utilizes whatever he can of the techniques of publicity that, at the same time, permit him to remain concealed. He works through the various secondary means of communication, the press, printed forms in general, radio, pictures, inspired rumors, and the like. As he must appeal to large groups, there is a premium upon simplicity, emotional appeals and direct suggestions. He seeks to exert social pressures but works indirectly. His aim is the widespread acceptance of his conclusions. But he is limited by his own inadequacies, by the existing "field structure," by existing ignorances, by popular prejudices, by the limitations upon his control of and his access to the various media of communication and by his opportunities to obtain a monopoly by the silencing of oppositions by censorship. Finally, the more success-

---

[1] See the discussion of the methods of making complex and abstract meanings simple and concrete in Bonney, M. E., *Technique of Appeal and of Social Control*, thesis, Columbia University, 1937.

[2] Casey, R. D., "Republican Propaganda in the 1936 Campaign," *Pub. Opin. Quar.*, 1: 2: 27–43.

On the danger and fallacies in the popular use of statistics, see: Cohen, M. R., and Nagel, E., *An Introduction to Logic and Scientific Method*, pp. 316–323, 1934; Lehman, H. C., and Witty, P. A., "Statistics Show," *Jour. Ed. Psychol.*, 19: 175–184.

ful propagandists usually are able to convince themselves. A part of the technique of propaganda consists of the ways in which the propagandist manipulates his own attitudes and values. If he cannot integrate his own position, he usually lacks zeal. Skillful propagandists may have doubts, but these doubts must not loom too large in their daily work. The personal characteristics of the propagandist have not yet been adequately limned.[1]

MEDIA AND CHANNELS OF COMMUNICATION

The propagandist uses all the media of communication to which he can obtain access and which are adapted to his appeals in a particular campaign. Printed materials, newspapers, speeches, symbolic insignia, motion pictures, radio and all other ways of transmitting appeals are used. In the course of our discussions of the newspaper, motion pictures, graphic arts and radio in the later chapters of this work we shall consider illustrations of the activities of propagandists in those fields.

Methods are adapted to the situation in the particular propaganda campaign. During the last year of the World War the French invented a hand grenade that carried leaflets 600 feet in a favorable wind. The British developed a shell that would carry leaflets 10 miles into the enemy lines. During the last year the English manufactured over 2000 propaganda balloons per week. Each of these balloons carried 1000 leaflets into Germany. In a single month, October, 1918, Lord Northcliffe's propaganda department dropped 5,360,000 leaflets in Germany.[2]

Let us illustrate the propagandist's use of the various channels of communication in a single campaign, that of the utility companies between 1924 and 1930. The utility propaganda probably did more harm than good to the cause of the privately owned utilities. But that was because of the exposé of the utility propaganda by the Federal Trade Commission. The propaganda campaign itself was extensive and intensive. We cannot follow the tortuous trail of the utility companies' special pleading. But we may note a few items on their use of various means of communication. There were extensive speaking campaigns with speakers whose association with the utility companies often was not disclosed. In one year, 1927, there were 2450 talks given in Oklahoma to audiences estimated at 250,000; in Texas, 1525 talks to audiences of 125,000; Louisiana, 410 talks to 45,000 people; Arkansas, 65 speeches to 6000 people; Mississippi, 55 speeches to 5000 listeners; in Illinois, Michi-

[1] Lasswell, H. D., has tentatively approached this problem in, "The Person: Subject and Object of Propaganda," *Ann. Am. Acad. Pol. Soc. Sci.*, 179: 187–193.

[2] Viereck, *op. cit.*, p. 205.

gan, Wisconsin and Indiana, 7147 speeches to 1,309,762 people.[1] Clubs and organizations of various kinds were furnished speakers, special literature and motion pictures and were approached in other ways. Women's clubs and farm organizations were studied and appealed to in an organized fashion. Domestic-science teachers explained cooking, but also defended rates and spoke for private ownership. Pamphleteering was extensive. There were booklets entitled *Government Ownership Advocates Shade from Deepest Red to Mauve, Russia Tried It Too, Utility Securities Are Pronounced Best, Six Hundred and Sixty City-owned Plants Abandoned,* and scores of others. Newspapers were bribed, bought and bluffed.[2] Mr. B. J. Mullaney of the Insull publicity organization wrote, "We are trying to promulgate the idea rapidly among the newspapers that public utilities offer a very fertile field for developing regular, prompt-paying customers of their advertising columns. When that idea penetrates the United States, unless human nature has changed, we will have less trouble with the newspapers than we had in the past."[3] In 1927, the electric light and power companies planned to spend no less than ten million dollars for newspaper advertising, and the utilities in general, around twenty-eight million dollars. A large section of the press succumbed to the utility advertising and threats.

The schools were invaded extensively. The objective was to convince students, especially in the secondary schools, of the superiority of private over public ownership. To do this, the utilities managed to insinuate special textbooks and pamphlets into the public schools of many states. A *Utilities Catechism* was used in 76 schools in Connecticut. In Texas, 82,000 items were sent to high schools in one year. In New York, 44,191 copies of one pamphlet were sent to 490 schools.[4] In Ohio, a utility information committee published a textbook entitled *Aladdins of Industry,* of which 190,000 copies were distributed in the schools. The record of many universities and colleges is none too savory in relation to the extensive utility drives of 1925 to 1930. These campaigns made effective use of radio talks and programs to publicize private-ownership arguments. A few motion pictures dealing with rural electrification were made, but these were not an important part of the utility propaganda. Gossip campaigns and rumors spread by utilities' employees were sometimes used. There were even songs favoring private ownership which were used in some public meetings, and especially in the meetings of the employees of the utility companies. All possible means of communication were utilized, and most of the possible appeals were

[1] Gruening, E., *The Public Pays*, p. 132, 1931.
[2] Seldes, G., *Freedom of the Press*, Chap. 4, 1935.
[3] Gruening, *op. cit.*, p. 166.
[4] Levin, J., *Power Ethics*, p. 144, 1931.

made.   The Federal Trade Commission reports on the methods of these propaganda campaigns are worthy of a more widespread perusal than has been accorded to them.

We shall not attempt at this point to illustrate the role of propaganda in the various channels of communication.   But we shall comment briefly on propaganda in education and in literature.

PROPAGANDA AND THE EDUCATIONAL SYSTEM

The practitioners and directors of special pleading have long since recognized the importance of impressing upon the young their arguments, suggestions and partial information.   Condition the very young to respond to the symbols of your special cause, teach him your "truths" and in adult life he will be likely to view them as self-evident.   The leaders of the Roman Catholic church have often spoken of the importance of inculcation of responses to religious symbols during the first few years of life and have adapted parts of their religious training to this end. Lenin said, "Give me four years to teach the children, and the seed I have sown will never be uprooted."   Mussolini writes that the textbook and the musket make the perfect Fascist.   Authoritarian leaders have ever been preoccupied with the indoctrination of the young.   But the freer political systems have as the avowed objective of education, the development of the intellect, however far short they may fall from this ideal in practice.   That people must think and think for themselves, and that they can be trained to do so, is the assumption and the faith of democracy.   But "fascism is war on intellectualism," says G. Gentile, philosopher of authoritarianism.   Regardless of the underlying educational philosophy, it is obviously true that every educational system indoctrinates, at least in part, the prevailing values within each culture. Nationalism, the prevailing economic system, the traditional history, the popular ethical values and democratic institutions are inculcated in American schools.   Any formal systematic training of the young will, perforce, have some frame of reference.   But under the freer systems, some diversity of presentation occurs, whereas systems controlled by authoritarian states regulate the minutiae.   There is an essential difference between inculcating a general philosophy and indocrinating details.

Some propagandistic indoctrination occurs in every formal school system.   Indeed, the part played by propaganda has been increasing since the Reformation.   The Jesuits, acquiring control over education, perfected techniques of indoctrination.   The Protestants did likewise. In the eighteenth century, revolutionary propaganda, nationalistic appeals and the taking of sides on the Napoleonic issue created additional special pleading.[1]   With the development of democracies, the values of

[1] Russell, B., *Education and the Modern World*, p. 209, 1932.

the general population were increasingly impressed upon education. Legislative control of curriculums increased, based on the theory that the taxpayers have the right to decide what should be taught. This led to a series of struggles between teachers and legislators. One of the recent expressions of this struggle is the teachers'-oath laws. Over a score of states in America have such statutes. But a gap appears between the values of the professional educator and those of the general public on many subjects other than that of nationalism. One of the more combative university presidents has recently denounced the popular quest for vocational training rather than for training in how to think.[1] Then, there are the numerous special interest groups, patriotic, reform, professional and economic, which have attempted partly to control curriculum content. The problem is ever more involved under democracies.

Educators intermittently attempt to resist the organized interest groups and the advertisers. They declare that education aims at independence of judgment. One group of educators has argued that: (1) The propagandist and the educator represent two extremes. The purpose of the propagandist is to teach what to think, whereas the guiding purpose of the educator is to teach how to think. The function of the school in developing the child's critical powers will be hopelessly hindered if its doors are left open to the propagandist. Children lack power of critical judgment. This must be developed in them. (2) The schools of America are founded upon the principle of control by all the people rather than by classes or groups. (3) The present course of study is already overcrowded. (4) There is an imperative need for an adult citizenry capable of protecting itself from the appeals of propaganda. The schools must prepare students to deal discriminatingly with information.[2] It is likely that courses of study directed toward the unmasking of propaganda will shortly appear in the secondary schools.[3] Propaganda is a form of attempted exploitation. Many teachers are eager to unmask at least a part of the propaganda appeals, the part with which they do not agree.

The best historical sketches of special interests in the schools have been written by B. L. Pierce and B. Raup.[4] In her latest book, Dr.

[1] Hutchins, R. M., "We are Getting No Brighter" (first of a series of four articles), *Sat. Eve. Post*, Dec. 11, 1937.

[2] Report of the Wisconsin Teachers' Association, 1930.

[3] The Institute for Propaganda Analysis, a small subsidized group studying propaganda methods, now sends a monthly newsletter to teachers. In the first issue this group stated, "There are three possible ways to deal with propaganda. You can suppress it, meet it with counter propaganda, or analyze it and try to see how much truth there is in it."

[4] Pierce, B. L., *Public Opinion and the Teaching of History*, 1926; *Citizens' Organizations and the Civic Training of Youth*, 1933.

Raup, B., *Education and Organized Interests in America*, 1936.

Pierce reports briefly on some 204 organizations; Raup discusses 95, of which 41 duplicate the Pierce list. There are patriotic organizations, military groups, peace organizations, business and labor groups, prohibition and antiprohibition organizations and others, all of whom have attempted or are attempting to carry on special pleading in the schools, often by means of propaganda. Many economic groups have used the schools for advertising or for pleading a special cause. Of these, the utility companies have received the most notoriety. Today, most administrators scrutinize more carefully than they did in the past the swelling tide of propaganda materials. However, all too frequently our superintendents give way before the pressures of well-organized groups. The media of propaganda in the schools have been listed by the Wisconsin Teachers' Association as follows:

1. Visual Education Materials:
   a. Posters developing some slogan or principle.
   b. Wall-charts, intended to help explain the operation or use of tools, machinery, etc.
   c. Motion picture films.
   d. Lantern Slides.
   e. Exhibits.
   f. Clipsheets and other bulletin board materials.
2. Free School Supplies:
   a. Book covers. These are often supplied free and carry advertising of various types.
   b. Calendars.
   c. Rulers, pens, pencils, blotters, and a large variety of small inexpensive school supplies. These generally carry advertising of the agency which supplies them.
3. Books and Pamphlets:
   a. Pamphlets and catechisms describing values, use, or manufacture of various products, or urging the adoption of certain ideas, or supplying information about various organizations.
   b. Study helps and teachers' manuals.
   c. Books and magazines for teachers.
4. Contests:
   a. Essay contests.
   b. Oratorical contests.
   c. Poster-making contests.
   d. Health contests.
   e. Penmanship contests.
   f. Typing contests.
   g. Music contests.
   h. Spelling contests.
   i. Athletic contests of certain types.
   j. Salesmanship contests.

   k. Thrift contests.

   l. Soap sculpture contests.[1]

It is evident that a great deal of propaganda has been injected into the school systems by special interest groups. Educators have been increasingly agitated by a growing awareness of this fact and, latterly, have been attempting to study the propagandist's activities. Dr. Pierce's survey was carried on under the direction of the Commission on the Social Studies which was set up by the American Historical Association. A number of state educational associations have prepared reports on this topic. The Social Science Research Council has created a Committee on Propaganda. The National Educational Association has prepared rules for the guidance of teachers and executives.[2]

The educators are in revolt against much of the propaganda of special interest groups. But what of the educators themselves? Should they become propagandists for viewpoints of which they approve? Should they organize counterpropaganda? Should they, in so far as possible, teach their students techniques for discovering and resisting propaganda?

The traditional American view has been that education consisted primarily of the acquisition of knowledge, the purveying and learning of facts. In practice there often has been but little opportunity for critical analysis and enlightened skepticism. So-called "objective" and "impartial" teaching has usually presented but a selected part of the "facts" on controversial issues. But, in theory, an allegiance to an educational philosophy of objectivity has predominated in the utterances of American educators. Latterly, there is some division in the educational ranks. A small but growing minority has become convinced that the educator must become a propagandist for programs that he considers to be in the public interest. Let us briefly examine the statements of their spokesmen.

In 1928, R. L. Finney discussed the problem of achieving followership of the duller intellects.[3] He declared, "The leadership of the wise and good has never been anything but a beautiful wish." Yet "successful democracy demands the ascendency of the wise and the good." How is this to be achieved? The usual formula is: Teach the people to think. Train them to discern false appeals, the pitfalls of logic, the wiles of the

---

[1] Report of the Wisconsin Teachers' Association, 1929; quoted by Lumley, F. E., *The Propaganda Menace*, p. 317. Quoted here by permission of the Wisconsin Teachers' Association.

[2] See the "Report of the Committee on Propaganda of the N.E.A.," *Addresses and Proceedings*, 67: 204–217. Complete report may be secured from National Educational Association, 1201 16th St., N. W., Washington, D. C.

[3] Finney, R. L., *A Sociological Philosophy of Education*, Chap. 20, 1928. By permission of The Macmillan Company, publishers.

special pleader. But Prof. Finney questions whether the average man, as represented by the barber, with an I.Q. of 78, according to the Army tests, can be taught to think fruitfully about social issues. When this "average man" does enunciate worth-while "truths," he does so because he has learned these from his intellectual betters. "The truth seems to be that a mere echo is the best which can ever be expected from the duller half of the population." And so, "in the present crisis the race is between those who would selfishly exploit the masses and those who would teach and thereby liberate them." But the teachers are hampered by the need of making rational appeals. Therefore, says Prof. Finney, on decisive social issues, the teachers should present special pleading, using all means of appeal, and should propagandize in the public interest. "It is not enough that we teach children to think, we must actually force-feed them with the concentrated results of expert thinking." As the "followership of the masses can be secured only by memoristic drill on the epitomized philosophy of the leaders," the schools are the natural training ground. Needless to say, Prof. Finney's position was not acclaimed by the professional educators of a decade ago. But the variety of conflicts since that time and the popular confusion, arising from the special pleading of numerous special interest groups, have caused an increasing number of educators to espouse seriously the principle of indoctrination.

The most outspoken leader of the avowed indoctrinators has been G. S. Counts.[1] Prof. Counts is prepared to defend the thesis that all education contains a large element of impositions, that this process is inevitable and that the teachers are the best judges of what should be indoctrinated. Simply stated, the arguments of the indoctrinators are as follows: (1) The schools indoctrinate anyway; the times impress values on the schools, and the teachers impress these on the young. (2) Students are incapable of fruitful thinking and rational judgments, since education has been popularized ("Now, few persons in the first twenty or thirty years of their lives, even if given access to the world's fund of knowledge and Socrates for a tutor, could evolve a workable conceptual scheme of society of their own into which to fit themselves");[2] (3) United social action demands a common base in thought. The problem of the schools is to outfit people with such a base. The defenders of indoctrination declare that the teacher knows that the majority of pupils lack the ability to imbibe anything but simple shibboleths and realizes

[1] See Counts, G. S., *Dare the School Build a New Social Order*, 1932, and the issues of *Soc. Frontier*, especially January, 1936, entitled, "Shall the Schools Indoctrinate."
Also, Scott, R. R., "In Defense of Propaganda," *Jour. Am. Assoc. Univ. Women*, January, 1938, pp. 68–71.
[2] Dennis, L., in *Soc. Frontier*, 1: 13.

the futility of attempting to train the majority for anything other than the acceptance of simple conclusions.

The arguments of the opponents of indoctrination are as follows: (1) In a changing social order, propaganda in the schools tends to stop the process and makes for a static society. "The indoctrination may be so artificial and wooden that in a changing world it may be dangerous. What has been too rapidly taught may be hard to apply to a new situation unforeseen at the time of the indoctrination."[1] (2) Indoctrination is based on the assumption that the propagandist has an adequate truth, so as to make its inculcation worth while. Enthusiasts may think that they have such a truth. The students of cultural history would disagree. A doctrine is a fixation. It defines a stopping place. "Whether the doctrine be the 'American dream,' the Christian scheme of salvation, the Fascist hierarchy, the Hitlerite sadist-ocracy, or the salvational drama of materialist dialectic—to mention only a few among the alternative candidates for a monopoly of orthodoxy—it can be final, indefeasible, infallibly efficacious only to hearts at least as sentimental and heads at least as romantic as those that stake their country's salvation on progressive education."[2] (3) This does not mean that the schools will not have definite objectives. Though eschewing a particular content, they may aim at general objectives, for instance, the development of an attitude favorable to the experimental method. "Education could become, under other auspices, one source of progress, if it were free to treat the future experimentally."[3] The opponents of further indoctrination in the schools do not deny the existence of indoctrination for nationalistic and economic programs at the present time. They note that such is unfortunately the fact. But they do not believe that the cure is to be found in counterpropaganda or new indoctrinations. Rather, they would "indoctrinate to end indoctrinations." And they would not have education purposeless. But they would teach inclusive aims, rather than specific programs and particular indoctrinations.[4]

The position that one assumes in this controversy depends upon faith: faith in the ability of the common man, or distrust of his capacity; faith in the principles of freedom, or in a particular doctrine as the way of salvation; faith in the values of a plural, diversified, changing, competitive order, or in a relatively static society governed by a doctrine; faith

---

[1] Merriam, C. E., *Political Power*, p. 307, 1934.

[2] Kallen, H. M., *Education versus Indoctrination*, 1934. This pamphlet is a devastating criticism of propaganda in the schools. Quoted by permission of University of Chicago Press.

[3] Tugwell, R. G., *Redirecting Education*, vol. I, p. 91, 1934–1935.

[4] Fraser, M. G., *The College of the Future*, pp. 262 ff.

For another criticism of indoctrination in education, see Gideonse, H., "National Collectivism and Charles A. Beard," *Jour. Pol. Econ.*, 43: 778 ff.

in intelligence, or in mass regimentation. In each dichotomy, the author chooses the first alternative.

LITERATURE AND PROPAGANDA

The problem of the influence of the literary, pictorial or musical artist upon popular opinion and beliefs is discussed perennially. Since the commentaries upon the artist by Plato and Aristotle, the philosophers of every age have dealt with the problem of the artist's influence. In periods of fervid social controversy, the political leaders and the artists themselves analyze the artist's products and his influence from the sociological point of view. The selection of literature for popular consumption in the interests of propaganda for a special viewpoint is advocated by Plato, who declares that there must be "a censorship of the writers of fiction, and let the censors receive any tale of fiction which is good and reject the bad."[1] The poets tell lies, says Plato. Although the intentional lie might be politically expedient, Plato would regulate the literary lies that were not expedient. Further, he objected to the poets because they made popular instruction by the philosophers more difficult and aroused human passions. Plato enunciated the propaganda role of literature and declared censorship necessary, so as to restrict all but the state propagandist poet. "Aristotle limits the political control of the arts to the regulation of them in the education of young children. He says no more, however, than that their governors and preceptors 'should take care of what tales and stories it may be proper for them to hear.'"[2] Aristotle states that fiction and literature may be viewed from the political and moral points of view but that they may also be considered psychologically in their uses for purgation and diversion in popular thinking. Stressing as he does the function of literature in providing amusement, relaxation, and recreation, he would permit freedom to the literary artist to an extent not permitted by Plato. The discussion of the function of the artist, including the literary man, has in large part stemmed from the Platonic and Aristotelian positions. With the victory of Christianity, literature was increasingly valued in proportion as it was thought to inculcate moral values. "Art for art's sake" appeared in neither the Platonic nor the Christian traditions. With the development of printing, mass literacy begins and popular literature burgeons. By the eighteenth century, literatures of classes, groups and various subdivisions of society were emerging. Literature then portrayed the characteristics of subgroups within particular cultures, as well as of universal types. For example, there was a growing literature of the middle classes. In England and France, the portrayal of middle-class

[1] *Republic*, 377C.
[2] Adler, M. J., *Art and Prudence*, p. 42, 1937.

life, with the accompanying values of diligence, frugality and honesty, appeared in the writings of Defoe and Molière, John Bunyan and Jonathan Swift, Fielding and Richardson. In the nineteenth century Macaulay, Thackeray, Eliot, Dickens and a host of others carried on the representations of the middle classes.[1] Likewise, other societal groups were portrayed. Increasingly during the past three centuries the varieties of types, classes and groups in Western society have been portrayed in popular literature.

National and group literatures provide symbols for their adherents and opponents. "We may say of the great passages in a people's literature that they form, as it were, a national liturgy. There are passages in the Authorized Version, speeches and lyrics and single lines in Shakespeare, stanzas of Gray's *Elegy in a Country Churchyard*, and verses in some of our hymns, which exercise a dominion over the mind."[2] Such symbols evolve in the experience of a people. Now the propagandist is a manipulator of symbols, and the modern propagandist attempts the management of literary forms. Propagandist literature is that which is used by some special group to plead a cause. The author may or may not have intended that his product be used as propaganda. The author of *The Face on the Bar-room Floor* never intended that a generation of Anti-Saloon Leaguers should quote his poem. On the other hand, when a Herr Julius Streicher has a literary lieutenant turn out an anti-Semitic *Mother Goose* for German children we have direct literary manufacture.

In the nineteenth century, a growing number of reform groups selected or manufactured a literature to further their causes. One thinks at once of Charles Dickens' *Nicholas Nickleby* and the abuses of the private schools of England; of *Uncle Tom's Cabin* and the anti-slavery movement in the United States; of *Black Beauty* and the campaign against cruelty to animals; of the Socialist movement in America and the novels of Upton Sinclair, Frank Norris and Jack London; of the "muckrakers" and Lincoln Steffens' *Shame of the Cities;* of Upton Sinclair's *The Jungle* and the reform of the meat-packing industry through the Pure Food and Drug Act of 1906; of a host of second-rate novels, poems and essays and the Prohibition movement; of many other instances of privately organized reform movements and the literatures by which they plead their causes.

During the past twenty years the problem of propaganda literature has entered a new phase of both discussion and practice in the state-inspired propaganda literatures of Russia, Italy and Germany. "Until recently these varying conceptions of literatures, which may be traced

[1] Palm, F. C., *The Middle Classes*, Chaps. 9, 18, 19, 1936.
[2] Barker, E., *National Character*, p. 222, 1927.

from Plato to Cocteau, have proceeded on the whole undisturbed by authoritarian intrusion. The victory of the Bolsheviks over the White armies in 1920 and the subsequent consolidation of the U.S.S.R. have brought the question of literature out of the realm of theoretical abstraction and converted intellectual polemics into revolutionary partisan warfare."[1] The Bolsheviks attempted the organization of proletarian culture. The question of bourgeois literature was immediately to the fore. Although many of the earlier revolutionary leaders, especially Lenin, did not favor a too detailed control of literary output, the extremists soon won the day.[2] They clamored for a literary dictatorship. Literature was viewed as a handmaid of the state. "Only he is an artist," they claimed, "who at the present moment can instill in the minds of millions the conviction that a return to the past is impossible." During the past fifteen years, policies on the control of literature have fluctuated somewhat, but, in the main, literary output has been rather closely controlled. The Communists have insisted that the arts have always been propaganda for the dominant ideology. Preoccupied with the class struggle, organizations of the Communist enthusiasts, such as the Artists International, have declared that art renounces individualism and is to be collectivized, systemized, organized, disciplined and molded as a weapon. Within Russia, the Communist leadership has extensively propagandized for a political viewpoint through the selection of what people should read. Vast government printing houses have produced an amazing flood of printed materials. Since the revolution, over six billion copies of books have been printed. There are about 45,000 new titles each year. There are over 1800 Soviet periodicals. (Some of the selected writers are presented in enormous editions: 12 million copies of the works of Tolstoy, 32 million of Gorky's, and for his centennial a total of 8,150,000 copies of Pushkin's.[3]) Literature has been used in an organized way for the propaganda of cultural values. There has been systematic preparation of a children's literature. The old fairy tales and folk tales were considered harmful. In place of these a children's literature that reflects the values desired by the Communist leadership is being created.

As the authoritarian states appeared in Italy, Germany and elsewhere, the principle of state control of literature has spread. There has been an orgy of burning books and banishing authors. In the liberal democratic states, propaganda literature has been disseminated by special interest groups, not by the state. America has a propaganda literature of the slavery movement, the prohibition movement, the

---

[1] Lerner, M., and Mims, E., Jr., "Literature," *Ency. Soc. Sci.*, 9: 539.
[2] Eastman, M., *Artists in Uniform*, 1934.
[3] Williams, A. R., *The Soviets*, p. 377, 1937.
   See also Harper, S. N., *Civic Training in Soviet Russia*, Chap. 14, 1929.

muckraking days, and other crusades. There are only a few instances of state-sponsored literature. One illustration is that of the selection of reading material for the soldiery in the World War.[1]

But the most powerful special pleading is that which occurs without formal propaganda. There is always a selection of literary content in terms of the dominant values. For example, the Communist and Fascist leaders have selected a propaganda literature to high-light certain aspects of the class struggle and economic groups. But from the early nineteenth century onward a growing part of all literature in the Western cultures has been concerned with the class struggle and economic groups. As Sorokin has written, "In brief, in the nineteenth- and twentieth-century economic problems, economic motives, economic behavior, economic ideology, the economic interpretation of almost all the actions of the heroes of literary works, became a mania, an obsession, a fashion, the sign of a supposedly deep insight into human nature."[2] If a certain set of values is dominant in literature, these values may be instilled all the more effectively because certain minority positions are also stated. The propagandist may be too thorough in his selections and exclusions. Credulity may be strained. In Germany today the propaganda leadership is busy remaking the country's songs, literature and schoolbooks. In America, five small books called the *McGuffey Readers* were printed between 1836 and 1840. During the last half of the nineteenth century these readers were the standard textbooks of the rural schools of the American Middle West. Political, economic, ethical and religious values as reflected in the *McGuffey Readers* were inculcated in untold millions of pupils.[3] These readers were not propaganda disseminated by a self-conscious leadership or special interest group. They were selected on the basis of common beliefs and values that were widely diffused. They were read in a culture in which there were other and minority statements of position on these problems. They were contemporaries of Ingersoll. Yet it remains to be proved that state-inspired propaganda textbooks will be more effective in unifying values for school children than were the folk-selected *McGuffey Readers*. Propaganda literature may be effective if it fits into prejudices, beliefs, loyalties and self-interests that are already widely disseminated. Those who are already partially or entirely convinced of the truth of the material propagandized may be fortified in their beliefs. Others may remain unconvinced though forced to be quiescent. A folk-selected literature waxes in influence; it remains to be seen whether an imposed literature will have equal vitality.

[1] Hall, G. S., *Morale*, pp. 83 *ff.*, 1920.
[2] Sorokin, P. A., "Fluctuation of Forms of Art," in *Social and Cultural Dynamics*, vol. I, p. 641, 1937.
[3] Minnich, H. C., *William Holmes McGuffey and His Readers*, 1936.

The process of propaganda is inevitable in modern society. Indignant discussion of propaganda as a "social evil" or "menace" and the advocacy of programs to eliminate propaganda are futile. Propaganda is here to stay. That a great deal of propaganda has been directed toward ends that are harmful to the larger society or to special groups is obvious. Such propaganda cannot be entirely eliminated from the present order, except through a monopolistic control by governments of all the channels of communication. This substitutes official political propaganda for all other special pleadings, as has occurred in the authoritarian states. But under democracy the channels of communication must be kept open. However, there are many limitations upon the activity of contemporary propagandists under relatively free discussion.

The propagandist may be exposed, and a long-drawn-out and expensive campaign may prove a boomerang if a large public is incensed as a result of the exposure. The utilities campaign brought about such repercussions. Then, too, a propaganda campaign may create opposition and arouse a counterpropaganda movement. If the counterpropaganda movement taps widespread popular prejudices, the propagandist cannot be successful, even if he has access to large financial subsidies. The Republican propaganda of 1936 is a case in point. The propagandist is also hampered by regulations set up within the various means of communication. The rules imposed by both the broadcasting chains in 1936 hampered the propagandists of both political parties. Certain legal restrictions may be set up enforcing publicity of the sources of material disseminated in newspapers, motion pictures, radio and other channels of communication. Evasion would probably be easy, and the legal restrictions would need to be carefully worded to avoid interference with freedom of expression, but some regulation is possible. Further, as we have noted, the propagandist is always limited by the existing popular beliefs and prejudices. The best organized special pleading may shatter on a prejudice. In addition, the propagandist may be thwarted by popular stupidity, lack of interest or apathy.[1] Mental sluggishness may prove a defense against rapid modification of opinions at the behest of a special pleader. Again, the point is often made that the common man is at a disadvantage because propaganda costs money and special interests have the larger war chest. This is sometimes true, but it must not be forgotten that the general public has political defenders who delight in tilting a lance at special interests. The general public is not defenseless before an organized interest. And finally, the general public may be protected in part by an increased knowledge of the propaganda process. The educational system should equip the modern student with a knowledge of the most frequently used propaganda devices.

[1] Lumley, *op. cit.*, pp. 394 *ff.*

Adult education should likewise stress the popularization of knowledge of the propagandist's techniques.[1] If the common man can achieve enough insight into the propaganda process, he can thwart the special pleader who is advocating causes not in the general interest. General publics can also hamper the propagandists if they can select champions of the larger interests who will organize counterpropaganda. The propagandist is himself ruled and limited by his social milieu, and a part of that environment is the alertness, intelligence and critical ability of the publics with which he operates. Although propaganda is pervasive and will be persistent, it need not be fatal to intelligent popular decisions.

[1] In this connection two recent developments should be noted: (1) the founding of the Institute for Propaganda Analysis, to which we have already referred and (2) the *America's Town Meeting of the Air* program on propaganda methods. See their bulletin, vol. III, No. 24.

CHAPTER XIX

THE RADIO

"The Athenians gathering en masse at the Acropolis had an ideal agency of communication. They could all listen at once to their peerless leader, Pericles. Until radio was invented America lacked her Acropolis. . . . With radio an American Pericles can have his Acropolis and speak to all America at once."[1]

"Radio was to revolutionize education; it has not done so. It was to revolutionize politics; it has not done so. In my judgment it cannot do so. Radio is nothing but an acceleration in time and an enlargement in space of the vibrations of the human mentality."[2]

The prophets of the early 1920's quite generally overestimated the immediate influence of the radio on political and ideational life and underestimated its development as a purveyor of advertising and a new medium of mass entertainment. They exhibited a distorted vision of the daily preoccupations and interests of the common man and of the business interests. But even though, in America, the radio's potentialities for the dissemination of political and educational information have not been exploited so extensively as was anticipated, it is none the less true that the radio is the most important instrument for mass communication since the invention and development of printing. The diffusion of ideas, facts and personality elements has been greatly stimulated. But that which is diffused is, for the most part, the same content as is already provided in newspaper, periodical literature and the motion pictures.

Although the content of radio programs is quite similar to that of newspapers, popular literature and motion pictures, the nature of the instrument of communication has affected the presentation in many ways. For example, perception is modified in that there is a separation of ideation from visual perception. Hence, simplicity in the formulation of and statement of ideas is at a premium. Further, in talking into the microphone one is not addressing a public meeting but talking to individuals. Broadcasting techniques must be adapted to that fact. At the listening end, the home has been reinforced as a public-opinion forum, and discussion within families is stimulated.

This new means of communication is potentially capable of diffusing anything that the human voice or other sound may express. This may

[1] Glenn Frank.

[2] Hard, W., in *Education on the Air*, Radio in Education, Proceedings, 1935.

be accomplished almost instantaneously and diffused to scores of millions of people. Therefore, new and unsolved problems of control are presented. If information, opinions and entertainment may be diffused more widely than was previously possible, the questions of what information and whose opinions become ever more significant. Authoritarian states quickly settle that question; but the democracies debate. In America, although revolutionary changes in opinions about education and politics have not emerged thus far, popular opinion has been somewhat influenced on hundreds of topics. Opinions are developed, buttressed or changed in many fields. Advertising proclaims its wares. In entertainment, the supremacy of the romantic quest is declared in song and story. Opinions on the humorous are colored by the "wisecracks" of a ventriloquist's dummy. Musical tastes are slightly improved. In general, however, the radio thus far is but an extension of the content of other means of communication. Attention areas have widened, but that which is attended to has not changed greatly.

As a commercial venture, the wireless has existed for four decades, the radio for less than twenty years. Marconi's Wireless Telegraph Company was formed in Great Britain in 1897 and incorporated in America in 1899. From the time when Marconi startled the world by broadcasting intelligible coded messages by wireless, many inventors devoted themselves to the problems of radiobroadcasting the human voice and other sounds. As early as 1904, a Danish engineer Poulsen had developed the first wireless telephone, and many other systems simultaneously created by other inventors soon appeared. However, all this apparatus was crude, uncertain and inefficient, so that popular programs were impossible. It was thought that the wireless telephone would be usable in war and in emergency situations. Apparently the inventors had no inkling of the contemporary radio industry with its commercial and entertainment interests. The vacuum tube, first used to increase the range of telephone conversations, provided the necessary basis for reliable broadcasting. On Nov. 2, 1920, KDKA of Westinghouse Electric Company of East Pittsburgh opened as a broadcasting station. The first program presented the returns of the Harding election. After this, KDKA broadcast for an hour every evening. Their objective was to interest the public so that the company might sell parts for the amateur construction of receiving sets. At first the radio was a novelty, and program content was not so important, as the listeners were primarily concerned with achieving clarity of reception, eliminating static and keeping the receiving set in working order for a few minutes at a time. Music, notable singers and speakers were the principal features. By 1922, occasional afternoon programs were being offered, and general news, weather forecasts, children's hours and time signals had been added. Interest in the radio programs developed rapidly, and hundreds of stations were established during each of the early years. By 1927 there were 694 stations, which number decreased each year until 1933, when there were 598. Newspapers, churches, equipment companies, schools and private broadcasters established stations. The U. S. Department of Commerce allotted wave lengths. Relative chaos reigned for a time with wave jumpers broadcasting on the time of other stations. This was ended on Feb. 28, 1927, when the Radio Control Bill was passed by Congress and the Federal Radio Commission was formed.[1]

The radio industry has grown phenomenally. The investment in radio equipment, stations and factories was estimated at over two billion dollars in 1934. In 1922, there were about 60,000 receiving sets in the United States, whereas in 1935 there were over twenty-one million sets.[2] The United States has approximately four-fifths of the world's supply of receiving sets. Certainly the radio has been invented, developed, perfected, popularized and diffused in an amazingly short time. It is a dramatic illustration of the mechanical efficiency that has been attained in the centers of western culture.

BROADCASTING STATIONS AND RECEIVING SETS IN THE UNITED STATES

In America, the early development of the radio was for the most part unorganized and unplanned. Inasmuch as receiving sets were not licensed, as they have been abroad, accurate statistics on their number and distribution do not exist. In the census of 1930, householders were asked about the ownership of sets. Census enumerators reported that 12,078,345 families owned radio sets. But some of these families had more than one set. In 1935, the Columbia Broadcasting System estimated that there were 21,455,799 sets in the United States. In Table IV, Chapter IX, are listed by states the percentages of families provided with radio sets at the time of the 1930 census. The large percentages of sets owned in the New England, Middle Atlantic, East North Central and Pacific areas may be noted from this table. In sharp contrast to these, the relatively small distribution of sets in the East South Central and West South Central states evidences not only economic but cultural insufficiency.

There are now somewhat less than 600 broadcasting stations in the United States. In the relatively chaotic and uncontrolled field of radio broadcasting during the early 1920's, scores of new stations began to broadcast each year. The problems of interference were soon acute, as

[1] An early study of radio development is Goldsmith, A. N., and Lescarboura, A. C., *This Thing Called Broadcasting*, 1930.

[2] Quoted from Columbia Broadcasting Company statistics by Eisenberg, A. L., *Children and Radio Programs*, p. 3, 1936.

there are but ninety-six air channels for North America.   The record of the number and ownership of stations until 1930 appears in Table IX.

TABLE IX.—NUMBER OF BROADCASTING STATIONS IN THE UNITED STATES, WITH SELECTED TYPES OF OWNERSHIP AND OPERATION, AS OF EACH JUNE 30, 1922–1930*

Year	Commercial broadcasting companies	Educational institutions	Churches	Newspapers and publishers	Electric and radio stores and service companies	Miscellaneous	Total
1922	10	45	6	48	126	147	382
1923	7	90	22	60	180	214	573
1924	15	86	31	38	125	240	535
1925	21	110	50	33	91	266	571
1926	31	89	41	38	72	257	528
1927	101	91	42	38	64	358	694
1928	120	82	48	41	71	329	691
1929	152	66	38	34	55	269	614
1930	223	52	30	36	37	234	612

* Table prepared for the Commission on Social Trends by Willey, M. M., and Rice, S. A., reported in *Communication Agencies and Social Life*, p. 196, 1933.   Quoted by permission of the McGraw-Hill Book Company, Inc.

The trends to be noted in Table IX, notably the growth of commercial broadcasting companies and the decrease of stations owned by churches, newspapers, electrical companies and educational institutions, continue to the present.   The nuisance value of a station may be twenty to thirty times its effective broadcasting range.   With the organization of the Federal Radio Commission in 1927 (now included in the Federal Communications Commission) a plan to create national, regional and local stations and greatly to reduce the total number of stations was announced. The original intention was to reduce the total number of stations to 315.[1] The courts interfered with this drastic reduction, recognizing vested interests in the use of wave lengths.   Some reduction was accomplished, but there is still an enormous waste of broadcasting facilities, inasmuch as the great chains preempt a number of effective channels, providing the same program over a number of national channels at the same time. The most effective channels are used to broadcast entertainment and commercial advertising.   Technical and legal obstacles have prevented the imposition of a more rational allocation of wave lengths.

BROADCASTING FACILITIES ABROAD

The number of radio stations, receiving sets and listeners in the United States exceeds that in the rest of the world today.   The number

[1] Reported in Orton, W. A., *America in Search of Culture*, p. 249, 1933.

TABLE X.—RECEIVING SETS AND BROADCASTING STATIONS IN VARIOUS COUNTRIES

Country	Number of receiving sets in use, 1932*	Number of receiving sets per thousand population	Number of broadcasting stations, 1932*
Alaska	1500	25.4	
Canada	571,898	55.1	77
Cuba	35,000	8.7	58
Mexico	100,000	6.0	50
United States	16,679,253	135.8	571†
Argentina	400,000	32.3	39
Brazil	150,000	3.3	21
Chile	35,000	8.1	27
Uruguay	50,000	25.7	28
Venezuela	9000	2.9	4
Austria	450,272	68.1	5
Belgium	199,000	24.2	12
Czechoslovakia	397,591	27.0	6
Denmark	476,214	129.2	4
France	2,000,000	47.8	31
Germany	3,980,852	60.3	30
Hungary	317,600	35.6	3
Italy	250,000	5.9	12
Netherlands	278,891	33.3	7
Norway	101,901	36.1	13
Poland	308,000	9.2	6
Spain	550,000	19.1	13
Sweden	550,000	88.5	31
United Kingdom	4,329,754	96.6	16
Russia	554,000	3.2	77
China	30,000	0.08	13
India	8,000	0.02	4
Japan	1,000,000	14.4	17
Australia	347,555	55.3	54
New Zealand	75,351	12.7	35
Africa (all of)	49,637	0.28	24
Algeria	10,000	1.5	2
Union of South Africa	26,025	2.7	5
Vatican City			1

* Source: Batson, L. D., *Radio Markets of the World, 1932*, Bureau of Foreign and Domestic Commerce, Trade Promotion Series, No. 136.
† *World Almanac.*

of sets, the number per thousand population and the number of broad-casting stations abroad have been compiled from various sources and are shown in Table X.[1]

It will be noted that Denmark, the United Kingdom, Sweden, and Holland have by far the largest proportions of licensed sets and that such large areas as Brazil, India, China and Russia have relatively very few receiving sets. The locations of the broadcasting stations of the world may be noted on Figs. 3 and 4, in Chapter IX on Geographic Distribution of Group Opinion.

The numbers equipped to listen to broadcasts are increasing rapidly. It is estimated that approximately twenty million additional persons per year have acquired radio facilities in the past five years. However, statistics in this field become obsolete almost as rapidly as they are compiled.

FOREIGN RADIO SYSTEMS[2]

In the United States, radio stations are privately owned and managed, subject to the licensing powers of the Federal Communications Commission. Although among the other countries of the world, great differences exist in the systems of ownership, management and control of stations and in the ways of licensing receiving sets, the systems are all so generally controlled by governments that one is justified in contrasting the American system with radio control in the rest of the world. In general, more or less autocratic governmental control provides the ultimate authority abroad. Let us briefly summarize certain pertinent facts regarding the radio in various important nations.

Great Britain.—From 1922 to 1926 the British Broadcasting Company was a privately owned limited liability company, to be controlled by the government only in case of emergency. In 1927, after a governmental commission had reported on the importance of broadcasting in national life, the British Broadcasting Corporation was established. The BBC is privately owned, but with regulated profits. It is administered by five governors who are appointed by the postmaster general for terms of five years. The corporation must broadcast whatever the government departments may require. Income is provided from a listeners' fee of ten shillings ($2.49) and from the sale of printed publications. The government receives this revenue, except for the regulated payments to

---

[1] A table on the licenses per thousand population abroad in 1934 will be found in *Education on the Air*, p. 304, 1935.

[2] The materials of this summary are abstracted from: Burrows, A. R., in *Ann. Am. Acad. of Pol. and Soc. Sci.*, 177: 29–42; a bulletin of *Education by Radio*, 2: 7; various other articles. Cantril, H., and Allport, G. W., *The Psychology of Radio*, p. 37, 1935, was also consulted.

stockholders. National programs are broadcast, and at the same time the regional stations broadcast programs adapted to the various areas. Some experimenting with programs is possible, so that audiences may be built up for programs that at first have few listeners. Educational broadcasts have been developed to an extent not possible under private control. Of course, the management is subject to popular demands, but considerable flexibility of program content is possible.

Germany.—Government ownership and control under the Ministry of Propaganda. License fees of two reichsmarks (eighty cents) per month are collected from owners of sets, by the postman on his rounds. Restricted advertising is permitted. Until 1933 the programs were primarily for entertainment, education and information. However, the National Socialist Party, during its first year in office, devoted most of the radio time to political propaganda. Since 1934, other types of programs have been allotted increased time. As liberalism has been supplanted by a state philosophy which proclaims that state interest precedes individual interest, authoritarian leaders have expressed no qualms about the diversion of radio programs into propaganda channels.

France.—At the present writing there are thirteen government and seventeen private stations. The government stations are supported by a license fee on receiving apparatus. This varies with the type of set, but the most common fee is fifty French francs ($3.29) per year. The private stations are maintained by advertising, local subsidies and fees obtained from the sale of their time. It is likely that there will soon be no private stations in France. Probably the condition of the government budget accounts for their being permitted to persist during the past few years. The principal development of radio in France is occurring in the government stations.

Italy.—Broadcasting equipment and service is a private monopoly under detailed state control. A supervisory commission controls the program activities. This supervisory commission works with the Ministry of Propaganda. Operating funds are provided by a tax on receiving sets (about $3.60), a municipal tax and a limited amount of advertising fees. The most important recent development in Italian broadcasting is the building of a number of short-wave stations to propagandize in Italian colonies and to create disturbances in French and English colonies.

Russia.—The All-Union Commission on Radiofication and Radio Broadcasting, a government commission, controls the radio. There are about eighty broadcasting stations, including the first 500-kilowatt transmitter in the world. In 1934, a system of license fees on receivers was instituted. The commission's executive committee, composed of the director and two assistants, administers the national broadcasts, determines their content and hours and also supervises the programs arranged by the sixty-seven regional committees, for broadcasting over regional stations. In Russia, the relatively small number of receiving sets does not accurately measure the number of listeners, because groups of people habitually listen at one receiving set. It is estimated that there are over ten million listeners using the 1,500,000 sets existing in 1935.

Japan.—Ownership of the radio by a chartered corporation, the Broadcasting Corporation of Japan (about 6000 stockholders). The corporation is controlled by the Department of State. Income is provided by a tax on receiving sets. The corporation provides upkeep and repair of these sets. Although program content is quite varied, the entire radio system is at the disposal of various government departments for propaganda broadcasts.

Among the other nations of the world, there is government ownership or control, support by public funds or license fees and little or no advertising, in Australia, Belgium, Canada (five stations), Denmark, Mexico, Finland, Austria, Czechoslovakia, Hungary, Irish Free State, Poland and Rumania. Stations are privately owned, with all revenues from advertising or by group subsidy, in the United States, Argentina, Brazil, Chile, Mexico (thirty-nine stations) and all the Canadian stations not yet nationalized.

PROBLEMS OF RADIO CONTROL

During the past decade the problems of governmental versus private ownership and control of radio have been discussed widely and debated frequently in the United States by educators, broadcasters and politicians.[1] Private ownership of radio stations, modified by an increasingly strict supervision by government bodies and by the creation of a number of national, state and municipal broadcasting stations, offers the best system for the development of diverse opinions and of an active opinion process in the United States. The average American listener has not yet considered the problems of radio control. Listeners have been dissatisfied and have expressed dislike of certain types of advertising, of some programs, of this and of that, but they have not seriously considered the possibility of changing the basis of ownership

---

[1] Private ownership has been perfervidly defended in a book distributed by the National Association of Broadcasters, *Broadcasting in the United States*, 1933; in a summary by Harris, E. H., "Shall the Government Own, Operate, and Control Radio Broadcasting in the United States?", *Radio and Education*, pp. 83–115, 1934; in scores of articles. Modifications of our private-ownership system have been suggested in Orton, *op. cit.*, Chap. 13, 1933; Cantril and Allport, *op. cit.*, Chap. 3; Brindze, R., *Not To Be Broadcast*, 1937, Bliven, B., in *Radio and Education*, pp. 76–83, 1934; in numerous bulletins published by *Education by Radio* (National Committee on Education by Radio, 1201 Sixteenth Street, N. W., Washington, D. C.).

and control. A great many of the intellectuals who have advocated government ownership and control have apparently had in mind control by the kind of government they would like to have. In revulsion against the business process they have jumped to another extreme. But although vested interests may desire a minimum of control and the simpleminded may demand complete control, it is possible that more closely controlled private stations and the creation of some publicly owned stations would provide the best system for "the American way."

Divisions of the Federal government now do considerable broadcasting but do not own stations. But the Federal Communications Act, Section 301, states, "It is the purpose of this Act, among other things, to maintain the control of the United States over all the channels of interstate and foreign radio transmission, and to provide for the use of such channels, but not the ownership thereof, by persons for limited periods of time, under licenses granted by Federal Authority, and no such license shall be construed to create any right, beyond the terms, conditions and periods of the license." Hence, private companies do not, in any irrevocable sense, "own" the air. States and municipalities maintain stations. Why should not the Federal government reserve some desirable wave lengths for its own use and provide programs of an educational, political and informational type that the private stations are loath to develop? At the present time, the stations of states and municipalities and other nonprofit stations are subject to continual attacks. This might be changed. The commission could exercise its power. J. G. Kerwin has stated, "A new policy must aim at the restriction or elimination of commercialism. Greater control must be lodged in the federal authorities to exercise discriminating severity, adequate regulation, and to provide some yardstick of measurement to keep the public constantly aware of the best that is possible in broadcasting. Let us realize the best possibilities of private enterprise. Let us provide efficient supervisory administration. To accomplish these ends the federal government should take over from five to ten frequencies within the 500 to 1000 kilocycle range."[1] Such increased governmental control, itself, somewhat limited by the pressures of private stations, might provide the best balance of power in radio control.

Owing to the insistence of vested interests the present distribution and power of broadcasting stations provide an inefficient coverage for the United States. Moreover, at the moment, minorities and financially weak applicants are at a disadvantage in comparison with dominant economic groups in the allocation of broadcasting time and power.

[1] Kerwin, J. G., *The Control of Radio*, p. 26, Public Policy Pamphlets, No. 10, University of Chicago Press, 1934. Quoted by permission of University of Chicago Press.

Present-day radio advertising is blatant. It intrudes upon programs and is often of questionable honesty. The general level of programs is low, and the sponsored program will be adapted to existing tastes rather than to educative efforts in music and entertainment. None the less, the retention of private ownership, modified by the creation of some government stations, appears politically desirable at the moment. The radio remains available as a potential instrument to mobilize opinion against the excesses of government and of the party in power in crisis situations. The liberal, even in his disgruntled moments must not forget the history of government.

Yet this great agency of mass impression must not be irresponsibly used by commercial broadcasters. Government regulation should check excesses. In addition to commercial stations and some government stations, the allocation of good wave lengths so that powerful stations could be maintained by a few universities or responsible endowed institutions would provide a diversity of control and ownership. It is essential that this basic means of communication should not be too closely controlled by any group.

The Content of Programs

Radio listeners, tuning in on the commercial broadcasting stations, find a considerable variety of programs. There are sponsored programs and sustaining programs, that is, those paid for by commercial sponsors and those supplied by the stations. At different periods of the day, the proportion of each varies. H. Cantril notes that, in one large station, the proportion of time sold is:

Time	Per cent	Time	Per cent	Time	Per cent
9:00–10:00 P.M.	72.0	10:00–11:00 A.M.	52.0	11:00–12:00 P.M.	30.0
7:00– 8:00 P.M.	70.0	5:00– 6:00 P.M.	48.0	4:00– 5:00 P.M.	29.0
8:00– 9:00 P.M.	63.0	9:00–10:00 A.M.	39.0	12:00– 1:00 P.M.	22.0
6:00– 7:00 P.M.	58.0	3:00– 4:00 P.M.	39.0	2:00– 3:00 P.M.	10.0

with lesser percentages for the other hours of the day.[1]

Most of the programs are primarily for entertainment and amusement rather than for instruction, although the proportion of time spent in instruction has increased slightly during the past few years.[2]

Some idea of the variety of American programs may be obtained from an examination of the various studies of program content. In

[1] Cantril and Allport, *op. cit.*, p. 77.

[2] The experience of educators with NBC is reported by Reed, T. H., "Commercial Broadcasting and Civic Education," *Pub. Opin. Quar.*, 1: 3: 57–68.

Chapter III on Communication we have noted the results of several small studies.[1] The author essayed a much more extensive and detailed classification in the study that is reported on the following pages.[2] Though but a small proportion of the program content deals with political or economic issues, all programs are of significance with regard to some type of opinion. Judgments of the worth of various kinds of music and stories, the significance of market reports, of various features and of economic goods result from radio listening.

In an attempt to find the principal trends in program content, we studied the programs from 1925 to 1935 of nine American and one English broadcasting station. The sources were the daily newspaper listings of programs; the classifications were according to the dominant characteristic of the program; the unit of record was the time devoted to a given program; and the results were worked out in percentages of the total time. Before turning to these results, we shall indicate briefly the chief problems encountered and the methods used.

1. There are three sources from which radio programs may be studied: some printed record, such as the daily newspaper listings or periodicals like the Chicago *Radio Guide;* the log books of stations; "listening in" to programs. For a detailed analysis, listening in would be best, but this limits the record to present or present and future programs. The records of the radio stations are not available, not, at any rate, unless one examines them at the stations. The periodicals dealing with radio programs are of recent vintage, dealing only with the past few years, and, moreover, do not cover the entire field. We therefore used daily newspapers from the cities in which the stations were located. For a few periods the listings were not complete in one newspaper, but we completed these by using other papers. One source of error in such a record is the variable accuracy of listings for various years. No doubt in the early years there was more changing of programs after they were printed in the papers than there has been of late years. With a considerable body of data, however, we need not regard this as a serious inaccuracy

2. The unit of measurement was the number of minutes devoted to a type of program. Within these time intervals there may be infinite variation in content. The effect of five minutes of one kind of dance music is not that of five minutes of another. But we are comparing the relative amount of time devoted to types of programs in a time series.

3. The categories for program classification were not arbitrarily devised. The twenty-seven types that may be noted in Table XI were

[1] The reports of G. A. Lundberg, C. Kirkpatrick, *Ventura Free Press* and H. Cantril and G. W. Allport are summarized in Chapter III, pp. 45–46.

[2] The bulk of the remainder of this section is adapted from Albig, W., "The Content of Radio Programs, 1925–1935," *Soc. Forces*, 16: 3: 338–349.

gradually developed from the program listings. Beginning with a few general types, which were later modified, examining a sample from the various years of the period recorded, so that the types would be inclusive of almost all the programs during the entire period, we developed this final list. Most of the small residue of miscellaneous items could have been classified, but the resultant list would have been unwieldy. The types are for the most part self-explanatory. The foreign programs are those originating abroad. The continued plays were separated from the plays presented in a single program because these continued plays have latterly won a distinct following. In this type were included all the continued plays except those for children, as these were already included in the children's classification. The star programs were those developed about a speaker, actor or commentator whose name was given for a regular program. This was exclusive of the persons featured in music or as exclusively news or political commentators.

4. The programs were usually listed in the newspapers by time categories; that is, all the stations broadcasting from 9:00 to 9:10 would be listed together with the names of their programs. This necessitated the selection of the programs of the stations we were classifying. The number of minutes devoted to the various programs of our stations were then recorded on a large data sheet. One such sheet was used for each week of the programs of the selected stations. There was classification of programs by program type, by station and by sections of the day—that is, from 6:00 A.M. to noon, noon to 6:00 P.M., 6:00 P.M. to the closing of the station. Figures indicating the number of minutes of a type of program were inscribed in the appropriate classification column. These small figures, showing number of minutes of a single program, were then totaled and worked out in percentages of the total for each program type, for each of the three periods of the day, for each station, for a weekly total.

5. Sampling tests indicated four weeks out of each year for each station as adequate. So the programs for Feb. 1–15 and July 18–31 were classified. These periods were selected to minimize the intrusion of holidays, also to include winter and summer programs. The stations classified were: WEAF, WOR and WJZ of New York from 1925 through 1934; WABC of New York from 1927 through 1934; WGN of Chicago from 1925 through 1934; WMAQ, KYW, WBBM of Chicago from 1929 through 1934; WDAF of Kansas City from 1925 through 1934; the London National of the BBC. from 1925 through 1934. Here is a sample of powerful stations in large cities. A parallel study of low-power stations in small towns and cities would be desirable. These would no doubt be found to have differed from one another, especially in the early period, more than do the large stations.

6. The relatively small samples of program-content analysis that have so far been published have not indicated either the consistency of individual classification, if one person did the judging, or the comparative uniformity of classification, if more than one was involved. C. Kirkpatrick, in the study already referred to, is an exception. In the early stages of our study, the four classifiers conferred together to some extent on the meaning of certain program titles, examined the columns of the radio pages for comments on or references to those programs, so as to determine what their classification should be. After that they worked independently. Well through the classification, each classified the same sample week. Their results were compared for each category in our list of types of programs. The coefficient of correlation was .93 $\pm$ .0178.

Our results provided a score or more of tables on which the classifications of program types for each station by yearly totals appeared. Further, there are tables in which the averages of the American stations are shown. Then, there are tables showing the classification by stations of the various program types. And, finally, those on which the range of percentages among the American stations for program types by years are noted. Of this bulk of material only a limited selection of general tables may be exhibited here. Table XI gives the percentages of time devoted to various types of programs. It is based on the averages of nine American stations. Table XII provides comparable results for the London National of the BBC. These tables present averages. However, the stations differ considerably from one another in the proportions of time devoted to any type program. The comparison of the American with the London National programs may be made by comparing Tables XI and XII. Extensive comment on the results is impossible within the limits of this volume. For convenience in thinking of the meaning of percentage differences it may be noted that, as most of the stations are on the air from 6:00 A.M. to at least 1:00 A.M., 1 per cent of broadcasting time is between eleven and twelve minutes per day. Hence, a change of as much as 3 per cent means at least a half hour more or less of that type of program every day.

In the results of this study we have a general survey and comparison that purport to show certain large trends and changes. The reader may note the trends by studying the tables. Our study does not reveal the important qualitative changes within the program types. Many of these also may be examined in an organized fashion. The most valuable use of studies of content, not only of radio programs but also of other media of communication, is in noting trends and changes in content. Systems of classification may be inadequate and unstandardized. Nevertheless, if a system is used consistently over a time period, valuable facts may appear.

TABLE XI.—PERCENTAGES OF TIME DEVOTED TO VARIOUS TYPES OF PROGRAMS—AVERAGES OF NINE AMERICAN BROADCASTING STATIONS, 1925–1935

Types of Programs	1925		1926		1927		1928		1929		1930		1931		1932		1933		1934	
	Feb.	July	Feb.	July	Feb.	July	Feb.	July	Feb.	July	Feb.	July	Feb.	July	Feb.	July	Feb.	July	Feb.	July
Dance music	22.85	19.50	20.27	28.53	19.70	26.37	23.29	24.95	23.15	28.42	23.90	25.47	26.89	29.57	23.45	25.17	19.81	25.89	23.40	24.74
String ensemble	10.05	8.71	8.35	12.58	14.50	11.56	8.76	9.99	3.02	5.11	6.41	6.59	6.12	2.67	3.26	7.07	4.20	5.43	3.98	4.27
Concert orchestra	4.33	16.64	9.62	12.89	12.01	7.39	9.80	7.85	8.01	7.77	13.54	7.70	10.45	6.37	8.35	9.33	5.40	10.07	5.02	8.22
Soloists	7.60	4.87	6.24	6.02	7.03	4.17	2.39	3.86	5.81	3.63	5.34	3.77	4.15	4.59	4.53	4.90	5.02	4.74	4.42	4.90
Combination	14.10	9.83	10.49	5.39	4.79	4.60	10.96	10.10	8.11	6.44	5.19	7.04	6.50	3.27	3.62	3.04	4.52	3.06	3.47	3.89
Vocal	8.06	8.84	10.11	7.79	9.14	7.80	6.62	7.63	5.55	6.02	6.53	6.27	7.00	11.23	13.06	12.80	16.62	13.71	16.72	14.37
Sacred	0.99	0.24	0.22	0.50	0.42	1.57	0.41	0.28	0.27	0.29	0.39	0.36	0.47	0.24	0.63	0.39	0.45	0.80	0.58	0.61
Victrola	0.00	0.00	0.01	0.00	0.33	0.36	2.51	1.31	3.52	3.19	4.21	5.35	5.75	3.42	3.24	3.21	4.31	2.48	3.47	3.49
Miscellaneous	3.36	2.16	2.97	2.67	4.30	7.00	8.10	8.13	10.04	6.51	2.71	4.24	2.04	6.06	3.99	3.35	6.16	2.43	5.39	5.64
Total	71.34	70.78	68.28	76.37	72.22	70.82	72.84	74.10	67.48	67.38	68.22	66.79	69.37	67.42	64.13	69.26	66.49	68.61	66.45	70.13
Women's	2.35	2.42	2.98	2.83	2.81	3.48	4.08	3.65	8.12	4.86	5.14	3.62	3.60	4.22	4.89	3.99	3.48	3.39	3.05	2.45
Feature	0.69	3.09	3.15	1.89	1.99	2.40	4.54	1.29	1.68	3.17	3.54	2.70	3.59	3.91	3.99	2.27	1.93	3.61	5.45	3.19
Education	4.93	1.26	4.39	1.99	3.88	1.42	2.38	2.03	4.94	3.89	5.19	3.11	6.04	3.04	7.21	4.79	4.65	3.56	4.01	2.83
Sports	0.23	3.82	0.85	2.91	0.15	5.32	0.89	4.12	0.79	4.80	0.41	4.52	0.71	6.04	1.71	4.79	3.99	3.56	0.56	4.72
News	0.68	0.70	3.10	1.90	1.52	2.19	1.93	1.24	1.34	1.56	1.33	1.98	1.03	1.11	1.20	0.48	1.25	0.81	1.07	1.54
Weather	0.34	0.75	0.57	0.65	1.25	0.99	0.63	0.37	0.49	0.47	0.40	0.29	0.24	0.39	0.09	0.16	0.14	0.20	0.10	0.19
Church service	3.14	1.72	2.21	1.43	2.80	2.39	2.60	1.92	3.31	1.80	2.34	2.05	3.12	1.39	2.23	1.95	2.38	1.85	2.22	1.29
Market reports	3.61	2.75	1.71	1.49	1.34	1.28	1.29	1.76	1.41	1.16	1.28	2.01	0.65	0.39	0.52	0.61	0.33	0.35	0.39	0.26
Political	1.80	0.69	1.33	0.64	0.22	0.02	0.33	0.45	0.59	0.44	0.95	0.38	1.21	0.11	1.38	1.03	0.99	1.05	0.72	0.21
Health exercises	1.81	6.59	4.02	3.28	2.34	2.73	1.78	2.36	1.59	1.79	1.06	1.21	1.63	1.61	0.61	0.00	0.12	0.12	0.41	0.11
Miscellaneous	4.92	0.49	1.14	0.12	3.01	0.82	0.29	1.13	2.45	0.51	0.70	0.51	0.15	0.04	0.44	0.15	2.84	0.05	1.16	0.68
Total	24.50	24.28	25.45	19.13	21.31	23.04	20.38	20.32	26.71	24.45	22.34	22.38	21.97	22.25	24.27	20.22	18.56	18.98	19.14	17.47
Foreign	0.00	0.00	0.47	0.00	0.26	0.26	0.16	0.00	0.10	0.00	0.44	0.23	0.99	0.69	0.46	0.41	0.16	0.20	0.25	1.17
Children's	3.72	2.45	4.21	3.34	3.76	2.35	1.89	1.64	2.45	2.30	2.82	2.54	1.86	2.44	3.52	2.32	3.62	3.85	3.74	2.34
Plays	0.04	0.79	0.10	0.69	0.27	1.11	2.79	1.13	1.11	1.48	1.64	1.42	1.69	1.31	1.19	0.59	1.76	2.00	1.70	1.81
Continued plays and readings	0.09	0.00	0.71	0.05	0.48	0.76	0.63	1.23	0.12	0.26	0.79	0.22	1.69	1.33	1.91	1.71	1.57	2.66	1.04	1.50
Sketches	0.00	1.53	0.64	0.16	1.23	0.90	0.81	0.56	1.27	1.69	2.07	2.51	1.76	2.87	3.27	4.19	5.71	2.49	5.77	4.65
Star	0.00	0.00	0.06	0.00	0.35	0.12	0.12	0.00	0.41	0.55	0.70	0.79	0.89	0.97	0.84	0.78	1.29	0.74	1.40	0.89
Total	3.85	4.77	6.19	4.24	6.09	5.50	6.40	4.56	5.46	6.28	8.46	7.71	8.30	9.61	11.19	10.00	14.11	11.94	13.93	12.36
Miscellaneous	0.19	0.00	0.00	0.15	0.19	0.47	0.05	0.86	0.63	1.64	0.87	3.06	0.09	0.55	0.21	0.43	0.69	0.44	0.36	0.00
Total	99.78	99.84	100.12	99.89	99.81	99.83	99.91	99.84	100.28	99.75	99.89	99.94	99.73	99.83	99.80	99.91	99.85	99.97	99.88	99.96

TABLE XII.—PERCENTAGES OF TIME DEVOTED TO VARIOUS TYPES OF PROGRAMS—LONDON NATIONAL OF THE BBC, 1925–1935

Types of Programs	1925 Feb.	1925 July	1926 Feb.	1926 July	1927 Feb.	1927 July	1928 Feb.	1928 July	1929 Feb.	1929 July	1930 Feb.	1930 July	1931 Feb.	1931 July	1932 Feb.	1932 July	1933 Feb.	1933 July	1934 Feb.	1934 July
Dance music	11.69	20.47	30.93	26.57	19.30	13.19	18.63	19.67	14.86	22.72	15.30	18.87	16.44	23.81	10.32	20.76	22.40	20.18	17.58	20.89
String ensemble	4.50	6.58	1.95	3.37	2.11	6.26	7.16	5.16	1.90	1.11	0.77	1.86	2.35	0.00	2.12	0.88	1.28	1.13	2.70	0.77
Concert orchestra	17.68	8.62	9.59	16.26	10.31	9.21	9.18	4.48	5.63	5.84	17.44	10.94	11.94	10.18	16.72	15.50	9.73	23.44	17.13	25.39
Soloists	2.77	1.37	6.63	6.90	1.53	1.67	9.65	6.06	6.37	4.51	11.54	10.64	7.11	7.26	12.14	13.25	13.28	8.32	8.60	10.12
Combination	10.51	13.19	2.55	3.38	9.77	18.26	5.57	9.86	12.55	9.82	2.56	4.68	5.04	9.54	2.06	6.74	5.66	8.96	3.78	2.29
Vocal	8.13	6.84	7.38	7.13	5.91	9.00	8.27	8.92	2.80	3.25	4.61	11.07	5.35	5.39	3.97	3.79	1.11	1.66	1.98	7.07
Sacred	1.08	0.88	2.91	0.40	0.40	3.08	0.99	5.64	1.67	2.37	1.68	1.74	5.45	4.71	1.11	1.00	0.00	0.69	0.45	1.15
Victrola	1.96	7.03	3.37	4.46	2.23	2.01	3.87	9.27	8.00	9.19	7.05	4.91	2.41	4.46	2.09	4.67	3.07	8.95	2.85	2.72
Miscellaneous	0.00	0.44	0.00	0.00	1.54	1.23	0.00	0.00	3.88	1.70	0.59	0.34	0.00	0.00	2.00	0.00	2.92	0.98	0.84	0.14
Total	58.32	65.42	65.31	68.47	57.75	63.91	63.22	69.06	57.66	60.51	61.54	65.05	56.09	65.35	52.53	66.59	59.45	74.31	55.71	70.54
Women's	0.76	0.95	0.18	0.55	0.45	0.55	0.31	0.57	2.07	3.17	1.54	1.38	0.82	0.87	0.86	0.79	0.41	1.03	0.42	0.71
Feature	10.03	7.67	7.51	7.21	7.51	8.22	4.82	6.50	0.13	0.00	7.53	5.59	5.94	5.94	5.78	6.07	0.00	0.00	0.00	3.01
Education	9.69	3.87	7.51	1.39	9.48	3.97	8.60	3.60	11.74	9.84	6.44	1.62	10.99	1.97	12.83	1.20	12.30	0.69	7.14	0.60
Sports	0.91	0.44	0.39	0.44	3.71	4.87	2.26	0.63	2.45	0.75	2.00	1.84	2.64	1.19	1.30	0.15	2.56	1.33	3.29	3.90
News	4.40	2.93	3.27	3.32	2.23	2.81	2.46	2.74	2.32	2.78	3.65	3.35	2.40	3.72	3.18	4.02	3.30	2.60	3.51	4.45
Weather	1.73	1.35	1.33	1.62	1.39	1.34	1.90	1.99	1.34	3.57	3.23	3.87	1.15	1.21	1.16	1.19	1.64	1.53	3.05	3.20
Church service	0.76	0.98	1.24	1.97	1.65	2.67	3.98	3.86	4.65	3.33	3.12	5.23	4.46	3.31	6.48	4.34	4.45	4.60	3.83	4.21
Market reports	0.00	0.29	0.40	0.81	0.32	0.12	0.37	0.45	3.09	0.79	0.70	1.27	3.15	4.48	5.54	4.31	3.65	3.45	0.40	0.00
Political	0.25	0.44	0.52	0.00	2.61	0.00	0.31	0.00	0.51	0.19	0.00	0.46	1.18	0.00	0.70	0.61	0.13	0.00	0.65	0.00
Health exercises	0.00	0.00	0.00	0.00	0.00	0.00	0.00	0.00	0.00	0.00	0.00	0.00	0.00	0.00	0.00	0.00	0.00	0.00	0.00	0.00
Miscellaneous	1.01	1.83	1.42	0.63	1.16	1.09	2.30	0.92	2.77	3.65	0.09	0.29	0.80	1.04	1.28	1.04	2.90	1.67	1.77	0.05
Total	29.54	20.75	21.76	17.68	30.51	23.64	27.31	21.71	31.07	28.07	28.30	24.90	33.57	23.73	39.11	23.72	31.34	17.12	34.49	20.13
Foreign	0.33	0.00	0.36	0.77	0.77	0.73	0.77	0.00	0.77	0.00	0.54	0.00	0.34	2.93	0.19	0.73	0.20	0.46	0.00	1.85
Children's	9.38	8.45	7.07	8.12	5.45	6.66	6.27	6.32	5.59	5.88	6.25	5.89	7.00	5.40	5.90	5.57	5.71	5.64	5.19	5.42
Plays	0.00	4.33	2.21	1.37	2.11	1.18	2.35	2.31	4.01	4.31	1.81	3.48	1.35	2.15	1.47	1.84	2.64	1.91	3.60	1.39
Continued plays and readings	0.00	0.00	0.00	1.42	0.57	0.37	0.14	0.00	0.77	0.64	0.00	0.00	0.55	0.34	0.00	1.50	0.24	0.50	0.00	0.00
Sketches	1.99	1.07	2.14	1.82	2.17	0.86	0.33	0.39	0.51	0.12	1.49	0.40	0.23	0.00	1.26	0.00	0.00	0.00	0.92	0.65
Star	0.42	0.44	0.59	0.89	0.00	0.00	1.10	0.00	0.00	0.00	0.00	0.00	0.69	0.00	0.00	0.00	0.00	0.00	0.00	0.00
Total	2.41	5.84	4.94	5.50	4.85	2.41	3.92	2.70	5.29	5.07	3.30	3.88	2.82	2.49	2.73	3.34	2.88	2.41	4.52	2.04
Miscellaneous	0.00	0.00	0.00	0.00	0.00	0.00	0.00	0.00	0.34	0.44	0.00	0.00	0.01	0.00	0.00	0.00	0.30	0.00	0.00	0.00
Total	99.98	100.46	99.44	99.77	99.33	99.35	100.72	99.79	99.95	99.94	99.93	99.72	99.83	99.83	100.46	99.95	99.88	99.94	99.91	99.98

The Listeners

Who listens to these programs; when and how long do they listen; what are the listeners' likes and dislikes; how are their attitudes, opinions and behavior affected by what they hear? As such questions are obviously of commercial significance to the broadcasters and also pique the curiosity of academic probers, a very considerable body of information has already been collected on these problems. Though a great deal of it reposes in the files of commercial broadcasting companies, there have been some published reports during the past few years, as indicated by the 732 items of the excellent bibliography appended to the volume *Measurement in Radio*, by F. H. Lumley.

Most American families now have access to radio sets. Almost three-quarters of all homes are supplied with receiving sets of some kind. Here is an unprecedented audience; huge, diverse in ways of life, age, sex, training and knowledge. It is reported that in large cities 93 per cent of all homes have receiving sets; in cities of 25,000 to 250,000, some 92 per cent; in cities of 1000 to 25,000, about 88 per cent are equipped; towns under 1000 inhabitants are well supplied, with 77 per cent; and 34 per cent of all the homes in the open country have radios.[1] Repeated and continuous surveys, by questionnaire, canvassing, telephone inquiry and analysis of mail response, are made in order to determine the characteristics of the listening publics. Radio ownership and audiences have been determined for income groups. As might be expected, the middle income groups listen most assiduously.

There have been many studies to determine when different groups listen in and when they prefer to listen. The evening hours are generally best, audience peak being reached from 7:00 to 10:00 P.M.[2] As would be expected, women listen more often during the morning hours, children after school, and farmers tune in from 12:00 noon to 2:00 P.M. Various studies have established that the average radio is operated from four to five hours a day. Sunday and Friday evenings are preferred; on Saturday evenings the sets are less generally used. In the summer months there is a decrease of about 10 per cent in comparison with the remainder of the year.[3] One method of noting the size of the audience tuning in on major broadcasts is the record of thousands of kilowatt hours of electricity consumed in running the sets. In a few cases, listening audiences have been requested to turn off one electric light and then turn it on again after a few seconds. From the change in amount of electricity consumed the size of the audience has been calculated.

[1] Cantril and Allport, *op. cit.*, p. 86. These authors summarized from a report of CBS.

[2] Lumley, F. H., *Measurement in Radio*, p. 194, 1934.

[3] *Ibid.*, p. 197.

The diversified radio audience has many preferences in types of programs. Moreover, these tastes have varied greatly from year to year since the popularization of radio. In general, music, comedy, dramatic programs and sport broadcasts head the list. Preferences are canvassed by questionnaires, by telephone calls to homes, asking which radio programs are being listened to, and by analysis of "fan mail." The mail responses are now considered a much less significant indicator of popular taste than was thought a few years ago. Letter writers are usually not typical. Will Durant decided from a sample of fan mail that the letters were written by invalids, lonely people, the very young and the very old and mischievous children.[1] Much mail response has been solicited by prizes, contests and free offers. The usefulness of mail response in gathering information about the listeners naturally depends somewhat on the type of program they are writing about. Response to colorful personalities may be similar to that of the fan mail of movie stars. Radio stars receive gifts and personal contributions of many types, from food to cough medicine. Guy Lombardo once received 193 yards of violin strings when he complained about one of the strings on his instrument.[2] Mail response and gifts are psychologically significant but are of but limited value in determining the likes and dislikes of typical radio fans.[3] Surveys have made it abundantly clear that the mass of listeners in America want to be, not educated, but entertained. But radio audiences have diversified tastes in entertainment, and the broadcasters attempt to meet the varied demands by giving a little of everything.

Something is known of the effects of radio programs on buying habits. Department stores have used "radio specials" to determine the extent to which buying depends upon radio advertising. Experiments, based on territories with and without radio advertising, have been made. Popular opinions about various types of products have been modified by radio appeals. But what are the results of radio discussion of controversial political and social problems? Father Coughlin had a large radio audience, but apparently he did not greatly influence the vote. Whether or not radio audiences are influenced greatly on such issues has not, except in a few limited cases, been subjected to experimental test. E. S. Robinson created a test of 120 statements on unemployment, each of which was preceded by a rating classification of five points. This was given to 419 persons (League of Women Voters members and friends). The subjects later gathered weekly for four successive weeks and listened

[1] *Ibid.*, p. 50.

[2] *Ibid.*, p. 167.

[3] Space does not permit a summary of even the more important studies of listeners' preferences. Examine the excellent summaries in Lumley, *op. cit.*, pp. 274–284, and Cantril and Allport, *op. cit.*, pp. 89–95.

to radio discussions of unemployment. An unexposed group was also tested. Both groups were retested after the series of radio lectures. Those who had listened to the lectures evidenced an increase in certainty regarding the statements with which they agreed before the lectures. That is, if inclined toward agreement, the subjects became more certain. Those who favored governmental action on unemployment had their beliefs fortified by the lectures, although the lecturers were selected to represent both positions. The opposite tendency was not evidenced. The listeners became more certain of what they did believe but did not become surer of what they did not believe.[1] Utilizing the very crude tests that the social psychologist has at his disposal at the present time, the influence of the broadcaster upon the opinions of listeners on political and social problems will no doubt be tested in the next few years.

THE INFLUENCE OF RADIO UPON GROUP OPINION

The effects of broadcasting upon interests, attitudes and opinions are so numerous, varied and subtle, and, thus far, so ill-understood, that we shall not commit the absurdity of attempting to list such consequences. They defy analysis of any complete and exact kind. Moreover, most of these effects are indirect and unintended, but by no means incidental. The contents of radio programs reflect the prevailing "climate of opinion." However, we shall comment on some of the more general relationships.

The rapid development of mechanical innovation in radio equipment may be roughly indicated by noting that the number of patents issued in this field from 1916 to 1920 was 50; from 1921 to 1925 there were 443, and from 1926 to 1930 the government office lists 1061 patents.[2] No similarly rapid change has occurred in our understanding of its implications as a new means of communication or in experimental explorations of its potentialities for distributing information and modifying public opinion. It is understandable, but ironical, that the nation which most vociferously espouses democracy should have been so laggard in the use of the radio to enrich and broaden the knowledge and thought life of the masses of its citizens. Although large groups cannot be made intelligent by fiat or through any one channel of communication, it is an axiom of democracy that they may be more or less gently led to more mature values. Commercial broadcasting, preoccupied with the size of its audiences, has had no incentive to provide a gradually rising standard of programs in an attempt to refine popular taste. We have already discussed the need for other and effective competing systems for the performance of this function. Thus far, American broadcasting has been

---

[1] Robinson, E. S., "Are Radio Fans Influenced," *Survey Graphic*, 68: 546–547.

[2] Sorokin, P. A., *Social and Cultural Dynamics*, vol. II, p. 166, 1933.

essentially but the amplification, repetition and diffusion of existing tastes, standards and interests. That the simpler provincial standards may be expanded into the values requisite to the "great society" is the faith of democracy.[1] Such a viewpoint assumes the development of taste and knowledge of values in any field as the result of training within a culture. In so far as American leadership remains permeated with this faith, it will not persistently ignore the potentialities of the radio.

Speed of communication accelerates the processes of opinion and of public decision at many points. It may be that in a fundamental way the popular fashions in thought will change more rapidly. Achieving integration in large publics has usually been a slow process. With the radio, a new and effective agency is provided for those bent upon building up or tearing down popular viewpoints. Political change will be accelerated. The defense of administrations and attacks upon them achieve a more immediate hearing. There is already evidence of a more rapid fashion change in demagogues. Preferences for popular songs, slang, slogans and other language forms are built up and outmoded at an increasing tempo. If there existed a widely diffused and stable framework of values, such speeding up of the opinion process and of decision might be desirable. With values in transition, however, instability, confusion and disintegration now occur at many points. Confusion may be merely increased by the multiplicity of impressions and viewpoints presented to a people inadequately implemented with measuring rods of stable value.

We have elsewhere discussed something of the increased diffusion resulting from the radio.[2] That impressions are more widely scattered is an obvious fact. But as Lewis Mumford notes, "As with all instruments of multiplication the critical question is as to the function and quality of the object one is multiplying."[3] Another basic question relates to the amount of psychological regimentation resulting from widespread diffusion. All the mass agencies of communication have some such blanketing effect, but, in a preoccupation with such standardization, the commentator must not minimize the beliefs, interests and attitudes developed from other means of communication or the particular viewpoints resulting from membership in class, regional, racial and other groups. Words, spoken in conversation or over the radio, cannot readily change such attitudes.

One function that the radio may perform in the opinion field is to inspire interest and indicate controversies. Those special groups which

---

[1] See Odum, H. W., in *Educational Broadcasting*, pp. 100–102, for a discussion of the radio and enrichment of rural life.

[2] Chap. III.

[3] Mumford, L., *Technics and Civilization*, p. 21, 1934.

have access to a richer and more diversified fare than that offered by the radio may listen infrequently. But that which may be simple or platitudinous to the expert or the better informed may be stimulating and inspire interest among the mass of listeners. President Sproul of California states, "The great need of our people today is not improved facilities for making known and available the materials of culture, but better means for interesting them in living more abundant lives. Adult education suffers no lack of facilities or matter for life-long learning: it does suffer from a dearth of consumers and of consumer psychology. In order to change that situation we must arouse in the average citizen a desire for intellectual and spiritual growth."[1] If the rule of the average man is to be maintained relatively uninvaded by special interests, at least a sizable minority must be constantly stimulated to an interest in public affairs. The radio may be used to inspire interest in a special viewpoint, ardently propagandized, or in a truly debated issue. Hence, radio systems effectively serve autocracy or liberal democracy.

Inasmuch as the radio reaches large audiences of the literate and the illiterate, of the learned and the ignorant, it may be an effective instrument of mass education or of propaganda to the millions. It is evident that the nature of the instrument does not determine that one type of appeal has a permanent advantage over the other. The radio provides a new forum for the discussions of popular democracy, but it has also proved a most powerful means of mass control by the dictators. Day after day under the government-controlled radio systems of Europe the listening audience receives either unabashed government propaganda or a minimum of political news.[2] Under the American system a mass of frequently confused and confusing counsel is provided. There is some informal censorship of extreme political and economic doctrines. Under the most free of democratic systems the difficult problem of allocation of time to small minority groups with a small following would remain. Public indifference applies its own censorship to such programs. Moreover, under relatively free discussion, the appeal of the demagogue, especially in crises, frequently outweighs the appeal of reason. But that is implicit in democracy, inescapable and persistent. Broadcasting has not made it so. Radio merely emphasizes and diffuses the existing systems, but the very extension of appeals to ever larger groups makes it a constantly more powerful agency for popular information or error, realistic knowledge or distortion.

Whether it is used to propagandize a special cause or develop opinion through discussion, the radio is the great unifying agency of modern life.

---

[1] Sproul, R. G., in *Radio and Education*, p. 32, 1934.
[2] See Hard, W., "Radio and Public Opinion," *Ann. Am. Acad. Pol. Soc. Sci.*, 177: 105 *ff*.

By means of radio and sound pictures, appeals may be made to large publics. Issues are carried to ever larger groups, and the processes of discussion and decision have increased their tempo. There is a degree of national unity that is requisite for the functioning of the state and of economic processes. Modern life also requires speed of decision at many points. If large publics are to be consulted frequently in the maintenance of a democracy adapted to other aspects of modern life and if diverse publics are to be unified, the radio is a most opportune invention.

LEADERSHIP AND THE RADIO

Though speech over the radio is less personal than in face-to-face situations, it is obviously much more so than appeals by printed words. The wide experience of the average man with personal relationships gives to these a reality that far surpasses any impersonal stimulus. In his radio speech the day after the banks were closed in 1933, President Roosevelt instilled a widespread confidence that could not have been achieved by written proclamation. During his first year in office the President addressed 38,000 words to approximately sixty million listeners. Radio has brought a reemphasis upon the appeal of speech for persuasion. During the past ten years much of the controversy between representatives of the press and the radio has centered on the division of advertising fees. Important though this may be to the present owners of newspapers and radio stations, the essential conflict is between written and spoken appeals. The authority of print is challenged by the persuasiveness of speech.[1]

Through long experience the rules of oratory have been more or less exactly formulated. The principles of effective radio speech have been less exactly stated. There are differences, however, which make it difficult to speak to an audience and into the microphone at the same time. Effective leadership by means of radio speeches is an art. It is possible to make a few generalizations about radio speaking, but these do not encompass the essential appeal of the great speaker. In addressing large publics it is desirable that the speaker should avoid local or sectional inflections and vocabulary. These distract and alienate a part of the listening public. Clarity is essential. "Radio talks seem to require more concrete illustration and more repetition, apparently because the listener's mind is not acting as creatively as in the face-to-face situation."[2] In radio speech, simplicity is at a premium. Of President Roosevelt, it is said, "He speaks right out with no 'high-falutin' words. There is

[1] Educational psychology has been concerned over this problem for many years. Some recent experiments on the relative effectiveness of listening versus reading are summarized in Cantril and Allport, *op. cit.*, Chap. 9.

[2] *Ibid.*, p. 157.

not much chance of Americans failing to get the meaning in such expressions as 'killing two birds with one stone'; 'we cannot ballyhoo ourselves back to prosperity'; 'the kind of prosperity that will lead us into another tail spin'; 'I have no expectation of making a hit every time I come to bat.' "[1] Brevity is requisite. Radio listeners are more readily tired than is an audience that can occupy itself with the personal characteristics of a speaker. In oratory, the finer shadings of emotional expression are in part presented by facial expression and gesture. The radio speaker must cultivate a greater variety of tone and inflection to communicate these. Emotional appeals can be made in radio speaking, but the technique differs from that of the orator. In the early days of the radio, commentators declared that the demagogue was outmoded. Since then we have had many radio demagogues. The traditional tricks of platform demagoguery were largely outmoded, but new types of demagogues, implemented with new varieties of emotional appeal, have appeared. However, in general, radio speaking has been characterized by more frequent appeals to logical thinking than has popular oratory. Political controversy over the radio has appeared to have a more rational tone than have the oratorical efforts of spellbinders swinging round the circle. During the 1936 campaign, Father Coughlin, an exception to this rule, had large audiences of listeners but apparently had very little effect in changing voting habits.

The art of radio leadership has already produced quite diverse types. The radio-listening multitude will project its tastes upon new types of leaders, and they in turn will mold anew the tastes of the listeners. In another decade it may be possible to limn more sharply the characteristics of the effective radio speaker.

THE RADIO IN POLITICS

The successful operation of political democracy depends largely upon the interest and intelligence of the electorate and upon close contact between the voters and their chosen executives. Commentators agree that there has been some increased interest in political discussion and in public affairs since the popularization of broadcasting. Persons who are not politically minded will not become so immediately after buying a receiving set. However, many people who would not go to a political meeting do tune in on some political talks. It is probable that a part of the recent increase in voting in national elections may be ascribed to interest aroused by radio talks and to the broadcasting of nominating conventions. In the national elections of 1856, 1860 and 1864 the percentages of the eligible vote that were cast were, respectively, 83.51, 84.19 and 84.85. The figures remained at about 80 per cent until 1900.

[1] Dunlap, O. E., *New York Times Mag.*, June 18, 1933, p. 17.

In 1904, 68.0 per cent of those eligible voted; in 1912, 61.95 per cent; in 1920, 52.36 per cent. This was the low point. In 1928, 63.86 per cent voted; in 1932, 65.13 per cent; in 1936, almost 70.0 per cent of the eligible voters appeared at the polls.[1] Of course, the emotion-arousing nature of the issues in the last three campaigns is primarily responsible for the widespread popular interest, but radio discussion of these issues was an important stimulant.

Increased contact with national and state leaders and a greater familiarity with certain political processes have resulted from broadcasting. Not only can the political executive explain his position to listeners, but he can bring and has brought pressure to bear on the legislative branches through an aroused popular response. Moreover, men of influence and ability, other than political leaders, have been induced to talk over the radio. Such men, often unaccustomed to public speaking, would be unwilling to face large audiences. Such increased contact with leaders can promote the ends of dictators and authoritarians but may also vivify the democratic process. Interest in political functioning is stimulated by the broadcasting of political events and meetings, especially of the nominating conventions. Some political commentators have achieved large radio audiences, notably Boake Carter, H. V. Kaltenborn, F. W. Wile, William Hard and David Lawrence. Some types of popularization of politics have been forbidden by radio officials, as witness the refusal of both large chains to broadcast political skits in the last election. The companies contended that they should permit only straightforward statements of fact and opinion by responsible spokesmen. However, some dramatization of events inevitably occurs through the descriptions by announcers. The public functioning of personalities is high-lighted.

Radio audiences are isolated as individuals and small groups. Although emotional appeals may be made over the radio, there can be no arousal of the mob feeling characteristic of the traditional political rally. The increasing importance of appeal to radio listeners is indicated by the fact that the chains sold 43 per cent more time for radio speeches in 1936 than in 1932. There were national hookups for over 200 hours of speaking in the last presidential campaign.

Owing largely to the radio, local influences are increasingly transcended in politics. Important speeches are heard in every section of the country and by all classes of people. Local and sectional appeals are decreased. Of the local leaders in Middletown, the Lynds state, "These men own Middletown's jobs and they largely own Middletown's press. . . . The one important channel of communication which they

[1] Figures taken from table in Barnes, H. E., *The History of Western Civilization*, vol. II, p. 864, 1935.

could not control was the national radio networks, which brought the other side before local voters, notably in President Roosevelt's own speeches."[1]

Political discussion is largely canalized through the administrative offices of the great chains. A. N. Holcombe has recently queried as to whether it is compatible with proper freedom of the air to: (1) refuse to sell time to political committees except between conventions and elections, (2) refuse to permit broadcasting of dramatic political sketches, (3) insist on allocating free time for the discussion of controversial issues according to the editorial judgment of company executives and (4) exercise power of shutting off from the air at any time any portion of a speech that seems to the executives to be prejudicial to the best interests of the public.[2] If private ownership of the radio is retained, it is evident that there are many problems to be clarified regarding the selection of broadcasting content.

New evidences of the influence of radio upon government and politics appear every year. The following list, though admittedly incomplete, presents those relations which appeared most important to W. F. Ogburn in 1932.[3]

On Government and Politics

In government, a new regulatory function necessitated.
Censorship problem raised because of charges of swearing, etc.
Legal questions raised beginning with the right to the air.
New specialization in law; four air law journals existing.
New problems of copyright have arisen.
New associations created, some active in lobbying.
Executive pressure on legislatures, through radio appeals.
A democratizing agency, since political programs and speeches are designed to reach wide varieties of persons at one time.
Public sentiment aroused in cases of emergencies like drought.
International affairs affected because of multiplication of national contacts.
Rumors and propaganda on nationalism have been spread.
Limits in broadcasting bands foster international arrangements.
Communication facilitated among belligerents in warfare.
Procedures of the nominating conventions altered somewhat.
Constituencies are kept in touch with nominating conventions.
Political campaigners reach larger audiences.
The importance of the political mass meeting diminished.
Presidential "barnstorming" and front porch campaign changed.

---

[1] Lynd, R. S., and Lynd, H. M., *Middletown in Transition*, p. 361, 1937.

[2] Summarized from Holcombe, A. N., *Radio and Education*, p. 118, 1936.
 See also, Denison, M., "Editorial Policies of Broadcasting Companies," *Pub. Opin. Quar.*, 1: 1: 64–83.

[3] *Recent Social Trends*, list on pp. 155-156.

Nature of campaign costs affected.

Appeal to prejudice of local group lessened.

Campaign speeches tend to be more logical and cogent.

An aid in raising campaign funds.

Campaign speaking by a number of party leaders lessened.

Campaign promises over radio said to be more binding.

High government officers who broadcast are said to appear to public less distant and more familiar.

BROADCASTING AND INTERNATIONAL RELATIONS

The broadcasting of programs between nations has made not only for international understanding and amity, but also for misunderstanding and disruption of relations. The BBC has for its motto "Nation shall speak peace unto nation." But newspaper headlines read, "Tension in Egypt Kept Up by Radio," and "Britain Starts War of Tongues on Air Lane Foes." One reads that *Brave New World* is the title of a new series of broadcasts by the Educational Radio Project of the U. S. Department of Education. The aim of the series is to promote further the good-neighbor policy of this country toward Latin America. But one also reads "Europe Wages a War of Electric Words," "The Battle of Radio Armaments," "The Frontiers Are Ignored" and "Secret Broadcasts in Europe Defy Dictator's Efforts to Rule Radio, Historian Ferrero Says." Potentially, the radio can promulgate understanding of the culture, the life ways, standards and values of divergent peoples. A French ambassador has recently declared, "Still more useful in my opinion than a purely theoretical knowledge, than a mere knowledge of the book, is the comprehension of the psychology peculiar to each country, the awareness of its modes of living, the grasp of its conception of life, which until now was the privilege solely of the traveller."[1] However, it requires no great stretch of the imagination to conceive of an ambassador furious and baffled by the intrusion of a free, frank and democratic discussion of an issue that had been traditionally dealt with by diplomatic ritual. Radio can bring increased understanding, but thus far it has primarily accentuated narrow nationalistic differences.

International communication was revolutionized by the invention of the wireless and radiobroadcasting. The political control of cable routes was no longer so important, nor did their ownership assure such monopolistic control of communication, as had previously been the case. But new struggles for power and national advantage began at once. The problem of allocation of wave lengths has been most vexatious. By 1925, interference caused by various stations on the same wave lengths had become intolerable. Abroad, the BBC called a conference in London

---

[1] De Laboulaye, Ambassador A., *Educational Broadcasting*, p. 128, 1936.

of the principal European broadcasters. The International Radiophone Union was formed. This organization has no official standing with the governments concerned, but it allocates wave lengths. Enforcement is in the control of the various governments. The union reallocated wave lengths on the basis of population, area and educational needs of the various states. The International Radiophone Union was based on mutual understanding, and it was hoped that the nations would adhere to their allotted wave lengths. They did not do this. In 1929, a new allocation agreement, known as the Plan of Prague, became effective in Europe. European powers have not all observed this compact either. They have evaded it for various reasons. States that had not built many stations before the agreement now feel that the distribution is unjust. States in which several languages are spoken feel the need of numbers of stations disproportionate to their areas and population. States with propaganda missions feel the need of powerful stations to appeal to neighboring peoples and have constructed such stations. Control of radio facilities in Europe is still very confused.[1] In North America, the confusion was alleviated by the agreement between Canada and the United States in 1926. Canada was allotted the exclusive use of six, and the partial use of eleven, of the 96 available channels. Some United States stations did not respect the agreement, and an epidemic of wave jumping lasted until the formation of the Radio Commission in 1927. Canada is not at present satisfied with this arrangement, maintaining that it should have at least twelve exclusive channels, whereas the United States point of view is that Canada has no legitimate need for additional channels, owing to her small population. However, the American controversy is simple in comparison with the chaotic conditions prevailing abroad.

Much more vital than the disputes over wave lengths in Europe are the battles over invasion by propaganda. In the spring of 1930, the 100-kilowatt station in Moscow began to broadcast talks in German, beginning with the statement "Police and soldiers of Germany, remember you are proletarians in uniform." A protest by the German government elicited the explanation that the Russians were broadcasting to the German settlers of the Volga basin. There were also a number of broadcasts to English workers. Radio has no frontiers. Thus, alien propaganda can be countered only by developing powerful stations capable of getting on the same wave length and making reception difficult or impossible in the invaded area. Hence, in 1930, governments started what can be described as a race in radio armaments. Germany has broadcast into Austria. The Czechoslovak government forbade its

[1] Biro, S., "International Aspects of Radio Control," *Jour. Radio Law*, 2: 56 *ff.* (1932).

citizens to tune in on German stations. Russia has made the reception of talks from the Vatican impossible in large sections of Germany and Poland. From Strasbourg, broadcasts—in German with a French accent —report news accounts that do not appear in German newspapers. What can governments do? They can forbid, and in a number of cases have forbidden, their subjects to listen to the alien broadcasts. They can encourage the distribution of weak receiving sets that are efficient only over small areas. The Germans have done this on a large scale, while at the same time they have built more and more powerful stations, certainly not for use exclusively within their own borders. And governments can create a system of powerful stations to counter those of other countries. Therefore it is no accident that along the boundaries of Silesia four rival stations stand within forty miles of one another, or that there is a 150-kilowatt station in Luxemburg. For broadcasting within the United States, it is maintained that a 50-kilowatt station is ample, but Hungary has a station of 120 kilowatts, Poland's latest station is 156 kilowatts, Vienna has a 120-kilowatt station and Russia has recently completed a 500-kilowatt transmitter. In 1933 the *New York Times* reported that in 1926 there were only about 100 kilowatts of broadcasting power in all of Europe, in 1929 there were 2000 and in 1933 there were 7500 kilowatts.[1] Today there are several thousand additional kilowatts. Costly systems of powerful broadcasting stations have been built during the past few years, strategically placed for interference with the broadcasts of other powers, but inefficient and ill-placed in terms of their own centers of population. The radio has rapidly been transformed into an instrument of war or of national or ideological prestige. During the year 1937, at 11:00 P.M., a mysterious wave length, the 29-meter wave length, carried to Italian and German citizens a virulent attack upon fascism and nazism.[2] The location of the transmitting station is unknown.

International incidents have occurred over the transmitting of commercial broadcasts, over ideological interpenetrations, over the broadcasting of news that had been censored within the country and over radio agitation among the colonial peoples of another power. England does not have commercial advertisements in its broadcasting. But the powerful 150-kilowatt Luxemburg transmitter hurls forth commercial broadcasts in English, French and German. Ideological and news invasions of other countries occur nightly. And the Mediterranean basin is the arena of daily conflicting propagandas to colonial peoples. Lawless confusion increases through this means of communication which was to unite peoples. The BBC announced on Nov. 2, 1937, that they would begin to broadcast in Spanish, Portuguese, Arabic and Afrikaans in

[1] *New York Times Mag.*, p. 6, Sept. 10, 1933.
[2] Report by Ferrero, G., in *St. Louis Post Dispatch*, June 6, 1937.

order to counter widespread anti-British propaganda. The areas and points of conflict increase, as does the tempo of appeals and counterappeals.

Unfortunately for the psychological, and perhaps physical, peace of the world, the outlines of a system of control have not clearly emerged. Gentlemen's agreements as to wave lengths are not binding. Lately Russia has been broadcasting to Germany by changing the wave lengths at unexpected intervals for such Germans as care to listen in. It takes some time for the German stations to find out what the wave length is and adjust their equipment in order to counter it. International friction is constantly increased. Some national cohesion may be achieved by authoritarian government at the cost of international chaos. But there are limits to the effectiveness of propaganda by radio—limits of human apathy, experience and credulity, which we have already discussed as applicable to all propaganda. We are fortunate in the United States, in that, though the general public has been guided in its choice of economic goods and children have been led to demand certain foods and psychologically exploited by horror stories, we have not experienced as yet the full persuasive power of the radio in propagating an exclusive economic or political doctrine.

CHAPTER XX

MOTION PICTURES

"The greatest problem of the motion picture today, Box Office successes and how to get them."[1]
"I look upon the cinema as a pulpit and use it as a propagandist."[2]

As an agency of mass impression the motion picture is now considered by many as of greater importance than printing. Such commentators refer to the superiority of pictorial forms over printed forms in conveying impressions to the common man. Although these comparisons as to relative importance of print and picture are futile, it is evident that motion pictures have enormously vivified communication. In America, the bulk of popular pictorial stereotypes and personal symbols are acquired in the motion-picture theater. The rise of the motion picture and the radio during the last forty years has realigned the processes of communication, developed new publics and stimulated the dissemination of varied life ways, standards and values. It is indeed a rash commentator who becomes dogmatic as to their present or future effects and influence. The glib prophets of yesteryear appear today to have been somewhat bemused.

The motion picture came into being as a result of a series of inventions made public in rapid succession in the early nineties. For a time it was exploited as a kind of carnival novelty, a peepshow. When its commercial possibilities were realized, it was seized upon and developed into a tremendous business. American motion pictures can be understood only on the basis of their economic history which is a vivid record of commercial exploitation for dramatically large profits and losses.

The Kinetoscope, first patented by Edison in 1891, was publicly shown in New York on Apr. 14, 1894. Only one person at a time could watch the picture.[3] The projector and screen were developed by Thomas Armat, who exhibited motion pictures for the first time in 1895. The motion-picture cameras, film and projectors were rapidly improved by scores of inventions until, in 1928, the industry was equipped to produce and exhibit sound pictures.

[1] The topic sentence introducing a chapter by Mr. J. L. Lasky on the motion pictures in Saylor, O. M., *Revolt in the Arts*, 1930.
[2] J. Grierson.
[3] Dale, E., *How to Appreciate Motion Pictures*, p. 31, 1933.

At first the pictures were very short, the first public exhibition lasting four minutes. Subject matter of the films was of less importance than the novelty of the exhibition. The first real movie story was produced in 1905 in a one-reel, 1000-foot film. One- or two-reel pictures were then distributed until 1912, when an eight-reel picture *Quo Vadis* was made in Italy. In the meantime, methods of distribution and exchange of films had been worked out, and the motion picture as a commercial enterprise was fairly launched. Techniques of production were likewise rapidly developed. In 1907, D. W. Griffith evolved a screen technique of "close-up," "cutback" and "fade-out." The star system was popularized by Adolph Zukor. Sarah Bernhardt appeared on the screen in 1912. The essential outlines of what the motion pictures were to be —until the introduction of sound—had appeared before the World War. During the war, European production was stopped, while the industry in the United States developed rapidly. American producers emphasized the star system, thus diverting attention from the content of the motion picture to the personal characteristics of actors. Slapstick comedies, open-air Westerns, social comedies and historical romances were the mainstay of the producers of that time.[1] Later, more diversified types appeared.

During the past twenty years, the authoritarian states of Europe have controlled and directed motion-picture content in the interests of political and economic propaganda. Dictators would inculcate the significant pictorial symbols. The techniques of their directors have usually been crude, owing to the immaturity of motion pictures as an art form and to the huge diverse audience to whom they must appeal. However, some propaganda techniques have been subtle, as Eisenstein's famed dramatizations of mass rather than the individual. Politicians, businessmen, educators, artists and literary commentators have divergent definitions of the most significant role of the motion picture in contemporary life. This cleavage is widening as new uses are undertaken. The authoritarian rulers would utilize the motion picture and all the arts as agencies of mass impression. Businessmen exploit this means of popular entertainment. Educators and scientists find it an invaluable aid for recording and portraying physical and life processes. Some groups of artists plead for the development of a creative art that will do more than mirror life or engage in special pleading, maintaining that "the motion picture has not yet

[1] The history of the motion picture is sketched in the *Ency. Soc. Sci.;* the *Ency. Brit.;* Lewis, H. T., *The Motion Picture Industry,* 1933.

For detailed accounts see especially: Ramsaye, T., *A Million and One Nights,* 1926; Hampton, B., *History of the Movies,* 1931.

An elaborate record is to be presented in the forthcoming *Ency. Cinema,* sponsored by the International Institute of Intellectual Cooperation of the League of Nations.

understood, with rare exceptions, that its future does not lie in a faithful and automatic reproduction of a purely material reality, but rather in the creative search for authentic truth."[1] The cinema is many things to many men, but its nature, its content and its effects on various groups have not been thoroughly and experimentally explored. There are many kinds of motion pictures for entertainment, for instruction and for propaganda. Paul Rotha, eminent English director of documentary films, has suggested the following classification:[2]

I. Films of Fiction
  1. Adventure and Melodrama
    Early Films and Serials
    Westerns
    Crime and Gangster
    Adventure in Distant Lands
  2. Comedy
    Slapstick
    Comedy of Manners
    Satire
  3. Romance
    Modern
    Historical
    Musical
  4. Historical and Chronicle

  5. Fantasy
    Folk Tales and Sagas
    Prophecy
    Macabre
  6. Drama
    Personal Stories
    Sociological
  7. Epic
II. Films of Fact
  1. Newsreel, Record and Magazine
  2. Travel Films
  3. Instructional Films
III. Avant-Garde and Trick Films
  1. Avant-garde
  2. Trick Films

Mass production and distribution of the motion picture have created the fourth largest industry in the United States. The approximate weekly attendance in the United States during 1936 was 80 million to 85 million, and world attendance was 215 million. The world capital investment was approximately $2,650,000,000 of which over 2 billion was in the U. S. Admissions produced income of from 720 million to 1 billion dollars annually. There were 272,500 persons directly employed in this industry in the United States, and there were produced in the United States, during 1936, about 65 per cent of the volume and 85 per cent of the value of the world's films.[3] From 50 to 250 prints are made of each feature picture. These are distributed to exhibitors through some twenty-five film exchanges. The individual and small chain exhibitors bargain with the exchanges for their films; the large chains usually bargain direct with the production companies. There are no standard prices.

[1] Daniel-Rops, E., "Cinema, Reality and Life," *Intercine*, 7: 5.

[2] Rotha, P., *Movie Parade*, 1936; quoted by Thrasher, F. M., *Jour. Ed. Soc.*, 10: 133. Permission to quote granted.

[3] The data in this paragraph are selected from the *International Motion Picture Almanac*, 1936–1937.

The films are exhibited in theaters ranging in value from a few hundred to millions of dollars. There were 20,500 theaters in the United States; 27,379 in Europe; 3981 in Latin America; 3976 in the Far East; 1100 in Canada; 755 in Africa; 52 in the Near East. These figures, although but a few years old, are already much changed.[1] The attendance at the theaters in the United States is variously estimated at from 77 million to 115 million weekly. The Motion Picture Producers and Distributors of America estimated weekly attendance as 40 million in 1922, 48 million in 1925 and 115 million in 1930.[2] The recent Payne Fund Studies developed an estimate of 77 million for 1932. This was calculated from questionnaires circulated among 55,000 children and from clocking attendance at fifteen theaters in Columbus, Ohio, over a 3-month period.[3] On the basis of this sample, E. Dale calculated that children above seven years of age attended the movies once a week; from eight to ten years, 27 per cent of the boys and 21 per cent of the girls attended two or more times weekly. Of the audiences whose attendance was clocked, 3.1 per cent were under seven; 13.7 per cent were seven to thirteen; 20.8 per cent were fourteen to twenty; 62.4 per cent were over twenty-one years of age. It was estimated that 11 million under fourteen years of age attended each week and that 28 million of the total of 77 million were minors. Of the school children, about 80 per cent stay for one showing, 18 per cent see the feature twice, 20 per cent watch the newsreel twice and 26 per cent stay to see the comedy over again.

THE CONTENT OF MOTION PICTURES

The production and distribution of the commercial motion pictures is an industrial process. The industry with its chains of theaters, its production companies, its large capital investment and clamorous stockholders must produce some hundreds of feature pictures every year to provide continuous entertainment for millions of people. The subject matter of the films is determined by what the producing companies believe their audiences want. There is no conscious long-range plan. The producers adapt themselves to changes in the social scene, the productions of their competitors and the tried and true formulas. Economic motivation is conspicuous in the growth of this business and the selection of themes. Although the producer occasionally makes a film with a selective appeal, he must aim more often at the widest mass patronage. As a result, only a few of the six hundred feature pictures

[1] Source: *Census of Distribution of Motion Pictures*, p. 6, U. S. Bureau of the Census, 1932.

[2] Data taken from Willey, M., and Rice, S. A., *Communication Agencies and Social Life*, table, p. 179, 1933.

[3] Dale, E., *Children's Attendance at Motion Pictures*, 1933.

produced yearly in the United States are commended by the selective critic, the intellectual or the pictorial artist. But the producer knows that during the past fifteen years the largest total rentals have been paid for the following: of the silent pictures, *Four Horsemen of the Apocalypse, Ben Hur, The Big Parade, The Birth of a Nation, The Covered Wagon, The Gold Rush, The Kid, The Ten Commandments, The Sea Hawk, Way Down East;* of the sound pictures, *The Singing Fool, The Jazz Singer, Sunny Side Up, Broadway Melody, The Cock-eyed World, Whoopee, 42nd Street, Gold Diggers of Broadway* and *Grand Hotel.*[1] *The Singing Fool* is reputed to have returned five million dollars to the producers. The competition for these grand prizes has led producers to ignore special types of audiences, the minorities with some critical standards. Perhaps, even under the present system of production, these groups will have pictures produced for them when the industry is convinced that these audiences are large enough and when dollars for the industry are more elusive than has been true for the past thirty years. Thus far, the themes, artistry, personality types, photography and ideology of American motion pictures have usually been conventional.

As in the case of the newspaper, the motion pictures are usually popularly discussed in terms of a few items out of their content. The prevalence of sex, violence and crime arouses controversy whereas hundreds of dull, insipid, childish, naïve and unreal themes escape unattacked. We shall consider a few of these general discussions of content before turning to the experimental attempts to record film content.

From time to time the moralist is outraged by the motion-picture treatment of the relationships between the sexes. Certainly it is a central theme of American films, as it is of popular literature, periodicals, advertising, and other means of communication. This is inevitable. It is a mass preoccupation. But that the moving pictures emphasize sex less, and present it in a more conventional way than do either legitimate plays or novels, is the conclusion of a committee of the American Association of University Professors.[2] To this the censor replies that the movies reach a larger and more unselected audience. But the audiences express by their attendance a persistent interest in this theme. "In 1930 it was calculated that one out of every seven pictures shown was built around sex as its dominant feature, as compared with one out of every ten round war, horror, and mystery, and one out of every four round crime."[3] Romance, in the cheapest meaning of the word, is pervasive. "Everything they have to say about love has to be expressed

[1] *International Motion Picture Almanac,* 1937, p. 834.
[2] Bulletin of that association, 16: 148.
[3] *For Filmgoers Only,* p. 66, British Institute of Adult Education, 1935.

in such terms that people of all levels and almost all ages can understand them, and moreover, these terms have to be such as can be used in large public gatherings."[1] Of necessity, there results a naïve oversimplification of personal-character types and of simplified moral categories.

There have been cycles of feminine types in the pictures of the past twenty years. One remembers the adventurous girl of the serials and the Westerns: the incredible, voluptuous, adventurous girl of the Theda Bara "vamp" type; the "it" girl of the late twenties; those pained ladies who didn't seem to know what the male animals of their pictures were talking about; the numerous contemporary actresses of more frankly physical appeal. "Woman has appeared as the siren, as the tomboy, the shrinking virgin, and only within the last few years as a partner in man's sexual pleasure."[2] In observing the experiences of these actresses, millions have achieved in vicarious experiences a natural outlet for passions and emotions. Paralleling these more unusual feminine types have been scores of "sweet, simple and girlish" actresses, the objects of simple romantic attraction, frequently pursued under idyllic conditions. The conditions of courtship, especially in the great urban areas of America, are far from idyllic. There is a vast field for compensatory idealization. In dealing with such relatively simple character stereotypes, the attitudes and opinions of audiences are usually simply canalized.

Critics have deplored an overemphasis on displays of violence and action in the motion pictures. Moralists have indignantly denounced certain idealizations of the desperado, the criminal and the gangster. But the technique of the motion picture, especially in its development before the sound pictures, was better adapted to show action and movement than to portray psychological nuances. In addition, action had a more universal appeal. Hence the Westerns, the adventure pictures and the melodrama, the war pictures, the crime, gangster, detective and action pictures in general. And action leaps beyond the humanly possible in the animated cartoons. Much action has taken the form of violence. Indeed, there is much more violence in the pictures than in the ordinary life of the picture-goers. This is likewise true of the bulk of periodical literature. In the traditions of American culture, successful violence has been esteemed. If there is much less violence in everyday life today than there was on the roistering frontier, the tradition of violence is maintained, and the movies perform a compensatory function. Even the extremes of violence appear with surprising frequency in the pictures. In reporting a recent survey of 115 pictures, E. Dale notes, "Murder, the most extreme form of violence, is at the top in the number of crimes committed, as well as in the number attempted. Assault and battery is second, and is

[1] Rotha, P., *Celluloid, The Film Today*, p. 116, 1933.
[2] *Ibid.*, p. 116.

committed in 32 pictures. Forty-three crimes are attempted and 406 committed. Further, we note that 97 of the 115 pictures or 84 per cent contain some form of crime or violence."[1] There is a great and persistent demand for pictures containing violence. The motion pictures meet the demand. American culture values, not the pictures, are to be indicted.

The critics bewail the distortion of reality in the "happy ending," so characteristic of the American motion pictures. To the common man such endings do not appear so unreal as they do to the intellectual. Fantastically good things in the realm of economic achievement and of personal adventure have happened in American experience during the nineteenth century. If they have happened less frequently than is commonly supposed, statistical analysis of life and mathematical portrayal of reality have not yet reached the common man. There is still a large residue of optimism and hopefulness. Such attitudes welcome even the most preposterous happy ending, and it has been woven into the artistic conventions of the American motion picture. Recently producers have been experimenting with audience response to endings. *Beloved Enemy* was shown for several weeks as a tragedy in which the hero died and his assailant committed suicide. Another ending in which both lived was used in the succeeding weeks.[2] The common man projects his wishes in demanding the happy ending. But the intellectual who criticizes the happy ending is also frequently motivated by attitudes that are not entirely based on objective descriptions of reality. "The intellectuals have been remarkably hospitable to all the great European systems of damnation—damnation by sex by Freud, by economics by Marx, by history by Spengler."[3]

The Russian films are avowedly propagandistic, the German and Italian films in part so. In Italy, propaganda films are directed and controlled by the government, and other pictures are censored and restricted, a distinct division being made between propaganda and other commercial films. To what extent has propaganda been introduced into American feature films? It is generally agreed that the commercial motion pictures have usually fought shy of obvious propaganda. The objectives have been box-office returns and entertainment, not instruction and special pleading. A few years ago, out of 840 films examined, only 15, or 1.7 per cent, were classified as propagandist. Critical comment on the existing societal order is rare. However, the very content of most of the pictures, in fortifying popular attitudes, makes powerful, if unintended, special pleading for the existing social and economic order. The

---

[1] Dale, E., *The Content of Motion Pictures*, p. 139, 1935.

[2] *New York Times*, Jan. 17, 1937, motion-picture page.

[3] Seldes, G. V., *Mainland*, p. 111, 1936.

national government sponsored a dozen propaganda films during the World War; and, in a few other instances, such as the cooperation between producers and the Navy, some feature films have been used for propaganda purposes. The motion pictures are a powerful potential medium for propaganda, but the feature pictures have been so used only incidentally.

The newsreel, however, has been quite widely used for propaganda purposes. For example, in 1934 the producers were in agreement as to the undesirability of Upton Sinclair as governor of California. By selection of personality types, the pro-Merriam supporters appeared as decent respectable citizens, whereas the pro-Sinclair speakers were funny, bleary-eyed, shabby men and women who stammered and squawked before the camera. Indeed, political propaganda has become notorious in the newsreels. There has been a considerable amount of "big-Navy," anti-prohibition, anti-communism and anti-strike propaganda. This does not mean that the newsreels are pro-Fascist propaganda, as a certain radical group has latterly protested. But they do reflect the political and economic ideology of their producers. And the content of these pictures follows a rather simple and incomplete pattern of news reporting.[1] A League of Nations committee, deploring the intensely nationalistic propaganda of most newsreels, has recently made extensive recommendations for the injection of more international propaganda into them.[2]

The cycle of war pictures was produced because of the melodramatic appeal of this intensely exciting human activity. Although some producers may have been motivated by a sincere opposition to the brutality of war, the primary motive was the exploitation of the dramatic possibilities of war situations. Millions of people in the Western nations have seen these films. The results on attitudes and opinions toward war will vary with age groups and with the culture backgrounds of the audiences. For example, a simple questionnaire study of responses of 25,042 children by a subcommittee of the League of Nations indicates that, in general, children under fifteen are not influenced toward peace by such pictures. The children respond primarily to the dramatic personal situations and the excitement of the war pictures. The responses from various national groups varied considerably, however. A child in Italy, trained on the slogan "Better live one day like a lion than a hundred years as a sheep," sees glory in these pictures; whereas the son of an English socialist may have his pacifism fortified. Adults are reported to indicate more often a greater pacifist sentiment after seeing war pictures. Suffering, horror, physical cruelty are more evident to

[1] See survey of content in Dale, *op. cit.*, Chap. 12.
[2] "The Cinema in International Life; Report of the International Institute of Intellectual Cooperation," *Int. Rev. Ed. Cinematography*, 6: 391.

them than to the children.   However, the question of the influence of war pictures on the creation of pacifist sentiment is in general undecided. The way in which they are produced is all-important.

Another and very popular field of the motion picture is the animated cartoon.   There is an enthusiastic popular demand of international scope for *Mickey Mouse* and *Silly Symphonies*.   The sheer fanciful, humanized play of these strange creatures provides imaginative flight from realities of time and place.   And Mickey Mouse has not become a propagandist. "It is not our job to teach, implant morals or improve anything. . . . Mickey is never mean or ugly . . . he never lies and cheats and steals— he never takes advantage of the weak and we see to it that nothing ever happens that will change his faith in the transcendent destiny of one Mickey Mouse or his convictions that the world is just a big apple pie."[1] The animated cartoons reflect values diffused through contemporary culture, but apparently there is no conscious propaganda.

There has been widespread discussion of motion-picture content by those who have approached the subject from some special interest. Classifications of content have until recently been very simple.   For example, A. M. Mitchell asked 10,052 school children to indicate prefer- ences for Western, comedy, adventure, mystery, romance, sports, historical, war, tragedy and educational pictures.[2]   These types are not mutually exclusive, children could not adequately differentiate them and such classification is evidently worthless.   E. Dale and associates recently conducted an admirably organized survey of motion-picture content based on classification of 1500 descriptions of pictures, the analysis of 115 pictures and the detailed analysis of 40 pictures.[3]   Comparing the types of motion pictures produced in 1920, 1925 and 1930, he achieves the summary indicated in Table XIII.

Classifiers, observing the films of 115 pictures, then checked on large data sheets the content of these pictures as to the following points: locale and setting of the pictures (country, area, building, room, etc.); age of characters, economic status and occupation of characters; types of clothing worn in the pictures; circumstances of meeting and love- making (frequency, where and when—and the intentions); crime in the movies (types, murder techniques, punishment, etc.); vulgarity in the pictures; the goals sought by the leading characters.   This excellent survey is more objective than anything attempted thus far.   None the less it could deal only with a limited number of selected items of motion-picture content; and, of course, such selection will

---

[1] Disney, W., "The Cartoon's Contribution to Children," *Overland*, 91: 138. Quoted by permission of the author.

[2] Mitchell, A. M., *Children and Movies*, Chap. 11, 1929.

[3] For methods used, see Chap. XIX.

depend upon the research director's objectives. Certainly the reader
gathers from this study that the movies are peopled by smartly attired
individuals with ignoble goals in life, but the investigator's system
of classification is in itself the projection of his attitudes. Social-science
methodology wallows in so many subjective factors.

TABLE XIII.—COMPARISON OF THE TYPES OF MOTION PICTURES PRODUCED IN 1920,
1925 AND 1930*

(Number and per cent of pictures of each type as shown by a 500 sample each year)

Type of picture	Release date					
	1920		1925		1930	
	Number	Per cent	Number	Per cent	Number	Per cent
Crime...............	120	24.0	148	29.6	137	27.4
Sex.................	65	13.0	84	16.8	75	15.0
Love...............	223	44.6	164	32.8	148	29.6
Mystery............	16	3.2	11	2.2	24	4.8
War................	10	2.0	11	2.2	19	3.8
Children...........	2	.4	4	.8	1	.2
History............	0	0.0	6	1.2	7	1.4
Travel.............	1	.2	7	1.4	9	1.8
Comedy............	59	11.8	63	12.6	80	16.0
Social propaganda.......	4	.8	2	.4	0	0.0
Total.............	500	100.	500	100.	500	100.

* Dale, *op. cit.*, p. 17.   By permission of The Macmillan Company, publishers.

How do the action and the implied attitudes and standards of motion-
picture characters compare with the prevailing mores in various social
groups in contemporary society?   C. C. Peters attempted to answer this
fundamental and intriguing question about motion-picture content.[1]
Prof. Peters developed a large number of brief paragraphs descriptive of
action in current movies on four basic themes: (1) aggressiveness of a
girl in lovemaking; (2) democratic attitudes and practices; (3) kissing and
caressing in the pictures; (4) the treatment of children by parents.   These
brief descriptions of scenes from actual motion pictures were then submitted to some thirteen groups of twenty-five to thirty-five members each
for statements of approval or disapproval of the action.   The results were
then developed by means of elaborate statistical techniques.   But in a
very real sense the study goes entirely outside the limits of its problem at
the very first step.   For the response to the stimulus of a situation in the
motion picture is a very different thing from the response to a written
description of that situation.   However, the sections of this study in

[1] Peters, C. C., *The Motion Pictures and Standards of Morality*, 1933.

which comparison is made between practices in certain social groups and the conduct displayed in the movies is a valuable contribution to studies of the motion picture. But the problem of the mores remains unanswered. How far do the motion pictures diverge from the prevailing mores? To what extent do they influence those standards which are incorporated into individual attitudes?

MOVIES AND CONDUCT

It is obvious that the motion pictures influence conduct over a wide range of behavior, such as participation in styles and fads, mannerisms, impersonation of actors, amatory techniques, speech forms and scores of other types of action. Buying habits are known to be influenced. In Japan, English imports decrease almost in proportion to the increase of imports from the United States, and the opinion of many resident Englishmen is that this is due to the influence of American films. Our films have been sales agents in many countries. The varieties of behavior thought to be influenced by the motion pictures have been indicated in thousands of articles and scores of books during the past twenty-five years. But, with the possible exception of parts of the *Payne Fund Studies* and the recent report on the effects of the film compiled by the chief inspector of the London County Council,[1] there are no valid and convincing data on the influence of pictures on behavior. Most of the materials on this problem are mere expressions of opinion, unsubstantiated by data.

However, the motion pictures may influence conduct in many ways. There may be the copying of specific behavior, there may be a transfer of some emotional state by which subsequent conduct is influenced or the movie theme as a whole may affect the individual's attitudes. Later these attitudes motivate behavior. Impersonation of movie characters in children's play is obviously widespread. To what extent does this affect subsequent behavior? Imitation of dress, mannerisms and the amorous techniques of favorite stars is widely noted. Models for imitation must be provided somewhere. Parents are not generally desirable as sartorial models or for purveying gestures which indicate that life is dominated and lived with zest. Some of the really important effects of pictures on behavior are not usually discussed at all. For example, children reared on motion pictures have become film-conscious and pictorially minded. Their behavior in dealing with advertising pictures, pictured news, and indeed, fundamentally, their behavior toward individuals, racial groups, and the like, is profoundly modified by motion-picture stereotypes and symbols. Attitudes and behavior toward a wide range of phenomena that the individual would not otherwise experience are developed by the pictures.

[1] *School Children and the Cinema*, London, 1932.

Motion Pictures and International Life

Various items of material culture, clothing, household equipment and the thousand gewgaws of Western civilizations are being disseminated and copied elsewhere, in part because of the models presented in motion pictures. Subjective elements, the folkways, attitudes, standards and values, are also being modified by this agency. The motion-picture version of American culture is more widely diffused than that of any other group. It is true that effusive overstatements of these effects have frequently been made during the past twenty years and also that there is no detailed knowledge of the influence of the pictures.

The motion picture in its simpler aspects, bringing action into pictorial forms, may be appreciated beyond the culture and nation of its origin. In cultures other than that of their origin the various art forms, painting, music and drama, are in general understood by cultivated minorities only. But the motion picture, more than any other popular art, became almost universal in its mass appeal. This was especially true of the silent pictures. In them, simple pantomime was most readily understood by alien cultures and by simple peoples both abroad and at home. The backbone of the early nickelodeon trade in America was the audience of newly arrived immigrants. "Love, hate, desolation, despair, joy, ecstasy, defeat, triumph—these are universal emotions. Conveyed solely by words, as drama conveys them, they may offer difficulties to remote and various peoples. But conveyed by movements of the human face and body, by smiles and tears, troubled brows and dejected shoulders, sparkling eyes and fluttering hands, they are immediately recognizable. Dancing feet, a laugh, or a sob is the same the world over. They need not words to explain them."[1] This statement is not entirely true, but it is clear that gesture is more often universal communication than is speech.

But the various aspects of culture determine in part the individual's perceptions, interpretations and memories of any pictorial stimulus. For example, a political, economic or general ideology provides one frame of reference from which a film is viewed. Not only will an avowed Communist or a State Socialist, in contrast to an American Republican, differently interpret a film of the romantic quest in the upper economic strata, but he will also perceive certain elements, such as physical types, clothing, setting and speech, in a quite different fashion. The pacifist will miss the beauty of a fleet in battle formation on the sparkling Pacific in his revulsion at its purpose. Also, general values in a culture are constantly involved in responses to films. Representations in the films of mechanical routines of the modern factory, which often prove so repulsive to the liberal intellectual, arouse admiration in the Russian

[1] *Ency. Brit.* (14th ed.), 15: 865.

Communist. One learns that Janet Gaynor is by all odds the movie favorite of the Chinese, both young and old. This actress has no such preeminent position in America. But the high value of sweetness and tenderness in the female under the standards of Chinese culture dictates this choice. In his propaganda for fecund females, Mussolini has censored the pictures of women in the Italian press, eliminating the slender type. Would this have no effect on an Italian audience viewing Mae West and Katherine Hepburn? In the transfer of pictures between cultures there is the fundamental problem of meaning. It is vital to understand other people's mentality, points of view, attitudes, national and race cultural values. Unfortunately the effects of culture upon psychological processes have not been systematically studied even by the crude methods available to the contemporary social psychologist. Indeed, it is a problem so fundamental not only for pictures but for all media of communication that it is all the more remarkable that general psychology has so long practically ignored the existence of cultural differences as modifying the various mental processes. Some attention has been given to this problem recently.[1]

Although much of the content of motion pictures is either misunderstood or distorted when they are exhibited abroad, the international distribution of films became a large business in the years immediately after the World War. American films have had the largest foreign markets. This has been due to the advantage gained by American producers in building up the industry here during the World War; to the technical superiority of American films; to the large capital holdings of American producers who alone could finance the lavish spectacle pictures, so popular abroad and at home during the 1920's; to the large home market of the American producers which had provided the competitive advantage in the first place; to the star system and the American policy of hiring many stars from abroad; to the ownership or control of theaters abroad by American companies. Although the proportion of revenue obtained from foreign distribution of American films varies from year to year, during the past fifteen years from 20 to 30 per cent of the total revenue of American producers has come from abroad.[2] As the capital expenditures on films increased, an even wider market was needed, and the foreign market seemed indispensable to American producers.

It has become increasingly difficult for producers to maintain the American dominance over foreign film markets, and changes are now

---

[1] Bartlett, F. C., *Remembering*, 1931.
  Mannheim, K., *Ideology and Utopia*, 1936.
  Sherif, M., *The Psychology of Social Norms*, 1936.
  Numerous works of Gestalt psychologists.
[2] Lewis, *op. cit.*, p. 393.

occurring very rapidly. In the silent film a picture could be retitled in any language for $2000 or $3000. But it has cost from $20,000 to $50,000 to make a foreign version of sound pictures.[1] "Dubbing" (that is, the substitution of one sound column for another) is often difficult to synchronize with the action, and special foreign versions using principals of foreign-language groups are often too expensive to produce. The producer also has much more difficulty in finding a common denominator of interests and formulas that will standardize the inoffensive. In pantomime this was not so difficult, but the susceptibilities of peoples are more often wounded by the spoken word. Among different groups, fundamental conceptions, modes of life, and beliefs are seen to be much more at variance at the speech level. Further, the

TABLE XIV.—MARKETS FOR AMERICAN FILMS

Country	1925	1931	1935
	Per cent of American foreign revenues	Per cent of American films to total films*†	Per cent of American films to total films‡	Per cent of American films to foreign films¶
United Kingdom..................	35.	95.	72.	71.7
Germany........................	10.	16.	27.9	24.8
Australia and New Zealand........	8.	95.	89.	
Scandinavia.....................	6.	85.	60.5	
Argentina.......................	5.	90.	90.	88.
Canada.........................	5.	95.	94.7	95.
France.........................	3.	70.	48.5	53.6
Japan..........................	3.	30.	11.6	35.1
Brazil..........................	3.	75.	77.4	

* In terms of percentage of American films to total number of feature films exhibited.
† Lewis, H. T., *The Motion Picture Industry*, p. 397.
‡ Lewis, *ibid.*, p. 425.
¶ Compiled from *International Motion Picture Almanac*, 1936.

intensified political and economic conflicts of the past few years have caused leaders to scent propaganda in every medium of communication. This has resulted in the exclusion of many pictures and led to the formulation of general policies of national cultural autarchy. Monetary problems of exchange have also complicated the exchange of pictures. The fiscal policy of Germany during 1936 practically destroyed the market there. Mussolini has ruled that not more than 25 per cent of the profits of any American film shown in Italy can be taken out of the country, and other nations have multiplied regulation.

[1] Lewis, *op. cit.*, p. 401.

Although the trend is downward, Americans still distribute the bulk of the world's films.

For 1936 it is reported that "motion pictures made in the United States continued to hold their supremacy in foreign lands, though there was an unusual amount of political and taxational disturbance. . . . in Spain, France, Italy, Germany and Russia the political trend was toward giving artificial impetus to home production. In Japan, too, the national spirit was reflected in movements toward centralization of film control."[1] The importation of pictures to the United States has gradually increased but, as yet, the foreign pictures do not have a large audience, although there were 125 brought in during 1931 and 123 during 1932.[2]

In terms of the present capital organization and system of distribution the foreign market is very important to the American industry. The good will of foreign exhibitors and publics is often sought by changing the content of films, deleting offensive sections. It is reported that production of *It Can't Happen Here* was stopped, because Italy and Germany would have taken offense at its anti-Fascist theme; that the negative of *The Devil Is a Woman* was destroyed, because of a Spanish protest at the disrespectful treatment of the Civil Guard; that all mention of the War of 1812 was omitted from *Lloyd's of London*, because of the English audience; that *The Forty Days of Musa Dagh* was halted, in Turkey's interest. In many other cases films have been censored for home consumption as well as for foreign distribution.[3]

Although space does not permit of an elaborate description, a few comments on the motion-picture situation in several European countries may aid our understanding of the problems involved. We shall consider briefly the film in England, France, Germany and Russia. The English films, like the American, are dominated by commercial objectives, but their industry, handicapped by the war years and by the cautiousness of British capital, has developed slowly. During 1936 only 28.3 per cent of the features and 17.3 per cent of the shorts exhibited in the 4500 English theaters were made in Great Britain. Most of the others were made in the United States. Yet in the past two years, production in England has boomed owing to a protective Films Act and more adventurous capital. Critics of the English film note that most feature films produced in England are merely transpositions of stage successes and that their producers have not mastered the techniques of other kinds of feature films. The supposed influence of the American films is indicated by the variety of charges made against them. Educators assert that

---

[1] *International Motion Picture Almanac*, 1936–1937, p. 1077.

[2] Lewis, *op. cit.*, p. 428.

[3] Illustrations taken from *New York Times*, Jan. 24, 1937.

children learn American slang from them and that their attitudes and moral values are distorted by them; businessmen maintain that these films stimulate the taste for American styles and products; colonial government officials in Africa and India plead yearly for a stricter censorship, declaring that the white man has lost prestige with the natives owing to movie themes and acting.   Hindu leaders question "whether it is possible to feed peoples' imaginations for any length of time on jazz rhapsodies without seriously undermining the authority of Manu, and whether encouraging a taste for provocative nudity, which characterizes the cabaret world of Harlem and Manhattan would not eventually have devastating, perhaps fatal, repercussions on such time honored institutions as Purdah."[1]   It is concluded that the films have already had marked effects on native folkways and culture and that Western standards of behavior and values have been widely diffused.   Leaders in Great Britain and various parts of the empire quite generally deplore the influence of American pictures, although there are few studies to indicate just what these influences are.   But countless numbers of regular cinema patrons demand the American films.

The French do not attend the motion pictures so regularly, especially in the provinces.   It is estimated that only 7 to 10 per cent of the population of France are regular patrons.[2]   Those who did attend the 4600 theaters saw, during 1935, some 463 feature pictures, of which 112 were produced in France, 248 in America, 60 in Germany and 19 in Great Britain.   More than any other nation, the French have resented this cultural invasion, especially as the majority of first-class motion-picture houses in France are owned or controlled by American interests. Various special interest, patriotic and cultural groups have agitated and lobbied for many years against American films.   In addition, French producers naturally want protection.   For ten years the regulations have been changed almost every year.   In 1928, a quota law limited the importation of films by demanding the exhibition of one French film to every seven foreign films.   A fierce controversy the following year led finally to the retention of this quota for another year.   Then the sound pictures came.   In the early days of sound pictures there were not enough "dubbed" pictures to fill the demand, and the quota was abolished.   In 1933, a film decree made compulsory the dubbing of the pictures in France and, in 1934, limited the number of dubbed films to 140 yearly. The French cinema owners vociferously oppose this regulation, for they well know the popularity of American films and of many American stars with that section of the population which does attend regularly.   These theater owners are the most severe critics of their own motion-picture

[1] Singh, I. G. P., "Hollywood and India," *Spectator*, 155: 1064.
[2] Hayes, C. J. H., *France, a Nation of Patriots*, p. 182, 1930.

industry.   Latterly, French feature-film production has been decreasing;
there were 157 such films in 1932, 143 in 1933 and 126 in 1934.[1]   The
French are not equipped to produce their own films, but French leadership
is keenly aware of the cultural diffusion brought about by motion pictures.
They are acutely dissatisfied with the film products of any other
country.

The German motion-picture industry is next to that of the United
States in technical development, in production and in exports and in
many respects surpasses the American film in experimental inventiveness,
settings, photography and emotional acting—at least, according to
numerous critics.[2]   Despite a large home industry, they import many
films.   The record of feature films of recent years is as follows:[3]

Year	German	American	Other foreign films
1933	94	50	57
1934	122	37	37
1935	121	65	27

Under the Nazi regime there are, of course, a close censorship of the
films and also the injection of a large propaganda element into their
content.   During 1935 thirty-six German films and nineteen foreign films
were banned.   There has been considerable experimental audacity in the
output of German producers during the last fifteen years.   A French critic
notes that "the American cinema is life in movement, the Russian is the
propagation of an idea, the French cinema has usually been concerned
with making money, while only the German cinema is real art in the best
and worst senses of the term."[4]   The Germans were the first to introduce
into the cinema the mental drama in distinction to simple action.   Latterly, the German use of the motion picture for propaganda purposes has
interfered somewhat with its development as an art form.   The Nazi
code of morals is not limited to political themes.

The Russian film has a mission.   In this far-flung state of diverse
culture groups, a way of life is propagandized in 10,041 regular urban
theaters and 19,650 rural theaters.   Naturally almost all the features are
made in Russia under careful political supervision.   In 1935, the Russians
produced films of the following types:[5]

[1] *International Motion Picture Almanac*, 1936, pp. 1117–1119.
[2] Cheronnet, L., "The German Cinema," *Living Age*, 343: 443.
[3] Compiled from *International Motion Picture Almanac*, 1936.
[4] Petsche, M., "The French Cinema," *Living Age*, 349: 243.
[5] *International Motion Picture Almanac*, 1936, p. 1098.

Recently a few foreign films have been permitted in Russia. Last year ten American feature films were imported. Of course they were carefully censored. The development of a state-owned and -controlled motion-picture industry has freed the director for technical experimentation but bound him to a propaganda theme. In the Russian propaganda films, the appeal is to a large, undifferentiated audience. Naturally the themes are presented in simple, elementary and unsubtle terms. To a considerable extent this repels the sophisticated observer. Maurice Hindus states, "In the past half dozen years very few Soviet pictures have commanded the attention of the outside world or aroused excitement in Russia, simply because of the dullness which has resulted from an excess of political sermonizing. The scenarios are of stereotyped pattern. . . . "[1] A few American left-wing critics have sung paeans of praise about the Russian film, but one suspects that they have seen at most a half-dozen Russian films by Eisenstein and other eminent producers and compared these with the worst 590 out of the 600 or more produced in an American film year. Most English and American observers consider the Soviet film very dull. The motion pictures perform several major functions in modern life. They instruct and inform, they entertain and they should be a creative art form in their own right. If the American film can be criticized for a too great emphasis on entertainment, it is likewise certain that the Russian films have not provided satisfactory entertainment to the Soviet masses and have overemphasized political information and propaganda.

There have been many effusive overstatements written about the world-wide influence of the motion pictures during the past thirty years. There are not exact studies of that influence in which convincing methodology has been used.[2] Studies using whatever techniques the social psychologist has at his command should be made at once. However,

---

[1] Hindus, M., *The Great Offensive*, p. 266, 1933.

[2] Scattered through the issues of the *Int. Rev. Ed. Cinematography* (*Intercine* since 1936) there are a number of reports based on questionnaires given to school children in various parts of the world under this organization of the League of Nations. They are based on simple questionnaires and are reliable neither as information nor as opinion tests. It is unfortunate that a more sophisticated methodology has not been attempted.

neither the commercial producers and distributors, the political leaders, nor the international agencies appear to be eager for such attempts to evaluate the influence of the pictures. Of course the problem has become infinitely more complex since the development of sound pictures. Certainly most of the results of the international distribution of films have been unintended. But, as C. H. Cooley has said, "most of the evil of the world is done by the elbows, not by the fists." American films have been evangelical for a way of life that emphasizes among other things individual freedom, lack of discipline, youthful lack of restraint and a thoroughgoing and avid consumption of economic goods. All this has been of vastly more weight in influencing opinion in different parts of the world than has all the conscious propaganda ever attempted. One notes the report that a feeling of opposition to the emancipation of women has been provoked among Mussulmen by their having seen pictures produced in America. They have not liked the behavior of our female screen characters. In India, the governing classes and Buddhist reformers have been led to organize a campaign for film censorship to safeguard the morals and religious tradition of the Hindus. The elders of Budapest bewail that the boys and girls want to dance to jazz because America has sent in films that become the criteria of modern life. It is reported that Chinese youth, to the distress of the elders, have learned to "wisecrack" as a form of humor. The unintended results have thus far been much more important than those brought about by the conscious propaganda of a few Russian films scattered elsewhere in the world, or of Mussolini's attempt to proselyte for fascism in Paris with a film called *Blackshirt*, or of the project of the Empire Marketing Board of Great Britain when it makes and distributes internationally a few propaganda films.

The motion pictures, though increasing understanding between cultures, have been also a great distorting medium. Neither the unintentional nor the conscious distortions can be corrected by law. Relatively truthful rendering and presentation can be assured only if there exist among producers and distributors fundamental good will and honesty. As this means of communication becomes more mechanically perfect, illusions, rather than truth, may be spread. For example, television will give a sense of reality never before achieved. The more convincing the medium, the greater the increase in the dangerous illusion that seeing means knowing. Yet the television camera could easily select, distort and fake. Formal rules do not now solve the problem, nor will they do so in the future.

The International Institute of Intellectual Cooperation of the League of Nations poses certain fundamental questions with regard to the motion pictures:

1. How shall we by means of the cinema facilitate the bringing together and mental comprehension of people with people? How shall we utilize to the utmost this instrument of reproduction and diffusion and the infinite resources it offers to spread useful knowledge, to broaden the crowd's field of intuition, to supply new grounds of opinion and give scope for the formation of a general concept of the world's life and its necessities?

2. How shall we prevent this means of drawing nations together from being employed for the opposite purpose, not merely deliberately as a dangerous propaganda, but also through ignorance or disregard of certain foreign civilizations and mentalities?

3. How shall we prevent those isolation reactions which are so frequent today and which might lead to the closing of frontiers to films of real interest? How, we might add, shall we bring about an intellectual protection which will assure the free circulation of those works of the mind which should be known all over the world?

4. How, lastly, shall we make the best use of the cinema to raise the intellectual level of the public, to develop its sense of beauty, to accustom it to appreciate the masterpieces of thought? How shall we increase the intellectual functions of the cinema and its task of forming the mind?[1]

EFFECTS ON ATTITUDE AND OPINION

The motion pictures are obviously a powerful agent for fixing or modifying individual attitudes as well as those attitudes which are widely diffused among masses of people. To be sure, the importance of the pictures in affecting attitudes varies greatly as between age groups, classes of intelligence and personality types. But pictorial stimuli are amazingly vital for most persons. One may appreciate the infinite variation in individual effects and the bewildering complexity of individual reponses, and at the same time note certain uniformities in social attitudes and behavior resulting from attendance at the motion pictures. To enumerate these results in any formal way would imply a completeness of analysis that no one has the right to assume in the present state of knowledge about motion-picture effects. However, in the following paragraphs we shall discuss a number of relationships.

It is frequently stated that the motion pictures tend to discourage logical thinking and reflective thought. Indeed, this charge is made with regard to all the modern means of communication for the masses: the popular newspaper, most plays, the bulk of periodical literature and radio programs. It is claimed that the very mass of communicated material in contemporary pictures, print and sound occupies and diverts the mind, rather than instigating reflective thought. There is some truth in this

---

[1] "The Cinema in International Life," *Int. Rev. Ed. Cinematography*, 6: 388.

assertion. The average mind is incapable of selection and rejection of the stimuli to which it is subjected, and indeed the well-organized, critical mind also is overwhelmed by the mass of the claims for attention. Moreover, the content of motion pictures is usually not such as to give rise to reflective thought. It is for the most part noncontroversial. Much of the content deals with life situations, values, standards and mores with which the majority of popular audiences are in complete accord. And then, much of the content of the motion pictures in the United States has been sheer spectacle: throngs, crowds, wide spaces, masses of objects, troupes of dancers, the routine of modern musical shows, and the like. This may entertain; it does not provoke reflective thought. The degeneration of the Roman theater as it proceeded from thoughtful tragedy and comedy to spectacles for the masses has often been traced. The motion picture has provided such entertainment almost from its beginning.

One of the fundamental characteristics of modern thought is a time sense.[1] There are, not only a heightened awareness of the passage of time, but also widely diffused attitudes toward culture forms of the past, and to a lesser extent toward the future. The motion picture accentuates this process by preserving a record of passing events in the news pictures, by creating and modifying attitudes toward the past in historical films and by providing an occasional prophetic film of the future. Films of the past and the future have been used for propaganda purposes in Russia, Germany and Italy. Popular attitudes toward culture elements of the past have so far been exploited only incidentally in the American pictures, as in the newsreel portrayal of past clothing styles, cars and other objects for humorous purposes. Historical films dealing with legendary personages have not strayed far from the prevalent stereotypes. As the pictures become more vivid and convincing, there are obvious possibilities for modifying attitudes toward the past and thereby affecting opinion and action in the present. Utopian presentations may also be influential in motivating present behavior. The influence of present press campaigns may be relatively unimportant in comparison with a future motion-picture and television campaign. Although there is relatively little of conscious intent in these fields of contemporary commercial pictures in America, they have already greatly affected popular attitudes about historic events. The extension of the time sense is inevitable, and the attitudes resulting therefrom will be woven into the fabric of popular opinion.

Vicarious experience has been enormously increased by the motion pictures. Print made possible a great extension of such experience for masses of mankind, but the pictures provided a vivid and personal

[1] Lewis, W., *Time and Western Man*, 1927.

imagery.   As such experience increased, aspects of life previously not discussible were portrayed, new controversies and heightened tensions thus were created.   Values in transition were high-lighted.   A Sunday newspaper supplement provides a page of description of the life and experiences of Gypsy Rose Lee, once the premier strip-teaser of America. She is presented as an outstanding example of successful sex exploitation for large rewards.   As a result of her preeminence in display of epidermis, she was queen of the Columbia Senior Prom, star of the Follies, and something of a social lioness.   This is not the success story that Minnie Jones, aged fifteen, read in the *McGuffey Readers* of 1880.   And a motion-picture presentation of a cabaret career may provide a far more vivid vicarious experience for this adolescent than does a newspaper account.

The picture audience lives in hundreds of roles during the course of a year.   To be sure, these roles are largely standardized, but new elements do appear.   The veteran producer Mr. Adolph Zukor notes, "As for audiences themselves, their essential desires and tastes, there is little change from twenty-five years ago.   Audiences like to project themselves on the screen and live there in one role or another for the time they are in the theatre."[1]   The extent to which vicarious experience at the motion pictures serves to widen the individual's understanding and sympathy for the behavior and emotional experience of others will depend upon his choice of pictures.   He may see more and more of the same thing; but for most persons the pictures widen the horizons of life.

Of late years the term "compensation" has come into semitechnical use referring to action or thinking which "shall make amends for some lack or loss in personal characteristic or status."[2]   Especially for the adult audiences, the motion pictures perform an important function in providing the materials for compensation.   The pictures have developed during several decades in which masses of mankind in the Western world have been in especial need of fantasy, idealizations and delightful dream material to take them away from the successive crises of reality in economics, politics and religion.   There are many maladjustments, and, as Lewis Mumford notes, "vital organs of life, which have been amputated through historic accident, must be restored at least in fantasy."[3]   So, "the motion picture has found a distinct function in creating for us a fantasy world which is extremely popular and satisfying . . . the gorgeous settings . . . luxurious homes, servants, limousines, beautiful women and strong men . . . it is a conventional outlet for our unfulfilled desires and our unrequited heartaches."[4]   The lavish settings

[1] Zukor, A., in *New York Times Mag.*, Feb. 28, 1937.
[2] English, H. B., *A Student's Dictionary of Psychological Terms*, 1934.
[3] Mumford, L., *Technics and Civilization*, p. 286, 1934.
[4] Young, K., *Social Psychology*, p. 549, 1930.

of the long-popular DeMille pictures or the settings of modern musical romances illustrate fantasy in dealing with objects and the economic world. A thousand vagaries of the amorous quest as portrayed in the movies of three decades illustrate the popular demand for variety of titillation and for compensatory ideal adjustments in the relations between the sexes. In part, the pictures have been able to satisfy this demand because of the technical flexibility of camera portrayals. The camera moves about at all angles, as well as close up or far away. Nuances of emotional portrayal may certainly be registered on a face that is perhaps a dozen feet in width when thrown on the screen. However, the compensatory function of the motion pictures is a variable with class and age groups. Small children are bored by the pictures conveying vicarious compensation to middle-aged housewives.

Children and youth, if they do not so frequently use the motion pictures for vicarious compensation, do obtain therefrom ideas and images for fantasy and daydreaming. In a study of motion-picture autobiographies, Blumer records that of 458 high-school students, 66 per cent gave distinct evidence of the influence of the pictures on daydreaming and fantasies, 24 per cent gave no information and 10 per cent denied such influence.[1] The adolescents, especially, create a dream world from movie materials dealing with luxury, possessions, amorous experience, adventure, travel, and so on. Such thinking may be a satisfying end in itself, providing vicarious satisfactions and relieving the tensions of everyday life. Or it may lead to attempts at behavior similar to that seen in the films. Or it may profoundly modify general attitudes toward the conditions, the action, and the values and standards of everyday life.

Students' reports indicate that general ideas, schemes of life and opinions about values are greatly influenced by the movies.[2] From pictures dealing with the life of modern youth many students derived attitudes toward freedom, relations to parents and conduct toward associates. Attitudes toward love and sex relations that were modified by the movies were reported in over half the autobiographies. Comparison of the ways of life in the movies and the students' own experience at home led to unrest and dissatisfaction on the part of 22 per cent of those writing autobiographies. In 12 per cent of the accounts there was some mention of rebellious feelings toward parental control as a result of comparison with the movie portrayals of the relations between parents and children. According to 59 per cent of the autobiographies, the pictures stimulated a desire to travel and come in contact with other peoples. Further instances of how the motion pictures may help to shape schemes of life and attitudes were recounted in the reports on the

[1] Blumer, H., *Movies and Conduct,* 1933.
[2] *Ibid.,* Chap. 10.

influence of pictures on ambitions. Themes of family affection, religious duty and courage stimulated desires "to be good" in many students. Quite diverse individual responses to the same picture were frequently noted. Moreover, the influence of the movies on students ranges from rather complete "emotional possession" of the individual to the development of a considerable degree of emotional detachment.

As the attention areas of modern man have widened, he has had need for more and more stereotypes. The motion pictures, as the most vivid pictorial record to which millions have access, have provided many of the new personal stereotypes and profoundly influenced the earlier national and large-group stereotypes. Relations between nationalities, class groups, occupational groups, character groups, and the like, are modified by the opinions of one another prevalent in these groups. To a considerable extent the motion pictures have determined how people visualize these types and the opinions they express about them. Motion-picture characters provide the symbolic models. Thus, film stars have become an important part of modern legendry and mythology. Not only is there an interest in them as persons, but also they serve as symbols of groups, classes and various types. Because of the number of such groups that the broadened attention areas have revealed to the general public, there is an increased need for personal symbolism. The actual persons of the individual's environment are increasingly inadequate to fill these roles. Motion-picture characters often do so.

In addition, these stereotypes influence opinions about real persons as they are encountered in face-to-face contact, in still pictures of the newspaper and elsewhere and in the motion-picture record of real persons. Thus the adolescent girl forms opinions about the possible charm and amorous capabilities of the youth she has just met as compared with those of the reigning screen heroes, and the adult audience adversely judges the statesman, economic advisor, scientist and businessman of the newsreel on a scale of personality symbols developed in part from the feature pictures. And the individual may be imbued with a firm conviction of the truth and reality of his stereotypes because they are vivid, personal and reiterated—he may have seen Warner Oland as Charlie Chan in ten pictures, thus fixing his stereotype of Chinese. Such personal stereotypes are convincing to the common man. Printed descriptions are rarely so vivid. And it is just this sense of reality that may be so dangerous to logical analysis and the reexamination of one's opinions. Thus, distortions may become even more permanent than heretofore.

Superficiality may be disarmingly convincing when provided in pictorial forms. There is a sense of completeness and profundity that is not actually justified. A contemporary historical analysis of the great events of history must consider scores of important factors. The usual motion-picture interpretation is almost entirely in personal terms.   Yet this personal motivation so definitely fits into the preconceptions of the common man that he finds no incongruity and complacently augments his preferences for personal interpretations.   In a sense, the speed of motion-picture action makes for another type of superficiality.   A situation is pictorially presented; a few seconds later it is whisked away, and attention is directed toward something else.   In reading, even at the lowest levels, one may stop to think, or just stop, at any point.   In the pictures, the tempo of portrayal is mechanically controlled outside the individual.   Analysis is thereby discouraged and, indeed, often frustrated.   The individual is more a passive recipient than is the case in other means of communication.

The potency of the motion picture in influencing the thought and opinions of large publics in the fields of politics and economics has not yet been thoroughly tested.   Interest groups of various kinds have been ineffectual in influencing motion-picture content in America.   This is because producers view their product as entertainment and eschew provocative and controversial themes.   To be sure, there are exceptions to this in the case of a few pictures.   And no political group has thus far controlled the entire industry.   Where political propaganda has been dominant (Italy, Germany and Russia), the industry has not been so well developed as in the United States; directorial capacities have not been so diverse and matured in the tricks of affecting audiences; the people have not been assiduous motion-picture "fans."   At the present time the full power of the pictures to influence and control opinion could be tested only in the great democracies, in England or the United States.

CHAPTER XXI

THE NEWSPAPER

The modern newspaper is the most important medium of communication for the distribution of news and opinions to large publics. This is true despite the fact that the majority of the voting public in the last two national elections in the United States has assumed a position contrary to the stand of over 80 per cent of the newspapers. But these elections were a special case and a special situation. Steadily, day after day, the press influences public opinion on various issues, on what types of goods one should buy, on the financial trends and economic ideology, on European and foreign politics, on spectacular public trials, on fashions and beauty standards, on cooking and food values, on popular science, and the like. The news is so various, the influence of the press so pervasive and the results of many types of news so controversial that the author has hesitated to attempt to discuss these problems within the limits of a chapter in this general volume on public opinion.[1]

The Development of the Newspaper

To trace the development of the newspaper is beyond the scope of this chapter. We shall content ourselves with an historical note. The newspaper is a modern method for satisfying an old need—that of distributing news and informing publics as to the events of the day. Primitive and folk peoples, living in communities of a few hundreds or thousands, distributed information and news by word of mouth. In the early civilizations, Egyptian, Greek and Roman, there was the gossip of the public square, neighborhoods and baths, and placards were posted in public places. There were also formal newsmongers and newsletters. These same methods were used to distribute news through the Middle Ages. Printing was developed in the fifteenth century, but the regular newspaper did not appear until two centuries later. The early and effective use of pamphleteering by the Protestants during the Reformation convinced those in authority of the disruptive possibilities of the printed

[1] See: Lee, A. M., *The Daily Newspaper in America*, 1937; Desmond, R. W., *The Press and World Affairs*, 1937; Mott, F. L., and Casey, R. D. (ed.), *Interpretations of Journalism*, 1937; Irwin, W., *Propaganda and the News*, 1936; Rosten, L. C., *The Washington Correspondents*, 1937; Keezer, D. M., "Press," *Ency. Soc. Sci.*, 12:325–344. Salmon, L. M., *The Newspaper and the Historian*, 1923. See also the author's forthcoming volume of studies on newspaper content, *The Newspaper and Public Opinion*.

page. "Thus when a *Weekly Newes* was launched in England in 1622 as the first contribution of the press in that country, it was restricted to the reporting of foreign news, presumably on the theory that news of developments far removed is relatively innocuous."[1] But the early English newspapers were relatively uninfluential in comparison with the gossip of the coffee houses in London and the newsletters that were distributed to subscribers in the provinces. In France, the *Gazette de France* was founded in 1631.[2] The news presented in these early papers was selected by those in governmental authority. Richelieu directed the policy of the *Gazette de France*. In England, the press did not become an independent political power for two centuries. " 'The development of the Press as an independent political power,' says Pebody, 'dates from the Reform Bill in 1831. Till then the newspapers had never thought of discussing the principles of Government in their broadest sense.' "[3] A few years later the press was a potent power in public decision. "It is therefore not surprising to find that Cobden's famous struggle against the tariff on grain (1838–1846) was already completely fought outside Parliament and through the press. . . . After 1860 the press entered upon its new career and commenced to rival Parliament as a platform of political discussion."[4] In France, governmental restrictions persisted until the revolution and were revived by Napoleon. The most dramatic stroke for freedom by the French press was the revolt of the editors in 1830. In America, the ideal of freedom from political control had been stated long before the American Revolution.

During the seventeenth and eighteenth centuries, newspapers were small, limited in content, personally edited and had few readers. It was a handicraft industry. The mass circulations that were achieved in the nineteenth century were based upon inventions that made rapid duplication of large numbers of copies possible, upon the developing literacy of the masses, upon the popularization of the content of the papers and upon the development of the newspaper as an advertising medium for the distribution of consumers' goods. In 1814, the *London Times* applied steam to its printing presses, thus speeding up the production. In the United States, the popularization of the press occurred under the aegis of a succession of dramatic personalities. In 1833, Benjamin Day started a penny paper *The Sun*, which achieved a circulation of 30,000 daily within four years of its founding. Day wrote for laborers and emphasized the formula of police news and crime.[5] In 1835, the elder James Gordon

---

[1] Keezer, *op. cit.*, 12: 346.
[2] Salmon, *op. cit.*, p. 10.
[3] *Ibid.*, p. 34.
[4] Friedrich, C. J., *Constitutional Government and Politics*, p. 427, 1937.
[5] Keezer, *op. cit.*, 12: 328.

Bennett started to publish the *New York Herald*. Editors were previously more concerned with molding opinion than with presenting news. Bennett went after news, human-interest stories, personal intimacies, fashion news, business deals, and the like. He demonstrated the popular appeal of such items, aiming his paper at the masses and caring little if he outraged fashionable folk. The mid-nineteenth century was a period of personal journalism, of strong personal editorial opinion. Horace Greeley, who founded the *New York Tribune* in 1841, was the dean of the personal journalists. He sought to improve society through his editorials. He achieved wide circulations by building up a personal following, as well as by presenting a diversity of news items. But Greeley avoided the sensationalism of the Bennetts. To the popularization of the newspaper, Charles A. Dana contributed "original, clever, concise writing, seeking to develop an American style in contrast to the heavier English news style, the imitation of which had persisted in American papers."[1] The next important stage in the development of popular journalism was the purchase of the *New York World* by Joseph Pulitzer in 1883. Pulitzer renewed the sensationalism of the Bennetts. He created news by starting crusades and reforms. He emphasized sensational news, political cartoons and illustrations and, after a few years, the comics, and spectacular headlines. Indeed, the term "yellow journalism" was coined in connection with a comic character colored yellow. This was in 1897. By that time, Pulitzer was engaged in a titanic struggle with William Randolph Hearst, who in 1896 had purchased the *New York Journal*. Hearst emphasized emotional appeals, and his papers have been unequaled in sensationalism in both news content and make-up. Circulations increased rapidly, and the urban daily newspaper became a great business enterprise. Yellow journalism was impudent, impertinent, inaccurate and emotion arousing. Yet lower depths were plumbed by the tabloids. In 1919, the *Chicago Tribune* started a tabloid paper in New York City called the *Daily News*. The tabloids are smaller papers, five columns wide instead of eight and with an unusually large number of illustrations. The *Daily News* reached a million circulation in a few years. The rival papers, the *Mirror* and the *Graphic*, have smaller circulations. The tabloids featured spectacular and dramatic stories, the public trials, the Hall-Mills and Snyder-Gray murder cases, and the like, used flamboyant make-up, large headlines, numerous photographs (some faked) and sensational language. They have been the last stage in the progressive cheapening of the press.

As the newspaper was popularized, it became "big business." Its organization and ownership changed. Chains were instituted or combined. E. W. Scripps started a chain in 1887. By 1900, the various

[1] Mott, G. F. (ed.), *An Outline Survey of Journalism*, p. 23, 1937.

chains circulated from 12 to 15 per cent of the daily circulation. Group ownership increased rapidly thereafter. In 1910, thirteen chains operated 52 papers. In 1926, there were fifty-five chains with 228 daily papers. In 1935, there were fifty-nine chains with 329 dailies. In 1933, the chains controlled 37.4 per cent of the daily newspaper circulation and 45.9 per cent of the Sunday circulations.[1] Newspapers were becoming, not only big business, but increasingly centralized business.

CIRCULATION

The number of daily and of weekly newspapers increased through the nineteenth century and until 1915. After that year the number of papers published declined rather sharply. In the century preceding 1915, there was a continuous expansion of the number of towns and cities, and new papers were formed to serve these areas. But after 1915, although the total population continued to increase, the number of urban places declined. Further, newspaper consolidations were occurring, and the more powerful urban papers were extending their territories and eliminating weaker rivals. The number of daily and weekly newspapers is presented in Table XV.

TABLE XV.—TOTAL NUMBER OF DAILY AND WEEKLY NEWSPAPERS PUBLISHED IN THE UNITED STATES AND TERRITORIES

Year	Daily	Weekly
1881	956	8,207
1885	1207	10,241
1890	1662	13,562
1900	2200	15,681
1905	2377	16,152
1910	2467	16,200
1915	2502	16,323
1916	2494	16,091
1920	2398	14,008
1925	2348	13,439
1930	2299	11,205
1935	2084	10,675

But the trends in circulation show a continued increase until 1930, after which, through the depression years, there was a decline of approximately 10 per cent. The number of copies of newspapers issued daily and the number of copies as compared with the population figures have increased enormously during the past eighty years. "In eighty years, between 1850 and 1930, the number of people in the United States for

[1] Lee, *op. cit.*, p. 216.

each daily paper issued dropped from 31.0 to 2.9. In the same period, daily newspaper subscribers soared from 4.6 to 43.1 per cent of the population ten years of age and older. In sixty years, between 1870 and 1930, subscribers mounted from 11.5 to 45.0 per cent of the literate population."[1] The total circulations of daily and Sunday papers and the circulation per 100 population by years for the past fifteen years is given in Table XVI.

TABLE XVI.—NUMBER OF DAILY AND SUNDAY ENGLISH LANGUAGE NEWSPAPERS AND TOTAL AND PER CAPITA CIRCULATION, UNITED STATES, 1920–1935*

Year	Daily newspapers			Sunday newspapers		
	Number	Circulation, thousands	Circulation per 100 population	Number	Circulation, thousands	Circulation per 100 population
1920	2042	27,791	26.1	522	17,084	16.0
1921	2028	28,424	26.3	545	19,041	17.6
1922	2033	29,780	27.1	546	19,713	17.9
1923	2036	31,454	28.2	547	21,463	19.2
1924	2014	32,999	29.2	539	22,220	19.6
1925	2008	33,739	29.4	548	23,355	20.3
1926	2001	36,002	30.9	545	24,435	21.0
1927	1949	37,967	32.1	526	25,469	21.5
1928	1939	37,973	31.7	522	25,771	21.5
1929	1944	39,426	32.4	528	26,880	22.1
1930	1942	39,589	32.1	521	26,413	21.4
1931	1923	38,761	31.2	513	25,702	20.7
1932	1913	36,408	29.2	518	24,860	19.9
1933	1911	35,175	28.0	506	24,041	19.1
1934	1929	36,709	29.0	505	26,545	21.0
1935	1950	38,156	30.0	518	28,147	22.1

* From: Waples, D., *Research Memorandum on Social Aspects of Reading in the Depression*, p. 80, Social Science Research Council, Bulletin 37, 1937. Quoted by permission of Social Science Research Council.

The daily newspaper has been primarily an urban institution. But during the last three decades the dailies have steadily increased the number of their subscribers and readers who live outside the urban boundaries. But the penetration of the urban daily outside the corporate limits of the city depends upon the type of population living in the area. "One interesting fact the study of the distribution of newspaper circulation has brought out: the man in the small city reads the metropolitan in preference to the local paper. But the farmer, it seems, still gets his news

[1] Lee, *op. cit.*, p. 70. See Lee, *ibid.*, Chap. 4; *The International Year Book Numbers of Editor and Publisher;* Wilson, L. R., *The Geography of Reading*, 1938.

from the same market in which he buys his groceries."[1]   Therefore, urban-rural composition of the population of various states, as well as factors of literacy, wealth and transportation facilities, accounts for the great differences in the distribution of newspapers by states.   Massachusetts has 563.6 daily papers per 1000 population; New York has 561.9; Missouri, 448.0; Illinois, 413.1.   In the middle group Wisconsin has 246.0; Maine, 243.5; Texas, 221.0; New Jersey, 207.8.   But, in South Carolina only 86.0 newspapers are distributed daily per 1000 population, 82.7 in Arkansas and 58.2 in Mississippi.

General figures on newspaper circulation indicate trends for the nation and for various subdivisions.   At the same time, we must remember that such figures indicate nothing as to the average number of readers per copy; the amount of time spent thereon; which sections are read; the relative influence of what is read at different times, in different sections of the paper and in various papers upon the readers' opinions.

NEWSPAPER READING HABITS

The number of papers that are distributed daily as reported by the newspaper-circulation figures does not indicate how many people are reading papers.   The circulation of daily newspapers decreased about 10 per cent and of Sunday papers about 12 per cent, through the depression years.   The circulation of daily newspapers per hundred population was 32.6 in 1925; 35.0 in 1927; 34.6 in 1929; 33.3 in 1931; 29.9 in 1933; 32.1 in 1935.[2]   However, there were undoubtedly more readers per copy in 1933 than was true of the earlier years.   At the depth of the depression there was more borrowing of papers.   When several families were crowded into a single dwelling, one paper often sufficed for the entire group.   Urban families, accustomed to the daily paper, borrowed a paper if they did not buy it, and an increasing percentage, as reported by librarians, read the library copies.   In 1933, a sample of Chicago adults showed that 90 per cent read the daily paper, yet no such percentage of individuals bought a paper.   There are virtually no valid data on newspaper-reading habits in the depression.   Yet the intense interest in economic and political affairs and the increased leisure of the unemployed must have increased the number of readers, though the newspaper circulations decreased.

Summarizing the data extant in 1929, Gray and Munroe conclude that 98 per cent of the men read papers on the average of 45.1 minutes a day and 93 per cent of the women read on the average of 28.7 minutes per day.

[1] Park, R. E., "Urbanization as Measured by Newspaper Circulation," *Am. Jour Sociol.*, 35: 75.

[2] Waples, *op. cit.*, p. 84.

TABLE XVII.—TIME SPENT IN NEWSPAPER READING BY AGE, OCCUPATIONAL, AND EDUCATIONAL CLASSES*

Age	Per cent reading	Average number of minutes per day	Occupational	Per cent reading	Average number of minutes per day	Educational	Per cent reading	Average number of minutes per day
Under 30.	96.0	36.1	Professional.........	100.0	34.7	Graduate training....	100.0	26.4
30–40....	97.8	39.3	Clerical.............	100.0	41.0	College or university		
40–50....	96.0	41.8	At home............	96.7	32.3	graduate.........	100.0	39.3
50–60....	97.0	47.3	Managerial..........	100.0	45.0	Some college training.	100.0	47.5
Over 60..	100.0	52.6	Commercial.........	96.7	45.4	High school graduate.	98.5	50.6
			Trades and labor.....	91.7	41.7	Some high-school		
			Public and personal			training...........	100.0	42.5
			service............	84.6	25.0	Eighth grade........	93.3	31.9
			Proprietors..........	100.0	55.0	Less than eighth grade	91.0	39.5
			Agriculture..........	100.0	....	Foreign—no schooling		
						in America........	100.0	33.8

* Compiled from Gray, W. S., and Munroe, R., *The Reading Interests and Habits of Adults*, Tables 8, 11, 12, 1929. By permission of The Macmillan Company, publishers.

TABLE XVIII.—NEWS FEATURES PREFERRED AS SHOWN BY FOUR STUDIES GIVING ORDER OF PREFERENCE*

News features	546 business and professional men in New York City, per cent	988 male college students in New York City, per cent	91 male clerical workers in New York City, per cent	Chicago business and professional men, per cent
General news................	19.30 (1)	19.72 (1)	16.88 (1)	7.2 (6)
Finance.....................	16.78 (2)	9.95 (4)	4.18 (9)	11.3 (3)
Editorials...................	11.53 (3)	14.72 (2)	16.40 (2)	9.0 (5)
Politics.....................	11.16 (4)	11.38 (3)	8.20 (5)	15.8 (2)
Foreign news................	10.01 (5)	6.08 (6)	8.99 (3)	9.5 (4)
Sports......................	7.59 (6)	8.76 (5)	8.91 (4)	5.8 (8)
Local news..................	4.24 (7)	3.36 (9)	4.97 (7)	17.8 (1)
Business page...............	3.14 (8)	3.55 (8)	2.29 (10)	
Special arts.................	2.70 (9)	4.72 (7)	5.99 (6)	4.3 (9)
Cartoons....................	2.39 (10)	2.34 (10)	4.50 (8)	4.3 (9)

* Kingsbury, S. M., Hart, H., *et al.*, *Newspapers and the News*, p. 155, 1937. Reprinted by permission of Susan M. Kingsbury and Mildred Fairchild. Published by G. P. Putnam's Sons.

The city people read an average of 2.29 papers; town dwellers, 2.03 papers; rural dwellers, 0.57 papers.

There are a number of studies of readers' preferences, but most of these are unpublished, having been made for particular newspapers or by advertising agencies. Relatively little data have been published. Ross observed passengers on a New York subway. Of 1837 passengers counted, 765 were reading. Of these, 701 were reading newspapers. He noted what materials were being read by 253 passengers.[1] But most of the studies have been questionnaire records or ranking tests. Such records seldom have a high validity. Hart has summarized several studies of this type.

THE CONTENT OF NEWSPAPERS

The newspapers report the world only in part—they are selective in emphasis. This selection occurs on the basis of the standards and interests of governments, publishers and the reading public. The student of the press must consider that: "(1) there is no government in the world not engaged in 'weighting' the news in its own interest; (2) that there are many news-gathering organizations some of which add their own bias to what they report; (3) that correspondents have what Mr. Justice Holmes called their 'inarticulate major premises' which necessarily color the reports they send; and (4) that the editorial offices have also their own special values to contribute to the work of selection and presentation of the news."[2] He must further consider that the contemporary newspaper in America is a "big business" with the biases of the economic viewpoints of publisher, editor and advertiser. And he must then consider the selective influence of reader interest, the demand for the personal, the incidental and the ephemeral. When he reads, "Rabbit Pulls Trigger, Kills Man Hunting Him," "A Man Goes Fishing, Gets Caught by Fish," the reader is responsible for the selection of such news. When the "Black Panther of Newdealism" stalks through the cartoons of the *Chicago Tribune*, the publisher is somewhere in the background. When the Panay incident is played down after a short period of spectacular reporting, the U.S. State Department has reported that there are vital national interests at stake. Of course, the reader realizes to some extent the partial nature of news reporting. Otherwise he would feel very insecure, indeed, in a world as reflected in the newspaper accounts.

Critics of the modern newspaper usually discuss and attack only a small portion of the total content of the paper. A typical comment by a philosopher declares:

[1] Ross, C. L., "Interests of Adults and High School Pupils in Newspaper Reading," *School and Society*, 27: 212–214.

[2] Laski, H., in Introduction to Desmond, *op. cit.*, 1937. Quoted by permission of D. Appleton-Century Company, Inc.

All the news of all the world! But whose world? The world of politics, too dirty, mongrel, and mad for a clean and intelligent person to besmear himself with. There is the world of scandal, the enlightening and savory details of which never get into print. There is the world of vulgar and violent crime. The worlds of beauty and of truth that come to stir one through the senses or the passions of the mind, these are never news for the millions, and never will be. Science is not news until it screams in a death ray or a gland operation for the restoration of youth. Poetry is not news until a poet runs away with a stockbroker's wife. Art is not news until a picture is slashed by a maniac or sold for a million dollars. Philosophy does not break into the public prints until it sponsors infanticide or vegetarianism or throws some oblique speculation on the Holy Ghost.[1]

Such attacks ignore perhaps 95 per cent of the column-inch content of this morning's paper.[2]

Another approach to the consideration of the newspaper's content is the measurement of the number of column inches devoted to various types of news. We have already discussed the uses and limitations of such studies.[3] They are primarily helpful in making comparisons between different time periods so that one may say something about the trends in content. However, such studies have not as yet been extensively employed in this way.[4] The most useful summary of quantitative and qualitative newspaper analyses is that of Kingsbury and Hart.[5]

THE PRESS ABROAD

The newspapers of the world cannot be classified according to national types. There are great similarities among the modern large newspapers of various countries as well as great differences. One distinction that cuts across national lines is that of "opinion" newspapers or "information" newspapers. The French papers are primarily opinion newspapers, the American newspapers are information newspapers. Yet in many ways the numerous small provincial dailies of France are very similar in content to the small city dailies of the United States. But the Parisian papers, whose circulation is built around the political outlook of their

[1] Edman, I., *Richard Kane Looks at Life*, p. 148, 1926. Quoted by permission of Houghton Mifflin Company.

[2] Strunsky, S., *The Rediscovery of Jones*, Chap. 2, 1931.

[3] Chap. III.

[4] The only examples of comparative studies of this kind are: the duplication of the Willcox study of 1899 by White, P. W., in 1924; "What Do You Read," *The Nation*, June 25, 1924; a comparison of news content in 1878, 1888, and 1898 reported in Schlesinger, A. M., *The Rise of the City*, pp. 199 ff., 1933.

[5] Kingsbury, Hart, *et al.*, *op. cit.*, 1937. The first part of this volume is devoted to the creation of a spectrum analysis of newspaper sensationalism and standards; Part II is a summary of previous objective studies of newspapers.

editors, are unlike any newspapers in the United States. This type of French press is frankly and openly a press of opinion. Most articles are signed. Advertising income is relatively small; subsidies from individuals or groups are the rule. This press is notoriously corrupt. Subsidies and bribes play a large part in winning adherence to the causes of numerous special interest groups and nationalities. It has often been proved that foreign governments had made payments to this sector of the French press. Indeed, it would appear that certain French papers are founded in order to receive bribes. This makes the French press a complicated pattern of sponsoring personalities, causes, parties and national interests, to understand which a detailed knowledge of French political life is required. The opinion papers are the most characteristically French newspapers, but there are five great commercial dailies published in Paris which resemble American newspapers in their interest in circulation and in their types of news content.

In contrast to the opinion press are the government-controlled newspapers of the authoritarian states, especially Russia, Germany, Italy and Japan. In Russia, the papers are owned either by the unions, the party or the government, but they are controlled by the government and the Communist party. Committees are responsible for the direction of particular papers. Newspapers are widely distributed and widely read. Their combined circulations are over twelve times that of the newspapers of Czarist Russia. *Pravda*, a Communist organ, has a circulation of over 1,700,000, and the government paper *Isvestia*, has a circulation of 1,600,000. The growth of these papers has been so rapid that their circulations have been restricted for the time being. There are now 4162 newspapers published in Russia, as compared with 500 in 1923 and 600 in 1929.[1] The content of these papers is determined by Communist ideology. Gossip and sensationalism are not allowed. Salacious news is not permitted; crime news appears only after the perpetrators have been detected. The public, not the private, acts of leaders are reported in the press. Local and foreign correspondents disregard the unique, the accidental and the subjective. There is the attempt to present the essential economic or political aspect of events. Although government-controlled, the Soviet press permits considerable criticism. It has been estimated that over one-quarter of the content of the newspaper is critical.[2] There is some popular demand for a less severely propagandist press. The afternoon *Moscow*, reporting events of the day in the city, has achieved a circulation of over one million. Persistent human interest in gossip, personalities and unusual incidents achieve some expression, even under communism.

[1] Bess, D., *Christian Science Monitor*, May 7, 1934.
[2] Keith, L., "Vom Wesen der Sowjetpresse," *Nord u. Süd*, 53: 7: 806.

R. R. Barlow has distinguished four systems of governmental control of the press.

These systems may be called: first, the free press systems of the United States, the British Commonwealth of Nations, Switzerland, Holland, and the Scandinavian countries; second, the autocratic system of control, characterized by a limited amount of freedom of the press, in operation in Japan, Germany in the days of the Kaiser, most of the South American countries, and small nations elsewhere; third, the proletarian press system espoused in Russia; and fourth, the Fascist or state press system set up in recent years in Italy, Germany, and other totalitarian states.[1]

Freedom of the press is increasingly an issue in the modern world. Under authoritarian states it has been largely eliminated in the interests of a political ideology and a central government, whereas in the democracies the concept of a free press has often been a "red herring" drawn across the trail of economic reforms.

THE NEWSPAPER AND PUBLIC OPINION

Not all of the newspaper content deals with material that is controversial and therefore the subject of opinion. Weather reports, factual accounts, a part of the news reports on the financial page, some human interest stories, many feature sections, serial novels, the announcement of radio programs, most obituary accounts, a part of the factual information on the women's page, and the like, are not primarily concerned with the controversial. Other sections of the paper have considerable indirect influence upon opinion. The moral and cultural standards are reflected in and influenced by the comics, the news of divorce, scandal and crime, the reporting of spectacular trials and numerous unslanted news accounts. But other parts of the paper are directed to the modifying of popular opinion. The editorials are avowedly opinion material. Cartoons; letters to the editor; a part of the space utilized by the columnists; the making and breaking of the reputations of motion-picture actors and actresses, financiers and other public figures; the blurb about beauty into which is woven the names of products favored by the paper; parts of the financial page which are directed at the influencing of investors; deliberately slanted news accounts—all these are intentionally partial. The half of the paper devoted to advertising is avowedly directed to the swaying of opinions regarding economic goods. But to what extent does the press mold public opinion, and how far is the content of the newspaper a reflection of popular opinion? This is a long-disputed point.

[1] Mott, *op. cit.*, p. 270, 1937. Quoted by permission of Barnes & Noble, Inc.

The influence of the press varies greatly in different cultures. The newspaper must be understood in terms of its development and its relation to various aspects of a society. No one is in a position to generalize accurately on the newspaper and popular opinion in all nations. The relationships are often subtle, and the true inwardness of such interaction may be discerned only after long and intimate study. Even then, there is only partial and incomplete knowledge, for, as yet, the newer and more exact methods of social psychology have not been applied to this problem. The content of the press and its influence on popular opinion are quite different in the authoritarian states, where regimentation and the selection and slanting of the news are under centralized control, than in the democracies, where news accounts and interpretations and opinion manipulation are kept somewhat distinct. Although news accounts are slanted in American newspapers, especially on economic issues, the process is by no means complete, even in the most partial papers with the most definite policies. And then, opposing viewpoints are expressed in other papers, although these are usually papers of small circulation. Although American theory and practice regarding the press have changed greatly since the days of the early classic libertarians and although there is today much less faith in the essential rationality of the common man, civil liberties are much prized, and the American press is the freest in the world. There is still something of the spirit, if not the hopefulness, of Thomas Jefferson. "If left to me to decide whether we should have a government without newspapers, or newspapers without a government, I should not hesitate for a moment to prefer the latter." He believed that the people in possession of the facts would reach reasonable conclusions. Today, "facts" are more complicated, issues more varied and there is a "glut of occurrences." To a far greater extent, the newspaper must select its news. There are partisan, independent and neutral papers. There is no central control, and the press is not viewed as "a great organ on which the Leader must play."

The modern daily paper is a great commercial institution directed toward the making of profits. It must hold its readers, increase its circulation. Therefore, the press reflects certain reader attitudes and tastes. The reader has interest in the immediate and in the local values and standards, which he would apply to the larger world. He quests for the personal, the "human interest," the anecdotal account, the little, dramatized conflict, and the like. The supply meets the demand. The readers' interests and values determine the content of large sections of the daily paper, especially those sections which they read carefully. The publisher's interest may be quite influential in determining the news content provided by his Washington correspondents, but he may find that only about 10 per cent of his subscribers read the Washington correspondents.[1] It is said that "the popular commercial press of the 19th century escaped from the tutelage of government only to fall under the tutelage of the masses. It found support and profit in serving the whims and curiosity of the people."[2] Certainly there has been a catering to simple tastes in the struggle for circulations. But there are many newspaper publics to which a quite varied press has accommodated itself.

POLITICS AND THE PRESS

When the owners, publishers or editors attempt to direct public opinion they are by no means always successful, although the results are not always exactly known. In those cases where public decision follows closely upon a newspaper campaign, something of the effects of the newspaper's pleading can be known. The effects of newspaper advertising on the sale of goods have been exactly shown in numerous studies. Election results have been compared with the position of the press in a few instances. However, there is no basis for generalization from these few incidental studies, as most elections are complicated situations in which the position of the press is but one factor. There are dramatic situations in which candidates have won in spite of a very general opposition of the newspapers. After the World War, the Labor party in England gained electoral successes in spite of an overwhelmingly conservative press. The Roosevelt majority of 1936 was obtained despite the opposition of over 80 per cent of the daily newspapers of the United States. In France, many regular readers of the conservative press vote Socialist. In a study made in Seattle in 1926, G. A. Lundberg asked 840 newspaper readers which papers they regularly read and how they had voted in the preceding elections. On the City Manager Plan, the *Seattle Times* was opposed, and 42 per cent of its readers in Lundberg's sample voted for the plan; the *Post Intelligencer* was favorable, and 40 per cent of its readers voted against the plan; the *Star* was for the plan, and 55 per cent of the readers voted against it. The Skagit Project, an extension of municipal power, was opposed by the *Times*, and 75 per cent of the readers voted for the project; the *Post Intelligencer* was friendly to the project, and 72 per cent of its readers voted for it; the *Star* was for the project, and 79 per cent of its readers voted for it.[3]

From a much more extensive study of newspaper position on candidates and election results in Chicago, Harold Gosnell concludes, "While a number of candidates have carried the second largest city of the

[1] Gallup, G., "Guesswork Is Eliminated in New Method of Determining Reader Interest," *Editor and Publisher*, 62: 38: 55.

[2] Lippmann, W., "Two Revolutions in the American Press," *Yale Rev.*, 20: 3: 437.

[3] Lundberg, G. A., "The Newspaper and Public Opinion," *Soc. Forces*, 4: 7: 5.

United States in the face of a bitter and overwhelming press opposition, this does not mean that the press is without influence or that its relative effectiveness is rapidly declining."[1] In this study, the home coverage of the various newspapers was shown by areas; the content of the newspapers on various candidates was shown by column-inch measurement of news devoted to candidates, by editorials and by cartoons; the voting record over a number of elections was obtained by areas, and intercorrelations of variables related to newspaper home coverage and voting behavior in Chicago, 1930–1936, were determined.[2]

There are many difficulties confronting any attempt to record newspaper influence. How can the complex variables be separated and related? On the basis of the few simple studies that have thus far been made, it would appear that the press remains extremely effective in influencing voters with regard to those candidates about whom the voters know little or about those issues on which the electorate is either uninformed or indifferent. However, when voters believe that self-interest is involved or when the readers have considerable information that differs from that provided by their daily newspapers, they will vote contrary to the program or candidates advocated by the papers. As the newspaper increased in importance and circulation during the nineteenth century, the belief developed among societal leaders that control of the press meant control of public opinion. This has proved to be true only in part. The press has failed to direct its readers in numerous crisis situations. But it retains an enormous influence over its readers in their day-to-day decisions on issues about which they are not aroused.

THE NEWS FROM WASHINGTON

The press has become more important in political affairs as the role of government in life has proportionately increased. Under authoritarian states, the newspaper is a publicity organ of the state, and, under American democracy, the amount of political news has increased. Such news is provided by press-association stories; by local, county and state reporters; by the Washington correspondents and columnists. The Associated Press and United Press each lease elaborate networks of wire for the transmission of domestic news. They maintain staffs at key centers, and at less important points their local newspapers serve as correspondents. The news from Washington has increased in importance during the last twenty years. The functions performed by the national government have rapidly multiplied, and public attention is now more often directed to the capital; Washington is a rich news center. In 1871, there were 143 correspondents who covered Congress and Washing-

---

[1] Gosnell, H., *Machine Politics: Chicago Model*, p. 181, 1937.
[2] *Ibid.*, Chap. 8.

ton news for 130 newspapers and 6 press associations.[1] In 1937, there were 504 accredited newspaper and magazine correspondents in the capital.[2] These men and women have access to conferences with the officers of the government from the president of the United States down. There are conferences with the president, cabinet heads, and heads of departments. There are the official press bureaus, now rapidly increasing in number. The correspondents gather information from the lobbies and various private organizations. The correspondents also have various private sources of information. The "glut of news" in Washington and the deluge of facts have led during the past twenty years to the development of signed articles by political interpreters and during the past decade to the rise of the columnists. These attempt to provide clear, simple and interpretive accounts of the facts. Naturally, professional purveyors of Washington news are not always clear as to the meaning of events nor are they always unbiased. Certain limitations of these correspondents are evident: they frequently present only partial accounts; they yearn to "make a story"; many have been trained to write of the "game of politics" and not of the larger social implications of legislation; they sometimes write for their editors and not for their readers.[3] These correspondents are remarkably accurate in reporting facts but they are often limited in perspective.

The scope of the publicity services of various government departments may be indicated by the numbers of their employees who devote their entire time to publicity activities. The U. S. Treasury Department has 15; Agriculture, 78; War, 5; FHA, 25; WPA, 32; AAA, 46; Social Security, 61; HOLC, 16; Commerce, 13; and so on.[4]

The following generalizations on Washington news are presented by L. C. Rosten. "Newspapers get the type of reporting which they encourage; publishers get the kind of Washington correspondents that they deserve; and the public receives Washington correspondence of a character which the newspaper publishers, and ultimately they alone, make possible."[5] But what are the results of Washington news on public opinion? No one knows exactly. How many newspaper readers carefully read the Washington reports? The estimate is 10 per cent.

---

[1] Lee, *op. cit.*, p. 510.

[2] Rosten, *op. cit.*, 1937.

Knebel, F., "Washington Press Conference," *Ken*, July 28, 1938, p. 74.

Rosten, L. C., "President Roosevelt and the Washington Correspondents," *Pub. Opin. Quar.*, 1: 1: 36–53.

[3] Kiplinger, W. M., "What Can You Believe," *Today*, 3: 5: 3.

[4] *Editor and Publisher*, 70: 40, Part 1.

An oversensationalized account of government publicity will be found in Michael, G., *Handout*, 1937.

[5] Rosten, L. C., *The Washington Correspondents*, p. 304, 1937.

Of those who read the reports, some are undoubtedly swayed by the Washington correspondents, but others are swayed by their own interests, when they can determine what those interests are.

FOREIGN NEWS

The bulk of the world's news is provided for the individual newspapers by the great press associations. Some newspapers in the great cities receive foreign news cabled to them from their correspondents abroad. There are three American news agencies and seven great American newspapers that collect news in Europe. About 300 men are engaged as full-time correspondents.

There are many press associations in the world.[1] The great systems are: the Agence Havas of France (established 1840); Reuter's of England (established 1851—the most extensive and important association in the world); Deutsches Nachrichten Büro (Germany); for the United States the Associated Press (a mutual nonprofit organization serving 1400 member newspapers), the United Press (a privately owned corporation serving 1200 newspapers, founded in 1907 by E. W. Scripps) and the International News Service of W. R. Hearst with some 700 other clients. These press associations have transmitted the bulk of their news by cable; hence the importance of the national control of cable lines during the nineteenth century. But, with the development of radio, control of the cables no longer had such strategic importance in crises. Of course, a great many feature stories are sent by mail, but this is not "hot" news. The major news-gathering associations of the world, some thirty in addition to Havas, Reuter's, A.P. and D.N.B., have been associated in the so-called "ring combination." The affiliated members exchange news. But, owing to the rising tide of nationalism, the agreements of the ring combination broke down in 1932. News is still exchanged, but A.P., Reuter's, D.N.B. and Havas now invade one another's territory. The great associations are attempting to develop independent world coverage.[2]

The foreign correspondent selects news. He is limited by the press that he serves and, as the large American daily newspapers are a big business, he reports economic affairs in large part in terms of his employer's interests. There is a tendency to defend the *status quo*. There is a demand for "spot" news, and his accounts are often hurried and incomplete. He must keep on good terms with the sources of his news, which is increasingly difficult amidst the rampant nationalisms and

[1] Desmond, *op. cit.*, pp. 66 *ff.*
[2] Desmond, *op. cit.*, pp. 50–75.
Riegel, O. W., *Mobilizing for Chaos*, Chap. 5.
Keezer, D. M., "Press," *Ency. Soc. Sci.*, 12: 325–344.

clashing ideologies of the modern world.   And then, "the sensationalism required by the home office exaggerates conflict and reduces the complicated relations of international life to the stereotyped heroics of nineteenth century melodrama."[1]   He cannot gather the bulk of his news himself, so is dependent upon foreign newspapers, ticker services, official government news, the purchase of exclusive rights to certain news such as interviews and his sources among his personal friends and contacts.[2]   He sometimes draws upon his imagination and guesses.   He faces the problems of propaganda and censorship.   "The miracle is that so much sound journalism from Europe does manage to appear.   The organization is slipshod, the personnel is miscellaneous, and the technic extremely helterskelter."[3]   Nonetheless, in the United States the newspaper reader has access to more accurate foreign news than he has elsewhere in the world.   At the same time, he has fewer opinions, sound or unsound, about foreign affairs than is true of the citizen of any other great power.   Perhaps 5 per cent of the column-inch content of the great dailies is foreign news, a much smaller percentage in the smaller papers.   The newspaper reader could have more and better foreign news if he evinced interest in it.   American readers have more facts, but they make less use of them.   Many a powerful American daily provides better foreign news (in spite of biases on some topics) than its readers demand or appreciate.   The first factor necessary for a better informed popular opinion on foreign affairs is a public that desires to be informed.

Columnists

News reporting has become impersonal.   Since 1900, the editorial has become increasingly impersonal.   But personal journalism achieved a new expression in the rise of columnists.   There are columns by news commentators, political commentators, sports writers, beauty specialists, essayists; gossip purveyors of the news of the town, political personages and movie stars; advisors of the lovelorn, rhyming philosophers, humorists, and the like.   Notable contributors are Walter Lippmann, Boake Carter, the late Will Rogers, Arthur Brisbane, and former president Coolidge, Frank R. Kent, Paul Mallon, Heywood Broun, Grantland Rice, Westbrook Pegler, Damon Runyon, Pierson and Allen, Walter Winchell, the late O. O. McIntyre, Louella Parsons, Edgar Guest, Dorothy Thompson, Ray Clapper and Mrs. Roosevelt.   Some of these columns are widely syndicated.   Pierson and Allen's *Merry-Go-Round* appears in over 300 papers, and Paul Mallon in over 200 daily papers.

[1] Riegel, *op. cit.*, p. 140.
[2] Gunther, J., "Funneling the European News," *Harpers*, April, 1930.
[3] *Ibid.*, p. 41.

It is impossible, as yet, to evaluate in any definite way the influence of these commentators upon popular opinion. Some of them have very large followings numbered in hundreds of thousands or millions. They represent a significant return to personal journalism. That the columnists are believed to be influential is evidenced by the restive plaints of major political leaders that these interpreters frequently distort the news.

The political columnists are of relatively recent vintage, the older type being the gossipmongers. A century ago Anne Newport Royall was writing Washington gossip.[1] Forty years ago Dorothy Dix (Mrs. E. M. Gilmer) began her fabulous career as a "sob sister." She has had many imitators. Twenty years ago O. O. McIntyre began a new type of round-the-town gossip column. Many of the columns are characterized by strikingly original methods of presentation and unconventional language, if not unusual ideas.

The "glut of news" has led to the demand for simplifiers. There is a rising demand for explanations. All daily papers carry a number of such columns. As the columnist has grown in influence and his role in the daily paper has become more obvious, it is important that his personal philosophy, his biases and prejudices, his sources of news; his chief sponsor; the groups to which he is allied; and other questions about him be systematically studied. As yet this has not been done. Nor has there been any adequate study and evaluation of his readers or of his influence.

Editorials

Theoretically, the American newspaper makes a sharp division between the news and the interpretation of news. Naturally, in the news columns there is selection, distortion and slanting at many points. But in theory, there is a divorce of news and opinion. The editorial page is the traditional forum for the expression of opinion. In the editorial columns the policy of the paper is expressed. M. W. Brown has written that the function of editorials is to inform the reader of details omitted from the news columns; to explain the news columns; to interpret as to the real significance of an event; to argue with logical analysis of cause and effect; to urge action; to conduct crusades; to lead by persuasion, often by emotional appeals; to announce policies; to offer entertainment.[2]

For over a century there have been editorials in American newspapers. Nathan Hale purchased the Boston *Advertiser* in 1814, and was the first

---

[1] Brown, D., "Godmother of Columnists," *Coronet*, July, 1938, pp. 79–81.

[2] Mott, *op. cit.*, pp. 254 *ff.*

editor to write editorials on events of public interest.[1] In that period of partisan journalism the editor expressed himself. He was the boss. In the 1830's the popularization of the newspapers began. Although the strong editorial writer continued to have a large following and, indeed, spectacular editorial leaders waxed in influence for fifty years thereafter, the commercial aspects of the new type of paper presaged his eclipse. Income became more dependent upon advertising, advertising upon circulation, and circulation upon the purveying of news, not views.[2] However, the editor remained as a dramatic figure, a controversialist, a crusader and a dramatic oracle until about 1880. The day of greatest influence of the editorial writer was the Civil War period and the following decade. Through this bitter period—confused, chaotic and frenzied —the anxious reader found solace in his allegiance and loyalty to his favored editors and in denunciatory name-calling directed toward those editors with whom he differed. It was the "golden era of personal journalism." The editor canalized the opinions of his readers. The editor was a good hater and a vivid controversialist. It was during this period that the rule developed among newspapermen that every paper should have one good hate about which to editorialize at least once a week. There should be a controversy close at home and one directed toward something at a distance. One editor solved his second problem by regularly writing about the outrageous piracy against fur-bearing seals in the Kamchatka Inlet. But the importance of the editorial declined toward the end of the nineteenth century. Personal ownership of newspapers was being succeeded by corporate ownership. The commercial interests of the paper became dominant. The business office and the news staff attacked the editor and limited the range of his discussions. Great news-collecting agencies were being developed, and attention centered more and more upon their product. Experts, foreign correspondents, political writers and columnists usurped much of the field of the editorial. Editorial boards limited the personal flair of the individual writer. The monthly magazines, rapidly increasing their circulation from 1900 onward, contained much controversial material. The era of the muckrakers, 1900–1910, was dominated by magazine publishers such as McClure. These men led crusades that fifty years earlier would have been started in newspaper editorials. Also, the public had access to new sources of information—latterly, the radio. The editorial fell into disrepute; popular confidence in the infallibility of editorial writers waned. Following the 1936 election, Capt. Joseph Medill Patterson wrote, "This election demonstrated that the power of

[1] Douglass, P. F., *The Newspaper and Responsibility*, p. 79, 1931.
[2] Allen, E. W., "Economic Influences and Editorial Influence," *Jour. Quar.*, September, 1931.

the press to sway public opinion in this country is dying, if not dead— that people read newspapers these days to get facts—baseball and football and stock market scores, weather reports, facts from the fighting fronts and the war medicine distilleries, shopping tips—but they either don't read or they don't rely on editorials."[1] The editorial has become more factual, more informative, less controversial, and less influential. The depression years have brought more acrimonious dispute over political personages and policies into the editorial columns, but there is no evidence to show that the editorial has increased its influence over popular opinion and public decision.

THE PROBLEMS OF CONTROL

During the eighteenth and nineteenth centuries the struggle for freedom of the press was directed against the domination of newspapers by the state. In varying degrees the press in the Western nations achieved such independence. In the United States and in England the maximum of freedom was obtained. In America the Colonial press agitated against political domination by England, and a number of press martyrs, notably John Peter Zenger, played dramatic roles. In the national Bill of Rights of 1791, freedom for the press was legally stated. "Congress shall make no law abridging the freedom of speech or of the press." The essence of that freedom was also defined in popular catchwords and slogans. In the early nineteenth century, newspapers were founded in every growing center of population. They were private enterprises, representing diverse viewpoints and interests. A paper could be founded with very little capital. In the 1840's the elder Bennett started with $500. But technological changes raised the costs of production, and by the end of the century the daily newspaper had become a very big business. Capital requirements were large, and control became more centralized. Weaker rivals were purchased, consolidations occurred and chains developed. In 1931, there were fifty-six chains, the largest being the Scripps-Howard group with twenty-five newspapers and Hearst with twenty-one papers.[2] "The relatively monopolistic nature of the daily newspaper properties is indicated by the fact that in 1936, the 1560 evening papers of general circulation were located in about 1430 cities; the 1950 morning and evening dailies of this sort in 1457 cities. While only 9.3 per cent of all dailies, in 1929, were located in cities with 500,000 or more inhabitants, these papers controlled 45.4 per cent of the total daily circulation."[3] The newspaper, as a business

---

[1] *Time*, Nov. 16, 1936, p. 65.

[2] Keezer, *op. cit.*, 12: 344.

[3] Lee, A. M., in *Studies in the Science of Society*, Presented to A. G. Keller (Murdock, G. P., ed.), p. 368, Yale University Press, 1937.

enterprise, had its own interests. In general, the larger papers shared the interests and purposes of big business. They became increasingly dependent upon advertising, as advertising pays, on the average, four-fifths of the costs of newspaper production. So the press naturally reflects present-day commercial interests. Although the spectacular charges of direct dictation by powerful advertisers have no doubt been exaggerated by newspaper critics, the large dailies do reflect the general interests of the business groups. The papers themselves are part of the process. In the contemporary struggles over economic issues, a number of powerful newspaper owners and publishers have utilized the old and reputable slogans about freedom of the press to divert attention from the partiality of certain of the causes that they advocate and the positions that they wish to maintain. By this spurious appeal for press freedom, they may have alienated considerable popular support, so that when a real issue of press freedom from governmental interference arises it may be more difficult to arouse the readers.

The commercially dominated daily press exhibits bias on controversial issues between capital and labor. When one industry dominates a community, such as the steel industry in the Pittsburgh area or copper in Montana, the distortion of the news at crises is most flagrant. However, this is a capitalistic society, and there is no ready solution for this problem. A class press on the other side is not the answer, for the labor papers are not only small in circulation, but also equally biased in the other direction.

As a business, newspapers seek circulation. This has led to the providing of crime and salacious news, to the shocking invasion of the privacy of men and women in public and private life, to the romanticizing of daring but illegal exploits and to an overemphasis on personalities. It is these aspects of newspaper content which the critics most often deplore. There are some papers that ignore such news, notably the *Christian Science Monitor*. But most daily newspapers select the unusual, the spectacular, the criminal and the salacious items far out of proportion to the statistical frequency of such behavior in society. Under authoritarian control, as in Russia, such news may be excluded by fiat. But in a democratic state with privately owned newspapers there are only three ways of improvement. The first and most general is the raising of the standards of readers by general education and intelligence; the second is educational work among editors and the raising of professional standards at the behest of their own associations and societies; and the third is the restriction of certain types of news by law. Though newspaper publishers would at once cry "censorship" and declare that freedom of the press was invaded, it is possible that additional legal curbs on the publication of certain types of material would benefit the press in the long run. Newspaper associations should canalize the attacks, directing them toward known and admitted abuses, and should advocate reasonable legislation. It is highly unlikely that they will do so.

Leaving the control of the press in private hands, the standards of news content might be bettered by the legalized outlawing of certain types of news and the setting up of judicial bodies to deal with infractions of the rules and the assignment of penalties. Increasing social control of the press is imperative. The technical and legal problems are difficult, but perhaps not insurmountable. If the press is to be free, and that is imperative for democracy, it must be responsible. Wise publishers would lead the reform. But the newspapers, as indeed other social institutions, have grown without plan, making immediate, selfish and often shortsighted adaptations to an immediate problem. A continuance of this process may mean a far more extensive governmental invasion of publishing than is desirable in the interests of real freedom. The control of the press by government spreads rapidly once the dikes are breached. When Napoleon took over the control of Paris newspapers, there were seventy-three political papers. Only four survived and these were placed under rigid censorship. Contemporary authoritarian states, Communistic, Fascist and Nazi, have achieved complete control of the press. In America, today, the press is acutely sensitive to any suggestion of political restriction. Newspapermen are complaining about government "handouts." Some of these objections are intensively partisan, exaggerated and even hysterical. But it is well to be suspicious. At the same time, some regulation of nonpolitical news content, if advocated by publishers themselves, might stem the rising tide of popular criticism of the press. The appeals of the political advocate of extensive press control would be less influential, should such a movement develop. By abusing their present "freedom," newspaper publishers are strengthening the possibility of political interference with that freedom.

The American press should be critical of the political process, but a too unselected and partisan criticism may be unwise at the present moment. "The premium which journalism places upon an attack and the spurious daily 'crises' which clutter the pages of the newspapers, tend to (1) overemphasize the errors and inefficiencies of representative government at a time when democratic agencies should concern themselves with buttressing its prestige; (2) deaden the perception of the public in advance to genuine crises which may arise; (3) heighten tensions and foster an impatience with democratic government which demagogues may use to their advantage."[1]

The sources of news should be more explicitly stated, and the responsibility for opinion material should be personally assigned. Twenty years

---

[1] Rosten, *op. cit.*, p. 300. Quoted by permission of Harcourt, Brace & Company.

ago Walter Lippmann suggested that the reader should know the names of the principal members of the newspaper staff and their affiliations; that articles should be signed and documented; that the sources of news in reports by the great news agencies, press bureaus or reporters' accounts should be stated; that false documentation should be illegal.[1] These suggestions are still valid. Newspapermen are extremely critical of advice from nonprofessional sources, but they are sadly in need of a program to save themselves and their product from popular and official attack. Perhaps the American Society of Newspaper Editors' canons of newspaper ethics should be taken seriously by editors, and other professional standards of product and personnel should be developed.

Standards of accuracy of news reports have been bettered by the competition of the radio, especially of the radio news commentators. This is in the public interest. The more channels of communication, the more diverse the control, the greater the possibility of accuracy of report. But both the newspaper and radio aim at the largest popular audience, and hence neither is active in promulgating the unpopular truth or bringing out the unpopular fact. There is no remedy for this. A growth in popular wisdom could emerge only with a higher level of general intelligence.

It has been suggested that there will be two types of newspapers in the future. One will deal with trivialities and be designed chiefly to entertain; the other will be a journal of interpretation, will be manned by experts in sifting news and will appeal to the serious reader.[2] There is another possibility. Within the same daily paper there is already a great diversity in levels of news and interpretation. The devotees of sports news, of gossip, of the business page, of the comics, of political and foreign news have their favorite fare prepared for them by writers greatly alien to one another in intelligence. Certain political interpretations and commentaries on foreign news have achieved a relatively high level of excellence. If these are not so widely read as the more popular sections of the paper, at least they are there to be read, when and if the reader develops an interest in them.

The modern newspaper, when the self-interest of the publisher is not involved, is about as good as could be expected. It is easier to criticize the private ownership of the press than to find the plans for a better system in terms of the public interest. Under private control, the better representatives of the American press system and the better English newspapers, notably the *Manchester Guardian*, provide a quality of news such as has never before existed. The American press is an industry

[1] Lippmann, W., *Liberty and the News*, 1920.
[2] Bent, S., "The Future Newspaper," *Century*, January, 1929, pp. 342–348.

and as such has developed distortions and biases due to the demands for circulation and profit.   It is an agency for distributing news, and in this function it has performed with amazing efficiency and a relatively high degree of accuracy.   It is a forum for the discussion of controversial issues, but in this role most newspapers have been flamboyant, superficial or dull.

CHAPTER XXII

THE GRAPHIC ARTS AND PUBLIC OPINION

The graphic arts, especially certain paintings and statues that have become symbols for groups; the drawings, cartoons and caricatures that provide comments on the passing scene; and, latterly, the welter of selected photographs that illustrate the newspaper and periodical, are

Fig. 13.—Cartoon by Herbert Johnson. (*Reprinted by special permission from Sat. Eve. Post. Copyright, 1934, by Curtis Publishing Company.*)

very influential in modifying popular opinion. Significant art from the viewpoint of popular opinion is that which can be widely understood, that which conveys impressions and is functionally significant in the larger publics.

"Pictures have always been the surest way of conveying an idea, and next in order, words that call up pictures in memory."[1] The pictures may be individually remembered scenes, situations, persons and incidents,

[1] Lippmann, W., *Public Opinion*, p. 162, 1922.

or they may be actual prints, photographs, and the like, which are reproduced and distributed among masses of people. This is widely recognized today, and now, in greater degree than ever before, all social movements are lavishly equipped with pictorial symbols. The Russian government, during the past twenty years, has utilized the most extensive poster campaigns ever attempted in any social movement. The various symbols are spread broadcast. Even in designing textiles for clothing, there has been an attempt to popularize designs containing hammers, sickles, tractors, the red star, automobiles, and the like, in place of the "bourgeois" flowers and other conventional designs. The American NRA immediately developed the blue eagle. In the Nazi campaign for a rising birth rate, advertising artists were recently informed that they should present families of four children in their pictures. Pictorial stimuli are ever more carefully supervised, for today societal leaders recognize, as did General von Ludendorff, that "pictures and films and illustrations in poster form strike home more and produce greater effects than writing, and these have greater effects on the masses." Last year the state of Georgia duly commissioned an official cartoonist.

However, a recognition of the effectiveness of pictorial forms in simplifying issues and in making emotional appeals to the masses is not new. Confucius said, "One picture is worth ten thousand words." During the past two centuries, since cartooning and caricaturing have made their mass appeals, many a public man could bear testimony to their effectiveness. Gillray plagued Napoleon with his numerous caricatures of "little Boney." A generation ago, Boss Tweed of Tammany, bedeviled by the caricatures drawn by Thomas Nast, is reported to have said, "Let's stop them damned pictures. I don't care so much what the papers write about me—my constituents can't read—but, damn it, they can see the pictures."

But before pictorial forms could be effectively used to influence popular opinion, certain prerequisites and accompanying culture complexes were necessary. Among these were: (1) The development of the means of communication, especially of newspapers and periodicals, in which pictures could be reproduced. (2) The technical developments making possible duplicate pictorial reproduction. In 1833, the *New York Sun* published its first illustration, printed from a wood engraving. In the 1870's, crude photoengraving appeared. This made possible the reproduction of photographs. In the 1890's, four-color rotary newspaper presses were produced. In the 1920's, the rotogravure processes were applied to newspaper publishing.[1] (3) The building up of large circulations of newspapers and magazines which made possible the influencing of large publics by means of pictures as well as print. The great cari-

[1] Lee, A. M., *The Daily Newspaper in America*, pp. 129 *ff.*, 1937.

caturists of the end of the eighteenth century issued their drawings in small booklets which were published by private booksellers. At most, the circulation of these booklets was a few thousand. (4) No development in culture can be thoroughly understood merely in terms of external factors that play upon it; the development of the thing itself is a factor. The present widespread use of pictorial forms can be further understood in terms of fashions in their use.

Historical records must be approached cautiously. As the anthropologist has often pointed out, there may or may not be a functional similarity between items of different ages that appear to be similar. A historical record of caricature begins with a few illustrations in primitive drawing and then notes the caricatures of ancient India, especially those ribald pictures of the god Krishna. "In an ancient Hindu drawing we see Krishna on his travels, the god is mounted on an elephant, and the elephant, rollicking along joyously, is constructed of the various accommodating young ladies that make up the god's harem."[1]   After that, the record provides some illustrations from ancient Egypt (one of the earliest known humorous drawings is that of servants carrying their drunken master home from a banquet in the Egypt of 3000 years ago). There are some illustrations from Greece and Rome. The next significant period is that of the numerous Gothic caricatures. Modern caricature begins in the middle of the eighteenth century. But is the functional significance of a humorous scrawl on an ancient Hindu temple the same as that of this morning's cartoon in the *Chicago Tribune?* The historic record is significant if there is an evolutionary development of the designs and of the pictorical techniques or if the pictorializing processes have the same functional relationships in the publics of different ages. There has been a historic evolution of designs and techniques which may profitably be traced. However, the only historic record that is significant in a discussion of the functional relationships among cartoons, caricatures, pictures and publics is that of the period since 1750. In this period, the large publics emerged, modern communication developed, mass reproductions became possible, issues multiplied and the technique of pictorial presentations was developed in relation to the growing need to influence large publics. Our "historical mindedness" is also illustrated in connection with the evolution of particular symbols. As soon as the swastika became an emblem of the Nazi party, their opponents at once pointed out that this design was an ancient sex emblem. This fact then became of significance, as it could be used in the political conflict to depreciate the emblem. Otherwise, it was of no significance.

There is a great stir in the graphic arts today, because there is increasing need for the communication of ideas. The uses of modern

[1] Ashbee, C. R., *Caricature*, p. 6, 1928.

photographs, sketches, posters, cartoons and caricatures for the conveying of ideas and the influencing of opinions are evident on every hand.
Most contemporary muralists are using the wall spaces at their disposal
to propagandize for something. The most notorious of these artists is
Diego Rivera. "One needs no assistance in understanding the murals
that the Mexican painters have been turning out. One may or may not
like them. They may or may not be what the previous generation
meant when it looked down its nose and talked about art. But a child
of six can get their meaning."[1] Of the mile or more of wall covered with
frescoes in the Mexican Ministry of Education, A. L. Strong writes, "The
infinite struggling strength of man, the worker, was seen in the under-
ground miner with powerful pick, his body bent by seams of earth; the
infinite humiliation of man in that peon with uplifted arms, searched by
mine inspectors; the infinite endurance of women, pounding their grain,
patient for ages . . . "[2] Such art can be powerfully influential in providing social symbols, emphasizing types, kindling sympathy and
arousing emotional responses.[3] Rivera's murals in Rockefeller Center
were censored by the owners. "For art is not innocuous; images have
the power to stir men, and beliefs and attitudes may be expressed in
painting and sculpture that would be easily recognized and suppressed
if they were stated in so many words."[4] But the meaning of most
contemporary mural art is easily intelligible, and so, during recent years,
there have been numerous controversies between authorities and artists.
One limitation of a too blatantly propagandist art is that it alienates
and angers the "nonbelievers."

The care with which modern authoritarian rulers are scrutinizing the
pictorial symbols of our day may be indicated by the fact that Mickey
Mouse has been censored in several countries. "Yugoslavia suspects
him of communistic and revolutionary designs, the Soviet thinks he
represents the meekness and mildness of the masses under capitalism,
and has countered by creating a Russian Mickey, known as Yozh, or the
Porcupine, an animal favorite of the Soviet children."[5] Commercial
concerns have used the Mickey Mouse symbol to transfer children's
loyalties to Mickey Mouse clothing, hats, sundaes, and the like. Popular
suspicion is not so evident as is that of political and economic leaders.

The subject matter of contemporary graphic arts changes rapidly
with the increasing tempo of fashion change in thought and theory.

[1] O'Brien, H. V., *Notes for a Book about Mexico*, p. 154, 1937.
[2] Strong, A. L., *I Change Worlds*, p. 244, 1935.
[3] Ross, E. A., *Social Control*, pp. 257 ff., 1901.
[4] Mumford, L., "Social Significance of Contemporary Art," *Soc. Frontier*, December, 1935, p. 77.
[5] Russell, H., "An Inquiry into a Plot of World Wide Scope," *New York Times
Mag.*, Dec. 26, 1937, p. 4.

Sorokin maintains that this is characteristic of all modern visual art. "Since the Visual Art depicts, not the lasting but the passing visual aspect of things, an incessant novelty, change, and variety in its pictures and sculptures are its traits also; otherwise, the same thing becomes sensuously boring, too familiar, devoid of a sense of novelty. The Visual Art must change incessantly; therefore it is and must be an art of mode and fashion and fad; the more variety the more enjoyment."[1]

CHARTS AND GRAPHS

One way of showing the relationships of quantities to one another is to present them in charts and graphs. These are intended to make intelligible at a glance relationships that otherwise would have to be described at great length. Straight-line graphs, cumulative charts, bar charts, maps, circle charts, various designs of comparable size, and the like, are presented to newspaper and magazine readers with increasing frequency. Promoters in various fields use graphs to present information. Advertisers, government bureaus and special interest groups display graphs and charts to the reader or to the audience. If the data are accurate and unbiased, these may be extremely useful tools for transmitting ideas. However, many publics have become far too credulous as to the accuracy of graphic displays. Graphs and charts may be manipulated so as to distort the truth, and interest groups often do so. In addition, it is evident that a fashion element pervades the means of popular pleading and that numerous agencies use graphic methods of presentation because these methods are popular with the expert. Graphs may be used when the data are of such simplicity that they could be adequately stated in a few figures or a few descriptive phrases.

THE CARTOON AND CARICATURE

As the range of values and the variety of human interactions which the artist attempts to portray have increased and as the publics to which he appeals have broadened, popular art forms have become more explicit and expressive. The cartoon and caricature are mediums well suited to the conveying of ideas. The cartoon simply limns the essentials of its subject. As popular conflict has increased, as the variety of topics with which general publics concern themselves have multiplied, self analysis and group analysis have become more evident in the themes of the artist.[2] The modern age of cartoon and caricature has paralleled the controversies and the intellectual ferment of the past two centuries. Prof. Sorokin has described this trend statistically. Referring to the growth of cari-

[1] Sorokin, P. A. *Social and Cultural Dynamics*, vol. I, p. 261, copyright. Quoted by permission of American Book Company.
[2] Bernard, L. L., *Social Psychology*, pp. 471–473, 1926.

cature, he states, "A glance at Table 27 shows that the religious—ancient and medieval—art does not have it at all; that in secular art up to the seventeenth, and for most European countries even up to the eighteenth century, the caricature portrait is practically lacking in the temple of the grand art. It is a satellite of the Sensate mentality. As such it functions as friendly humor, as a weapon in the social and political struggle with opponents and enemies, as 'fun', and so on. Emerging in the seventeenth century, it stays in the field of art with some fluctuation."[1] The modern pictorial artists address large publics on common themes. Daumier said, "One must be of his time," and the modern cartoonist is often not only of his time, but of his day and week.

"The difference between caricature and cartoon is perhaps best suggested by M. H. Spielmann who implies that the caricature has been a weapon of venomous attack, used as an instrument for the manufacture of public opinion, while the cartoon 'has come to be regarded as an humorous or sarcastic comment upon the topic uppermost in the nation's mind.' "[2] The caricature is a subtle exposing of the individual's physical peculiarities or idiosyncrasies of manner, whereas the "cartoon, in the modern sense, is—with or without humor—a forceful presentation by means of exaggeration of a topical political or moral issue."[3] The caricature is an instrument of satirical and sometimes spiteful personal attack. The cartoon is simply a pictorial crystallization of a current thought. The drawing may or may not be humorous. Originally, a cartoon was simply a full-scale drawing to be used as a model for a mural painting or other work of art. In the early 1840's, the English humorous periodical *Punch* labeled some illustrative drawings "cartoons," and the term has been used since that time to designate any drawing that illustrates a social issue. A rigid distinction between cartoon and caricature is not always possible. Often the intention of the artist would have to be the deciding factor, and this is not always evident.

The forerunners of the present-day cartoonist are the caricaturists of the eighteenth and early nineteenth centuries. William Hogarth (1697–1764) was the first of the great English caricaturists. He had many emulators. F. G. Stephens has compiled for the British Museum a catalogue of satirical prints preceding 1770, which contains over 4000 items.[4] During the Hogarth period, caricatures and cartoons were printed, not in newspapers, but on handbills or posters, in booklets and sometimes in magazines. Hogarth drew an amazing number of pictures:

---

[1] Sorokin, *op. cit.*, vol. I, p. 490, copyright. Quoted by permission of American Book Company.

[2] Salmon, L. M., *The Newspaper and the Historian*, p. 389, 1923.

[3] Murrell, W., *A History of American Graphic Humor*, vol. I, p. 4, 1933.

[4] *Graphic Arts* (volume of selected articles from *Ency. Brit.*), p. 17, 1929.

illustrations, moral and satiric commentaries, caricatures and grotesques. There are a number of famous series of pictures: "A Harlot's Progress," "A Rake's Progress," "Marriage à la Mode" and "Industry and Idleness."[1] Hogarth's moral pictures were extremely popular, and, although the number of copies was limited, these vivid, simple pictorial stories were passed around and had great influence upon the moral "climate of opinion" of their day. Hogarth caricatured the great of his day, the political leaders, aristocrats and clergy, as well as thieves, harlots, gamblers, drunkards, musicians, poets, housewives and other types. He portrayed a half century of London life. Following Hogarth, there are two great English cartoonists Thomas Rowlandson (1756–1827) and James Gillray (1757–1815). Their caricature was exceedingly coarse, but it was a vivid commentary on the life of their time. Gillray was the first great political caricaturist. His drawings were of the gutter, and the mob could understand them. His pencil was extremely influential in arousing England against Napoleon, and for years he kept alive the hatred of the English masses.[2] Today, in leafing through a collection of Gillray prints, one is struck by the persistence of the same political and economic problems: militarism, the dictator, recruiting, the problem of the gold standard, the chicanery of leaders, the marriage of convenience, the stupidity of the military, and the like. Gillray, with vitriolic and frequently obscene caricature, portrayed them all. Although modern cartooning stems from these sources, as well as from the French Charles Philipon, "the father of comic journalism," the modern product is, for the most part, tame in comparison. Most modern cartooning is merely illustrative, lacks the personal-attack quality and is largely shorn of coarse obscenity. This is primarily due to the size and diversity of the groups viewing the modern product. It has been necessary to find a common denominator of the inoffensive in the newspaper cartoons. Latterly, some American periodicals are once more purveying vigorous personal caricature.

The cartoonist may effectively use humor. At crisis situations a humorous cartoon may be especially effective in influencing opinions. The laughter provides a welcome release from tensions. At times, the cartoonist plays the role of court jester. But not all modern cartoons are funny. There has been a marked decrease in the number of humorous cartoons since 1900. Laughter varies greatly from period to period, and humor is an infinitely varied and subtle element in culture. It is often difficult thoroughly to understand the humorous cartoons and caricatures

---

[1] For a description of the separate plates of the series, see Bowen, M., *William Hogarth*, pp. 121–184, 1935.

[2] Berryman, C. K., "Development of the Cartoon," University of Missouri Bulletin, Journalism Series, No. 41, 1926.

of a past age. Used effectively, humor is one of the greatest appeals of the cartoonist. However, the contemporary cartoonist is facing ever greater difficulty in utilizing humor for some of the political and economic topics that he is called upon to illustrate.

THE CARTOON IN THE UNITED STATES

Although cartoons are widely used in controversial discussion in England and on the Continent, the political cartoon has been more generally used in the United States than in any other country. One of the earliest American cartoons was produced by Franklin, who, "urging the colonies to unite against their common foe, published in the *Pennsylvania Gazette*, May 9, 1754, the famous snake cartoon. This wood block depicted a snake cut into eight pieces presumably representing the colonial divisions then eligible to send delegates to the Albany Congress. . . . The caption was 'Join or Die.' "[1] There were a few cartoons during the period of the War of 1812, but "the 'Era of Good Feeling' which followed the War of 1812 was marked by an almost complete dearth of cartoons. Controversy is the cartoonist's staff of life; he starves in times of brotherly love."[2] During the 1830's and 1840's, there was a slow growth of illustrative humorous drawing which was a kind of graphic reporting, providing commentaries on American customs. Some of the best work came from abroad. A. Hervieu illustrated Mrs. Trollope's *Domestic Manners of the Americans* (1832) with a series of drawings of Uncle Sam in his shirt sleeves, elevating his feet when seated, spitting, etc.[3] Whittling, tobacco-chewing, hands-in-pockets, lounging rural dwellers were mildly ridiculed. Clothing styles were commented on. The elaborate boot fashions of the women of the 1850's, bloomers and crinolines were caricatured. The large skirts were depicted as sweeping the streets, as having utility in protecting children during showers or as saving the wearer from drowning.[4] However, we may note that the political controversy of the thirty years preceding the Civil War produced very little significant cartoon art. The cartoons of this period were issued separately as engravings or lithographs. During the pre-Civil-War period there were some propaganda cartoons, notably those produced during the 1840's for the Washingtonians, a temperance organization.[5] The various representations of the drunkard's progress from the first glass to the grave were no doubt influential in affecting youths' opinions on temperance.

---

[1] Johnson, I. S., "Cartoons," *Pub. Opin. Quar.*, 1: 3: 33.

[2] *Ibid.*, p. 35.

[3] Weitenkampf, F., "Social History of the United States in Caricature," *Critic*, 47: 136.

[4] *Ibid.*, p. 137.

[5] *New York Times Mag.*, pp. 10 *ff.*, Dec. 7, 1930.

The Civil War period was not especially prolific in cartoon pictures, although there are a considerable number that deal with the problems of enlistment and of war profiteering, with army contractors and conditions of camp and field and that caricature prominent persons. Thomas Nast was a boy of twenty-one when the war started, but by the end of the war he had produced so many effective cartoons that Abraham Lincoln said, "Thomas Nast has been our best recruiting sergeant."[1] It was during this period that the cartoon appeared in the periodicals. "During the 1860's and 70's the cartoon in this separate form began to disappear. Cartoons then became an eagerly awaited feature of the illustrated magazines such as *Harper's Weekly, Frank Leslie's, Vanity Fair, Puck, Judge,* and the *Wasp.*"[2]

The first great period of American cartooning began in the early 1870's. The "Tweed Ring" was in control of New York City. In *Harper's Weekly,* Thomas Nast began a series of vitriolic attacks upon Boss Tweed and his lieutenants. These were extremely effective in arousing opinion against the ring, and Thomas Nast has been credited by historians as the major force that started the campaign which led to the exposure and disgrace of the ring. During 1871, Thomas Nast was paid $8000 for his pictures, but it is said that he was offered bribes of a hundred times that amount to desist from his drawing.[3] It was during the 1870's that Nast produced the principal symbols of our political cartooning. The cartoon in which the elephant first appeared as an emblem of the Republican party was drawn by Nast in 1874. Three years before that he had produced the Tammany tiger. Nast tried the figures of a tiger, of a fox, and of a wolf for the Democratic party, but none of them caught the public fancy. He had used the donkey as a symbol for certain Democratic politicians as early as 1869. But Nast did not consistently use the donkey in this role. "It is not at all certain that Nast deserves the credit for enlisting the donkey permanently in the Democratic ranks, though one of his cartoons, published early in 1878, was probably the first in which the elephant and the donkey appeared in the same cartoon to signify the two major parties."[4] These animals evolved and became eloquently expressive. Other animals appeared as symbols— the American eagle, the bull moose of Theodore Roosevelt's day, the goat of the Populist party and many others.

An increasing stream of pictorial commentary on social life and customs in the United States was produced during the last thirty years of the nineteenth century. There were many cartoons dealing with

[1] Paine, A. B., *Thomas Nast,* p. 69, 1904.
[2] Johnson, *op. cit.,* p. 35.
[3] Paine, *op. cit.,* p. 206.
[4] *New York Times Mag.,* Nov. 27, 1932, p. 9.

fashionable life, the aping of English customs, the problems of urbanization and life in the crowded quarters of the "flat" and the boarding house, speed and recklessness on bicycles, a steady output of commentary on styles, fads, fashions, and the like.

The second great period of American cartooning was from 1900 to 1910. This was a time of social reform—the era of the muckrakers, the "trust-busting" days of Theodore Roosevelt. In that period a number of skillful cartoonists, notably Homer Davenport, F. B. Opper, Floyd Campbell and DeMar were enlisted on the side of reform. Their work had vigor as they were motivated by an aggressive zeal. Davenport developed the symbol of the trusts, that huge, overgrown, monstrosity of a man bulging in all directions. Opper was a master of humorous interpretation. Floyd Campbell was the terror of the corrupt ring of Philadelphia. DeMar was a master caricaturist. Many leaders writhed under the skillful attacks of these artists. It was the heyday of baiting. The plight of certain economic leaders, notably J. D. Rockefeller, was not enviable. "The cartoonists, or the knights of brush and pencil, whose brains are dedicated to righting the wrongs of the age and the merciless unmasking of the enemies of society, are today among the foremost influences battling for the overthrow of the ring, the machine and the corruptionists, who have impaired municipal and national integrity, and brought shame and dishonor on the great republic."[1] During this period, Theodore Roosevelt and the issues that he personalized provided a veritable field day for the cartoonist.

After 1910, vigorous personal attacks in the cartoons declined. The cartoon was syndicated. W. R. Hearst made much of drawings in his string of papers, and outside papers sought to buy the output of his cartoonists and comic artists. A syndicate was started. Then others were formed, and by 1925 there were at least fifty organizations offering syndicated material to the papers. All newspapers used such material. "The syndicate, having to serve all sorts of papers in all sorts of communities has softened the attack quality in most of this product so that the result has been a more or less negative, qualified picture which is guaranteed to offend no one and therefore has lost most of its pungency. Lacking that virility, it has come to be simply a thing of entertainment."[2]

As the interpretations of the social process maintained by intelligent men became somewhat less simple and explicit, the cartoonist, among other interpreters, was often aware of complexities. Abstract and complex economic problems were difficult to portray simply. The election

[1] Flower, B. O., "Floyd Campbell: A Knight of Municipal Honor," *Arena*, 34: 372 (1905).

[2] Shaffer, L. F., *Children's Interpretations of Cartoons*, Teachers College Contributions to Education, No. 429, p. 3, 1930.

of 1932 was a low point of effective cartoon interpretation. The average cartoonist was largely thwarted by the gold standard, war debts, a balanced budget, credit inflation, change, etc.[1] But the quality of cartooning has been improved during the last few years as the lines of controversy have become more clearly drawn.

In Table XIX on Cartoon Symbol Types some data on the trends of cartoon symbols from 1900 to 1935 are presented. Some eighty or more cartoons from each of four or five metropolitan dailies for each year of the period are analyzed. Space does not permit either an extensive description of the methods of selection or classification or analysis of results.

COMIC STRIPS

During the later half of the nineteenth century, various series of humorous drawings began to appear in the back pages of American magazines. But it was well toward the close of the century before the now popular "comic strip" was presented in the newspaper. *"The New York Daily News* used one of the first comic strips in its special Saturday edition of August 16, 1884. It presented a humorous situation in six pictures. . . . On November 18, 1894, then, the *New York World* printed the first colored Sunday comic, the product of R. F. Outcault."[2] In 1895, W. R. Hearst hired Outcault, and the regular production of comic strips was established. The theme of the early strips, the Yellow Kid, Katzenjammer Kids, Buster Brown, and Captain and the Kids, was primarily the playing of practical jokes of a crude slapstick variety. These picture comics were indigenous to America, bearing little resemblance to anything in the European tradition. They became popular very rapidly and are now regularly read by some twenty to thirty million people.

There have been many types of strips, offering slapstick comedy, satire on manners and customs, trenchant commentary on daily life, popular philosophy and dealing with local-color types, occupational groups, nationality and racial characteristics; lately we have had those strips which are simply little pictured continued stories. At what points have these comics been most influential in molding popular opinion? There is very little of direct political commentary. Also, there has been very little direct advocacy of economic doctrine or practice. The exception to this is the use of the comics for the advertising of economic goods since 1931. However, indirectly, these popular pictures must have been enormously effective in modifying opinions and creating stereotypes. The diversified national backgrounds of Americans have led to a wide-

---

[1] There is a description of the most significant 1932 cartoons in *Time*, Oct. 24, 1932, pp. 25–32.

[2] Lee, *op. cit.*, p. 401.

TABLE XIX.—CARTOON
(Trends in cartoon symbols in five metropolitan daily newspapers expressed

	1900	1901	1902	1903	1904	1905	1906	1907	1908	1909	1910	1911	1912
Number of papers	2	2	2	1	1	1	1	1	1	4	5	5	5
Number of cartoons, average per paper	84.5	83.0	80.5	57.0	84.0	84.0	84.0	84.0	84.0	66.7	68.8	84.0	77.8
Percentage for	4.1	4.7	11.9	7.0	2.4	5.9	0.0	2.4	15.5	4.1	4.6	6.9	12.0
Percentage against	25.8	27.4	13.7	7.0	3.6	21.4	17.9	1.2	22.6	4.6	18.6	15.0	13.3
Percentage illustrative	70.0	67.8	74.4	86.0	94.1	72.6	82.1	96.4	61.9	90.8	76.9	78.1	74.7
Average number of symbols per cartoon	4.1	4.3	4.6	6.2	5.8	5.9	5.7	3.4	4.5	4.6	4.5	5.3	5.0
Average number of symbols labeled	2.6	2.7	3.6	3.4	3.0	3.0	1.7	1.5	2.4	2.3	2.7	3.0	2.9
Percentage of cartoons in which no symbols labeled	23.5	17.5	8.0	26.3	21.4	15.5	43.9	45.2	17.9	23.0	25.2	30.0	17.1
Percentage of cartoons in which loops were used	2.9	9.1	21.1	28.0	17.9	7.1	14.3	26.2	38.1	30.7	26.0	35.7	40.7
Average number of loops used	2.5	1.1	1.1	3.6	2.2	1.5	1.0	3.7	3.5	2.7	2.4	2.4	1.8
Percentage of cartoons made up of series of pictures	1.1	3.6	1.8	50.0	34.5	21.4	22.6	44.0	35.7	6.4	11.2	14.3	12.3
Average number of pictures in series	2.5	2.9	1.0	4.0	3.6	3.1	2.9	4.0	4.2	3.4	3.6	3.6	1.7
Symbol types:													
1. Personal symbols—Totals, %	44.3	43.9	45.1	49.3	60.6	55.7	49.5	64.8	67.4	48.5	55.4	53.0	53.9
For group, party, etc.	8.8	14.4	13.4	32.6	29.8	23.3	31.6	48.9	20.4	20.3	16.6	25.9	20.6
Anonymous (Boy	0.0	0.1	0.0	1.1	0.0	0.8	0.0	0.0	0.0	1.3	1.1	0.7	0.1
Man	0.7	0.5	0.1	4.5	1.0	4.1	0.0	0.3	2.1	4.9	7.9	3.3	1.3
Girl	0.0	0.0	0.1	0.6	0.2	0.4	0.0	0.3	0.3	0.0	0.0	0.1	0.0
Woman	0.0	0.6	0.1	0.0	0.4	0.6	0.2	0.7	0.5	1.5	2.3	1.5	0.6
Crowd	0.0	0.3	0.4	0.0	0.0	0.6	0.0	0.3	0.0	1.4	1.8	0.7	0.2
For country or other governmental unit	8.1	8.4	9.0	0.8	4.7	5.9	0.8	2.1	1.6	3.7	2.8	5.3	4.3
For abstract quality	2.5	2.6	3.8	0.3	2.0	2.0	4.8	2.4	0.8	5.6	3.9	3.9	4.1
Personalized animate being	0.0	0.3	2.0	0.0	0.4	0.0	0.2	0.0	0.5	0.0	0.1	0.3	0.0
Some recognizable or labeled person	23.2	16.6	15.3	8.8	21.7	16.8	10.2	9.8	39.4	9.5	17.8	10.8	22.0
Miscellaneous	1.0	0.1	0.9	0.6	0.0	1.2	1.7	0.0	1.8	0.4	1.1	0.5	0.7
2. Animals as symbols—Totals, %	7.9	6.3	5.7	7.7	1.8	2.4	4.7	2.0	3.2	3.7	4.5	3.7	5.1
For nation	1.5	0.5	0.6	0.0	0.0	0.4	0.2	0.0	0.0	0.1	0.1	0.2	0.2
For political party	1.9	0.0	1.2	0.6	0.0	0.0	0.4	0.7	1.8	0.2	2.0	0.6	2.6
For other special group	2.7	3.8	0.2	5.7	0.0	0.2	0.0	0.0	0.3	0.2	0.4	0.4	0.6
For abstract quality	1.7	0.4	0.7	0.0	0.4	0.6	0.6	0.3	0.0	1.1	0.3	0.9	1.2
Miscellaneous	0.1	1.6	3.0	1.4	1.4	1.2	3.5	1.0	1.1	2.1	1.7	1.6	0.5
3. Objects as symbols—Totals, %	41.3	40.9	42.0	38.9	32.6	39.4	42.0	30.8	26.9	43.5	36.5	40.1	37.7
Buildings	3.6	3.6	3.0	8.5	5.9	3.9	7.5	4.5	5.0	4.8	3.8	5.4	3.4
Roadways	0.0	1.2	1.5	0.0	0.0	0.4	0.4	0.7	0.5	0.4	0.1	0.3	0.8
Containers	2.2	3.4	1.5	2.0	0.8	0.0	2.3	0.0	1.1	4.0	2.6	3.2	3.2
Weapons, clubs, missiles, etc	4.3	3.2	3.1	2.8	1.4	3.6	1.9	1.0	3.2	0.9	0.8	3.4	1.9
Scrolls, documents, etc	3.0	2.8	4.7	5.1	4.7	6.3	4.4	10.1	5.0	8.2	8.3	6.1	8.4
Vehicles	2.2	3.4	1.4	2.0	3.2	1.2	3.5	3.5	1.1	4.7	2.8	3.0	1.8
Money	0.7	0.9	1.0	0.0	1.4	0.6	0.6	1.0	0.5	0.7	0.8	0.7	0.7
Pictures	0.9	0.5	0.2	0.3	1.4	0.6	0.2	0.0	0.5	0.5	0.8	0.5	0.4
Flags	1.1	1.2	1.9	0.3	0.4	0.6	0.0	0.0	0.0	1.5	1.0	0.4	0.4
Furniture	1.5	0.9	0.0	0.0	1.2	1.4	1.9	0.0	2.6	1.4	0.8	1.5	0.7
Articles of clothing	0.9	1.1	0.2	0.3	1.4	0.4	1.9	0.3	0.5	0.7	0.3	1.0	2.0
Food	0.9	0.2	0.5	0.6	1.2	0.4	1.2	0.3	0.5	0.9	0.6	1.2	0.6
Writing equipment	0.0	0.1	0.0	0.0	0.2	0.4	0.4	0.0	0.3	0.2	0.2	0.2	0.1
Boundaries (fences, lines, etc.)	0.6	1.0	0.4	0.0	0.0	0.2	1.2	0.0	0.5	0.2	0.2	0.8	0.9
Signs	6.1	6.2	3.6	8.8	4.3	9.9	9.4	2.4	0.5	5.1	4.8	4.0	3.5
Miscellaneous	13.3	11.2	19.0	8.2	5.1	9.5	5.2	7.0	5.6	9.3	8.6	8.4	8.9
4. Nature symbols—Totals, %	6.0	8.5	6.7	4.3	4.3	2.0	3.4	1.6	1.9	3.8	2.1	3.0	3.2
Trees	0.6	0.5	0.2	0.6	0.0	0.0	0.8	0.0	0.0	0.2	0.1	0.3	0.2
Rocks	0.4	0.7	0.0	0.0	0.2	0.0	0.2	0.0	0.0	0.1	0.2	0.1	0.1
Water	1.2	3.5	1.0	0.6	0.4	0.0	1.2	1.0	0.8	1.0	0.1	1.0	0.5
Hill	0.0	0.2	0.5	0.3	0.8	0.6	0.2	0.3	0.0	0.2	0.1	0.2	0.3
Wind	0.0	0.2	0.3	0.0	0.0	0.0	0.2	0.3	0.8	0.0	0.0	0.0	0.3
Vegetation	0.3	0.3	1.4	0.0	0.0	0.8	0.8	0.0	0.3	0.2	0.3	0.4	0.2
Miscellaneous	3.5	3.1	3.3	2.8	2.9	0.6	0.0	0.0	0.0	2.1	1.3	1.0	1.6

SYMBOL TYPES
in percentages of the total number of cartoon symbols examined for each year)

1913	1914	1915	1916	1917	1918	1919	1920	1921	1922	1923	1924	1925	1926	1927	1928	1929	1930	1931	1932	1933	1934	1935
5	5	5	4	4	5	5	5	5	4	4	4	4	5	5	5	5	5	5	5	5	5	5
82.2	80.2	76.6	84.0	84.0	84.0	81.2	77.6	78.4	83.5	84.0	84.0	82.2	83.6	82.4	83.8	84.0	84.0	84.0	84.0	84.0	84.0	79.8
12.6	4.6	8.6	6.8	15.8	12.6	14.2	9.3	16.2	5.7	4.5	9.8	11.7	12.9	6.0	5.7	8.1	4.8	11.7	6.4	11.9	10.5	3.1
12.2	11.1	14.4	29.2	28.3	30.2	18.8	17.8	41.2	20.4	15.5	18.4	20.8	22.6	17.9	16.9	18.8	21.9	18.1	30.5	25.9	38.1	59.8
75.2	84.3	76.8	63.9	55.9	57.1	67.0	72.8	42.6	73.8	80.1	71.5	67.5	64.5	76.2	77.4	72.9	73.3	70.2	63.1	62.1	51.4	37.0
3.9	4.4	3.9	4.6	5.1	6.0	4.8	6.7	5.4	6.2	6.2	6.5	4.4	4.8	5.1	5.7	4.9	5.3	4.3	5.3	5.2	4.2	5.9
2.2	2.7	2.4	2.2	2.6	3.4	3.5	4.6	2.9	3.8	4.1	4.3	3.1	3.5	3.6	3.8	3.3	4.0	3.1	3.8	3.8	3.2	3.8
15.3	19.9	18.2	26.5	15.8	14.5	8.5	6.6	12.9	5.4	7.4	5.6	12.0	7.9	9.9	4.5	8.1	7.4	7.1	5.7	5.5	4.5	3.5
53.8	38.8	33.4	38.1	40.8	28.1	46.8	48.5	42.1	44.6	44.0	45.5	39.9	52.6	55.5	50.4	47.6	58.1	46.9	46.7	48.1	55.2	48.4
1.8	1.8	1.5	2.0	1.9	1.5	1.9	2.0	1.7	1.9	2.3	1.9	1.4	1.8	1.7	1.5	1.6	1.9	1.9	1.5	1.8	1.7	1.6
18.3	11.5	12.7	14.9	14.3	12.9	17.7	22.6	17.0	14.4	13.9	17.6	9.8	18.3	20.2	10.2	16.1	15.5	17.1	13.6	12.1	13.3	5.1
2.3	3.0	3.3	3.5	3.4	3.1	2.9	3.0	2.9	2.4	3.2	3.0	3.3	2.8	2.7	2.6	3.4	2.8	2.8	2.9	2.6	2.9	3.3
58.2	53.5	48.9	49.8	55.4	49.0	55.0	56.0	56.1	48.8	52.6	48.5	51.7	51.3	49.5	46.2	47.9	50.0	52.8	46.9	50.6	49.4	38.0
25.0	18.3	14.8	21.0	18.2	17.2	18.1	20.6	23.4	17.6	21.2	19.3	25.8	24.6	18.7	19.0	19.3	15.0	21.8	20.4	17.5	22.4	21.2
1.1	0.3	0.9	0.0	0.7	0.1	0.3	0.2	0.6	0.7	0.4	0.1	0.1	0.0	0.2	0.4	0.1	0.5	0.7	0.0	0.2	0.3	0.0
2.2	2.3	1.8	0.2	2.2	0.3	1.3	0.8	0.8	1.2	1.2	1.2	1.3	0.3	1.7	1.0	1.5	2.4	1.0	0.3	0.8	0.5	0.6
0.3	0.2	0.1	0.0	0.1	0.0	0.0	0.0	0.0	0.1	0.2	0.1	0.0	0.0	0.1	0.0	0.0	0.0	0.0	0.0	0.0	0.0	0.0
1.1	0.6	0.6	0.0	0.7	0.2	0.4	0.2	0.4	0.6	0.6	0.2	0.2	0.2	0.6	0.4	0.6	0.4	0.2	0.0	0.4	0.2	0.1
0.1	1.6	0.1	0.0	0.3	0.0	1.7	1.1	0.2	0.6	0.2	0.7	0.0	0.1	1.8	0.1	0.5	1.7	2.0	0.0	0.1	0.4	0.0
7.7	11.2	14.6	9.4	17.8	12.1	13.1	8.2	11.6	11.7	9.3	7.2	8.0	8.0	8.0	6.6	8.7	10.8	8.6	7.0	10.8	8.7	3.6
5.8	7.2	6.2	6.6	5.9	8.3	13.1	7.1	10.6	8.9	9.9	8.9	8.6	11.4	7.7	8.6	8.8	10.2	10.6	9.3	13.1	8.6	6.7
0.2	0.0	0.1	0.3	0.3	0.1	0.2	0.3	0.7	0.1	0.9	0.0	0.3	0.1	0.8	0.0	0.4	0.1	0.4	0.3	0.6	1.4	0.2
13.9	10.7	9.4	12.1	7.9	10.1	5.5	16.8	6.9	6.4	8.2	9.7	6.6	5.5	8.1	8.6	5.9	8.2	6.5	9.3	5.7	5.4	5.5
0.8	1.1	0.3	0.2	1.3	0.6	1.3	0.7	0.9	0.9	0.5	1.1	0.8	1.1	1.8	1.5	2.2	0.7	0.9	0.3	1.4	1.5	0.1
4.5	3.9	5.8	4.6	4.0	5.7	4.7	8.5	5.1	6.2	6.7	6.3	5.8	5.8	6.7	9.6	6.0	8.5	9.6	10.4	7.9	9.7	7.2
0.1	0.5	1.2	0.7	0.8	1.2	0.6	0.1	0.2	0.4	1.3	0.3	0.4	0.2	0.3	0.1	0.4	0.8	0.3	0.3	0.2	0.4	0.0
0.5	0.2	0.7	1.5	0.1	0.2	0.8	3.6	1.2	0.6	1.7	2.2	1.0	1.9	2.4	5.1	0.9	2.4	2.8	4.2	1.0	1.8	1.4
1.3	1.1	2.0	0.2	0.2	0.5	0.7	0.6	0.2	0.9	0.4	0.3	0.9	0.7	1.2	1.0	1.0	1.3	1.0	1.1	0.8	1.3	1.1
1.0	1.3	1.2	1.0	2.1	2.5	1.9	3.3	2.7	3.6	2.3	2.6	2.1	1.9	1.5	1.5	2.3	2.6	3.1	3.2	4.0	4.6	3.6
1.6	0.8	0.7	1.2	0.8	1.3	0.7	0.9	0.7	1.0	0.9	1.4	1.1	1.3	1.9	1.5	1.4	2.4	1.6	1.9	1.6	1.6	1.1
34.0	40.1	39.7	42.2	37.4	41.5	36.5	30.8	35.1	38.8	35.2	40.3	37.1	36.9	38.8	39.2	40.9	35.8	31.0	36.3	36.2	36.3	46.8
4.3	3.0	3.5	3.2	2.7	2.3	3.7	3.0	4.4	4.0	3.9	3.8	4.3	4.7	3.0	3.4	4.4	3.3	3.2	4.5	3.0	3.0	5.0
0.9	0.4	0.7	0.5	0.1	0.3	0.5	0.3	1.3	0.7	1.0	0.4	1.1	0.9	0.3	1.0	0.5	0.7	1.3	0.7	0.3	0.4	1.4
2.5	2.4	2.6	2.8	3.4	3.3	3.0	2.5	2.7	4.6	3.3	4.2	3.0	3.7	2.7	4.0	2.0	2.6	2.7	5.3	3.7	3.4	4.4
1.5	3.2	2.9	3.9	3.1	5.6	2.0	0.9	2.6	2.1	1.3	2.3	3.0	1.6	2.5	1.3	1.5	2.2	1.4	2.3	2.6	2.1	2.6
6.9	7.8	6.8	7.0	6.4	5.6	5.9	3.5	4.2	4.6	3.6	4.7	4.4	4.1	5.6	5.2	6.0	6.2	3.5	4.1	3.4	4.0	5.2
3.8	2.3	4.2	3.1	2.0	3.1	2.1	3.3	3.8	3.6	4.5	4.1	4.9	3.7	3.5	3.3	4.6	3.2	4.2	3.3	2.8	2.9	3.5
1.3	1.0	0.8	0.3	0.7	0.8	1.0	1.1	0.8	0.8	0.7	0.7	1.6	0.9	0.6	0.7	1.4	0.5	1.1	1.2	1.2	1.6	0.8
0.1	0.8	0.3	0.6	0.4	0.5	0.4	0.3	0.6	0.4	0.7	0.4	0.5	0.2	0.7	0.4	1.0	0.3	0.2	0.9	0.3	0.5	0.5
0.2	0.8	1.8	2.2	3.1	1.9	0.7	0.9	0.3	0.5	0.4	0.6	0.3	0.4	0.5	0.9	0.5	0.6	0.3	0.4	0.9	1.1	0.7
0.4	0.3	1.6	1.5	1.5	1.0	1.2	0.9	1.5	1.2	0.8	1.2	0.9	0.6	0.6	1.2	0.9	0.8	0.7	0.9	0.6	0.8	1.4
1.5	0.6	0.9	1.3	1.7	0.9	1.0	0.2	1.4	1.4	1.2	1.3	0.2	0.5	1.0	1.9	1.2	0.6	0.5	0.5	0.5	0.7	0.6
1.0	1.1	0.8	0.3	1.6	1.4	0.7	1.0	1.4	0.6	0.4	0.5	0.7	1.6	1.3	0.9	1.0	0.7	1.0	0.7	0.1	1.1	0.9
0.1	0.2	0.1	0.1	0.1	0.2	0.1	0.1	0.0	0.1	0.0	0.1	0.0	0.2	0.2	0.1	0.2	0.0	0.0	0.2	0.1	0.1	0.3
0.3	0.1	0.8	0.7	0.3	0.4	0.5	1.0	0.6	0.9	0.7	0.2	0.8	1.1	0.3	1.0	0.6	0.5	0.3	0.6	1.0	1.4	1.2
1.8	4.0	3.5	3.2	2.6	4.6	3.3	4.4	3.7	3.1	3.2	4.5	1.7	1.7	5.1	4.0	4.5	4.3	2.0	3.0	3.6	3.8	4.6
7.4	12.1	8.4	11.5	7.7	9.2	10.4	7.4	5.8	10.3	9.5	11.3	9.7	11.0	10.9	9.9	10.6	9.3	8.6	7.7	12.1	9.4	13.7
3.0	2.3	5.5	3.6	3.4	3.3	3.6	3.8	3.9	6.1	6.0	4.5	5.3	6.0	4.9	5.0	4.6	5.5	6.6	5.7	4.8	5.4	7.7
0.0	0.0	0.2	0.1	1.0	0.6	0.4	0.3	0.3	0.3	0.4	0.4	0.5	0.7	0.6	0.4	0.7	1.3	0.7	0.9	0.4	0.6	0.5
0.1	0.1	0.6	0.0	0.2	0.2	0.4	0.5	0.0	0.9	0.8	1.2	0.5	0.3	0.3	0.5	0.1	0.6	0.2	0.6	0.4	0.2	0.4
0.5	0.5	1.6	1.4	0.7	1.2	0.7	0.7	0.9	1.6	1.4	1.3	1.6	1.2	1.1	1.6	0.8	1.6	1.4	1.8	1.4	0.8	2.2
0.2	0.1	0.1	0.3	0.2	0.5	0.5	0.8	0.5	0.3	0.5	0.4	0.5	0.9	0.3	0.2	0.1	0.3	0.3	0.2	0.4	0.7	0.5
0.3	0.0	0.1	0.0	0.1	0.0	0.0	0.0	0.3	0.0	0.0	0.1	0.0	0.1	0.2	0.0	0.1	0.2	0.0	0.0	0.1	0.6	0.0
0.4	0.5	0.4	0.4	0.2	0.1	0.2	0.6	0.4	0.3	0.4	0.4	0.4	0.5	0.7	0.3	0.2	0.5	0.4	0.5	0.4	0.8	0.3
1.5	1.1	2.5	1.4	1.0	1.1	1.4	0.9	1.5	2.7	2.5	0.7	1.8	2.3	1.7	2.0	2.6	1.0	3.6	1.7	1.7	1.7	3.8

spread interest in national characteristics. National types were presented in the comics in such strips as "The Katzenjammer Kids," "Mr. Jiggs," "Abie the Agent," "Alphonse and Gaston," and many others. Economic standards were portrayed in the mishaps of the newly rich (Jiggs), in the economic objectives of the stenographer, in the tramplike ingenuity of roomers and adventurers (the Hall-room Boys), in the successful inventive genius of several characters, and the like. Standards as between parents and children, husband and wife, male and female are constantly portrayed. Of F. Opper's drawings, it is said "The husbands he pictures never have the strength or even the willingness, to stand firm against the seductions of actresses and chorus ladies. He has never shown us a male eye that could remain undistracted by the ample beauties of the bathing girls he can draw so well."[1] There are ethical values portrayed in funny-paper philosophy, notably in R. L. Goldberg's "Boob McNutt," "Life's Little Jokes," "It's All Wrong, Alf," or in Briggs's "Ain't It a Grand and Glorious Feeling." Lately, since the comic strip has come to be devoted so largely to purveying pictured stories, often not humorous, the range of stereotypes acquired from them has widened. Children's ideas of life in the jungle, life on Mars, life in the twenty-fifth century, life as a gangster or a detective, and so on, must have been influenced by these pictures. However, thus far, the influence of the comics has not been carefully studied.

There are over 300 comic strips now appearing in American newspapers. Every sizable newspaper, except the *New York Times* and the *Christian Science Monitor*, runs at least a page of them daily. There are many syndicates distributing this pictorial product. International distribution is increasing. Pearson and Allen recently stated, "Seldom weighed in the scales of Pan-Americanism is the bond made by the comic strips. Well-known U. S. comics are syndicated in South American countries under various Spanish names."

The Poster

A publicly exhibited printed, written or illustrated announcement is a poster. The most widespread contemporary use of posters is in economic advertising and in political announcements and propaganda. Although poster publicity is an ancient art, such announcements in the form of wall paintings and mural decorations having been used by the Egyptians at least 5000 years ago, the modern versions began in France in 1867.[2] "The poster, as it is known today did not exist in the United States previous to 1889, except for the theatrical and circus posters made

---

[1] Brennecke, E., "The Real Mission of the Funny Paper," *Century*, 107: 5: 670.
[2] *Graphic Arts*, p. 34.

by Matt Morgan."[1]   The earliest posters used here advertised magazines and books.   In the 1890's, business groups began to use the poster for advertising consumers' goods.   In the World War period, posters were widely used to stimulate recruiting.   There are a number of collections of World War posters from various nations in American libraries, notably the collection in the Princeton University Library.   It would be interesting to classify the types of appeal used in the various campaigns. Since the war, the authoritarian states of Europe have made extensive use of the poster in various publicity campaigns.   Soviet Russia has carried on literally hundreds of poster campaigns for increased industrial efficiency, for farm programs, for the creation of popular stereotypes about other nationality groups, for the army, for aviation, for health programs, for education, for organizing opposition to the priests, and the like.   The poster is especially well adapted to the distribution of appeals to a semiliterate population, in the absence of other adequate means of communication.   There are no unique psychological principles involved in the construction of or in the types of appeals used in the poster.   It is merely another channel for modern organized communication.

PHOTOGRAPHS

"Photographs have the kind of authority over imagination today, which the printed word had yesterday, and the spoken word before that. They seem utterly real.   They come, we imagine, directly to us without human meddling, and they are the most effortless food for the mind conceivable."[2]   Photographs do seem real, often more so than the cartoon which is obviously the artist's product.   But the photograph as purveyed by newspaper or periodical today does not come to us without human meddling.   Pictures are published every day that tell untrue stories.   A public convinced that the camera does not lie is in a credulous state.   First, there is the process of selection.   In taking numerous pictures of public men, especially with small cameras, it is possible to get a wide variety of expression.   The publisher then selects that negative which most nearly fits the impression he desires to convey.   This is done constantly, but the most notorious and most publicized instance was a photograph of President Roosevelt.   On the President's fifty-fourth birthday the photographers were admitted and snapped many pictures. When the cameramen appeared to be finished, the President relaxed and rubbed his eyes, strained by the numerous flashes from magnesium bulbs. One cameraman took another photograph in which the President then appeared as a tired and discouraged man.   The photograph was captioned "Pensive President Ponders Problems," and the accompanying account

[1] *Ibid.*, p. 34.
[2] Lippmann, *op. cit.*, p. 92.

reported that this photograph was taken shortly after he had conferred with Secretary Wallace about the AAA. After that incident the photographers were requested to use cameras on tripods, so that photographs might be posed.

There is the selection of individuals as representatives of groups, so as to create popular impressions. In the newspaper photography dealing with Townsend conventions, Prohibition conventions, labor meetings, and the like, the leaders photographed are not necessarily typical of their groups but may have been selected because they have certain physical characteristics that identify them in the reader's mind with the "lunatic fringe." In the English coronation proceedings, the photographers were warned not to take any "unseemly or untoward" pictures. One anonymous picture has recently been widely circulated in the South. It is an enlarged flashlight of J. L. Lewis and Associate Justice Hugo Black. The caption intimates that they are intimate friends. Actually the photograph was taken at a Senate hearing, and the others appearing in the picture have been blacked out. These are instances of selection.

Then, there is intentional distortion. Any competent news cameraman can caricature anyone by getting the right angles. But caricatures can also be made from an ordinary negative by tilting the enlarging easel. Negatives can be retouched in various ways. There are the instances of outright fabrication of pictures. This became very common in the early 1920's in connection with the rise of the tabloids. Certainly the methods of creating illusions by pictures exist. And certainly popular opinion has been extensively influenced by selected, distorted or fabricated pictures. Persons constantly in the public eye have some recourse. They can retaliate upon the offending cameraman in various ways, by refusing to pose, by discriminating against him, by personal violence. Or they may partially correct one bad impression by other pictures. This problem of the impressions created by photographs is becoming acute. G. Seldes has suggested a law containing the following regulations: (1) no pictures to be used without consent of the subject except photographs taken at public meetings or where the subject has voluntarily put himself in the public eye; (2) surreptitious candid-camera pictures not taken in public meetings to be actionable; (3) no picture to be changed or faked without the consent of the subject.[1] However, though it might be possible to eliminate some of the gravest personal abuses by law, the public personage would remain at the mercy of the photographer under most situations. Legal restrictions would be difficult to formulate and to enforce. The intent of the photographer is crucial.

This problem of selective impressions by photography will become very much more involved with the popularization of television. A short

[1] Smith, H. L., "The News Camera on Trial," *Forum*, 98: 270.

time ago the first television cameraman photographing outside the studio shocked the people in the studio by sending back a picture of a suicide falling six stories. Imagine what a cameraman could do by a selective broadcast of a riot, a battle, a political meeting, a public event. Obviously, the intent of those in control of these potent means of communication becomes all important.

CHAPTER XXIII

PUBLIC OPINION AND REALITY

We have considered the nature of opinion and have indicated something of the opinion process. Opinion—expression on a controversial point—and beliefs have been related to the processes of communication. Communication may distort the transmitted material, because of the psychological processes of individuals, because of the nature and limitations of the systems of communication or because of selective influences, as when special interest groups censor and propagandize. However incomplete the data supplied to members of groups, group opinions are formed, after a process of interaction, on controversial issues. And the number of issues on which the common man is expected to express opinions has increased as the attention areas of modern man have been widened by communication. Furthermore, the opinions of the members of large publics are increasingly solicited, and there are extensive attempts to manipulate those opinions. How do these popular opinions relate to reality?

"Reality" is one of those concepts which, like progress, has been variously defined, depending upon the frame of reference of the theorist. The nature of reality is a fundamental metaphysical problem. It is a very old philosophical problem. Plato and Aristotle posed the problem, and the most famous philosophical dispute of the Middle Ages concerned nominalism-realism. The scholastic doctrine maintained that universals had a more real existence than things. We are not concerned here with the metaphysical problem of ultimate reality. But we may note briefly some of the concepts of reality posited by various types of theorists.

"The original intention of the term realism is to assert the existence of real things as opposed to the products of the mind; which, in so far as they are fancies and imaginations, are considered not to be real things."[1] From one viewpoint the real things are the objects of the material environment. The geographic determinists declared reality to exist in the directive and limiting force of the material environment upon human culture. It is obvious that objective physical reality places limits on man, regardless of his opinions or beliefs regarding it. "The difference between facts which are what they are independent of human desire and endeavor and facts which are to some extent what they are because

[1] Joad, C. E. M., "Realism," *Ency. Soc. Sci.*, 13: 140.

of human interest and purpose, and which alter with alteration in the latter, cannot be got rid of by any methodology."[1] The cartographers of the Middle Ages believed that the world was flat; the German people may believe that the food supply of the Russians is less than it actually is; the peoples of the world may be erroneously informed as to the monetary supply or the oil resources of their rivals; these beliefs do not change the objective reality. Certainly the material environment is one realm of reality, but there are other levels. We cannot explain the social order, the philosophic thought forms or the psychological processes on the basis of environmental reality.

Plato and the philosophers in the platonic tradition have posited reality in a conceptual realism of thought forms. "The forms were conceived by Plato to constitute the real world, a world of immaterial logical entities, permanent, perfect and changeless, standing in immutable relations to one another."[2] In the *Republic* (Book VII), Plato presents the famous image of the cave. The world is a cave in which men sit fettered with their backs to a fire. They can see only shadows cast on the farther wall of the cave, shadows cast by moving objects behind them but in front of the fire. These shadows man takes for realities. But the shadows are illusions; man's perception of the physical world is unreal and untrue. Yet man, clinging to his erroneous beliefs and opinions, resists the philosopher who would lead him into the light of day and reality. From this viewpoint, reality is to be found in following the philosopher's construction of logical thought forms. The universals are the realities. Opinion is depreciated as transient, untrue and unreal.

Again it will be maintained that the realities are to be found in the social order, the systems and institutions of society. The social philosophers of the nineteenth century maintained the reality of the social organism.

The psychologist declares, as do the common man and the societal leader, that beliefs, ideas and opinions are real. Reality, for the psychologist, is also to be found in the functioning of the organism in relation to the objective environment. The degree of reality of an experience may be stated in terms of the persistence of its effect on the organism. As such experiences exist with differing degrees of clarity and of persistence of effect, the psychologist may differentiate between levels or degrees of reality on these bases. One way in which the degree of reality may be stated is in terms of the memory value of an experience or thought, in terms of any form of persistence of effect or in terms of the degrees of potency of a stimulus. "A daydream, a vague hope, has in general less reality than an action; an action sometimes has more reality

[1] Dewey, J., *The Public and Its Problems*, p. 7, 1927.
[2] Joad, *op. cit.*, 13: 141.

than speech; a perception more than an image; a faraway 'ideal goal' is less real than a 'real goal' that determines one's immediate action. Action itself can be of very different degrees of reality."[1] For the psychologist, popular opinions are one form of reality.

"Philosophers have long differed as to the way in which beliefs influence social evolution. Deterministic theories minimize their importance; beliefs are said to be only the ideologic reflections of the physical environment, of the racial inheritance, of the system of production, of the interests of the dominant class, or of irrational emotions and feelings."[2] But in social practice, men have persistently acted "as if" beliefs were important. They have indoctrinated, proselyted and attempted to convince their fellows. They have promulgated illusions and rational doctrines with equal fervor and have used illogical and logical methods of appeal. The view that *preponderant* beliefs and opinions have greater reality than those less widely held grew out of rationalism and the emphasis on the individual. During the past four centuries, the powerful currents of Protestantism and of political democracy, an economy oriented more and more toward the wants of the individual consumer and, latterly, the psychologizing of learning—all have made the individual the central value. This preoccupation with the individual finds expression in the laboring with the person's psychological processes. Change his beliefs, modify his opinions, argue, proselyte, plead, save his soul, gently guide his wants by advertising, present problems for him to solve under a democratic system; and, if he is then found to be somewhat confused, turn him over for repairs to the psychologist and psychiatrist, the mental cults, the movies or *The Voice of Experience*. The harried soul may even find a haven in astrology.

Popular opinions may agree more or less with the reality of the physical environment, the reality of the social organizations and processes and the reality of the psychological processes of those about whom the opinions are formed. Thinking that does coincide with reality is called "realistic" thinking; popular opinions may be based on realistic thinking. The individual, as a member of large publics, may think realistically, but often he does not do so because of the limitations of his own psychological processes or because of the inadequacy, fallaciousness or incompleteness of his data. The aim of the special pleader is to manipulate man's beliefs and opinions, often irrespective of objective realities. To be sure, the propagandist has often overestimated the response to his special pleading. "Evidently human beings have been living to a considerable degree in a real world rather than in a Plato-Lippmann's den, and have

---

[1] Lewin, K., *Principles of Topological Psychology* (English trans.), p. 196, 1936.
[2] Cohen, M. R., "Belief," *Ency. Soc. Sci.*, 2: 501.

reacted principally to the real environment, rather than to the shadows of the pseudo-environment which they see from the bottom of the den."[1]

The liberal desires to increase the amount of realistic thinking. He believes that the opinions of the common man can be made more realistic by providing more accurate data about objective facts; by presenting more detailed and less simple descriptions of the ideas and ideologies, the beliefs and opinions of other groups; by equipping him with more adequate methods of thinking. The liberal believes that intelligence can replace ignorance, the traditional beliefs and unquestioning followership. The science of material things is substituting verified facts for erroneous beliefs; and the liberal believes in the possibility of a science of social relations. "Instead of accepting experience, science discriminates between the experience of truth and the experience of illusion. Not all reality, but only a reality free from ugliness and confusing incoherence is the aim of art. Conduct, science, and art thus depend on rational discrimination."[2] Systems of social values should be created rationally, and in so far as possible these should be transmitted by logical discussion. Only thereby can popular opinion achieve a relatively high degree of realism. Leaders and experts can accelerate this process when their objectives are understanding and guidance of the common man, not his exploitation. A well-intentioned liberal leadership may be inefficient in dealing with certain aspects of society, but it will preserve values that are vital to the elevation of the individual. Unfortunately, the authoritarian leaders of the modern world are not thus well-intentioned.

[1] Sorokin, P. A., *Contemporary Sociological Theories*, p. 709, 1928.
[2] Cohen, M. R., *Reason and Nature*, p. 457, 1931.

SELECTED REFERENCES

It is the author's contention that extended reference lists are justified only when they are functionally useful. In English, there is no other work of academic vintage on Public Opinion, with the exception of W. B. Graves' *Readings in Public Opinion* published a decade ago. Therefore, the author believes that this somewhat lengthy list may be useful to students and scholars.

CHAPTERS I AND II

THE NATURE AND DEVELOPMENT OF PUBLIC OPINION

Albig, W.: *Group Opinion and the Mexican*, Ph.D. thesis, University of Michigan, 1929.

Allport, F. H.: *Institutional Behavior*, 1933.

————: *Social Psychology*, pp. 395 *ff.*, 308 *ff.*, 1924.

————: "Toward a Science of Public Opinion," *Pub. Opin. Quar.*, 1: 1: 7–23.

Angell, N.: *The Public Mind*, 1926.

Arnold, T. W.: *The Folklore of Capitalism*, Yale University Press, 1937.

Bagehot, W.: *Physics and Politics*, Chap. 5, 1875.

Bain, R.: "Theory and Measurement of Attitudes and Opinion," *Psychol. Bull.*, 27: 357–379.

Bartlett, F. C.: "Group Organization and Social Behavior," *Int. Jour. Ethics*, 35: 346–367.

Bauer, W.: *Die öffentliche Meinung in der Weltgeschichte*, Potsdam, 1929.

Beard, C. A.: *The Discussion of Human Affairs*, 1936.

Bentley, A. F.: *The Process of Government*, Chaps. 3, 8, 1908.

Bernard, L. L.: *An Introduction to Social Psychology*, Chaps. 26–31, 1926.

Bernays, E. L.: *Crystallizing Public Opinion*, 1923.

Binkley, R. C.: "The Concept of Public Opinion in the Social Sciences," *Soc. Forces*, 6: 389–396.

Bogardus, E. S.: *Social Psychology*, Chap. 25, 1917.

Bryce, J.: *American Commonwealth*, 1889.

Carr, L. J.: "Public Opinion as a Dynamic Concept," *Sociol. Soc. Res.*, 13: 18–30.

Clark, C. D.: "The Concept of the Public," *Southwest. Soc. Sci. Quar.*, 13:311–321.

Cooley, C. H.: *Social Organization*, Chaps. 12, 13, 1909.

————: *Social Process*, Chap. 31, 1918.

Coyle, G. L.: *Social Process in Organized Groups*, 1930.

Deherme, G.: *Les Forces à règler: le nombre et l'opinion publique*, 1919.

Delaisi, F.: *Political Myths and Economic Realities*, 1925.

Dewey, J.: "New Paternalism, Molding Public Opinion," *New Republic*, Dec. 21, 1918.

————: *The Public and Its Problems*, 1927.

Dicey, A. V.: *Lectures on the Relation between Law and Public Opinion in England during the 19th Century*, 1905.

Ellwood, C. A.: *The Psychology of Human Society*, Chap. 7, 1925.

Encyclopaedia of the Social Sciences, The Nature of Public Opinion: "Belief," "Casuistry," "Consensus," "Crises," "Culture," "Custom," "Doctrinaire,"

"Dogma," "Folklore," "Folkways," "Mores," "Public Opinion," "Sanction—Social."

The Development of Public Opinion: "Absolutism," "Agitation," "Balance of Power," "Compromise," "Democracy," "Dictatorship," "Dictatorship of the Proletariat," "Education," "Education—Primitive," "Fascism," "Goodwill," "Hedonism," "Individualism," "Intellectuals," "Majority Rule," "Masses," "Materialism," "Minority Rights," "Social Mobility," "Nihilism," "Progress," "Puritanism," "Radicalism," "Rationalism," "Reformation," "Revolution and Counter-Revolution," "Socialism," "Tradition," "Traditionalism," "Utopia."

Faris, E.: *The Nature of Human Nature*, Chap. 12, 1937.

Ginsberg, M.: *The Psychology of Society*, pp. 137–148, 1921.

Godkin, E. L.: "Growth and Expression of Public Opinion," *Atlantic*, 81: 1–15, 1898.

Graves, W. B. (ed.): *Readings in Public Opinion*, Chaps. 1, 2, 3, 4, 1928.

Hackett, F. W.: "Sources of Public Opinion," *Independent*, 52: 1603–1604.

Jordan, E.: *Theory of Legislation: An Essay on the Dynamics of the Public Mind*, 1930.

Kent, F. R.: *Political Behavior*, 1928.

King, C. L.: *Public Opinion as Viewed by Eminent Political Theorists*, University of Pennsylvania Public Lectures, 1916.

Laird, J.: *Knowledge, Belief, and Opinion*, 1930.

Lippmann, W.: *Public Opinion*, pp. 3–114, 1922.

———: *The Phantom Public*, 1925.

Lowell, A. L., *Conflicts of Principle*, 1932.

———: *Public Opinion and Popular Government*, 1913.

———: *Public Opinion in War and Peace*, 1923.

Lundberg, G. A.: "Public Opinion from a Behavioristic Viewpoint," *Am. Jour. Sociol.*, 36: 387–405.

Lundholm, H.: *The Psychology of Belief*, Duke University Press, 1936.

McDougall, W.: *The Group Mind*, 1920.

Mackinnon, W. A.: *Public Opinion*, 1828.

MacPherson, W.: *The Psychology of Persuasion*, 1920.

Mannheim, K.: *Ideology and Utopia* (English trans.), 1936.

Martin, B. K.: *The Triumph of Lord Palmerston: A Study of Public Opinion in England before the Crimean War*, London, 1924.

Martin, E. D., "Some Mechanisms Which Distinguish the Crowd from Other Forms of Social Behavior," *Jour. Abn. Soc. Psychol.*, 18: 188–203.

———: *The Behavior of Crowds: A Psychological Study*, 1920.

———: *The Conflict of the Individual and the Mass in the Modern World*, 1932.

Mead, M.: "Public Opinion Mechanisms among Primitive Peoples," *Pub. Opin. Quar.*, 1: 3: 5–17.

Mecklin, J. M.: *An Introduction to Social Ethics*, Chap. 9, 1920.

Meier, N. C.: "Public Opinion," *Am. Jour. Sociol.*, 31: 199–212.

Odegard, P. H.: *The American Public Mind*, 1930.

Palmer, P. A.: *Concepts of Public Opinion in the History of Political Thought*, Ph. D. thesis, Harvard University, 1933.

Park, R. E., and Burgess, E. W.: *Introduction to the Science of Sociology*, Chap. 12, 1921.

Perry, R. B.: "Is There a Social Mind?" *Am. Jour. Sociol.*, 27: 561–572, 721–736.

Ross, E. A.: *Social Control*, Chap. 10, 1901.

Schanck, R. L.: *A Study of a Community and Its Groups and Institutions Conceived of as Behaviors of Individuals*, Psychol. Mon., (1932).

Sedman, V. R.: "Some Interpretations of Public Opinion," *Soc. Forces*, 10: 339–350.

Sheffield, A. D.: *Joining in Public Discussion*, 1922.

Sorokin, P. A.: *Social and Cultural Dynamics*, vol. II (Fluctuation of Systems of Truth, Ethics and Law), 1937.

Stratton, G. M.: *Social Psychology of International Conduct*, 1929.

Tarde, G.: *L'Opinion et la foule*, Paris, 1901.

Tocqueville, A. de: *Democracy in America*, 1898.

Tönnies, F.: *Kritik der öffentlichen Meinung*, 1922.

Vaihinger, H.: *The Philosophy of "As If"* (English trans.), 1924.

Wilson, F. G.: "Concepts of Public Opinion," *Am. Pol. Sci. Rev.*, 27: 371–391.

———: *The Elements of Modern Politics*, Chaps. 10, 11, 1936.

Wright, Q. (ed.): *Public Opinion and World Politics*, University of Chicago Press, 1933.

Young, K.: *Social Psychology*, Chap. 24, 1930.

Young, K. (ed): *Source Book for Social Psychology*, Chap. 25, 1927.

CHAPTER III

COMMUNICATION

American Directory of Newspapers and Periodicals, N. W. Ayer and Son.

Annual Reports of the Postmaster General (materials on postal communication).

Bancroft, G., and Jewett, F. B.: "Telephone Communications System of the United States," *Bell System Tech. Jour.*, 9: 1–100 (1930).

Bernard, L. L.: *An Introduction to Social Psychology*, pp. 465–495, 1926.

Bickel, K. A.: *New Empires*, 1930.

Bostwick, A. E.: *The American Public Library*, 4th ed., 1929.

Carter, T. F.: *The Invention of Printing in China*, Columbia University Press, 1925.

Census of Electrical Industries: Telegraphs, Bureau of the Census, 1902, 1907, 1909, 1912, 1917, 1922, 1927.

Census of Manufactures, 1904, 1909, 1914, 1919 (and biennially thereafter).

Chapin, F. S.: *Cultural Change*, pp. 279–331, 1928.

Cooley, C. H.: *Social Organization*, pp. 61–107, 1909.

———: "Theory of Transportation," pp. 17–118 in *Social Theory and Social Research* (Angell, R. C., ed.), 1930.

Duffus, R. L.: "Printing," *Ency. Soc. Sci.*

Editor and Publisher: International Year Book Number (January edition of each year).

Encyclopaedia of the Social Sciences, "Ceremony," "Communication," "Copyright," "Diffusionism," "Fairs," "Isolation," "Literacy and Illiteracy," "Printing," "Public Libraries," "Telephone and Telegraph," "Theater."

Haserot, F. S., *Essays on the Logic of Being* (1st section on Communication), 1932.

Hiller, E. T., *Principles of Sociology*, Chaps. 6, 7, 8, 9, 1933.

Kaempffert, W. B., *Modern Wonder Workers*, pp. 289 *ff.* (Development of Telegraph), 1931.

Laguna, T. de: *The Factors of Social Evolution*, pp. 277–302, 1926.

The Magic of Communication, American Telephone and Telegraph Co., Information Department Pamphlets.

Markey, J. F.: *The Symbolic Process*, 1928.

Vendryes, J.: *Language, a Linguistic Introduction to History*, 1925.

Willey, M. M., and Rice, S. A.: *Communication Agencies and Social Life*, 1933.

Woodbury, D. O.: *Communication*, 1931.

CHAPTER IV

PSYCHOLOGICAL PROCESSES AND OPINION

Allport, F. H.: *Social Psychology*, 1924.

Angell, N.: *The Public Mind*, 1926.

Bartlett, F. C.: *Remembering*, 1932.

Bentham, J.: *The Theory of Fictions* (Introduction by Ogden, C. K.), London, International Library of Psychology, Philosophy, and Scientific Method, 1932.

Bentley, A. F.: *The Process of Government*, Chaps. 1, 2, 1908.

Bernard, L. L.: *An Introduction to Social Psychology*, 1926.

———: *Instinct*, 1924.

Biddle, W. W.: "The Relationship between Knowledge and a Measure of Autistic Thinking on Certain International Problems," *Jour. Soc. Psychol.*, 2: 493–496.

Boas, G.: *Our New Ways of Thinking*, 1930.

Branford, V.: "The Purpose of Liturgy," *Sociol. Rev.*, 20: 1–17.

Brown, J. F.: *Psychology and the Social Order*, 1936.

Brown, W. O.: "Rationalization of Race Prejudice," *Int. Jour. Ethics*, 43: 294–306.

Burrough, T.: *The Social Basis of Consciousness*, 1927.

Burtt, E. A.: *Principles and Problems of Right Thinking*, Chaps. 1, 2, 3, 1928.

Clarke, B. L.: "On the Difficulty of Conveying Ideas," *Sci. Mon.*, 27: 545–551.

Clarke, E. L.: *The Art of Straight Thinking*, Chaps. 1, 2, 3, 1929.

Cooley, C. H.: *Human Nature and the Social Order*, Chaps. 2, 3, 1902.

Denison, J. H.: *Emotional Currents in American History*, 1932.

Dewey, J.: *Human Nature and Conduct*, 1922.

———: "Knowledge and Speech Reaction," *Jour. Phil.*, 19: 561–570.

Doob, L. W.: *Propaganda*, 1935.

Dorsey, M. F., and Hopkins, L. T.: "The Influence of Attitude upon Transfer," *Jour. Ed. Psychol.*, 21: 410–417.

Dunbar, H. F.: *Symbolism in Mediaeval Thought*, Yale University Press, 1929.

Eaton, R. M.: *Symbolism and Truth*, 1925.

Elliott, H. S.: *The Process of Group Thinking*, 1928.

Encyclopaedia of the Social Sciences, "Adjustment," "Boom," "Collective Behavior," "Crowd," "Expert Testimony," "Fictions," "Habit," "Identification," "Imitation," "Logic," "Mental Tests," "Mob," "Morale," "Panics," "Psychoanalysis," "Rationalization."

English, H. B.: "The Emotional Short-Circuiting of Thought," *Jour. Abn. Soc. Psychol.*, 36: 402–404.

Frank, J.: *Law and the Modern Mind*, Chaps. 3, 8, 1930.

Freeman, E.: *Social Psychology*, 1936.

Fülöp-Miller, R.: *Leaders, Dreamers, and Rebels*, Chaps. 1, 2, 1935.

Garrett, H. E., and Fisher, T. R.: "The Prevalence of Certain Popular Misconceptions," *Jour. Appl. Psychol.*, 10: 411–420.

Ginsberg, M.: *The Psychology of Society*, 1921.

Glover, E.: "Sublimation, Substitution and Social Anxiety," *Int. Jour. Psychoanalysis*, 12: 263–297.

Goblet d'Alviella, E., *The Migration of Symbols*, 1894.

Graves, W. B. (ed.): *Readings in Public Opinion*, Chap. 1, 1928.

Hamill, R. C.: "The Role of the Risqué Story," *Jour. Abn. Soc. Psychol.*, 16: 269–273.

Hart, H.: "The Transmutation of Motivation," *Am. Jour. Sociol.*, 35: 588–600.

Hollingworth, H. L.: *The Psychology of Thought*, Chaps. 5, 11, 15, 1926.

House, S. D.: "Psychologies of the Unconscious," *Psychoanalytic Rev.*, 15: 1–26.

Hurlock, E. B.: "Motivation in Fashion," *Arch. Psychol.*, No. 3, 17: 1–71.

Hutchins, R. M., and Slesinger, D.: "Some Observations on the Law of Evidence," *Harvard Law Rev.*, 41: 860–873.

Jastrow, J.: *The Psychology of Conviction*, 1918.

Jones, E.: "The Theory of Symbolism," *Brit. Jour. Psychol.*, 9: 181–229.

Josey, C. C.: *The Social Philosophy of Instinct*, 1922.

Judd, C. H.: *The Psychology of Social Institutions*, 1926.

Jung, C. G.: *Psychological Types*, 1923.

Kantor, J. R.: *Principles of Psychology*, vol. II, Chaps. 16, 17, 1926.

Katz, D. and Braley, K.: "Racial Stereotypes of One Hundred College Students," *Jour. Abn. Soc. Psychol.*, 28: 280–290.

Klein, M.: "The Importance of Symbol-Formation in the Development of the Ego," *Int. Jour. Psychoanalysis*, 11: 24–39.

Kosok, P.: *Modern Germany*, Chap. 16, 1933.

Laird, D.: "The Influence of Likes and Dislikes on Memory as Related to Personality," *Jour. Exper. Psychol.*, 6: 294–303.

LaPiere, R. T., and Farnsworth, P. R.: *Social Psychology*, Chaps. 4, 5, 9, 10, 1936.

Lasswell, H. D.: *Politics*, Chap. 2, 1936.

——: *Psychopathology and Politics*, 1930.

——: *World Politics and Personal Insecurity*, Chap. 10, 1935.

Lehman, H. C., and Witty, P. A.: "Sex Differences in Credulity," *Jour. Abn. Soc. Psychol.*, 23: 356–368.

Lévy-Bruhl, L.: *How Natives Think*, Parts 1 and 3, 1926.

Lewis, W.: *The Art of Being Ruled*, 1926.

Lippmann, W.: *Public Opinion*, Chaps, 4, 5, 6, 7, 8, 10, 1922.

Litterer, O. F.: "Stereotypes," *Jour. Soc. Psychol.*, 4: 59–69.

Lorden, D. M.: "Mob Behavior and Social Attitudes," *Sociol. Soc. Res.*, 14: 324–331.

Lowell, A. L.: *Public Opinion and Popular Government*, 1913.

Lund, F. H.: *Emotions of Men*, 1930.

McDougall, W.: *An Introduction to Social Psychology*, 1926.

——: *The Group Mind*, 1920.

McGill, K. H.: "The School Teacher Stereotype," *Jour. Ed. Sociol.*, 4: 642–650.

Mackenzie, D. A.: *The Migration of Symbols*, 1926.

Maier, N. R. F.: "Reasoning and Learning," *Psychol. Rev.*, 38: 332–346.

Mannheim, K.: *Ideology and Utopia* (English trans.), 1936.

Markey, J. F.: *The Symbolic Process*, 1928.

Martin, E. D.: *The Behavior of Crowds*, 1920.

Meltzer, H.: "Personification of Ideals in Problem Children," *Am. Jour. Orthopsychiatry*, 2: 384–399.

Merriam, C. E.: *Political Power*, pp. 37 *ff.*, 105 *ff.*, 310 *ff.*, 1934.

More, A.: "The Theory of Fictions," *Psyche*, 9: 31–38.

Morris, C. W.: *Pragmatism and the Crisis of Democracy*, Public Policy Pamphlet No. 12, University of Chicago Press, 1934.

——: "The Concept of the Symbol," *Jour. Phil.*, 24: 253–262, 281–291.

Murchison, C. A. (ed.): *A Handbook of Social Psychology*, Chap. 17, 1935.

Murphy, G., and Murphy, L. B.: *Experimental Social Psychology*, Chap. 11, 1931.

Odegard, P. H.: *The American Public Mind*, Chap. 1, Columbia University Press, 1930.

Pareto, V.: *The Mind and Society* (English trans.) vols. II and III, 1935.

Rice, S. A.: *Quantitative Methods in Politics*, Chap. 5, 1928.

Rignano, E.: *The Psychology of Reasoning*, pp. 71–140, 1923.

Robinson, J. H.: *The Mind in the Making*, 1921.

Schanck, R. L.: *A Study of a Community and Its Groups and Institutions Conceived of as Behaviors of Individuals*, *Psychol. Mon.*, 1932.

Schneider, H. W.: *The Puritan Mind*, 1930.

Schweisinger, G. C.: *Heredity and Environment*, 1933.

Shankle, G. E.: *State Names, Flags, Seals, Songs, Birds, Flowers, and Other Symbols*, 1934.

Sharpe, E. F.: "Certain Aspects of Sublimation and Delusion," *Int. Jour. Psycho-analysis*, 11: 12–24.

Silberer, H.: *Problems of Mysticism and Its Symbolism*, 1917.

Slesinger, D., and Pilpel, E. M.: "Legal Psychology," *Psychol. Bull.*, 26: 677–692.

Sorokin, P. A.: *Contemporary Sociological Theories*, Chaps. 11, 12, 1928.

Starch, D., Stanton, H. M., and Koerth, W.: *Controlling Human Behavior*, Chaps. 4, 6, 7, 1936.

Stratton, G. M.: *Social Psychology of International Conduct*, 1929.

Taylor, W. S.: "Rationalization and Its Social Significance," *Jour. Abn. Soc. Psychol.*, 17: 410–418.

Thouless, R. H.: *Straight and Crooked Thinking*, Chaps. 1, 5, 7, 1930.

Wallas, G.: *Human Nature in Politics*, Chaps. 1, 3, 1909.

———: *The Great Society*, Chaps. 6, 7, 9, 10, 1914.

Wallis, W. D.: "Mental Patterns in Relation to Culture," *Jour. Abn. Soc. Psychol.*, 19: 179–184.

Whipple, G. M.: "The Psychology of Testimony," *Psychol. Bull.*, 12: 221–224.

Whitehead, A. N.: *Symbolism*, 1927.

Wingfield-Stratford, E. C.: *New Minds for Old*, pp. 271–375, 1935.

Witty, P. A., and Lehman, H. C.: "Some Dangers of Over-Simplification," *Ed. Rev.*, 76: 150–161.

Young, K.: *Social Psychology*, Chap. 8, 1930.

Young, K. (ed.): *Source Book for Social Psychology*, Chap. 6, 8, 12, 1927.

CHAPTER V

LANGUAGE AND PUBLIC OPINION

Adams, S., and Powers, F. F.: "The Psychology of Language," *Psychol. Bull.*, 26 241–260.

Arnold, T. W.: *Symbols of Government*, 1935.

———: *Folklore of Capitalism*, 1937.

Bloomfield, L.: *An Introduction to the Study of Language*, 1914.

Brown, H. C.: "The Use and Abuse of Language," *Jour. Phil.*, 26: 533–541.

Buck, C. D.: "Language and the Sentiment of Nationality," *Am. Pol. Sci. Rev.*, 10: 44–69.

Chase, S.: *The Tyranny of Words*, 1938.

Dewey, J.: "Knowledge and Speech Reaction," *Jour. Phil.*, 19: 561–570.

Eastman, M.: "The Cult of Unintelligibility," *Harper's*, 158: 632–639.

Encyclopaedia of the Social Sciences, "Dialect," "Language."

Frank, J.: *Law and the Modern Mind*, Chaps. 3, 7, 10, 1930.

Gillette, J. M.: "Extent of Personal Vocabularies," *Sci. Mon.*, 29: 451–457.

Huse, H. R.: *The Illiteracy of the Literate*, 1933.

Jespersen, O.: *Language, Its Nature, Development and Origin*, 1922.

Kantor, J. R.: *The Principles of Psychology*, vol. II, Chap. 23, 1926.

Lumley, F. E.: *Means of Social Control*, Chaps. 7, 12, 14, 1925.

MacDougall, R.: "The 'Colored Words' of Art," *Psychol. Rev.*, 20: 505–516.

Mencken, H. L.: *The American Language*, 1936 edition.

Murchison, C. (ed.): *Handbook of Social Psychology*, Chap. 11, 1935.

Ogden, C. K., and Richards, I. A.: *The Meaning of Meaning*, 1923.

Paget, R.: *Human Speech*, London, 1930.

Palmer, H. E.: "Word Values," *Psyche*, 9: 13–28.

Pareto, V.: *The Mind and Society*, (English trans.) vol. III, Sections 1543–1686, 1935.

Perry, C. M.: "Language and Thought," *Monist*, 38: 211–231.

Pillsbury, W. B., and Meader, C. L.: *The Psychology of Language*, 1928.
Roback, A. A.: "Writing Slips and Personality," *Character and Personality*, 1: 137–146.
Sapir, E.: *Language, an Introduction to the Study of Speech*, 1921.
Schweisinger, G. C., *The Social-Ethical Significance of Vocabulary*, Teachers College Contributions to Education, No. 211, 1926.
Urban, W. M.: "The Philosophy of Language," *Psychol. Bull.*, 26: 324–334.
Vendryes, J.: *Language, a Linguistic Introduction to History*, 1925.
Wingfield-Stratford, E.: *New Minds for Old*, pp. 271–307, 345–375, 1935.
Wright, Q. (ed.): *Public Opinion and World Politics*, pp. 116–137, 1933.
Young, K.: *Social Psychology*, Chaps. 10, 16, 1930.
Young, K. (ed.): *Source Book for Social Psychology*, pp. 328–346, 1927.

CHAPTER VI

THE LEADER AND PERSONAL SYMBOLISM

Allport, G. W.: *Personality* (Discussion of Traits), 1937.
Arnet, C. E., Davidson, H. H., and Lewis, H. N.: "Prestige as a Factor in Attitude Changes," *Sociol. Soc. Res.*, 16: 49–55.
Bartlett, F. C.: "The Social Psychology of Leadership," *Jour. Nat. Inst. Indus. Psychol.*, 3: 188–193.
Bernard, L. L.: *An Introduction to Social Psychology*, Chaps. 33, 34, 1926.
Bogardus, E. S.: "Balance in Leadership," *Sociol. Soc. Res.*, 15: 344–351.
———: *Leaders and Leadership*, 1934.
Bowman, L. E.: "An Approach to the Study of Leadership," *Jour. Appl. Psychol.*, 2: 315–321.
Bryce, J.: *The American Commonwealth*, 1889.
Burr, W.: *Community Leadership*, 1929.
Carlyle, T.: *Heroes and Hero Worship*, 1900.
Clark, L. P.: "Unconscious Motives Underlying the Personalities of Great Statesmen and Their Relation to Epoch-making Events," *Psychoanalytic Rev.*, 8: 1–21.
Cooley, C. H.: *Human Nature and the Social Order*, Chaps. 4, 9, 1902.
———: *Social Process*, Chap. 10, 1918.
Cowley, W. H.: "The Traits of Face-to-face Leaders," *Jour. Abn. Soc. Psychol.*, 26: 304–313.
———: "Three Distinctions in the Study of Leaders," *Jour. Abn. Soc. Psychol.*, 23: 144–157.
Cox, C. M.: *The Early Mental Traits of Three Hundred Geniuses*, Chaps. 2, 3, Stanford University Press, 1926.
Coyle, G. L.: *Social Process in Organized Groups*, Chap. 5, R. R. Smith, 1930.
Elliott, H. S.: *The Process of Group Thinking*, 1928.
Encyclopaedia of the Social Sciences, "Authority," "Leadership."
Fearing, F.: "Psychological Studies of Historical Personalities," *Psychol. Bull.*, 24: 521–539.
Gowin, E. B.: *The Executive and His Control of Men*, Chaps. 4, 6, 1915.
Graves, W. B. (ed.): *Readings in Public Opinion*, Chaps. 14, 22, 23, 24, 1928.
Hart, H.: *The Science of Human Relations*, Chap. 10, 1927.
Hocking, W. E.: "Leaders and Led," *Yale Rev.*, 13: 625–641.
Kent, F. R.: *The Great Game of Politics*, 1923.
Lasswell, H. D.: *Psychopathology and Politics*, 1930.
———: "Types of Political Personalities," *Pub. Am. Sociol. Soc.*, 22: 159–169.
LeBon, G.: *The Crowd: A Study of the Popular Mind*, Part II, Chap. 2, 1900.
Leopold, L.: *Prestige*, T. Fisher Unwin, 1913.

Michels, R.: *Political Parties*, Parts II and III on Leadership, 1915.

Munro, W. B.: *Personality in Politics*, 1924.

Nafe, R. W.: "A Psychological Description of Leadership," *Jour. Soc. Psychol.*, 1: 248–266.

Pigors, P. J.: *Leadership or Domination*, 1935.

Sheffield, A. D.: *Creative Discussion; A Statement of Method for Leaders and Members of Discussion Groups and Conferences*, 1927.

Sorokin, P. A.: "Leaders of Labor and Radical Movements in the United States and Foreign Countries," *Am. Jour. Sociol.*, 33: 382–411.

Spiller, G.: "The Dynamics of Greatness," *Sociol. Rev.*, 21: 218–232.

Tait, W. D.: "Psychology of Leadership and Democracy," *Jour. Abn. Soc. Psychol.*, 22: 27–32.

————: "The Menace of the Reformer," *Jour. Abn. Soc. Psychol.*, 21: 343–353.

Taussig, F. W., and Joslyn, C. S.: *American Business Leaders*, 1932.

Webb, B., and Webb, S.: *Soviet Communism*, Chap. 5, 1936.

Young, K., (ed.): *Source Book for Social Psychology*, Chaps. 20, 21, 1927.

Zink, H.: *City Bosses in the United States*, Duke University Press, 1930.

A Few Illustrative Biographies and Autobiographies of Significant Popular Leaders, or of Leaders Who Have Greatly Influenced Popular Leaders

(A selected list of biographies dealing with men prominent in journalism will be appended to the Selected References for Chapter XXI on The Newspaper.)

Leaders in Social Adventure, Russell Sage Foundation, 1930.

Men of Turmoil: Biographies by Leading Authorities of the Dominating Personalities of Our Day, Milton, Balch & Co., 1935.

Addams, J.: *Twenty Years at Hull House*, 1910.

————: *Second Twenty Years at Hull House*, 1930.

Beer, T.: *Hanna*, 1929.

Bowers, C. G.: *Jefferson and Hamilton*, 1925.

————: *Jefferson in Power*, 1936.

Bradford, G.: *D. L. Moody*, 1927.

Broun, H., and Leech, M.: *Anthony Comstock*, 1927.

Busbey, L. W.: *Uncle Joe Cannon*, 1927.

Chitambar, J. R.: *Mahatma Gandhi: His Life, Work and Influence*, 1933.

Clark, C.: *My Quarter Century of American Politics*, 2 vols., 1920.

Cole, G. D. H.: *The Life of William Cobbett*, New York, William Collins Sons & Co., Ltd., 1924.

Coudray, H. du: *Metternich*, 1936.

Dakin, E. F.: *Mrs. Eddy: The Biography of a Virginal Mind*, 1929.

Darrow, C.: *Story of My Life*, 1932.

Dodd, W. E.: *Woodrow Wilson and His Work*, rev. ed., 1932.

Gandhi, M. K.: *The Story of My Experiments with Truth*, 2 vols., Ahmedabad, Navajivan Press, 1927–1929.

Gandhi, M. K., Andrews, C. F. (ed.): *Mahatma Gandhi: His Own Story*, 1930.

————: *Mahatma Gandhi at Work; His Own Story, Continued*, 1931.

Gosnell, H. F.: *Boss Platt and His New York Machine*, University of Chicago Press, 1924.

Hall, G. S.: *Jesus, the Christ, in the Light of Psychology*, 2 vols., 1917.

Hibben, P.: *Henry Ward Beecher: An American Portrait*, 1927.

———— and Grattan, C. H.: *The Peerless Leader, William Jennings Bryan*, 1929.

Hitler, A.: *Mein Kampf,* or the expurgated English edition, *My Battle,* 1933.

Howe, F. C.: *Confessions of a Reformer,* 1925.

Levine, I. D.: *Stalin,* 1931.

Linn, J. W.: *Jane Addams,* 1935.

Lynch, D. T.: *"Boss" Tweed,* 1927.

Mackinnon, J.: *Calvin and the Reformation,* 1936.

Mayer, G.: *Friedrich Engels,* 1936.

Merriam, C. E.: *Four American Party Leaders,* 1926.

Murray, D. L.: *Disraeli,* 1927.

Mussolini, B.: *My Autobiography,* 1928.

Nevins, A. (ed.): *American Political Leaders.* Biographies of the following political
   leaders have been published in this series: Rutherford B. Hayes, Thomas B.
   Reed, James A. Garfield, John G. Carlisle, Carl Schurz, Grover Cleveland, John
   Hay, James G. Blaine, Chester A. Arthur.

Nye, F. W.: *Bill Nye, His Own Life Story,* 1926.

Parkes, H. B.: *Jonathan Edwards,* 1930.

Pringle, H.: *Theodore Roosevelt,* 1931.

Raymond, E. J. (pseud.): *Mr. Lloyd George,* 1922.

Restarick, H. B.: *Sun Yat Sen, Liberator of China,* 1931.

Rühle, O.: *Karl Marx; His Life and Work* (trans. Paul, E., and Paul, C.), 1929.

Sanger, M.: *My Fight for Birth Control,* 1931.

Steffens, J. L.: *The Autobiography of Lincoln Steffens,* 1931.

Steuart, J.: *Wayne Wheeler, Dry Boss: An Uncensored Biography,* Fleming H. Revell
   & Company, 1928.

Street, C. J. C.: *Thomas Masaryk of Czechoslovakia,* 1930.

Ware, L.: *Jacob A. Riis, Police Reporter, Reformer, Useful Citizen,* 1938.

Webb, B.: *My Apprenticeship,* 1926.

Wells, H. G.: *Experiment in Autobiography,* 1934.

Werner, M. R.: *Brigham Young,* 1925.

White, W. A.: *Forty Years on Main Street,* 1937.

————: *Woodrow Wilson, The Man, His Times, and His Task,* 1924.

Wortham, H. E.: *Mustapha Kemal of Turkey,* 1931.

CHAPTER VII

LEGENDS AND MYTHS

Abraham, K.: *Dreams and Myths,* 1913.

Arnold, T. W.: *The Folklore of Capitalism,* 1937.

Bartlett, F. C.: "Psychology in Relation to the Popular Story," *Folk-lore,* 31: 264–293.

Berkman, A.: *The Bolshevik Myth,* 1925.

Delaisi, F.: *Political Myths and Economic Realities,* 1925.

Encyclopaedia of the Social Sciences, "Diabolism," "Folklore," "Hero Worship,"
   "Myth."

Garçon, M., and Vinchon, J.: *The Devil,* 1930.

Graf, A.: *The Story of the Devil* (English trans.), 1931.

Guerard, A. L.: *Reflections on the Napoleonic Legend,* 1924.

Harrison, J. E.: *Themis,* 1912, 2d ed. rev., 1927.

Hocart, A. M.: "Myths in the Making," *Folk-lore,* 33: 57–71.

Lewis, L.: *Myths after Lincoln,* 1929.

Malinowski, B.: *Myth in Primitive Psychology,* 1926.

Pareto, V.: *The Mind and Society* (English trans.), vol. 1, Sections 650 *ff,* 1935.

Read, C.: *Man and His Superstitions,* Cambridge University Press, 1925.

Rogers, C.: *The Legend of Calvin Coolidge*, 1928.
Ross, E. A.: *Social Control*, Chap. 12, 1901.
Rudwin, M. J.: *The Devil in Legend and Literature*, 1931.
Sorel, G.: *Reflections on Violence*, 1912.
Sparkman, C. F.: "Satan and His Ancestors from a Psychological Standpoint," *Jour. Relig. Psychol.*, 5: 218–225.
Taylor, E. C.: "Shelley as Myth-Maker," *Jour. Abn. Psychol.*, 14: 64–89.
Thompson, R. L.: *The History of the Devil*, 1929.
Todd, A. J.: *Theories of Social Progress*, Chap. 29, 1918.
Young, K.: *Social Psychology*, Chap. 17, 1930.

The literary record of the folk myths of the American frontier may be found in such volumes as:

Blair, W., and Meine, F. J.: *Mike Fink, King of Mississippi Keelboatmen*, 1933.
Boatwright, M. C.: *Tall Tales From Texas*, 1934.
Bradford, R.: *John Henry*, 1931.
Holbrook, S. H.: *Holy Old Mackinaw*, 1938.
McCormick, D. J.: *Paul Bunyan Swings His Axe*, 1936.
Stevens, J.: *Paul Bunyan*, 1925.

CHAPTER VIII

VIOLENCE AND PUBLIC OPINION

Adamic, L.: *Dynamite* (revised ed.), 1936.
Bovet, P.: *The Fighting Instinct*, 1923.
Brissenden, P. F.: *The I. W. W.*, 1919.
Cadoux, C. J.: "Ethics of Coercion," *Contemp.*, 145: 688–697.
Case, C. M.: *Non-violent Coercion*, 1923.
Chamberlin, W. H.: "Evolution of Soviet Terrorism," *Foreign Affairs*, 13: 113–121.
———: "Government by Terror," *Atlantic*, 154: 410–420.
Conway, M.: *The Crowd in Peace and War*, 1915.
Coulton, G. G.: *The Inquisition*, 1929.
Crook, W. H.: *The General Strike*, 1931.
Cutler, J. E.: *Lynch Law*, 1905.
Dewey, J.: "Force and Coercion," *Int. Jour. Ethics*, 26: 359–367.
Encyclopaedia of the Social Sciences, "Abduction," "Agent provocateur," "Assassination," "Atrocities," "Capital Punishment," "Coercion," "Corporal Punishment," "Coup d'état," "Direct Action," "Duelling," "Feuds," "Gangs," "Humanitarianism," "Impressment," "Imprisonment," "Intimidation," "Lynching," "Mass Expulsion," "Mutiny," "Piracy," "Punishment," "Racketeering," "Riot," "Sabotage," "Strikes and Lockouts," "Terrorism," "Violence."
Finer, H.: *Mussolini's Italy*, 1935.
Gambs, J. S.: *The Decline of the I. W. W.*, 1932.
Gregg, R. B.: *The Power of Non-violence*, 1934.
Hiller, E. T.: *The Strike*, 1928.
Hunter, R.: *Violence and the Labor Movement*, 1914.
Kitchin, G.: *Prisoner of the OGPU*, 1935.
Langhoff, W.: *Rubber Truncheon*, 1935.
Lasswell, H. D.: *Politics*, Chap. 3, 1936.
Ludovici, A. M.: *Violence, Sacrifice, and War*, 1933.
Machiavelli, N., *The Prince* (English trans., Thompson, N. H.) 3d ed., Oxford, 1913.
Malaparte, C.: *Coup d'état: The Technique of Revolution*, 1932.
Maycock, A. L.: *The Inquisition*, 1927.
Mead, M.: *Sex and Temperament in Three Primitive Societies*, 1935.

Merriam, C. E.: *Political Power*, pp. 220–228, 299 *ff.*, 1934.

Novicow, J.: *War and Its Alleged Benefits* (trans., 1911). (Original ed., 1894.)

Pareto, V.: *The Mind and Society* (English trans.), vol. IV, Sections 2182–2193, 1935.

Perlman, S., and Taft, P.: *History of Labor in the United States*, 1896–1932, vol. IV, Labor Movements, 1935.

Prince, S. H.: *Catastrophe and Social Change*, Columbia University Studies in History, Economics, and Public Law, No. 212, 1920.

Roper, A.: *The Tragedy of Lynching*, 1933.

Schuman, F. L.: *The Nazi Dictatorship*, 1935.

Seger, G.: *A Nation Terrorized*, 1935.

Sorel, G.: *Reflections on Violence*, 3d ed., B. W. Huebsch, 1912.

Sorokin, P. A.: *Contemporary Sociological Theories*, Chap. 6, 1928.

——: *Social and Cultural Dynamics*, Vol. 3, Chaps. 9–14, pp. 149–153 (see numerous tables and charts), 1937.

Spiridovitch, A. I.: *Histoire du terrorisme russe*, 1886–1916, Paris, Payot, 1930.

Trotter, W. F.: *Instincts of the Herd in Peace and War*, 1916.

Trotsky, L.: *The Defense of Terrorism*, London, 1921.

Vacandard, E.: *The Inquisition*, 1908.

White, W. F.: *Rope and Faggot*, 1929.

CHAPTER IX

GEOGRAPHIC DISTRIBUTION OF GROUP OPINION

Albig, W.: "A Comparison of Methods of Recording Urban Residential Mobility," *Sociol. Soc. Res.*, 21: 226–233.

——: "A Method of Recording Trends in Urban Residential Mobility," *Sociol. Soc. Res.*, 21: 120–127.

——: "The Mobility of Urban Population: A Study of Four Cities of 30,000 to 40,000 Population," *Soc. Forces*, 11: 351–367.

Bailey, T. A.: "The West and Radical Legislation (1890–1930)," *Am. Jour. Sociol.*, 38: 603–611.

Bittner, W. S.: "The Relation of the Local Community to the Principal Factors of Public Opinion," *Soc. Forces*, 7: 98–101.

Bogardus, E. S.: *Immigration and Race Attitudes*, 1928.

——: *The New Social Research*, 1926.

Chapin, F. S.: *Cultural Change*, pp. 361–376, 1928.

Encyclopaedia of the Social Sciences, "Cosmopolitanism," "Decentralization," "Ecology—Human," "Neighborhood," "Regionalism," "Sectionalism."

Lundberg, G. A.: "The Demographic and Economic Basis of Political Radicalism and Conservatism," *Am. Jour. Sociol.*, 32: 719–732.

McMackin, D. L.: *The Correlation of Newspaper Circulation and Votes Cast on Selected Issues in Illinois* (unpublished M. A. thesis), University of Illinois, 1931.

Miller, P. G.: "Contemporary Observations of American Frontier Political Attitudes: 1790–1840," *Int. Jour. Ethics*, 39: 80–92.

Mumford, L.: *The Culture of Cities*, 1938.

Neprash, J. A.: *The Brookhart Campaigns in Iowa*, 1920–1926: *A Study in the Motivation of Political Attitudes*, Columbia University Studies in History, Economics, and Public Law, No. 366, 1932.

Odum, H. W.: *Southern Regions*, 1936.

—— and Moore, H. E.: *American Regionalism*, 1938.

Paullin, C. O.: *Atlas of the Historical Geography of the United States*, 1932.

Rice, S. A.: *Farmers and Workers in American Politics*, pp. 143–183, 1924.

——: *Quantitative Methods in Politics*, Chaps. 10, 11, 12, 1928.

Sorokin, P. A.: *Social Mobility*, Chap. 3, 1927.
Turner, F. J.: *The Significance of Sections in American History*, 1932.
Tylor, W. R.: "The Process of Change from Neighborhood to Regional Organization and Its Effect on Rural Life," *Soc. Forces*, 16: 530–542.
Vance, R. B.: *Human Geography of the South*, University of North Carolina Press, 1932.
Visher, S. S.: "Ecology of American Notables," *Human Biol.*, 1: 544–554.
———: "The Comparative Rank of American States," *Am. Jour. Sociol.*, 36: 735–757.
Wilson, L. R.: *The Geography of Reading*, published jointly by American Library Association and University of Chicago Press, 1938.
Wooddy, C. H., and Stouffer, S. A.: "Local Option and Public Opinion," *Am. Jour. Sociol.*, 36: 175–205.
Zimmerman, E. W.: *World Resources and Industries*, 1933.

CHAPTER X

ATTITUDE AND OPINION

Allport, G. W.: "Attitudes," in *A Handbook of Social Psychology* (Murchison, C. A., ed.), Chap. 7, 1935.
Cantril, H.: "General and Specific Attitudes," *Psychol. Mon.*, vol. XLII, No. 5, 1932.
Clarke, H. M.: "Conscious Attitudes," *Am. Jour. Psychol.*, 22: 214–249.
Droba, D. D.: "The Nature of Attitude," *Jour. Soc. Psychol.*, 4: 444–463.
Encyclopaedia of the Social Sciences, "Attitudes—Social."
Faris, E.: "Attitudes and Behavior," *Am. Jour. Sociol.*, 34: 271–281.
———: *The Nature of Human Nature*, Chaps. 10, 11, 1937.
———: "Social Attitudes," in *Social Attitudes* (Young, K., ed.), pp. 3–17, 1931.
Folsom, J. K.: *Social Psychology*, Chap. 11, 1931.
Frank, L. K.: "The Management of Tensions," *Am. Jour. Sociol.*, 33: 705–736.
Hollingworth, H. L.: "Sensuous Determinants of Psychological Attitude," *Psychol. Rev.*, 35: 93–117.
Krueger, E. T., and Reckless, W. C.: *Social Psychology*, Chaps. 9, 10, 1931.
Pintner, R.: "A Comparison of Interests, Abilities, and Attitudes," *Jour. Abn. Soc. Psychol.*, 27: 351–357.
Symonds, P. M.: "What is an Attitude?" *Psychol. Bull.*, 24: 200 ff.
Thomas, W. I., and Znaniecki, F.: *The Polish Peasant in Europe and America*, vol. I, pp. 1–86, 1918.
Tuttle, H. S.: "Habit and Attitude," *Jour. Ed. Psychol.*, 21: 418–428.
Williams, J. M.: *Our Rural Heritage*, 1925.
Young, K., (ed.): *Social Attitudes*, 1931.

CHAPTERS XI AND XII

THE PROBLEM OF MEASUREMENT AND MEASUREMENT OF OPINION

Albig, W.: "The Measurement of Opinion," *Pub. Mich. Acad. Sci.*, 10: 103–115 (1928).
Allport, G. W.: "Attitudes," in *A Handbook of Social Psychology* (Murchison, C., ed.), pp. 798–839, 1935.
Bain, R.: "An Attitude on Attitude Research," *Am. Jour. Sociol.*, 33: 940–951.
Bogardus, E. S.: "Measuring Public Opinion," *Sociol. Soc. Res.*, 17: 465–469.
Droba, D. D.: "Methods for Measuring Attitudes," *Psychol. Bull.*, 29: 309–323.
———: "Methods Used for Measuring Public Opinion," *Am. Jour. Sociol.* 37: 410–423.

Encyclopaedia of the Social Sciences, "Case Method," "Voting."

Fearing, F.: "The Experimental Study of Attitude, Meaning and the Processes Antecedent to Action, by N. Ach and others in the Würzburg Laboratory," in *Methods in Social Science* (Rice, S. A., ed.), pp. 715–730, 1931.

Gosnell, H. F.: "Statisticians and Political Scientists," *Am. Pol. Sci. Rev.*, 27: 392–403.

Guilford, J. P.: "The Method of Paired Comparisons as a Psychometric Method," *Psychol. Rev.*, 35: 494–506.

———: "Some Empirical Tests of the Method of Paired Comparisons," *Jour. Gen. Psychol.*, 5: 64–77.

Lehman, H. C., and Witty, P. A.: "Statistics Show . . . ," *Jour. Ed. Psychol.*, 19: 175–184.

Knight, F. B., and Franzen, R. H.: "Pitfalls in Rating Schemes," *Jour. Ed. Psychol.*, 13: 204–213.

Likert, R.: "A Technique for the Measurement of Attitude," *Arch. Psychol.*, No. 140, 1932.

Lundberg, G. A.: *Social Research*, Chap. 9, 1929.

Murphy, G., and Likert, R.: *Public Opinion and the Individual*, Chaps. 1, 3, 1938. (This book arrived after the present author's discussion had been sent to the printers. Otherwise this excellent study would have been discussed in the body of these chapters.)

——— and Murphy, L. B.: *Experimental Social Psychology*, Chap. 11, 1931.

———, ——— and Newcomb, T. M.: *Experimental Social Psychology*, Chap. 13, 1937. (The revision of the Murphys' *Experimental Social Psychology* which includes the excellent Chap. 13 on Social Attitudes and Their Measurement (by Newcomb, T. M.) was received by this author after his own chapters had been sent to the printer. Therefore, he did not have the benefit of this summarizing chapter. The student should consult this well-organized material.)

Rice, S. A.: "Social Attitudes and Public Opinion," *Pub. Am. Sociol. Soc.*, 24: 242–250.

Rice, S. A. (ed.): *Statistics in Social Studies*, 1930.

Sherman, M.: "Theories and Measurement of Attitudes," *Child Development*, 3: 15–28.

Stouffer, S. A.: "Experimental Comparison of a Statistical and a Case History Technique of Attitude Research," *Pub. Am. Sociol. Soc.*, 25: 154–156.

Thurstone, L. L.: "Attitudes Can Be Measured," *Am. Jour. Sociol.*, 33: 529–554.

———: "A Mental Unit of Measurement," *Psychol. Rev.*, 34: 416–423.

———: "Commentary," in *Statistics in Social Studies* (Rice, S. A., ed.), pp. 192–196, 1930.

———: "The Method of Paired Comparisons for Social Values," *Jour. Abn. Soc. Psychol.*, 21: 384–400.

———: "Theory of Attitude Measurement," *Psychol. Rev.*, 36: 226–241.

———: "Three Psychophysical Laws," *Psychol. Rev.*, 34: 424–432.

Types of Opinion Tests

This is by no means a complete bibliography of opinion tests. The purpose of this selected bibliography is to provide illustrations of our classifications of types. In each case the study is classified according to the principal method used.

TYPE I

Yes-or-no: True-or-false: and Cross-out Tests

Bain, R.: "Religious Attitudes of College Students," *Am. Jour. Sociol.*, 32: 762–770 (1927).

Cavan, R. S., and Cavan, J. T.: "The Attitudes of Young Business Women toward Home and Married Life," *Rel. Ed.*, 22: 817–820 (1927).

Frederick, R.: "An Investigation into Some Social Attitudes of High School Pupils," *Sch. Soc.*, 25: 410–412 (1927).

Gilliland, A. R.: "A Study of the Superstitions of College Students," *Jour. Abn. Soc. Psychol.*, 24: 472–479.

Kornhauser, A. W., and Sharp, A. A.: "Employee Attitudes: Suggestions from a Study in a Factory," *Personnel Jour.*, 10: 393–404 (1932).

Moore, H. T.: "Innate Factors in Radicalism and Conservatism," *Jour. Abn. Soc. Psychol.*, 20: 234–244 (1925–1926).

Symonds, P. M.: "A Social Attitudes Questionnaire," *Jour. Ed. Psychol.*, 16: 316–322.

Watson, G. B.: "The Measurement of Fair-mindedness," Teachers College Contributions to Education, No. 176, 1925. (Also includes use of Types III and IV.)

Willey, M. M., and Rice, S. A.: "William J. Bryan as a Social Force," *Soc. Forces*, 2: 338–344 (1924). (Also includes use of Type II.)

Willoughby, R. R.: "A Sampling of Student Opinion," *Jour. Soc. Psychol.*, 1: 164–169.

Wooddy, C. H.: "Local Option and Public Opinion," *U. S. National Commission on Law Observance and Enforcement, Official Records*, 5: 61–89.

Zeleny, L. D.: "A Measure of Social Opinions of Students," *Jour. Appl. Sociol.*, 11: 56–64.

TYPE II

Essay Type or Case Method

Albig, W., *Group Opinion and the Mexican*, Chaps. 6, 7, 8, 9, Ph.D. thesis, University of Michigan, 1929.

Alexander, H. B.: "Negro Opinion and Amos and Andy," *Sociol. Soc. Res.*, 16: 345–354 (1932).

Baumgarten, F., and Prescott, D. A.: "Why Children Hate: An Experimental Investigation of the Reactions of School Children of Poland to the Enemy Occupation," *Jour. Ed. Psychol.*, 19: 303–312 (1928).

Bogardus, E. S.: "American Attitudes toward Filipinos," *Sociol. Soc. Res.*, 14: 59–69 (1929).

———: "Filipino Immigrant Attitudes," *Sociol. Soc. Res.*, 14: 469–479 (1930).

———: *Immigration and Race Attitudes*, 1928. (Also includes use of Type IV.)

———: "Social Distance and Its Origins," *Jour. Appl. Sociol.*, 9: 216–226 (1924–1925). (Also includes use of Type V.)

Lasker, B.: *Race Attitudes in Children*, 1929.

Leuba, J. H.: *The Belief in God and Immortality*, 1916.

Merriam, C. E., and Gosnell, H. F.: *Non-voting: Causes and Methods of Control*, 1924. (Also includes use of Types III and VII.)

Penningroth, P. W.: *A Study of Public Opinion in International Relations in Certain Communities*, 1932.

Vaughan, W. F.: "An Experimental Study of Political Prejudice," *Jour. Abn. Soc. Psychol.*, 25: 268–274 (1930).

Willey, M. M., and Rice, S. A.: "William J. Bryan as a Social Force," *Soc. Forces*, 2: 3: 338–344. (Also includes use of Type I.)

Young, P. V.: "Occupational Attitudes and Values of Russian Lumber Workers," *Sociol. Soc. Res.*, 12: 543–553 (1928).

Zimmerman, C. C., and Black, J. D.: *The Marketing Attitudes of Minnesota Farmers*, 1926.

TYPE III

Multiple-choice Tests

Allport, G. W.: "The Composition of Political Attitudes," *Am. Jour. Sociol.*, 35: 220–238.

Bogardus, E. S.: "Measuring Social Distance," *Jour. Appl. Sociol.*, 9: 299–308 (1924–1925).

Hall, O. M.: "Attitudes and Unemployment," *Arch. Psychol.*, No. 165, 1934.

Hart, H.: *Test of Social Attitudes and Interests*, University of Iowa Studies, No. 4, 1923.

Jasper, H. H.: "Optimism and Pessimism in College Environment," *Am. Jour. Sociol.*, 34: 856–873 (1929).

Likert, R.: "A Technique for the Measurement of Attitudes," *Arch. Psychol.*, No. 140, 1932. (Also includes use of Types IV and VI.)

Lockhart, E. G.: *The Attitudes of Children Toward Law*, Ph.D. thesis, University of Iowa Studies in Character, vol. III, No. 1, 1930.

Manry, J. C.: *World Citizenship: A Measurement of Certain Factors Determining Information and Judgment of International Affairs*, Ph.D. thesis, University of Iowa Studies in Character, vol. I, No. 1, 1927.

Merriam, C. E., and Gosnell, H. F.: *Non Voting: Causes and Methods of Control*, 1924. (Also includes use of Types II and VII.)

Van Wagenen, M. J.: *Historical Information and Judgment in Pupils of Elementary Schools*, 1919.

Vetter, G. B.: "The Measurement of Social and Political Attitudes and Other Related Personality Factors," *Jour. Abn. Soc. Psychol.*, 25: 149–189 (1930). (Also includes use of Type VI.)

Watson, G. B.: *The Measurement of Fair-mindedness*, Teachers College Contributions to Education, No. 176, 1925. (Also includes use of Types I and IV.)

TYPE IV

Rating Tests

Allport, F. H., and Hartman, D. A.: "The Measurement and Motivation of Atypical Opinion in a Certain Group," *Am. Pol. Sci. Rev.*, 19: 735–760 (1925). (Also includes use of Type VI.)

Bogardus, E. S.: *Immigration and Race Attitudes*, 1928. (Also includes use of Type II.)

Carter, T. M.: "Ethical Attitudes of 623 Men and Women," *Int. Jour. Ethics*, 43: 279–294 (1933).

Chen, W. K. C.: *The Influence of Oral Propaganda Material upon Students' Attitudes*, Ph.D. thesis, Columbia University, *Arch. Psychol.*, No. 150, 1933.

Clark, W. W.: "The Measurement of Social Attitudes," *Jour. Appl. Sociol.*, 8: 345–354 (1924).

Droba, D. D.: "Effects of Various Factors on Militarism-Pacifism," *Jour. Abn. Soc. Psychol.*, 26: 141–153. (Also includes use of Type VI.)

Dudycha, G. J.: "The Moral and Popular Beliefs of College Freshmen," *Sch. Soc.*, 32: 69–72 (1930).

Garrison, K. C., and Mann, M.: "A Study of the Opinions of College Students," *Jour. Soc. Psychol.*, 2: 168–178 (1931).

Guthrie, E. R.: "Measuring Student Opinion of Teachers," *Sch. Soc.*, 25: 175–176 (1927). (Also includes use of Type V.)

Harper, H. R.: *What European and American Students Think on International Problems: A Comparative Study of the World-mindedness of University Students*, Ph.D. thesis,

Columbia University, 1931. Studies of the International Institute of Teachers College, No. 12.

Jones, E. S.: "The Opinions of College Students," *Jour. Appl. Psychol.*, 10: 428–436.

Kornhauser, A. W.: "Changes in the Information and Attitudes of Students in an Economics Course," *Jour. Ed. Res.*, 22: 288–298 (1930).

Likert, R.: "A Technique for the Measurement of Attitudes," *Arch. Psychol.*, No. 140, 1932. (Also includes use of Types III and VI.)

Lund, F. H.: "The Psychology of Belief," *Jour. Abn. Psychol.*, 20: 63–81.

Neumann, G. B.: *A Study of the International Attitudes of High School Students*, Teachers College Contributions to Education, No. 239, 1926.

Rice, S. A.: "Differential Changes of Political Preference Under Campaign Stimulation," *Jour. Abn. Soc. Psychol.*, 21: 297–303.

Robinson, E. S.: "Are Radio Fans Influenced? An Experiment in Measuring Changes in Public Opinion," *Survey*, 68: 546–547 (1932).

Watson, G. B.: *The Measurement of Fair-mindedness*, Teachers College Contributions to Education, No. 176, 1925. (Also includes use of Types I and III.)

TYPE V

Ranking Tests

Albig, W.: *Group Opinion and the Mexican*, Chap. 5, Ph.D. thesis, University of Michigan, 1929.

Anderson, W. A.: "The Occupational Attitudes and Choices of a Group of College Men," *Soc. Forces*, 6: 278–283 (1927), 6: 467–473 (1928).

Bogardus, E. S.: "Social Distance and Its Origins," *Jour. Appl. Sociol.*, 9: 216–226 (1924–1925). (Also includes use of Type II.)

Brogan, A. P.: "Problems and Methods in Statistical Ethics," *Pub. Am. Sociol. Soc.*, 21: 174–177.

Davis, J.: "Testing the Social Attitudes of Children in the Government Schools of Russia," *Am. Jour. Sociol.*, 32: 947–952.

Guilford, J. P.: "Racial Preferences of 1,000 American University Students," *Jour. Soc. Psychol.*, 2: 179–204 (1931). (Also includes use of Type VII.)

Guthrie, E. R.: "Measuring Student Opinion of Teachers," *Sch. Soc.*, 25: 175–176 (1927). (Also includes use of Type IV.)

Young, D.: "Some Effects of a Course in American Race Problems on the Race Prejudice of 450 Undergraduates at the University of Pennsylvania," *Jour. Abn. Soc. Psychol.*, 22: 235–242 (1927).

TYPE VI

An Attitude Scale

Allport, F. H., and Hartman, D. A.: "The Measurement and Motivation of Atypical Opinion in a Certain Group," *Am. Pol. Sci. Rev.*, 19: 735–760 (1925). (Also includes use of Type IV.)

Droba, D. D.: "Effects of Various Factors on Militarism—Pacifism," *Jour. Abn. Soc. Psychol.*, 26: 141–153. (Also includes use of Type IV.)

Harper, M. H.: "Social Beliefs and Attitudes of American Educators," Teachers College Contributions to Education, No. 294, 1927.

Katz, D., and Allport, F. H.: *Student Attitudes*, a report of the Syracuse University Reaction Study, 1931.

Likert, R.: "A Technique for the Measurement of Attitudes," *Arch. Psychol.*, No. 140, 1932. (Also includes use of Types III and IV.)

Moore, G., and Garrison, K. C.: "A Comparative Study of Social and Political Attitudes of College Students," *Jour. Abn. Soc. Psychol.*, 27: 195–208 (1932).

Vetter, G. B.: "The Measurement of Social and Political Attitudes and Other Related Personality Factors," *Jour. Abn. Soc. Psychol.*, 25: 149–189. (Also includes use of Type III.)

TYPE VII

The Thurstone Scale

Allport, F. H., and Hartman, D. A.: "A Technique for the Measurement and Analysis of Public Opinion," *Pub. Am. Sociol. Soc.*, 32: 241–244.

Beyle, H.: "A Scale for the Measurement of Attitude toward Candidates for Elective Governmental Office," *Am. Pol. Sci. Rev.*, 26: 3: 527–545 (1932).

Carlson, H. B.: "Attitudes of Undergraduate Students," *Jour. Soc. Psychol.*, 5: 202–213.

Guilford, J. P.: "Racial Preferences of 1,000 American University Students," *Jour. Soc. Psychol.*, 2: 179–204 (1931). (Also includes use of Type V.)

Hinckley, E. D.: "The Influence of Individual Opinion on Construction of an Attitude Scale," *Jour. Soc. Psychol.*, 3: 283–296.

Lentz, T. F., Jr.: "Reliability of Opinionaire Technique Studied Intensively by the Retest Method," *Jour. Soc. Psychol.*, 5: 338–364.

Likert, R., and Roslow, S., and Murphy, G.: "A Simple and Reliable Method of Scoring the Thurstone Attitude Scales," *Jour. Soc. Psychol.*, 5: 228–238.

Pintner, R., and Forlano, G.: "The Influence of Attitude upon Scaling of Attitude Items," *Jour. Soc. Psychol.*, 8: 39–45.

Remmers, H. H., and Silance, E. B.: "Generalized Attitude Scales," *Jour. Soc. Psychol.*, 5: 298–312.

Rosander, A. C.: "An Attitude Scale Based upon Behavior Situations," *Jour. Soc. Psychol.*, 8: 3–15.

Seashore, R. H., and Hevner, K.: "A Time-saving Device for the Construction of Attitude Scales," *Jour. Soc. Psychol.*, 4: 366–372.

Thurstone, L. L., and Chave, E. J.: *The Measurement of Attitude*, 1929. (Professor Thurstone and his students have constructed scales and developed tests on more than a score of topics. Tests on Militarism-Pacifism, Prohibition, Movies, Law, etc., can be obtained from the University of Chicago Press.)

Uhrbrock, R. S.: "Attitudes of 4430 Employees," *Jour. Soc. Psychol.*, 5: 365–377.

Whisler, L. D.: "Multiple-factor Analysis of Generalized Attitudes," *Jour. Soc. Psychol.*, 5: 283–297.

TYPE VIII

Behavior Records and Opinion

English, G. H.: "What Lies behind Our Votes: Records of Progress," *Int. Rev.*, 12: 78–90.

Faris, E.: *The Nature of Human Nature*, Chap. 12, 1937.

LaPiere, R. T.: "Attitudes vs. Actions," *Soc. Forces*, 13: 230–237.

——: "Race Prejudice: France and England," *Soc. Forces*, 7: 101–111.

Lundberg, G. A.: "The Demographic and Economic Basis of Political Radicalism and Conservatism," *Am. Jour. Sociol.*, 32: 790–799.

Meier, N. C.: "Motives in Voting: A Study in Public Opinion," *Am. Jour. Sociol.*, 31: 199–212.

Merriam, C. E., and Gosnell, H. F.: *Non-voting: Causes and Methods of Control*, 1924. (Also includes use of Types II and III.)

Ogburn, W. F., and Goltra, I.: "How Women Vote," *Pol. Sci. Quar.*, 34: 413–433.

Robinson, C. E.: *Straw Votes*, 1932.

Tibbitts, C.: "Majority Votes and the Business Cycle," *Am. Jour. Sociol.*, 36: 596–607.

Willcox, W. F.: "Attempts to Measure Public Opinion about Repealing the 18th Amendment," *Jour. Am. Stat. Assoc.*, 26: 243–261.

Unclassified Studies Relating to Opinion Tests

Achilles, P. S.: *The Effectiveness of Certain Social Hygiene Literature*, 1923.

Hart, H.: "Changing Opinions about Business Prosperity: A Consensus of Magazine Opinion in the United States," *Am. Jour. Sociol.*, 38: 665–688.

Hartshorne, H., and May, M.: *Studies in Deceit*, 1928.

—— and ——: "Testing the Knowledge of Right and Wrong," *Rel. Ed. Ass. Mon.*, No. 1, 1927.

Hayes, S. P., Jr.: "Occupational and Sex Differences in Political Attitudes," *Jour. Soc. Psychol.*, 8: 87–113.

Jones, V.: "Ideas of Right and Wrong among Teachers and Children," *Teachers College Rec.*, 30: 529–541.

Kolstad, A.: *A Study of Opinions on Some International Problems*, Teachers College Contributions to Education, No. 555, 1933.

Lacey, J. M.: *Social Studies Concepts of Children in the First Three Grades*, Teachers College Contributions to Education, No. 548, 1932.

Lockhart, E. G.: *The Attitudes of Children toward Law*, University of Iowa Studies in Character, vol. III, No. 1, 1930.

Peterson, R. C., and Thurstone, L. L.: *Motion Pictures and the Social Attitudes of Children*, 1933.

Thurstone, L. L.: "An Experimental Study of Nationality Preferences," *Jour. Gen. Psychol.*, 1: 405–425.

Vetter, G. B.: "The Study of Social and Political Opinions," *Jour. Abn. Soc. Psychol.*, 25: 26–39.

Washburne, J. N.: "Experimental Study of Various Graphic, Tabular, and Textual Methods of Presenting Quantitative Material," *Jour. Ed. Psychol.*, 18: 361–376, 465–476.

Williamson, E. G., and Darley, J. G.: "The Measurement of Social Attitudes of College Students: II. Validation of Two Attitude Tests," *Jour. Soc. Psychol.*, 8: 231–242.

Witmer, H. L.: *The Attitudes of Mothers toward Sex Education*, 1929.

Woolston, H.: "Stepbrothers; A Study of Prejudice and Convention," *Soc. Forces*, 6: 368–375.

Zimmerman, C. C.: "Types of Farmers' Attitudes," *Soc. Forces*, 5: 591–596.

CHAPTER XIII

OPINION CHANGE

Allport, G. W.: "The Composition of Political Attitudes," *Am. Jour. Sociol.*, 35: 220–238.

Annis, A. D., and Meier, N. C.: "The Induction of Opinion through Suggestion, by Means of Planted Content," *Jour. Soc. Psychol.*, 5: 65–81.

Arnet, C. E., *et al.*: "Prestige as a Factor in Attitude Changes," *Sociol. Soc. Res.*, 16: 49–55.

Baker, W. J., and McGregor, D.: "Conversation as a Reflector of Social Change," *Jour. Soc. Psychol.*, 8: 487–490.

Bernays, E. L.: "Manipulating Public Opinion," *Am. Jour. Sociol.*, 33: 958–971.

Biddle, W. W.: *Propaganda and Education*, Teachers College Contributions to Education, No. 531, 1932.

Binnewies, W. G.: "Measuring Changes in Opinion," *Sociol. Soc. Res.*, 16: 143–148.

Blythe, I. T.: "The Textbooks and New Discoveries, Emphases and Viewpoints in American History," *Historical Outlook*, 23: 395–402.

Bogardus, E. S.: "Analyzing Changes in Public Opinion," *Sociol. Soc. Res.*, 9: 372–381.

————: "Mutations in Social Distance," *Jour. Appl. Sociol.*, 11: 77–83.

Campbell, D. W., and Stover, G. F.: "Teaching International-mindedness in the Social Studies," *Jour. Ed. Sociol.*, 7: 244–248.

Carr, L. J.: "Public Opinion as a Dynamic Concept," *Sociol. Soc. Res.*, 13: 18–30.

Chen, W. K. C.: "The Influence of Oral Propaganda Material upon Students' Attitudes," *Arch. Psychol.*, No. 150, 1923.

Cherrington, B. M., and Miller, L. W.: "Changes in Attitude as the Result of a Lecture and Reading Similar Materials," *Jour. Soc. Psychol.*, 4: 479–484.

Crossley, A. M.: "Straw Polls in 1936," *Pub. Opin. Quar.*, 1: 24–36.

Encyclopaedia of the Social Sciences, "Arbitration—Commercial, Industrial, International," "Boycott," "Mediation," "Pressures—Social."

Gardiner, I. C.: "Effect of a Group of Social Stimuli upon Attitudes," *Jour. Ed. Psychol.*, 26: 471–479.

Ghoshal, U. N.: "Hindu Political Ideas of Today," *Scientia*, 20: 111–120.

Griffin, H. C.: "Changes in the Religious Attitudes of College Students," *Rel. Ed.*, 24: 159–164.

Hart, H.: "Changing Opinions about Business Prosperity: A Consensus of Magazine Opinion in the United States," *Am. Jour. Sociol.*, 38: 665–688.

Hershey, R. A.: "Periodical Changes in Male Workers," *Jour. Personnel Res.*, 77: 459–464.

Jenness, A.: "Changing Opinion regarding a Matter of Fact," *Jour. Abn. Soc. Psychol.*, 27: 279–296.

————: "Social Influences in the Change of Opinion," *Jour. Abn. Soc. Psychol.*, 27: 29–34.

Knower, F. H.: "Experimental Studies in Changes in Attitudes, I. A Study of the Effect of Oral Argument on Changes of Attitude," *Jour. Soc. Psychol.*, 6: 315–347. "II. A Study of the Effect of Printed Argument on Changes in Attitude," *Jour. Abn. Soc. Psychol.*, 30: 522–532. "III. Some Incidence of Attitude Changes," *Jour. Appl. Psychol.*, 20: 114–127.

Kornhauser, A. W.: "Changes in Information and Attitudes of Students in an Economics Course," *Jour. Ed. Res.*, 22: 288–298.

Lasswell, H. D.: "The Theory of Political Propaganda," *Am. Pol. Sci. Rev.*, 31: 627–631.

Paget, E. H.: "Sudden Changes in Group Opinion," *Soc. Forces*, 7: 438–444.

Peterson, R. C., and Thurstone, L. L.: *Motion Pictures and the Social Attitudes of Children*, 1933.

Prince, S. H.: *Catastrophe and Social Change*, 1920.

Ravitch, J.: "Relative Rate of Change in Customs and Beliefs of Modern Jews," *Proc. Am. Sociol. Soc.*, 19: 171–176.

Robinson, C. E.: "Recent Development in the Straw-poll Field," Part I, *Pub. Opin. Quar.*, 1: 3: 45–56; Part II, 1: 4: 42–52.

Robinson, E. S.: "Are Radio Fans Influenced?" *Survey*, 68: 546–547.

Rosenthal, S. P.: "Change of Socio-economic Attitudes under Radical Motion Picture Propaganda," *Arch. Psychol.*, No. 166, 1934.

Thurstone, L. L.: "Influence of Motion Pictures on Children's Attitudes," *Jour. Soc. Psychol.*, 2: 291–305.

Vreeland, F. M.: "The Process of Reform with Especial Reference to Reform Groups in the Field of Population," Ph.D. thesis, University of Michigan, 1929.

Walser, F.: *The Art of Conference*, 1933.

Wheeler, J. H.: "Change of Individual Opinion to Accord with Group Opinion," *Jour. Abn. Soc. Psychol.*, 24: 203–206.

White, W. A., and Myer, W. E.: *Conflict in American Public Opinion*, 1925.

Young, D.: "Some Effects of a Course in American Race Problems on the Race Prejudice of 450 Undergraduates at the University of Pennsylvania," *Jour. Abn. Soc. Psychol.*, 22: 235–242.

Chapters XIV and XV

Censorship

Bibliographies on Censorship

Beman, L. T. (compiler): *Selected Articles on Censorship of Speech and the Press*, 1930.

Childs, H. L.: *A Reference Guide to the Study of Public Opinion*, pp. 65–68, 1934.

Lasswell, H. D., *et al.*: *Propaganda and Promotional Activities*, pp. 382–401, 1935.

Schroeder, T. A.: *Free Speech Bibliography*, New York, H. W. Wilson Company, 1922.

Young, K., and Lawrence, R. D.: *Bibliography on Censorship and Propaganda*, University of Oregon Publication, Journalism Series, 1928.

Encyclopaedia of the Social Sciences, "Alien and Sedition Acts," "Assembly—Right of," "Blacklist," "Blacklist—Labor, War," "Blasphemy," "Censorship," "Civil Liberties," "Freedom," "Freedom of Association," "Freedom of Speech and of the Press," "Heresy," "Inquisition," "Intolerance," "Liberalism," "Liberty," "John Locke," "John Stuart Mill," "Sedition."

Liberalism, Freedom and Censorship

Acton, J. E.: *The History of Freedom*, 1919.

Annals of the American Academy of Political and Social Science, vol. CLXXX, July, 1935.

Bates, E. S.: *This Land of Liberty*, 1930.

Becker, C. L.: "New Liberties for Old," *Jour. Soc. Phil.*, 1: 101–121.

Benett, W.: *Freedom and Liberty*, Oxford University Press, 1920.

Bentham, J.: *On the Liberty of the Press and Public Discussion*, 1821.

Buell, R. L.: *Contemporary French Politics*, Chap. 9, 1920.

Bury, J. B.: *History of Freedom of Thought*, 1913.

Chafee, Z.: *Freedom of Speech*, 1920.

Chapin, F. S.: *Cultural Change*, pp. 279–312, 1928.

Cooley, C. H.: *Social Organization*, Chaps. 7, 8, 9, 10, 1909.

Dewey, J.: *Liberalism and Social Action*, 1935.

Ernst, M. L., and Seagle, W.: *To the Pure: A Study of Obscenity and the Censor*, 1928.

Freedom of Communication, Pub. Am. Sociol. Soc., 1915.

Graves, W. B. (ed.): *Readings in Public Opinion*, Chap. 31, 1928.

Haynes, E. S. P.: *The Decline of Liberty in England*, Chap. 5, 1916.

Hays, A. G.: *Let Freedom Ring*, 1928.

Kallen, H. M.: *Indecency and the Seven Arts*, 1930.

Laski, H. J.: *The Rise of European Liberalism*, London, 1936.

Lippmann, W.: *The Good Society*, 1937.

Logan, G. B.: *Liberty in the Modern World*, 1928.

Mill, J. S.: *Essay on Liberty*, 1912 edition.

Neilson, W. A.: "The Theory of Censorship," *Atlantic*, 145: 13–16.

Odegard, P. H.: *The American Public Mind*, Chap. 9, 1930.

Putnam, G. H.: *The Censorship of the Church of Rome*, 1906.

Riegel, O. W.: *Mobilizing for Chaos*, 1934.

Seagle, W.: *Cato, or the Future of Censorship*, London, 1930.

Seldes, G.: *The Vatican: Yesterday, Today, Tomorrow*, Chap. 11, 1934.

Smith, T. V.: *The Promise of American Politics*, Chap. 2, 1936.

Whipple, L.: *The Story of Civil Liberty in the United States*, 1927.

Young, K.: *Social Psychology*, Chap. 26, 1930.

Books

Adcock, A.: "Books That Have Been Banned," *Bookman*, 74: 26–28.

Calverton, V. F.: *The Liberation of American Literature*, 1932.

Darling, Lord, *et al.*: "The Censorship of Books," *Nineteenth Cent.*, 105: 433–450.

Gillett, C. R.: *Burned Books*, 2 vols., 1932.

Mussey, H. R.: "The Christian Science Censor. II. 'Obnoxious Books,'" *Nation*, 130: 175.

Records of the International Conference for the Suppression of the Circulation of and Traffic in Obscene Publications, 1923 (C.734.M.299, 1923. IV). *Suppression of the Circulation of and Traffic in Obscene Publications*. Summary of Reports Received from Governments (Ser. L.o.N.P. 1928. IV. 6).

Stewart, H.: "Is Censorship Necessary?" *Sat. Rev. Lit.*, 154: 218.

"What Russians May and May Not Read," *Lit. Digest*, 30: 27–28.

The Press

Bent, S.: "Freedom of Speech, Conscience and the Press," in *Freedom in the Modern World* (Kallen, H. M., ed.), 1928.

Dawson, S. A.: *Freedom of the Press*, 1924.

Lippmann, W.: *Liberty and the News*, 1920.

Park, R. E.: *The Immigrant Press and Its Control*, 1922.

Salmon, L. M.: *The Newspaper and Authority*, Chap. 2, 1923.

Schofield, H.: "Freedom of the Press in the United States," *Proc. Am. Sociol. Soc.*, 9: 67–116.

Seldes, G.: *Freedom of the Press*, 1935.

Siebert, F. S.: *The Rights and Privileges of the Press*, 1934.

The Nation: Series of articles: "Thought Control in Japan," 112: 290 (1921). "The Authors' Bureau of Censorship," 113: 40 (1921). "'Dangerous Thoughts' in Japan," 117: 251 (1923). "The Fascisti Guarantee Freedom of the Press," 116: 280 (1923). "Bayonet Rule for Our Colonial Press," 116: 267 (1923). "Gagging the Press in Italy," 119: 269 (1924). "Censorship in Bulgaria," 121: 524 (1925). "Free Speech in China," 122: 253 (1926). "Mussolini Chokes the Press," 124: 34 (1927). "The Indecency of Censorship," 124: 162 (1927). "Japan Dams 'Dangerous Thoughts,'" 127: 504 (1928). "Censorship in Ireland," 128: 570 (1929). "The Myth of a Free Press," 128: 576 (1929). "Modern Spain, III. Censorship," 129: 50 (1929). "The Christian Science Censor: III. The Freedom of the Press," 130: 241 (1930). "Censorship in the Irish Free State," 133: 49 (1931). "Red Menace and Yellow Journalism," 132: 602 (1931).

Wickwar, W. H.: *The Struggle for the Freedom of the Press*, 1928.

Wildes, H. E.: *Japan in Crisis*, 1934.

——: "Press Freedom in Japan," *Am. Jour. Sociol.*, 32: 601–614.

The Motion Picture

Beman, L. T.: *Selected Articles on Censorship of the Theater and Moving Pictures* (Bibliography), New York, H. W. Wilson Company, 1931.

Clements, T.: "Censoring the Talkies," *New Republic*, 59: 64–66.

Ernst, M. L., and Lorentz, P.: *Censored: The Private Life of the Movie*, 1930.

Hays, W. H.: "Motion Pictures and their Censors," *Rev. of Rev.*, 75: 393–398.

Levenson, J.: "Censorship of the Movies," *Forum*, 69: 1404–1414.

Lewis, H. T.: *The Motion Picture Industry*, Chap. 12, 1933.

Lowry, E. G.: "Reform in the Movies," *World's Work*, 50: 329–333, 429–437.

Merz, C.: "Morals and the Movies," *New Republic*, 33: 179.

Montagu, I.: *The Political Censorship of Films*, London, 1929.

Oberholtzer, E. P.: "Moving Picture: Obiter dicta of a Censor," *Yale Rev.*, 9: 620–632.

Perlman, W. J.: *The Movies on Trial*, 1936.

Quirk, J. R.: "Wowsers Tackle the Movies," *Am. Mercury*, 11: 349–356.

Robson, W. A.: "British Films are Pure," *Nation*, 131: 547.

Seabury, W. M.: *The Public and the Motion Picture Industry*, pp. 143–159, 1926.

What Shocked the Censors, National Council on Freedom from Censorship, 1933.

CHAPTER XVI

SPECIAL INTEREST GROUPS

For an extended bibliography on national groups, local institutions, political parties, professional groups, labor groups, agrarian groups, sex and age groups, ecclesiastical groups, racial groups and business groups, see Lasswell, H. D., *et al.*: *Propaganda and Promotional Activities*, pp. 67–161.

A Directory of Organizations Engaged in Governmental Research, Government Research Association, 1935.

Beales, A. C. F.: *History of Peace*, 1931.

Bernard, L. L.: *An Introduction to Social Psychology*, pp. 418 *ff.*, 1926.

Breckenridge, S. P.: *Women in the Twentieth Century*, 1933.

Brown, J. F.: *Psychology and the Social Order*, Chaps. 6–12, 1936.

Brownlow, L. (ed.): *A Directory of Organizations in the Field of Public Administration*, 1932.

Catt, C. C. and Shuler, N. R.: *Woman Suffrage and Politics*, 1923.

Chambers, M. M.: *Youth-Serving Organizations: National Non-governmental Associations*, 1937.

Childs, H. L.: "Pressure Groups and Propaganda," Chap. 6, in *The American Political Scene* (Logan, E. B., ed.), 1936.

Commercial and Industrial Organizations of the United States, U. S. Department of Commerce Publication, 1931.

Curti, M. E.: *The American Peace Crusade*, Vol. I, 1929.

Davis, J.: *Contemporary Social Movements*, 1930.

Directory of Youth Organizations, National Youth Administration, 1937.

Encyclopaedia of the Social Sciences, "American Legion," "American Protective Association," "Caste," "Class," "Class Consciousness," "Clubs—Political," "Constituency," "Cults," "Faction," "Group," "Lobby," "Minorities—National," "Political Parties," "Patriotism," "Revivals—Religious Sects," "Trade Associations."

Organized Social Movements: "Abolition," "Anticlericalism," "Antimilitarism," "Antiradicalism," "Anti-Saloon League," "Antisemitism," "Back-to-the-Land Movements," "Benefit Societies," "Birth Control," "Boys' and Girls' Clubs," "Chautauqua," "Cruelty to Animals," "Emancipation," "Farm Bloc—U. S.," "Farm Bureau Federation—American," "Fraternal Orders," "Grange," "Ku Klux Klan," "Labor Movement," "Messianism," "Pacifism," "Peace Movements," "Prohibition," "Reformism," "Socialist Parties," "Temperance Movements," "Trade Unions," "Youth Movements."

Everett, S.: *Democracy Faces the Future*, Chap. 8, 1935.

Ferguson, C. W.: *Fifty Million Brothers*, 1937.

Foth, J. H.: *Trade Associations*, 1930.

Freeman, E.: *Social Psychology*, Chap. 20, 1936.

Friedrich, C. J.: *Constitutional Government and Politics*, Chap. 24, 1937.

Graves, W. B. (ed.): *Readings in Public Opinion*, Chaps. 17, 19, 20, 1928.

Handbook of International Organizations, League of Nations, 1929, and *Supplement*, 1931.

Handbook of Learned Societies and Institutions, Carnegie Institute of Washington, 1908.

Handbook of Scientific and Technical Societies and Institutions of the United States and Canada, National Research Council, 1937.

Herring, E. P.: *Group Representation Before Congress*, 1929.

————: *Public Administration and the Public Interest*, 1936.

Lasswell, H. D.: *Politics*, Chap. 7, 1936.

MacIver, R. M.: *Society*, Chap. 13, 1937.

Macy, J.: *The Anti-slavery Crusade*, Yale University Press, 1919.

Naylor, E. H.: *Trade Associations: Their Organization and Management*, 1921.

North, C. C.: *Social Differentiation*, 1926.

Odegard, P. H.: *Pressure Politics*, 1928.

Pendry, E. R.: *Organizations for Youth*, 1935.

Phelps, C.: *Anglo-American Peace Movement in the Mid-nineteenth Century*, Columbia University Press, 1930.

Pierce, B. L.: *Citizens' Organizations and the Civic Training of Youth*, 1933.

Preuss, A.: *A Dictionary of Secret and Other Societies*, 1924.

Raup, B.: *Education and Organized Interests in America*, 1936.

Savord, R. (compiler): *Directory of American Agencies concerned with International Affairs*, Council on Foreign Relations, Inc., 1931.

Standards Yearbook, 1933, Bureau of Standards Miscellaneous Publication, No. 139.

Timmons, B. F.: *Personnel Practices among Ohio Industries*, Ohio State University Press, Bureau of Business Research Monographs, No. 18, 1931.

————: "Group Insurance in 189 Ohio Industrial Firms," *Sociol. Soc. Res.*, 16: 39–48.

Tönnies, F.: *Gemeinschaft und Gesellschaft*, pp. 1–32, Berlin, K. Curtius, 1926.

World Almanac, pp. 393–405, 1937.

CHAPTERS XVII AND XVIII

THE NATURE AND ART OF PROPAGANDA

There are three bibliographies which are extremely useful to the student of the nature, techniques, and results of modern propaganda. They are:

Young, K., and Lawrence, R. D.: *Bibliography on Censorship and Propaganda* University of Oregon Publication, Journalism Series, 1928.

Childs, H. L.: *A Reference Guide to the Study of Public Opinion*, Princeton University, 1934.

Lasswell, H. D., Casey, R. D., and Smith, B. L.: *Propaganda and Promotional Activities*, University of Minnesota Press, 1935.

Achilles, P. S.: *Psychology at Work*, Chap. 7, 1932.

Adler, M. J.: *Art and Prudence*, 1937.

Bagehot, W.: *Literary Studies*, vol. V, pp. 422–437, London, R. H. Hutton, 1884.

Baster, A. S. J.: *Advertising Reconsidered*, London, P. S. King & Son, Ltd., 1935.

Beaglehole, E.: "Some Aspects of Propaganda," *Australian Jour. Psychol. Phil.*, 6: 93–110.

Bernays, E. L.: *Propaganda*, 1928.

Bernstorff, Count J. von: *My Three Years in America*, 1920.

Biddle, W. W.: "A Psychological Definition of Propaganda," *Jour. Abn. Soc. Psychol.*, 26: 283–295.

————: *Propaganda and Education*, Teachers College Contributions to Education, No. 531, 1932.

Bliven, B.: "Let's Have More Propaganda," *World Tomorrow*, December, 1926.

Brown, J. M.: "Propagandist Theatres," *Theatre Arts Mon.*, 8: 129–142.

Bruntz, G. C.: "Propaganda As an Instrument of War," *Cur. Hist.*, July, 1930.

Caldwell, O. W.: "Science, Truth, or Propaganda," *Sch. Soc.*, 37: 169–174.

Cantril, H., and Allport, G. W.: *The Psychology of Radio*, pp. 59–64, 1935.

Carr, W. G.: "School Child and Propaganda," *National Conference of Social Work Proceedings*, pp. 597–605, 1931.

Carter, J.: "Propaganda—As Seen in Recent Books," *Outlook and Independent*, July 23, 1930.

Chase, S.: *The Tragedy of Waste*, Chap. 7, 1925.

Childs, H. L. (ed.): *Propaganda and Dictatorship*, 1936.

Clarke, E. L.: *The Art of Straight Thinking*, Chap. 13, 1929.

Conclusions and Recommendations of the Commission, Report of the Commission on the Social Studies, American Historical Association, 1934.

Creel, G.: *How We Advertised America*, 1920.

Desmond, R. W.: *The Press and World Affairs*, pp. 154–169, 1937.

Dickinson, H. W.: *Crying Our Wares*, 1929.

Doob, L. W.: *Propaganda*, 1935.

Durstine, R. S.: *This Advertising Business*, 1928.

Ellis, E. (ed.): *Education against Propaganda*, 7th Yearbook, National Council for the Social Studies, 1937.

Encyclopaedia of the Social Sciences, "Advertising," "Business Ethics," "Literature," "Promotion," "Propaganda," "Publicity."

Finney, R. L.: *A Sociological Philosophy of Education*, Chap. 20, 1928.

French, G.: *20th Century Advertising*, 1926.

Gaus, J. M.: *Great Britain, A Study in Civic Loyalty*, 1929.

Gibbs, P. H.: *More That Must Be Told*, 1921.

————: *Now It Can Be Told*, 1920.

Graves, W. B. (ed.): *Readings in Public Opinion*, 1928.

Gruening, E.: "Power and Propaganda," *Am. Econ. Rev. Supplement*, March, 1931.

————: *The Public Pays*, 1931.

Hapgood, N. (ed.): *Professional Patriots*, 1927.

Harper, S. N.: *Civic Training in Soviet Russia*, Chaps. 14, 15, 1929.

Herring, E. P.: *Group Representation before Congress*, 1929.

Hotchkiss, G. B.: *An Outline of Advertising: Its Philosophy, Science, Art, and Strategy*, 1933.

Huxley, A.: "Notes on Propaganda," *Harper's*, 174: 32–41.

Irwin, W. H.: *Propaganda and the News*, 1936.

Jacobson, C.: "Exploitation of the Public Schools by Outside Organizations," *Ed. Res. Record*, 1: 91–98.

Jordan, E.: *Theory of Legislation*, Indianapolis, Progress Publishing Co., 1930.

Jorgensen, E. O.: *Betrayal of Our Public Schools*, Educators Protective Association of America, 1344 Altgeld Ave., Chicago, Ill., 1930.

Kallen, H. M.: *Education Versus Indoctrination in the Schools*, Public Policy Pamphlet No. 13, University of Chicago Press, 1934.

Kaltenborn, H. V.: "Propaganda Land," *Century*, 114: 678–687.

Kenner, H. J.: *The Fight for Truth in Advertising*, 1936.

Kent, F. R.: *The Great Game of Politics*, 1923.

Lasswell, H. D.: *Propaganda Technique in the World War*, 1927.

———: "The Function of the Propagandist," *Int. Jour. Ethics*, 38: 258–268.

———: "The Theory of Political Propaganda," *Am. Pol. Sci. Rev.*, 21: 627–631.

Lenin, N.: *Agitation and Propaganda*, Vienna, Marxistische Bibliothek, vol. VIII, 1929.

Levin, J.: *Power Ethics*, 1931.

Lumley, F. E.: *The Propaganda Menace*, 1933.

Lutz, R. H.: "Studies of World War Propaganda, 1914–1933," *Jour. Mod. Hist.*, 5: 496–516.

MacPherson, W.: *The Psychology of Persuasion*, London, 1920.

Martin, E. D.: *The Meaning of a Liberal Education*, Chap. 3, 1926.

Merriam, C. E.: *Political Power*, pp. 307 *ff.*, 1934.

———: *The Making of Citizens*, 1931.

Michels, R.: *Political Parties*, 1915.

Miller, C. R.: "Propagandist in the Public School," *School Executives Mag.*, 50: 217–219.

Millis, W.: *The Martial Spirit*, 1931.

Minnich, H. C.: *William Holmes McGuffey and His Readers*, 1936.

Mott, F. L., and Casey, R. D. (eds.): *Interpretations of Journalism*, Chaps. 46, 47, 48, 1937.

Motvani, K. L.: "Propaganda in Mahatma Gandhi's Movement," *Soc. Forces*, 8: 574–581.

Overstreet, H. A.: *Influencing Human Behavior*, 1925.

Palm, F. C.: *The Middle Classes Then and Now*, Chaps. 9, 18, 19, 28, 1936.

Parker, H. L.: "Plan for Sifting Propaganda in the Schools," *Elementary Sch. Jour.*, 33: 277–282.

Pierce, B. L.: *Citizens' Organizations and the Civic Training of Youth*, 1933.

———: *Public Opinion and the Teaching of History*, 1926.

Poffenberger, A. T.: *Psychology in Advertising*, 1925.

Ponsonby, A.: *Falsehood in Wartime*, 1928.

"Pressure Groups and Propaganda," *Ann. Am. Acad. Pol. Soc. Sci.*, vol. CLXXIX.

Rassak, J.: *Psychologie de l'opinion et de la propagande politique*, Paris, 1927.

Report of the Committee on Propaganda in the Schools, National Education Association, 1929.

Riegel, O. W.: *Mobilizing for Chaos: The Story of the New Propaganda*, Yale University Press, 1934.

Rorty, J.: *Our Master's Voice, Advertising*, 1934.

Russell, B. R.: *Education and the Modern World*, 1932.

———: *Free Thought and Official Propaganda*, 1922.

Salmon, L. M.: *The Newspaper and Authority*, Chap. 12, 1923.

————: *The Newspaper and the Historian*, Chap. 4, 1923.

Schultze-Pfaelzer, G.: *Propaganda, Agitation, Reklame*, Berlin, Stilke, 1923.

Squires, J. D.: *British Propaganda at Home and in the United States*, 1914–1917, Harvard University Press, 1935.

Stern-Rubarth, E.: *Die Propaganda als politisches Instrument*, Berlin, Trowitzsch, 1921.

Stewart, F. M.: "Propaganda Methods of the National Civil Service Reform League," *Southwest. Pol. Soc. Sci. Quar.*, 9: 15–37.

Thimme, H.: *Weltkrieg ohne Waffen*, Stuttgard, 1932.

Thompson, C. D.: *Confessions of the Power Trust*, 1932.

Thouless, R. H.: *Straight and Crooked Thinking*, 1930.

Van Loon, H.: "Napoleon as a Propagandist," *Nation*, Apr. 5, 1919.

Viereck, G. S.: *Spreading Germs of Hate*, 1930.

Weeks, A. D.: *The Control of the Social Mind*, 1923.

Wilkerson, M. M.: *Public Opinion and the Spanish-American War*, 1932.

Willis, I. C.: *England's Holy War*, 1928.

Wreford, R.: "Propaganda, Evil and Good," *Nineteenth Century*, 1923.

Wright, Q. (ed.): *Public Opinion and World Politics*, 1933.

Young, K.: Social Psychology, Chap. 27, 1930.

CHAPTER XIX

THE RADIO

In F. H. Lumley's *Measurement in Radio* there is a bibliography of 732 items.

Air Law Review, published since 1930.

Albig, W.: "The Content of Radio Programs, 1925–1935," *Soc. Forces*, 16: 338–349.

Beuick, M. D.: "The Limited Social Effect of Radio Broadcasting," *Am. Jour. Sociol.*, 32: 615–622.

Bickel, K. A.: *New Empires*, 1930.

Broadcasting and Peace, Intellectual Cooperation Series, Institute of Intellectual Cooperation, League of Nations, 1931.

Buehler, E. C. (compiler): *American versus British System of Radio Control*, H. W. Wilson Company, 1933.

Cantril, H., and Allport, G. W.: *The Psychology of Radio*, 1935.

Clark, K.: *International Communications*, Columbia University Press, 1931.

Commercial Radio Advertising, Federal Radio Commission, Government Printing Office, 1932.

Davis, S. B.: *The Law of Radio Communication*, 1927.

Dunlap, O. E.: *Radio in Advertising*, 1931.

Education by Radio, National Committee on Education by Radio, Pamphlets published from 1930 to 1938.

Education on the Air, Yearbooks of the Institute for Education by Radio, Ohio State University Press, 1930–1936. (Now combined with *Radio and Education*, University of Chicago Press.)

Eisenberg, A. L.: *Children and Radio Programs*, Columbia University Press, 1936.

Encyclopaedia of the Social Sciences, "Radio."

Goldsmith, A. N., and Lescarboura, A. C.: *This Thing Called Broadcasting*, 1930.

Graves, W. B. (ed.): *Readings in Public Opinion*, Chap. 15, 1928.

Harper, S. N.: *Civic Training in Soviet Russia*, Chap. 15, 1929.

Hettinger, H. S.: *A Decade of Radio Advertising*, 1933.

————: *Study of Habits and Preferences of Radio Listeners in Philadelphia*, 21 pp., Philadelphia, Universal Broadcasting Company, 1930.

———: *The Summer Radio Audience,* 48 pp., Philadelphia, Universal Broadcasting Company, 1931.

International Radio Telegraph Conference, Madrid, 1932, *Publications,* 2 vols., Berne, Switzerland, 1932.

Kerwin, J. G.: *The Control of Radio,* Public Policy Pamphlets, No. 10, University of Chicago Press, 1934.

Kirkpatrick, C.: *Report of a Research into the Attitudes and Habits of Radio Listeners,* Webb Book Publishing Company, 1933.

Listening Areas, Second Series, Columbia Broadcasting System, 1933.

Lumley, F. H.: *Children's Preferences for Children's Programs,* Ohio State University, Bureau of Educational Research, Monograph No. 19, 1934.

———: *Measurement in Radio,* 1934.

National Advisory Council on Radio in Education, various publications, New York.

Odegard, P. H.: *American Public Mind,* pp. 223–238, 1930.

Orton, W. A.: *America in Search of Culture,* Chap. 13, 1933.

Publications of the National Broadcasting Company and the Radio Corporation of America.

Radio: The Fifth Estate, Ann. Am. Acad. Pol. Soc. Sci., vol. CLXXVII, 1935.

Riegel, O. W.: *Mobilizing for Chaos,* Yale University Press, 1934.

Robinson, E. S.: "Are Radio Fans Influenced?" *Survey Graphic,* Nov. 1, 1932.

Rorty, J.: *Order on the Air,* 1934.

Rutherford, G. W.: "Radio as a Means of Instruction in Government," *Am. Pol. Sci. Rev.,* 27: 264–273.

Schmeckebier, L. F.: *The Federal Radio Commission; Its History, Activities, and Organization,* Brookings Institution, 1932.

Segal, P. M., and Spearman, P. D.: *State and Municipal Regulation of Radio Communication,* Government Printing Office, 1929.

The BBC Yearbook (yearly), British Broadcasting Company.

"The Freedom of Radio Speech," *Harvard Law Rev.,* 46: 987–993, 1933.

The Importance of Broadcasting, Geneva, Switzerland, International Broadcasting Union, 1932.

The Journal of Radio Law, published since 1931.

Waldrop, F. C., and Borkin, J.: *Television, A Struggle for Power,* 1938.

Willey, M. M., and Rice, S. A.: *Communication Agencies and Social Life,* 1933.

Zollman, C.: *Cases on Air Law,* 1930.

CHAPTER XX

MOTION PICTURES

Arrington, R. E.: "Some Technical Aspects of Observer Reliability as Indicated in Studies of the Talkies," *Am. Jour. Sociol.,* 38: 409–417.

Barry, I.: *Let's Go to the Pictures,* London, Chatto & Windus, 1926.

Beman, L. T.: *Selected Articles on Censorship of the Theater and Moving Pictures,* 1931.

Betts, E.: *Heraclitus: or, The Future of Films,* 1928.

Blumer, H.: *Movies and Conduct,* 1933.

Bollman, G.: *Motion Pictures for Community Needs,* 1922.

Bryher, W.: *Film Problems of Soviet Russia,* London, Pool Publications, 1929.

Buchanan, A.: *Films; the Way of the Cinema,* 1932.

Carter, H.: *The New Spirit in the Cinema,* London, Harold Shaylor, Ltd., 1930.

Charters, W. W.: *Motion Pictures and Youth: A Summary,* 1933.

Chase, W. S.: *The Case for Federal Supervision of Motion Pictures,* 36 pp., Washington, International Reform Federation, 1927.

Conrad, H. S., and Jones, H. E.: "Rural Preferences in Motion Pictures," *Jour. Soc. Psychol.*, 1: 419–423.

Dale, E.: *The Content of Motion Pictures*, 1935.

———: *Children's Attendance at Motion Pictures*, 1935.

Dysinger, W. S., and Ruckmick, C. A.: *The Emotional Responses of Children to the Motion Picture Situation*, 1933.

Encyclopaedia of the Social Sciences, "Motion Pictures."

Ernst, M. L., and Lorentz, P.: *Censored: The Private Life of the Movie*, 1930.

Freeman, F. N., and Hoefer, C.: "An Experimental Study of the Influence of Motion Picture Films on Behavior," *Jour. Ed. Psychol.*, 22: 411–425.

Galliard, O.: "Le Place du cinéma dans la vie sociale," *Musée Sociale*, 38: 297–324.

Geiger, J. R.: "Effect of Motion Pictures on the Mind and Morals of the Young," *Int. Jour. Ethics*, 34: 69–83.

Gould, K. M.: "Cinepatriotism," *Soc. Forces*, 7: 120–129.

Graves, W. B. (ed.): *Readings in Public Opinion*, Chap. 10, 1928.

Hampton, B. B.: *History of the Movies*, 1931.

Harper, S. N.: *Civic Training in Soviet Russia*, Chap. 15, 1929.

Hill, E. C.: *The American Scene*, Chap. 22, 1933.

Holaday, P. W., and Stoddard, G. D.: *Getting Ideas from the Movies*, 1933.

LaPierre, M.: *Le Cinéma et la paix*, Paris, Valois, 1932.

Lashley, K. S., and Watson, J. B.: *Psychological Study of Motion Pictures in Relation to Venereal Disease Campaigns*, 1922.

Le Role Intellectuel du Cinéma, International Institute for Intellectual Cooperation, League of Nations, 1937.

Lewis, H. T.: *The Motion Picture Industry*, 1933.

Mirsky, D. S.: "The Soviet Films," *Virginia Quar. Rev.*, 7: 522–531.

Mitchell, A. M.: *Children and Movies*, 1929.

Montagu, I. G. S.: *The Political Censorship of Films*, London, Victor Gollancz, Ltd., 1929.

Notcutt, L. A., and Latham, G. C. (eds.): *The African and the Cinema*, Edinburgh House Press, 1937.

Odegard, P. H.: *The American Public Mind*, 1930.

Peters, C. C.: *Motion Pictures and Standards of Morality*, 1933.

Peterson, R. C., and Thurstone, L. L.: *Motion Pictures and the Social Attitudes of Children*, 1933.

Publications of the Motion Picture Division, Bureau of Foreign and Domestic Commerce, United States Department of Commerce.

Pudovkin, V. I.: *On Film Technique*, London, Victor Gollancz, Ltd., 1930.

Rotha, P.: *Celluloid, The Film To-day*, 1931.

———: *The Film Till Now*, London, Jonathan Cape, Ltd., 1930.

Seabury, W. M.: *The Public and the Motion Picture Industry*, 1926.

See the forthcoming *Encyclopaedia Cinema*, sponsored by the International Institute of Intellectual Cooperation of the League of Nations.

Seldes, G. V.: *The Seven Lively Arts*, 1924.

Shuttleworth, F. K., and May, M. A.: *The Social Conduct and Attitudes of Movie Fans*, 1933.

The Cinema, 34 pp., Geneva, Child Welfare Committee, League of Nations, 1928.

The Film Daily Yearbook of Motion Pictures, New York, The Film Daily, since 1918.

The Film in National Life (with bibliography), Commission on Educational and Cultural Films, London, Allen & Unwin, Ltd., 1932.

The International Journal of Educational Cinematography, 1930–1935, since then titled *Intercine*.

The International Motion Picture Almanac, 1936–1938.

The Motion Picture in its Economic and Social Aspects, **Ann. Am. Acad. Pol. and Soc. Sci.,** vol. CXXVIII, November, 1926.

The Motion Picture Almanac.

The Public Relations of the Motion Picture Industry, Federal Council of the Churches of Christ in America, 1931.

Willey, M. M., and Rice, S. A.: *Communication Agencies and Social Life,* 1933.

Wood, L.: *The Romance of the Movies,* London, William Heinemann, 1937.

CHAPTER XXI

THE NEWSPAPER

Bibliographies on the Newspaper

Bömer, K.: *Internationale Bibliographie des Zeitungswesens,* Otto Harrassowitz, 1932.

Cannon, C. L.: *Journalism, A Bibliography,* New York Public Library, 1924.

Childs, H. L.: *A Reference Guide to the Study of Public Opinion,* pp. 38–42, 1934.

Desmond, R. W.: *The Press and World Affairs,* pp. 379–393, 1937.

Lasswell, H. D., *et al.: Propaganda and Promotional Activities,* pp. 279–312, 1935.

The Journalism Quarterly frequently publishes bibliographies on various topics in Journalism.

General References

Abbot, W. J., Bent, S., and Koenigsberg, M.: *The Press: Its Responsibility in International Relations,* Foreign Policy Association, 1928.

Allen, C. L., *Country Journalism,* 1928.

Angell, N.: *The Press and the Organization of Society,* London, Labour Publishing Co., 1922.

Benét, S. V.: "The United Press," *Fortune,* 7: 67–80.

Benson, I.: *Fundamentals of Journalism,* 1932.

Bent, S.: *Ballyhoo: The Voice of the Press,* 1927.

———: "Newspaper Truth," *Scribner's,* 88: 399–406.

———: "The Future Newspaper," *Century,* 117: 342–348.

Bickel, K. A.: *New Empires: The Newspaper and the Radio,* 1930.

Blake, G.: *The Press and the Public,* London, Faber & Faber, Ltd., 1930.

Bleyer, W. G.: *Main Currents in the History of American Journalism,* 1927.

Brown, F. J.: *The Cable and Wireless Communications of the World,* 2nd rev. ed., London, 1930.

Bush, C. R.: *Editorial Thinking and Writing,* 1932.

Chisholm, H.: "Newspapers," in *Ency. Brit.,* 19: 577.

Cook, E.: *The Press in War-Time,* 1920.

Cole, V. L.: "The Newspaper and Crime," *University of Missouri Bulletin,* Vol. 28, No. 4.

Corbin, C. R.: *Why News Is News,* 1928.

Desmond, R. W.: *The Press and World Affairs,* 1937.

Douglass, P. F., and Bömer, K.: "The Press as a Factor in International Relations," *Ann. Am. Acad. Pol. Soc. Sci.,* 162: 241–272.

Encyclopaedia of the Social Sciences, "Foreign Language Press," "Journalism," "Newspapers," "Press."

Flint, L. N.: *The Conscience of the Newspaper: A Case Book in the Principles and Problems of Journalism,* 1925.

Gosnell, C. B., and Nixon, R. B.: *Public Opinion and the Press*, Atlanta, Emory University Press, 1933.
Gosnell, H. F.: *Machine Politics: Chicago Model*, Chap. 8, 1937.
Graves, W. B. (ed.): *Readings in Public Opinion*, Chap. 9, 1928.
Gray, W. S., and Munroe, R.: *The Reading Interests and Habits of Adults*, 1929.
Gunther, J.: "Funneling the European News," *Harpers*, April, 1930.
Herd, H.: *The Making of Modern Journalism*, London, Allen & Unwin, Ltd., 1927.
———: *The Newspaper of Tomorrow*, London, Allen & Unwin, Ltd., 1930.
Hyde, G. M.: "Public Opinion and the Press," *Jour. Quar.*, 8: 73–83.
Irwin, W.: *Propaganda and the News*, 1936.
Kawabé, K.: *The Press and Politics in Japan*, 1921.
Kingsbury, S. M., Hart, H., et al.: *Newspapers and the News*, 1937.
Lee, A. M.: *The Daily Newspaper in America, The Evolution of a Social Instrument*, 1937.
Lee, J. M.: *History of American Journalism*, 1923.
Lehman, H. C., and Witty, P. A.: "Ethics and the Press," *Int. Jour. Ethics*, 38: 191–203.
Lin Yutang: *History of the Press and Public Opinion in China*, 1936.
Lippmann, W.: *Liberty and the News*, 1920.
———: "Press and Public Opinion," *Pol. Sci. Quar.*, 46: 161–170.
———: *Public Opinion*, Chaps. 21, 22, 23, 24, 1922.
———: *The Phantom Public*, 1925.
Lloyd, A. H.: "Newspaper Conscience: A Study of Half-truths," *Am. Jour. Sociol.*, 27: 197–210.
Lundberg, G. A.: "The Newspaper and Public Opinion," *Soc. Forces*, 4: 709–715.
McKenzie, R. D.: "Community Forces: A Study of the Non-partisan Municipal Election in Seattle," *Soc. Forces*, 2: 226–273, 415–421, 560–568.
Mott, F. L., and Casey, R. D. (eds.): *Interpretations of Journalism*, 1937.
Mott, G. F., et al.: *An Outline Survey of Journalism*, New York, Barnes and Noble, Inc., 1937.
Nevins, A.: *American Press Opinion from Washington to Coolidge: A Documentary Record of Editorial Leadership and Criticism, 1785–1927*, 1928.
Ockham, D.: *Stentor: or, The Press of Today and Tomorrow*, 1928.
Odegard, P. H.: *The American Public Mind*, Chap. 5, 1930.
Orton, W.: "News and Opinion," *Am. Jour. Sociol.*, 33: 80–93.
Park, R. E.: *The Immigrant Press and Its Control*, 1922.
———: "The Natural History of the Newspaper," *Am. Jour. Sociol.*, 29: 273–289.
———: "Urbanization as Measured by Newspaper Circulation," *Am. Jour. Sociol.*, 35: 60–79.
——— and Burgess, E. W.: *The City*, Chap. 4, 1925.
Perry, S. H.: "The Press Under Fire," *University of Mo. Bull.*, 29: 2–17.
Ratcliffe, S. K.: "The Revolution in Fleet Street," *Nineteenth Century*, 108: 15–24.
Riegel, O. W.: *Mobilizing for Chaos*, 1934.
Rosten, L. C.: *The Washington Correspondents*, 1937.
Salmon, L. M.: *The Newspaper and Authority*, 1923.
———: *The Newspaper and the Historian*, 1923.
———: "The Newspaper and Research," *Am. Jour. Sociol.*, 32: 217–226.
Seldes, G.: *You Can't Print That! The Truth behind the News, 1918–1928*, 1929.
Sharp, E. W.: *International News Communication*, University of Missouri, 1927.
Sinclair, U. B.: *The Brass Check*, 1919.
Steed, W.: *Journalism*, London, Ernest Benn, Ltd., 1928.

Strunsky, S.: *The Rediscovery of Jones*, 1931.
The Journalism Quarterly.
Villard, O. G.: *The Press Today*, 1930.
Watson, E. S.: *A History of Newspaper Syndicates in the United States—1865–1935*, Chicago, Publishers' Auxiliary Publication, 1936.
Wilson, L. R.: *The Geography of Reading*, Chap. 9, 1938.
Woodward, J. L.: *Foreign News in American Morning Newspapers*, Columbia University Press, 1930.
Yarros, V. S.: "The Press and Public Opinion," *Am. Jour. Sociol.*, 5: 372–382.
Young, K.: *Social Psychology*, Chap. 25, 1930.

Histories of Particular Newspapers, and Biographies of Journalists

Ayer, N. W., & Son: *Directory of Newspapers and Periodicals*, yearly.
Barrett, J. W.: *The World, the Flesh, and Messrs. Pulitzer*, 1931.
Bates, E. S., and Carson, O.: *Hearst, Lord of San Simeon*, 1936.
Bowman, W. D.: *The Story of The Times*, 1931.
Carson, W. E.: *Northcliffe, Britain's Man of Power*, 1918.
Chamberlin, J. E.: *The Boston Transcript: A History of Its First Hundred Years*, 1930.
Cochran, N. D.: *E. W. Scripps*, 1933.
Davis, E. H.: *History of the New York Times, 1851–1921*, 1921.
Downey, F. D.: *Richard Harding Davis; His Day*, 1933.
Duranty, W.: *I Write As I Please*, 1935.
Farson, N.: *The Way of a Transgressor*, 1936.
Fowler, G.: *Timber Line*, 1933.
Fyfe, H. H.: *Northcliffe, An Intimate Biography*, 1930.
Gardner, G.: *Lusty Scripps*, 1932.
Harris, J. C.: *Joel Chandler Harris*, University of North Carolina Press, 1931.
Lundberg, F.: *Imperial Hearst, A Social Biography*, 1936.
McClure, S. S.: *My Autobiography*, 1914.
MacKenzie, F. A.: *Beaverbrook, An Authentic Biography*, 1931.
Nevins, A.: *The Evening Post: A Century of Journalism*, 1922.
O'Brien, F. M.: *The Story of The Sun*, 1918.
Pemberton, M.: *Lord Northcliffe, A Memoir*, 1922.
Rosebault, C. J.: *When Dana Was The Sun*, 1931.
Ross, I.: *Ladies of the Press*, 1936.
Seitz, D. C.: *Horace Greeley, Founder of the New York Tribune*, 1926.
———: *Joseph Pulitzer, His Life and Letters*, 1924.
———: *The James Gordon Bennetts*, 1928.
Sheean, V.: *Personal History*, 1935.
Steffens, J. L.: *The Autobiography of Lincoln Steffens*, 1931.
Villard, O. G.: *Some Newspapers and Newspapermen*, 1923.
Winkler, J. K.: *W. R. Hearst, An American Phenomenon*, 1928.

CHAPTER XXII

THE GRAPHIC ARTS AND PUBLIC OPINION

Ashbee, C. R.: *Caricature*, 1928.
Avenarius, F.: *Das Bild als Narr*, 1918.
Berryman, C. K.: *Development of the Cartoon*, University of Missouri Bulletin, Journalism Series, No. 41, 1926.
Bowen, M.: *William Hogarth*, 1936.

Brinton, C. C.: "Revolutionary Symbolism in the Jacobin Clubs," *Am. Hist. Rev.*, 32: 737–752.

Burtt, H. E., and Crockett, T. S.: "A Technique for Psychological Study of Poster-board Advertisements and Some Preliminary Results," *Jour. Appl. Psychol.*, 12: 43–55.

Byrnes, J. E.: *A Study of Thomas Nast in Relation to His Times*, A. M. thesis, University of Illinois Library, 1935.

"Campaign Cartoons," *Time*, pp. 25–32, Oct. 24, 1932.

Downey, F. D.: *Portrait of an Era as Drawn by C. D. Gibson*, 1936.

Everitt, G.: *English Caricaturists and Graphic Humourists of the 19th Century*, 1886.

Farnsworth, P. R.: "Suggestion in Pictures," *Jour. Gen. Psychol.*, 2: 362–366.

Gibson, C. D.: "Cartoons and Cartoonists from Hogarth to the Present Day," *Mentor*, 11: 1–18.

Graphic Arts, a selection of articles from the 14th edition of the *Ency. Brit.*, Britannica Booklet No. 4.

Graves, W. B. (ed.): *Readings in Public Opinion*, Chap. 13, 1928.

Hardie, M., and Sabin, A. K. (eds.): *War Posters Issued by Belligerent Nations and Neutral Nations*, 1914–1919, 1920.

Hiatt, C.: *Picture Posters*, London, 1895.

Johnson, I. S.: "Cartoons," *Pub. Opin. Quar.*, 1: 3: 21–44.

Jones, S. R.: *Posters and Their Designers*, 1924.

Kauffer, E. M.: *The Art of the Poster*, 1924.

Kirby, R.: *Highlights*, 1931.

Lynch, J. G. B.: *A History of Caricature*, 1927.

Maurice, A. B.: "Cartoons That Have Swayed History," *Mentor*, 18: 22–25.

——: *History of 19th Century in Caricature*, 1904.

Maurier, G. du: *Social Political Satire*, 1898.

Mellinger, B. C.: *Children's Interests in Pictures*, Teachers College Contributions to Education, No. 516, 1932.

Murrell, W.: *A History of American Graphic Humor*, vol. I, 1933.

Paine, A. B.: *Thomas Nast, His Period and Pictures*, 1904.

Ross, E. A.: *Social Control*, Chap. 20, 1904.

Salmon, L. M.: *The Newspaper and the Historian*, Chap. 14, 1923.

Seldes, G. V.: *The Seven Lively Arts*, pp. 213–249, 1924.

Shaffer, L. F.: *Children's Interpretations of Cartoons*, 1930.

Weitenkampf, F.: *American Graphic Art*, 1924 edition.

——: "Inwardness of the Comic Strip," *Bookman*, 61: 574–577.

Wright, T.: *Caricatures and Grotesque in Art*, Chatto & Windus, 1875.

Young, A. H.: *On My Way*, 1928.

——: *The Best of Art Young*, 1936.

NAME INDEX

A

Abbot, W. J., 461
Abraham, K., 441
Ach, N., 170, 445
Achilles, P. S., 450, 456
Acton, J. E., 452
Adamic, L., 145n., 154n., 442
Adams, J., 126
Adams, S., 287, 289, 438
Adcock, A., 453
Addams, J., 440, 441
Addison, J., 245
Adler, M. J., 328n., 456
Albig, W., 46n., 81n., 156n., 185n., 190n.,
    197n., 344n., 433, 444, 446, 448, 458
Alexander VI, 33, 243
Alexander, H. B., 446
Allee, W. C., 98n.
Allen, C. L., 461
Allen, E. W., 162n., 405n.
Allen, R. S., 109n.ff., 403, 424
Allport, F. H., 4n., 6, 6n., 18, 18n., 102,
    102n., 185, 185n., 193, 193n., 199,
    199n., 202, 204n., 205, 205n., 269n.,
    433, 435, 447, 448, 449
Allport, G. W., 46, 46n., 104, 104n.,
    105n., 170n., 173n., 175n., 193, 193n.,
    339n., 341n., 343n., 344n., 349n.,
    350n., 354n., 439, 444, 447, 450, 456,
    458
Anaxagoras, 243
Anderson, N., 79n.
Anderson, W. A., 448
Andrews, C. F., 440
Angell, N., 433, 435, 461
Angell, R. C., 3n., 435
Angello, F., 37
Annis, A. D., 221, 221n., 450
Annunzio, G. d', 245
Antony, 288
Aristotle, 9, 119, 210, 328, 428
Armat, T., 362

Arnet, C. E., 439, 450
Arnold, B., 126
Arnold, T. W., 15n., 90n., 118, 119n.,
    433, 438, 441
Arrington, R. E., 459
Arthur, C. A., 441
Arthur, King, 119
Ashbee, C. R., 413n., 463
Avenarius, F., 463
Ayer, N. W., 35n., 272, 435, 463

B

Bacon, F., 13, 80n.
Bagehot, W., 3n., 433, 456
Bagnold, E., 66n.
Bailey, T. A., 443
Bain, R., 185n.–187n., 433–445
Baker, W. J., 450
Bakunin, M., 152
Ball, J., 81
Bancroft, G., 435
Bara, T., 367
Barker, E., 329n.
Barlow, R. R., 397
Barnes, H. E., 356n.
Barrett, J. W., 463
Barry, I., 459
Bartlett, F. C., 54n., 71n., 74n., 374n.,
    433, 436, 439, 441
Basler, R. P., 130n.
Baster, A. S. J., 456
Bates, E. S., 452, 463
Batson, L. D., 338
Bauer, W., 3n., 20n., 433
Baumgarten, F., 446
Beach, R., 58
Beaglehole, E., 286n., 456
Beales, A. C. F., 454
Beard, C. A., 273, 273n., 289n., 327n., 433
Beard, M., 20n.
Beaverbrook, Lord, 463
Becker, C. L., 13n., 452

465

SUBJECT INDEX

A

Actress, motion picture, types of, 367
Advertising, appeals in, 306, 307
  attacks on, 306–309
  defined, 305
  expenditures on, 306
  as science, 311
Affirmative response preferred, 232
Antirationalism, 11
Anti-Saloon League, 276
Appeals, to fear, 65, 66
  and propaganda, 313
Areas, geographic, 156, 157
Attention areas, 49, 385
Attitude, and behavior, 205–208
  classification of, 178, 179
  columnists reflect, 231
  conscious, 177
  definitions of, 173
  general, 176
  group, 174
  individual, 174
  and motion pictures, 222–226
  and opinion, 179
  periodicals as index to, 225–226
  and propaganda, 317, 318
  specific, 175
  unconscious, 177
  voting and, 226, 227
Attitude scales, 199, 200
Attitude testing, limitations of, 184
Authority, 92–95
  institutional, 95
  personal, 93, 94

B

Bandwagon effects, 233
Beliefs, 8
  and reality, 430
Books, numbers of, 34, 36, 38

C

Caricature, 415–418
  defined, 416
  subjects of, 417
Cartoon, 415–421
  as attack, 420
  defined, 416
  and humor, 417
  as illustration, 420
  limitations of, 420, 421
  symbols, 422, 423
  syndicates, 420
  in the United States, 418–421
Censorship, of books, 257–260
  by the Catholic Church, 242, 243
  the church and, 241–245
  as conflict, 241
  defined, 238
  freedom of speech and, 246–248
  infallibility and, 239
  of motion pictures, 260–267
  and personal morality, 258–260
  popular values and, 240
  of the press, 249–257
  and propaganda, 312, 313
  and prosecutions, 259
  trends in, 249
Chamber of Commerce, 274
Charts and graphs, 415
Climate, and folk beliefs, 156
  of opinion, 14
Coercion, nonviolent, 140, 141
Collective representations, 72–77
Collective unconscious, 70–72
  psychoanalysts' concepts of, **71**
Columnists, 403–404
  and press control, 256
Comic strips, 421–424
Communication, and community size, 47
  definition of, 26
  face-to-face, 27
  and graphic arts, 411, 412
  individual's ability for, 28

481